THE GOOD HOTEL GUIDE 2013

GREAT BRITAIN & IRELAND

Editors:
Desmond Balmer
and Adam Raphael

Editor in chief:
Caroline Raphael

Founding editor:
Hilary Rubinstein

THE GOOD HOTEL GUIDE LTD

The Good Hotel Guide Ltd

This edition first published in 2012 by
The Good Hotel Guide Ltd
1 3 5 7 9 10 8 6 4 2

Contributing editors:
Bill Bennett
Nicola Davies
Veronica Lee
Aileen Reid
Astella Saw

Production: Hugh Allan
Managing editor: Alison Wormleighton
Designer: Lizzy Laczynska
Text editor: Daphne Trotter
Researcher: Sophie MacLean
Computer consultant: Vince Nacey
Website design and development: HeadChannel Ltd, London

A CIP catalogue record for this book may be found in the British Library.

ISBN 978 0 9549404 7 8

Cover photograph: *Scarista House*, Scarista

Photographs on pp16, 18, 20, 28, 34, 36, 38, 41, 65, 339, 413, 459 and 465 © iStockphoto.com

Printed and bound in Spain by Graphy Cems

Hilary Rubinstein 1926–2012

We were sad to hear of the death this summer of the *Good Hotel Guide*'s founding editor, Hilary Rubinstein, at the ripe old age of 86. Only days before, he had sent us a hotel report, written in his inimitable style. Hilary espoused the cause of the small, owner-managed hotel, but he never lost sight of the *Guide*'s maxim:

'A good hotel is where the guest comes first'

Gliffaes, Crickhowell

CONTENTS

INTRODUCTION

The printed edition of the *Good Hotel Guide* is the cornerstone on which our multimedia applications depend. This is because the editors select the hotels on merit alone, offering unbiased advice on the best hotels in Great Britain and Ireland. Hotels do not pay to be included in the printed *Guide*: no money changes hands, freebies are not accepted.

Readers play a crucial role. They recommend new hotels and report on their experiences at existing entries. These comments are filtered by the editors who make a balanced judgment, backed where necessary by an anonymous inspection. A majority of reports come via email or the *Guide*'s website. There are report forms at the back of the book for those who prefer pen and paper.

The *Guide*'s thriving website works in tandem with the printed edition. It carries the full entries for many, but not all, of our selected hotels. Unlike the printed *Guide*, hotels pay a fee for inclusion on the website. If they choose not to pay, their hotel remains listed, but without the detail and photographs published in the print edition. The *Guide* is also available as an ebook and we have a popular iPhone app. The website has many tempting special offers from *Guide* hotels. It also has a growing selection of good hotels in mainland Europe.

The hotels we select are as independent as we are. Most are small, family owned and family run. They are places of character, who give a warm welcome, and flexible service. Diversity is the key to the selection: simple B&Bs are listed alongside grand country houses and city hotels.

Desmond Balmer and Adam Raphael
July 2012

HOW TO USE THE *GOOD HOTEL GUIDE*

MAIN ENTRY

The 457 main entries, which are given a full page each, are those we believe to be the best of their type in Great Britain and Ireland.

Colour bands identify each country; London has its own section.

An index at the back lists hotels by county; another index lists them by hotel name.

Hotels are listed alphabetically under the name of the town or village.

The maps at the back of the book are divided into grids for easy reference. A small house indicates a main entry, a triangle a Shortlist one.

Some entries carry a NEW symbol, indicating that a hotel is making its first appearance, is returning after an absence, or is upgraded from the Shortlist.

This hotel has agreed to give *Guide* readers a discount of 25% off their normal bed-and-breakfast rate for one night only; subject to availability, terms and conditions apply.

We name readers who have endorsed a hotel; we do not name inspectors, readers who ask to remain anonymous, or those who have written a critical report.

The panels provide the contact details, number of bedrooms and facilities.

450 WALES

PWLLHELI Gwynedd

Map 3:B2

THE OLD RECTORY

NEW

In a large 'cared-for' garden, this 'handsome' former Georgian rectory stands near the church of a village in the 'beautiful' Lleyn peninsula. It is run as a B&B by new owners Gary and Lindsay Ashcroft: 'They clearly love the place and what they are doing,' says a trusted reporter in 2012, restoring *The Old Rectory* to the *Guide*. 'They wanted to make the house their own and have completed a successful refurbishment; everything from the furniture, to the pictures, to the pretty cups on the tea tray in the bedroom has been chosen with care.' All the bedrooms have views of the grounds: 'Ours was not large but was cosy, with a built-in wardrobe, a dressing table and an armchair. It had a light, airy feel; pristine white bedlinen, an immaculate bathroom.' Breakfast, at a communal table in a dining room which catches the morning sun, has help-yourself juices, cereals and yogurts: 'Highly recommended are the creamy porridge and the full Welsh, which has bacon cured by a butcher just down the road.' The Ashcrofts recommend local restaurants: 'We were late and he gave us a lift'. Dogs are welcomed; they stay in a 'classy, well-built and sheltered kennel'. (*Sarah Thomas, Jane Forshaw*)

25% DISCOUNT VOUCHERS

Boduan
nr Pwllheli LL53 6DT

T: 01758-721519
E: theashcrofts@theoldrectory.net
W: www.theoldrectory.net

BEDROOMS: 3, also self-catering cottage.
OPEN: all year except Christmas.
FACILITIES: drawing room, dining room, 3½-acre grounds, walking, riding, sailing.
BACKGROUND MUSIC: none.
LOCATION: 4 miles NW of Pwllheli.
CHILDREN: all ages welcomed.
DOGS: not allowed in house (kennel and run available).
CREDIT CARDS: MasterCard, Visa.
PRICES: [2012] B&B £45–£90 per person, seasonal offers, 1-night bookings refused high season and bank holidays.

www.goodhotelguide.com

We give the range of prices per person for 2013, or the 2012 prices when we went to press. If a price for dinner is given, it is for (as full alc) the cost of three courses with wine.

HOW TO USE THE *GOOD HOTEL GUIDE*

SHORTLIST ENTRY

The Shortlist includes untested new entries and places we think should be appropriate in areas where we have limited choice. It also has some hotels about which we have not had recent reports. There are no photographs; many of these hotels have chosen to be included on our website, where pictures are carried.

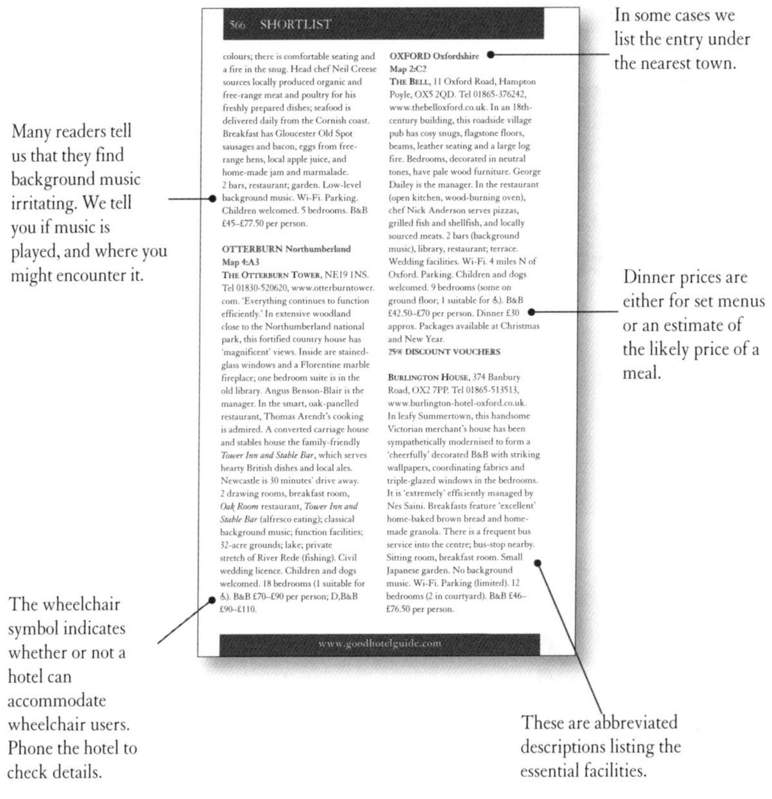

566 SHORTLIST

colours; there is comfortable seating and a fire in the snug. Head chef Neil Creese sources locally produced organic and free-range meat and poultry for his freshly prepared dishes; seafood is delivered daily from the Cornish coast. Breakfast has Gloucester Old Spot sausages and bacon, eggs from free-range hens, local apple juice, and home-made jam and marmalade.
2 bars, restaurant; garden. Low-level background music. Wi-Fi. Parking. Children welcomed. 5 bedrooms. B&B £45–£77.50 per person.

OTTERBURN Northumberland
Map 4:A3
The Otterburn Tower, NE19 1NS. Tel 01830-520620, www.otterburntower.com. 'Everything continues to function efficiently.' In extensive woodland close to the Northumberland national park, this fortified country house has 'magnificent' views. Inside are stained-glass windows and a Florentine marble fireplace; one bedroom suite is in the old library. Angus Benson-Blair is the manager. In the smart, oak-panelled restaurant, Thomas Arendt's cooking is admired. A converted carriage house and stables house the family-friendly *Tower Inn and Stable Bar*, which serves hearty British dishes and local ales. Newcastle is 30 minutes' drive away.
2 drawing rooms, breakfast room, *Oak Room* restaurant, *Tower Inn and Stable Bar* (alfresco eating); classical background music; function facilities; 32-acre grounds; lake; private stretch of River Rede (fishing). Civil wedding licence. Children and dogs welcomed. 18 bedrooms (1 suitable for ♿). B&B £70–£90 per person; D,B&B £90–£110.

OXFORD Oxfordshire
Map 2:C2
The Bell, 11 Oxford Road, Hampton Poyle, OX5 2QD. Tel 01865-376242, www.thebelloxford.co.uk. In an 18th-century building, this roadside village pub has cosy snugs, flagstone floors, beams, leather seating and a large log fire. Bedrooms, decorated in neutral tones, have pale wood furniture. George Dailey is the manager. In the restaurant (open kitchen, wood-burning oven), chef Nick Anderson serves pizzas, grilled fish and shellfish, and locally sourced meats. 2 bars (background music), library, restaurant; terrace. Wedding facilities. Wi-Fi. 4 miles N of Oxford. Parking. Children and dogs welcomed. 9 bedrooms (some on ground floor; 1 suitable for ♿). B&B £42.50–£70 per person. Dinner £30 approx. Packages available at Christmas and New Year.
25% DISCOUNT VOUCHERS

Burlington House, 374 Banbury Road, OX2 7PP. Tel 01865-513513, www.burlington-hotel-oxford.co.uk. In leafy Summertown, this handsome Victorian merchant's house has been sympathetically modernised to form a 'cheerfully' decorated B&B with striking wallpapers, coordinating fabrics and triple-glazed windows in the bedrooms. It is 'extremely' efficiently managed by Nes Saini. Breakfasts feature 'excellent' home-baked brown bread and home-made granola. There is a frequent bus service into the centre; bus-stop nearby.
Sitting room, breakfast room. Small Japanese garden. No background music. Wi-Fi. Parking (limited). 12 bedrooms (2 in courtyard). B&B £46–£76.50 per person.

www.goodhotelguide.com

CÉSARS 2013

We give our *César* award to the ten best hotels of the year. Named after César Ritz, the most celebrated of hoteliers, these are the Oscars of hotel-keeping.

B&B NEWCOMER OF THE YEAR

NUMBER THIRTY EIGHT CLIFTON, BRISTOL

Adam Dorrien-Smith has given his luxury B&B, a Georgian house on the edge of Clifton Downs, a stunning contemporary interior; the staff are charming and cheerful.

CORNISH HOTEL OF THE YEAR

THE OLD QUAY HOUSE, FOWEY

'Simply spot-on, chic and comfortable', this former seamen's mission has been turned by owners Jane and Roy Carson into a stylish hotel that is 'an absolute delight from start to finish'.

NEWCOMER OF THE YEAR

THE FEATHERED NEST, NETHER WESTCOTE

In a quiet village on a Cotswold hillside, this country pub has been renovated with a sure touch into a smart restaurant-with-rooms by owners Tony and Amanda Timmer. The service is outstanding.

CITY HOTEL OF THE YEAR

JESMOND DENE HOUSE, NEWCASTLE

'A country house almost in the city', Terry Laybourne and Peter Candler's Arts & Crafts mansion is in a wooded suburb. They have created a 'very good hotel with attentive service from a young staff'.

SUFFOLK INN OF THE YEAR

THE CROWN AND CASTLE, ORFORD

'A very good example of a *Good Hotel Guide* hotel', this old red brick inn in a peaceful village (owned by TV presenter Ruth Watson, her husband, David, and Tim Sunderland) 'is a joy to return to'.

PUB-WITH-ROOMS OF THE YEAR

THE BLACK SWAN, RAVENSTONEDALE

Alan and Louise Dinnes's restored Victorian pub, which they have made the hub of village life, is 'warm, friendly and very well run'. 'They are hands-on owners; the staff are interested in their guests.'

DINING PUB OF THE YEAR

THE STAGG INN, TITLEY

The cooking is as 'easy-going as the surroundings' in Steve and Nicola Reynolds's unpretentious village pub, which has 'a good feeling; excellent food and interesting bedrooms'.

SCOTTISH HOTEL OF THE YEAR

BOATH HOUSE, AULDEARN

One of the finest Regency houses in Scotland has been stylishly restored by Wendy and Don Matheson who have given it a 'real feeling of warmth'. The manager, Jonny Ross, is 'a huge asset'.

WELSH INN OF THE YEAR

THE FELIN FACH GRIFFIN, FELIN FACH

Brothers Charles and Edmund Inkin and their manager, Julie Bell, have created 'an extraordinary haven' at their old inn near Brecon which they run as a relaxed dining pub.

IRISH COUNTRY HOUSE OF THE YEAR

SALVILLE HOUSE, ENNISCORTHY

On a quiet hilltop near Wexford, Gordon and Jane Parker's Victorian country house has long been liked by readers for the warmth of the welcome, the sense of style and the exceptional cooking.

THE ORIGINAL HEROES

Only four hotels, two in England and two in Ireland, have had an entry in every edition of the *Good Hotel Guide*. Here we pay tribute to these enduring favourites, each of which is still run by the same family, by printing extracts from the first (1978) edition of the *Guide* and from this, the 36th edition.

ROTHAY MANOR
Ambleside

1978 There are hotels which offer a particularly friendly ambience, others which are in an exhilarating location, and others again which concentrate on *haute cuisine*. Hotels which combine all three virtues are comparatively rare, but the *Rothay Manor* belongs to this class. The Nixons have managed to preserve the atmosphere of a private house. 'The cooking is imaginative (though a bit on the rich side if you are staying for a long time) and the service excellent.'
Terms: B&B £11. Dinner £6.25.

2013 'The chief glory of *Rothay Manor* is the staff,' says a visitor in 2012 to the Nixon family's traditional hotel near the head of Lake Windermere. 'Under the relaxed supervision of the owner, Nigel Nixon, every one of them evinces a real pleasure in helping guests.' The cooking of the long-serving chef, Jane Binns, is also praised this year: 'The food is simply cooked but very attractively served.'
B&B £82.50–£117.50 per person, D,B&B £112.50–£152.50, set dinner £39.

LASTINGHAM GRANGE
Lastingham

1978 'My husband and I have stayed here many times over the last 11 years, at first with our three children, and we have never failed to enjoy it. It is a true English country house hotel, dating back to the 17th century, run by a family, and situated in a charming village within yards of superb walking country. The menus are limited but usually excellent.'
Terms: B&B £7.50, half-board £11.50.

2013 'You cannot help but love *Lastingham Grange*; you are so well looked after by the pleasant staff from early-morning tea to the five-course dinner.' There are many returning visitors to the 'hard-working' Wood family's traditional hotel. Bertie Wood is helped by his mother, Jane, and brother, Tom. At dinner, chef Paul Cattaneo serves a daily-changing menu of 'good, plain English cooking'.
B&B £75–£100 per person, D,B&B £90–£140.

CURRAREVAGH HOUSE
Oughterard

1978 'The Hodgson family have been living in this mid-Victorian country house on the banks of Lough Corrib for five generations, and June and Harry Hodgson now run it as an unstuffy, personal hotel. There are no keys to the bedrooms. The decor hasn't changed much since 1900. The food is good plain home cooking; excellent home-made brown bread for breakfast, for instance.'
Terms: full board £13.

2013 'An absolute delight,' a returning visitor's praise for this early Victorian manor house which has been run as a hotel by the Hodgson family since 1890. Henry Hodgson is assisted front-of-house by his mother, June; his wife, Lucy, is the chef. 'We run it as a private country house without pretension,' they say; there are no keys to the bedroom doors. 'Lucy's cooking is seriously good.' Breakfast has home-made soda bread. B&B €75–€85 per person, D,B&B €110–€130.

BALLYMALOE HOUSE
Shanagarry

1978 'It's a beguiling place. The Allen family who run it are in evidence everywhere. Mrs Allen is in the kitchen, various children driving tractors on the Home Farm, helping in the office, etc. The service is efficient and relaxed. The menus are very imaginative, and make full use of fish caught in Ballycotton Bay nearby. The home-made bread is out of this world.'
Terms: B&B £6.25. Dinner £5.50.

2013 '*Ballymaloe* remains as lovely as ever; a genuine country house hotel without pretension and a true family affair.' Founded by Myrtle Allen more than 40 years ago, the hotel/restaurant is managed by her daughter-in-law, Hazel; another daughter-in-law, Darina, runs the famous cookery school. 'Myrtle came to chat during dinner and was much in evidence at other times.' B&B €85–€130 per person, D,B&B €155–€200.

REPORT OF THE YEAR COMPETITION

Readers' contributions are the lifeblood of the *Good Hotel Guide*. Everyone who writes to us is a potential winner of the Report of the Year competition. Each year a dozen correspondents are singled out for the helpfulness of their reports. They win a copy of the *Guide*, and an invitation to our annual launch party in October. In addition, they are potential winners of our monthly competition for the best review. The prize is dinner, bed and breakfast for two at one of the *Guide*'s top hotels. The winner is announced in the monthly newsletter and also on the *Guide* website. This year's winners are:

Tony and Virginia Ayers of Hungerford
John Barnes of Reading
David Birnie of Fareham
Sophie Harrowes of London
Sara Hollowell of Pyrford
Jane Horovitch of Corwen
Shirley King of Berkhamsted
Andrew Laugharne of Bideford
Fiona Lorimer of Chislehurst
Frances Thomas of Hemel Hempstead
Penelope Visman of Folkestone
Barbara Watkinson of Shere

JOIN THE *GOOD HOTEL GUIDE* READERS' CLUB

Send us a review of your favourite hotel.

As a member of the club, you will be entitled to:

1. A pre-publication discount offer
2. Personal advice on hotels
3. Advice if you are in dispute with a hotel
4. Monthly emailed *Guide* newsletter

The writers of the 12 best reviews will each win a free copy of the *Guide* and an invitation to our launch party. And the winner of our monthly competition will win a free night, dinner and breakfast for two at one of the *Guide*'s top hotels.

Send your review via:

our website: www.goodhotelguide.com
or email: editor@goodhotelguide.com
or fax: 020-7602 4182
or write to:

In the UK
Good Hotel Guide
Freepost PAM 2931
London W11 4BR
(no stamp needed)

From abroad
Good Hotel Guide
50 Addison Avenue
London W11 4QP
England

EDITOR'S CHOICE

A visit to a hotel should be a special occasion. Here are some of our favourite hotels in various categories. Turn to the full entry for the bigger picture.

NUMBER THIRTY EIGHT CLIFTON
BRISTOL
Adam Dorrien-Smith has transformed this Georgian house on the edge of Clifton Downs into a luxury B&B. He has given it a stunning contemporary interior with striking sculptures and modern art. The bedrooms, on six floors, above and below the entrance, have wide bay windows, wooden floorboards and coir carpeting. A ground-floor lounge has sofas and armchairs, coffee tables with magazines, local information.
Read more, page 116.

THE PIG
BROCKENHURST
The co-founder of Hotel du Vin, Robin Hutson, has created a 'country house hotel with attitude' at this former hunting lodge in the New Forest. It is laid back and stylish: lounges have old stripped floorboards, squashy sofas, open fires, bookshelf wallpaper in alcoves. In the conservatory restaurant, a '25-mile menu' is 'great fun'. The bedrooms come in three sizes: 'snug', 'comfy' and 'spacious'.
Read more, page 119.

THE OLD RECTORY
MARTINHOE
In a hamlet in the Exmoor national park, this part-Georgian rectory is run as a small hotel by owners Huw Rees and Sam Prosser. 'Visible, friendly and calmly efficient', they have created an informal house-in-the-country atmosphere. 'Everything is new, bar a few antiques.' In a cosy lounge and conservatory, guests place their orders for Huw Rees's short 'delicious' menus.
Read more, page 222.

THE FEATHERED NEST
NETHER WESTCOTE
Friendly owners Tony and Amanda Timmer have renovated this country pub in a Cotswolds village 'with a sure touch'. It has stunning views of the Evenlode valley ('not a pylon in sight'). French doors in the bright restaurant open on to a terrace and garden. Chef Peter Eaton serves elaborate dishes: 'Every morsel was delicious.' The bar has a flagstone floor, a log fire. Everything is peaceful at night in the well-equipped bedrooms.
Read more, page 238.

THE WHEATSHEAF
NORTHLEACH
There is striking artwork throughout this old coaching inn which has been imaginatively restored by the owners, Sam and Georgie Pearman. The bar has a flagstone floor, a log fire, 'locals popping in for a drink'. The bedrooms have original features, massive beds, useful extras in a 'have-you-forgotten' bag. In the dining room, the menu has an 'interesting' mix of dishes.
Read more, page 250.

THE GUNTON ARMS
THORPE MARKET
In the middle of a deer park, this previously rundown hotel has been restored by art dealer Ivor Braka and his artist wife, Sarah Graham, into a relaxed restaurant/pub-with-rooms. They have given it a vibrant decor: stunning wallpapers, deep red rustic paintwork; an eclectic selection of artwork and unusual pieces. Chef Stuart Tattersall cooks on an open fire in the dining room.
Read more, page 314.

MILLERS64
EDINBURGH
Near the park in a quiet street in Leith, this Victorian town house is run as a small B&B by sisters Shona and Louise Clelland. They have decorated it in a clean, modern style with Oriental influences reflecting their childhood in Malaysia. The well-proportioned bedrooms have bold furnishings; Victorian detailing. Louise Clelland bakes daily specials for breakfast, taken at a communal table.
Read more, page 361.

GLENHOLME COUNTRY HOUSE
KIRKCUDBRIGHT
A civilised place with a delightful decor, this high Victorian mansion has been carefully restored by retired diplomat Laurence Bristow-Smith and his artist wife, Jennifer, who run it as an upmarket guest house. They have given the house 'a cultured feel': the guest sitting room is a library lined with bookshelves. The bedrooms have been decorated in Victorian style. Mr Bristow-Smith cooks a short no-choice dinner menu by arrangement.
Read more, page 381.

THE GROVE
NARBERTH
Facing the Preseli hills, this 18th-century mansion has been rescued from dereliction by Neil Kedward and Zoë Agar, who have turned it into an intimate hotel. Many of the staff are local as is much of the produce. The bedrooms are in the main house, a coach house and a 15th-century longhouse next to the main building.
Read more, page 444.

ARIEL HOUSE
DUBLIN
The McKeown family's hotel, a conversion of Victorian town houses, is a 'perfect *Guide* choice': it has 'a personal feel that is often missing in city hotels'. The family have renovated the buildings, retaining original fireplaces, cornices and stained-glass windows. 'Gracious' rooms in the main house have appropriate Georgian period furniture. Standard rooms in a simpler style are in a modern wing overlooking the garden.
Read more, page 481.

CHURCH STREET HOTEL
LONDON
On a busy street in Camberwell Green, this idiosyncratic hotel has been given a flamboyant Latin theme by Greek/Spanish brothers José and Mel Raido. It gives 'a more personal experience' than that encountered in a faceless chain hotel. A warren of steep staircases leads to the bedrooms, which have vibrant colours. Tapas meals are served in the 'excellent' *Angels & Gypsies* restaurant. B&B £45–£90 per person.
Read more, page 43.

THE FIELDING
LONDON
A 'simple, well-located place to stay', this small hotel is on a pedestrianised street near the Royal Opera House. Bedrooms, reached by flights of narrow stairs ('enlivened by pictures and mirrors'), are modestly decorated. Inspectors were pleased to find a 'comfortable' bed, 'plenty of storage space' and 'a neat, efficient shower room'. No public rooms; no breakfast; many eating places nearby. Room (*excluding VAT*) £90–£180.
Read more, page 49.

THE ABBEY HOUSE
ABBOTSBURY
Long a favourite with readers for the good value and warm welcome, this 14th-century house stands on the site of an 11th-century abbey. It is run as a small guest house by Jonathan and Maureen Cooke. The decor is traditional (chintz, knick-knacks). 'Comfortable' bedrooms vary greatly in size and style. B&B £35–£60 per person. Evening meals for house parties only.
Read more, page 66.

BROOKS GUESTHOUSE
BRISTOL
Close to the waterfront in the old town, this former hostel has been imaginatively converted into a hotel by Carla and Andrew Brooks. The small bedrooms have a contemporary decor; the quietest face a paved courtyard which has a mural by Banksy's friends. A large lounge/breakfast room has newspapers and magazines, an honesty bar. 'Exceptional value.' B&B £35–£49.50 per person.
Read more, page 114.

CASTLEMAN
CHETTLE
In an ancient Dorset village, Barbara Garnsworthy's restaurant-with-rooms is 'the most agreeable and best-value hotel we know'. The public rooms of the former dower house have high ceilings, ornate plasterwork; a 'faded gentility'. 'The food was exceptional, in a plain English style with an emphasis on local produce and game; the vegetables (so obviously fresh) were particularly good.' B&B £45–£65, dinner £30.
Read more, page 135.

THISTLEYHAUGH FARM
LONGHORSLEY
In a Georgian farmhouse on a large organic farm in rural Northumberland, Enid Nelless's 'hospitality and kindness continue to amaze'. The bedrooms in the old house, which has many original features, are priced according to size; they have 'excellent bedlinen'. Complimentary sherry is served before dinner, taken communally; the 'excellent' meal is based on seasonal produce from the farm. D,B&B from £70 per person.
Read more, page 207.

THE BLACK SWAN
RAVENSTONEDALE
In a beautiful village near Kirkby Stephen, this Victorian pub is run in exuberant style by hands-on owners Alan and Louise Dinnes. They have made the pub the hub of village life: the bars are popular with locals and a downstairs room has been turned into a community shop. Artisan dishes are served on a seasonal menu in two dining rooms. B&B £40–£70 per person. Dinner £26.
Read more, page 273.

HOWTOWN HOTEL
ULLSWATER
Without pretension or frills, this modest guest house (on the quieter eastern shore of Lake Ullswater) is liked by those who prefer a simpler life. There is no telephone, television or radio in the bedrooms. It is run by Jacquie Baldry and her son, David. Most of the bedrooms have lake views; four rooms have their private bathroom 'a hop across the corridor'. D,B&B £85 per person.
Read more, page 317.

BEALACH HOUSE
DUROR
Reached by a forestry track, Jim and Hilary McFadyen's 'handsome' guest house is the only dwelling in a glen between Oban and Fort William. Bedrooms, if not large, 'had everything we needed'. Guests eat together in the small dining room at dinner and breakfast. Hilary McFadyen is 'a great cook'; almost everything is home made. B&B £50–£60 per person, dinner £30.
Read more, page 357.

DALSHIAN HOUSE
PITLOCHRY
On the outskirts of the Victorian resort town, this 18th-century building is run as a B&B by Martin and Heather Walls. The house has 'lots of fine touches': well-equipped bedrooms have traditional furnishings, contemporary colours. Breakfast, 'a delight', has an extensive buffet, unusual home-made breads and preserves, interesting cooked options. B&B £35–£40 per person.
Read more, page 393.

THE EVESHAM HOTEL
EVESHAM
Children under 12 sharing a room with their parents are charged £2 for each year of their life at John and Sue Jenkinson's quirky, informal hotel. Younger visitors love the themed rooms (Alice and Wonderland, a family suite, has a play nook under the beams). Facilities include a swimming pool, a huge playroom, slides and a trampoline in the garden.
Read more, page 163.

AUGILL CASTLE
KIRKBY STEPHEN
Children are 'welcome guests' at Simon and Wendy Bennett's restored neo-Gothic Victorian castle. There are many diversions: a drawing room with toys and costumes; a children's cookery school; a fort in the forest; a tree house. In the evening, after an early supper, younger guests can watch films. Many of the bedrooms are big enough for a family.
Read more, page 192.

SWINTON PARK
MASHAM
There is much for children to do in the grounds of this mock-Gothic castle, the family home of Mark and Felicity Cunliffe-Lister. There are activity days, falconry displays, mountain biking. Indoors are a playroom, billiards, a TV projected on to a wall. A new family suite has been added this year. Nappies, wipes and baby powders are provided for families; decanters of spirits for adults.
Read more, page 223.

BEDRUTHAN STEPS HOTEL
MAWGAN PORTH
'They know exactly what families need, and have the space to provide it,' says a visitor to this large family hotel in a village above a golden beach in north Cornwall. There are indoor and outdoor swimming pools; 'a wonderful array of entertainment'; playgrounds, a jungle gym; tennis courts. The *Wild Café* has replaced the family restaurant; it has meals (including high tea) for all ages.
Read more, page 225.

CHEWTON GLEN
NEW MILTON
In a significant change of policy, children are now actively welcome at this luxurious country house hotel on

the edge of the New Forest. Children are given an activity pack; mini-bathrobes and slippers; baby wellington boots for beach walks. In school holidays, a supervised children's club is open twice a day. There are play stations and a cupboard full of games. Six new two-bedroom tree-house suites, which have been built in woodlands in the grounds, will appeal to families.
Read more, page 240.

SOAR MILL COVE HOTEL
SOAR MILL COVE
Busy with families in the school holidays, Keith Makepeace's hotel stands in extensive grounds above a sandy cove. 'We never impose rules but try our best to offer a range of options,' he says. These include a small swimming pool, indoor and outdoor play areas, activity packs, rock pooling on the beach. There are high teas and family dinner times; *Castaways* coffee bar is for 'muddy paws and boots and younger guests'.
Read more, page 298.

CALCOT MANOR
TETBURY
Adults and children 'co-exist happily together' at this 'civilised' Cotswold hotel. It combines a 'genuine welcome' for younger visitors with spa facilities and fine dining for their parents. Older children have the run of the *Mez*, which has games consoles, computers; a cinema and an outdoor swimming pool. Little ones have an Ofsted-registered *Playzone*, which has toys and a crèche. Special times are allocated for children in the spa and swimming pool.
Read more, page 313.

TREFEDDIAN HOTEL
ABERDYFI
Popular with families during the school holidays, the Cave family's traditional hotel overlooks a magnificent sweep of Cardigan Bay. Younger guests have an indoor games room, outdoor play area and early dinners. Families have use of a large lounge; children have their own supper menu. Baby-monitoring is available. In the large grounds are tennis and a pitch-and-putt course.
Read more, page 415.

PORTH TOCYN HOTEL
ABERSOCH
The Fletcher-Brewer family's 'laid-back, homely' hotel on the Lleyn peninsula has many facilitites for families. Children have a dedicated area with a cosy 'snug' (TV and DVDs) and a games room with table tennis. Younger children take high tea at 5.30 pm in the children's room; 'simple suppers' have been introduced for families seeking flexible dining.
Read more, page 417.

THE DRUIDSTONE
BROAD HAVEN
'Homely and welcoming', this late 19th-century stone house is run as an informal small hotel/family holiday centre by the Bell family. Visitors are encouraged 'to treat the place as a second home'. It stands on a cliff above a huge sandy beach (surfing, sailing, windsurfing and canoeing are available). Children have high tea around a big kitchen table.
Read more, 424.

HELL BAY HOTEL
BRYHER
On the western side of an island which can be reached only by boat, this small contemporary hotel stands by a sandy beach; there are more beaches within easy walking distance. Most of the bedrooms (mainly suites) have a sea view which can be seen from the bed; each has a sitting area and a terrace or a private balcony. Rooms are decorated in seaside colours.
Read more, page 121.

TREGLOS HOTEL
CONSTANTINE BAY
In landscaped gardens above the sandy crescent of Constantine Bay, this traditional seaside hotel has been run by the Barlow family for more than 40 years. There are lovely views of the bay from many of the bedrooms, which are decorated in blue and beige. Many activities for adults and children are provided at the hotel and on the beach.
Read more, page 141.

DRIFTWOOD HOTEL
PORTSCATHO
Steep steps in the grounds of this stylish hotel on the Roseland peninsula lead through woodland to a private beach (picnics can be provided). The interiors reflect the seaside setting: driftwood tables and lamps; colours are white with shades of blue. Almost all the bedrooms have a sea view. There is good walking in both directions on the Cornish Coast Path.
Read more, page 268.

SOUTH SANDS
SALCOMBE
The best bedrooms at this informal, contemporary hotel have views of the estuary. Almost on the beach, the building has a battleship-grey weatherboard exterior, marine pastels in the interior. Five two-bedroom beach suites are good for families (and dog owners). The beachside restaurant has a terrace for outdoor eating.
Read more, page 289.

SOAR MILL COVE HOTEL
SOAR MILL COVE
Surrounded by National Trust land, this single-storey stone and slate hotel stands above a sandy beach framed by cliffs (good rock pooling). It is popular with families during the school holidays: children can enjoy a small swimming

pool, a play area, activity packs. All bedrooms have French doors opening on to a patio.
Read more, page 298.

WATERSMEET
WOOLACOMBE
On a cliff above Woolacombe Bay, this traditional hotel has gardens (with a swimming pool) leading down to the sea. There are excellent views from the lounge and dining room from Hartland Point to Lundy. Tables are on three levels in the dining room ensure that every diner has the view. All but three of the bedrooms have a sea view. On Combesgate beach, below the hotel, children can go rock pooling, paddling, boogie boarding; there is good surfing at the neighbouring beach.
Read more, page 335.

TIGH AN DOCHAIS
BROADFORD
Guests can walk straight out on to the beach (when the tide is out) at this striking contemporary B&B, which was designed by award-winning architects to make the most of the views across Broadford Bay. The house is entered by a bridge to the upper floor. All three bedrooms (spacious and well equipped) on the ground floor enjoy the 'fantastic' views.
Read more, page 347

DUNVALANREE IN CARRADALE
CARRADALE
Sea tours can be arranged at this small hotel/restaurant in a fishing village on the Kintyre peninsula. It stands at the end of a quiet road with beaches on both sides. 'The brown and cream paintwork gives it an old-fashioned air, which is precisely its charm.' There are wonderful views across to the Isle of Arran. Local seafood is the highlight of the cooking. A ground floor room, which has French doors on to a patio with tables and chairs, has immediate access to the shore.
Read more, page 349.

THE COLONSAY
COLONSAY
'Relaxing and unpretentious', this is the only hotel on a lovely little Hebridean island (*pictured opposite*) which has more than a dozen beaches to choose from. The renovated mid-18th-century inn, on a hill above the harbour, has 'stunning views all round'. There are outdoor seating areas in the garden; locally brewed beer in the bar, which is popular with islanders. Grey seals, otters, dolphins, even whales can be spotted. At low tide, a mile-long stretch of sand joins Colonsay with the Isle of Oronsay.
Read more, page 350.

THE DRUIDSTONE
BROAD HAVEN
The informality and friendliness is liked at this 'family holiday centre' on a cliff-top above a huge sandy beach (safe for swimming). Surfing, sailing, canoeing and windsurfing are all available on the beach or nearby. Children's high tea is taken around a big kitchen table. Five bedrooms have en suite facilities; six share three bathrooms. There are bunk beds in one room.
Read more, page 424.

HARTWELL HOUSE
AYLESBURY
In beautiful gardens and parkland, this stately home (*pictured above*) has elegant public rooms with fine plasterwork, marble fireplaces, and antique furniture. It is run by Richard Broyd's Historic House Hotels for the National Trust. A staircase with Jacobean carvings leads to bedrooms in the main house; other rooms are in a converted stable block. There is a swimming pool, a bar and a café in a separate spa building.
Read more, page 78.

FARLAM HALL
BRAMPTON
Sheltered by tall trees in a landscaped garden, this manorial house is run in traditional, courteous style by the Quinion family. There are open fires in the ornate public rooms, which have patterned wallpaper, knick-knacks and Victoriana. Smart dress is expected in the huge dining room where Barry Quinion serves a short daily-changing menu of 'imaginative dishes with unusual combinations'.
Read more, page 109.

GIDLEIGH PARK
CHAGFORD
Andrew and Christina Brownsword's luxurious country house hotel stands in extensive grounds on the banks of the North Teign river. Panelled public rooms have Arts and Crafts features; bedrooms, all different, have antiques, paintings, prints, flowers; executive chef Michael Caines has two *Michelin* stars for his classic French menus.
Read more, page 132.

HAMBLETON HALL
HAMBLETON
'Everything about this country house hotel is a class act,' says a reader about Tim and Stefa Hart's mansion on a peninsula jutting into Rutland Water. Mrs Hart has designed the interiors in classic style (fine fabrics, antiques, 'sumptuous' sofas). In the newly renovated restaurant, chef Aaron Patterson has a *Michelin* star for his classic cooking with modern touches.
Read more, page 175.

LIME WOOD
LYNDHURST
'Worth the expense for the unashamed luxury', this laid-back country house hotel

stands in extensive grounds in the New Forest. The Regency manor house has been styled with 'wit, flair and humour'; fine period furniture and antiques stand alongside quirky modern pieces. Bedrooms are in the main house and three 'eye-catching' garden lodges. A 'memorable' breakfast buffet had all kinds of fruit, yogurts, breads; ham on the bone.
Read more, page 218.

CHEWTON GLEN
NEW MILTON
On the edge of the New Forest, this luxurious country house hotel is an 'absolute treat' thanks to 'attention to detail, courteous staff and a calm atmosphere'. The restaurant has been relaunched as as *Vetiver*, with a contemporary decor. Bedrooms in the main house have antiques, modern fabrics; most have a terrace, balcony or private garden. Six two-bedroom tree-house suites have been built in the grounds.
Read more, page. 240.

GILPIN HOTEL AND LAKE HOUSE
WINDERMERE
The Cunliffe family are hands-on owners at their Edwardian country house in extensive grounds within the Lake District national park. 'All those little touches that make a place spot-on' are evident. The individually decorated bedrooms vary in size and view. In the restaurant, the new chef, Phil Cubin, serves an 'appetizing' menu.
Read more, page 331.

GLENAPP CASTLE
BALLANTRAE
Overlooking Ailsa Craig, this classic example of a 19th-century Scottish baronial castle (the former seat of the earls of Inchcape) is run as a luxurious hotel by owners Graham and Fay Cowan. The castle has intricate plasterwork, an Austrian oak-panelled entrance and staircase; it has been furnished with fine paintings, Middle Eastern rugs, antiques. Adam Stokes, the 'innovative and confident' *Michelin*-starred chef, serves 'beautifully presented' dishes on a daily-changing dinner menu.
Read more, page 344.

THE LAKE
LLANGAMMARCH WELLS
There are good walks through woodland and in the countryside at this 19th-century hunting and fishing lodge which is run as a country house and spa retreat. Lounges in the half-timbered building have antiques and paintings, lots of seating on large sofas and armchairs. Bedrooms in the main house have rich fabrics and wallpaper; suites in the lodge have a more contemporary decor and an open-plan sitting room.
Read more, page 440.

MARLFIELD HOUSE
GOREY
The Bowe family's fine Regency mansion (once the Irish residence of the earls of Courtown) is run by sisters Margaret and Laura Bowe as a sophisticated country house hotel. Antiques and pictures abound in the elegant building: a grand marble hall, a lounge with an open fire, spectacular flower displays. The best bedrooms have antiques, dramatic wallpaper and curtains, a marble bathroom.
Read more, page 486.

THE ZETTER
LONDON
The former Zetter Pools building (originally a 19th-century warehouse) has been converted into a contemporary hotel full of retro styling. The bedrooms are decorated with wit (dark pink walls, olive fittings, a citrus yellow rug). They have all the necessary technology (television, radio, iPod docks, free Wi-Fi). The smallest rooms are compact. The crescent-shaped restaurant, *Bistrot Bruno Loubet*, overlooks St John's Square (where tables are laid in summer).
Read more, page 46.

THE ZETTER TOWNHOUSE
LONDON
Modelled on the imagined jumble (portraits, stuffed animals, Staffordshire china dogs, etc) found in the home of an eccentric aunt, this intimate town house has been decorated with flair and humour. The lounge/bar is 'zany and attractive; huge vases of flowers; entertaining pieces on every surface'. The bedrooms have an equally eclectic mix of furnishings. Cocktails and small tapas-style dishes are served in the bar.
Read more, page 47.

COVENT GARDEN HOTEL
LONDON
Kit Kemp, who owns the small Firmdale group with her husband, Tim, has given this boutique hotel a dramatic interior fitting for its position in London's theatreland. An opulent drawing room on the first floor is like a stage set: it has panelling, vivid upholstery, a French stone fireplace. Some of the individually designed bedrooms have views over the city rooftops; bathrooms are dressed in granite and mahogany.
Read more, page 48.

THE ROCKWELL
LONDON
Two white-stucco town houses have been turned into a modern hotel (*pictured above*) with a calm contemporary feel. The high-ceilinged lounge/lobby has big sofas, an open fire, bold wallpaper. The bedrooms have bright modern colours, light oak fitted furnishings; modern bathrooms have under-floor heating, a powerful shower. A south-facing courtyard garden is a suntrap.
Read more, page 50.

THE ARCH
LONDON
The public areas of this stylish conversion of Georgian town houses near Marble Arch are decorated with striking modern artwork and installations by emerging British artists. The bar has Philippe Starck stools, curtained booths; the open kitchen has a wood-burning stove. The bedrooms, which have eye-catching colours, are comprehensively equipped: a Nespresso coffee machine, HD television, digital radio; a working desk and a laptop safe.
Read more, page 53.

THE QUEENSBERRY
BATH
Four 18th-century town houses form Laurence and Helen Beere's 'swishy' contemporary hotel on an elegant street just off the Circus. It is a 'model of how a hotel should be'. The bedrooms are spacious, decorated in muted tones, with splashes of colour in throws, spreads and wallpapers. The split-level *Olive Tree* restaurant in the basement has a light, bright decor.
Read more, page 87.

HOTEL DU VIN BIRMINGHAM
BIRMINGHAM
Giant pillars offset by trompe l'oeil stonework and a ceiling fresco form a dramatic entrance to this branch of the du Vin chain, a conversion of the city's former eye hospital. The building has a wonderful sweeping staircase, a lovely courtyard and a lively basement bar. The bedrooms, around a central courtyard with a retractable roof, have a dark decor (lots of black, a cream bedspread); state-of-the-art bathroom.
Read more, page 97.

DRAKES
BRIGHTON
On the seafront (within walking distance of The Lanes), Andy Shearer's conversion of two white stucco Regency town houses has a striking modern interior, mixing 'orientalism with a touch of decadence'. The better bedrooms, reached by a dramatic staircase, face the sea: all rooms have hand-made beds, contemporary ceiling mouldings, natural wood; colours are cream and brown.
Read more, page 112.

HART'S HOTEL
NOTTINGHAM
In a quiet cul-de-sac on the site of the city's medieval castle, Tim Hart's purpose-built hotel has modern lines with curved buttresses and lots of glass. The interiors (designed by Mr Hart's wife, Stefa) are equally striking: a brightly coloured ceiling, much art on the walls, vast windows in the lobby. The bedrooms, decorated in masculine colours, have well-planned lighting.
Read more, page 252.

OLD BANK
OXFORD
On the High, opposite All Souls, Jeremy Mogford's conversion of three old stone buildings is liked for the laid-back luxury and contemporary decor. The buzzy restaurant, *Quod*, is in the old banking hall, which is filled with Mr Mogford's extensive collection of modern art. The well-appointed bedrooms also have original artwork (including Stanley Spencer prints); bathrooms are ultra-modern.
Read more, page 257.

THE ZETTER TOWNHOUSE
LONDON
Surprisingly intimate for London, this small town house hotel is on peaceful St John's Square in Clerkenwell. Take a cocktail in the atmospheric bar/lounge before retiring to one of the characterful bedrooms. The club rooms are compact but colourful. Splash out on the apartment, which has a free-standing bath and 'oodles of space'; or the grand suite described as a 'veritable playground'.
Read more, page 47.

THE PORTOBELLO
LONDON
In an anonymous Victorian terraced house in Notting Hill, this small, bohemian hotel is the preferred choice of A-list celebrities (many from the music industry) seeking a discreet hideaway in London. Honeymooners choose room 16, which is dominated by a central circular bed and has a Moroccan lantern and muslin curtains; a Victorian bathing machine, and a dressing room.
Read more, page 57.

BURGH ISLAND HOTEL
BIGBURY-ON-SEA
Visitors arriving at high tide are transported by sea tractor across the tidal estuary to this white, Art Deco hotel which has been restored with a 'proper sense of period fun'. Dress for dinner and take to the dance floor when the jazz band strikes up. The Beach House, built as a writer's retreat for Agatha Christie and a favourite of Wallis Simpson and Edward Windsor, 'must be one of the most romantic rooms on the planet'.
Read more, page 93.

LINTHWAITE HOUSE
BOWNESS-ON-WINDERMERE
Sleep under the stars in the loft suite at this creeper-clad hotel overlooking Lake Windermere. Its sliding glass panel in the ceiling opens up to allow star-gazing; a telescope is provided. It has its own entrance, an open-plan design; the highlight is the bathroom, which has a huge free-standing Italian bath.
Read more, page 106.

HELL BAY
BRYHER
You can walk straight on to the beach from the terrace of a ground-floor suite at this contemporary hotel on the smallest of the inhabited Scilly islands. It is on an isolated bay on the island's wilder western coast (next stop America). The bedrooms, decorated in seaside colours, have a sitting area facing the sea. You can find a beach of your own on this quiet island.
Read more, page 121.

COMBE HOUSE
GITTISHAM
On a vast estate of woodland, meadows and pastures, Ken and Ruth Hunt's Grade I listed Elizabethan manor house is run in informal style. Public rooms have oak panelling, antiques, fresh flowers, 18th-century portraits. Book the spacious Linen suite, which has a 6ft diameter copper bathtub with an enormous central shower head: 'The closest you'll ever get to experiencing a warm Niagara.'
Read more, page 170.

LE MANOIR AUX QUAT'SAISONS
GREAT MILTON
Raymond Blanc brings a French intensity to the importance of romance at his celebrated domain in immaculate gardens in a pretty Oxfordshire village. He has collaborated with leading designers to create unusual themed suites. Blanc de Blanc, with a private garden, is layered in shades of white. Even standard rooms have a luxurious bathroom. The place for a special occasion, say readers.
Read more, page 173.

LAVENHAM PRIORY
LAVENHAM
Approached through a garden with herbs and old roses, this beautiful half-timbered house, originally a priory, has been restored in the style of the Elizabethan merchant's mansion it later became. The spacious 'bedchambers' have sloping beamed ceilings, massive oak floorboards (which inevitably creak); unusual beds (four-poster, sleigh or polonaise).
Read more, page 198.

THE OLD RAILWAY STATION
PETWORTH
Guests check in at the ticket desk of this disused railway station near Goodwood and be ushered along the platform to your bedroom, a converted Pullman railway car. This unusual B&B is a conversion of the station building and four converted carriages. Two bedrooms, the biggest, are in the building; the most romantic are in converted carriages. They have a comfortable bed, and a surprising amount of furniture (chairs, a chest of drawers), and a bathroom with a proper bath.
Read more, page 263.

ARDANAISEIG
KILCHRENAN
On the shore of Loch Awe, a converted boathouse makes a remote hideaway for lovers in the grounds of this baronial mansion, once voted Scotland's most romantic hotel. The boathouse is on two levels, with double-height windows and a deck facing the water. Guests can borrow bicycles to explore the woodland tracks.
Read more, page 375.

LITTLE BARWICK HALL
BARWICK
'It still sets the standard,' say visitors to Tim (the chef) and Emma Ford's restaurant-with-rooms (*pictured above*) near the Somerset/Dorset border. 'The personable Emma' runs front-of-house, showing an 'impressive' knowledge of the wine list. In the restaurant, her husband sources ingredients locally for his 'short but enticing' seasonal menu of modern English dishes, perhaps pink-roasted wild roe deer, braised red cabbage, beetroot purée, rösti potato.
Read more, page 81.

FISCHER'S BASLOW HALL
BASLOW
The innovative food and the faultless service attract praise at Max and Susan Fischer's restaurant-with-rooms on the edge of a village near the Chatsworth estate. In the formal dining room (redecorated this year), Mr Fischer and head chef Rupert Rowley have a *Michelin* star for their modern European cooking. Dishes might include Derbyshire ox cheek and sirloin, St Petersburg stout and malt jus, sweetcorn polenta, charred Grelot onion.
Read more, page 83.

SIMPSONS
BIRMINGHAM
Andreas Antona is the chef/patron at this Georgian mansion in a leafy suburb where a trusted correspondent departed 'savouring the memory of one of the best meals we have ever had'. Executive chef Luke Tipping and head chef Adam Bennett can be watched in the kitchen (behind glass) preparing their menus of seasonal dishes, perhaps sea bass, wild rice, squid, peppers, coriander, lime.
Read more, page 98.

36 ON THE QUAY
EMSWORTH
Ramon (the chef) and Karen Farthing's restaurant-with-rooms, a 17th-century former fishermen's inn on the harbour front in a quiet Hampshire town, has a 'thoroughly deserved' *Michelin* star. The cooking is 'high-quality, sophisticated, with a considerable emphasis on presentation' (say inspectors). A typical dish: new-season lamb, roasted garlic, broad beans and braised brisket of lamb, roast lamb sauce.
Read more, page 160.

READ'S

FAVERSHAM

David Pitchford has a *Michelin* star for his imaginative cooking at the fine Georgian house which he runs as a restaurant-with-rooms with his wife, Rona. The ambience in the 'elegantly dressed', candlelit restaurant is 'not spoiled' by background music. Fresh local ingredients 'come to the fore' in his dishes; perhaps slow-cooked belly of English pork, sweet and sour plums, celeriac purée and a spiced pork sauce.
Read more: page 166.

THE GREAT HOUSE

LAVENHAM

'Memorable'; 'immaculate'; 'wonderful'. Régis and Martine Crépy's restaurant-with-rooms, which they run with Gallic flair, has long been popular with readers. They have given the ancient building a cool modern look, adding a dining area with retractable canopy in a sheltered courtyard. The 'immaculate' cooking of chef Enrique Bilbault is often praised by visitors who might have enjoyed corn-fed Suffolk chicken, stuffed thighs, mushroom duxelle, port sauce.
Read more, page 197.

MR UNDERHILL'S

LUDLOW

In a conservation area, Christopher and Judy Bradley's restaurant-with-rooms (*Michelin* star) stands by a weir on the River Teme. His eight-course 'market' menu rarely fails to please with 'playful food combinations', perhaps hot fondant beetroot tart, carrot ice cream, pea custard, black pepper caramel. Breakfast bacon is steamed, then grilled ('a revelation').
Read more, page 214.

THE THREE CHIMNEYS

DUNVEGAN

'Better than anything else on the island', Eddie and Shirley Spear's acclaimed restaurant-with-rooms has a remote setting by Loch Dunvegan in north-west Skye. In the candle-lit restaurant (a converted crofter's cottage), Michael Smith's contemporary cooking is 'fresh, simple, not too quirky and absolutely convincing in its quality'. A typical dish: steamed half Moonen Bay lobster with crushed new potatoes, garden peas, carrots, shellfish and tarragon butter.
Read more, page 356.

THE PEAT INN

PEAT INN

Owner/chef Geoffrey Smeddle and his wife, Katherine, have made this old coaching inn near St Andrews 'deservedly popular, and a sought-after focus for foodies'. Mr Smeddle has a *Michelin* star for his 'imaginative' cooking of seasonal 'modern Scottish/ French' dishes like daube of beef, red cabbage, crushed turnips, bacon, cauliflower, red wine sauce.
Read more, page 391.

PLAS BODEGROES

PWLLHELI

'Helpful, caring staff' and 'excellent, imaginative cooking' bring visitors to Chris and Gunna Chown's white Georgian manor house on the remote Lleyn peninsula. His daily-changing menu of 'beautifully presented' classically based dishes might include line-caught local sea bass, crab, ginger and pak choy, lemongrass sauce.
Read more: page 451.

THE VICTORIA
LONDON
Liked for its 'village feel', this pub-with-rooms near Richmond Park is run by celebrity chef Paul Merrett. An ambassador for Compassion in World Farming, he uses only suppliers 'who take an ethical view'. 'The food is good' in the handsome conservatory restaurant. A typical dish: oak-smoked trout risotto, new season peas and broad beans, poached egg, pea shoots. Children have a 'jolly' menu.
Read more, page 56.

THE BILDESTON CROWN
BILDESTON
James Buckle, a Suffolk farmer, owns this old coaching inn on the main street of a Suffolk village: his herd of Red Poll cattle supplies the kitchen with beef. The 'exceptional' cooking of chef Chris Lee continues to impress. Try peppered beef, pickled vegetables from his tasting menu; or Suffolk ham, duck egg and chips, mustard sauce from his Crown Classics.
Read more, page 96.

THE HORSE AND GROOM
BOURTON-ON-THE-HILL
In a honey-stone Cotswold village, this old Georgian coaching inn is run by brothers Tom and Will (the chef) Greenstock. Vegetables come from the inn's garden, other produce from local farms, for Will's blackboard menus of dishes like sweet potato and cumin soup; roasted beetroot, thyme jus, horseradish cream. The open-plan bar and restaurant have ancient beams, wooden floors.
Read more, page 104.'

THE TROUT AT TADPOLE BRIDGE
BUCKLAND MARSH
Gareth and Helen Pugh's old stone pub (*pictured above*), a 'warm and friendly' place, is popular with locals. By a narrow bridge over the River Thames (where boats can moor), it has part-timbered walls and original fireplaces. Pascal Clavaud, the chef, serves an interesting menu, supplemented by a good specials board, with dishes like a plate of Kelmscott pork (belly, cheek, fillet and black pudding), bubble and squeak, cider sauce.
Read more, page 123.

THE SUN INN
DEDHAM

The cooking of the chef, Ugo Simonelli, has a distinct Italian influence at Piers Baker's yellow-painted old coaching inn opposite the church on Dedham's main street. On his daily-changing menu taken in an open-plan dining room (old floorboards, log fires) you might find Sutton Hoo chicken roasted with peppers, tomatoes, garlic, onion, thyme, grilled polenta. 'Worth seeking out by any serious food lover.'
Read more, page 152.

THE WHEATSHEAF
NORTHLEACH

'Imaginatively' restored by the owners, Sam and Georgie Pearman, this old coaching inn is on the main street of a small Cotswolds market town. The menu promises 'simple, rustic food without pretension'. 'Standards are high,' said *Guide* inspectors who enjoyed twice-baked cheese soufflé; sea bass with chorizo, girolles, and haricot beans.
Read more, page 250.

THE THREE HORSESHOES
RADNAGE

Simon Crawshaw is the chef/patron of this country inn and restaurant, a renovated 18th-century pub in a 'truly rural village' in the less populated eastern Chilterns. In the restaurant, in a handsome south-facing extension, he serves an 'extensive, ambitious' menu of modern British dishes, perhaps roast Barbary duck breast, butternut squash purée, savoy cabbage ball, red wine jus.
Read more, page 271.

THE GURNARD'S HEAD
ZENNOR

In an isolated coastal position near Land's End, Charles and Edmund Inkin's laid-back inn is 'just how a pub should be'. The menus of chef Bruce Rennie are 'driven by what our suppliers bring to our back door; fish from day boats, greenery from small growers'. Typical dishes: sweetcorn, apple, duck egg, leaves; gurnard, mashed potato, smoked haddock, leeks, curry. The home-baked soda bread is 'the best outside Ireland'.
Read more, page 338.

THE FELIN FACH GRIFFIN
FELIN FACH

On the road between the Brecon Beacons and the Black Mountains, this old inn is managed by Julie Bell for brothers Charles and Edmund Inkin. Its organic kitchen garden provides chef Ross Bruce with ingredients for his modern menus, which might include potato gnocchi, wild rabbit, corn, pancetta; rump of Welsh lamb, with grilled vegetables, couscous, black olives
Read more, page 432.

THE BELL AT SKENFRITH
SKENFRITH

The bar of Janet and William Hutchings's white-painted 17th-century coaching inn in a village in the Welsh Marches has flagstone floors, an inglenook fireplace, comfortable seating. The inn's organic kitchen garden supplies vegetables, herbs, salads and soft fruits for the modern menus which might include garden pea soup, Bower farm crème fraiche; braised shin of beef, creamed parsnip, bacon and onion sauce.
Read more, page 454.

BLAGDON MANOR
ASHWATER
Cassia and Mace, the resident chocolate Labradors, 'always look forward to welcoming new friends', say Liz and Steve Morey at their 17th-century manor house in rolling north Devon countryside. 'Your best friend will be welcomed with a fleece blanket, dog bowl and treats to make their stay as comfortable as yours.' There is good walking in open fields leading from the garden.
Read more, page 75.

COMBE HOUSE
GITTISHAM
'I like the way they welcome dogs. They asked for our dog's name when we booked, and she was greeted by name on arrival.' A reader recommends Ken and Ruth Hunt's Grade I listed Elizabethan manor house on a large estate of woodland and pastures. Guests are given an illustrated booklet of dog-friendly walks. These have been found by Toby (a Dalmatian) and his 'best friend' Alan. A thatched cottage in the grounds has a walled garden where pets can safely play.
Read more, page 170.

OVERWATER HALL
IREBY
'Well-behaved' dogs are 'genuinely welcomed, on or off the leash' at this castellated Georgian mansion in an isolated part of the northern Lake District. Pets are allowed in the bedrooms and one of the lounges (but no sitting on chairs). They can enjoy (unleashed) the 18-acre grounds, including a woodland boardwalk. A dog-sitting service is offered 'for rainy days when you want to visit an art gallery'.
Read more, page 189.

THE COTTAGE IN THE WOOD
MALVERN WELLS
'We were touched to find a mat, a bowl and a treat in the room when we arrived,' said a visitor to the Pattin family's hotel on the side of the Malvern hills. Dogs are allowed (up to two in a room) in the ground-floor rooms in *The Pinnacles*, 100 yards from the main building, which are large and have the best views.
Read more, page 219.

THE BOAR'S HEAD
RIPLEY
Dogs are allowed in two courtyard rooms at Sir Thomas and Lady Ingilby's

old inn in a village on their castle estate. These rooms may be smallish, but 'a bone is placed in their basket, and water bowls are provided'. Owners must be 'well trained'. Dogs are allowed in the lounge area.
Read more, page 277.

PLUMBER MANOR
STURMINSTER NEWTON
'Dogs love it here,' say the Prideaux-Brune family at their 17th-century manor house in extensive grounds with well-kept gardens. Canine visitors are allowed in four courtyard bedrooms 'with direct access to the gardens and easy access to the car park, so you can take your dog out for a quick walk whenever necessary'. There is good country walking from the door.
Read more, page 305.

THE BONHAM
EDINBURGH
'The demand for pooch-friendly hotels' is recognised at this town house hotel in a quiet square near the West End. A 'doggy dreams' package includes a welcome toy and treat, a dog bed, and advice from the concierge on local parks, walks, pet shops and grooming parlours (appointments can be made). Chefs will prepare a 'luxury' bowl of meat, vegetables and gravy for an 'in-room meal'.
Read more, page 360.

KILCAMB LODGE
STRONTIAN
The outdoor life of the Highlands 'simply has to be shared with your best pal', say Sally and David Ruthven-Fox, whose old stone lodge is on the shore of Loch Sunart. They provide many extras to help visiting pets enjoy their holiday: extra towels for drying dogs after swimming from the hotel's own beach; mats for feeding bowls in the room; doggy bags; dog sitting by arrangement. The extensive loch-side grounds are 'perfect for dogs; no dangers from traffic, no roads to cross'.
Read more, page 403.

TRIGONY HOUSE
THORNHILL
Adam and Jan Moore's small country hotel is 'extremely' dog-friendly, says a *Guide* inspector, who warns: 'Your pooch may have to take second place to the doe-eyed resident Labrador, Rosie.' A welcome pack has a map of the best local walks and gourmet dog treats. Dogs are allowed in public rooms except the dining room ('should you want to eat with your dog, you are more than welcome in the bar').
Read more, page 406.

RATHMULLAN HOUSE
RATHMULLAN
A superior doggy room in a courtyard extension with a patio door leading to the garden is provided at the Wheeler family's handsome white mansion. Dogs have a 'room within a room', with a bed and toys, and a doormat decorated with patterns of paws. They also have an outdoor area to run around in. 'Company is on hand', courtesy of resident pooches, Jack Russells Odie and Brushie, as well as Suzie, a golden retriever.
Read more, page 502.

Each of these hotels has a tennis court (T) and/or a swimming pool (S)

LONDON
One Aldwych (S)

ENGLAND
Hartwell House,
Aylesbury (T,S)
Bath Priory,
Bath (S)
Park House,
Bepton (T,S)
Burgh Island,
Bigbury-on-Sea (T,S)
Blakeney,
Blakeney (S)
Frogg Manor,
Broxton (T)
Hell Bay,
Bryher (S)
Gidleigh Park,
Chagford (T)
Tor Cottage,
Chillaton (S)
Treglos,
Constantine Bay (S)
Corse Lawn House,
Corse Lawn (T,S)
Rectory,
Crudwell (S)
Dart Marina,
Dartmouth (S)
Old Whyly,
East Hoathly (T,S)
Summer Lodge,
Evershot (T,S)
Evesham,
Evesham (S)
Stock Hill House,
Gillingham (T)
Hambleton Hall,
Hambleton (T,S)
Pheasant,
Harome (S)
Esseborne Manor,
Hurstbourne Tarrant (T)
Augill Castle,
Kirkby Stephen (T)
Feathers,
Ledbury (S)
Lime Wood,
Lyndhurst (S)
Bedruthan Steps,
Mawgan Porth (T,S)
Scarlet,
Mawgan Porth (T)
Budock Vean,
Mawnan Smith (T,S)
Eshott Hall,
Morpeth (T)
Mullion Cove,
Mullion Cove (S)
TerraVina,
Netley Marsh (S)
Chewton Glen,
New Milton (T,S)

Newick Park,
Newick (T,S)
Old Rectory,
Norwich (S)
Hotel Penzance,
Penzance (S)
Ennys,
St Hilary (T,S)
Star Castle,
St Mary's (T,S)
Tides Reach,
Salcombe (S)
Soar Mill Cove,
Soar Mill Cove (T,S)
Plumber Manor,
Sturminster Newton (T)
Launceston Farm,
Tarrant Launceston (S)
Calcot Manor,
Tetbury (T,S)
Nare,
Veryan-in-Roseland (T,S)
Gilpin Hotel and Lake House,
Windermere (S)
Holbeck Ghyll,
Windermere (T)
Watersmeet,
Woolacombe (S)
Middlethorpe Hall,
York (S)

SCOTLAND
Glenapp Castle,
Ballantrae (T)
Isle of Eriska,
Eriska (T,S)
Inverlochy Castle,
Fort William (T)
Ardanaiseig,
Kilchrenan (T)
New Lanark Mill,
Lanark (S)
Kirroughtree House,
Newton Stewart (T)
Skirling House,
Skirling (T)

WALES
Trefeddian,
Aberdyfi (T,S)
Porth Tocyn Hotel,
Abersoch (T,S)
Glangrwyney Court,
Crickhowell (T)
Gliffaes,
Crickhowell (T)
Bodysgallen Hall and Spa,
Llandudno (T,S)
St Tudno,
Llandudno (S)
Lake,
Llangammarch Wells (T,S)
Portmeirion Hotel,
Portmeirion (S)

CHANNEL ISLANDS
White House,
Herm (T,S)
Atlantic,
St Brelade (T,S)
Longueville Manor,
St Saviour (T,S)

IRELAND
Cashel House,
Cashel Bay (T)
Marlfield House,
Gorey (T)
Shelburne Lodge,
Kenmare (T)
Rosleague Manor,
Letterfrack (T)
Currarevagh House,
Oughterard (T)
Rathmullan House,
Rathmullan (T,S)
Coopershill,
Riverstown (T)
Ballymaloe House,
Shanagarry (T,S)

Each of these hotels has at least one bedroom equipped for a visitor in a wheelchair. You should telephone to discuss individual requirements

LONDON
Alma
Arch
Goring
Montague on the Gardens
One Aldwych
Victoria
Zetter

ENGLAND
Wentworth, Aldeburgh
Rothay Manor, Ambleside
Hartwell House, Aylesbury
Bath Priory, Bath
Park House, Bepton
Bildeston Crown, Bildeston
Millstream, Bosham
White Horse, Brancaster Staithe
du Vin Birmingham, Birmingham
Brooks, Bristol
Frogg Manor, Broxton
Hell Bay, Bryher
Northcote Manor, Burrington
Pendragon Country House, Camelford
Blackmore Farm, Cannington
Gidleigh Park, Chagford
Montpellier Chapter, Cheltenham
Beech House & Olive Branch, Clipsham
Treglos, Constantine Bay
Bay, Coverack
Hipping Hall, Cowan Bridge
Clow Beck House, Croft-on-Tees
Coach House at Crookham, Crookham
Dart Marina, Dartmouth
Dedham Hall, Dedham
Summer Lodge, Evershot
Evesham, Evesham
Le Manoir, Great Milton
Byfords, Holt
Salthouse Harbour, Ipswich
Northcote, Langho
Lime Wood, Lyndhurst
Cottage in the Wood, Malvern Wells
Swinton Park, Masham
Bedruthan Steps, Mawgan Porth
Scarlet, Mawgan Porth
Meudon, Mawnan Smith
Manor House, Moreton-in-Marsh
Redesdale Arms, Moreton-in-Marsh

TerraVina,
Netley Marsh
Chewton Glen,
New Milton
Jesmond Dene House,
Newcastle upon Tyne
Three Choirs Vineyards,
Newent
Newick Park,
Newick
Beechwood,
North Walsham
Hart's,
Nottingham
Grange at Oborne,
Oborne
Old Bank,
Oxford
Old Parsonage,
Oxford
Elephant,
Pangbourne
Old Railway Station,
Petworth
Black Swan,
Ravenstonedale
Burgoyne,
Reeth
South Sands,
Salcombe
Seaview,
Seaview
Rose & Crown,
Snettisham
Titchwell Manor,
Titchwell
Nare,
Veryan-in-Roseland
Holbeck Ghyll,
Windermere
Watersmeet,
Woolacombe
Middlethorpe Hall,
York

SCOTLAND
Boath House,
Auldearn
Dunvalanree in Carradale,
Carradale
Killoran House,
Dervaig
Three Chimneys and House Over-By,
Dunvegan
Bonham,
Edinburgh
Lovat,
Fort Augustus
New Lanark Mill,
Lanark
Langass Lodge,
Locheport
Craigatin House,
Pitlochry
Green Park,
Pitlochry
Viewfield House,
Portree
Skirling House,
Skirling
Torridon,
Torridon

WALES
Harbourmaster,
Aberaeron
Ye Olde Bulls Head,
Beaumaris
Penbontbren,
Glynarthen
Hand at Llanarmon,
Llanarmon Dyffryn Ceiriog
Tyddan Llan,
Llandrillo
Bodysgallen Hall and Spa,
Llandudno
Lake,
Llangammarch Wells
Hafod Elwy Hall,
Pentrefoelas
Portmeirion,
Portmeirion

IRELAND
Mustard Seed at Echo Lodge,
Ballingarry
Stella Maris,
Ballycastle
Seaview House,
Ballylickey
Quay House,
Clifden
Rayanne House,
Holywood
No. 1 Pery Square,
Limerick
Sheedy's,
Lisdoonvarna
Rathmullan House,
Rathmullan

LONDON

Clock Tower, Palace of Westminster

BLOOMSBURY

Map 2:D4

THE MONTAGUE ON THE GARDENS

'The sort of place that redeems your faith in London', this Georgian town house hotel near the British Museum is managed by Dirk Crokaert for the Red Carnation group. The nominator enjoyed the personal touch: 'The staff don't speak like trained robots.' Snacks and light meals can be taken in the *Terrace* bar (where a pianist plays most evenings); it opens on to a wood-decked terrace which becomes a cigar lounge from 5 pm. Martin Halls is the head chef, serving a seasonal menu in the informal *Blue Door* bistro (candlelit at night) with modern dishes like crab and avocado cocktail, gazpacho dressing; duck cottage pie, spring vegetables. The public rooms are ornate (bold colours, crystal chandeliers, antique side tables). The themed bedrooms are equally extravagant: extra touches ('unusual at this price range') include complimentary mineral water, 'proper' coffee, fresh fruit; in the wardrobe are robes, slippers. Visiting children are not forgotten; they have bathrobes, games and toys. Pets are welcomed: dogs are given a bed, food and a water bowl and a goodie bag (dog-sitting and -walking available).

15 Montague Street
London WC1B 5BJ

T: 020-7637 1001
F: 020-7637 2516
E: infomt@rchmail.com
W: www.montaguehotel.com

BEDROOMS: 100, 1 suitable for ♿.
OPEN: all year.
FACILITIES: lobby, lounge, 2 conservatories, *Terrace* bar, *Blue Door* bistro, civil wedding licence, terrace.
BACKGROUND MUSIC: in public areas, pianist in *Terrace* bar in evening except Sun.
LOCATION: Bloomsbury, underground Russell Square.
CHILDREN: all ages welcomed.
DOGS: allowed.
CREDIT CARDS: all major cards.
PRICES: [2012] room (*excluding VAT*) £255–£640, breakfast £19.50, set meals £19.50–£25.50, full alc £60, website offers, Christmas/New Year packages.

SEE ALSO SHORTLIST

CAMBERWELL GREEN

Map 2:D4

CHURCH STREET HOTEL

An 'unusual' choice, this idiosyncratic hotel with a flamboyant Latin theme is on a busy street in less than fashionable Camberwell Green in south London. It is owned by Greek/Spanish brothers José and Mel Raido, who give 'a more personal experience' than that encountered in faceless chain hotels. There are bright colours, interesting posters, artwork and ornaments in the public areas. The 'excellent' *Angels & Gypsies* restaurant (exposed brickwork, legs of Iberico ham hanging from the ceiling) serves tapas meals at lunch and in the evening: 'Really tasty, reasonably priced dishes; quick, friendly service.' A warren of steep staircases leads to the bedrooms, which have vibrant colours, Mexican tiles in the bathroom, 'a quality bed and good linen'. Eight of the smaller rooms have shared bathrooms. Some walls are thin, and noise may be heard; 'double glazing limits traffic noise'. The Havana lounge has a 'welcome' honesty bar; complimentary tea and coffee is available in the breakfast room. In the morning, Mexican oil cloths cover communal tables: 'Good croissants, pains au chocolat and almond pastries; fresh juice, toast and free-range eggs.' (*CB*)

29–33 Camberwell Church Street
London SE5 8TR

T: 020-7703 5984
F: 020-7385-8377
E: info@churchstreethotel.com
W: www.churchstreethotel.com

BEDROOMS: 28.
OPEN: all year, restaurant closed 24/25 Dec, Mon lunch.
FACILITIES: lounge/breakfast room, restaurant, unsuitable for ♿.
BACKGROUND MUSIC: 'easy listening' in public areas.
LOCATION: Camberwell Green, underground Oval.
CHILDREN: all ages welcomed.
DOGS: not allowed.
CREDIT CARDS: Amex, MasterCard, Visa.
PRICES: B&B £45–£90 per person, weekend deals, Christmas/New Year packages.

SEE ALSO SHORTLIST

CHELSEA

Map 2:D4

THE DRAYCOTT

Converted from three brick-faced Edwardian houses on a quiet garden square, this luxury hotel, part of Adrian Gardiner's Mantis group, has 'lots of character', said inspectors. 'Not the least bit designerish; the decor gives a lived-in, though not at all shabby, feel.' The atmosphere is that of a 'comfortable country house', where efficient staff ensure that 'every request is rapidly met'. High-ceilinged public rooms have antiques and prints; the drawing room, where complimentary tea, champagne and hot chocolate are served, was refurbished by Nina Campbell in 2012. The absence of background music is applauded. Many bedrooms have a working fireplace; rear rooms have a view of the private garden and, in season, cherry trees in bloom. Kean, a large room, has 'a beautifully moulded ceiling, floor-to-ceiling windows with heavy curtains, a table and chairs for meals'. Guests' names are written on a card and placed outside room doors 'like at an Edwardian house party'. There is no restaurant, but 24-hour room service is available. Breakfast, charged extra, is served in a 'small, light room'; it has loose-leaf teas and 'good marmalade, jam and honey'.

22–26 Cadogan Gardens
London SW3 2RP

T: 020-7730 6466
F: 020-7730 0236
E: reservations@draycotthotel.com
W: www.draycotthotel.com

BEDROOMS: 35, 4 that allow smoking.
OPEN: all year.
FACILITIES: drawing room, library, breakfast room, 1-acre garden, unsuitable for ♿.
BACKGROUND MUSIC: none.
LOCATION: Chelsea, underground Sloane Square.
CHILDREN: all ages welcomed.
DOGS: not allowed in public rooms.
CREDIT CARDS: all major cards.
PRICES: [to 31 Mar 2013] room (*excluding VAT*) £165–£798, breakfast £17.50–£21.95, special breaks.

SEE ALSO SHORTLIST

CHELSEA

Map 2:D4

SAN DOMENICO HOUSE

NEW

The Italian ownership is evident at Marisa Melpignano's small hotel spread over two Victorian red brick houses west of Sloane Square. She has furnished it in opulent style, with plush fabrics, paintings and antiques. The staff are Italian. 'It has a most pleasing and relaxing ambience, and an emphasis on comfort and service,' says a *Guide* inspector this year, upgrading *San Domenico* to a full entry. 'My large rectangular bedroom was red: carpets, full-length curtains, tablecloths, and patterned light shades all shared this harmonising feature. It had an oriental theme with beautiful antique furniture – a carved bedhead, a painted chest of drawers, a mirror with a gilded frame. The pillows on the king-size bed were soft and comfortable; a well-lit bathroom.' Gallery bedrooms have a mezzanine sitting area which looks down on a silk-canopied bed. There is no restaurant; a room-service menu is available. Service is 'prompt and courteous' at breakfast, taken in a smallish basement room; it has freshly squeezed orange juice, 'good' coffee and bacon. There is a small, sunny roof terrace. 'High class; worth the money.'

25% DISCOUNT VOUCHERS

29–31 Draycott Place
London SW3 2SH

T: 020-7581 5757
F: 020-7584 1348
E: info@sandomenicohouse.com
W: www.sandomenicohouse.com

BEDROOMS: 16.
OPEN: all year.
FACILITIES: lounge, breakfast room, roof terrace, unsuitable for ♿.
BACKGROUND MUSIC: classical in lounge.
LOCATION: Chelsea, underground Sloane Square.
CHILDREN: all ages welcomed.
DOGS: occasionally by arrangement, not in public rooms.
CREDIT CARDS: all major cards.
PRICES: [2012] (*excluding VAT*) room £255–£390, breakfast £12–£18, special breaks.

SEE ALSO SHORTLIST

CLERKENWELL

Map 2:D4

THE ZETTER

Restaurateurs Mark Sainsbury and Michael Benyan have converted the former Zetters Pools building into a contemporary hotel, full of retro styling in keeping with this trendy part of London in which it's situated. 'The staff were exceptional; friendly at all times, going out of their way to help,' said inspectors. The bedrooms vary considerably in size but come with all the necessary technology; television, radio, iPod docks, free Wi-Fi; spring water from the hotel's own borehole. The smallest rooms are compact. A 'spacious' corner room facing Clerkenwell Road (shutters and secondary glazing to minimise noise) was 'decorated with wit': dark pink walls, pale olive fittings; a citrus-yellow rug on the large bed; a powerful walk-in shower in the bathroom. The crescent-shaped restaurant, *Bistrot Bruno Loubet*, has a 'wonderful outlook on St John's Square' (and tables there in summer); the menu ('imaginative without pretension') might include pan-fried fillet of sea bream, brandade piquillo pepper, Grenobloise butter. Breakfast ('greatly enjoyed') has 'fresh bread; excellent pastries; interesting cooked dishes'. The sister *Zetter Townhouse* is across the square (see next entry).

86–88 Clerkenwell Road
London EC1M 5RJ

T: 020-7324 4444
F: 020-7324 4445
E: info@thezetter.com
W: www.thezetter.com

BEDROOMS: 59, 2 suitable for ♿.
OPEN: all year.
FACILITIES: 2 lifts, ramps, cocktail bar/lounge, restaurant, 2 function/meeting rooms.
BACKGROUND MUSIC: 'low-volume' eclectic mix.
LOCATION: Clerkenwell, by St John's Sq, NCP garage 5 mins' walk, underground Farringdon.
CHILDREN: all ages welcomed.
DOGS: only guide dogs allowed.
CREDIT CARDS: Amex, MasterCard, Visa.
PRICES: [2012] room £185–£438, full English breakfast £9.50, full alc £45, Christmas package.

SEE ALSO SHORTLIST

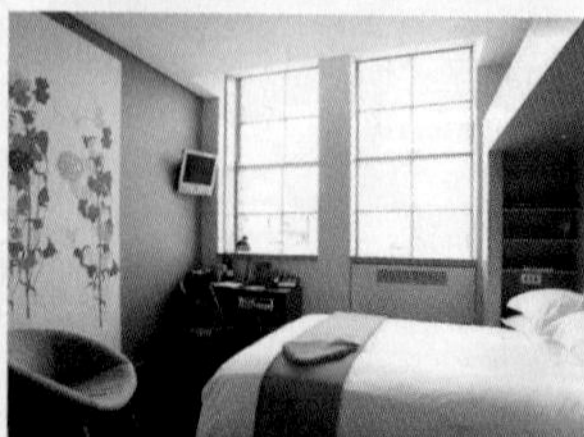

CLERKENWELL

Map 2:D4

THE ZETTER TOWNHOUSE

César award in 2012

'Decorated with flair', this 'intimate' town house hotel is modelled on the imagined jumble (portraits, stuffed animals, Staffordshire china dogs) found in the home of an eccentric aunt. 'We enjoyed our stay very much,' said visitors (*Guide* hoteliers) this year. Inspectors were impressed by the 'huge attention to detail in colour and fittings' throughout, and by the 'outstanding service'. The lounge/bar is 'zany and attractive; huge vases of flowers; entertaining pieces on every surface'. The bedrooms have an equally eclectic mix of furnishings. A compact club room has a 'wildly colourful headboard made from a fairground merry-go-round; a chest of drawers painted to match; an antique walnut wardrobe'. 'Interesting' cocktails and small tapas-style dishes are served in the bar; in the basement are board games, table tennis, Wii, etc. There is a 24-hour room service menu. Breakfast, often included in direct bookings, can be taken in the room or the lounge. Under the same ownership (Michael Benyan and Mark Sainsbury) as *The Zetter* (see previous entry) across the square. (*Chris and Jenny Mullen*)

49–50 St John's Square
London EC1V 4JJ

T: 020-7324 4567
F: 020-7324 4456
E: reservations@thezetter.com
W: www.thezettertownhouse.com

BEDROOMS: 13.
OPEN: all year.
FACILITIES: cocktail lounge, private dining room, games room.
BACKGROUND MUSIC: in public areas.
LOCATION: Clerkenwell, underground Farringdon.
CHILDREN: all ages welcomed.
DOGS: not allowed.
CREDIT CARDS: Amex, MasterCard, Visa.
PRICES: [2012] room (*excluding VAT*) £205–£400, breakfast £9.50–£17.50, special breaks, New Year package, 1-night bookings rarely refused.

SEE ALSO SHORTLIST

COVENT GARDEN

Map 2:D4

COVENT GARDEN HOTEL

Liked for the 'superb comfort and fantastic service', this 'wonderfully central' hotel is well placed for theatre-goers who can take a pre- or post-performance supper at the in-house *Brasserie Max*. It is part of Tim and Kit Kemp's small Firmdale group (see also *Number Sixteen*). Kit Kemp is responsible for the contemporary design – the lobby has been compared to a stage set, and there is a leather-seated screening room on the lower ground floor. The 'excellent' brasserie meals have a 'light European touch', with dishes like Old Spot pork schnitzel stuffed with Parma ham and Gruyère. The menus are available on room service, which 'is so fast it is unbelievable'. The 'lovely, comfortable' bedrooms are individually designed and have views over the rooftops of London; four-poster rooms have a king-size bed; bathrooms are dressed in marble and mahogany; many have a walk-in shower. An opulent drawing room on the first floor has panelling, vivid upholstery, a French stone fireplace. There is an honesty bar in the adjoining library. Breakfast (charged extra) has 'so much choice'. 'A super capital treat; expensive but worth every penny.' (*JL*)

10 Monmouth Street
London WC2H 9HB

T: 020-7806 1000
F: 020-7806 1100
E: covent@firmdale.com
W: www.coventgardenhotel.co.uk

BEDROOMS: 58.
OPEN: all year.
FACILITIES: drawing room, library, bar, restaurant, meeting room, screening room, gym.
BACKGROUND MUSIC: none.
LOCATION: Covent Garden, underground Covent Garden, Leicester Square.
CHILDREN: all ages welcomed.
DOGS: not allowed.
CREDIT CARDS: all major cards.
PRICES: [2012] room (excluding VAT) £260–£1,450, breakfast £21, set dinner £23.50–£25.

SEE ALSO SHORTLIST

COVENT GARDEN

Map 2:D4

THE FIELDING

Steps away from the Royal Opera House, on a pedestrianised street that still has 19th-century gas lamps, this small hotel is 'a delightful, comfortable' place to stay, says a visitor in 2012. Olive trees and window boxes flank its entrance; at night, fairy lights lend a 'romantic' air. The entire hotel was renovated in 2011. There is no lift: upstairs bedrooms are reached via flights of narrow stairs ('enlivened by pictures and mirrors'). Rooms are modestly decorated in shades of sage, cream and burgundy; all are air conditioned and come with tea- and coffee-making facilities and bottles of mineral water. Inspectors were pleased to find a 'comfortable' bed, 'plenty of storage space' and 'a neat, efficient shower room with decent-sized towels and plenty of soaps'. 'Our window overlooked a quiet area and at night there was little noise' – despite the hotel's central location in an animated part of the city. The hotel has no public rooms and no meals are provided; there are many eating places in the neighbourhood. Guests have free access to a nearby health centre, with gym, swimming pool and spa. 'The perfect complement to a night at the opera.' (*Matthew Caminer*)

4 Broad Court
Bow Street
London WC2B 5QZ

T: 020-7836 8305
F: 020-7497 0064
E: reservations@thefieldinghotel.co.uk
W: www.thefieldinghotel.co.uk

BEDROOMS: 25.
OPEN: all year.
FACILITIES: no public rooms, unsuitable for ♿.
BACKGROUND MUSIC: none.
LOCATION: central, underground Covent Garden.
CHILDREN: all ages welcomed.
DOGS: not allowed.
CREDIT CARDS: all major cards.
PRICES: [2012] room (*excluding VAT*) £90–£180.

SEE ALSO SHORTLIST

EARLS COURT

Map 2:D4

THE ROCKWELL

Two classic, stucco-fronted Earls Court town houses on the busy Cromwell Road ('double glazing kept out road noise') have been turned into a 40-room hotel with 'a clean modern look and informal vibe' by owners Michael Squire (an architect) and Tony Bartlett. Ocky Paller is the manager: staff were 'friendly and efficient'; 'a porter was on hand to help with luggage'. The 'fine high-ceilinged' lounge/lobby has big sofas, an open fire, bold wallpaper. The bedrooms (some singles are compact) have bright modern colours, light oak fitted furnishings; modern bathrooms have under-floor heating, powerful shower. Split-level mezzanine suites have bed space and sitting area on separate levels, joined by a curving staircase. A 24-hour room-service menu is available. Bistro-type meals can be taken in an attractive dining room ('bold colours again'), eg, salmon fillet on red lentils with spinach. In summer, meals and drinks are served in the south-facing courtyard garden ('a suntrap' with bamboo plants and olive trees in pots). Breakfast (extra charge) has freshly baked bread, salamis, cheese and hams. The cooked menu includes eggs Benedict and Florentine; pancakes.

181 Cromwell Road
London SW5 0SF

T: 020-7244 2000
F: 020-7244 2001
E: enquiries@therockwell.com
W: www.therockwell.com

BEDROOMS: 40, 1 on ground floor.
OPEN: all year.
FACILITIES: lift, ramps, lobby, lounge, bar, restaurant, conference room, garden.
BACKGROUND MUSIC: jazz in lobby and library.
LOCATION: 1 mile SW of Marble Arch, opposite Cromwell Hospital, underground Earls Court.
CHILDREN: all ages welcomed.
DOGS: not allowed.
CREDIT CARDS: Amex, MasterCard, Visa.
PRICES: room £130–£230, breakfast £10.50–£12.50, full alc £35, website offers, Christmas/New Year packages.

SEE ALSO SHORTLIST

KNIGHTSBRIDGE

Map 2:D4

THE CAPITAL

César award in 2008

'One hundred and twenty-seven footsteps from Harrods', and just a few more to Hyde Park and nearby museums, David Levin's town house hotel has a 'convenient' location from which to explore the city. Mr Levin's daughter, Kate, is the manager. Calling itself a 'grand hotel in miniature', it has a traditional feel, and is filled with original artwork from the family's collection. The formality is observed in the compact wood-panelled dining room where 'tables are well spaced for private conversation'. A reader this year enjoyed Jérôme Ponchelle's French-inspired cooking: 'Good, plump scallops, first-class peppery celeriac purée'; 'generous and gamey pheasant with rich truffle macaroni'. The wine list is 'comprehensive but at SW1 prices'; it has bottles from Mr Levin's organic vineyard in the Loire valley; service was 'attentive, almost over-zealous'. Lighter meals can be taken in the bar. The bedrooms are individually styled. One recent visitor praised a 'luxurious' junior suite; another felt 'a few extra touches' were required. Minibars can be customised. Mr Levin also owns *The Levin*, next door (see entry). (*RG, and others*)

22–24 Basil Street
London SW3 1AT

T: 020-7589 5171
F: 020-7225 0011
E: reservations@capitalhotel.co.uk
W: www.capitalhotel.co.uk

BEDROOMS: 49.
OPEN: all year.
FACILITIES: lift, sitting room, bar, restaurant, brasserie/bar next door, 2 private dining rooms, only restaurant suitable for ♿.
BACKGROUND MUSIC: soft jazz in bar in evenings.
LOCATION: central, underground Knightsbridge, private car park (£6 an hour, £30 a day).
CHILDREN: all ages welcomed.
DOGS: small dogs, on request.
CREDIT CARDS: all major cards.
PRICES: [2012] room (*excluding VAT*) £250–£500, breakfast £16–£19.50, full alc £65 (*plus 12½% discretionary service charge*), various packages – see website.

SEE ALSO SHORTLIST

KNIGHTSBRIDGE

Map 2:D4

THE LEVIN

'Peaceful, comfortable and quiet', this tall terraced town house is the baby sister of David Levin's 'more opulent' *Capital* next door (see previous entry). 'There is less show, and a stronger domestic sense here,' says a *Guide* inspector this year. It is managed by Harald Duttine; the young staff are 'courteous, friendly'. Guests are welcomed in a small pistachio-coloured lobby; a 'spectacular' 18-metre-long light installation cascades down the stairwell of the spiral staircase leading to the bedrooms. An east-facing room had 'an urban prospect of town house rooflines; tasteful, minimalist furniture; a very comfortable bed; good lighting; and 30 Penguin classics to choose from'. A champagne minibar stocks only the ingredients needed for guests to mix cocktails. In the 'compact' *Le Metro* bar and bistro, chef Marcin Kosinski serves a grazing menu of small plates (crispy squid, garlic aïoli; cumin kofte, minted yogurt dip) with larger classics (burgers; haddock and chips). There is a 'varied' breakfast buffet – 'freshly squeezed red grapefruit juice, good yogurt, conserves in white china pots' and 'excellent scrambled eggs served on a well-heated plate'.

28 Basil Street
London SW3 1AS

T: 020-7589 6286
F: 020-7823 7826
E: reservations@thelevinhotel.co.uk
W: www.thelevinhotel.co.uk

BEDROOMS: 12.
OPEN: all year, restaurant closed Sun after 5.30 pm.
FACILITIES: lobby, library, honesty bar, bar/brasserie (*Le Metro*), access to nearby health club/spa, unsuitable for ♿.
BACKGROUND MUSIC: in restaurant.
LOCATION: central, underground Knightsbridge (Harrods exit), private car park (£40 a night).
CHILDREN: all ages welcomed.
DOGS: not allowed.
CREDIT CARDS: all major cards.
PRICES: [2012] B&B (continental, *excluding VAT and 5% 'discretionary' service charge*) £122.50–£260 per person, full alc £40, seasonal offers, Christmas/New Year packages.

SEE ALSO SHORTLIST

MARBLE ARCH

Map 2:D4

THE ARCH

Within sight of Marble Arch, this stylish modern hotel (Pride of Britain) 'has an intimate feel for its size', say *Guide* inspectors in 2012, who found 'much to like'. A conversion of seven Georgian town houses and two mews homes, it is owned by Abraham Bejerano; Grant Powell is now the manager. 'The staff were unfailingly helpful, ordering taxis, looking up information on the Internet for us.' The public areas are decorated with striking artwork and installations by emerging young British artists. The bedrooms have eye-catching colours: 'Our standard room was small but comprehensively equipped: good storage, well-thought-through details (a light in the wardrobe, proper coat-hangers, good lighting by the bed for those who want to read); a Nespresso machine, fresh milk and complimentary soft drinks. It overlooked a mews and was peaceful at night.' Quinton Bennett, the chef in the informal *HUNter 486* brasserie, has introduced a new menu (dishes like oven-baked duck egg, cumin-scented brown shrimp; Suffolk chicken casserole). Breakfast is 'delicious', with 'especially good home-made muesli', a bowl of fresh-cut fruit; 'eggs on chunky sourdough toast'.

25% DISCOUNT VOUCHERS

50 Great Cumberland Place
London W1H 7FD

T: 020-7724 4700
F: 020-7724 4744
E: info@thearchlondon.com
W: www.thearchlondon.com

BEDROOMS: 82, 2 suitable for ♿.
OPEN: all year.
FACILITIES: lobby, bar, brasserie, library, champagne salon, gym.
BACKGROUND MUSIC: jazz in lounge.
LOCATION: near Marble Arch, underground Marble Arch.
CHILDREN: all ages welcomed.
DOGS: allowed.
CREDIT CARDS: Amex, MasterCard, Visa.
PRICES: [2012] room (*excluding VAT*) £205–£545, breakfast £17–£22, set menu £17.50–£20, full alc £35–£45, weekend rates (including breakfast), Christmas/New Year packages.

SEE ALSO SHORTLIST

MARBLE ARCH

Map 2:D4

THE GRAZING GOAT

In a chic enclave behind Marble Arch, this pub with-rooms lies within the Portman Estate; its name derives from Lady Portman's allergy to cow's milk – she grazed her goats in the area. An 'unusual venture for central London', it is owned by the small Cubitt House group. The atmosphere is 'youthful and informal', said inspectors. The downstairs bar, 'busy with after-work drinkers', has iron beams, a long bar with stools, lots of French oak. In the panelled first-floor dining room (light thanks to windows at both ends), English bistro dishes are served, perhaps chicken and ham hock pie. The 28-day-aged Castle of Mey steaks are 'particularly recommended'. The eight bedrooms are on the three top floors (no lift). 'They have a country feel, with wooden floorboards, well-made wooden fittings (doors, window sills, cupboards and wardrobes); grey-green walls, subtle fabric colours. Our room had a huge bed with a wooden headboard, a ceiling-height freestanding mirror.' An à la carte breakfast has 'good' cooked dishes (eg, boiled eggs and soldiers); 'shame about the tea – just a tea bag with hot water'.

6 New Quebec Street
London W1H 7RQ

T: 020-7724 7243
E: reservations@thegrazinggoat.co.uk
W: www.thegrazinggoat.co.uk

BEDROOMS: 8.
OPEN: all year.
FACILITIES: bar, dining room, unsuitable for ♿.
BACKGROUND MUSIC: in bar and dining room.
LOCATION: central, underground Marble Arch.
CHILDREN: all ages welcomed.
DOGS: not allowed.
CREDIT CARDS: Amex, MasterCard, Visa.
PRICES: [2012] room £195–£225, cooked breakfast from £7.50, full alc £48.

SEE ALSO SHORTLIST

MARYLEBONE

Map 2:D4

DURRANTS

César award in 2010

'Pleasingly old-fashioned: the type of personal, slightly eccentric hotel we like.' Praise in 2012 from visitors to the Miller family's conversion of four terraced houses with a Georgian facade, 'a hop and a skip' from Marylebone High Street. 'It did not seem to have changed a bit since our last visit 40 years ago; we mean this as a compliment.' Ian McIntosh is the long-serving manager: the staff are 'very friendly', said a guest who 'enjoyed an excellent last-minute deal on the hotel's website'. Porters take luggage from the taxi to the bedrooms, which vary considerably in size and style (some are 'small and dark'): 'Ours was quiet, well kitted out, with a comfortable bed.' Rooms at the front might suffer from traffic noise in summer when the windows are open. The panelled lounges have leather settees and chairs, original paintings, antiques, prints and engravings. 'We loved the cosy bar with its coal fire.' In the *Grill Room*, Cara Baird is now the chef, cooking a short menu of international dishes. 'We enjoyed the properly cooked breakfast (not the ubiquitous buffet).' (*Robert Cooper, CJ*)

26–32 George Street
London W1H 5BJ

T: 020-7935 8131
F: 020-7487 3510
E: enquiries@durrantshotel.co.uk
W: www.durrantshotel.co.uk

BEDROOMS: 92, 7 on ground floor.
OPEN: all year, restaurant closed 25 Dec evening.
FACILITIES: lifts, ramp, bar, restaurant, lounge, 5 function rooms.
BACKGROUND MUSIC: none.
LOCATION: off Oxford Street, underground Bond Street, Baker Street.
CHILDREN: all ages welcomed.
DOGS: only guide dogs allowed.
CREDIT CARDS: Amex, MasterCard, Visa.
PRICES: [2012] room (*excluding VAT*) from £174, full alc £50 (*excluding 'optional' 12½% service charge*), last-minute website deals, weekend offers.

SEE ALSO SHORTLIST

MORTLAKE

Map 2:D4

THE VICTORIA

Close to East Sheen Common, this pub-with-rooms is liked for the 'nice local atmosphere in a neighbourhood with a pleasant village feel'. It is owned by celebrity chef Paul Merrett and his business partner, Greg Bellamy, who is the manager. Inspectors were impressed with the ethos of the chef, who is an ambassador for Compassion in World Farming, and only uses suppliers 'who take an ethical view'. 'The food is good' in the handsome conservatory restaurant: 'We enjoyed pea soup; a garlic and mushroom risotto; best of all, delicious sliced blood oranges in a Campari sauce.' A garden barbecue menu is available on summer Sunday evenings; meals can be taken on a large terrace. The simple bedrooms, in a separate building reached by a covered walkway, are decorated in cool shades of lilac, biscuit and sea green; they have an 'efficient' shower. Children are positively encouraged, with a jolly menu and a play area with swings and a climbing frame. Mortlake station, ten minutes' walk away, is 25 minutes by train from London Waterloo.

10 West Temple Sheen
London SW14 7RT

T: 020-8876 4238
F: 020-8878 3464
E: bookings@thevictoria.net
W: www.thevictoria.net

BEDROOMS: 7, 3 on ground floor, 1 suitable for ♿.
OPEN: all year.
FACILITIES: bar, restaurant, garden.
BACKGROUND MUSIC: 'easy listening' throughout.
LOCATION: Mortlake (10 mins' walk) to Waterloo/Clapham Jct, car park.
CHILDREN: all ages welcomed.
DOGS: allowed in bar.
CREDIT CARDS: MasterCard, Visa.
PRICES: [2012] B&B (continental) £65–£120 per person (higher in Wimbledon weeks), cooked breakfast from £6.50, full alc £35, special breaks, Christmas/New Year packages.

SEE ALSO SHORTLIST

NOTTING HILL

Map 2:D4

THE PORTOBELLO

In an outwardly anonymous Victorian terrace house on a residential street in Notting Hill, this small, eccentric hotel has 'a real sense of character'. It is owned by Tim and Cathy Herring with partner Johnny Ekperigin (who manages it with Hanna Turner). It remains popular with A-list celebrities who like the combination of eccentricity and discretion. Rooms vary considerably in size and style: regulars recommend the 'special' rooms, which should be 'discussed before booking'. 'Cabins', with a shower room, can be compact; larger rooms are decorated with carpets, plants, unusual fittings. A first-floor room has a balcony overlooking gardens, and a high four-poster bed from Hampton Court Palace, accessible via a step stool; another room has a bay window and, in the bathroom, an antique gold-leaf roll-top bath draped with muslin curtains. Breakfast (with 'freshly squeezed juice, slabs of butter, excellent tea and coffee, but tiny pots of preserves') can be taken in bedrooms or in the garden-facing drawing room. No restaurant (guests get a discount at nearby *Julie's*, under the ownership); a simple room-service menu is available 24 hours a day. More reports, please.

22 Stanley Gardens
London W11 2NG

T: 020-7727 2777
F: 020-7792 9641
E: info@portobellohotel.com
W: www.portobellohotel.com

BEDROOMS: 21 (smoking allowed in 6).
OPEN: all year except 24–28 Dec.
FACILITIES: lift, small bar, foyer/lounge, access to nearby health club, unsuitable for ♿.
BACKGROUND MUSIC: none.
LOCATION: Notting Hill, meter parking, underground Notting Hill Gate.
CHILDREN: all ages welcomed.
DOGS: allowed in bedrooms.
CREDIT CARDS: Amex, MasterCard, Visa.
PRICES: [2012] B&B (continental, *excluding VAT*) £97.50–£160 per person, full alc £25.

SEE ALSO SHORTLIST

SHOREDITCH

Map 2:D4

BOUNDARY

NEW

On a cobbled street in Shoreditch, this Victorian warehouse has been converted by Sir Terence Conran into a café, restaurant, rooftop bar and bedrooms. *Guide* inspectors were 'delighted with the experience' this year. Most of the ground floor is taken up by the *Albion* café, a shop and a bakery. The bedrooms are reached by a 'modest' side entrance with a desk and lifts. 'The staff were charming at all stages.' Each of the rooms has been given bespoke furniture, interesting pieces. 'The British room is a lovely bright space with a high ceiling, original brick pillars and two sash windows facing the street. It was as well thought out as it was stylish. The patchwork bedhead and matching chair came from Squint; a bookcase had interesting design literature; proper hangers in the fitted wardrobes; lighting was excellent; the bathroom was modern and well equipped.' Five suites on the upper floors are on two levels. Hotel guests are given priority seating in the popular café. Breakfast, not included in the rates, is 'not cheap but good fun; interesting cooked dishes, nice tea and coffee'.

2–4 Boundary Street
London E2 7DD

T: 020-7729 1051
F: 020-7729 3061
E: rooms@theboundary.co.uk
W: www.theboundary.co.uk

BEDROOMS: 17.
OPEN: all year.
FACILITIES: lift, restaurant, café, restaurant, rooftop grill and bar.
BACKGROUND MUSIC: in all public areas.
LOCATION: Shoreditch, underground Liverpool Street, Old Street.
CHILDREN: all ages welcomed.
DOGS: not allowed.
CREDIT CARDS: Amex, MasterCard, Visa.
PRICES: [2012] room (*excluding VAT*) £220–£500, set meals (restaurant) £19.50–£24.50, full alc £65.

SEE ALSO SHORTLIST

SOHO

Map 2:D4

DEAN STREET TOWNHOUSE

In a Grade II listed Georgian building (once owned by the Novello family), this hotel and restaurant is part of Nick Jones's Soho House group. Though many of the details are modern, the renovation has given the building a timeless feel. 'It lives up to expectations, with a friendly atmosphere, well-furnished rooms, and excellent food,' said inspectors. Early booking is necessary to secure a table at the busy restaurant, which is next door: it has a 'real buzz'; a wooden floor, a bar running almost the length of the room, red banquettes. The menu is English comfort food: dishes like lemon-soused scallops with fennel; pork faggot, red cabbage, Bramley apple mash. The bedrooms come in four sizes and prices: tiny, small, medium and bigger. A 'tiny' room was 'filled by an enormous bed; best for visitors on the move'; a 'small' room had 'loads of character; a folksy feel with sage-patterned wallpaper and a soft seagrass carpet; a generous selection of extras – earplugs, toothpaste and brush, flip-flops for slippers'. An à la carte breakfast was 'superb'.

69–71 Dean Street
London W1D 3SE

T: 020-7434 1775
E: hotel@deanstreettownhouse.com
W: www.deanstreettownhouse.com

BEDROOMS: 39.
OPEN: all year.
FACILITIES: lifts, lobby, dining room, private dining room suitable for ♿.
BACKGROUND MUSIC: in Reception, dining room.
LOCATION: Soho, underground Piccadilly Circus.
CHILDREN: all ages welcomed.
DOGS: only guide dogs allowed.
CREDIT CARDS: Amex, MasterCard, Visa.
PRICES: [2012] room from £110–£300, breakfast from £5.50, full alc £40, Christmas package.

SEE ALSO SHORTLIST

SOHO

Map 2:D4

HAZLITT'S

César award in 2002

'More like a private club than a hotel', this discreet property, named after the radical essayist who lived here in the 19th century, occupies a group of historic Georgian houses in busy Soho. Guests ring a bell to enter; the 'welcoming' foyer sets the tone with gilt-framed paintings and painted panelled walls. Bedrooms – also with panelled walls – are 'furnished with style': each has either a 17th-century carved oak bed or a Georgian four-poster, antiques, pictures, rugs. Some rooms retain their sloping, creaking floorboards. Inspectors praised the 'superb bedlinen and supremely comfortable mattress', and thoughtful details such as 'proper hangers', though their 'cosy-in-winter' room lacked natural light. Bathrooms have restored fittings; many have a roll-top bath. Breakfast is served in the bedroom or in the library. 'We enjoyed the freshest of squeezed juice, a big bowl of berries, and a delicious bacon panini.' The oak-panelled library has an honesty bar and a fireplace; this is where author guests often leave a signed copy of their work. There is no restaurant, but the room-service menu includes classics such as bangers and mash.

6 Frith Street
London W1D 3JA

T: 020-7434 1771
F: 020-7439 1524
E: reservations@hazlitts.co.uk
W: www.hazlittshotel.com

BEDROOMS: 30, 2 on ground floor.
OPEN: all year.
FACILITIES: lift, 2 sitting rooms, meeting room, unsuitable for ♿.
BACKGROUND MUSIC: none.
LOCATION: Soho (front windows triple glazed, rear rooms quietest), NCP nearby, underground Tottenham Court Road, Leicester Square.
CHILDREN: all ages welcomed.
DOGS: not allowed.
CREDIT CARDS: all major cards.
PRICES: [2012] room (*excluding VAT*) £185–£750, breakfast £11.95.

SEE ALSO SHORTLIST

SOUTH KENSINGTON

Map 2:D4

NUMBER SIXTEEN

César award in 2011

Part of Tim and Kit Kemp's small group of London hotels, this white stucco town house has been given a lively modern look by Mrs Kemp, who was responsible for the interiors. On a tree-lined street (quiet at night) near South Kensington underground station, it is 'handy for just about everything'. The bedrooms, which have bold colours and prints, an oversized headboard, are well equipped: automatic lighting in a large wardrobe; a full-length mirror; 'excellent' reading lights; a writing desk and an iPod docking station; quality bedlinen on a 'supremely comfortable' bed. Downstairs is a 'colourful, modern' drawing room; a well-stocked honesty bar in the library, and a conservatory which opens on to a lush private garden. There is no restaurant, but a room-service menu can be taken in the conservatory or the bedroom. In warm weather drinks and afternoon tea are served alfresco. Breakfast, normally charged extra, can be continental, 'healthy' or a choice of cooked dishes. Families of 'all shapes and sizes' are welcomed: children have their own menu, bathrobe and toiletries; babysitting can be arranged.

16 Sumner Place
London SW7 3EG

T: 020-7589 5232
F: 020-7584 8615
E: sixteen@firmdale.com
W: www.numbersixteenhotel.co.uk

BEDROOMS: 42, 5 on ground floor.
OPEN: all year.
FACILITIES: drawing room, library, conservatory, civil wedding licence, garden.
BACKGROUND MUSIC: none.
LOCATION: Kensington, underground South Kensington.
CHILDREN: all ages welcomed.
DOGS: not allowed.
CREDIT CARDS: all major cards.
PRICES: [2012] room (*excluding VAT*) £140–£300, breakfast £18–£24.50, special offers, Christmas/New Year packages.

SEE ALSO SHORTLIST

STRAND

Map 2:D4

ONE ALDWYCH

César award in 2005

'Friendly' and 'accommodating' staff are consistently praised at this 'cool' hotel opposite Waterloo bridge. The grand Edwardian exterior (the building was once home to the *Morning Post*) opens on to an 'ultra-modern' interior, where vast flower arrangements on Perspex plinths rise into the double-height lobby. The bedrooms have 'excellent beds', 'fantastic pillows'; all the latest technology and free Wi-Fi; Nintendo Wii consoles are available upon request. Housekeeping is commended: 'They came to clean the room three times a day, and, at turn-down, left helpful notes with the next day's weather forecast.' Children are welcomed with child-sized bathrobe and slippers, and an evening treat at turn-down. Two restaurants: the informal *Indigo*, on a balcony, serves modern European dishes (perhaps tempura of soft-shell crab, grilled scallop, saffron-cured sea bass); *Axis*, on the lower ground floor, which was being given a new look and a fresh menu as the *Guide* went to press. Eco-friendly policies are followed throughout. (*BL, and others*)

1 Aldwych
London WC2B 4BZ

T: 020-7300 1000
F: 020-7300 0501
E: reservations@onealdwych.com
W: www.onealdwych.com

BEDROOMS: 105, 6 suitable for ♿.
OPEN: all year, *Axis* closed Sun/Mon.
FACILITIES: lifts, 2 bars (live DJ Sat evening), 2 restaurants, function facilities, screening room, health club (18-metre swimming pool, spa, sauna, gym), civil wedding licence.
BACKGROUND MUSIC: in *Axis*, lobby bar.
LOCATION: Strand (windows triple glazed), valet parking, underground Covent Garden, Charing Cross, Waterloo.
CHILDREN: all ages welcomed.
DOGS: only guide dogs allowed.
CREDIT CARDS: all major cards.
PRICES: [2012] rooms and suites (*excluding VAT*) £250–£1,430, breakfast £23, pre- and post-theatre menu £18.75–£21.75, Christmas/New Year packages.

SEE ALSO SHORTLIST

VICTORIA

Map 2:D4

THE GORING

César award in 1994

Now in its second century, this grande dame – in 1910 the first hotel in the world to have private bathrooms – is loved for its air of Englishness. Near Victoria Station and Buckingham Palace (as royal watchers know), it is still a family-run concern (chief executive Jeremy Goring is the fourth generation to be in charge). Many of the staff are long serving: bowler-hatted doorman Peter Sweeney has greeted guests for almost 50 years. David Morgan-Hewitt is the managing director. Opulent, individually designed bedrooms have rich fabrics and bespoke furnishings; many overlook the private garden (some have a private terrace). Six 'silk' rooms have hand-woven Gainsborough silk wall coverings based on designs in British palaces; two have wardrobes that open to reveal hand-painted silk birds within. The royal suite occupies the entire top floor. In the David Linley-designed dining room, which has glass chandeliers by Swarovski, chef Derek Quelch serves classic dishes, eg, Scottish lobster omelette; beef Wellington served from the trolley. Breakfast has a selection of fruit; kippers among the cooked dishes.

Beeston Place
Grosvenor Gardens
London SW1W 0JW

T: 020-7396 9000
F: 020-7834 4393
E: reception@thegoring.com
W: www.thegoring.com

BEDROOMS: 69, 2 suitable for ♿, 35 that allow smoking.
OPEN: all year.
FACILITIES: lifts, ramps, lounge bar, terrace room, restaurant, function facilities, civil wedding licence.
BACKGROUND MUSIC: none.
LOCATION: near Victoria Station, garage, mews parking, underground Victoria.
CHILDREN: all ages welcomed.
DOGS: not allowed.
CREDIT CARDS: all major cards.
PRICES: [2012] room (*excluding VAT*) £239–£5,250, breakfast from £20, set lunch £36.00, set dinner £48.50, full alc £80, Christmas/New Year packages.

SEE ALSO SHORTLIST

WANDSWORTH

Map 2:D4

THE ALMA

Behind a popular Victorian pub, this old metalworks has been turned by Young's Brewery into a striking modern hotel. The brick and glass building, with its own entrance down a cobbled alley, has a smart lobby with a seating area; 'we were greeted whenever we passed,' said inspectors. The spacious bedrooms have bold wallpapers, bespoke furniture. 'Our room was thoughtfully put together with high-quality fittings; good reading lights and switches by the bed; London-related art on the walls. We were particularly impressed with our huge bathroom, with bath and separate walk-in shower.' Three top-floor rooms have floor-to-ceiling windows, views of the streets around; a suite (two bedrooms and two bathrooms) has a private garden with outdoor seating. Original features (a plasterwork frieze, mosaics) have been restored in the pub. In the separate dining area, chef Martin Nugent serves 'typical gastropub fare', perhaps Parma ham with quail's egg salad; lamb's liver and mash, bacon and mushroom jus. Breakfast is served until 11 am at weekends. No parking: visitors are encouraged to travel by train (15 minutes to Waterloo from the nearby station).

499 Old York Road
Wandsworth
London SW18 1TF

T: 020-8870 2537
E: alma@youngs.co.uk
W: www.thealma.co.uk

BEDROOMS: 23, 2 on ground floor suitable for ♿.
OPEN: all year.
FACILITIES: bar, restaurant, function room, civil wedding licence.
BACKGROUND MUSIC: in bar and restaurant.
LOCATION: by Wandsworth Town railway station.
CHILDREN: all ages welcomed.
DOGS: not allowed in bedrooms or restaurant.
CREDIT CARDS: all major cards.
PRICES: [2012] B&B £69.50–£129 per person, full alc £35.

SEE ALSO SHORTLIST

ENGLAND

Knaresborough, North Yorkshire

ABBOTSBURY Dorset

Map 1:D6

THE ABBEY HOUSE

In gardens with wide lawns which slope down to a millpond ('very quiet, no traffic noise'), Jonathan and Maureen Cooke's guest house 'has a wonderful outlook' over the fragments of an 11th-century abbey. The house (itself 14th-century) has much character: flagstone floors, panelled doors, original windows. The decor is traditional – lots of chintz and knick-knacks. Visitors praise the 'very professional' outlook of the owners. Bedrooms vary in size and style: St Catherine has a half-tester bed and is south-facing, with views of the garden; Abbot, an attic room, has a beamed sloping ceiling, a king-size brass and iron bed, and a view of St Catherine's chapel. Monks has a private bathroom across the corridor. 'Rooms were very comfortable.' The 'excellent' breakfast, served in a room believed to have been the abbey infirmary, has fruit juices, home-made muesli; cooked dishes include free-range eggs, smoked haddock and grilled kippers. In summer, light lunches and cream teas are served in the garden. The village is noted for its ancient swannery and subtropical gardens. More reports, please.

Church Street
Abbotsbury DT3 4JJ

T: 01305-871330
E: info@theabbeyhouse.co.uk
W: www.theabbeyhouse.co.uk

BEDROOMS: 5.
OPEN: all year, tea room open for lunches Apr–Sept, dinners for house parties only.
FACILITIES: reception, lounge, breakfast/tea room, 1½-acre garden (stage for opera), sea 15 mins' walk, unsuitable for ♿.
BACKGROUND MUSIC: classical, sometimes.
LOCATION: village centre.
CHILDREN: not under 12.
DOGS: not allowed.
CREDIT CARDS: none.
PRICES: B&B £35–£60 per person, New Year package, 1-night bookings sometimes refused.

ALDEBURGH Suffolk

Map 2:C6

THE WENTWORTH

A stone's throw from the shingle beach in this musical town on the Suffolk coast, this traditional hotel has been owned by the Pritt family since 1920. Michael Pritt, who has been in charge since 1975, 'keeps a personal eye on what is happening and is usually around', say visitors. There has been much renovation: the reception area now has new wallpaper and a hand-built desk; the conservatory lounge, which has new sofas and Lloyd Loom chairs, has been arranged to allow light meals to be taken. The seven bedrooms in *Darfield House* have been given light-oak fitted furniture; neutral colours; a modern bathroom. Binoculars are provided in those bedrooms in the main house which have sea views. 'It may have been modernised but old-fashioned aspects remain,' is a comment. 'Housekeeping was immaculate in our lovely spacious room.' In the 'well-managed' dining room, there are mixed reports on the cooking of chef Tim Keeble. One visitor thought the food had 'improved'; another was disappointed. The fresh fish is recommended. (*Simon Rodway, Jennifer Davis*)

25% DISCOUNT VOUCHERS

Wentworth Road
Aldeburgh IP15 5BD

T: 01728-452312
F: 01728-454343
E: stay@wentworth-aldeburgh.co.uk
W: www.wentworth-aldeburgh.com

BEDROOMS: 35, 7 in *Darfield House* opposite, 5 on ground floor, 1 suitable for ♿.

OPEN: all year except possibly short period Jan.

FACILITIES: ramps, 2 lounges, bar, restaurant, private dining room, conference room, 2 terrace gardens, shingle beach 200 yds.

BACKGROUND MUSIC: none.

LOCATION: seafront, 5 mins' walk from centre.

CHILDREN: all ages welcomed.

DOGS: not allowed in restaurant.

CREDIT CARDS: all major cards.

PRICES: B&B £62–£139 per person, D,B&B £74–£152, set dinner £24, weekend/midweek breaks, Christmas/New Year packages, 1-night bookings refused Sat.

SEE ALSO SHORTLIST

ALKHAM Kent

Map 2:D5

THE MARQUIS AT ALKHAM

In a pretty village at the southern end of the Kent Downs, this 200-year-old inn has been turned into a 'busy, trendy' restaurant-with-rooms. 'It is professional and well run,' says a visitor in 2012. Modern fabrics, exposed brickwork, wooden flooring give a contemporary touch to the interiors of the old building. All bedrooms have views across the Alkham valley, a designated area of outstanding natural beauty. They have a Nespresso coffee machine, flat-screen TV and DVD-player; a monsoon shower in the bathroom. The Sir Thomas Berridge Suite has a black-and-yellow colour scheme, floor-to-ceiling windows. 'Our spotless room was small but well equipped, and it had a big shower.' Rooms at the back are 'quieter'. The chef, Charles Lakin, promises 'produce from the valley and the best of the forager's basket' for his modern menus. 'Good modern cooking, small portions.' Breakfast has croissants and home-made jam, 'beautifully presented cooked dishes'. Close to Dover and the Channel Tunnel, the *Marquis* is well placed for an overnight break for travellers to and from the Continent. (*JS and F Waters*)

25% DISCOUNT VOUCHERS

Alkham Valley Road
Alkham
CT15 7DF

T: 01304-873410
F: 01304-873418
E: reception@themarquisatalkham.co.uk
W: www.themarquisatalkham.co.uk

BEDROOMS: 10, 3 in cottages 3 mins' drive away.

OPEN: all year, restaurant closed Mon lunch.

FACILITIES: bar, lounge, dining room, civil wedding licence, small garden.

BACKGROUND MUSIC: ambient in public areas.

LOCATION: 4 miles W of Dover.

CHILDREN: all ages welcomed, not under 8 in restaurant after 6 pm.

DOGS: not allowed.

CREDIT CARDS: Amex, MasterCard, Visa.

PRICES: [2012] B&B £49–£125 per person, D,B&B £79–£199, full alc £57.50, special breaks, Christmas/New Year packages.

ALSTON Cumbria

Map 4:B3

LOVELADY SHIELD

'The setting is lovely; the local staff were pleasant and homely,' say visitors this year to Peter and Marie Haynes's country hotel. It stands on the site of a 13th-century convent on the banks of the River Nent. There are unrestricted views of the countryside from the large gardens of the white-fronted Georgian building, which is approached by a tree-lined drive. A visitor, who was unimpressed by the red carpet in the hallway, liked her 'beautiful' bedroom: 'The curtains were sumptuous and tasteful. Excellent tea- and coffee-making facilities, including a cafetière.' In the dining room, chef Barrie Garton serves 'well-presented and interesting' dishes on a seasonal menu. His style is British 'with continental influences', perhaps truffled goat's cheese, wild mushrooms, pine nut and nettle salad; duo of Alston spring lamb, pomme purée, spinach and girolles. Recommended wines accompany a seven-course gourmet menu. The lounge and bar have a traditional country house decor ('no sign of trendy designer bleak'). Breakfast is 'excellent, with lots of choice'. There is good walking on marked footpaths from the door. 'Good value.' (*Barbara Watkinson*)

25% DISCOUNT VOUCHERS

Lovelady Lane
nr Alston CA9 3LX

T: 01434-381203
F: 01434-381515
E: enquiries@lovelady.co.uk
W: www.lovelady.co.uk

BEDROOMS: 12.
OPEN: all year.
FACILITIES: 2 lounges, bar, restaurant, conference facilities, civil wedding licence, 2-acre grounds (river, fishing, croquet, woodland walks), unsuitable for ♿.
BACKGROUND MUSIC: 'definitely not'.
LOCATION: 2 miles N of Alston on A689.
CHILDREN: all ages welcomed.
DOGS: not allowed in public rooms.
CREDIT CARDS: Amex, MasterCard, Visa.
PRICES: B&B £55–£110 per person, D,B&B £85–£140, set dinner £27.50–£32, special breaks, Christmas/New Year packages.

AMBLESIDE Cumbria

Map 4: inset C2

THE REGENT

Offering 'exceedingly good value', Christine Hewitt's white-fronted, creeper-clad lakeside hotel is managed by her son, Andrew. 'The food is first class and the service is excellent,' says a visitor. This year the bar and lounges have been redecorated. In the airy split-level restaurant, chef John Mathers serves dishes like Morecambe Bay shrimps with poached egg; confit shin of fell-bred beef, creamy mash. The bedrooms vary considerably in size: rooms with direct access to the courtyard are suitable for guests with children or dogs. Each of the five first-floor garden rooms ('which feel more like a suite') has a private balcony. The nautically themed Sail Loft has a terrace with views of Waterhead Bay and Lake Windermere. Breakfast, which is served from 8 am until noon, is a generous affair: on a buffet table is a selection of fruit, yogurts, and porridge with heather honey and cream. The cooked menu has a dozen choices (including Devereau kippers and 'notable' scrambled eggs). The swimming pool has been closed because of a rise in the lake's water table. (*PC, and others*)

25% DISCOUNT VOUCHERS

Waterhead Bay
Ambleside LA22 0ES

T: 015394-32254
F: 015394-31474
E: info@regentlakes.co.uk
W: www.regentlakes.co.uk

BEDROOMS: 30, 10 in courtyard, 5 in garden, 7 on ground floor.
OPEN: all year, except Christmas.
FACILITIES: ramp, lounge, sun lounge, bar, restaurant, courtyard, ¼-acre garden, on Lake Windermere.
BACKGROUND MUSIC: classical/modern in public rooms.
LOCATION: on A591, S of centre, at Waterhead Bay.
CHILDREN: all ages welcomed.
DOGS: not allowed in public rooms.
CREDIT CARDS: MasterCard, Visa.
PRICES: [2012] B&B £52–£79 per person, D,B&B £79–£114, full alc £42.95, website offers, New Year package.

SEE ALSO SHORTLIST

AMBLESIDE Cumbria

Map 4: inset C2

ROTHAY MANOR

César award in 1992

'The chief glory of *Rothay Manor* is the staff,' says a visitor in 2012 to the Nixon family's traditional hotel near the head of Lake Windermere. 'Under the relaxed supervision of the owner, Nigel Nixon, every one of them evinces a real pleasure in helping guests.' The cooking of the long-serving chef, Jane Binns, is also praised this year: 'The food is simply cooked but very attractively served: we particularly enjoyed plaice stuffed with salmon mousseline; guineafowl, lamb and mallard were also excellent.' The bedrooms are spacious: 'Our front-facing room, recently decorated, was a decent size and met all our needs.' 'Ours had a balcony on which I spent many happy hours reading.' The bar, lounge and main dining room are 'a pleasure to use'; afternoon tea, 'a favourite treat for families in the area, is wonderfully relaxing in the garden in fine weather'. Breakfast 'sets you up for the whole day'. Children are welcomed (they have their own menu in a family dining room). 'Disabled guests are well and unobtrusively looked after.' (*Michael Barnett, Margaret Box, Anthony Bradbury*)

25% DISCOUNT VOUCHERS

Rothay Bridge
Ambleside LA22 0EH

T: 015394-33605
F: 015394-33607
E: hotel@rothaymanor.co.uk
W: www.rothaymanor.co.uk

BEDROOMS: 19, 2 in annexe, 2 suitable for ♿.

OPEN: all year except 2–18 Jan.

FACILITIES: ramp, 2 lounges, bar, 2 dining rooms, meeting/conference facilities, 1-acre garden (croquet), free access to local leisure centre.

BACKGROUND MUSIC: no.

LOCATION: ¼ mile SW of Ambleside.

CHILDREN: all ages welcomed.

DOGS: not allowed.

CREDIT CARDS: Amex, MasterCard, Visa.

PRICES: [2012] B&B £82.50–£117.50 per person, D,B&B £112.50–£152.50, set dinner £39, special breaks, Christmas/New Year packages, 1-night bookings refused Sat.

SEE ALSO SHORTLIST

AMPLEFORTH North Yorkshire

Map 4:D4

SHALLOWDALE HOUSE

César award in 2005

On a sheltered south-facing hillside on the edge of the North York Moors national park, this small guest house has spectacular views across a valley to the Howardian hills. It is run in personal style by Phillip Gill and Anton van der Horst, who 'may be enormously professional but know how to treat their guests as if they are friends rather than customers'. They have many returning visitors: 'Everyone we have introduced to *Shallowdale* seems to share our enthusiasm.' There are picture windows in the three first-floor bedrooms, which have large bed, good storage, and binoculars. Two rooms are en suite, one has a private bathroom across the corridor. 'Housekeeping is perfect.' There is a drawing room on the ground floor and a sitting room on the first floor. In summer, afternoon tea can be taken on a terrace in front of the house. A four-course no-choice dinner is taken at 7.30 pm; the menu (discussed in advance) might include duck breasts with endives and Marsala. The 'best cooked breakfasts we know' have Whitby kippers, Cumbrian dry-cured bacon, home-made preserves. (*Andrew Warren, Richard Creed*)

West End, Ampleforth
nr York, YO62 4DY

T: 01439-788325
F: 01439-788885
E: stay@shallowdalehouse.co.uk
W: www.shallowdalehouse.co.uk

BEDROOMS: 3.
OPEN: all year except Christmas/New Year, occasionally at other times.
FACILITIES: drawing room, sitting room, dining room, 2½-acre grounds, unsuitable for ♿.
BACKGROUND MUSIC: none.
LOCATION: edge of village.
CHILDREN: not under 12.
DOGS: not allowed.
CREDIT CARDS: MasterCard, Visa.
PRICES: B&B £52–£65 per person, set dinner £39.50, 1-night bookings occasionally refused weekends.

ARLINGHAM Gloucestershire

Map 3:D5

THE OLD PASSAGE

In an 'idyllic' position on an ox-bow bend of the River Severn, this old green-painted inn is run as a restaurant-with-rooms by Sally Pearce. It is well placed for watching the Severn Bore; special breakfasts and dinners are held to coincide with the passage of the wave upstream. The bedrooms, each named after a fish, have a 'grandstand view of the river'. 'Ours, Tuna, was a smallish, pretty room with double-aspect windows, an unfussy decor, and a light and pleasing bathroom.' Downstairs, most of the space is given over to 'well-kept' dining areas where local artwork is displayed. The chef, Mark Redwood, has a classic style (with innovative touches); seafood is a speciality of his menus, which might include potted shrimps with coriander, pickled cucumber salad; whole roasted lemon sole, new potatoes and curly kale. To drink: 'We chose the reasonably priced English house wine from the nearby Three Choirs Vineyards.' Breakfast has porridge, boiled eggs with sourdough soldiers, fruit, muesli, toast and preserves. Alternatives, such as wild mushrooms with Parmesan on toast, are available at an extra cost. More reports, please.

25% DISCOUNT VOUCHERS

Passage Road
Arlingham GL2 7JR

T: 01452-740547
E: oldpassage@btconnect.com
W: www.theoldpassage.com

BEDROOMS: 3.

OPEN: all year except 25/26 Dec, restaurant closed Sun night/Mon, open for lunch only 28 Dec–1 Jan.

FACILITIES: sitting room, restaurant, 2-acre garden, only restaurant suitable for ♿.

BACKGROUND MUSIC: low-key in restaurant.

LOCATION: ¼ mile W of Arlingham.

CHILDREN: all ages welcomed (lunch time only in restaurant).

DOGS: allowed by arrangement, not in restaurant.

CREDIT CARDS: Amex, MasterCard, Visa.

PRICES: [2012] B&B £40–£65 per person, full alc £50.

ARUNDEL West Sussex

Map 2:E3

THE TOWN HOUSE

At the top of the steep High Street, opposite Arundel Castle, owner/chef Lee Williams runs this restaurant-with-rooms with his wife, Katie. They and their staff are 'friendly and accommodating', and the cooking is 'excellent', says one visitor. A surprising feature of the Grade II listed Regency building is a 16th-century carved and gilded walnut-panelled ceiling, which was imported from Italy. The atmosphere, however, is informal: 'We aim to attract a relaxed clientele,' say the Williamses; there is 'no dress code; stuffiness is taboo'. Mr Williams uses seasonal and local produce for his modern menus, which have five choices for each course, eg, wild mushroom soup, truffle cheese; fillet of lamb, pesto mousse, dauphinoise potato. The four bedrooms (two on the first floor, two on the second) are individually furnished; one has a balcony overlooking the castle, two have a four-poster bed. Breakfast is continental or full English; 'good bacon and poached eggs'; bread is home baked. No lounge, so 'best for a short stay'. Arundel is an attractive Georgian market town with narrow streets; visits to the castle and the Wildfowl & Wetlands Trust sanctuary are recommended.

25% DISCOUNT VOUCHERS

65 High Street
Arundel BN18 9AJ

T: 01903-883847
E: enquiries@thetownhouse.co.uk
W: www.thetownhouse.co.uk

BEDROOMS: 4.
OPEN: all year except 25/26 Dec, 1 Jan, 2 weeks Easter, 2 weeks Oct, restaurant closed Sun/Mon.
FACILITIES: restaurant, unsuitable for ♿.
BACKGROUND MUSIC: 'easy listening' in restaurant.
LOCATION: top end of High Street.
CHILDREN: all ages welcomed.
DOGS: not allowed.
CREDIT CARDS: Diners, MasterCard, Visa.
PRICES: [2012] B&B £47.50–£65 per person, D,B&B (midweek) £67.50–£85, set dinner £23.50–£29.00, 1-night bookings refused weekends in high season.

SEE ALSO SHORTLIST

ASHWATER Devon

Map 1:C3

BLAGDON MANOR

César award in 2006

'No detail has been missed by Liz and Steve Morey, who have put a lot of thought into making their small restaurant-with-rooms perfect. We could not fault anything.' A former hotelier's praise this year for this ever-popular Grade II listed mansion in countryside with panoramic views towards Dartmoor. 'They keep high standards, yet the manor maintains its air of complete relaxation,' said earlier visitors. Mr Moray is the acclaimed chef, serving 'exquisite' modern dishes, eg, galantine of rabbit and pigeon, sesame-coated chicken wings, date sauce; pan-fried sea bass, chargrilled courgettes, olives and tiger prawns. 'We enjoyed seven first-class fish dishes in three days. Service is well judged; times are staggered at dinner to avoid delays.' The house has many original features (oak beams, slate flagstones, walk-in fireplaces). The bedrooms, individually decorated, vary in size and view. 'Our very comfortable room had everything we needed, from sherry, chocolates and fruit to a clothes brush, and candle and matches in case of a power cut.' Dogs are welcomed. 'Country walks are on their doorstep and the coast is not far away.' (*Sue Lyons, GC*)

25% DISCOUNT VOUCHERS

Ashwater EX21 5DF

T: 01409-211224
E: stay@blagdon.com
W: www.blagdon.com

BEDROOMS: 7.

OPEN: all year Wed–Sun, except Jan.

FACILITIES: ramps, lounge, library, snug, bar, conservatory, restaurant, private dining room, 20-acre grounds (3-acre gardens, croquet, giant chess, gazebo, pond), unsuitable for ♿.

BACKGROUND MUSIC: none.

LOCATION: 8 miles NE of Launceston.

CHILDREN: not under 12.

DOGS: not allowed in restaurant, £8.50 charged per night.

CREDIT CARDS: MasterCard, Visa.

PRICES: [2012] B&B £72.50–£102.50 per person, set dinner £55–£60, midweek winter breaks, 1-night bookings refused Christmas.

AUSTWICK North Yorkshire

Map 4:D3

AUSTWICK HALL

'A lovely old house lovingly brought back to life', this Elizabethan manor is run as a small hotel by Michael Pearson and Eric Culley. 'They are great company; their enthusiasm for their home is obvious,' says a visitor in 2012. Inspectors were impressed with the location (a village on the edge of the Yorkshire Dales) and the 'interesting' interiors. The house is filled with antiques, family heirlooms and ethnic artwork collected on the owners' travels. A huge entrance hall has a central staircase which opens on to two landings; a modern stained-glass window contributes to the 'wow factor'. There are original features in the bedrooms: 'Eric showed us to a grand room which had an equally grand bathroom.' All rooms are provided with complimentary wine, teas and coffee; free Wi-Fi. In a 'beautiful' Regency-panelled dining room, Mr Pearson serves a short seasonal menu (two choices for each course), which might include wild mushrooms pan-fried with garlic; rack of lamb, hot mint sauce. 'Good home-like cooking; we enjoyed everything we were given.' Breakfast is a 'relaxed affair from 9 am'. (*Jennifer Davis, and others*)

Townhead Lane
Austwick LA2 8BS

T: 01524-251794
E: austwickhall@austwick.org
W: www.austwickhall.co.uk

BEDROOMS: 5.
OPEN: all year except 3–31 Jan.
FACILITIES: hall, sitting room, drawing room, dining room, civil wedding licence, 13-acre gardens, unsuitable for ♿.
BACKGROUND MUSIC: none.
LOCATION: edge of village.
CHILDREN: not under 16.
DOGS: not allowed.
CREDIT CARDS: MasterCard, Visa.
PRICES: [2012] B&B £77.50–£92.50 per person, D,B&B £101.50–£116.50, set menus £29–£36, New Year package, 1-night bookings refused weekends.

AUSTWICK North Yorkshire

Map 4:D3

THE TRADDOCK

In a charming village in the Yorkshire Dales, this 'lovely old manor house' is run as a small, 'friendly' hotel by the Reynolds family. 'Delightful: lots of welcoming public rooms with deep sofas to slump into,' says a returning visitor in 2012. 'The staff are efficient as well as friendly; the cooking is of a high standard.' The bedrooms are individually styled: 'Mine had attractive traditional furnishings, lots of character; nice touches like home-made shortbread, fruit and a Thermos of cold milk. The spotless bathroom had fluffy towels.' Four rooms have been refurbished this year. There are tables and chairs in the pretty garden. The chef, John Pratt, sources local produce for his modern British dishes (perhaps twice-baked soufflé of Whitby crab; slow-roasted shoulder of sucking pig). 'Very well cooked, using flavourful local produce; those with a big appetite won't be disappointed,' is one comment (a dissenter was less keen). The 'fantastic' breakfast has freshly baked bread, made-to-order smoothies; 'an enormous full English with lots of tastes and flavour'. Many visitors come for the excellent walking from the door (packed lunches are provided). (*Jim Grover, and others*)

25% DISCOUNT VOUCHERS

Austwick, Settle
LA2 8BY

T: 01524-251224
F: 01524-251796
E: info@austwicktraddock.co.uk
W: www.thetraddock.co.uk

BEDROOMS: 12, 1 on ground floor.
OPEN: all year.
FACILITIES: 3 lounges, bar, 2 dining rooms, function facilities, 1½-acre grounds (sun deck), only public rooms accessible to ♿.
BACKGROUND MUSIC: in 2 lounges and dining rooms.
LOCATION: 4 miles NW of Settle, train Settle, bus.
CHILDREN: all ages welcomed.
DOGS: allowed in bedrooms, public rooms on lead, not in restaurant.
CREDIT CARDS: MasterCard, Visa.
PRICES: [2012] B&B £45–£95 per person, D,B&B £75–£125, full alc £52, Christmas/New Year packages, 1-night bookings refused weekends in season.

AYLESBURY Buckinghamshire

Map 2:C3

HARTWELL HOUSE

César award in 1997

Set in 'beautiful grounds', this stately home is run by Richard Broyd's Historic House Hotels for the National Trust; Jonathan Thompson is the long-serving manager. It is 'highly recommended' by a visitor this year: 'The bedrooms are comfortable and well equipped; the four drawing rooms are sumptuous, and the food is excellent.' An earlier comment: 'The staff, from the manager down, were charming.' The elegant public rooms have fine plasterwork, marble fireplaces, many antiques. A staircase with Jacobean carvings leads to 30 bedrooms in the main house ('ours was the size of a tennis court'). Some of the rooms in a converted stable block are split-level. The chef, Daniel Richardson, serves British dishes in the candlelit dining room, eg, pork and sage risotto; paupiette of plaice with salmon mousse. The only let-down: 'Flabby toast at breakfast.' Various treatments are available in a spa which has a 'lovely' swimming pool. 'Good snack lunches' and dinner can be taken in the informal spa café/bar. *Middlethorpe Hall*, York, *Bodysgallen Hall*, Llandudno, Wales (see entries) are also owned by the National Trust. (*Zara Elliott*)

25% DISCOUNT VOUCHERS

Oxford Road
nr Aylesbury HP17 8NR

T: 01296-747444
F: 01296-747450
E: info@hartwell-house.com
W: www.hartwell-house.com

BEDROOMS: 46, 16 in stable block, some on ground floor, 2 suitable for ♿.

OPEN: all year.

FACILITIES: lift, ramps, 4 drawing rooms, bar, 3 dining rooms, conference facilities, civil wedding licence, spa (swimming pool, 8 by 16 metres), 90-acre grounds (tennis).

BACKGROUND MUSIC: none.

LOCATION: 2 miles W of Aylesbury.

CHILDREN: not under 4.

DOGS: allowed in some bedrooms.

CREDIT CARDS: Amex, MasterCard, Visa.

PRICES: [to 31 Mar 2013] B&B £102.50–£350 per person, D,B&B from £125, set dinner £23.75, full alc £52, special breaks, Christmas/New Year packages.

BABBACOMBE Devon

Map 1:D5

THE CARY ARMS

'We had an excellent welcome from the young staff,' say visitors this year to Lana de Savary's nautically themed hotel. It sits below a steep, sheltered hillside overlooking a wide bay. All bedrooms have sea views; some have a terrace or balcony. 'We had a lovely large room with light wood-panelled walls, New England-style, and a big, comfy bed; a stick of rock left on each pillow during turn-down; a second bedside light would have been useful.' The bar/dining area has stone walls, wood and slate floor, wooden tables in small alcoves; a conservatory dining area section. Chef Ben Kingdon's 'good gastropub food' is served by candlelight. 'We ate seared scallops in chilli jam with pea shoots, prawn and crayfish cocktail with pickled lemons, garlic-infused lamb (cooked perfectly pink as requested), and sea bass with caper sauce.' The 'very good' breakfast has fruit, cereals and yogurts, ham cut from the bone; many cooked options; 'real toast, home-made marmalade, and slabs of butter'. The garden overlooks the bay, beach and quay; there is alfresco dining in warm months. (*Carol Jackson*)

Beach Road
Babbacombe TQ1 3LX

T: 01803-327110
F: 01803-323221
E: enquiries@caryarms.co.uk
W: www.caryarms.co.uk

BEDROOMS: 8, 2 on ground floor.
OPEN: all year.
FACILITIES: lounge, bar, restaurant, conservatory, civil wedding licence, garden, terrace, treatment room.
BACKGROUND MUSIC: radio in bar.
LOCATION: by beach.
CHILDREN: all ages welcomed.
DOGS: not allowed in conservatory.
CREDIT CARDS: Amex, MasterCard, Visa.
PRICES: [2012] B&B £80–£135 per person, full alc £38, Christmas/New Year packages, 1-night bookings refused weekends.

BARNSLEY Gloucestershire

Map 3:E6

BARNSLEY HOUSE

In a Cotswold village, this Grade II listed William and Mary house is run as a luxury hotel by the owners of *Calcot Manor*, Tetbury (see entry); it is managed by Michele Mella. Once the home of gardener Rosemary Verey and her family, it has been sensitively restored as a 'lusciously peaceful, plumply upholstered haven'. The *Potager* restaurant has been given a facelift this year, creating a more contemporary look, with natural textures and earthy tones to reflect the garden, which can be seen from the windows. Graham Grafton, the chef, serves modern dishes, using vegetables and herbs from the gardens. Typical dishes: vegetable tempura with Thai dipping sauce; Vincisgrassi (baked pasta with Parma ham, porcini and truffles from an 18th-century recipe). The bedrooms (six are in buildings in the garden and six in a converted stableyard) are individually decorated in a minimalist style with splashes of colour. Several have a private garden or terrace. The garden has been restored, retaining Rosemary Verey's signature informality. A wilderness path 'makes a tranquil route' to the spa, which has a heated outdoor hydrotherapy pool.

Barnsley, nr Cirencester
GL7 5EE

T: 01285-740000
F: 01285-740925
E: reception@barnsleyhouse.com
W: www.barnsleyhouse.com

BEDROOMS: 18, 6 in stableyard, 5 in courtyard, 1 in cottage, 1 on ground floor.

OPEN: all year.

FACILITIES: lounge, bar, restaurant, meeting room, civil wedding licence, terrace, 11-acre garden (spa), unsuitable for ♿.

BACKGROUND MUSIC: in restaurant.

LOCATION: 5 miles NE of Cirencester.

CHILDREN: not under 12 in restaurant, not under 14 in spa.

DOGS: allowed in stableyard rooms, not in grounds.

CREDIT CARDS: all major cards.

PRICES: [2012] B&B £137.50–£260 per person, full alc £50, special breaks, Christmas/New Year packages, 1-night bookings sometimes refused Fri/Sat.

SEE ALSO SHORTLIST

BARWICK Somerset

Map 1:C6

LITTLE BARWICK HOUSE

César award in 2002

'As good as ever; it still sets the standard.' Praise from a visitor returning this year to Tim and Emma Ford's restaurant-with-rooms, a listed Georgian dower house close to the Somerset/ Dorset border. 'The personable Emma' runs front-of-house with two long-serving assistants; her husband is the much-admired chef; their teenage sons (Ben and Olly) help in the kitchen. The 'welcoming and comfortable ambience and attentive service' are often praised. Arriving visitors are served tea and cake in a drawing room. In the restaurant, Mr Ford sources ingredients locally for his 'short but enticing' seasonal menu of 'well-presented' modern English dishes, which might include parsley and ham hock soup; roasted saddle of wild roe deer. Emma Ford has 'an excellent knowledge' of her wine list. The bedrooms vary in size (some are small). 'It's the touches that go to make the whole: complimentary mineral water; fresh milk with the tea and coffee; checking whether you prefer duvet or blankets on your bed; turn-down in the evening.' A 'first-class' breakfast has a wide choice of cooked dishes. (*Mary Blaxall*)

25% DISCOUNT VOUCHERS

Barwick, nr Yeovil
BA22 9TD

T: 01935-423902
F: 01935-420908
E: reservations@barwick7.fsnet.co.uk
W: www.littlebarwickhouse.co.uk

BEDROOMS: 6.

OPEN: all year except Christmas–end Jan, restaurant closed Sun evenings, midday on Mon and Tues.

FACILITIES: ramp, 2 lounges, restaurant, conservatory, 3½-acre garden (terrace, paddock), unsuitable for ♿.

BACKGROUND MUSIC: none.

LOCATION: ¾ mile outside Yeovil.

CHILDREN: not under 5.

DOGS: allowed in public rooms subject to other guests' approval.

CREDIT CARDS: MasterCard, Visa.

PRICES: [2012] B&B £70–£92.50 per person, D,B&B £100–£140, set dinner £37.95–£43.95, 2-night breaks, 1-night bookings sometimes refused.

BASLOW Derbyshire

Map 3:A6

THE CAVENDISH

César award in 2002

The staff 'go out of their way to be helpful' at this traditional country hotel on the Chatsworth estate, which is run for the Devonshire trustees by Eric Marsh and Philip Joseph (the manager). A visitor with mobility problems was given 'unobtrusive support'. Mr Marsh, who also owns *The George Hotel*, Hathersage (see entry), 'remains the perfect host and is there for long hours'. The entrance hall and gallery have 'a smart design that fits the era'; huge settees, upholstered chairs, antique desks. Mike Thompson is now the chef, cooking modern dishes and 'revised classics' for the *Gallery* restaurant and the conservatory *Garden Room*. 'Our meals were very satisfactory,' says a returning visitor. 'An excellent country terrine came with a delicious chutney and toasted fruit loaf; Cornish turbot was moist and fresh.' The hotel is on a busy road but the bedrooms are at the back. 'Our room, though not large, was delightful, with all that one needed.' Breakfast has 'a good selection of prepared fruits, decent juices, pastry and toast'; cooked dishes are 'substantial'. (*Padi Howard, Susan Wilmington, Donald Reid*)

Church Lane
Baslow DE45 1SP

T: 01246-582311
F: 01246-582312
E: info@cavendish-hotel.net
W: www.cavendish-hotel.net

BEDROOMS: 24, 2 on ground floor.
OPEN: all year.
FACILITIES: lounge, bar, 2 restaurants, 2 meeting rooms, ½-acre grounds (putting), river fishing nearby.
BACKGROUND MUSIC: classical in *Garden Room* restaurant.
LOCATION: on A619, in Chatsworth grounds.
CHILDREN: all ages welcomed.
DOGS: not allowed.
CREDIT CARDS: all major cards.
PRICES: [2012] room £133–£286, breakfast £9.70–£18.90, set meals £45 (*5% 'service levy' added to all accounts*), midweek breaks, Christmas/New Year packages, 1-night bookings sometimes refused.

BASLOW Derbyshire

Map 3:A6

FISCHER'S BASLOW HALL

César award in 1998

'The welcome is always warm; the food is innovative and the service faultless.' New praise for Max and Susan Fischer's restaurant-with-rooms on the edge of a village near the Chatsworth estate. In the formal dining room (redecorated in early 2012), Mr Fischer and head chef Rupert Rowley have a *Michelin* star for their modern European cooking (typical dishes: tempura of quail breast, pressed leg confit; fillet of sea bass, mandarin and star anise purée, spinach. 'Impeccable service and food,' says a visitor in 2012. 'Superbly cooked, beautifully presented,' is another comment. The bedrooms are 'warm and comfortable, with good-quality linen, mattresses and pillows'; two bathrooms have been renovated. The rooms in the main house are traditionally styled; *Garden House* rooms are contemporary. All now have a tea and coffee tray. The turn-down service is appreciated, as is the free Wi-Fi. An 'impeccable' breakfast has freshly squeezed juices, fresh fruit, home-made granola; a 'comprehensive' basket of bread and pastries. (*John and Haf Davies-Humphreys, Donald Reid*)

Calver Road
Baslow DE45 1RR

T: 01246-583259
F: 01246-583818
E: reservations@fischers-baslowhall.co.uk
W: www.fischers-baslowhall.co.uk

BEDROOMS: 11, 5 in *Garden House*.
OPEN: all year except 25/26 and 31 Dec evening.
FACILITIES: lounge/bar, breakfast room, 3 dining rooms, function facilities, civil wedding licence, 5-acre grounds, unsuitable for ♿.
BACKGROUND MUSIC: none.
LOCATION: edge of village.
CHILDREN: not under 12 in restaurant after 7 pm.
DOGS: not allowed.
CREDIT CARDS: Amex, MasterCard, Visa.
PRICES: [2012] B&B £77.50–£112.50 per person, set dinner £48–£72, full alc £100, mid-week breaks, 1-night bookings refused for superior rooms Sat in season.

BASSENTHWAITE LAKE Cumbria

Map 4: inset C2

THE PHEASANT

'The ever-present manager, Matthew Wylie, cares greatly for the well-being of guests and maintains a lovely atmosphere.' Much praise this year for this 16th-century whitewashed coaching inn (owned by the trustees of the Inglewood estate), which is at the unspoilt northern end of the Lake District. 'Charming; altogether to be recommended,' is another comment. The 'welcoming' lounges have log fires; the bar ('full of atmosphere') is popular with locals. There is a choice of dining styles. In *The Fell* restaurant, chef Alan O'Kane 'scales new heights' with his daily-changing menu, which might include ballottine of confit duck, crispy duck egg, date and orange compote; roast fillet of pork, glazed pig's cheek, red wine sauce. 'Always enjoyable', the food is 'beautifully presented'. Visitors who prefer 'less elaborate' cooking enjoyed 'ample and tasty' dishes in the bistro. Bedrooms vary in size, but all have views over the gardens or surrounding woodlands. Suites have a sitting area and extras (CD-player, iPod/iPhone dock). 'We had a most pleasant room, good bathroom and attractive furnishings.' Breakfast 'is full of choices'; the home-made porridge is 'super'. (*Clive T Blackburn, Mariana Lampert*)

25% DISCOUNT VOUCHERS

Bassenthwaite Lake
nr Cockermouth
CA13 9YE

T: 017687-76234
F: 017687-76002
E: info@the-pheasant.co.uk
W: www.the-pheasant.co.uk

BEDROOMS: 15, 2 on ground floor in lodge.

OPEN: all year except 25 Dec.

FACILITIES: 3 lounges, bar, dining room, bistro, 10-acre grounds, lake 200 yds (fishing), unsuitable for ♿.

BACKGROUND MUSIC: none.

LOCATION: 5 miles E of Cockermouth, ¼ mile off A66 to Keswick.

CHILDREN: not under 8.

DOGS: allowed in lodge bedrooms and public rooms.

CREDIT CARDS: MasterCard, Visa.

PRICES: [2012] B&B £75–£110 per person, D,B&B £105–£140, set dinner £35, midweek breaks, New Year package, 1-night bookings sometimes refused Sat.

BATH Somerset

Map 2:D1

APSLEY HOUSE

The welcome is 'impeccable' at Claire and Nicholas Potts's elegant Georgian house, built by the Duke of Wellington for his mistress. 'Excellent; great service – we were greeted in the car park,' says a visitor. The Pottses have appointed new managers this year: Stephanie and David Cowley. The 'delightful' house is furnished with antiques and fine paintings. The 'spacious' lounge, with tall windows overlooking the garden and distant countryside, has an honesty bar; guests can gather here for pre-dinner drinks before heading out to Bath (a 20-minute walk away) – or a nightcap on their return. The 'well-appointed' bedrooms have a 'modern bathroom': the Beau has a carved four-poster bed and a private entrance via the garden; Mornington, a lower-ground room, was 'very light, thanks to French windows opening on to the garden'. The house, set back from a busy road, was found 'very quiet' at night. No dinner: the hosts provide an extensive list of recommended restaurants. Mornings see an 'excellent' breakfast: a buffet is set out on a large dresser, and there is a 'good choice' of cooked dishes. (*Robert Hatcher, and others*)

141 Newbridge Hill
Bath BA1 3PT

T: 01225-336966
F: 01225-425462
E: info@apsley-house.co.uk
W: www.apsley-house.co.uk

BEDROOMS: 12, 1 on ground floor, plus 1 self-catering apartment.
OPEN: all year except 24/25/26 Dec.
FACILITIES: drawing room, bar, dining room, ¼-acre garden.
BACKGROUND MUSIC: Classic FM in dining room.
LOCATION: 1¼ miles W of city centre.
CHILDREN: all ages welcomed (under-2s free).
DOGS: only guide dogs allowed.
CREDIT CARDS: Amex, MasterCard, Visa.
PRICES: [2012] B&B £45–£90 per person, 1-night bookings refused weekends.

SEE ALSO SHORTLIST

BATH Somerset

Map 2:D1

THE BATH PRIORY

'Like a country house although it is on the edge of the city', this luxury hotel (Relais & Châteaux) is part of Andrew and Christina Brownsword's small but growing group of hotels, which includes *Gidleigh Park*, Chagford (see entry). The Georgian house, which stands in extensive gardens, is 20 minutes' walk (through Royal Victoria Park) from the city centre. 'The staff are formal but friendly, the lounges are elegant and relaxing, and the cooking is of the highest quality,' said inspectors. The best bedrooms overlook the gardens; a smaller room at the front 'had everything we needed, a smart bathroom'. Six Crescent suites in an adjacent building opened in May 2012: they have handcrafted furniture, wooden panelling, garden views. There are two dining rooms; Sam Moody, the head chef who works under the guidance of executive chef Michael Caines, has a modern European style, eg, ravioli of Cornish lobster, roast crown of squab pigeon, broad bean and mushroom fricassée. Children are welcomed (toy boxes, high teas, babysitting) as are dogs (bowl and basket provided). A spa has a small indoor pool, treatment rooms.

Weston Road
Bath BA1 2XT

T: 01225-331922
F: 01225-448276
E: mail@thebathpriory.co.uk
W: www.thebathpriory.co.uk

BEDROOMS: 33, 6 in annexe, 3 on ground floor, 1 suitable for ♿.

OPEN: all year.

FACILITIES: ramps, lounge bar, library, drawing room, 2 dining rooms, civil wedding licence, spa (heated indoor pool, 9 by 5 metres), 4-acre grounds (heated outdoor pool, 11 by 4 metres).

BACKGROUND MUSIC: none.

LOCATION: 1½ miles W of centre.

CHILDREN: no under-8s in restaurant at night.

DOGS: allowed in 2 bedrooms, not in public rooms.

CREDIT CARDS: All major cards.

PRICES: [2012] B&B £105–£600 per person, D,B&B £150–£675, full alc £100, special breaks, Christmas/ New Year packages, 1-night bookings sometimes refused.

SEE ALSO SHORTLIST

BATH Somerset

Map 2:D1

THE QUEENSBERRY

'Rather good and swishy,' say 2012 visitors to an 'exemplary' conversion of four 18th-century town houses in a grand street just off the Circus. Owners Laurence and Helen Beere have renovated in contemporary style. 'The staff could not have been more helpful, a model of how a hotel should be,' is another comment. The bedrooms are spacious, decorated in muted tones, with splashes of colour in throws, spreads and wallpapers. 'Fantastic room, very comfortable bed with crisp Egyptian linens, fluffy towels – it was how I would want my home to be.' In the *Olive Tree* restaurant (split-level in the basement), chef Nick Brodie serves modern dishes. 'We had a memorable meal of pigeon, fillet of beef, and caramel mousse. All well presented with an excellent mix of flavours.' Lighter meals (sandwiches, snacks) are available in the *Old Q* bar, and guests can eat in one of the four terraced gardens in fine weather. Breakfast is a 'well-presented selection of pastries, coffee and cooked breakfast. My full English was perfection.' (*Robin and Sue Hodges, Mark Woolfenden*)

25% DISCOUNT VOUCHERS

4–7 Russel Street
Bath BA1 2QF

T: 01225-447928
F: 01225-446065
E: reservations@thequeensberry.co.uk
W: www.thequeensberry.co.uk

BEDROOMS: 29, some on ground floor.

OPEN: all year, restaurant closed Mon lunch.

FACILITIES: lift, 2 drawing rooms, bar, restaurant, meeting room, 4 linked courtyard gardens, unsuitable for ♿.

BACKGROUND MUSIC: in restaurant and bar.

LOCATION: near Assembly Rooms.

CHILDREN: all ages welcomed.

DOGS: not allowed.

CREDIT CARDS: Amex, MasterCard, Visa.

PRICES: [2012] B&B £75–£135 per person, set dinner £38.50, full alc £55, 1-night bookings sometimes refused Sat.

SEE ALSO SHORTLIST

BATH Somerset

Map 2:D1

TASBURGH HOUSE

In 'a peaceful setting with wonderful views', Susan Keeling's red brick Victorian guest house stands in a row of imposing mansions lining the slope of a hill facing Bath. 'It might be outside the city, but it is a nice walk along the canal by day and a short taxi ride at night,' says an inspector. 'Susan, an elegant and kind hostess, offers to help in any way, booking taxis, providing drinks; when she is absent, her daughter, Antonia, is there to maintain the personal touch. Everyone was kind and friendly.' The bedrooms, named after famous writers, are all different. George Eliot has antique-style furnishings; Charlotte Brontë, on the first floor, has a garden view; Tennyson, in green and gold, has an original fireplace. Music plays all day in the 'charming' lounge and the conservatory, where breakfast is taken. A continental buffet, included in the price, has freshly squeezed orange juice, yogurt, 'lots of cereals', fruit. Cooked dishes cost extra. Three-course evening meals are provided, by arrangement, for groups of four or more.

25% DISCOUNT VOUCHERS

Warminster Road
Bath BA2 6SH

T: 01225-425096
F: 01225-463842
E: stay@tasburghhouse.co.uk
W: www.tasburghhouse.co.uk

BEDROOMS: 12, 2 on ground floor.
OPEN: 14 Jan–21 Dec.
FACILITIES: drawing room, dining room, conservatory, terrace, 7-acre grounds (canal walks, mooring), unsuitable for ♿.
BACKGROUND MUSIC: 'when appropriate'.
LOCATION: on A36 to Warminster, ½ mile E of centre.
CHILDREN: not under 8.
DOGS: only guide dogs allowed.
CREDIT CARDS: MasterCard, Visa.
PRICES: B&B (continental breakfast) £60–£95 per person, cooked breakfast £8.50, set dinner (Mon–Thurs for groups of 4 or more) £37.50, special breaks, 1-night bookings sometimes refused Sat.

SEE ALSO SHORTLIST

BEAMINSTER Dorset

Map 1:C6

BRIDGEHOUSE

'A very comfortable old inn', Mark and Joanna Donovan's small hotel stands by a bridge in this 'interesting' market town. The 13th-century building was once a priest's house; the public rooms in the oldest part of the building have thick walls, mullioned windows, inglenook fireplaces, oak beams; 'lots of books to browse'. The largest bedrooms are in the main house: the quietest face a large walled garden. Four smaller rooms and a family suite (children are welcomed) are in a converted coach house at the back. 'Our pleasant room was decorated in modern style; the bathroom was excellent,' said a visitor this year. In the *Beaminster Brasserie*, an elegant Georgian dining room (with an Adam fireplace), chef Stephen Pielesz cooks imaginative dishes, perhaps Jurassic Coast beef loin carpaccio with pickled beetroot; Lyme Bay brill, sea bass and scallop, sautéed potatoes and spinach. 'An excellent meal served by friendly, helpful staff.' Breakfast and light lunches are taken in a conservatory by the walled garden. Mapperton Gardens, close by, are worth a visit. (*Celia Gregory, and others*)

25% DISCOUNT VOUCHERS

3 Prout Bridge
Beaminster DT8 3AY

T: 01308-862200
F: 01308-863700
E: enquiries@bridge-house.co.uk
W: www.bridge-house.co.uk

BEDROOMS: 13, 4 in coach house, 4 on ground floor.
OPEN: all year.
FACILITIES: hall/reception, lounge, bar, conservatory, restaurant, civil wedding licence, ¼-acre walled garden, alfresco dining.
BACKGROUND MUSIC: light jazz and classical.
LOCATION: 100 yds from centre.
CHILDREN: all ages welcomed.
DOGS: allowed in coach house, in bar except during food service.
CREDIT CARDS: Amex, MasterCard, Visa.
PRICES: [2012] B&B £63–£108 per person, full alc £55, special breaks, Christmas/New Year packages, 1-night bookings refused weekends and bank holidays.

BEAULIEU Hampshire

Map 2:E2

MONTAGU ARMS

'A beautiful old building in a lovely village', this brick-faced and wisteria-clad hotel is on the site of an 18th-century inn in the New Forest. Visitors this year praised the 'friendly' staff. 'We were addressed by name at all times and given a very personal service.' The much-extended building has oak-panelled public rooms with old brick fireplaces, 'comfy' armchairs and sofas; a conservatory faces the formal gardens. Bedrooms vary considerably in size and price; all are individually decorated in traditional style. 'Our superior room, which overlooked the garden, had a settee; it was if anything over-furnished for its size; less would have been more.' Matthew Tomkinson, the chef, uses local organic ingredients, many from the hotel's kitchen garden, for his dishes in the *Michelin*-starred *Terrace* restaurant. 'Perfectly cooked, with generous portions.' Typical dishes: white onion and Parmesan velouté; roast saddle of venison, parsnip purée, crispy venison croquette. Less formal meals can be taken in *Monty's* bar/brasserie. 'Excellent' breakfasts have home-made pastries; eggs, from the hotel's hens, were 'a joy to eat'. (*Peter Anderson, Monty Knight-Olds*)

Palace Lane
Beaulieu SO42 7ZL

T: 01590-612324
F: 01590-612188
E: reservations@montaguarms.co.uk
W: www.montaguarmshotel.co.uk

BEDROOMS: 22.

OPEN: all year, Terrace restaurant closed Mon.

FACILITIES: lounge, conservatory, bar/brasserie, restaurant, civil wedding licence, garden, access to nearby spa, only public rooms suitable for ♿.

BACKGROUND MUSIC: none.

LOCATION: village centre.

CHILDREN: all ages welcomed (under-3s stay free).

DOGS: not allowed.

CREDIT CARDS: Amex, MasterCard, Visa.

PRICES: [2012] B&B £74–£174 per person, D,B&B £114–£214, full alc £72, special breaks, Christmas/New Year packages, 1-night bookings refused Sat in season.

BEELEY Derbyshire

Map 3:A6

THE DEVONSHIRE ARMS AT BEELEY

NEW

In a village on the Chatsworth estate, this 17th-century coaching inn is run by chef/patron Alan Hill for the Duke and Duchess of Devonshire. It returns to the *Guide* after positive reports in 2012 from regular correspondents. 'Delightful; first-class service and accommodation; a pleasant stay.' The original bar has oak beams, flagged floors, log fires; the brasserie extension and the bedrooms (in the main building and *Brookside House*, next door) are more contemporary. 'Housekeeping was excellent; a good bathroom with a shower over the bath.' Six new rooms were being added as we went to press, in *Dove Cottages*, across the road from the inn. 'The cooking has improved,' say returning visitors: 'We enjoyed a generous portion of fresh-as-a-daisy haddock in a crisp, light batter; line-caught sea trout in a delicate fish broth was so good that I had it a second time.' A guest who would have liked 'more variety after two nights' thought breakfast 'was the best ever: unusual dishes like French toast with Greek yogurt and berries; Derbyshire oatcakes with chorizo'. (*Jennifer Davis, Padi and John Howard*)

Devonshire Square
Beeley, nr Matlock DE4 2NR

T/F: 01629-733259
E: enquiries@devonshirebeeley.co.uk
W: www.devonshirebeeley.co.uk

BEDROOMS: 8, 4 in annexe, 2 on ground floor.
OPEN: all year.
FACILITIES: bar, brasserie, malt vault.
BACKGROUND MUSIC: light jazz/classical in brasserie.
LOCATION: 5 miles N of Matlock, off B6012.
CHILDREN: all ages welcomed.
DOGS: allowed in Brookside bedrooms, not in public rooms.
CREDIT CARDS: all major cards.
PRICES: [2012] B&B £64.50–£109.50 per person, full alc £40, special breaks, Christmas/New Year packages.

BEPTON West Sussex

Map 2:E3

PARK HOUSE

'Small and luxurious, but never imposing or stuffy', this country hotel at the foot of the South Downs is managed by Rebecca Coonan for the O'Brien family. The Victorian house (with medieval roots) was renovated at the turn of the Millennium: 'smart and comfortable', it stands in gardens and grounds 'worthy of Chelsea'. There is much praise from regular correspondents this year: 'A good place to relax and enjoy the wonderful facilities and fabulous views.' 'Everything was of the highest quality for our golden wedding party; the attention to detail was remarkable.' The 'well-kept' bedrooms are in the main house and three cottages in the grounds: 'Our double-aspect room overlooked the croquet lawn and the South Downs; large and roomy, it had a lovely bathroom and a fabulous bed.' In the formal dining room and a conservatory, chef Kyle Coleman serves modern dishes, perhaps watercress and wild nettle soup; roast rump of lamb, smoked garlic mash, sage and redcurrant coulis. 'When my husband went for an early-morning stroll, the night porter gave him coffee and pastries.' (*Valerie Durkan, Mary Woods*)

Bepton Road
Bepton
Midhurst GU29 0JB

T: 01730-819000
F: 01730-819099
E: reservations@parkhousehotel.com
W: www.parkhousehotel.com

BEDROOMS: 21, 5 on ground floor, 1 suitable for ♿, 9 in cottages in grounds.
OPEN: all year.
FACILITIES: drawing room, bar, dining room, conservatory, civil wedding licence, 9-acre grounds, spa, indoor and outdoor swimming pools (both heated, 15 metres), tennis, pitch and putt.
BACKGROUND MUSIC: in dining room.
LOCATION: 2½ miles SW of Midhurst.
CHILDREN: all ages welcomed.
DOGS: allowed in 2 bedrooms, not in dining room.
CREDIT CARDS: Amex, MasterCard, Visa.
PRICES: [2012] B&B £67.50–£180 per person, D,B&B £117.50–£220, set dinner £37.50, seasonal breaks, 1-night bookings refused weekends.

BIGBURY-ON-SEA Devon

Map 1:D4

BURGH ISLAND HOTEL

César award in 2012

'Quirky, but magnificent when one gets with it,' says a visitor in 2012 to this Devon landmark, which has been restored to its 1930s glamour by owners Tony Orchard and Deborah Clark. 'It is an Art Deco tour de force, run with a proper sense of period fun,' was a reporter's comment. 'The spectacular island setting adds to the buzz.' The bedrooms are individually decorated and vary greatly. The largest suite has two bathrooms; a snug double has a slipper bath with uninterrupted view of sea and sky. The Beach House 'must be one of the most romantic rooms on the planet, with its stunning views'. The public rooms 'help you forget everyday life and drift back to a bygone era'. Guests are encouraged to dress for dinner (but black tie is not obligatory) in the candlelit dining room. Chef Timothy Hall's daily-changing menu of local ingredients might include Brixham fish soup; slow-roast beef fillet, Armagnac prune, Merlot reduction. 'When the jazz band strikes up in the ballroom, it's no surprise that everyone gets up to dance.' (*Margaret West, Richard Axford*)

Burgh Island
Bigbury-on-Sea TQ7 4BG

T: 01548-810514
E: reception@burghisland.com
W: www.burghisland.com

BEDROOMS: 25, 1 suite in Beach House, apartment above *Pilchard Inn*.

OPEN: all year.

FACILITIES: lift, sun lounge, *Palm Court* bar, dining room, ballroom, children's games room, spa, civil wedding licence, 12-acre grounds on 27-acre island (30-metre natural sea swimming pool, tennis).

BACKGROUND MUSIC: 1930s in public areas, live Wed, Sun with dinner.

LOCATION: 5 miles S of Modbury, private garages on mainland.

CHILDREN: not under 5, no under-12s at dinner.

DOGS: only guide/hearing dogs allowed.

CREDIT CARDS: MasterCard, Visa.

PRICES: [to 31 Mar 2013] D,B&B £200–£320 per person, special events, Christmas/New Year packages, 1-night booking sometimes refused Sat.

BIGBURY-ON-SEA Devon

Map 1:D4

THE HENLEY

César award in 2003

'Even better than before,' says a visitor returning this year to Martyn Scarterfield and Petra Lampe's 'perfect' hotel above the Avon estuary on the south Devon coast. 'Small, homely and relaxing', the Edwardian holiday villa has seating areas with Lloyd Loom chairs, books and magazines, and binoculars for guests' use. There are five simple bedrooms: the largest has 'stunning views of the sea and hills behind; a big bathroom with an excellent shower'. 'Petra is a wonderful front-of-house, always helpful.' Over pre-dinner drinks in the lounge, she 'recites the dinner menu with flair'. Martyn Scarterfield's 'small but consistently good' menu, which might include rack of lamb and gratin of mixed fish, uses local produce where possible. 'The food is outstanding, with a different local fish every night.' Breakfast, served at a time of the guest's choice, is thought 'excellent'. The hosts' young daughter, Marika, 'entertained us every day'. 'Our two dogs were made so welcome, as we were.' A cliff path, recently reopened after repair, descends to a 'superb' beach. (*Simon Rodway, John and Christine Moore*)

Folly Hill
Bigbury-on-Sea TQ7 4AR

T/F: 01548-810240
E: thehenleyhotel@btconnect.com
W: www.thehenleyhotel.co.uk

BEDROOMS: 5.

OPEN: mid-Mar–Oct.

FACILITIES: 2 lounges, bar, conservatory dining room, small garden (steps to beach, golf, sailing, fishing), Coastal Path nearby, unsuitable for ♿.

BACKGROUND MUSIC: jazz, classical in the evenings in lounge, dining room.

LOCATION: 5 miles S of Modbury.

CHILDREN: not under 12.

DOGS: well-behaved dogs in lounge only.

CREDIT CARDS: Amex, MasterCard, Visa.

PRICES: [2012] B&B £60–£85 per person, D,B&B (3 nights min.) £85–£110, set dinner £36, 1-night bookings sometimes refused weekends.

BIGGIN-BY-HARTINGTON Derbyshire

Map 3:B6

BIGGIN HALL

In open countryside within the Peak District national park, James Moffett's Grade II* listed 17th-century building has long been liked by ramblers for its relaxed simplicity and 'amazingly good value'. Some visitors comment on 'imperfections' (plastic flower arrangements, 'impersonal service'). 'Let's rejoice in the price and enjoy it for what it is,' says an enthusiast this year who will return. The 'attractive' stone building has mullioned windows, massive stone fireplaces: there are two sitting rooms and a library. 'The mealtime routine is strict but not impossible': guests gather at 6.30 pm to give their orders from a 'well-designed and cooked' menu, served promptly at 7 pm in the candlelit dining room. The traditional dishes might include leek and potato soup; braised Derbyshire beef in red wine. 'A sideboard loaded with local cheeses was an unexpected bonus,' said a visitor in 2012. Breakfast, served between 8 and 9 am, is 'first rate', with a hot and cold buffet. The simple bedrooms are in the main house, the courtyard, the 'bothy' and the lodge. 'An excellent base for walks in the noble countryside of Dovedale.' Packed lunches are provided. (*Michael and Patricia Blanchard, and others*)

Biggin-by-Hartington
Buxton SK17 0DH

T: 01298-84451
E: enquiries@bigginhall.co.uk
W: www.bigginhall.co.uk

BEDROOMS: 20, 12 in annexes, some on ground floor.
OPEN: all year.
FACILITIES: sitting room, library, dining room, meeting room, civil wedding licence, 8-acre grounds (croquet), River Dove 1½ miles, unsuitable for ♿.
BACKGROUND MUSIC: classical, in dining room.
LOCATION: 8 miles N of Ashbourne.
CHILDREN: not under 12.
DOGS: allowed in courtyard and bothy bedrooms, not in public rooms.
CREDIT CARDS: MasterCard, Visa.
PRICES: [2012] B&B £43–£71 per person, D,B&B £59–£87, set dinner £22.50, Christmas/New Year packages, 1-night bookings sometimes refused.

BILDESTON Suffolk

Map 2:C5

THE BILDESTON CROWN

On the main street of a pretty Suffolk village, this 'handsome' 15th-century coaching inn has been restored by James Buckle, a local farmer whose herd of Red Poll cattle supplies the kitchen with beef. The 'exceptional' cooking of chef Chris Lee (whose wife, Hayley, is manager) has impressed readers and *Guide* inspectors. 'The accommodation is excellent; the staff are courteous, and the meals are well presented.' They can be taken in the bar, with wooden tables and chairs, beamed ceiling, which has a 'classics' menu (eg, ham, duck eggs and chips). The restaurant has been refurbished this year (white linens and dark leather chairs) and renamed *Ingrams*. Guests can choose between a 'select' and a tasting menu (typical dishes: cumin-roasted scallop, smoked eel, carrot; canon of Semer lamb, sweetbreads, watercress and turnip). The bedrooms, reached by a winding corridor with a tartan carpet, are modern: 'Our room was decorated in yellow, with a pale green carpet; thick cream-striped curtains; a well-equipped bathroom with a shower over the bath.' Breakfast is served at table (no buffet). (*RG, and others*)

104 High Street
Bildeston IP7 7EB

T: 01449-740510
E: reception@thebildestoncrown.com
W: www.thebildestoncrown.com

BEDROOMS: 12, 1 suitable for ♿.
OPEN: all year, except 25 Dec (when restaurant is open for lunch).
FACILITIES: lift, bar, lounge, restaurant, 2 meeting rooms, civil wedding licence, courtyard.
BACKGROUND MUSIC: none.
LOCATION: village centre.
CHILDREN: all ages welcomed.
DOGS: allowed (£10 charge).
CREDIT CARDS: MasterCard, Visa.
PRICES: [2012] B&B £70–£120 per person, set meals £35–£70, full alc £60, New Year package, special breaks.

BIRMINGHAM West Midlands

Map 2:B2

HOTEL DU VIN BIRMINGHAM

NEW

An artful conversion of Birmingham's red brick eye hospital, this 'fine old building' houses the Birmingham branch of the du Vin chain. 'It is an impressive building with a wonderful sweeping staircase, a lovely courtyard and a lively basement bar,' said an inspector. 'When I booked, I was asked how I would like to be addressed and if I had any special requests (I did, sheets and blankets instead of a duvet, which were provided). The welcome from smart young men was courteous; my bags were taken to my room while I had lunch.' The bedrooms are around a central courtyard which has a retractable roof. 'The decor is masculine; my spacious room had lots of black (wardrobe, curtains) but a cream bedspread; shiny white tiles in the large bathroom, a slipper bath and a huge shower area. Room service was prompt when I ordered a drink.' The 'charming' bistro has round and square wooden tables with candles and shining glasses, a wooden floor, lots of pictures. 'A good meal of sea bream with spaghetti vegetables; a delicious custard tart; a superb glass of Shiraz.'

25 Church Street
Birmingham B3 2NR

T: 0121-200 0600
E: info.birmingham@hotelduvin.com
W: www.hotelduvin.com

BEDROOMS: 66, 3 suitable for ♿.
OPEN: all year.
FACILITIES: lift, bistro, 2 bars, billiard room, civil wedding licence, spa, courtyard.
BACKGROUND MUSIC: in public areas.
LOCATION: central, near St Philip's Cathedral.
CHILDREN: all ages welcomed.
DOGS: not allowed in bar/bistro.
CREDIT CARDS: Amex, MasterCard, Visa.
PRICES: [2012] room £140–£340, breakfast £12.50–£14.95, full alc £45, special breaks.

BIRMINGHAM West Midlands

Map 2:B2

SIMPSONS

NEW

In leafy Edgbaston, this Georgian mansion is run as a restaurant-with-rooms by chef/patron Andreas Antona, who has a *Michelin* star for his classic French cooking. It returns to the *Guide* after a period without feedback, thanks to a positive report from a trusted correspondent. 'We were very happy with our stay; the staff were welcoming and helpful. We are still savouring the memory of one of the best meals we have ever had.' Executive chef Luke Tipping and head chef Adam Bennett can be watched in the kitchen (behind glass) from one of the relaxed dining areas which open on to a terrace where alfresco meals can be taken. Typical dishes on the seasonal menu: crispy duck egg, white beans, chorizo; Iberico pork chop, parsnip purée, black pudding, mustard sauce. The four bedrooms (available from Tuesday to Saturday) are themed: French has ornate furniture; Venetian has velvet, reds and gold. 'It was lovely to retreat to our very comfortable and well-equipped room.' The continental breakfast was 'delicious as dinner: freshly squeezed orange juice, fruit salad, home-made yogurt, all beautifully presented'. (*Virginia Lynch*)

20 Highfield Road
Edgbaston
Birmingham B15 3DU

T: 0121-454 3434
F: 0121-454 3399
E: info@simpsonsrestaurant.co.uk
W: www.simpsonsrestaurant.co.uk

BEDROOMS: 4.

OPEN: all year except bank holidays, restaurant closed Sun evening, accommodation Tues–Sat only.

FACILITIES: lounge, 3 restaurant areas, private dining room, cookery school, terrace (alfresco dining), garden, only restaurant suitable for ♿.

BACKGROUND MUSIC: none.

LOCATION: 1 mile from centre.

CHILDREN: all ages welcomed (no special facilities).

DOGS: only guide dogs allowed.

CREDIT CARDS: Amex, MasterCard, Visa.

PRICES: [2012] B&B (continental) £80–£112.50 per person, full alc £55.

BLAKENEY Norfolk

Map 2:A5

THE BLAKENEY HOTEL

On a quayside of a tidal estuary, this large, traditional hotel attracts many returning visitors (families during the school holidays and an older generation off-season). It is owned by the Stannard family; Anne Thornalley is the manager. It has many fans: 'The management is obvious and hands-on; the staff seem happy, which makes for happy guests,' says a visitor in 2012. There are two lounges: a ground-floor room has huge settees and beige armchairs; a first-floor lounge has a fine view of the estuary (it is designated as a quiet area; but a rare dissenter this year complained of 'noisy non-residents'). The best bedrooms have the view; others face the garden. 'My room at the back was quiet; tons of pillows on a firm bed; exceptional lighting.' In the dining room, which 'runs like clockwork', Martin Sewell's daily-changing menu might include seared fillet of black bream on crushed potatoes. Light meals are served in the bar and on the terrace. Breakfast has 'a great variety of cereals, fruit, croissants, juices, and excellent marmalade'.
(*CT Blackburn, Moira Jarrett, and others*)

Blakeney
nr Holt NR25 7NE

T: 01263-740797
F: 01263-740795
E: reception@blakeneyhotel.co.uk
W: www.blakeneyhotel.co.uk

BEDROOMS: 63, 16 in *Granary* annexe opposite, some on ground floor.
OPEN: all year.
FACILITIES: lift, ramps, lounge, sun lounge, bar, restaurant, function facilities, heated indoor swimming pool (12 by 5 metres), steam room, sauna, mini-gym, games room, ¼-acre garden.
BACKGROUND MUSIC: none.
LOCATION: on quay.
CHILDREN: all ages welcomed.
DOGS: allowed in some bedrooms, not in public rooms.
CREDIT CARDS: all major cards.
PRICES: [2012] B&B £79–£141 per person, D,B&B £91–£159, alc £29.50–£44, activity breaks, Christmas/New Year packages, 1-night bookings sometimes refused Fri/Sat, bank holidays.

BLEDINGTON Oxfordshire

Map 3:D6

THE KING'S HEAD INN

Built as a cider house, Archie and Nicola Orr-Ewing's 16th-century Cotswold stone inn sits on a village green with a stream running through it. There are low ceilings, flagstone floors, open fireplaces, wooden tables and chairs in the bar, which is popular with locals. 'There is a great atmosphere in the evening,' said inspectors. Six bedrooms are in the original building; they have a mix of antiques, junk-shop finds and painted furniture. The courtyard bedrooms are larger: 'Ours had a feature wall with a bold metallic design, black bedside lamps, and shiny-black-framed prints; a functional bathroom. The chef, Steven Brookes, has joined from the nearby *Swan Inn*, Swinbrooke (see Shortlist), which is managed by the Orr-Ewings. He serves an English/French menu 'with a modern edge'. Typical dishes: Upton smoked pigeon Caesar salad; venison cottage pie, braised red cabbage. The food is mostly organic and locally sourced; the Aberdeen Angus beef comes from Mr Orr-Ewing's uncle's nearby farm. Breakfast 'is served with less of a flourish'; a basic buffet with packaged yogurt, butter and jams; a choice of cooked dishes.

25% DISCOUNT VOUCHERS

The Green
Bledington OX7 6XQ

T: 01608-658365
F: 01608-658167
E: info@kingsheadinn.net
W: www.thekingsheadinn.net

BEDROOMS: 12, 6 in annexe, some on ground floor.
OPEN: all year except 25/26 Dec.
FACILITIES: 2 bars, restaurant, courtyard.
BACKGROUND MUSIC: occasionally in bar.
LOCATION: on village green.
CHILDREN: all ages welcomed.
DOGS: not allowed in bedrooms.
CREDIT CARDS: MasterCard, Visa.
PRICES: B&B £35–£60 per person, full alc £40, winter midweek packages, 1-night bookings refused Sat.

BLOCKLEY Gloucestershire

Map 3:D6

LOWER BROOK HOUSE

In a converted 17th-century silk mill of 'great character', this 'homely' small hotel is run by owners Julian and Anna Ebbutt. Downstairs, a small dining room and two sitting areas have original flagstone floors, exposed oak beams; an open fire in the larger room, books about the area, magazines, and 'a medley of personal objects'. Mrs Ebbutt, 'a competent cook', serves traditional dishes (eg, beef, ale and mushroom pie, carrot mash) on a supper menu that can be taken in the dining room, 'the comfort of your bedroom', or in warm weather in the garden. The bedrooms, each named after a member of the family who once lived in the house, vary considerably in size and style. Snugborough has a pitched, beamed ceiling, a compact shower room; Northwick, on the top floor, has a four-poster bed and a large bathroom. Daddy Lowe is 'small but pleasant, decorated in the modern plain style; thoughtfully equipped; plenty of towels and good toiletries'. The 'very good' breakfast has a buffet with freshly pressed orange juice, various mueslis; 'good, thickly cut toast, heavenly preserves'; a choice of cooked dishes.

25% DISCOUNT VOUCHERS

Lower Street
Blockley GL56 9DS

T: 01386-700286
F: 01386-701400
E: info@lowerbrookhouse.com
W: www.lowerbrookhouse.com

BEDROOMS: 6.

OPEN: all year except Christmas, dining room closed Sun night.

FACILITIES: lounge, restaurant, 1-acre garden, unsuitable for ♿.

BACKGROUND MUSIC: in restaurant at night.

LOCATION: centre of village.

CHILDREN: not under 10.

DOGS: not allowed.

CREDIT CARDS: MasterCard, Visa.

PRICES: [2012] B&B £55–£95 per person, full alc £35, midweek packages, 1-night bookings usually refused Sat.

BOSCASTLE Cornwall

Map 1:C3

THE OLD RECTORY

In a fold in a valley near the north Cornwall coast, this 'beautiful' slate-hung house is run as an eco-friendly B&B by Chris and Sally Searle. Visitors commend the 'comfort and cleanliness', the owners' 'flexibility in accommodating the needs of guests', and the attention to detail. The house has a strong literary resonance: here in 1870 Thomas Hardy met Emma Gifford, the rector's sister, who became his wife. Her death forty years later triggered some of his best poetry. Hardy memorabilia is displayed in the house. The well-equipped bedrooms are individually decorated in period style with dark woods: Emma's room has an original fireplace with turquoise tiles, blue brocade curtains, a pine four-poster bed; an old thunderbox lavatory. Guests have a sitting room with tea- and coffee-making facilities and a fridge with fresh milk. Mrs Searle cooks evening meals by arrangement (guests are asked to provide their own alcohol); they are in the restored Victorian greenhouse. Breakfast has eggs from hens and ducks in the garden, and bacon and sausages from the Searles' pigs, which roam in nearby pasture. (*MW, and others*)

St Juliot, nr Boscastle
PL35 0BT

T: 01840-250225
E: sally@stjuliot.com
W: www.stjuliot.com

BEDROOMS: 4, 1 in stables (linked to house).

OPEN: mid-Jan–mid-Dec.

FACILITIES: sitting room, breakfast room, conservatory, 3-acre garden (croquet lawn, 'lookout'), unsuitable for ♿.

BACKGROUND MUSIC: none.

LOCATION: 2 miles NE of Boscastle.

CHILDREN: not under 12.

DOGS: only allowed in stables.

CREDIT CARDS: MasterCard, Visa.

PRICES: [2012] B&B £35–£49 per person, 1-night bookings refused weekends and high season.

SEE ALSO SHORTLIST

BOSHAM West Sussex

Map 2:E3

THE MILLSTREAM

On the road leading to the harbour in a historic West Sussex village, this converted manor house has a manicured garden with a millstream and gazebo. It has long been managed by Antony Wallace. Praise comes this year from an extended family: 'Our rooms were attractive, the food is good, and service continues to be excellent.' Another returning visitor was pleased to find 'an old friend as good as ever. In an understated way, it gets a lot of things right: a silent fridge with mineral water and fresh milk; a face flannel is a nice extra; pity about the captive coat-hangers.' Mr Wallace tells us that several more bedrooms have been renovated this year. A guest in a wheelchair was impressed by a fully equipped bedroom; a dissenter was less impressed with his ground-floor room. In the restaurant the chef, Neil Hiskey, serves a modern British menu with dishes like seared wild scallops, pea and mint salad; breast of guineafowl, white beans, shiitake mushrooms.' *Marwick's*, a 'more casual dining experience', opened in 2012.
(Shirley King, Peter Jowitt, and others)

Bosham Lane
Bosham, nr Chichester
PO18 8HL

T: 01243-573234
F: 01243-573459
E: info@millstreamhotel.com
W: www.millstreamhotel.com

BEDROOMS: 35, 2 in cottage, 7 on ground floor, 1 suitable for ♿.
OPEN: all year.
FACILITIES: lounge, bar, restaurant (pianist Fri and Sat), brasserie, conference room, civil wedding licence, 1¼-acre garden (stream, gazebo), Chichester Harbour (sailing, fishing) 300 yards.
BACKGROUND MUSIC: classical 10.30 am–10.30 pm in lounge and restaurant.
LOCATION: 4 miles W of Chichester.
CHILDREN: all ages welcomed.
DOGS: only guide dogs allowed.
CREDIT CARDS: all major cards.
PRICES: [2012] B&B £77.50–£95 per person, D,B&B (min. 2 nights) £92–£119, set dinner £25–£32.50, Christmas/New Year packages, 1-night bookings refused Sat.

BOURTON-ON-THE-HILL Gloucestershire Map 3:D6

THE HORSE AND GROOM

César award in 2012

Found 'excellent on all counts' by a visitor, this former coaching inn is run as a pub-with-rooms by brothers Tom and Will Greenstock. Other praise (in 2012): 'We thoroughly enjoyed our stay, and would certainly go again.' The honey-coloured building has an open-plan bar and restaurant. Guests order from Will Greenstock's blackboard menu in the bar: 'We enjoyed spicy soup, excellent pork, and real vegetables in a separate dish; red cabbage just as it should be.' Vegetables come from the pub's garden, other produce from local farms. The bedrooms are spacious: 'Mine had a mirrored chest of drawers, and was twice the size you would expect in a pub,' said a reporter. 'Our recently decorated room was spacious and comfortable, with a large bathroom.' The A44 runs by the pub, but is quieter at night ('heavy curtains provided good soundproofing'). The 'first-rate' breakfast has milk and butter from a local farm ('where all the cows have a name'). 'The home-made croissants were a delight, warm, buttery, flaky.' Check-in is before 3 pm or after 6 pm. (*Michael Mackenzie, Jill and Mike Bennett*)

25% DISCOUNT VOUCHERS

Bourton-on-the-Hill
nr Moreton-in-Marsh
GL56 9AQ

T/F: 01386-700413
E: greenstocks@horseandgroom.info
W: www.horseandgroom.info

BEDROOMS: 5.
OPEN: all year except 25/31 Dec, restaurant closed Sun eve.
FACILITIES: bar/restaurant, 1-acre garden, unsuitable for ♿.
BACKGROUND MUSIC: none.
LOCATION: village centre.
CHILDREN: all ages welcomed.
DOGS: not allowed.
CREDIT CARDS: MasterCard, Visa.
PRICES: [2012] B&B £48–£85 per person, full alc £30, midweek discounts, 1-night bookings refused weekends.

BOWNESS-ON-WINDERMERE Cumbria Map 4: inset C2

LINDETH FELL

César award in 2009

'That comfortable feeling of being at home remains; you know that the guest comes first.' Praise in 2012 comes again from returning visitors to this traditional hotel owned and run in personal style by Diana Kennedy and her daughter, Sheena. The long-serving manager, Linda Hartill, has retired: 'Mrs Kennedy is still much in evidence talking to guests every evening, and Sheena is now the very efficient manager.' Another comment: 'The furnishings might take you back in time; a reminder of what to like about an era of old-fashioned personal service; you are well looked after.' Julian Ankers, the new chef, 'has introduced interesting dishes, nicely presented; guineafowl was very good as were the venison and lamb'. The bedrooms, all of which have been refurbished, are 'beautifully furnished, clean and welcoming; beds are supportive, thank goodness'. 'Our superior room was modestly sized, and well appointed, with a modern, elegant, bathroom.' Many have views of Lake Windermere. (*Jill and Mike Bennett, Alan and Edwina Williams, Ian and Francine Walsh*)

25% DISCOUNT VOUCHERS

Lyth Valley Road
Bowness-on-Windermere
LA23 3JP

T: 015394-43286
F: 015394-47455
E: kennedy@lindethfell.co.uk
W: www.lindethfell.co.uk

BEDROOMS: 14, 1 on ground floor.

OPEN: all year except Jan.

FACILITIES: ramp, hall, 2 lounges, dispense bar, 3 dining rooms, 7-acre grounds (gardens, croquet, putting, bowls, tarn, fishing permits).

BACKGROUND MUSIC: none.

LOCATION: 1 mile S of Bowness on A5074.

CHILDREN: all ages welcomed, but no under-7s in dining rooms in evening.

DOGS: only assistance dogs allowed.

CREDIT CARDS: MasterCard, Visa.

PRICES: [2012] B&B £70–£105 per person, D,B&B £100–£140, set dinner £36, special breaks, Christmas/New Year packages, 1-night bookings sometimes refused weekends, bank holidays.

SEE ALSO SHORTLIST

BOWNESS-ON-WINDERMERE Cumbria Map 4: inset C2

LINTHWAITE HOUSE

Built in 1900 as a private home, this creeper-covered white and stone house has fine views across landscaped gardens to Lake Windermere. Owned by Mike Bevans, it is managed by Andrew Nicholson. 'Excellent; lovely staff and much attention to detail,' writes a visitor this year. The public rooms have oriental rugs, potted plants, memorabilia; an enclosed veranda faces the water. Smart casual dress is required in the candlelit restaurant, where Chris O'Callaghan is now the chef: he cooks modern British dishes, perhaps lightly cured and poached salmon, pickled baby beetroots; poached and roasted tenderloin of pork, smoked celeriac purée, white beans. Bedrooms, which have a 'calm, chintz-free' decor, vary in size and outlook; larger rooms overlook the lake, others have a garden view; one room has an outdoor hot tub; the Loft Suite has a separate lounge, a retractable glass roof panel (which closes automatically if it rains), and a telescope. Breakfast has a buffet of cereals, fruit, creamy yogurt, compotes; home-made croissants; a choice of nine cooked dishes. (*Sue Tunstall*)

25% DISCOUNT VOUCHERS

Crook Road
Bowness-on-Windermere
LA23 3JA

T: 015394-88600
F: 015394-88601
E: stay@linthwaite.com
W: www.linthwaite.com

BEDROOMS: 30, some on ground floor.

OPEN: all year.

FACILITIES: ramp, lounge/bar, conservatory, 3 dining rooms, function facilities, civil wedding licence, 14-acre grounds.

BACKGROUND MUSIC: light music in bar and dining room.

LOCATION: ¾ mile S of Bowness.

CHILDREN: no under-7s in dining rooms after 7 pm.

DOGS: allowed in two bedrooms.

CREDIT CARDS: Amex, MasterCard, Visa.

PRICES: [2012] B&B £97.50–£277 per person, D,B&B £141–£320, full alc £47.50, special breaks, Christmas/New Year packages, 1-night bookings sometimes refused.

SEE ALSO SHORTLIST

BRADPOLE Dorset

Map 1:C6

ORCHARD BARN

On the site of an old Dorset farm, Nigel and Margaret Corbett's B&B stands in 'tranquil' gardens on the banks of the River Asker. Hoteliers for 50 years (most recently as owners of *Summer Lodge*, Evershot, see entry), they have a loyal following who admire the 'five-star care and accommodation'. Guests are welcomed with tea and home-made cake in a sitting room with a gallery constructed from timbers of an old barn; French windows open on to the south-facing garden where tea can be taken in summer. The bedrooms are in a separate wing of the house. The ground-floor Mews Room, which has its own front door and lobby, can be accessed by a secret entrance from the sitting room. There are many good places to eat in the area; or a light supper (perhaps quiche lorraine, new potatoes and salad), served on a tray in front of the fire, can be ordered in advance. Breakfast has a help-yourself buffet, which has River Cottage yogurts, home-prepared muesli; cooked options include West Country white pudding. Bread, jam and marmalade are home made.
(*Mr and Mrs GT*)

Bradpole
nr Bridport DT6 4AR

T/F: 01308-455655
E: enquiries@lodgeatorchardbarn.co.uk
W: www.lodgeatorchardbarn.co.uk

BEDROOMS: 3, 1 on ground floor.
OPEN: all year except Christmas/New Year.
FACILITIES: lounge, dining room.
BACKGROUND MUSIC: none.
LOCATION: off A35, via Lee Lane, in village adjoining Bridport.
CHILDREN: all ages welcomed.
DOGS: allowed in public rooms subject to other guests' approval.
CREDIT CARDS: none accepted.
PRICES: B&B £67.50–£72.50 per person, snack supper £5.95–£25, 1-night bookings sometimes refused Sat.

BRAITHWAITE Cumbria

Map 4: inset C2

THE COTTAGE IN THE WOOD

Within England's only mountain forest, this converted 17th-century coaching inn is run as a restaurant-with-rooms by Kath and Liam Berney. Guests have a cosy sitting room with a wood-burner, walking magazines, books and games; in summer they can sit on a terrace or in the small garden. In the conservatory restaurant, which has views down the valley, Ryan Blackburn is now the chef, using local and foraged produce for his modern daily-changing menus. Typical dishes: seared breast of wood pigeon, wild mushroom tortellini; pan-roasted brill, pig's trotter, cockle vinaigrette. We would welcome reports on his cooking. The bedrooms vary in size: smaller rooms are decorated in cottage style with brass and light oak fittings; Tree Tops, in the loft, has a large bathroom with a roll-top bath and a walk-in shower; the Garden Room has a wet room and a sitting area. Breakfast includes fruit juices, cereals, yogurt and a choice of a full Cumbrian, grilled Craster kippers or smoked salmon with scrambled eggs. Viewing points for the Bassenthwaite ospreys are nearby; Keswick is a ten-minute drive. (*J and TB, and others*)

25% DISCOUNT VOUCHERS

Magic Hill
Whinlatter Forest
Braithwaite CA12 5TW

T: 017687-78409
E: relax@thecottageinthewood.co.uk
W: www.thecottageinthewood.co.uk

BEDROOMS: 10, 1 on ground floor.
OPEN: Feb–Dec, restaurant closed Mon.
FACILITIES: lounge, bar, restaurant, 5-acre grounds (terraced garden).
BACKGROUND MUSIC: none.
LOCATION: 5 miles NW of Keswick.
CHILDREN: not under 10.
DOGS: not allowed.
CREDIT CARDS: Amex, MasterCard, Visa.
PRICES: B&B £50–£90 per person, D,B&B £80–£120, set menus £36–£52, full alc £40, midweek breaks, Christmas/New Year packages, 1-night bookings refused weekends.

BRAMPTON Cumbria

Map 4:B3

FARLAM HALL

César award in 2001

'The courtesy of the owners and the helpfulness of the staff is outstanding,' says a visitor this year to the Quinion family's traditional country hotel (Relais & Châteaux). The former Borders manor house stands sheltered by tall trees in an 'immaculate' landscaped garden. Its ornamental lake has an 'entrancing' fountain. There are open fires in the ornate public rooms, which have patterned wallpaper, lots of knick-knacks and Victoriana. Bedrooms, priced according to size, are liked: 'Ours couldn't have been more comfortable,' is a typical comment. In the evening, 'smart dress is preferred': drinks and canapés are served before dinner in the two drawing rooms. The huge dining room has floor-to-ceiling windows that overlook the garden. The chef, Barry Quinion, serves a short daily-changing menu of 'imaginative dishes with unusual combinations', perhaps terrine of partridge, herb and pistachio; breast of guineafowl, ginger risotto, plum and orange sauce. The 'lovely' breakfast had 'proper toast and conserves; beautifully cooked scrambled egg; tender sweet bacon'. Hadrian's Wall and the M6 are within easy reach. (*Dr Gillian Todd*)

25% DISCOUNT VOUCHERS

Brampton CA8 2NG

T: 01697-746234
F: 01697-746683
E: farlam@farlamhall.co.uk
W: www.farlamhall.co.uk

BEDROOMS: 12, 1 in stables, 2 on ground floor.

OPEN: all year except 24–30 Dec, 3–13 Jan, restaurant closed midday (light lunches by arrangement).

FACILITIES: ramps, 2 lounges, restaurant, civil wedding licence, 10-acre grounds, unsuitable for ♿.

BACKGROUND MUSIC: none.

LOCATION: on A689, 2½ miles SE of Brampton (not in Farlam village).

CHILDREN: not under 5.

DOGS: not allowed unattended in bedrooms.

CREDIT CARDS: Amex, MasterCard, Visa.

PRICES: B&B £107–£137 per person, D,B&B £150–£180, set dinner £45–£47.50, special breaks, New Year package.

BRANCASTER STAITHE Norfolk

Map 2:A5

THE WHITE HORSE

There are panoramic views across tidal sea marshes from the conservatory restaurant and terrace of this relaxed inn on the north Norfolk coast. It is owned by Cliff Nye. Christina Boyle was appointed manager in June 2012. The bedrooms are decorated in seaside colours (blue, green, lavender and sand). Eight rooms are in a garden annexe which has a grass and sedum roof to blend with the marshland; having direct access to the garden, these are suitable for walkers, cyclists and dog owners (£10 charge). In the main building, the Room at the Top has a viewing balcony with a telescope. The public areas are open plan: scrubbed pine furnishings and photographs of local characters in the bar; there are Lloyd Loom sofas in a lounge area; the restaurant has pine tables and chairs. The modern menus of the chef, Aurum Frankel, are influenced by local produce, in particular fish and shellfish from the village (mussels are harvested at the bottom of the garden). Typical dishes: verrine of Letzer's smoked salmon, cucumber jelly, micro herbs; pea, butternut, Parmesan and truffle risotto, Norfolk pea shoots, crispy leeks.

Brancaster Staithe
PE31 8BY

T: 01485-210262
F: 01485-210930
E: reception@whitehorsebrancaster.co.uk
W: www.whitehorsebrancaster.co.uk

BEDROOMS: 15, 8 on ground floor in annexe, 1 suitable for ♿.
OPEN: all year.
FACILITIES: 2 lounge areas, public bar, conservatory restaurant, dining room, ½-acre garden (covered sunken garden), harbour sailing.
BACKGROUND MUSIC: none.
LOCATION: centre of village just E of Brancaster.
CHILDREN: all ages welcomed.
DOGS: allowed in annexe rooms (£10) and bar.
CREDIT CARDS: MasterCard, Visa.
PRICES: [2012] B&B £47–£110 per person, D,B&B (Nov–Mar only) £67–£105, full alc £42, off-season breaks, Christmas/New Year packages.

BRAY Berkshire

Map 2:D3

THE WATERSIDE INN

'The service is beyond reproach' at Alain and Michel Roux's restaurant-with-rooms in a prosperous Thames-side village. 'I cannot fault the meals, which were enhanced by the personal attention of the ever-smiling manager, Diego Masciaga, and Alain Roux,' says a visitor this year. The father and son owner/chefs have long held three *Michelin* stars for their classic French cuisine, which is taken in a glass-fronted restaurant overlooking the river. 'Though the unwary could be shocked at the cost, the food is as fabulous as you would expect. I would recommend the "menu exceptionnel".' This has to be ordered by the entire table: the dishes might include langoustine soufflé, cassoulet of langoustines scented with truffles; saddle of milk lamb stuffed with morels and served with baby vegetables. The wine list is 'pretty stratospheric'. A three-course 'menu gastronomique' is available at lunchtime. Pre-dinner drinks can be taken on a terrace. The 'impeccable' bedrooms, designed by Michel Roux's wife, Robyn, are also French in style. Two rooms share a balcony above the water. 'Breakfast is brought to the bedroom on a wicker tray.'

Ferry Road
Bray SL6 2AT

T: 01628-620691
F: 01628-789182
E: reservations@waterside-inn.co.uk
W: www.waterside-inn.co.uk

BEDROOMS: 10, plus 2 apartments in nearby cottage.
OPEN: Feb–Dec except 25/26 Dec, Mon/Tues.
FACILITIES: restaurant, private dining room (with drawing room and courtyard garden), civil wedding licence, riverside terrace (launch for drinks/coffee), unsuitable for ♿.
BACKGROUND MUSIC: none.
LOCATION: 3 miles SE of Maidenhead.
CHILDREN: not under 12.
DOGS: not allowed.
CREDIT CARDS: all major cards.
PRICES: [2012] B&B £110–£170 per person, suite/apartment £475–£750, set lunch £58–£74, tasting menu £147.50.

BRIGHTON East Sussex

Map 2:E4

DRAKES

On the seafront, in sight of the pier and within walking distance of The Lanes, this conversion of two white stucco Regency town houses, owned by Andy Shearer, is managed by Richard Hayes. It has a striking modern interior, mixing 'orientalism with a touch of decadence'. The better bedrooms, reached by a dramatic staircase, face the sea; others overlook gardens at the back. A triple-aspect circular room has a freestanding bath in front of the floor-to-ceiling windows (providing 'ridiculous pleasure'), a shower big enough for two, and a super king-size bed. All rooms have air conditioning, flat-screen TV, DVD/CD-player and Wi-Fi. In-room massage and treatments are available, and a personal shopper can be arranged. A cocktail bar/lounge on the ground floor is open to hotel guests at all times. In the basement restaurant, which has subtle lighting and exposed brickwork, chef Andrew MacKenzie serves modern dishes, eg, parsley root soup, poached quail's egg; roast squab pigeon, Alsace bacon, lentils and fondant potato. A five-course tasting menu and a vegetarian tasting menu are also available.

25% DISCOUNT VOUCHERS

43/44 Marine Parade
Brighton BN2 1PE

T: 01273-696934
F: 01273-684805
E: info@drakesofbrighton.com
W: www.drakesofbrighton.com

BEDROOMS: 20, 2 on ground floor.
OPEN: all year.
FACILITIES: ramp, lounge/bar/Reception, restaurant, meeting room, civil wedding/partnership licence, unsuitable for ♿.
BACKGROUND MUSIC: 'light music' in bar.
LOCATION: on seafront.
CHILDREN: all ages welcomed.
DOGS: not allowed.
CREDIT CARDS: Amex, MasterCard, Visa.
PRICES: room £115–£345, breakfast £6–£12.50, set menu £29.95–£49.95, tasting menu £55, full alc £55 (*12.5% 'discretionary' service charge added*), midweek packages, Christmas/New Year packages, 1-night bookings refused Sat, bank holidays.

SEE ALSO SHORTLIST

BRIGHTON East Sussex

Map 2:E4

HOTEL DU VIN BRIGHTON

Quirky original features (a carved staircase, bizarre gargoyles, a vault-ceilinged hall) have been retained in the imaginative conversion of these Gothic revival and mock Tudor buildings that form the Brighton branch of the Hotel du Vin chain. Between the cobbled streets of The Lanes and the seafront, it is a 'lively' place to stay ('my favourite in the city,' according to a trusted correspondent). The bedrooms (some of which are reached by steep staircases) are decorated in seaside fashion: Beachy Head has a two-seater sofa, a freestanding roll-top bath in a bay window; a twin shower in the bathroom. The Loft Suite, with sea views, has a small private terrace. 'The atmosphere in the bistro is lively and the food is as good as you get in Brighton.' Chef Robert Carr's menus might include potted crab, caper berry and egg salad; slow-roasted pork belly, celeriac purée, chorizo. The 'excellent' breakfast has a substantial continental buffet ('lovely fruit salad, nice croissants, good yogurts'); 'delicious' porridge; and 'well-presented cooked dishes'. (*WS, and others*)

2–6 Ship Street
Brighton BN1 1AD

T: 01273-718588
E: info.brighton@hotelduvin.com
W: www.hotelduvin.com

BEDROOMS: 49, 6 in courtyard, 11 in connected *Pub du Vin*.
OPEN: all year.
FACILITIES: lounge/bar, bistro, billiard room, function rooms, civil wedding licence, unsuitable for ♿.
BACKGROUND MUSIC: 'easy listening' in bar all day.
LOCATION: 50 yds from seafront.
CHILDREN: all ages welcomed.
DOGS: allowed.
CREDIT CARDS: Amex, MasterCard, Visa.
PRICES: [2012] B&B £125–£250 per person, breakfast £14.95, full alc £45, Christmas/New Year packages, special breaks, 1-night bookings sometimes refused in summer.

SEE ALSO SHORTLIST

BRISTOL

Map 1:B6

BROOKS GUESTHOUSE BRISTOL

NEW

In a 'great position' in the old town, 'seconds from the waterfront', this former hostel has been converted by owners Carla and Andrew Brooks into a 'stylish' modern hotel. It is upgraded to a full entry thanks to an enthusiastic report from a *Guide* hotelier. 'They have created a memorable experience, demonstrating flair, imagination and excellent staff interaction.' 'Impressive' wrought iron gates open to a large paved courtyard with, on a hot day, 'an almost Mediterranean feel'; it has an 'entertaining' mural by Banksy's friends. A front desk area leads to a lounge/dining room with sofas and armchairs, free Wi-Fi, newspapers and magazines; an honesty bar. The small bedrooms have a contemporary decor: 'My room had a good bed, excellent lighting; a quirky 1950s chair; no wardrobe – two wooden hangers sufficed.' Bedrooms facing the street might suffer from late-night noise; courtyard rooms are quieter. Breakfast has 'quality coffee, granary toast; a tasty blackcurrant compote; wonderful eggs Benedict; unobtrusive background music'. 'Exceptional value.' (*Rosemary Reeves, and others*)

Exchange Avenue
Bristol BS1 1UB

T: 0117-930 0066
F: 0117-929 9489
E: info@brooksguesthousebristol.com
W: www.brooksguesthousebristol.com

BEDROOMS: 22, 1 on ground floor suitable for ♿.
OPEN: all year except 23–27 Dec.
FACILITIES: lounge/dining room, courtyard garden.
BACKGROUND MUSIC: 'soft' in lounge.
LOCATION: central.
CHILDREN: all ages welcomed.
DOGS: not allowed.
CREDIT CARDS: MasterCard, Visa.
PRICES: B&B £35–£49.50 per person, New Year package.

BRISTOL

Map 1:B6

HOTEL DU VIN BRISTOL

An imaginative conversion of a group of Grade II listed buildings (one a former sugar warehouse) houses the Bristol branch of the Hotel du Vin chain. 'They push the right buttons for me,' said a fan: 'Minimalist lines, strong dark colours, large beds with good mattress, soft pillows.' Other visitors this year had reservations: 'My room had a dark feel; a wide wooden surround to the huge bed made it unnecessarily wide; but it was made up with sheets and blankets as requested; the splendid bathroom had a large separate shower and fluffy towels. Very quiet at night.' A spacious two-level room has a bath by the window. The large public areas have tables and potted plants, and a sweeping steel and oak staircase. A guest was 'well looked after' in the bistro which has a modern French menu (the plat du jour might be smoked haddock with crab velouté). Breakfast has a 'good buffet' (cereals, compotes, pain au chocolat, croissants, etc); 'nice kippers'. On a busy road: a secure car park has limited space. (*DB, and others*)

The Sugar House
Narrow Lewins Mead
Bristol BS1 2NU

T: 0117-925 5577
F: 0117-925 1199
E: info.bristol@hotelduvin.com
W: www.hotelduvin.com

BEDROOMS: 40.
OPEN: all year.
FACILITIES: lift, ramp, lounge, library/billiard room, 2 bars, bistro, 3 private dining rooms, civil wedding licence.
BACKGROUND MUSIC: 'easy listening' in bar.
LOCATION: city centre.
CHILDREN: all ages welcomed.
DOGS: allowed.
CREDIT CARDS: Amex, MasterCard, Visa.
PRICES: room £125–£330, breakfast £12.50–£14.95, full alc £60, special breaks, New Year package.

BRISTOL

Map 1:B6

NUMBER THIRTY EIGHT CLIFTON NEW

César award: B&B newcomer of the year

At the top of the city on the edge of Clifton Downs, this Georgian house has been transformed into a luxury B&B by Adam Dorrien-Smith. 'He has created a stunning contemporary interior with striking sculptures and modern art,' say inspectors in 2012. The managers are Jarek Eliasz and Shona Smillie, 'a charming and cheerful couple'. The ground-floor lounge has 'comfortable armchairs and sofas, coffee tables with magazines, local information'. The bedrooms are on six floors, above and below the entrance. 'Our huge room had wide bay windows; wooden floorboards and coir carpeting, smart linen fabrics, excellent lighting, plenty of storage. Its vast bathroom had a roll-top bath by the window, a separate power shower.' The breakfast room has well-spaced tables; fresh fruit, juices, cereals and pastries on a central pedestal table; 'good coffee and brown toast; excellent scrambled eggs'. No evening meals: drinks and snacks are served on a 'lovely' roof terrace which has plants, outdoor settees and chairs. Mr Dorrien-Smith's father, Robert, owns *Hell Bay Hotel*, Bryher (see entry).

38 Upper Belgrave Road
Clifton, Bristol BS8 2XN

T: 0117-946 6905
E: info@number38clifton.com
W: www.number38clifton.com

BEDROOMS: 10.
OPEN: all year.
FACILITIES: lounge, breakfast room, terrace, unsuitable for ♿.
BACKGROUND MUSIC: jazz at breakfast.
LOCATION: on edge of Clifton Downs.
CHILDREN: not under 12.
DOGS: not allowed.
CREDIT CARDS: all major cards.
PRICES: [2012] B&B £50–£87.50 per person.

BROAD CAMPDEN Gloucestershire

Map 3:D6

THE MALT HOUSE

'Beautifully decorated; a fine B&B with a very hospitable host.' Judi Wilkes's 16th-century, Grade II listed malt house with its two adjacent cottages (combined as a single building) has many fans. Other praise this year: 'Judi is full of useful advice and information about the area.' The house is entered through a 'delightful' garden, which has a terrace, summer house, croquet lawn and wisteria-draped wall. The two comfortable sitting rooms have open fire, armchairs, plenty of newspapers and magazines, and a small honesty bar. In fine weather, afternoon tea and early evening drinks can be taken in the garden. The bedrooms (all look over the garden) are well equipped with umbrella, spare toothbrushes, scissors, fresh milk for tea-making, current magazines. One has a four-poster, three have a private entrance. The 'delicious and generous' breakfasts have home-made breads, berries and rhubarb from the garden in season, freshly squeezed orange juice; bacon and eggs from Cotswold suppliers. There are many places to eat within a short distance. (*Paula and John Sloan, and others*)

25% DISCOUNT VOUCHERS

Broad Campden
nr Chipping Campden
GL55 6UU

T: 01386-840295
E: info@malt-house.co.uk
W: www.malt-house.co.uk

BEDROOMS: 7, 2 on ground floor, 3 with own entrance.
OPEN: all year except Christmas/New Year.
FACILITIES: 2 lounges, dining room, 3-acre garden (croquet, orchard, stream), unsuitable for ♿.
BACKGROUND MUSIC: none.
LOCATION: 1 mile S of Chipping Campden.
CHILDREN: all ages welcomed.
DOGS: not allowed.
CREDIT CARDS: MasterCard, Visa.
PRICES: B&B £65–£85 per person, special breaks.

BROADWAY Worcestershire

Map 3:D6

RUSSELL'S RESTAURANT

César award in 2006

'Wonderful; excellent staff, housekeeping and food.' New praise this year for Andrew Riley's restaurant-with-rooms. A chic contemporary conversion of the former showroom of Arts and Crafts furniture designer Sir Gordon Russell, it stands on the wide High Street of a Cotswold village. Inglenook fireplaces, beams and an old oak staircase are among the original features retained in the renovation. In the L-shaped restaurant (wooden tables, grey slate mats, modern cutlery and artwork), chef Damian Clisby serves modern British dishes (eg, pork terrine, pistachio; Cotswold white chicken, foie grass, cèpe sauce) on an extensive carte and a short fixed-price menu. A fine Russell table is the centrepiece of a small private dining room. The bedrooms are individually designed: 'Our well-equipped room had a walk-in shower and separate bath; a coffee machine was a welcome extra.' An 'exciting' room on two levels had two armchairs and 'a window on almost every wall'. Some rooms face the village (windows are double glazed). All have air conditioning, good linen, flat-screen TV and broadband Internet access. (*Simon Irving*)

The Green, 20 High Street
Broadway WR12 7DT

T: 01386-853555
E: info@russellsofbroadway.co.uk
W: www.russellsofbroadway.co.uk

BEDROOMS: 7, 3 in adjoining building, 2 on ground floor.

OPEN: all year, restaurant closed Sun night.

FACILITIES: ramp, residents' lobby, bar, restaurant, private dining room, patio (heating, meal service).

BACKGROUND MUSIC: 'ambient' in restaurant.

LOCATION: village centre.

CHILDREN: all ages welcomed.

DOGS: not allowed.

CREDIT CARDS: Amex, MasterCard, Visa.

PRICES: [2012] B&B £52.50–£150 per person, set menus £17.95–£24.95, full alc £42, seasonal breaks on website, 1-night bookings refused weekends.

BROCKENHURST Hampshire

Map 2:E2

THE PIG

NEW

Deep in the New Forest, this former hunting lodge has been given a modern make-over by Robin Hutson, co-founder of Hotel du Vin. 'He set out to create a country house hotel with attitude, and he has pulled it off,' said inspectors. 'The tone is laid-back and stylish.' The lounges have old stripped floorboards, squashy sofas, open fires, bookshelf wallpaper in alcoves, scented plants. Dinner in the 'beautifully styled' conservatory restaurant is 'great fun': the chef, James Golding, turns to the kitchen gardener and the forager to supply his 25-mile menu: 'We enjoyed delicious mushrooms from the "literally picked this morning" section; a rich risotto with chorizo; an outstanding crème fraîche with rose water and wild berries. Loud background music was soon drowned by the happy hum of conversation.' The bedrooms come in three sizes: 'snug', 'comfy' and 'spacious'. Those in the stable block by the kitchen garden have retained original features: 'The horse divider in our room separated the bed and bath space; old floorboards and brick walls remained.' The continental breakfast is 'especially good'. *The Pig* is the baby sister of *Lime Wood*, Lyndhurst (see entry).

Beaulieu Road
Brockenhurst SO42 7QL

T: 01590-622354
E: info@thepighotel.com
W: www.thepighotel.co.uk

BEDROOMS: 26, 10 in stable block (100 yds), some on ground floor.

OPEN: all year.

FACILITIES: 2 lounges, bar, restaurant, Potting Shed spa, kitchen garden, 14-acre grounds.

BACKGROUND MUSIC: in restaurant and lounges.

LOCATION: 2 miles E of Brockenhurst.

CHILDREN: all ages welcomed.

DOGS: allowed in some bedrooms, some public areas.

CREDIT CARDS: Amex, MasterCard, Visa.

PRICES: [2012] room £125–£220, breakfast £10–£15, full alc £42.50, 1-night bookings refused at weekends.

BROXTON Cheshire

Map 3:A5

FROGG MANOR

César award in 1997

'Wonderful, laid-back and relaxing.' More praise this year for John Sykes's 'totally eccentric' manor house in rural Cheshire. It has been described as a 'Marmite' hotel (guests either love it or hate it). 'Be prepared to take it as you find it,' is the advice of one visitor. Mr Sykes has dedicated the house to frogs: there are 'thousands of them' (ceramic, brass, straw, etc) in the extravagantly furnished public rooms. The genial owner might be seen 'padding around in bare feet', perhaps wearing a brown fedora. A visitor in 2012, who stayed in the 'sumptuous' Guinevere Suite (a tree house in the grounds), enjoyed 'a heavenly experience, literally; at the flick of a switch a solar system projector turned the ceiling into the Milky Way'. Other rooms are no less dramatic: the Wellington Suite has a crown-canopied bed, a dressing room, and a small secret door in the corner which opens through the bookcase into an upstairs lounge. Mr Sykes is the 'very good' chef, pricing his menus in guineas. (*Colin Holroyd, Janice Gleave, and others*)

25% DISCOUNT VOUCHERS

Nantwich Road
Broxton, Chester CH3 9JH

T: 01829-782629
F: 01829-782459
E: info@froggmanorhotel.co.uk
W: www.froggmanorhotel.co.uk

BEDROOMS: 8, 1 in tree house, 1 suitable for ♿.

OPEN: all year.

FACILITIES: ramp, lounge, bar lounge, restaurant, private dining room, conference/function facilities, civil wedding licence, 9½-acre grounds (tennis).

BACKGROUND MUSIC: 1930s–50s CDs in lounge, restaurant and bar lounge.

LOCATION: 12 miles SE of Chester.

CHILDREN: all ages welcomed.

DOGS: allowed in bedrooms, bar lounge.

CREDIT CARDS: all major cards.

PRICES: [2012] B&B (continental) £54.56–£138.37 per person, D,B&B £80.31–£157.26, set dinner £25.75–£37.75, full alc £41.65–£53.65, midweek discounts.

BRYHER Isles of Scilly

Map 1: inset C1

HELL BAY HOTEL

Built like a group of cottages beside a sandy beach, this is the only hotel on Bryher, the smallest of the inhabited Isles of Scilly. It is owned by Robert Dorrien-Smith, who has the lease for neighbouring Tresco. Visitors arrive by boat and are transported from the quay by Land Rover. The bar and large lounge have 'excellent sitting areas'; Mr Dorrien-Smith's 'wonderful' collection of modern Cornish art is displayed here ('it rivals Tate St Ives,' says a regular visitor). The accommodation is in suites in buildings around the courtyard and in the garden. Decorated in seaside colours, most have a sitting area. Many face the sea and have a balcony or a terrace: 'How lovely to lie in bed and look out across a rocky bay,' is a recent comment. Large canvases by local artist Richard Pearce (his studio is by the garden gate) hang in the dining room. Richard Kearsley joined as chef in 2012; his short modern menus might include Cornish scallops, thyme-scented rhubarb purée; oven-roast pork tenderloin, shoulder beignets, haricot blanc casserole. Mr Dorrien-Smith's son, Adam, runs the *César*-winning *Number Thirty Eight Clifton,* Bristol (see entry). (*AT, and others*)

Bryher, Isles of Scilly
Cornwall TR23 0PR

T: 01720-422947
F: 01720-423004
E: contactus@hellbay.co.uk
W: www.hellbay.co.uk

BEDROOMS: 25 suites, in 5 buildings, some on ground floor, 1 suitable for ♿.

OPEN: 15 Mar–2 Nov.

FACILITIES: lounge, games room, bar, 2 dining rooms, gym, sauna, large grounds (heated swimming pool, 15 by 10 metres, children's playground, par 3 golf course), beach 75 yds.

BACKGROUND MUSIC: none.

LOCATION: W coast of island, boat from Tresco (reached by boat/helicopter from mainland) or St Mary's.

CHILDREN: all ages welcomed (high tea at 5.30).

DOGS: not allowed in public rooms.

CREDIT CARDS: MasterCard, Visa.

PRICES: [2012] D,B&B £135–£320 per person, set dinner £35, short breaks, 1-night bookings refused weekends.

BUCKDEN Cambridgeshire

Map 2:B4

THE GEORGE

'We were warmly greeted as if we were old friends, despite never having been there before.' Praise from a reader in 2012 for this small hotel and brasserie on the main street of a pretty Cambridgeshire village. The 19th-century former coaching inn was renovated by owners Anne, Richard and Becky Furbank; Cynthia Schaeffer is the manager. 'The staff are delightful; the public areas are charming though the background music was noticeable,' said inspectors. The bedrooms are named after famous Georges (eg, Hanover, Eliot, Stephenson). 'Our spacious room had a masculine decor; a big bed, free-range hangers in a wardrobe, but no drawers other than the small ones in the bedside tables.' The road can be busy (windows are double glazed but rooms could be 'stuffy on a hot day'). Meals are served in the brasserie, alfresco on the terrace in summer, and in the bar and lounge. 'The conservatory-style dining room had shiny wooden tables, big white napkins, plates properly hot; meals promptly served by a caring staff.' José Graziosi is the chef: 'My soup (celeriac and chestnut with truffle oil) was delicious.' (*Neil Gershon, and others*)

25% DISCOUNT VOUCHERS

High Street
Buckden PE19 5XA

T: 01480-812300
F: 01480-813920
E: mail@thegeorgebuckden.com
W: www.thegeorgebuckden.com

BEDROOMS: 12.
OPEN: all year.
FACILITIES: lift, bar, lounge, restaurant, private dining room, civil wedding licence, courtyard.
BACKGROUND MUSIC: light jazz in all public areas.
LOCATION: village centre.
CHILDREN: all ages welcomed, baby-changing facilities.
DOGS: not allowed in public rooms.
CREDIT CARDS: Amex, MasterCard, Visa.
PRICES: B&B £45–£75 per person, D,B&B from £60, full alc £40.

BUCKLAND MARSH Oxfordshire

Map 2:C2

THE TROUT AT TADPOLE BRIDGE

'The staff are welcoming and the food is great,' says a visitor this year to Gareth and Helen Pugh's 'warm and friendly' 17th-century pub/restaurant beside a narrow bridge over the River Thames. The bar and eating areas, which have part-timbered walls and original fireplaces, are popular with locals. Mrs Pugh runs front-of-house 'with charm', and takes orders for dinner; Pascal Clavaud is the chef. 'His interesting menu is supplemented by a good specials board: we had bubble and squeak with a poached egg and hollandaise sauce, roast pheasant with caramelised pears.' The bedrooms are individually decorated in contemporary style: 'A lot of thought had gone into our room's design to ensure it provided comfort and functionality; a king-size bed, a well-lit dressing table, large wardrobe, cafetière and fresh milk, magazines; good-quality fittings and towels in the bathroom.' Breakfast 'is as good as dinner', with a selection of cooked dishes including fish, and a basket with croissants and toast'. Children and dogs are welcomed. 'Pretty good value.' (*Mrs EM Anderson, Ken and Priscilla Wilmslow, Peter Adam*)

Buckland Marsh
SN7 8RF

T: 01367-870382
F: 01367-870912
E: info@trout-inn.co.uk
W: www.trout-inn.co.uk

BEDROOMS: 6, 3 in courtyard.
OPEN: all year except 25/26 Dec.
FACILITIES: bar, dining area, breakfast area, 2-acre garden (river, moorings).
BACKGROUND MUSIC: none.
LOCATION: 2 miles N of A420, halfway between Oxford and Swindon.
CHILDREN: all ages welcomed.
DOGS: allowed.
CREDIT CARDS: MasterCard, Visa.
PRICES: [2012] B&B £65–£85 per person, D,B&B £95–£115, full alc £30, New Year package, 1-night bookings refused weekends.

BUDE Cornwall

Map 1:C3

THE BEACH AT BUDE

'Something out of the ordinary', Timothy Davis's luxury B&B stands out from more nondescript properties on a narrow street above the beach at this north Cornish resort. 'He has restored the building to the highest standard,' said a trusted reporter. It has a large conservatory and breakfast room with 'spectacular' views over Summerleaze beach; a library with books, magazines and newspapers; and a business centre; a sun terrace with wicker seating. The best bedrooms have sea views (five have a private terrace, others a Juliet balcony); they have a seating area, a bath and a separate walk-in shower. Standard rooms face a courtyard. All rooms are decorated in New England style: 'Fitted furniture in bleached oak, and the freestanding Lloyd Loom furnishings fitted into the seaside atmosphere. Our bathroom had a large tub, twin basins on a slate plinth, and a superb separate shower.' Breakfast has juices, yogurts, cereals, fresh croissants and a variety of cooked dishes. There is a storeroom for surfboards, and a warm outside shower for guests coming from the beach. Many eating places are nearby. (*PM*)

25% DISCOUNT VOUCHERS

Summerleaze Crescent
Bude EX23 8HL

T: 01288-389800
F: 01288-389820
E: enquiries@thebeachatbude.co.uk
W: www.thebeachatbude.co.uk

BEDROOMS: 15, 3 on ground floor.
OPEN: all year except 23–29 Dec.
FACILITIES: lift, conservatory, dining room, sunroom, library, terrace.
BACKGROUND MUSIC: at breakfast.
LOCATION: above Summerleaze beach.
CHILDREN: not under 12.
DOGS: not allowed.
CREDIT CARDS: MasterCard, Visa.
PRICES: [2012] B&B £55–£80 per person, special breaks.

BURFORD Oxfordshire

Map 2:C2

BURFORD HOUSE

On the main street of a 'wonderfully historic' Cotswold town, this handsome 17th-century house is run as a small hotel by Ian Hawkins and Stewart Dunkley (the chef). 'Thoroughly recommended; our place of choice in the area,' say visitors this year. The *Centre Stage* restaurant has 'immaculately dressed' tables, theatrical posters. ('The downside: songs from the shows are pumped out.') Lunch is served daily; dinner is available from Thursday to Saturday. The modern menu might include rillette of Barbary duck, home-smoked breast, rhubarb; Sauvignon poached turbot, samphire, brown shrimp, smoked pancetta. The staff are 'friendly and obliging'. A minor reservation: 'Meal times are inflexible.' The quietest bedrooms are at the back: 'Our large room was comfortable and well equipped.' A room at the top, reached by a steep staircase, had beams, a 'luxuriant' large bed; a 'capacious, well-lit' bathroom. 'Wooden shutters kept out the noise of the busy high street.' A 'faultless' breakfast has 'wonderful' freshly squeezed orange juice; cooked dishes to order ('perfect smoked haddock with a poached egg'). Street parking is limited; a public car park is a short walk away. (*Robert Gower, Angy Kirker*)

99 High Street
Burford OX18 4QA

T: 01993-823151
F: 01993-823240
E: stay@burfordhouse.co.uk
W: www.burfordhouse.co.uk

BEDROOMS: 8, 2 in adjoining coach house, 1 on ground floor.

OPEN: all year except 1 week in Jan, restaurant closed Sun–Wed nights.

FACILITIES: 2 lounges, restaurant, small courtyard garden, unsuitable for ♿.

BACKGROUND MUSIC: in lounges and restaurant.

LOCATION: central.

CHILDREN: all ages welcomed.

DOGS: only guide dogs allowed in bedrooms.

CREDIT CARDS: all major cards.

PRICES: [2012] B&B £89.50–£139.50 per person, set dinner £29.50–£35, special offers, Christmas/New Year packages, 1-night bookings normally refused weekends, bank holidays.

SEE ALSO SHORTLIST

BURFORD Oxfordshire

Map 2:C2

THE LAMB INN

On a leafy street in this medieval town, this mellow stone building is based on a clutch of 15th-century weavers' cottages which later became an inn. 'As you would expect from a very old building, it is comfortable, rather than stylish,' says a trusted reporter, who had 'a thoroughly enjoyable' stay this year. Managed by Bill Ramsay, it is part of a small Cotswold hotel group (see also *The Manor House*, Moreton-in-Marsh). The two lounges have flagstoned floor, beamed ceilings, settees and 'welcoming' log fires. A small public bar has an 'interesting' range of snacks and light lunches. Six bedrooms have been refurbished this year. 'Our first-floor room was a reasonable size, as was the bathroom; the lack of a full-length mirror was irritating.' In the light and airy restaurant, which has well-laid tables, good linen and glassware, Sean Ducie serves contemporary dishes, perhaps scallops and langoustines with crystallised seaweed; Cotswold fillet steak, truffled potatoes, shallot purée. 'The food was excellent as was the service from the mainly Central European staff.' Breakfast is thought 'good'. (*Bill Bennett, and others*)

25% DISCOUNT VOUCHERS

Sheep Street
Burford OX18 4LR

T: 01993-823155
F: 01993-822228
E: manager@lambinn-burford.co.uk
W: www.cotswold-inns-hotels.co.uk/lamb

BEDROOMS: 17.
OPEN: all year.
FACILITIES: 2 lounges, bar, restaurant, courtyard, ½-acre garden, unsuitable for ♿.
BACKGROUND MUSIC: 'gentle' in restaurant.
LOCATION: 150 yds from centre.
CHILDREN: all ages welcomed.
DOGS: allowed, on lead in restaurant.
CREDIT CARDS: all major cards.
PRICES: [2012] B&B £50–£145 per person, D,B&B £80–£180, tasting menu £49, full alc £59 (*10% service added to restaurant bills*), special breaks, Christmas/New Year packages, 1-night bookings sometimes refused Sat.

SEE ALSO SHORTLIST

BURRINGTON Devon

Map 1:C4

NORTHCOTE MANOR

'A delightful experience,' say visitors this year to Jean-Pierre Mifsud's 'near-perfect' 18th-century former manor house in the north Devon countryside. In a 'beautiful setting with extensive views over the Taw valley', the house is approached by a meandering, deeply wooded driveway. Beyond a spacious hall are a drawing room and a sitting room with a bay window; there are log fires, oriental rugs and large murals. Bedrooms (five have been added this year) come with 'many complimentary extras, such as a minibar with soft drinks, fresh milk in the fridge, a cafetière on the tray, free Wi-Fi and daily newspaper. Our bathroom was modern, with top-quality fittings.' In the elegant restaurant, chef Richie Herkes cooks a modern menu of dishes like oak-smoked salmon with Cornish crab cakes; breast of duckling, gratin potatoes, honey-roasted parsnips, venison gravy. A five-course gourmet menu, to be taken by the whole table, is available. Cooked dishes at breakfast (no buffet) are 'fresh and excellent'. Mr Mifsud also owns *The Lake*, Llangammarch Wells, Wales (see entry). (*Ken and Priscilla Winslow, George and Annette Crossley*)

25% DISCOUNT VOUCHERS

Burrington
Umberleigh EX37 9LZ

T: 01769-560501
F: 01769-560770
E: rest@northcotemanor.co.uk
W: www.northcotemanor.co.uk

BEDROOMS: 16, 1 suitable for ♿.
OPEN: all year.
FACILITIES: 2 lounges, bar, 2 restaurants, civil wedding licence, 25-acre grounds.
BACKGROUND MUSIC: classical.
LOCATION: 3 miles S of Umberleigh.
CHILDREN: all ages welcomed.
DOGS: not allowed in restaurants.
CREDIT CARDS: Amex, MasterCard, Visa.
PRICES: [2012] B&B £90–£170 per person, D,B&B £135–£210, full alc £70, special breaks, Christmas/New Year packages.

CAMELFORD Cornwall

Map 1:C3

PENDRAGON COUNTRY HOUSE

'The welcome was as warm as a day's sunshine,' says a visitor in 2012 to Sharon and Nigel Reed's guest house, a former Victorian rectory. 'They should be proud of what they have achieved,' says another guest. The 'unobtrusive, efficient' hosts have furnished the house with Victorian antiques. There are books and board games in the two lounges, log fires and a 24-hour honesty bar. Children are welcomed: baby monitors and a listening service are available. Bedrooms vary in size and decor: Bedivere has a solid cherry-wood king-size four-poster bed, a shower cabinet and roll-top bath big enough for two; Tristram, the largest, can accommodate four people and has a Cornish tin ceiling. A wheelchair user praised the accessibility of the house. Chef Nigel Reed's meals, taken in the *Orangery* dining room, are 'well balanced'. Typical dishes: carpaccio of venison, blackcurrant jus; trio of local fish en papillote, fennel, lemon and white wine. Breakfast has home-baked bread, freshly squeezed orange juice; 'the best ever' choice of cooked dishes (perhaps the special cheese sandwich with a runny poached egg). (*Shirley Beach, Sofia Dettman*)

25% DISCOUNT VOUCHERS

Davidstow
Camelford PL32 9XR

T: 01840-261131
E: enquiries@pendragoncountryhouse.com
W: www.pendragoncountryhouse.com

BEDROOMS: 7, 1 on ground floor suitable for ♿.
OPEN: all year except 24–26 Dec, restaurant closed Sun.
FACILITIES: sitting room, bar, *Orangery* breakfast/dining room, private dining room, civil wedding licence, 1¼-acre grounds.
BACKGROUND MUSIC: if requested.
LOCATION: 3½ miles NE of Camelford.
CHILDREN: all ages welcomed.
DOGS: allowed in downstairs bedroom.
CREDIT CARDS: all major cards.
PRICES: B&B £42–£65 per person, D,B&B £18.50 added, set meals £22.50, New Year package.

CAMPSEA ASHE Suffolk

Map 2:C6

THE OLD RECTORY

NEW

By the church in a village near the Suffolk coast, Sally Ball's 'elegant and comfortable' 18th-century rectory gains a full entry after several positive reports: 'A beautiful house in lovely gardens; a peaceful place to stay,' says a visitor in 2012. 'Very welcoming, with well above average food,' is a comment from a regular correspondent. There is an honesty bar in the 'spacious and agreeably furnished' lounge. A three-course set modern menu is served on three evenings a week (by arrangement for parties of eight or more on other nights). The 'beautifully cooked and well-presented dishes' might include rabbit salad, potato rösti; cod with a chickpea, chorizo and tomato cassoulet. 'Fresh, local and delicious.' A large room in the main house 'had windows on two sides overlooking the well-maintained garden'. A ground-floor room in a cottage beside the house has a sitting area (with a sofa bed) and a private terrace: a good room for a family. Breakfast (in a conservatory in warm months) has home-made preserves; eggs from the Balls's own hens. (*Margaret Hyde, Ruth West, and others*)

Station Road
Campsea Ashe
nr Woodbridge IP13 0PU

T: 01728-746524
E: mail@theoldrectorysuffolk.com
W: www.theoldrectorysuffolk.com

BEDROOMS: 7, 1 in garden cottage on ground floor, 1 in coach house.
OPEN: all year except Christmas/New Year, restaurant closed lunch, Sun/Tues/Thurs/Sat except for parties of 8 or more by arrangement.
FACILITIES: sitting room, dining room, conservatory, terrace, garden, unsuitable for ♿.
BACKGROUND MUSIC: none.
LOCATION: in village 8 miles NE of Woodbridge.
CHILDREN: all ages welcomed.
DOGS: allowed in garden cottage and coach house, not in main house.
CREDIT CARDS: MasterCard, Visa.
PRICES: [2012] B&B £45–£70 per person, set dinner £28, website offers, 1-night bookings refused weekends at busy times.

CANNINGTON Somerset

Map 1:B5

BLACKMORE FARM

This 15th-century Grade I listed manor house, run as a B&B, has oak beams, stone archways and huge open fireplaces. Its owners, Ann and Ian Dyer, are working farmers who have 850 acres of land with a large dairy herd and cereal crops. They also run a farm shop selling local produce, and a café serving light lunches and cream teas. 'They give wonderful value and excitement in their medieval farm,' says a returning visitor this year. An ancient front door opens on to the Great Hall, which has a long wooden refectory table (where a communal breakfast is served). The bedrooms in the house have considerable character: the West Room has views to the Quantock hills, a four-poster bed, original roof trusses and a cob-and-lime plaster wall. The intriguing Gallery has original wall panelling, a sitting room up a steep flight of steps; a small bathroom (lavatory in a medieval garderobe). Two bedrooms are in a converted barn. Breakfast includes fresh fruit salad, toast, croissants, and any combination of full English. Children 'will love the quirkiness, and the lack of formality'. (*David Humphreys*)

Blackmore Lane
Cannington
nr Bridgwater TA5 2NE

T: 01278-653442
E: dyerfarm@aol.com
W: www.dyerfarm.co.uk

BEDROOMS: 5, 2, in ground-floor barn, suitable for ♿.
OPEN: all year.
FACILITIES: lounge/TV room, hall/breakfast room, 1-acre garden (stream, coarse fishing).
BACKGROUND MUSIC: none.
LOCATION: 3 miles NW of Bridgwater.
CHILDREN: all ages welcomed.
DOGS: not allowed.
CREDIT CARDS: Diners, MasterCard, Visa.
PRICES: B&B £50 per person, 1-night bookings refused bank holiday weekends.

CARTMEL Cumbria

Map 4: inset C2

AYNSOME MANOR

César award in 1998

'*Aynsome* is not plush but it scores on other virtues: first-class food, a warm welcome and farewell (with cases carried), and exceptional value.' Praise again this year from returning visitors to the Varley family's traditional hotel, a 17th-century stone manor house between the fells and the sea in the Vale of Cartmel. Another view, from a guest who had 'a bad experience' at a nearby (unnamed) hotel: 'What a pleasant surprise; excellent and friendly.' It is owned by Chris and Andrea Varley, second-generation hoteliers; Ben and Antonia Shepherd are the resident managers. They tell us that this year the lounge has new carpets and seating. Bedrooms vary in size and view: 'Our room was excellent, well kitted out and comfortable.' Two rooms are in a cottage across the cobbled courtyard, which has its own sitting room. In the oak-panelled restaurant, chef Gordon Topp's daily-changing menu of dishes 'presented with imagination' might include escabeche of mackerel, apple and walnut salad and citrus dressing; roast chump of Cumbrian lamb with braised red cabbage, redcurrant and thyme jus. (*Ken and Mildred Edwards, Gwyn Morgan, and others*)

25% DISCOUNT VOUCHERS

Cartmel
nr Grange-over-Sands
LA11 6HH

T: 01539-536653
F: 01539-536016
E: aynsomemanor@btconnect.com
W: www.aynsomemanorhotel.co.uk

BEDROOMS: 12, 2 in cottage (with lounge) across courtyard.
OPEN: all year except 25/26 Dec, 2–25 Jan, lunch served Sun only, Sun dinner for residents only.
FACILITIES: 2 lounges, bar, dining room, ½-acre garden, unsuitable for ♿.
BACKGROUND MUSIC: none.
LOCATION: ½ mile outside village.
CHILDREN: no under-5s at dinner.
DOGS: not allowed in public rooms.
CREDIT CARDS: Amex, MasterCard, Visa.
PRICES: B&B £43–£65 per person, D,B&B £70–£85, full alc £36, New Year package, 1-night bookings sometimes refused bank holidays.

CHAGFORD Devon

Map 1:C4

GIDLEIGH PARK

The formal gardens of this luxurious country house hotel (Relais & Châteaux) are in dramatic contrast to the wildness of the surrounding countryside (within Dartmoor national park). It is managed by Andrew Foulkes for the owners, Andrew and Christina Brownsword. The Tudor-style building stands in a large estate with marked walks, and bridges over the North Teign river. The panelled public rooms have Arts and Crafts features. The bedrooms, all different, have 'supremely comfortable' bed; antiques, paintings, prints, flowers; welcoming touches include fresh fruit, mineral water, a decanter of Madeira. A small room at the top has a private hot tub on the roof; the thatched two-bedroom cottage in the garden is good for a family (children are welcomed, babysitting can be arranged). Dinner is the 'main focus': executive chef Michael Caines has two *Michelin* stars for his 'elaborate' cooking. Dishes on a carte or a tasting menu might include langoustine cannelloni, sauce vièrge; Dartmoor lamb, boulangère potato and confit shoulder, fennel purée. The Brownswords' small group of hotels includes *The Bath Priory*, Bath (see entry). (*LH, and others*)

Chagford TQ13 8HH

T: 01647-432367
F: 01647-432574
E: gidleighpark@gidleigh.co.uk
W: www.gidleigh.com

BEDROOMS: 24, 2 in annexe (75 yds), 2 in cottage (375 yds), 3 on ground floor, 1 suitable for ♿.

OPEN: all year.

FACILITIES: ramps, drawing room, hall, bar, loggia, conservatory, 3 dining rooms, civil wedding licence, 107-acre grounds (gardens, tennis).

BACKGROUND MUSIC: none.

LOCATION: 2 miles from Chagford.

CHILDREN: no under-8s at dinner.

DOGS: allowed in 3 bedrooms, not in public rooms.

CREDIT CARDS: all major cards.

PRICES: [2012] B&B £162.50–£587.50 per person, D,B&B £267.50–£692.50, full alc £150, special breaks, Christmas/New Year packages, 1-night bookings sometimes refused.

SEE ALSO SHORTLIST

CHAGFORD Devon

Map 1:C4

PARFORD WELL

'A superb place for strolls on Dartmoor', this small B&B (named after the village well) stands in a pretty walled garden overlooking countryside in the Teign valley. It run by the owner, Tim Daniel, 'who used to manage one of London's first townhouse hotels [*Number Sixteen*], and it shows', says a returning visitor. 'Everything is impeccable' in the house: the lounge has original paintings, sculptures, fresh flowers, books and a fire. Here, arriving guests are served tea and home-made cake. Mr Daniel, who lives in an adjacent cottage, 'passes the test' with breakfast, which he cooks to order. It is normally taken communally at a farmhouse table, though guests preferring privacy can choose to eat in a small room ('with antique furniture and a garden view') across the hall. There is fruit, yogurt with honey, cereals; all the produce is local for the cooked breakfast. 'It certainly sets us up for the day.' The three bedrooms overlook the garden; one has its own bathroom across the landing. There is a 'good, sensibly priced pub opposite' for evening meals. (*DC*)

Sandy Park
nr Chagford TQ13 8JW

T: 01647-433353
E: tim@parfordwell.co.uk
W: www.parfordwell.co.uk

BEDROOMS: 3.

OPEN: all year.

FACILITIES: sitting room, 2 breakfast rooms, ½-acre garden, unsuitable for ♿.

BACKGROUND MUSIC: none.

LOCATION: in hamlet 1 mile N of Chagford.

CHILDREN: not under 8.

DOGS: not allowed.

CREDIT CARDS: none.

PRICES: B&B £42.50–£50 per person, 1-night bookings sometimes refused weekends in season.

SEE ALSO SHORTLIST

CHELTENHAM Gloucestershire

Map 3:D5

MONTPELLIER CHAPTER NEW

In fashionable Montpellier, this handsome Regency building has been given a sleek make-over by the Hong Kong-based Swire group. *Guide* readers are enthusiastic: 'At last a hotel worthy of and convenient for the town's excellent festivals.' 'It exceeded expectations; excellent food, well-equipped rooms.' Inspectors agreed: 'Just right for a town hotel; the mood is lively, the smiling staff go out of their way to help.' The ground floor is a semi-open-plan space; no formal desk – check-in is paperless. The decor throughout is in shades of grey; interesting modern works of art hang in the corridors and the bedrooms, which vary in size and style. 'Our superior room, as high as it was wide, had lovely wooden fittings; all the expected high-tech stuff (an iPod touch information system, free Wi-Fi, Sky TV); a generous "yummy" section with a Nespresso machine.' A modern glass extension at the back brings light to the dining room, which has an open kitchen with a wood oven. 'The food was good: a standout dish was baked asparagus wrapped in Parma ham and pancakes.' (*Peter Stoakley, Peter Chance, and others*)

Bayshill Road
Cheltenham GL50 3AS

T: 01242-527788
E: montpellier@chapterhotels.com
W: www.themontpellierchapterhotel.com

BEDROOMS: 60, 3 on ground floor suitable for ♿.
OPEN: all year.
FACILITIES: lobby/lounge, sitting room/library, bar, garden room, restaurant, conservatory, terrace, spa.
BACKGROUND MUSIC: in public areas.
LOCATION: Montpellier.
CHILDREN: all ages welcomed.
DOGS: allowed by arrangement.
CREDIT CARDS: all major cards.
PRICES: [2012] B&B (continental) £60–£185 per person, set supper (Sun–Thurs) £15, full alc £40, special breaks, 1-night bookings refused weekends.

SEE ALSO SHORTLIST

CHETTLE Dorset

Map 2:E1

CASTLEMAN

César award in 2004

'The most agreeable and best-value hotel we know,' say fans returning to Barbara Garnsworthy's restaurant-with-rooms in a historic Dorset village. Further praise from guests in 2012: 'Excellent; super rooms, fine food and the most friendly staff.' The former dower house dates back to 1580 but was enlarged in the Regency and Victorian eras; the 'faded gentility' of the public areas is liked: they have high ceiling, ornate plasterwork, oak panelling. Mrs Garnsworthy's brother, Brendan, runs front-of-house, while she cooks with Richard Morris. 'The food was exceptional, in a plain English style with an emphasis on local produce and game; the vegetables (so obviously fresh) were particularly good.' The bedrooms vary in size and decor: 'Our large room had a sofa, desk and table; two windows gave lovely views across the fields; the spacious bathroom had an enormous old-fashioned bath with fast-flowing hot water.' Breakfast, served until 10 am, has 'more or less anything you ask'. The 'complete silence' and 'lack of rules' are appreciated. (*Leo Pilkington, Tim Messenger, Janet and Dennis Allom*)

Chettle
nr Blandford Forum
DT11 8DB

T: 01258-830096
F: 01258-830051
E: enquiry@castlemanhotel.co.uk
W: www.castlemanhotel.co.uk

BEDROOMS: 8 (1 family).
OPEN: Mar–Jan, except 25/26 Dec, 31 Dec, restaurant closed midday except Sun.
FACILITIES: 2 drawing rooms, bar, restaurant, 2-acre grounds (stables for visiting horses), riding, fishing, shooting, cycling nearby, only restaurant suitable for ♿.
BACKGROUND MUSIC: none.
LOCATION: village, 1 mile off A354 Salisbury–Blandford, hotel signposted.
CHILDREN: all ages welcomed.
DOGS: not allowed.
CREDIT CARDS: MasterCard, Visa.
PRICES: [2012] B&B £45–£65, full alc £30.

CHICHESTER West Sussex

Map 2:E3

ROOKS HILL

At their 'impeccably' restored brick-and-flint former farmhouse (Grade II listed), which they run as an upmarket B&B, Ron and Lin Allen set a 'very high standard'. The 'charming' hosts 'went out of their way, without being overpowering, to ensure we had everything we needed,' said one visitor. An inspector agreed, noting the warmth of the welcome; the quality of the furnishings, and the fresh flowers displayed throughout the house. Tea or coffee is served in the part-panelled lounge to arriving guests; help is given with baggage. The bedrooms are well equipped, and have a modern bathroom. 'Our room was sumptuous, with a really comfortable bed and plenty of space; we could have stayed for ever.' 'Sheets and blankets were provided as we requested.' Windows are triple glazed: 'Noise from the busy road was not a problem.' Breakfast, served in an oak-beamed, double-aspect room, was 'super'. There is home-baked bread, preserves made from organic fruit from the garden and a range of cooked dishes. The *Earl of March* pub opposite is recommended for meals; many places to eat are in nearby Chichester. (*GJ, and others*)

Lavant Road
Mid Lavant, Chichester PO18 0BQ

T: 01243-528400
E: info@rookshill.co.uk
W: www.rookshill.co.uk

BEDROOMS: 3, 1 on ground floor.
OPEN: all year.
FACILITIES: lounge, breakfast room, courtyard garden, unsuitable for ♿.
BACKGROUND MUSIC: classical in breakfast room.
LOCATION: 2 miles N of city centre.
CHILDREN: not under 12.
DOGS: not allowed.
CREDIT CARDS: Amex, MasterCard, Visa.
PRICES: [2012] B&B £50–£88 per person, special offers, 1-night bookings refused weekends Apr–Oct.

SEE ALSO SHORTLIST

CHILLATON Devon

Map 1:D3

TOR COTTAGE

The welcome is 'friendly' at Maureen Rowlatt's upmarket B&B which is reached by a bridle path in a private mid-Devon valley. Four of the five bedrooms are in the extensive grounds. Mrs Rowlatt tells us that all the rooms have been redecorated this year and given new reading lights, curtains and linen. Each of the garden rooms has been given an enhanced hospitality area with a fridge, microwave/grill and more spacious worktop and cupboard. Guests are encouraged to prepare ready meals or jacket potatoes in their room in the evening; a picnic platter of sandwiches, lemon posset and cheese can be provided by arrangement. An Art Deco room has a cabinet of collectibles which guests have contributed to, a small conservatory and a private terrace. Laughing Waters, by a stream, has Shaker furniture, a gypsy caravan, a hammock and a barbecue. The cottage wing in the main house also has a hospitality area. A welcome trug contains sparkling wine, chocolate truffles and fresh fruit. In summer, guests have access to a heated outdoor swimming pool. (*CT*)

Chillaton, nr Lifton
PL16 0JE

T: 01822-860248
E: info@torcottage.co.uk
W: www.torcottage.co.uk

BEDROOMS: 5, 4 in garden.
OPEN: Feb–Dec except Christmas/New Year, do not arrive before 4 pm.
FACILITIES: sitting room, large conservatory, breakfast room, 28-acre grounds (2-acre garden, heated swimming pool – 13 by 6 metres) May–Sept, barbecue, stream, bridleway, walks), river (fishing ½ mile), unsuitable for ♿.
BACKGROUND MUSIC: in conservatory.
LOCATION: ½ mile S of Chillaton.
CHILDREN: not under 14.
DOGS: only guide dogs allowed.
CREDIT CARDS: MasterCard, Visa.
PRICES: B&B (min. 2 nights) £70–£77.50 per person, picnic platter £16, autumn and spring breaks, 1-night bookings sometimes refused.

CLEE STANTON Shropshire

Map 3:C5

TIMBERSTONE

25% DISCOUNT VOUCHERS

'Charming hosts' Tracey Baylis and Alex Read give 'a warm welcome, excellent accommodation and food', according to a visitor in 2012. Their 'delightful' B&B is in a remote hamlet in the Clee Hills (just five miles from Ludlow). The traditional stone cottage, in well-tended gardens, has original beams, and has been 'lovingly' restored and extended. Two bedrooms, in the main house, have a big bed with an iron bedstead. Newer rooms, in an extension, have been 'beautifully crafted' with oak fittings; one has a freestanding bath in the room, and a small balcony. A large, light room which serves as both sitting room and dining room has floor-to-ceiling windows, rugs on an oak floor, big sofas; it is well stocked with CDs, DVDs, board games and jigsaw puzzles. Tracey Baylis, who worked with *Michelin*-starred chef Shaun Hill, cooks dinner by arrangement, offering dishes like local lamb on a pea and mint purée. 'It is worth dining in; wonderful food.' Breakfast has home-made preserves, toast and croissants, eggs from the owners' hens; vegetarian alternatives. *Timberstone* is difficult to find ('ask for directions, don't rely on satnav'). (*Paul Booth, Stuart Barnes*)

Lackstone Lane
Clee Stanton
Ludlow SY8 3EL

T: 01584-823519
E: timberstone1@hotmail.com
W: www.timberstoneludlow.co.uk

BEDROOMS: 4 (plus summerhouse retreat in summer).
OPEN: all year except 25 Dec and 1 Jan.
FACILITIES: lounge/dining room, ½-acre garden, treatment room, unsuitable for ♿.
BACKGROUND MUSIC: in lounge/dining room ('if guests request it').
LOCATION: 5 miles NE of Ludlow.
CHILDREN: all ages welcomed.
DOGS: not allowed.
CREDIT CARDS: MasterCard, Visa.
PRICES: [2012] B&B £47.50–£67.50 per person, full alc £30.50, winter breaks.

CLIPSHAM Rutland

Map 2:A3

BEECH HOUSE & OLIVE BRANCH

César award in 2012

In an attractive village near Stamford, this informal pub/restaurant-with-rooms is owned and run by Sean Hope and Ben Jones, who met when working at nearby *Hambleton Hall*, Hambleton (see entry). They have appointed Louise Williams as manager. In the restaurant, a series of rooms with beams and log fires, Mr Hope has a *Michelin* star for his modern cooking on a short set menu (perhaps trio of fish; braised shoulder of lamb, ratatouille) and a longer carte. 'Excellent; standards are maintained,' says a returning visitor this year. The bedrooms are in a Georgian house across the road. Berry, the largest room, on the ground floor, has antique walnut furniture, a separate dressing room. All rooms have a tea tray with home-made biscuits; fresh milk is provided in a fridge on the landing, and umbrellas are available for the short walk to the pub. A 'very good' breakfast, taken in a restored barn, has leaf tea, 'proper' sausages, crispy bacon; bread from the Hambleton bakery, and seasonal smoothies. A shop in the pub sells cured meats, home-made pickles, chutneys and jams.

25% DISCOUNT VOUCHERS

Main Street
Clipsham LE15 7SH

T: 01780-410355
F: 01780-410000
E: beechhouse@theolivebranchpub.com
W: www.theolivebranchpub.com

BEDROOMS: 6, 2 on ground floor, family room (also suitable for ♿) in annexe.

OPEN: all year.

FACILITIES: ramps, pub, dining room, breakfast room, small front garden.

BACKGROUND MUSIC: in pub.

LOCATION: in village 7 miles NW of Stamford.

CHILDREN: all ages welcomed.

DOGS: allowed in downstairs bedrooms and bar.

CREDIT CARDS: Diners, MasterCard, Visa.

PRICES: B&B £57.50–£97.50 per person, D,B&B £77.50–£107.50, set meals £21.50–£24.50, full alc £35, seasonal breaks.

COLWALL Worcestershire

Map 3:D5

COLWALL PARK HOTEL

'The really friendly staff made our short break feel special,' says a visitor in 2012 to Iain and Sarah Nesbitt's country hotel at the foot of the Malvern hills. The large Edwardian building, part red brick, part black-and-white timbered, is in the centre of a rural village. There are two residents' lounges, 'comfortable, but with uninspiring reading matter'. Bedrooms range in style from traditional to contemporary; all have flat-screen TV, free Wi-Fi, tea- and coffee-making facilities. 'Ours was clean and comfortable with a modern shower room.' A top-floor room was 'of good size; a slightly bland decor with floral curtains, a view of the gardens'. All agree about the 'excellence' of the cooking in the *Seasons* restaurant. James Garth serves modern British dishes, perhaps spiced salmon and crab cakes; roast breast of guineafowl, new potatoes, creamed leeks. The *Lantern Bar*, which is popular with locals, has a brasserie-style menu. Service is 'friendly' at breakfast, which is 'well presented, very tasty'. 'Ideal for walkers' with immediate access to the hills. (*Joanna Hartlen, Roland Cassam, Sue Lyons*)

25% DISCOUNT VOUCHERS

Colwall, nr Malvern
WR13 6QG

T: 01684-540000
F: 01684-540847
E: hotel@colwall.com
W: www.colwall.co.uk

BEDROOMS: 22.

OPEN: all year.

FACILITIES: ramp, 2 lounges (1 with TV), library, bar, restaurant, ballroom, business facilities, 1-acre garden, only public rooms suitable for ♿.

BACKGROUND MUSIC: blues in bar, jazz in restaurant.

LOCATION: halfway between Malvern and Ledbury on B4218, train Colwall.

CHILDREN: all ages welcomed.

DOGS: allowed in bar only.

CREDIT CARDS: MasterCard, Visa.

PRICES: [2012] B&B £65–£190 per person, D,B&B from £97.50, full alc £45, gourmet breaks, Christmas/New Year packages, 1-night bookings sometimes refused weekends.

CONSTANTINE BAY Cornwall

Map 1:D2

TREGLOS HOTEL

In landscaped gardens above the sandy crescent of Constantine Bay, this traditional seaside hotel (built in 1895) has been extended and renovated by Jim and Rose Barlow, owners for 40 years. The manager is Jonathan Summerfield. 'The staff were outstandingly pleasant, and the head housekeeper addressed minor problems most efficiently,' say visitors this year. 'It is exceedingly well run and we hope to return.' There are changes in the restaurant: men are asked to wear a jacket or a tie in the evening, though this is relaxed to 'smart casual' during school holidays. Carl Quible is the new chef, serving English dishes on a daily-changing menu, perhaps Cornish turbot mousse, smoked salmon and yellow pepper dressing; seared pigeon breast, duck liver terrine, mustard dressing. The public rooms are 'peaceful and well furnished'; bedrooms are decorated in blue and beige: 'Our spacious room had lovely views of the bay.' Some rooms face the gardens. Children are well catered for with a den and table tennis. The Barlow family also owns Merlin Golf and Country Club (ten minutes' drive away). (*Tony and Jenny Dawe*)

Constantine Bay
Padstow PL28 8JH

T: 01841-520727
F: 01841-521163
E: stay@tregloshotel.com
W: www.tregloshotel.com

BEDROOMS: 42, 1 on ground floor, 2 suitable for ♿.

OPEN: mid-Feb–end Nov.

FACILITIES: ramps, 2 lounges (pianist twice weekly), bar, restaurant, children's den, snooker room, beauty treatments, indoor swimming pool (10 by 5 metres), 3-acre grounds.

BACKGROUND MUSIC: in restaurant if quiet, piano in restaurant Tues/Thurs.

LOCATION: 4 miles W of Padstow.

CHILDREN: no under-5s in restaurant after 6.30 pm.

DOGS: not allowed in public rooms.

CREDIT CARDS: MasterCard, Visa.

PRICES: [2012] B&B £67.50–£103 per person, D,B&B £86.50–£122.50, full alc £32, special breaks and offers, 1-night bookings sometimes refused.

CORNHILL ON TWEED Northumberland

Map 4:A3

COLLINGWOOD ARMS

Popular with fisherfolk, golfers and walkers, this 18th-century stone-built coaching inn is owned by John Cook; Kevin Kenny is the 'hands-on' manager. The 'very friendly' hotel, which stands in 'magnificent countryside' just south of the Scottish border, has been meticulously renovated by local craftsmen. It takes its name from the merchant family who used to own it; a family member, Cuthbert Collingwood, was one of Nelson's vice-admirals (rooms are named after his 'van' at Trafalgar). There is a mix of traditional and modern in the interiors: comfy sofas and log fires in the 'spacious, well-kept' library/sitting room and the front hall; bedrooms have antiques, and there are 'large, comfortable' beds. Deluxe rooms have a roll-top bath. In the restaurant, where 'there is plenty of room between tables', chef Gordon Campbell's daily-changing menu uses local ingredients for dishes like salmon and scallop terrine; beef and venison pie, red wine gravy. The bar/brasserie has a simpler, seasonal menu. The 'first-rate' breakfast includes 'superb home-made lemon curd and raspberry jam'; 'the best kipper I have ever had'. There are kennels for dogs. (*M and PF*)

25% DISCOUNT VOUCHERS

Main Street
Cornhill on Tweed
TD12 4UH

T: 01890-882424
F: 01890-883098
E: enquiries@collingwoodarms.com
W: www.collingwoodarms.com

BEDROOMS: 15, 1 on ground floor.
OPEN: all year except Christmas Day.
FACILITIES: hall, library, bar/brasserie, dining room, small garden.
BACKGROUND MUSIC: in bar.
LOCATION: village centre.
CHILDREN: all ages welcomed.
DOGS: allowed in kennels.
CREDIT CARDS: MasterCard, Visa.
PRICES: [2012] B&B £60–£87.50 per person, set menus £22.50–£35.00, full alc £50, New Year package.

CORSE LAWN Gloucestershire

Map 3:D5

CORSE LAWN HOUSE

César award in 2005

Fronted by an ornamental pond (originally a coach wash into which a stage and four could be driven), this elegant Queen Anne Grade II listed building is set back from the village green on a busy road near Tewkesbury. It is owned and managed in personal style by Baba Hine as a hotel and restaurant; Gilles Champier is her French manager. 'A good experience, a pleasant welcome and fine dining,' says a visitor in 2012. The joint chefs, Andrew Poole and Martin Kinahan, serve 'above-average' French and English dishes in the informal brasserie and the more formal restaurant, where smart casual dress is required (regular visitors like the 'subdued elegance and refined ambience'). Typical dishes: Hereford snails with garlic butter; slow-cooked ox cheeks, mushrooms ` and shallots. The bedrooms are traditionally furnished with Hine family antiques ('like a spare room in a country house'); many are spacious and have a fridge with fresh milk for the tea and coffee tray, and a bowl of fresh fruit. There's an indoor swimming pool and a croquet lawn. Dogs are welcomed. (*Stuart Smith*)

25% DISCOUNT VOUCHERS

Corse Lawn GL19 4LZ

T: 01452-780771
F: 01452-780840
E: enquiries@corselawn.com
W: www.corselawn.com

BEDROOMS: 18, 5 on ground floor.
OPEN: all year except 24–26 Dec.
FACILITIES: lounge, bar lounge, bistro/bar, 2 restaurants, 2 conference/private dining rooms, civil wedding licence, 12-acre grounds (croquet, tennis, covered heated swimming pool, 20 by 10 metres).
BACKGROUND MUSIC: none.
LOCATION: 5 miles SW of Tewkesbury on B4211.
CHILDREN: all ages welcomed.
DOGS: on lead in public rooms.
CREDIT CARDS: all major cards.
PRICES: [2012] B&B £80–£100 per person, D,B&B from £95, set dinner £20–£35, short breaks, New Year package.

COVERACK Cornwall

Map 1:E2

THE BAY HOTEL

In a peaceful village on the Lizard peninsula, this solid, white-painted hotel is owned and managed by Ric and Gina House and their daughter, Zoë. 'Gina is very much in charge,' said a visitor this year. 'She welcomes guests (regulars were greeted like old friends), serves pre-dinner drinks, keeps an eye on dinner service,' say inspectors this year. A 'pleasant lounge, with beige and brown sofas in separate seating areas', overlooks the bay. Guests are asked to make their orders in advance when possible from Ric House's menu which has 'house dishes' supplemented by a changing list of specials (much local fish). 'We enjoyed the rich flavours of a generous plate of scallops and crab; an enormous whole plaice; best of all a pleasantly sharp lemon tart. Excellent service by a friendly East European couple. Many of the bedrooms have a view of the bay. A 'small room in the eaves had a sloping roof; good lighting over the small double bed; some noise from the neighbouring bathroom'. A ground-floor room has a huge bay window and a small patio.

North Corner, Coverack
nr Helston TR12 6TF

T: 01326-280464
E: enquiries@thebayhotel.co.uk
W: www.thebayhotel.co.uk

BEDROOMS: 15, 1 on ground floor suitable for ♿.

OPEN: Mar–Nov, Christmas/New Year.

FACILITIES: reception lounge, lounge, bar lounge, restaurant, 1-acre garden.

BACKGROUND MUSIC: none.

LOCATION: village centre, 10 miles SE of Helston.

CHILDREN: not under 11.

DOGS: not allowed in public rooms.

CREDIT CARDS: MasterCard, Visa.

PRICES: [2012] B&B £58–£130 per person, D,B&B £73–£145, set dinner £34.95, special offers, Christmas/New Year house parties.

COWAN BRIDGE Lancashire

Map 4: inset D2

HIPPING HALL

César award in 2008

'Smart but informal', this 17th-century house is run as a small hotel/restaurant by Andrew Wildsmith, 'a hands-on owner who looks after guests with great skill'. Shielded by woods, it stands in mature gardens beside a 'splendid church next to Ruskin's famous view over the Lune river'. The house has been renovated 'with great flair', say visitors returning in 2012. The bedrooms are furnished in rustic style: 'Our favourite room is spacious and light; a comfortable bed and armchairs with a view of the garden; a luxurious bathroom.' Downstairs, the sitting room is 'more traditional, with sofas and a stone fireplace'. Dinner is taken in the 15th-century Great Hall linked to the house by a conservatory. The chef, Brent Hulena, serves a three-course table d'hôte and a multi-course tasting menu: 'The well-presented modern dishes might include langoustines with belly pork; impressively juicy guineafowl, wild mushrooms, garlicky potato croquettes, sauce Albufera.' Breakfast 'eschews the tendency towards a predictable buffet; the full English is a generous plateful; juices are freshly squeezed, smoothies home made.' (*David and Kate Wooff*)

Cowan Bridge
nr Kirkby Lonsdale LA6 2JJ

T: 015242-71187
E: info@hippinghall.com
W: www.hippinghall.com

BEDROOMS: 9, 3 in cottage, 1, on ground floor, suitable for ♿.
OPEN: all year.
FACILITIES: lounge, bar, restaurant, civil wedding licence.
BACKGROUND MUSIC: classical/'easy listening' in dining hall.
LOCATION: 2 miles SE of Kirkby Lonsdale, on A65.
CHILDREN: all ages welcomed.
DOGS: allowed in 3 bedrooms.
CREDIT CARDS: MasterCard, Visa.
PRICES: [2012] B&B £60–£116 per person, D,B&B £40 added, set dinner £49.50–£65, seasonal breaks, Christmas/New Year packages, 1-night bookings normally refused Sat.

CROFT-ON-TEES Co. Durham

Map 4:C4

CLOW BECK HOUSE

César award in 2007

'We were met warmly and sent into the lounge where we were served coffee and home-made cake, to recover from our five-hour journey,' say visitors in 2012 to Heather and David Armstrong's small hotel and restaurant. Other praise: 'Everything as good as before; an excellent room and good food.' The bedrooms ('fresh and clean') are in stone outbuildings around the landscaped garden; some have their own small garden. There is a touch of eccentricity (giant pigs in the flowerbeds). Some of the rooms are as colourful as their names (Fleur, Foxglove, Lily). The large, beamed restaurant is on two levels. David Armstrong is the chef, cooking British dishes on an extensive menu (with many vegetarian options), perhaps spinach and ricotta tortellini; rack of Yorkshire lamb, a rich red wine minted gravy. 'It is good, wholesome food; a chunky prawn cocktail was memorable.' The award-winning gardens have been created by Mrs Armstrong from the surrounding farmland that has been in the family for nearly a century. There is 'excellent dog-walking from the door'. (*Robert and Helen Marks, Averil Wilkinson, David Innes*)

Monk End Farm
Croft-on-Tees
nr Darlington DL2 2SW

T: 01325-721075
F: 01325-720419
E: david@clowbeckhouse.co.uk
W: www.clowbeckhouse.co.uk

BEDROOMS: 13, 12 in garden buildings, 1 suitable for ♿.

OPEN: all year except Christmas/New Year.

FACILITIES: ramps, lounge, restaurant, small conference facilities, 2-acre grounds in 100-acre farm.

BACKGROUND MUSIC: classical in restaurant.

LOCATION: 3 miles S of Darlington.

CHILDREN: all ages welcomed.

DOGS: not allowed.

CREDIT CARDS: Amex, MasterCard, Visa.

PRICES: B&B £67.50–£85, full alc £37.

CROOKHAM Northumberland

Map 4:A3

THE COACH HOUSE AT CROOKHAM

'A lovely, welcoming, well-run country retreat.' More praise this year for Toby and Leona Rutter's informal guest house, a Grade II listed 17th-century dower house, and a series of renovated farm buildings. 'We enjoyed our stay, it was really excellent,' write other guests. A 'beautiful' beamed residents' lounge has an open fire and honesty bar; guests are given complimentary tea on arrival with 'Leona's delicious cakes'. The bedrooms are traditionally furnished: 'Our courtyard room, which was warm, spacious and comfortable, had a small fridge and a hospitality tray.' In the evenings, the 'ever-smiling' Mrs Rutter cooks a three-course dinner, served on tables dressed with crisp linen and fine china. There is a choice of starters but not of main course: 'All good home fare with fresh vegetables: we particularly enjoyed the roast lamb, and splendid chicken and tarragon cooked in a brandy and cream sauce.' Breakfasts have 'plenty of variety: lots of warm toast, excellent cooked dishes; the pot of fresh coffee was never empty'. (*Diane Westwell, Florence and Russell Birch, Paul Booth*)

Crookham
Cornhill-on-Tweed
TD12 4TD

T: 01890-820293
F: 01890-820284
E: stay@coachhousecrookham.com
W: www.coachhousecrookham.com

BEDROOMS: 11, 7 around courtyard, 3 suitable for ♿.

OPEN: Feb–Nov.

FACILITIES: lounge, 2 dining rooms, terrace, orchard.

BACKGROUND MUSIC: none.

LOCATION: On A697, 3 miles N of Milfield.

CHILDREN: all ages welcomed.

DOGS: not allowed in public rooms.

CREDIT CARDS: MasterCard, Visa (*2% surcharge*).

PRICES: B&B £30–£70 per person, set dinner £22.95, discount for two or more nights, 1-night bookings sometimes refused Fri/Sat.

CRUDWELL Wiltshire

Map 3:E5

THE RECTORY HOTEL

By the church in a Cotswold village, this former 18th-century rectory is 'a homely hotel with a quality finish', say visitors this year. It is owned by Jonathan Barry (formerly with Hotel du Vin) and antiques dealer Julian Muggridge. Jenna Halliday is the manager; the service is 'informal but attentive'. The 'peaceful' position is liked: the stone building stands in a walled garden with a heated outdoor swimming pool. Children are welcomed: 'Our young son loved roaming the grounds; he was well looked after at mealtimes, and a travel cot and baby monitor were provided.' In the wood-panelled dining room, chef Peter Fairclough's modern British menu might include oak-smoked wood pigeon, parsnip purée, caramelised chicory; blade of beef, Roquefort and sage mash, red onion tarte Tatin, port jus. 'Good quality and value.' Guests can also eat at the 'wonderful' *Potting Shed* pub nearby which is under the same ownership. Bedrooms, which vary in size and price, have muted colours; a 'well-appointed' bathroom. Breakfast has a 'great cold buffet, with home-made muffins and Bircher muesli; a full, cooked menu'. (*Gary Pearson*)

Crudwell, nr Malmesbury
SN16 9EP

T: 01666-577194
F: 01666-577853
E: info@therectoryhotel.com
W: www.therectoryhotel.com

BEDROOMS: 12.

OPEN: all year, restaurant closed lunchtime.

FACILITIES: lounge, bar, dining room, meeting facilities, civil wedding licence, 3-acre garden (heated swimming pool, 10 by 5 metres), unsuitable for ♿.

BACKGROUND MUSIC: 'low background' in bar and dining room.

LOCATION: 4 miles N of Malmesbury.

CHILDREN: all ages welcomed.

DOGS: not allowed in dining room.

CREDIT CARDS: Amex, MasterCard, Visa.

PRICES: B&B £47.50–£102.50 per person, set dinner £32.50, midweek breaks, Christmas/New Year packages, 1-night bookings refused bank holidays.

DARTMOUTH Devon

Map 1:D4

DART MARINA

'A thoroughly pleasant place to stay', Richard Seton's hotel has 'an excellent position' by the higher ferry across the River Dart, near the centre of this riverside town. Paul Downing is the new manager. The multinational staff 'have plenty of time to speak to guests; the wonderful porter has an encyclopedic knowledge of the town'. Much work has been done this year: the *River* restaurant has been enlarged and redesigned; 14 bedrooms have been renovated. 'The strong points are the excellent service and the air of calm in the spacious, smart public rooms,' said inspectors in 2012. In the river-facing restaurant, the 'high standards' of chef Tom Woods are praised: 'We enjoyed delicious ballottine of salmon with sauce gribiche; orange-glazed confit duck came with leek mash and red wine sauce.' 'There was, alas, muzak except at breakfast.' All the bedrooms overlook the river. 'They are beautiful and well equipped; housekeeping is faultless.' The best rooms have a balcony and wooden seating. The 'glorious' breakfast has 'good juices, croissants, freshly cut fruit salad, and generous cooked dishes'.
(PJ Kilmartin, Mary Woods, and others)

Sandquay Road
Dartmouth
TQ6 9PH

T: 01803-832580
F: 01803-835040
E: reception@dartmarina.com
W: www.dartmarina.com

BEDROOMS: 49, 3 on ground floor, 1 suitable for ♿.
OPEN: all year.
FACILITIES: lounge/bar, bistro, restaurant, river-front terrace, spa (heated indoor swimming pool, 8 by 4 metres, gym, treatments).
BACKGROUND MUSIC: jazz/pop/classic in restaurant.
LOCATION: on waterfront.
CHILDREN: all ages welcomed.
DOGS: in ground-floor rooms (£10), not during meal times in public rooms.
CREDIT CARDS: MasterCard, Visa.
PRICES: [2012] B&B £70–£150 per person, D,B&B £97–£177, full alc £50, special breaks, Christmas/New Year packages, 1-night bookings refused Sat.

SEE ALSO SHORTLIST

DARTMOUTH Devon

Map 1:D4

NONSUCH HOUSE

César award in 2000

'A haven of calm and good food atop one of Devon's steepest hills', this large Edwardian building is run as a guest house by Kit and Penny Noble. 'They have charm and gentility,' says a visitor in 2012. 'She is always ready to answer the many queries posed by guests.' The hilltop position guarantees panoramic views of the River Dart; the Nobles say there are 'gentle ways' of getting up and down. Guests can relax in the conservatory/dining room while watching the activity on the water, or sit in the lounge with its log fire, where they might be joined by 'one of the house's soppy Labradors'. All of the bedrooms have the view. 'They are well equipped and spacious; chilled water flasks and fresh milk are especially welcome.' Kit Noble cooks dinner on four nights a week: 'The menu may be limited, but from the canapés to the locally caught fish, everything is delicious.' Breakfast has 'wonderful home-made bread and proper tea'; jams, muesli and compotes are also home made; fish is home smoked; local produce is used for the cooked dishes. (*Sarah Hollowell*)

Church Hill, Kingswear
Dartmouth TQ6 0BX

T: 01803-752829
F: 01803-752357
E: enquiries@nonsuch-house.co.uk
W: www.nonsuch-house.co.uk

BEDROOMS: 4.

OPEN: all year except Jan, dining room closed midday, evening Tues/Wed/Sat.

FACILITIES: ramps, lounge, dining room/conservatory, ¼-acre garden (sun terrace), rock beach 300 yds (sailing nearby), membership of local gym and spa.

BACKGROUND MUSIC: none.

LOCATION: 5 mins' walk from ferry to Dartmouth.

CHILDREN: not under 12.

DOGS: not allowed.

CREDIT CARDS: MasterCard, Visa.

PRICES: [2012] B&B £55–£85 per person, D,B&B £37.50 added, special breaks, Christmas/New Year packages, 1-night bookings usually refused weekends.

SEE ALSO SHORTLIST

DEDHAM Essex

Map 2:C5

DEDHAM HALL & FOUNTAIN HOUSE RESTAURANT

'Quirky and all the better for it', this cluster of buildings is set around a 15th-century manor house in a pretty village in Constable country. It is run as a guest house/restaurant/art school by Jim and Wendy Sarton. 'The whole establishment is wonderfully warm; everyone who looked after us came from nearby,' say visitors this year. The lounge has oak beams, books, and paintings by artists attending art courses, which take place from February to November. Visitors on courses are accommodated in rooms around a converted 14th-century barn; rooms in the main house are traditionally furnished: dark wood, huge beds, and Persian rugs. Bathrooms have 'lashings of hot water'. In the *Fountain House* restaurant, the 'interesting' menu might include 'generous portions' of mushrooms in sour cream; roast guineafowl with herb stuffing and redcurrant gravy. Dinner is provided for hotel guests when the restaurant is closed. 'The route between our room and the restaurant took us through the kitchen where we were cheerfully greeted by staff who clearly had a pride in their workplace.' Flatford Mill is a two-mile walk along the River Stour. (*RJD*)

Brook Street, Dedham
nr Colchester CO7 6AD

T: 01206-323027
F: 01206-323293
E: sarton@dedhamhall.demon.co.uk
W: www.dedhamhall.co.uk

BEDROOMS: 20, 16 in annexe, some on ground floor, suitable for ♿.
OPEN: all year except Christmas/New Year, restaurant closed Sun/Mon.
FACILITIES: ramps, 2 lounges, 2 bars, dining room, restaurant, studio, 6-acre grounds (pond, gardens).
BACKGROUND MUSIC: none.
LOCATION: end of High Street.
CHILDREN: all ages welcomed.
DOGS: only guide dogs allowed.
CREDIT CARDS: MasterCard, Visa.
PRICES: B&B £55 per person, D,B&B £85, set menu £35, painting holidays (Feb–Nov).

DEDHAM Essex

Map 2:C5

THE SUN INN

Opposite the church in the village most associated with John Constable, this 15th-century coaching inn has been restored with elegance by its owner, Piers Baker. Public rooms have a traditional feel; old oak floorboards, log fires, window seats, club chairs and board games in the bar, and an oak-panelled lounge. Exposed beams separate the open-plan dining room, on two levels, from the bar. Bedrooms are decorated in a more modern style, with dark wood furnishings. Two rooms (added in 2011) are reached by an external Elizabethan staircase at the back of the building. Some rooms at the front might suffer from noise from the bar in late evening; compensation comes with the view of St Mary's church (the spire often seen in Constable's work). In the dining room, chef Ugo Simonelli serves Mediterranean food with a distinct Italian influence: his daily-changing menu might include potato dumplings, roast pumpkin, curly kale pesto, pecorino; rib-eye of beef, salsa d'erbe, baked borlotti beans, tomatoes and rocket. Tables are laid with white linen for breakfast, which has smoked fish of the day; hand-cut bread for toast.

High Street, Dedham
nr Colchester CO7 6DF

T: 01206-323351
E: office@thesuninndedham.com
W: www.thesuninndedham.com

BEDROOMS: 7.

OPEN: all year except 25/26 Dec.

FACILITIES: lounge, bar, dining room, 1-acre garden (covered terrace, children's play area), unsuitable for ♿.

BACKGROUND MUSIC: jazz/Latin/blues throughout.

LOCATION: central, 5 miles NE of Colchester.

CHILDREN: all ages welcomed.

DOGS: not allowed in bedrooms.

CREDIT CARDS: MasterCard, Visa.

PRICES: B&B £55–£80 per person, set meals £12.50–£15.50, full alc £30, New Year package, seasonal offers on website.

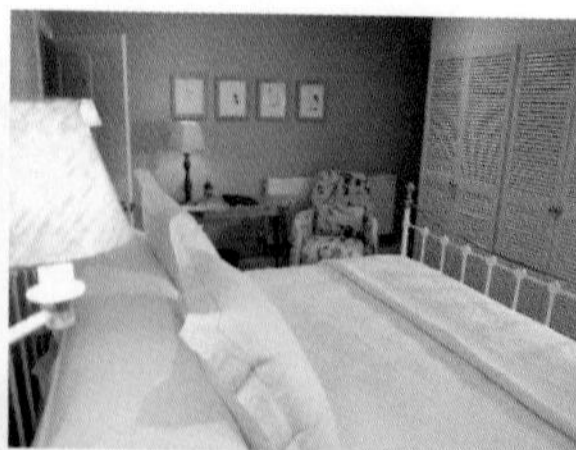

DODDISCOMBSLEIGH Devon

Map 1:C4

THE NOBODY INN

The co-owner, Sue Burdge, is 'a hands-on host, serving drinks, taking orders and chatting to guests' at this 16th-century inn in a hamlet in rolling Devon country near Exeter. A visitor in 2012 found 'a buzz of conversation and a wonderfully warm atmosphere, every table taken' in the two bars; 'its young staff were attentive, helpful'. It has cask beers, Devon ciders, more than 250 whiskies, and a wide choice of wines by the glass from a lengthy list, many supplied by wine merchant Nick Borst-Smith, who owns nearby *Town Barton* (see next entry). Meals can be taken in one of the bars or the adjoining restaurant. Adam Parnham joined as chef in 2012. He serves a menu of bar classics with daily specials: 'Rich flavours and generous helpings: we enjoyed scallops with crispy pork belly; sea bass with a lemon risotto.' The bedrooms, above the bar, have 'good bedding and lighting'; they are decorated in muted tones and are supplied with a decanter of sherry. A small room has its bathroom across the corridor. (*DB, and others*)

Doddiscombsleigh EX6 7PS

T: 01647-252394
F: 01647-252978
E: info@nobodyinn.co.uk
W: www.nobodyinn.co.uk

BEDROOMS: 5.
OPEN: all year, restaurant closed Sun/Mon evening.
FACILITIES: 2 bars, restaurant, small garden, patio, unsuitable for ♿.
BACKGROUND MUSIC: none.
LOCATION: in village 6 miles SW of Exeter.
CHILDREN: not under 14 in bar.
DOGS: not allowed in restaurant, bedrooms.
CREDIT CARDS: MasterCard, Visa.
PRICES: [2012] B&B £45 per person, full alc £40, special breaks.

DODDISCOMBSLEIGH Devon

Map 1:C4

TOWN BARTON

'What a treat; this is how a B&B should be run.' Praise from a trusted reporter in 2012 for Nick Borst-Smith's manor house in a Domesday village. 'It is a gem,' say other visitors. There are no public rooms but the four bedrooms are spacious. 'Our delightful room faced the medieval church; it had a large four-poster bed, two armchairs and a table. There were three sash windows, and a fourth in the bathroom. An electric stove ensured that the room was warm in mid-winter. There was a jug of distilled water, fresh milk in the fridge, two types of ground coffee and some fine teas.' Mr Borst-Smith will book a table for dinner at the nearby *Nobody Inn*, which he used to own (see previous entry). A cooked breakfast can be taken at the inn; or a continental tray can be left in the room. 'It has wrapped bread for the toaster; cereals in Kilner jars; decent orange juice; local honey.' The village is difficult to find (Henry VIII's troops missed it, so the church's medieval stained glass survives). (*DB, David M Horwitz*)

Doddiscombsleigh
nr Exeter EX6 7PT

T: 01647-252005
E: rooms@townbarton.co.uk
W: www.townbarton.co.uk

BEDROOMS: 4, 2 on ground floor.
OPEN: all year except 25/26 Dec.
FACILITIES: 4-acre gardens.
BACKGROUND MUSIC: none.
LOCATION: in village 6 miles SW of Exeter.
CHILDREN: all ages welcomed.
DOGS: not allowed.
CREDIT CARDS: MasterCard, Visa.
PRICES: [2012] room £50–£70, breakfast £5–£10.75.

EAST GRINSTEAD West Sussex

Map 2:D4

GRAVETYE MANOR

NEW

'Change without change' is the philosophy behind the extensive renovation of this luxury hotel (Relais & Châteaux). The creeper-clad Elizabethan manor house stands in wooded grounds and fine gardens designed by William Robinson, pioneer of the English natural movement. The owner, Jeremy Hosking (a fund manager and former guest), has appointed Andrew Thomason as managing director. *Guide* inspectors were impressed: 'The style remains that of a classic country house, but it has a relaxed air and is not at all stuffy; the staff were charming.' The smell of polish and wood smoke (from open fires) pervades the panelled public rooms 'which retain their Arts and Crafts feel; wonderful fresh flowers everywhere'. A log fire burns in the dining room (candles on well-spaced tables, no background music at dinner). The cooking of chef Rupert Gleadow is 'of the highest order: a tasty cup of crab and sweet potato; well-judged portions of smoked duck with prunes, pollack, garden leeks and broccoli'. All the bedrooms have been redecorated and given a new bathroom. The restoration of the gardens is 'impressive; thoughtful planting, exuberant colour'.

Vowels Lane
East Grinstead RH19 4LJ

T: 01342-810567
F: 01342-810080
E: info@gravetyemanor.co.uk
W: www.gravetyemanor.co.uk

BEDROOMS: 17.
OPEN: all year.
FACILITIES: 3 lounges, bar, restaurant, private dining room, civil wedding licence, 35-acre grounds, only restaurant suitable for ♿.
BACKGROUND MUSIC: in restaurant at breakfast.
LOCATION: 5 miles SW of East Grinstead.
CHILDREN: not under 7.
DOGS: not allowed.
CREDIT CARDS: all major cards.
PRICES: [2012] B&B £120–£450, set dinner £40, full alc £80, Christmas/New Year packages, special breaks, 1-night bookings sometimes refused Sat.

EAST HOATHLY East Sussex

Map 2:E4

OLD WHYLY

Within easy reach of Glyndebourne, this Grade II listed Georgian manor house has foundations dating back to the 12th century. It is run by owner Sarah Burgoyne as an upmarket B&B. 'The most elegant B&B of my experience,' said the nominator. It stands in extensive grounds with gardens that have a lake, an orchard, flowers and statuary. Visitors are greeted with 'home-made cake and tea in a beautiful drawing room'. The three bedrooms are individually decorated; two have facilities en suite, the other has a private bathroom. Dinner, prepared by Mrs Burgoyne by arrangement, is served in a 'charming' dining room. Trained in Paris, she uses local, 'if not home-grown', produce (including eggs from the hens and ducks in the grounds). Typical dishes: tuna carpaccio, ginger and rocket; South Downs spring lamb, baby vegetables. In fine weather, guests may eat under a vine-covered pergola. At the 'communal, but cheery' breakfast, everything is prepared to order; 'the marmalade is the best I've ever tasted'. Guests have access to a hard tennis court, and a wisteria-shaded swimming pool. More reports, please.

London Road
East Hoathly BN8 6EL

T: 01825-840216
E: stay@oldwhyly.co.uk
W: www.oldwhyly.co.uk

BEDROOMS: 3.
OPEN: all year.
FACILITIES: drawing room, dining room, 3-acre garden in 30-acre grounds, heated outdoor swimming pool (10 by 5 metres), tennis, unsuitable for ♿.
BACKGROUND MUSIC: none.
LOCATION: 1 mile N of village.
CHILDREN: all ages welcomed.
DOGS: not allowed.
CREDIT CARDS: none.
PRICES: [2012] B&B £47.50–£67.50 per person, set dinner £35.50, Glyndebourne hamper £35, 1-night bookings sometimes refused weekends in high season.

EAST LAVANT West Sussex

Map 2:E3

THE ROYAL OAK

'Popular and stylish', Charles Ullmann's 200-year-old flint-stone inn is in a village on the edge of the South Downs near Chichester. 'Excellent; it may look like a pub but the bedrooms are very comfortable and well fitted,' wrote a visitor this year. They are in the main building and in a converted cottage and barn which overlook fields behind the inn. They have inglenooks, exposed beams; modern bathrooms have 'lots of nice touches'. 'Our room, although fairly small, was smart.' In the restaurant (popular with locals, and with visitors to the Chichester Festival Theatre and Goodwood), the chef, Steve Ferre, serves modern European food on his seasonal menu. Typical dishes: red onion tarte Tatin with melted goat's cheese; slow-braised shoulder of lamb, celeriac and potato mash. There is a blackboard list of daily specials. The linen napkins were 'particularly appreciated'. 'Very good food,' said one visitor; another guest, with 'traditional tastes', commented that 'few vegetables were served'. Breakfast, which has 'lovely fresh fruit, accompanying a good choice of cereals', is 'excellent'. (*John Bickerdike, Dale Vargas*)

Pook Lane
East Lavant PO18 0AX

T: 01243-527434
E: rooms@royaloakeastlavant.co.uk
W: www.royaloakeastlavant.co.uk

BEDROOMS: 5, 3 in adjacent barn and cottage, 2 self-catering cottages nearby.
OPEN: all year, except 25 Dec.
FACILITIES: bar/restaurant, terrace (outside meals), small garden, unsuitable for ♿.
BACKGROUND MUSIC: jazz in restaurant.
LOCATION: 2 miles N of Chichester.
CHILDREN: all ages welcomed.
DOGS: not allowed in bedrooms.
CREDIT CARDS: All major cards.
PRICES: B&B £70–£142.50, full alc £50, winter breaks, 1-night bookings refused weekends.

EDENBRIDGE Kent

Map 2:D4

STARBOROUGH MANOR

In parkland opposite a small moated castle, this 'beautiful' old manor house is the home of Lynn and Jonathan Mathias and their teenage children. They welcome visitors on a B&B basis: a kitchen and dining room are available (£10 charge) for those who would prefer to prepare evening meals rather than dine out. The bedrooms are 'generously proportioned'. Two rooms, which share a bathroom, are let together as a family suite. Rooms are decorated and furnished in country/traditional style; all have a hospitality tray, mineral water, free Wi-Fi. Bathrooms are 'well equipped'. Guests have use of a first-floor sitting room, which has a television, a library of books to borrow, games and DVDs. A second sitting room/study is for those wanting to work or to read quietly. Breakfast, taken communally at a large oak table, is 'as good as it gets': generous portions of strawberries, blueberries, two types of melon, cereals and yogurts on the table; cooked dishes include kippers and smoked salmon and scrambled eggs. The grounds can be explored; a heated swimming pool is available in summer. (*AC, and others*)

Moor Lane, Marsh Green
Edenbridge TN8 5QY

T: 01732-862152
E: lynn@starboroughmanor.co.uk
W: www.starboroughmanor.co.uk

BEDROOMS: 4.
OPEN: all year.
FACILITIES: 2 sitting rooms, dining room, 14-acre grounds, unsuitable for ♿.
BACKGROUND MUSIC: none.
LOCATION: 1½ miles W of Edenbridge.
CHILDREN: all ages welcomed.
DOGS: not allowed.
CREDIT CARDS: MasterCard, Visa.
PRICES: [2012] B&B £70–£100 per person, 1-night bookings sometimes refused.

EGTON BRIDGE North Yorkshire

Map 4:C5

BROOM HOUSE

25% DISCOUNT VOUCHERS

'A comfortable and relaxing place to stay, with friendly, helpful staff.' David and Maria White's guest house is in a restored Victorian farmhouse near a village in the North York Moors national park. It is praised by a regular contributor this year. 'We were warmly welcomed, and given a key to allow 24-hour access.' The Whites have given the house 'a modern decor throughout'; the residents' lounge has 'comfortable sofas and an open fire, which was lit on a rainy evening'. Bedrooms, in the older part of the house and an extension, vary in size. 'Our smallish twin overlooked the garden; it had comfortable beds, good lighting, white furniture with lots of hanging and drawer space.' 'Quiet music' plays in the evening in *Whites* bistro, a large candlelit room with a wood burner. 'The food is good quality, plainish; we enjoyed ham hock terrine; slow-cooked lamb shoulder and lamb/mint sausage (twice).' Vegetarians are 'well catered for'. An 'excellent' breakfast has 'a good choice including Whitby kippers and smoked haddock'. Well placed for exploring the coast and the moors. (*GC, and others*)

Broom House Lane
Egton Bridge YO21 1XD

T: 01947-895279
F: 01947-895657
E: mw@broom-house.co.uk
W: www.egton-bridge.co.uk

BEDROOMS: 9, 1 on ground floor, 2 in cottage.
OPEN: Feb–Nov, restaurant closed Sun, Mon nights.
FACILITIES: lounge, dining room, restaurant, civil wedding licence, ½-acre garden.
BACKGROUND MUSIC: in restaurant.
LOCATION: ½ mile W of village.
CHILDREN: all ages welcomed.
DOGS: not allowed.
CREDIT CARDS: MasterCard, Visa.
PRICES: [2012] B&B £39.50–£72.50 per person, D,B&B £19.95 added, full alc £30, 1-night bookings sometimes refused weekends high season.

EMSWORTH Hampshire

Map 2:E3

36 ON THE QUAY

César award in 2011

'Sympathetically modernised to a high standard', Ramon and Karen Farthing's restaurant-with-rooms is a 17th-century former fishermen's inn on the harbour in a quiet town. Mrs Farthing runs front-of-house 'presiding over a quietly efficient operation with well-trained staff'; her husband has long had a *Michelin* star for his cooking, which visitors this year say is 'high-quality, sophisticated, with a considerable emphasis on presentation'. The dining room has 'beautifully laid tables and attentive service'. 'We had duck egg with Serrano ham and Puy lentils; slow-roasted Cotswold white chicken breast with confit leg on a fricassée of green spring vegetables; a trio of lemon desserts.' Bedrooms vary in size and view: 'Our large room, tastefully decorated, had a sitting area and view over the harbour.' The Vanilla Suite has a bay window seat, 'an exposed beam (challenging even for shorter guests), quality bedlinen'. A 'superb' continental breakfast can be taken in the bedroom or in a small breakfast room: 'Freshly squeezed fruit juice, muesli, cereals, yogurts, croissants.' (*Bryan and Mary Blaxall, Ken and Priscilla Winslow*)

47 South Street
Emsworth PO10 7EG

T: 01243-375592
E: bookings@36onthequay.co.uk
W: www.36onthequay.co.uk

BEDROOMS: 6, 1 in cottage (with lounge) across road (can be let weekly).

OPEN: all year except 24/25 Dec, 2 weeks Jan, 1 week May, 1 week Nov, restaurant closed Sun/Mon.

FACILITIES: lounge area, bar area, restaurant, terrace, only restaurant suitable for ♿.

BACKGROUND MUSIC: none.

LOCATION: on harbour.

CHILDREN: all ages welcomed.

DOGS: allowed in cottage, by arrangement.

CREDIT CARDS: Diners, MasterCard, Visa.

PRICES: [2012] B&B £50–£125 per person, set dinner £55.

ERMINGTON Devon

Map 1:D4

PLANTATION HOUSE

'We can only talk in superlatives: the owner, Richard Hendey, is very kind and his staff give you a warm welcome.' Dutch visitors found 'nothing we didn't like' this year at this Georgian rectory, now a small hotel and restaurant. Mr Hendey is the chef: 'Our main memory is the spectacular cooking,' say other guests. 'When we booked, he asked if we had any no-go food areas, and suggested he look after our menus. What a good decision: across three nights we enjoyed a stream of memorable dishes, including the freshest red mullet three ways; confit duck leg with a Spanish-style bean and tomato sauce.' The house has been decorated in plantation style: tropical plants, pale walls, cane furniture. 'Our immaculate and comfortable bedroom at the top had two easy chairs looking across the River Erme.' Mr Hendry tells us extra drawer space has been provided (following a comment last year). An 'outstanding' breakfast, which can be taken on a terrace or in bed, has home-smoked salmon, locally cured bacon. (*Hans and Alicia Winters, Tony and Ginny Ayers*)

25% DISCOUNT VOUCHERS

Totnes Road
Ermington, nr Plymouth
PL21 9NS

T: 01548-831100
E: info@plantationhousehotel.co.uk
W: www.plantationhousehotel.co.uk

BEDROOMS: 9.
OPEN: all year, restaurant closed midday, some Sundays.
FACILITIES: lounge/bar, 2 dining rooms, terrace, garden, unsuitable for ♿.
BACKGROUND MUSIC: if required.
LOCATION: 10 miles E of Plymouth.
CHILDREN: 'well-behaved' children welcomed.
DOGS: allowed in 1 bedroom, not in public rooms.
CREDIT CARDS: Amex, MasterCard, Visa.
PRICES: B&B £60–£115 per person, set dinner from £39, New Year package, 1-night bookings occasionally refused.

EVERSHOT Dorset

Map 1:C6

SUMMER LODGE

Deep in Thomas Hardy country, this 'quite grand' country house hotel and spa (Relais & Châteaux) stands in 'delightful, beautifully kept' grounds. It was built in 1798 as a dower house for the Earl of Ilchester, and was enlarged by Hardy, an architect by trade. Charles Lötter, the hands-on manager, is from South Africa; the international staff are 'friendly and polite'; not all have good English, say visitors. The public rooms are grandly decorated. The 'immaculate' bedrooms are awash with rich fabrics, antiques, bold prints and heavy drapes ('a little over the top'). One of Hardy's original rooms is now a suite with an open fireplace. In the restaurant, chef Steven Titman serves a French-influenced seasonal menu (with many organic ingredients), perhaps tartare of beef fillet; soy-infused loin of Exmoor venison, sweet potato, Szechuan pepper jus. The spa has a 'very good' swimming pool, aromatherapy and reflexology treatments. The less expensive *Acorn Inn* in the village is owned by the same group, Red Carnation, as is *The Montague on the Gardens* in London (see entry).

9 Fore Street
Evershot DT2 0JR

T: 01935-482000
F: 01935-482040
E: summerlodge@rchmail.com
W: www.summerlodgehotel.com

BEDROOMS: 24, 9 in coach house and courtyard house, 4 in lane, 1 on ground floor suitable for ♿.
OPEN: all year.
FACILITIES: ramps, drawing room, lounge/bar, restaurant, indoor swimming pool (11 by 6 metres), civil wedding licence, 4-acre grounds (garden, croquet, tennis).
BACKGROUND MUSIC: in lounge/bar.
LOCATION: 10 miles NW of Dorchester.
CHILDREN: all ages welcomed.
DOGS: allowed in some bedrooms.
CREDIT CARDS: all major cards.
PRICES: [2012] B&B £181.50–£308 per person, D,B&B £117–£338, set menu £30–£40, full alc £75, website offers, Christmas/New Year packages, 1-night bookings refused some weekends, bank holidays.

SEE ALSO SHORTLIST

EVESHAM Worcestershire

Map 3:D6

THE EVESHAM HOTEL

César award in 1990

Family friendly, idiosyncratic, 'relaxing'; John and Sue Jenkinson's small hotel has a loyal following. Guests enjoy the humour and the thoughtful service. Mr Jenkinson is a dominant presence, greeting visitors, serving drinks and meals, cracking jokes. Not everyone appreciates the jesting (improbable wooden ties, simulated fart noises in the lavatories). Those who do are enthusiastic: 'His humour was just right; he presented our grandchildren with three-foot-long drinking straws and advised them to put their drinks on the floor.' Other praise this year: 'Marvellous; once you enter, everything is taken care of; the staff are discreet but helpful.' The decor may be 'a little dated, but it doesn't matter a jot'. Mrs Jenkinson designed the bedrooms (many are themed). They are well equipped: a silent fridge with mineral water and fresh milk, 'washing line over the bath, liquid detergent, cool-air fan'. Children have an indoor swimming pool ('kept comfortably warm'), slides and a trampoline in the garden. Ben Whatcott has been promoted to chef: the menus have extensive choice (a vast buffet at lunch, 67 cereals at breakfast). (*John Dowling, Shirley King*)

25% DISCOUNT VOUCHERS

Cooper's Lane, off Waterside
Evesham
WR11 1DA

T: 01386-765566
F: 01386-765443
FP: 0800-716969 (reservations only)
E: reception@eveshamhotel.com
W: www.eveshamhotel.com

BEDROOMS: 39, 11 on ground floor, 2 suitable for ♿.

OPEN: all year except 25/26 Dec.

FACILITIES: 2 lounges, bar, restaurant, private dining room, indoor swimming pool (5 by 12 metres), 2½-acre grounds (croquet, putting, swings, trampoline).

BACKGROUND MUSIC: none.

LOCATION: 5 mins' walk from centre, across river.

CHILDREN: all ages welcomed.

DOGS: only guide dogs allowed in public rooms.

CREDIT CARDS: all major cards.

PRICES: B&B £68–£80 per person, D,B&B £76–£95, full alc £38, New Year package, 1-night bookings refused Sat for Cheltenham Gold Cup, New Year, often Sat at other times.

EXFORD Somerset

Map 1:B4

THE CROWN

With a 'comfortable, hospitable atmosphere', this 17th-century coaching inn is popular with 'country people'. Owned and managed by Sara and Dan Whittaker and her father, Chris Kirkbride, it stands in the centre of a pretty village in 'beautiful countryside'. It is close to the main shoots on Exmoor (a gun safe is available and shooting party rates are offered); dogs are welcomed and stabling can be provided for horses. 'A fire burns in the entrance hall and the welcome is friendly.' The 'homely feel' was liked by guests in 2012. There is 'good seating' in the lounge; the bar is 'a hub of conversation'. Olivier Certain is now the chef, serving modern dishes in the smart restaurant (perhaps slow-roasted pork belly, smoked champ creamed potatoes) and a separate menu in the bar (eg, 'excellent fish and chips'). The bedrooms vary in size: 'Ours had been nicely restored; two comfortable chairs were provided; a modest and well-laid-out bathroom.' At breakfast 'ham, cheese and salami are added to the usual cold offerings; good hot dishes'. (*Mrs M Mitchell, Kay and Peter Rogers*)

Exford
Exmoor National Park
TA24 7PP

T: 01643-831554
F: 01643-831665
E: info@crownhotelexmoor.co.uk
W: www.crownhotelexmoor.co.uk

BEDROOMS: 16.
OPEN: all year.
FACILITIES: lounge, cocktail bar, public bar, restaurant, meeting room, 3-acre grounds (trout stream, water garden, terrace garden), stabling, unsuitable for ♿.
BACKGROUND MUSIC: in bar and restaurant.
LOCATION: on village green.
CHILDREN: all ages welcomed.
DOGS: not allowed in restaurant.
CREDIT CARDS: MasterCard, Visa.
PRICES: [2012] B&B £57.50–£79.50 per person, full alc £45, special breaks, Christmas/New Year packages.

FARNINGHAM Kent

Map 2:D4

BEESFIELD FARM

NEW

In 'beautiful countryside' in the Darent valley, this 'idyllic' old farmhouse is run 'with much enthusiasm' as a B&B by owners Kim and Doug Vingoe. The house has a Victorian frontage added to a 16th-century Kentish long barn. The bedrooms are 'extravagantly' furnished in traditional style; 'the beds are comfortable and there are all the usual extras (tea/coffee tray, fresh milk in a flask, a television and good toiletries)', says the nominator. 'It all makes for a relaxing and comfortable stay.' The Cupid Room has a panelled wall and a half-tester bed; Granny's Room, the smallest, has oak beams, Victorian artefacts. In a 'gorgeous' dining room, breakfast is a 'five-star' meal: 'Large jugs of juice, wonderful bowls of fresh fruit (raspberries, strawberries, cherries, pineapple, etc); good thick brown and white toast as well as croissants; excellent preserves and marmalade; first-class ingredients in the full cooked.' The Vingoes keep bees and serve their own honey at breakfast; it can also be purchased. Although close to the M25, the valley is 'peaceful'; Hever Castle, Penshurst, Chartwell and Leeds Castle are nearby. (*CLH*)

Beesfield Lane
Farningham DA4 0LA

T/F: 01322-863900
E: kim.vingoe@btinternet.com
W: www.beesfieldfarm.co.uk

BEDROOMS: 4.
OPEN: all year except Christmas/New Year.
FACILITIES: lounge, dining room, garden, unsuitable for ♿.
BACKGROUND MUSIC: none.
LOCATION: 5 miles S of Dartford.
CHILDREN: not under 10.
DOGS: guide dogs only.
CREDIT CARDS: none.
PRICES: [2012] B&B £40–£65 per person.

FAVERSHAM Kent

Map 2:D5

READ'S

César award in 2005

'Hotel guests are anything but a second thought' at Rona and David Pitchford's restaurant-with-rooms, a 'beautiful' Georgian manor house. Trusted correspondents were impressed this year by the 'simultaneously classy and cosy interior, the attentive service, and the manageable scale of the place'. Mrs Pitchford, 'a warm, professional host who was consistently keen to help us', runs front-of-house; in the 'elegantly dressed', candlelit restaurant ('no background music to spoil the ambience') Mr Pitchford has a *Michelin* star for his 'imaginative' menu. 'The fresh local ingredients came to the fore: we enjoyed tiger prawns which were slightly overwhelmed by the orange-infused Puy lentils; chicken with a miniature wild mushroom and confit chicken lasagne; a wonderful dark chocolate and salted caramel délice.' The bedrooms have a 'traditional but not dated decor, with rich fabrics and warm colours'; the spacious Cedar Room has window seats and an 'extremely comfortable' bed. Breakfast has 'delicious home-pressed apple juice'; croissants, home-made jams; 'excellent' cooked choices. (*Anna and Bill Brewer*)

Macknade Manor
Canterbury Road
Faversham ME13 8XE

T: 01795-535344
F: 01795-591200
E: enquiries@reads.com
W: www.reads.com

BEDROOMS: 6.

OPEN: all year except 25/26 Dec, restaurant closed Sun/Mon.

FACILITIES: sitting room/bar, restaurant, private dining room, civil wedding licence, 4-acre garden (terrace, outdoor dining), only restaurant suitable for ♿.

BACKGROUND MUSIC: none.

LOCATION: 1 mile SE of Faversham.

CHILDREN: all ages welcomed.

DOGS: not allowed in public rooms.

CREDIT CARDS: Amex, MasterCard, Visa.

PRICES: [2012] B&B £82.50–£97.50 per person, D,B&B £135–£150, set dinner £58.

FOWEY Cornwall

Map 1:D3

THE OLD QUAY HOUSE

César award: Cornish hotel of the year

On the waterfront of a pretty old seaside town, this former seamen's mission has been turned into a stylish hotel by owners Jane and Roy Carson; Anthony Chapman is the hands-on manager. 'An absolute delight from start to finish; what lovely people,' said inspectors. Readers agreed in 2012: 'A well-presented hotel in beautiful surroundings'; 'Simply spot-on, chic and comfortable'. Because the town has narrow streets and tough parking restrictions, arriving visitors are asked to drop off baggage before parking 800 yards up the hill (cost included). 'The welcome is friendly, luggage already taken to the room. Ours was excellent, with a harbour view, large bed and nice touches: a folding umbrella, two smart rainproof jackets, white waffle bathrobes.' In the restaurant, the chef, Ben Bass, has a modern style with dishes like Cornish crab, pomegranate dressing; pan-seared fillet of Red Ruby beef, fondant potato, crispy shallots. 'A good meal; we could have done without the background music.' Breakfast was 'excellent; eggs Benedict came in three versions'. *(Hayley Gathercole, Natalie King, Stephen Cromie)*

28 Fore Street
Fowey PL23 1AQ

T: 01726-833302
F: 01726-833668
E: info@theoldquayhouse.com
W: www.theoldquayhouse.com

BEDROOMS: 11.

OPEN: all year.

FACILITIES: open-plan lounge, bar, restaurant with seating area, civil wedding licence, waterside terrace, unsuitable for ♿.

BACKGROUND MUSIC: 'low key' at mealtimes.

LOCATION: central, on waterfront.

CHILDREN: not under 13.

DOGS: not allowed.

CREDIT CARDS: Amex, MasterCard, Visa.

PRICES: B&B £90–£160 per person, D,B&B £35 added, set dinner £30–£37.50, full alc £53, seasonal breaks, Christmas/New Year packages, 1-night bookings refused high season weekends and bank holidays.

GATESHEAD Tyne and Wear

Map 4:B4

ESLINGTON VILLA

'A family-run place where you feel at home', Nick and Melanie Tulip's traditional hotel, formed from two large Victorian houses, is managed by Colin Edgar. *Guide* inspectors enjoyed the 'relaxed atmosphere' and praised the 'helpful, friendly' staff. Overlooking the Team valley, the hotel stands in large gardens with mature trees and shrubs, 'a pretty terrace with seating'. The main railway line to Newcastle runs at the bottom of the garden 'but is not particularly obtrusive'. In the public areas there are old photographs and modern artwork, antiques and Victorian decorative pieces; the bar has plenty of seating, sofas and upright chairs. In the traditional restaurant, the chef, Jamie Walsh, serves a modern British menu with a wide choice, eg, horseradish and potato salad; roast chicken breast, confit potato, cider sauce. Service was 'swift and friendly'. The bedrooms are named after trees and shrubs. 'Lilac had a more contemporary feel than the public rooms: the appropriate coloured patterned wallpaper, a bright blue carpet, a sofa in the window. A large bright bathroom was smartly tiled with a colourful border.' (*Judith Carruthers, and others*)

25% DISCOUNT VOUCHERS

8 Station Road, Low Fell
Gateshead NE9 6DR

T: 0191-487 6017
F: 0191-420 0667
E: home@eslingtonvilla.co.uk
W: www.eslingtonvilla.co.uk

BEDROOMS: 18, 3 with separate entrance on ground floor.

OPEN: all year except 25/26 Dec, 1 Jan.

FACILITIES: ramp, lounge/bar, conservatory, restaurant, private dining room, conference/function facilities, 2-acre garden (patio).

BACKGROUND MUSIC: jazz throughout.

LOCATION: 2 miles from centre, off A1.

CHILDREN: all ages welcomed.

DOGS: not allowed.

CREDIT CARDS: Amex, MasterCard, Visa.

PRICES: B&B [2011] £47–£79.50 per person, D,B&B £65–£105, set dinner £21–£25.

GILLINGHAM Dorset

Map 2:D1

STOCK HILL HOUSE

In 'lovely' landscaped grounds with 'huge' trees, lawns and flowerbeds, this imposing late Victorian house (once the summer home of cartoonist Osbert Lancaster) has long been run as a small hotel/restaurant by Nita and Peter Hauser. One of the two lounges is decorated in period style with stripped fabrics, a gilded mirror, Chinese figurines; the other, informal, has a log fire. Service is formal in the dining room, which faces the garden. Mr Hauser's daily-changing menu has English/French dishes with touches of his native Austria. It might include poached field mushroom ravioli, sweet red pepper coulis; escalope of beef rostbraten, onion and sour cream. Fish and shellfish come from the Dorset coast, vegetables and herbs from the walled kitchen garden. Vegetarians have an extensive menu. Bedrooms are individually decorated in eclectic style; they have 'good bed and bedding', antiques, curios, dark wood furniture, rich furnishings and fabrics in bold designs. An original Lancaster cartoon hangs in the breakfast room. Guests are encouraged to explore the gardens to 'guess what will be next on the menu'. More reports, please.

Stock Hill
Gillingham SP8 5NR

T: 01747-823626
F: 01747-825628
E: reception@stockhillhouse.co.uk
W: www.stockhillhouse.co.uk

BEDROOMS: 9, 3 in coach house, 3 on ground floor.
OPEN: all year.
FACILITIES: ramp, 2 lounges, restaurant, breakfast room, private dining room, 11-acre grounds (tennis, croquet, small lake), unsuitable for ♿.
BACKGROUND MUSIC: none.
LOCATION: 1 mile W of Gillingham.
CHILDREN: not under 7.
DOGS: not allowed.
CREDIT CARDS: MasterCard, Visa.
PRICES: [2012] D,B&B £132.50–£162.50 per person, set lunch £18.50–£30, dinner £45, Christmas/New Year packages.

GITTISHAM Devon

Map 1:C5

COMBE HOUSE

César award in 2007

In a 'splendid setting' on an extensive estate near a pretty village, Ken and Ruth Hunt's Grade I listed Elizabethan manor house continues to attract enthusiastic praise from *Guide* readers. Comments this year: 'Very, very good; the staff are charming and the cuisine is first class.' 'The staff genuinely seemed to care: a waitress put her tray down and ran to help my wife with her bag.' The reception hall (carved oak panelling, 18th-century portraits) is a 'conversation piece'. Bedrooms in the main house vary in size; some have panoramic views of the estate; all are decorated in rich colours and fabrics. 'Our spacious room was well furnished and equipped: we appreciated the choice between sheets and a duvet.' The chef, Hadleigh Barrett, uses vegetables and fruit from the kitchen garden for his modern menus. 'Top-quality cooking, with a succession of canapés and amuse-bouche; subtle tastes added interest to locally sourced lamb, pork and chicken; a good selection of wine.' Breakfast, served until 9.45 am, is 'equally commendable'. (*Ian Dewey, Ken and Mildred Edwards, David Hampshire, Richard Owen*)

25% DISCOUNT VOUCHERS

Gittisham
nr Honiton EX14 3AD

T: 01404-540400
E: stay@combehousedevon.com
W: www.combehousedevon.com

BEDROOMS: 16, 1 in cottage.

OPEN: all year.

FACILITIES: ramp, sitting room, Great Hall, bar, restaurant, private dining rooms, civil wedding licence, 10-acre garden in 3,500-acre estate (helipad), only public rooms suitable for ♿.

BACKGROUND MUSIC: occasionally in hall and bar.

LOCATION: 4 miles SW of Honiton.

CHILDREN: all ages welcomed.

DOGS: allowed in public rooms except restaurant, some bedrooms.

CREDIT CARDS: Amex, MasterCard, Visa.

PRICES: [2012] B&B £107.50–£212.50 per person, D,B&B from £159.50, full alc £75, special breaks, Christmas package, 1-night bookings sometimes refused Fri/Sat.

GRAFFHAM West Sussex

Map 2:E3

THE FORESTERS ARMS

In lovely countryside between Midhurst and Petworth, sheltered by the South Downs, Sarah and James Tippett-Iles's Grade II listed 17th-century inn delighted a *Guide* reader: 'It is a proper traditional English pub, with scrubbed tables and a roaring fire.' There are low beams and inglenook fireplaces in the bar and lounge. The food isn't 'gastropub pretentious'; seasonal produce is cooked in a British/Mediterranean style in dishes like salad of Sussex goat's cheese, char-grilled artichoke and confit beetroot; roast pork tenderloin with chive and Parmesan crust, cannellini and kidney beans, chorizo and red pepper. The 'interesting' wine list has 18 bottles at £20 or less. There are three bedrooms in a converted barn annexe, all with shower en suite, Freeview TV with DVD-player, cafetière coffee and tea-making equipment. 'Ours was charming, with a hefty wooden bed, and sheets of top-quality cotton; orchids on the window sill.' Breakfast has organic cereals (muesli is home made), porridge; cooked dishes; 'no plastic pots'. As Italian car enthusiasts themselves, the owners say that this is a car-club-friendly pub. Pets are welcome (notice must be given). (*JH*)

The Street
Graffham GU28 0QA

T: 01798-867202
E: info@forestersgraffham.co.uk
W: www.forestersgraffham.co.uk

BEDROOMS: 3 in annexe.
OPEN: all year.
FACILITIES: pub, restaurant, garden, unsuitable for ♿.
BACKGROUND MUSIC: mellow jazz.
LOCATION: 5 miles SW of Petworth.
CHILDREN: all ages welcomed.
DOGS: allowed.
CREDIT CARDS: Amex, MasterCard, Visa.
PRICES: [2012] B&B £35–£85 per person, full alc £32, Christmas/New Year packages, 1-night bookings sometimes refused.

GRASMERE Cumbria

Map 4: inset C2

OAK BANK

NEW

On a quiet road on the outskirts of the village, this small hotel is run by 'hands-on' owners Glynis and Simon Wood. 'Excellent; the staff are charming,' said a reader. *Guide* inspectors in 2012 admired the 'high standards that belie a modest appearance', recommending an upgrade from the Shortlist to a full entry. 'Simon Wood gave a cordial welcome, assisting with parking and carrying our bags to the room.' There is seating in the lobby and a lounge/bar, which has a wood fire in winter. 'Our small room, overlooking the garden, was smartly furnished with a modern decor. Excellent lighting allowed reading in bed without strain; a small two-seat settee and tea/coffee-making facilities; a good mirror and lots of hot water in the bathroom.' Three interconnecting rooms, one a conservatory, form the dining room; tables are well spaced. John Cook is the chef: 'We were pleased with the quality and the presentation: we greatly enjoyed a ballottine of salmon and an excellent rib-eye steak (justifying the small supplement). Efficient service; low background music.' Breakfast is 'superb'. 'Exceptional value.' (*David Palmer, and others*)

Broadgate
Grasmere LA22 9TA

T: 015394-35217
F: 015394-35685
E: info@lakedistricthotel.co.uk
W: www.lakedistricthotel.co.uk

BEDROOMS: 14, 1 on ground floor.
OPEN: all year except Christmas, 2–26 Jan.
FACILITIES: lounge, bar, dining room, conservatory dining room, unsuitable for ♿.
BACKGROUND MUSIC: during dinner in bar lounge and dining rooms.
LOCATION: outskirts of village.
CHILDREN: all ages welcomed.
DOGS: allowed in 3 bedrooms, 1 lounge.
CREDIT CARDS: MasterCard, Visa.
PRICES: [2012] B&B £40–£79 per person, D,B&B £60–£99, set dinner £32.50, full alc £45, special breaks, New Year package, 1-night bookings usually refused weekends.

SEE ALSO SHORTLIST

GREAT MILTON Oxfordshire

Map 2:C3

LE MANOIR AUX QUAT'SAISONS

César award in 1985

'A place for a really special occasion', Raymond Blanc's luxurious hotel (Relais & Châteaux) in an Oxfordshire village was given 'confident blessing' by the *Guide*'s late founder. Co-owned with Orient Express Hotels, it is managed by Philip Newman-Hall. M. Blanc's French-inspired cooking (with Gary Jones), which has two *Michelin* stars, continues to attract enthusiastic praise: 'The best meal I've ever had,' says a visitor this year on a birthday treat. There is a choice of menus in the conservatory restaurant: five- and seven-course set lunch 'experiences' (£75 and £120), and a seven-course dinner. A short carte is available at both meals. Hotel guests are met in the car park (luggage is taken to the room). The bedrooms, in the main house and in garden buildings, have 'wonderful' fresh fruit, a decanter of Madeira. Many are styled to a theme: Blanc de Blanc is layered in shades of white; Provence has a rustic feel with aubergine colours and an open wood-burning fireplace; Jade, in shades of green, has oriental features. The French breakfast has an impressive buffet; cooked dishes cost extra. (*HR, MF, and others*)

Church Road
Great Milton OX44 7PD

T: 01844-278881
F: 01844-278847
E: lemanoir@blanc.co.uk
W: www.manoir.com

BEDROOMS: 32, 22 in garden buildings, some on ground floor, 1 suitable for ♿.

OPEN: all year.

FACILITIES: ramps, 2 lounges, champagne bar, restaurant, private dining room, cookery school, civil wedding licence, 27-acre grounds.

BACKGROUND MUSIC: in the lounges.

LOCATION: 8 miles SE of Oxford.

CHILDREN: all ages welcomed.

DOGS: not allowed in house.

CREDIT CARDS: all major cards.

PRICES: [2012] B&B (French breakfast) £297.50–£840 per person, D,B&B (Sun–Thurs) £465–£1007.50, set dinner £150, full alc £200, special breaks, cookery courses, Christmas/New Year packages.

HALNAKER West Sussex

Map 2:E3

THE OLD STORE

The welcome with tea and cake in the garden pleased a regular correspondent who visited Patrick and Heather Birchenough's B&B this year with a group of friends. The 18th-century Grade II listed house, close to Chichester and the Goodwood estate, was once the village store and bakery. 'We were shown to our immaculate bedrooms. My single overlooked the main road, but triple-glazing cut out traffic noise. Fresh milk was provided in a Thermos flask.' One bedroom is on the ground floor; the other six are on two floors (up fairly steep stairs); a family room is large enough for four. 'We had two birthdays to celebrate and the Birchenoughs were happy to provide glasses, plates, and fridge space for our champagne.' Breakfast was 'excellent; not only full English, but pancakes with bacon and maple syrup, or a muffin with smoked salmon and scrambled egg'. The *Anglesey Arms*, across the road, is open for evening meals ('take a torch for the walk back'). *Field and Fork* at the Pallant Gallery in Chichester is also recommended. The village name is pronounced 'Hannaka'. (*Dr Heather Parry*)

Stane Street, Halnaker,
nr Chichester
PO18 0QL

T: 01243-531977
E: theoldstore4@aol.com
W: www.theoldstoreguesthouse.com

BEDROOMS: 7, 1 on ground floor.
OPEN: 17 Mar–22 Dec.
FACILITIES: lounge, breakfast room, ⅓-acre garden with seating, unsuitable for ♿.
BACKGROUND MUSIC: none.
LOCATION: 4 miles NE of Chichester.
CHILDREN: all ages welcomed.
DOGS: not allowed.
CREDIT CARDS: MasterCard, Visa.
PRICES: [2012] B&B £40–£50 per person (higher for Goodwood 'Festival of Speed' and 'Revival' meetings), 1-night bookings refused weekends in high season.

HAMBLETON Rutland

Map 2:B3

HAMBLETON HALL

César award in 1985

'Everything about this country house hotel is a class act: the location above Rutland Water, the decor, the service and the food and wine.' There is much praise from regular correspondents this year for Tim and Stefa Hart's luxury hotel (Relais & Châteaux), an imposing Victorian mansion. 'Our favourite; a benchmark against which we judge others,' say returning visitors. Mrs Hart is responsible for the interiors (the style is classic – fine fabrics, antiques, 'sumptuous' sofas and cushions). This year she has renovated the restaurant (with golden damask on the walls) and the bar (better lighting, more sparkle). The chef, Aaron Patterson, has a *Michelin* star for his classic cooking with modern touches (eg, sautéed langoustines, braised belly pork, rhubarb; hare Wellington, prune and Armagnac sauce). 'An excellent meal; faultless service.' The spacious bedrooms have a variety of styles; some have a floral decor; others a half-tester bed; the best overlook Rutland Water. Breakfast, a leisurely affair, has bread from Mr Hart's nearby bakery. He also owns *Harts*, Nottingham (see entry). (*Michael Raeside Auld, Roderic Rennison*)

Hambleton
Oakham LE15 8TH

T: 01572-756991
F: 01572-724721
E: hotel@hambletonhall.com
W: www.hambletonhall.com

BEDROOMS: 17, 2-bedroomed suite in pavilion.
OPEN: all year.
FACILITIES: lift, ramps, hall, drawing room, bar, restaurant, 2 private dining rooms, civil wedding licence, 17-acre grounds (swimming pool, heated May–Sept, tennis).
BACKGROUND MUSIC: none.
LOCATION: 3 miles SE of Oakham.
CHILDREN: only children 'of a grown-up age' in restaurant in evening.
DOGS: not allowed in public rooms, nor unattended in bedrooms.
CREDIT CARDS: all major cards.
PRICES: [2012] B&B (continental) £125–£210 per person, set dinner £38.50–£67, full alc £90, seasonal breaks, Christmas/New Year packages, 1-night bookings sometimes refused weekends.

HAROME North Yorkshire

Map 4:D4

THE PHEASANT

In a quiet village in the North Yorkshire moors, this conversion of a 17th-century village smithy and barns is owned by Jacquie Pern and Peter Neville, who used to be head chef at the *Michelin*-starred *Star Inn* (see next entry). The oak-beamed bar and lobby, decorated in country style, have exposed stone work. The large lounge opens on to a stone-flagged terrace. In an elegant dining room with subdued lighting, Mr Neville cooks modern dishes, perhaps pressed ham hock, fresh peas, pineapple and watercress; roast breast of wood pigeon, wild garlic risotto, preserved mushrooms. The bedrooms, which are grouped around a gravelled courtyard, are decorated in muted Shaker tones. 'Everyone was very helpful,' says a visitor this year (who was not so keen on the food). *Black Eagle Cottage* (with three bedrooms), a short stroll away, now belongs to *The Pheasant*. A room here was 'dark but comfortable; housekeeping was excellent, with an evening turn-down service'. A 'delicious' breakfast can be taken as a hamper at the cottage or in the conservatory at the *Pheasant*. (*Jennifer Davis, and others*)

Harome, nr Helmsley
YO62 5JG

T: 01439-771241
E: reservations@thepheasanthotel.com
W: www.thepheasanthotel.com

BEDROOMS: 18, 2 courtyard suites, 1 on ground floor, 3 in *Black Eagle Cottage*, nearby.
OPEN: all year.
FACILITIES: lounge, bar, dining room, conservatory, indoor swimming pool, courtyard, garden.
BACKGROUND MUSIC: classical/jazz in bar and restaurant.
LOCATION: village centre.
CHILDREN: all ages welcomed.
DOGS: in courtyard rooms only.
CREDIT CARDS: MasterCard, Visa.
PRICES: [2012] B&B £77.50–£100 per person, D,B&B £110–£132.50, set dinner £36, full alc £50, seasonal offers, Christmas package.

HAROME North Yorkshire

Map 4:D4

THE STAR INN

César award in 2004

Yorkshire-born chef Andrew Pern celebrates his northern roots at his restaurant-with-rooms, a thatched 14th-century longhouse in this village on the edge of the moors. He cooks modern Yorkshire dishes on a seasonal menu (perhaps Scarborough woof with marsh samphire; loin of Harome-shot hare, braised haunch tagliatelle). 'Exceptional: the duck was outstanding and the ginger pudding heavenly,' says a visitor this year. Meals can be taken in the informal restaurant, the bar, and alfresco in the garden in warm weather. An open-plan lounge 'has comfy sofas, a roaring fire, an honesty bar'. The decor is rustic modern in the bedrooms in *Cross House Lodge*, opposite. All have a 'well-stocked' tea tray, home-made biscuits, fruit and fudge. Several have a shower big enough for two. One reader complained of maintenance issues in her room; earlier visitors were pleased with theirs. Guests are 'invited to graze as long as they like' at breakfast taken communally around a huge circular table in a 'wonderful rustic room' in the lodge.

Harome, nr Helmsley
YO62 5JE

T: 01439-770397
F: 01439-771833
E: reservations@thestarinnatharome.co.uk
W: www.thestaratharome.co.uk

BEDROOMS: 8 in *Cross House Lodge* opposite, 3 on ground floor.
OPEN: all year, restaurant closed Sun evening, Mon lunch.
FACILITIES: lounge, coffee loft, bar, breakfast room, restaurant, private dining room, civil wedding licence, terrace, 2-acre garden, unsuitable for ♿.
BACKGROUND MUSIC: 'gentle jazz in public areas'.
LOCATION: village centre.
CHILDREN: all ages welcomed (children's menu).
DOGS: not allowed.
CREDIT CARDS: MasterCard, Visa.
PRICES: [2012] B&B £75–£120 per person, D,B&B £90–£135, market menu £20–£25, full alc £55, Christmas/New Year packages.

HARWICH Essex

Map 2:C5

THE PIER AT HARWICH

'A fine hotel with an excellent restaurant,' say visitors this year to Paul Milsom's conversion of two historic buildings on the quayside of this busy port. Richard Barnes is the manager (many of the 'competent' staff are long serving). The main building, once a waiting room for ferry passengers, houses the two restaurants and half of the bedrooms; the other rooms and a beamed lounge are in the adjacent former *Angel* pub, built in the 17th century. 'We stayed in the Mayflower Suite, a large room with a telescope for the splendid views over the water; a good bathroom.' 'We enjoyed watching the ferries come and go.' Tom Bushell has joined as chef from Mr Milsom's *Le Talbooth* at Dedham. In the first-floor *Harbourside* restaurant (minimalist decor, a polished pewter champagne and oyster bar), his speciality is locally landed seafood dishes, perhaps dressed crab, celery; skate wing, brown shrimp, capers and broad beans. Simpler dishes and sandwiches are served in the ground-floor *Ha' Penny* bistro. 'Highly recommended; there are many interesting things to see and do here.' The car park 'is a bonus'. (*Richard Lamb, and others*)

25% DISCOUNT VOUCHERS

The Quay
Harwich CO12 3HH

T: 01255-241212
F: 01255-551922
E: pier@milsomhotels.com
W: www.milsomhotels.com

BEDROOMS: 14, 8 in annexe, 1 on ground floor.
OPEN: all year.
FACILITIES: ramps, lounge (in annexe), restaurant, bistro, civil wedding licence, small front terrace.
BACKGROUND MUSIC: 'easy listening'.
LOCATION: on quay.
CHILDREN: all ages welcomed.
DOGS: not allowed in public rooms.
CREDIT CARDS: all major cards.
PRICES: [2012] B&B £57.50–£107.50 per person, full alc £41.50, special breaks, Christmas package.

HASTINGS East Sussex

Map 2:E5

BLACK ROCK HOUSE

This restored Victorian villa is on a side street, a 'steepish climb' up from the seafront. It has 'flamboyant turrets, handsome window casings, neatly clipped bay trees standing sentinel by the front entrance'. A stylish sitting room, with an open fire, has an honesty bar; drinks can be taken to a south-facing terrace. The five bedrooms are individually designed in contemporary colours. Braybrooke, in shades of grey, has a high ceiling and original mouldings; a marble wet room with a waterfall shower. The 'handsome' Garden Room, in a mix of browns and creams, has an 'opulent' bed, freestanding dark wood furnishings. Breakfast is served in a 'light and elegant' dining room. As we went to press we learned that *Black Rock House* had changed hands. We would welcome reports on the new regime. Some of the details on the right may no longer be accurate.

25% DISCOUNT VOUCHERS

10 Stanley Road
Hastings TN34 1UE

T: 01424-438448
E: enquiries@black-rock-hastings.co.uk
W: www.hastingsaccommodation.com

BEDROOMS: 5.
OPEN: all year.
FACILITIES: lounge, breakfast room, terrace, unsuitable for ♿.
BACKGROUND MUSIC: lounge and breakfast room.
LOCATION: central.
CHILDREN: not under 5.
DOGS: allowed on request.
CREDIT CARDS: MasterCard, Visa.
PRICES: [2012] B&B £49.50–£65 per person, 1-night bookings refused weekends.

HASTINGS East Sussex

Map 2:E5

SWAN HOUSE

In Hastings old town, where Tudor timbers blend with Victorian facades on the narrow streets, Brendan McDonagh and Lionel Copley run this white-painted, black-beamed 15th-century cottage as an up-market B&B. They have furnished it with a mix of antiques and bric-a-brac from their online business, an 'interiors emporium'. A long, oak-panelled lounge has settees and an inglenook fireplace; at the other end of the house is a breakfast room. One of the four bedrooms (the Garden Room) is on the ground floor and has oak doors leading to a patio garden. Upstairs, the Renaissance Suite is ideal for families; it has two large bedrooms and a shared en suite shower room. The Church Room, overlooking the 14th-century St Clement's church, has a king-size bed and a bathroom with shelled grotto bath panelling. The 'tranquil' Artisan Room, a former Victorian bakery, has a stained-glass ceiling window. Breakfast has Greek yogurt with prunes and honey, fruit smoothies; cooked dishes include pork sausages, scrambled eggs and home-made baked beans. A sister guest house, *The Old Rectory*, is in a nearby 18th-century building. More reports, please.

25% DISCOUNT VOUCHERS

1 Hill Street
Hastings, TN34 3HU

T: 01424-430014
E: res@swanhousehastings.co.uk
W: www.swanhousehastings.co.uk

BEDROOMS: 4, 1 on ground floor.
OPEN: all year except Christmas.
FACILITIES: lounge/breakfast room, courtyard garden, civil wedding licence, unsuitable for ♿.
BACKGROUND MUSIC: none.
LOCATION: in old town, near seafront.
CHILDREN: not under 5.
DOGS: not allowed.
CREDIT CARDS: all major cards.
PRICES: B&B £60–£95 per person, website offers.

HATCH BEAUCHAMP Somerset

Map 1:C6

FARTHINGS

25% DISCOUNT VOUCHERS

'Strongly recommended' this year, John Seeger's hotel/restaurant stands in large grounds with orchards and rose beds in a village near Taunton. 'We enjoyed a relaxing stay; the food is excellent,' is another comment. The white-painted Georgian house has 'many original features, with curved bays and shuttered windows; there was a log fire burning, and all the Sunday papers were to hand' in the large open lounge. Each of the 11 individually decorated bedrooms looks over the garden; they have antique furniture, pictures and porcelain. 'Ours was spacious, with a big lobby and large bathroom.' Sandalwood has a timbered ceiling; Magnolia has its own access to the front garden. In the yellow dining room, with subdued lighting, there is a large bay window looking over the garden. Chef Vincent Adeline uses local produce for his traditional menus: 'We had an excellent terrine of wild boar and a grilled half lobster'; 'delicious duck'. In season, vegetables and fruit are from the garden. Breakfast has freshly squeezed orange, apple and grapefruit juices, 'fine yogurt'; 'excellent fresh kippers'; good coffee. (*Lord Coleraine, Janet Walker*)

Hatch Beauchamp
nr Taunton TA3 6SG

T: 01823-480664
F: 01823-481118
E: farthingshotel@yahoo.co.uk
W: www.farthingshotel.co.uk

BEDROOMS: 12, 2 on ground floor.
OPEN: all year.
FACILITIES: bar, lounge, 3 restaurants, civil wedding licence, 3-acre garden.
BACKGROUND MUSIC: in bar and restaurant.
LOCATION: in village.
CHILDREN: all ages welcomed.
DOGS: not allowed in restaurant.
CREDIT CARDS: Amex, MasterCard, Visa.
PRICES: B&B £42.50–£110 per person, D,B&B £75–£95, full alc £50, special breaks, Christmas/New Year packages.

HATCH BEAUCHAMP Somerset

Map 1:C6

FROG STREET FARMHOUSE NEW

In peaceful Somerset countryside, this 15th-century longhouse is run as a small guest house by Louise and David Farrance, 'perfect hosts, friendly and accommodating'. 'She has given the house a fresh, contemporary look, while retaining the traditional character (exposed beams, Jacobean panelling, flagstone floors),' said an inspector. A reader found it 'comfortable and tastefully decorated'. A large sitting room has leather seating, Wi-Fi, a large television and a powerful wood-burning stove ('always lit when we returned from a day out'). 'Louise loves to cook and provides hearty three-course dinners if requested in advance; goat's cheese tart with salad; salmon, tarragon sauce, beautifully cooked vegetables.' The bedrooms are 'light and airy'; they have large bed, 'crisp linen'; good technology. The Willow Room has an exposed stone wall and beams, antique furniture, a double brass bedstead. The Garden Room has French-style furnishings. The Snug has its own entrance, a sitting room; a roll-top bath in the bathroom. Breakfast has home-made preserves, a selection of cereals, 'good' toast; eggs from the farm. 'Don't trust Satnav; ask for directions.' (*Jo Stevenson, and others*)

Hatch Beauchamp
nr Taunton TA3 6AF

T: 01823-481883
E: frogstreet@hotmail.com
W: www.frogstreet.co.uk

BEDROOMS: 4.
OPEN: all year except Christmas.
FACILITIES: 2 lounges, dining room, 150-acre grounds, unsuitable for ♿.
BACKGROUND MUSIC: optional.
LOCATION: 4 miles NW of Ilminster.
CHILDREN: all ages welcomed.
DOGS: not allowed.
CREDIT CARDS: MasterCard, Visa.
PRICES: B&B from £45 per person, dinner £22.50–£27.50.

HATHERSAGE Derbyshire

Map 3:A6

THE GEORGE HOTEL

'It is a very happy hotel, giving the impression that the staff really enjoy looking after their guests.' Praise from a trusted correspondent this year for Eric Marsh's 500-year-old grey-stone inn in a Peak District village. Mr Marsh also runs *The Cavendish* in Baslow (see entry); Philip Joseph is the manager of both. First-time visitors were 'made to feel most welcome'. The bedrooms (two have been added this year) have modern colours and fabrics: 'Our room was well decorated, spacious and quiet.' 'The ceiling lighting was excellent for reading; two good armchairs; a smallish bathroom with well-lit mirror and decent towels.' A small room ('nowhere to put the washing tackle') was less liked. In the dining room (candlelit, exposed brickwork), the cooking of chef Helen Heywood is 'a good reason to come'. 'The food is good: twice-baked basil and taleggio soufflé was light as a feather, and our lemon and parsley-crusted sea trout was moist, with a delicate flavour, most enjoyable.' A visitor in 2012 was disappointed when piped music in the dining room was not switched off when he asked. Breakfast has 'an excellent selection of fresh fruit, juices, etc'. (*Padi Howard, and others*)

Main Road
Hathersage S32 1BB

T: 01433-650436
F: 01433-650099
E: info@george-hotel.net
W: www.george-hotel.net

BEDROOMS: 24.
OPEN: all year.
FACILITIES: lounge/bar, restaurant, 2 function rooms, civil wedding licence, courtyard, Wi-Fi, only restaurant suitable for ♿.
BACKGROUND MUSIC: light jazz/blues in restaurant.
LOCATION: in village centre, parking.
CHILDREN: all ages welcomed.
DOGS: not allowed.
CREDIT CARDS: Amex, MasterCard, Visa.
PRICES: [2012] B&B £69.50–£99 per person, set dinner £29.25–£36.50, full alc £46.50, special breaks, Christmas/New Year packages, 1-night bookings occasionally refused.

HOLT Norfolk

Map 2:A5

BYFORDS

A 'posh B&B' is only part of the multifaceted business run by Iain and Clair Wilson at their conversion of a flint-fronted, Grade II listed house on the square of a charming Norfolk market town. An all-day continental-style café becomes a restaurant in the evening; a delicatessen sells bread, cakes and pastries baked on the premises (also frozen ready-meals and pizza takeaways). The 'higgledy-piggledy' building has narrow doorways, brickwork, oak floorboards. 'Our room was beautifully furnished.' Local materials (slate, leather, silk and linen) were used for the bedrooms, which have dark wood bedsteads and oak flooring; modern bathrooms are tiled in marble; many have a double-ended bath and drench shower. In the café/restaurant, a series of small interconnecting rooms, an extensive all-day menu has salads, pasta, 'posh pizzas', and 'grazing dishes' (eg, Binham Blue croquettes, Cley smokehouse-cured herrings). More substantial meals include Norfolk coast hotchpotch (fish and shellfish, fennel, leek and potato in a cream saffron broth). Breakfast has 'lots of choice'; home-made jam; filled croissants and wraps; smoked haddock and prawn kedgeree. More reports, please.

1–3 Shirehall Plain
Holt NR25 6BG

T: 01263-711400
E: queries@byfords.org.uk
W: www.byfords.org.uk

BEDROOMS: 16, 3 on ground floor, 1 suitable for ♿.

OPEN: all year.

FACILITIES: ramps, 5 internal eating areas, deli.

BACKGROUND MUSIC: jazz/'easy listening', live jazz on last Wed of every month.

LOCATION: central, private secure parking.

CHILDREN: all ages welcomed.

DOGS: only guide dogs allowed.

CREDIT CARDS: Amex, MasterCard, Visa.

PRICES: [2012] B&B £70–£115 per person, D,B&B £87.50–£133, full alc £35, winter offers, 1-night bookings refused Sat.

HOPE Derbyshire

Map 3:A6

UNDERLEIGH HOUSE

Down a narrow lane outside a village in the Hope valley, this popular B&B is well placed for walking in the Peak District. The owners, Vivienne and Philip Taylor, are 'wonderful' hosts; they greet guests with tea and home-made cake and are happy to 'point visitors in the right direction for sightseeing and walks'. The house is a conversion of a late 19th-century barn and cottages. The well-equipped bedrooms (some are small) have bottled water, tea- and coffee-making facilities, and fresh fruit. The Derwent suite has a lounge with dual-aspect windows overlooking Win Hill. The Thornhill suite has a stone staircase giving direct access from its lounge to the garden. A generous breakfast is taken communally at a long oak table: there are jugs of fruit juice, home-mixed muesli, home-baked bread and an array of Mrs Taylor's preserves. The cooked dishes include sausages and black pudding from the Hope butcher. Menus from local restaurants are displayed in the lounge with comments and suggestions. Maps and a packed lunch can be supplied for walkers. (*HRL, and others*)

Lose Hill Lane
off Edale Road
Hope S33 6AF

T: 01433-621372
F: 01433-621324
E: info@underleighhouse.co.uk
W: www.underleighhouse.co.uk

BEDROOMS: 5.
OPEN: All year except Christmas/New Year/7–31 Jan.
FACILITIES: lounge, breakfast room, ¼-acre garden, unsuitable for ♿.
BACKGROUND MUSIC: none.
LOCATION: 1 mile N of Hope.
CHILDREN: not under 12.
DOGS: allowed by arrangement.
CREDIT CARDS: MasterCard, Visa (*both 3% surcharge*).
PRICES: [2012] B&B £42.50–£85 per person, 3-night rates, 1-night bookings refused Fri/Sat, bank holidays.

SEE ALSO SHORTLIST

HUNTINGDON Cambridgeshire

Map 2:B4

THE OLD BRIDGE

Once a private bank, this creeper-clad 18th-century building stands by a medieval bridge over the River Ouse. Its owner, John Hoskins, also runs a wine shop on the premises; Nina Beaumond is the manager. The 'well-thought-out' bedrooms have been styled by Julia Hoskins: there are chaises longues, mosaic tiles. Three rooms have a four-poster bed; bathrooms are smart. The rooms that face the busy traffic system have triple glazing. Free Wi-Fi is available throughout. In the lively *Terrace* restaurant, which has an oval cupola, the chef, James Haydon, serves a monthly-changing menu with dishes like Serrano ham with chicory, celery and walnut salad; pan-fried fillet of John Dory, spinach, saffron potatoes and braised fennel. A snack menu, served from 12 noon to 10 pm, is also available. Many wines are available by the glass. Children are welcomed and have their own menu. Early morning tea is brought to the bedroom with a complimentary newspaper. Breakfast has 'plenty of choice, good orange juice, good service'. Wine dinners and a wine festival are held. Functions take place in a self-contained area. (*JG, and others*)

25% DISCOUNT VOUCHERS

1 High Street
Huntingdon PE29 3TQ

T: 01480-424300
F: 01480-411017
E: oldbridge@huntsbridge.co.uk
W: www.huntsbridge.com

BEDROOMS: 24, 2 on ground floor.
OPEN: all year.
FACILITIES: ramps, lounge, bar, restaurant, private dining room, wine shop, business centre, civil wedding licence, 1-acre grounds (terrace, garden), river (fishing, jetty, boat trips), unsuitable for ♿.
BACKGROUND MUSIC: none.
LOCATION: 500 yds from centre, parking, station 10 mins' walk.
CHILDREN: all ages welcomed.
DOGS: allowed.
CREDIT CARDS: MasterCard, Visa.
PRICES: B&B £75–£99.50 per person, D,B&B £95–£130, full alc £40, Christmas/New Year packages.

HURSTBOURNE TARRANT Hampshire

Map 2:D2

ESSEBORNE MANOR

In an 'idyllic setting with gardens and sheep grazing in meadows', this late Victorian house is run as an 'old-fashioned country hotel' by the owners, Lucilla and Ian Hamilton, and their son, Mark. The cream-painted house ('unpretentious yet stylish') is in a designated area of outstanding natural beauty in the North Wessex Downs. The bright sitting room ('we liked the blue and yellow theme') has comfortable chairs and a 'huge range of up-to-date magazines'. In the library and bar area 'an open fire was lit from early evening'. The bedrooms are divided between the main house, around a courtyard ('good for families') and garden cottages. 'They are of good size and reasonably furnished,' says a visitor this year. 'Everything was spotless and pleasant, despite some twee touches,' said inspectors. In the dining room, with its 'bold' red-patterned wallpaper (and quiet background music), Dennis Janssen is the new chef this year; he serves a short menu of modern dishes, perhaps salmon gravadlax, beetroot and yogurt; duo of beef (sous-vide fillet and slow-cooked shin), Béarnaise foam. We would welcome reports on his cooking. (*RJD, and others*)

25% DISCOUNT VOUCHERS

Hurstbourne Tarrant, nr Andover
SP11 0ER

T: 01264-736444
F: 01264-736725
E: info@esseborne-manor.co.uk
W: www.esseborne-manor.co.uk

BEDROOMS: 19, 6 in courtyard, 2 in cottages.
OPEN: all year, except Christmas.
FACILITIES: 2 lounges, bar, restaurant, function room, civil wedding licence, 3-acre grounds (formal gardens, tennis, croquet), arrangements with nearby golf club and fitness centre.
BACKGROUND MUSIC: in restaurant.
LOCATION: on A343, 7 miles N of Andover.
CHILDREN: all ages welcomed.
DOGS: not allowed in public rooms.
CREDIT CARDS: all major cards.
PRICES: B&B £55–£125 per person, D,B&B £20 added, set meals £20–£25, full alc £45, special breaks, New Year package.

IPSWICH Suffolk

Map 2:C5

SALTHOUSE HARBOUR HOTEL

On the waterfront at Neptune Marina, Robert Gough's stylishly converted Victorian warehouse has a clean, minimalist look. 'It is strong on the cool, hip image, but needs a little more attention to detail,' said a visitor in 2012 who had issues with Wi-Fi reception. The young staff are generally 'prompt and on the ball'; Lynn Cowan is the manager. The public areas are filled with a collection of quirky art, some of it commissioned by the hotel – contemporary urban paintings, suspended torsos, rugs, graffiti sculpture. Marina-facing rooms are recommended: you can watch the activity on the water and the distant Orwell Bridge. Modern bathrooms have separate power shower and bath. In the *Eaterie*, chef Simon Barker uses local produce for his modern dishes, eg, grilled mackerel, sweet-and-sour rhubarb; slow-cooked pig's cheeks, goat's cheese and walnut croquettes. 'Intrusive background music is not good.' Breakfast has 'light options' (croissants, fruit salad, etc) and 'more substantial' dishes, perhaps smoked salmon, poached egg and a bagel. Parking is limited. The Gough family also owns *The Angel*, Bury St Edmunds (see Shortlist). (*RG*)

Neptune Quay
Ipswich
IP4 1AX

T: 01473-226789
F: 01473-226927
E: reservations@salthouseharbour.co.uk
W: www.salthouseharbour.co.uk

BEDROOMS: 70, 4 suitable for ♿.
OPEN: all year.
FACILITIES: lounge, bar, *Eaterie*, conference rooms.
BACKGROUND MUSIC: eclectic mix in lounge, brasserie.
LOCATION: on waterfront.
CHILDREN: all ages welcomed.
DOGS: in lounge, bedrooms.
CREDIT CARDS: Amex, MasterCard, Visa.
PRICES: [2012] B&B £62.50–£150 per person, full alc £40, special offers.

IREBY Cumbria

Map 4: inset B2

OVERWATER HALL

Red squirrels have the run of the gardens and woodland surrounding this Grade II listed Georgian house in the quieter northern Lake District. It is run as a small, informal hotel by Adrian and Angela Hyde and Stephen Bore. 'They and their long-serving staff are very friendly,' says a visitor this year. The boldly decorated public rooms have 'comfortable furnishings, books, games'; a log fire burns in the high-ceilinged sitting room. 'Bedrooms are a good size, and well provisioned – including fruit liqueur.' A ground-floor room has a terrace leading to the garden; unusual turret rooms, with their curved walls and huge windows, are full of character. In the dining room, chef Adrian Hyde's 'excellent' modern British menus might include wild mallard, smoked bacon rösti, hedgerow jus; pan-roasted beef, crushed broad beans, oxtail ravioli. A children's high tea is served in the late afternoon, by arrangement. Morning coffee and afternoon tea come with home-made biscuits: 'The shortbread is superb.' The produce for breakfast (as that for dinner) is 'truly Cumbrian'. Dogs, who may sit with their owners in one lounge, are welcomed.
(*William Rankin*)

25% DISCOUNT VOUCHERS

Overwater, nr Ireby
CA7 1HH

T: 017687-76566
F: 017687-76921
E: welcome@overwaterhall.co.uk
W: www.overwaterhall.co.uk

BEDROOMS: 11, 1 on ground floor.
OPEN: all year.
FACILITIES: drawing room, lounge, bar area, restaurant, civil wedding licence, 18-acre grounds, Overwater tarn 1 mile.
BACKGROUND MUSIC: classical in restaurant.
LOCATION: 2 miles NE of Bassenthwaite Lake.
CHILDREN: not under 5 in restaurant (high tea at 5.30 pm).
DOGS: allowed except in 1 lounge, restaurant.
CREDIT CARDS: MasterCard, Visa.
PRICES: [2012] B&B £75–£120 per person, D,B&B £120–£165, set dinner £45, special breaks, Christmas/New Year packages, 1-night bookings refused Sat.

'S LYNN Norfolk

Map 2:A4

THE BANK HOUSE

Once a Georgian merchant's house, later the first bank of a founding father of Barclay's, this listed building stands on the quayside of a historic town. It has been rescued after years of neglect by Jeannette and Anthony Goodrich. 'They have done a good job, retaining original features while providing every facility we could need,' say visitors this year. 'Our very reasonably priced room was one of the biggest we've ever stayed in; the bathroom alone was larger than many doubles elsewhere.' There is no residents' lounge, but guests may sit in the large reception area, the smaller bar, and the old banking hall where tall armchairs face a quiet square. This is one of three dining areas; in summer, meals may also be taken under a sunshade sail on a riverside terrace. Chef Stuart Deuchars cooks classic English dishes (perhaps chicken liver parfait, spicy pear chutney) as well as more eclectic choices (pan-fried red mullet, Asian broth). 'Our evening meal was excellent, with efficient, friendly service.' The Goodriches also own *The Rose & Crown*, Snettisham (see entry). (*Robert and Shirley Lyne, and others*)

25% DISCOUNT VOUCHERS

King's Staithe Square
King's Lynn PE30 1RD

T: 01553-660492
E: info@thebankhouse.co.uk
W: www.thebankhouse.co.uk

BEDROOMS: 11.

OPEN: all year.

FACILITIES: bar, 3 dining rooms, private dining room, terrace, only dining rooms suitable for ♿.

BACKGROUND MUSIC: in bar and dining rooms.

LOCATION: central, opposite Custom House.

CHILDREN: all ages welcomed.

DOGS: not allowed.

CREDIT CARDS: all major cards.

PRICES: [2012] B&B £50–£120 per person, full alc £32.50, Christmas/New Year packages.

KIRKBY LONSDALE Cumbria

Map 4: inset C2

SUN INN

'A beautifully appointed small hotel with above-average food.' Praise from a regular correspondent this year for Lucy and Mark Fuller's white-painted 17th-century inn on the narrow street of a Cumbrian market town. 'The welcome couldn't have been warmer; this is an upmarket inn with a clean, contemporary style,' is a comment from a visitor in 2012. The Fullers are part of an 'excellent small team which knows how to make guests feel wanted'. The bar and restaurant have flagstone and oak floors, exposed beams, log fires, leather seating. In the restaurant, chef Charlotte Norfolk serves 'delicious' seasonal dishes like caramelised pear, Fine Fettle (Yorkshire feta cheese); slow-roasted belly of pork, creamed cabbage, toffee apple. The bedrooms have 'elegant' furnishings, modern bathroom. 'Our room was small but inviting; bright and light, it had a lovely view of the churchyard; it was well appointed (quality teas and coffees with home-made shortbread).' A 'delicious' breakfast has a 'good sideboard of home-made granola, freshly squeezed orange juice'; 'fine' cooked dishes brought to the table; 'toast when you want it'. (*Humphrey Norrington, Caroline Till*)

6 Market Street
Kirkby Lonsdale LA6 2AU

T: 015242-71965
F: 015242-72485
E: email@sun-inn.info
W: www.sun-inn.info

BEDROOMS: 11.
OPEN: all year, bar and restaurant closed Mon lunch.
FACILITIES: bar, restaurant.
BACKGROUND MUSIC: in bar.
LOCATION: town centre.
CHILDREN: all ages welcomed.
DOGS: allowed.
CREDIT CARDS: MasterCard, Visa.
PRICES: [2012] B&B £55–£81 per person, set dinner £25.95–£31.95, full alc £35, midweek breaks, Christmas/New Year packages, 1-night bookings refused weekends.

KIRKBY STEPHEN Cumbria

Map 4:C3

AUGILL CASTLE

From the turret wardrobes, to the 12-seat cinema (new this year), to the borrowable vintage MGB Roadster with picnic basket, there is plenty at this restored neo-Gothic Victorian castle to make it 'a remarkable experience'. 'We get away with mad things,' says Wendy Bennett, who owns the hotel with her husband, Simon. Visitors love the 'relaxed atmosphere' and family-friendly approach; children are 'welcome guests' given many diversions: a tree house, a drawing room with toys and costumes, a children's cookery school. 'All is excellent (staff, food, rooms),' says a visitor this year who 'enjoyed every single minute'. Bedrooms have bold wallpaper, antique furniture. A first-floor room has an Edwardian four-poster bed and a turn-of-the-century fireplace; a room wallpapered in pink and gold has a bathroom with stained-glass windows. A three-course dinner is available, by arrangement, in the striking blue dining room. Meals, eaten communally at a banquet-style table, might include chicken and leek terrine, chervil vinaigrette, nettle soup; Yorkshire Dales lamb, rosemary, redcurrants. Children are served an early supper. Breakfast is 'a leisurely affair'.

South Stainmore
nr Kirkby Stephen CA17 4DE

T: 01768-341937
E: enquiries@stayinacastle.com
W: www.stayinacastle.com

BEDROOMS: 14, 2 on ground floor, 4 in Stable House, 2 in Orangery.

OPEN: all year, dinner by arrangement, lunch for groups by arrangement.

FACILITIES: hall, cinema, drawing room, library (honesty bar), music (sitting) room, dining room, civil wedding licence, 15-acre grounds (landscaped garden, tennis).

BACKGROUND MUSIC: none.

LOCATION: 3 miles E of Kirkby Stephen.

CHILDREN: all ages welcomed.

DOGS: allowed in some bedrooms only, by arrangement.

CREDIT CARDS: Amex, MasterCard, Visa.

PRICES: [2012] B&B £80–£90 per person, set dinner £30, Christmas/ New Year packages, 2-night bookings preferred weekends.

SEE ALSO SHORTLIST

LACOCK Wiltshire

Map 2:D1

AT THE SIGN OF THE ANGEL

César award in 1989

Found 'first rate' by visitors this year, this 'enchanting' 15th-century inn has long been owned and run by Lorna and George Hardy. It is in an ancient National Trust village of lime-washed stone and half-timbered houses, much used as a location for films and television. 'Everyone is warm and friendly.' There are log fires in the public rooms, exposed beams, low doorways, stone fireplaces and flagstone floors. The bedrooms, all in the main building (cottage ones are no longer available), have large bed (one a four-poster, another a French tented bed), antiques, and rich-coloured fabrics and furnishings. The bathrooms are modern. 'Our room was a delight; so what if the floorboards creak and the doors are quaintly "off side"? Our comfy bed gently lulled us to sleep.' The smallest room, on the ground floor, has a large bathroom. In the three interconnecting dining rooms, guests dine by candlelight; the Hardys, who share chef duties, serve seasonal and mostly locally sourced food. Their traditional dishes might include individual steak and kidney pudding. Breakfast has eggs from the hens who roam the garden, Wiltshire bacon, home-made bread.

25% DISCOUNT VOUCHERS

6 Church Street
Lacock, nr Chippenham SN15 2LB

T: 01249-730230
F: 01249-730527
E: angel@lacock.co.uk
W: www.lacock.co.uk

BEDROOMS: 6.
OPEN: all year except 24–26 Dec, closed Mon lunch except bank holidays.
FACILITIES: ramps, lounge, bar, restaurant, civil wedding licence.
BACKGROUND MUSIC: none.
LOCATION: village centre, 3 miles S of Chippenham.
CHILDREN: all ages welcomed.
DOGS: not allowed in public rooms.
CREDIT CARDS: Amex, MasterCard, Visa.
PRICES: [2012] B&B £60–£85 per person, D,B&B £75–£115, full alc £37.50, New Year package.

LANGAR Nottinghamshire

Map 2:A3

LANGAR HALL

César award in 2000

'The complete antidote to faceless hotels; it feels like staying with friends in the country, except that the food is better.' Warm praise comes in 2012 from a regular *Guide* correspondent for Imogen Skirving's informal small hotel in the Vale of Belvoir. 'Quite a character, she is very much a hands-on owner,' is another comment. 'It is a tribute to her thoroughness that everything functions impeccably in her absence; the young staff have just the right level of cheerful attentiveness.' Stuccoed and apricot-washed, the late Georgian building has been in Mrs Skirving's family for over 150 years. The white sitting room has an open log fire, comfortable seating. Bedrooms are themed (Bohemia was once an artist's studio), or named after previous guests (Cartland, although no longer pink, is a 'romantic' room). Two bedrooms share a sitting room in a former gardener's cottage at the end of the lime avenue. In the pillared dining room, chefs Gary Booth and Ross Jeffrey serve 'very good' seasonal dishes. The marmite popcorn that accompanies pre-dinner drinks is not universally enjoyed. (*Peter Jowitt, Mrs Blethyn Elliott, and others*)

25% DISCOUNT VOUCHERS

Church Lane
Langar NG13 9HG

T: 01949-860559
F: 01949-861045
E: info@langarhall.co.uk
W: www.langarhall.com

BEDROOMS: 14, 1 on ground floor, 1 garden chalet, 2 in the *Lodge*.
OPEN: all year.
FACILITIES: ramps, sitting room, study, library, bar, garden room, restaurant, civil wedding licence, 20-acre grounds (gardens, children's play area, croquet, ponds, fishing), unsuitable for ♿.
BACKGROUND MUSIC: none.
LOCATION: 12 miles SE of Nottingham.
CHILDREN: all ages welcomed by arrangement.
DOGS: small dogs on a lead allowed by arrangement, not unaccompanied in certain bedrooms.
CREDIT CARDS: MasterCard, Visa.
PRICES: B&B £85–£140 per person, set dinner (2 courses) £20 (Tue–Fri), special offers, Christmas/New Year packages.

LANGHO Lancashire

Map 4:D3

NORTHCOTE

Chef/patron Nigel Haworth and his business partner, Craig Bancroft, have run their restaurant-with-rooms for 30 years in this 'beautiful' old house, a red brick, late Victorian/ Edwardian residence. In the wooded Trough of Bowland, the house has exceptional views across the Ribble valley. Mr Haworth and Lisa Allen have a *Michelin* star for their 'innovative' cooking served in the formal dining room: dishes on a tasting menu, which celebrates local ingredients, might include treacle salmon with ginger chilli, coriander, charred spring onions; Rowland hare with faggot, celeriac purée, wild mushrooms and roasted beets. Background music 'was not intrusive'. Many original features have been retained in the house (splendid wooden doors and windows). The bedrooms have rich fabrics, vibrant colours, unusual wall coverings. 'Our large room was well fitted; it had a fridge with soft drinks and fresh milk; a well-stocked tea/coffee tray had a cafetière and fresh coffee.' Some rooms have a private terrace. There is 'no boring buffet' at breakfast, which has fresh fruits and cereals, 'a good choice of cooked offerings'. Free Wi-Fi is available. (*PW*)

Northcote Road, Langho
nr Blackburn BB6 8BE

T: 01254-240555
F: 01254-246568
E: reception@northcote.com
W: www.northcote.com

BEDROOMS: 14, 4 on ground floor, 1 suitable for ♿.

OPEN: all year except 25 Dec.

FACILITIES: ramp, lounge, drawing room, cocktail bar, restaurant, private dining/meeting room, civil wedding licence, 2-acre garden.

BACKGROUND MUSIC: varied in restaurant.

LOCATION: 5½ miles N of Blackburn, on A59.

CHILDREN: all ages welcomed.

DOGS: not allowed.

CREDIT CARDS: Amex, MasterCard, Visa.

PRICES: B&B [2012] £115–£140 per person, set dinner £60–£85, gourmet breaks.

LASTINGHAM North Yorkshire

Map 4:C4

LASTINGHAM GRANGE

César award in 1991

'You cannot help but love *Lastingham Grange*; you are so well looked after by the pleasant staff from early-morning tea to the five-course dinner.' There are many returning visitors to the 'hard-working' Wood family's traditional hotel, which is one of only four places to have had an entry in every edition of the *Guide*. Bertie Wood is helped by his mother, Jane, and brother, Tom. The converted 17th-century farmhouse stands in large gardens and fields on the edge of the North Yorkshire Moors: 'You can be on the moor within five minutes from the front door – perfect for working up an appetite.' Afternoon tea, with hot scones, may be taken in the lounge or the rose garden; at dinner, chef Paul Cattaneo serves a daily-changing menu of 'good, plain English cooking'. 'Roast beef melts in the mouth; the Cointreau ginger log is scrumptious.' Comfortable bedrooms have 'all you need [tea- and coffee-making facilities, fresh milk and biscuits], and a lovely view of the garden'. Children are welcomed: there is an adventure playground, and special meals can be arranged. (*Carol Norris, and others*)

Lastingham YO62 6TH

T: 01751-417345
F: 01751-417358
E: reservations@lastinghamgrange.com
W: www.lastinghamgrange.com

BEDROOMS: 12, plus cottage in village.

OPEN: Mar–Nov.

FACILITIES: ramps, hall, lounge, dining room, laundry facilities, 12-acre grounds (terrace, garden, adventure playground, croquet, boules), unsuitable for ♿.

BACKGROUND MUSIC: none.

LOCATION: 5 miles NE of Kirkbymoorside.

CHILDREN: all ages welcomed.

DOGS: not allowed in public rooms.

CREDIT CARDS: Amex, MasterCard, Visa.

PRICES: [2012] B&B £75–£100 per person, D,B&B £90–£140, set dinner £39.75, full alc £46, special breaks, 1-night bookings refused Aug, Sept.

LAVENHAM Suffolk

Map 2:C5

THE GREAT HOUSE

César award in 2009

'Memorable: our room was lovely and the cooking wonderful as always.' Renewed praise in 2012 for this 'magnificent' Georgian house, which has been run for 25 years as a restaurant-with-rooms in distinctive French style by Gallic owners Régis and Martine Crépy. They have given the house a cool modern look: in 2012 they added an inner dining area in a sheltered courtyard, using stainless steel and opaque glass and a retractable canopy. 'Our attic room had all the modern knick-knacks fitted neatly among the ancient beams: the decor was neutral with bursts of colour and an aura of comfort; a bowl of fruit and decanter of sherry were complimentary. We slept well in a soft but supportive bed.' The candlelit dining room has panelled walls painted in French grey; modern artwork. The 'immaculate' cooking of chef Enrique Bilbault is often praised: 'Particularly good were bresaola and a spectacular tarte Tatin. Everything was impeccably served by the smart but friendly young French staff.' An 'excellent' breakfast has freshly squeezed orange juice, 'a wide range of cold meats and good cheese'.
(*Andrew and Moira Kleissner*)

Market Place
Lavenham CO10 9QZ

T: 01787-247431
F: 01787-248007
E: info@greathouse.co.uk
W: www.greathouse.co.uk

BEDROOMS: 5.
OPEN: Feb–Dec, restaurant closed Sun night, Mon, Tues midday.
FACILITIES: lounge/bar, restaurant, patio dining area, ½-acre garden, unsuitable for ♿.
BACKGROUND MUSIC: French.
LOCATION: by Market Cross, near Guildhall, public car park.
CHILDREN: all ages welcomed.
DOGS: not allowed.
CREDIT CARDS: MasterCard, Visa.
PRICES: [2012] B&B £62.50–£112.50 per person, D,B&B £94.50–£160.50, breakfast £15, dinner £31.95, full alc £56, special breaks, 1-night bookings sometimes refused Sat.

SEE ALSO SHORTLIST

LAVENHAM Suffolk

Map 2:C5

LAVENHAM PRIORY

César award in 2012

Once a Benedictine priory, this half-timbered Grade I listed medieval house has been sympathetically restored by owners Tim and Gilli Pitt in the style of the Elizabethan merchant's house it later became. The approach is through a garden with herbs and old roses: a massive door opens on to the 13th-century Great Hall, which has a huge inglenook fireplace, antiques and family photographs; a smaller lounge through a double arch has a wood-burner. Oak staircases lead to the spacious 'bedchambers'. There are sloping beamed ceilings, massive oak floorboards, and unusual beds (four-poster, sleigh or polonaise). 'It's a privilege to be able to sleep in such a historic building,' said a reporter this year: his room, the Painted Chamber, had traces of medieval wall paintings. Another comment (by an inspector): 'What a special room: the bed was large and comfortable.' Light sleepers might notice noise from several rooms facing a side road. Breakfast, taken around a large communal table in another beamed room, has a buffet of cereals and fruit; freshly squeezed orange juice; do-it-yourself toast; a wide choice of cooked dishes.

Water Street
Lavenham CO10 9RW

T: 01787-247404
F: 01787-248472
E: mail@lavenhampriory.co.uk
W: www.lavenhampriory.co.uk

BEDROOMS: 6.
OPEN: all year except Christmas/New Year.
FACILITIES: Great Hall/sitting room, snug, breakfast room, 3-acre garden (medieval courtyard, herb garden), unsuitable for ♿.
BACKGROUND MUSIC: none.
LOCATION: central.
CHILDREN: not under 10.
DOGS: not allowed in house.
CREDIT CARDS: MasterCard, Visa.
PRICES: [2012] B&B £60–£91 per person, winter midweek discount for 2 nights or more, 1-night bookings refused Sat.

SEE ALSO SHORTLIST

LEAMINGTON SPA Warwickshire

Map 2:B2

EIGHT CLARENDON CRESCENT

In a quiet street in 'picturesque' Leamington Spa, David and Christine Lawson run their Grade II listed Regency house as an upmarket B&B. 'Highly recommended' by trusted reporters, the 'grand' building is in 'immaculate' condition: 'They have kept the glorious original Regency features, and packed it with beautiful antique pieces they have collected.' The Lawsons are 'friendly' hosts: 'she was on hand to chat, never outstaying her welcome'. A 'sumptuous' drawing room, which overlooks the garden, has a baby grand piano 'which we would be delighted to hear you play', say the Lawsons. The four bedrooms are decorated in neutral colours; they have TV, Wi-Fi and beverage facilities. Three have an en suite bathroom; one has a private bathroom across the corridor and down a few stairs. 'Our spacious bedroom had dramatic bay windows overlooking the garden.' The breakfast, taken around an antique circular table, has home-made bread and preserves, fresh fruit, yogurt; a 'tasty' cooked full English. Coffee and tea are served in 'the finest silverware'. The town centre and the Royal Pump Rooms are a short walk away. (*A and BB*)

8 Clarendon Crescent
Leamington Spa CV32 5NR

T: 01926-429840
F: 01926-424641
E: lawson@lawson71.fsnet.co.uk
W: www.8clarendoncrescent.co.uk

BEDROOMS: 4.

OPEN: all year except Christmas, New Year, occasional holidays.

FACILITIES: drawing room, dining room, garden, 1-acre with private dell, unsuitable for ♿.

BACKGROUND MUSIC: none.

LOCATION: close to centre.

CHILDREN: all ages welcomed.

DOGS: not allowed.

CREDIT CARDS: none.

PRICES: [2012] B&B £40–£50 per person.

LEDBURY Herefordshire

Map 3:D5

THE FEATHERS

25% DISCOUNT VOUCHERS

High Street
Ledbury HR8 1DS

T: 01531-635266
F: 01531-638955
E: mary@feathers-ledbury.co.uk
W: www.feathers-ledbury.co.uk

BEDROOMS: 22, 1 suite in cottage, also self-catering apartments.
OPEN: all year.
FACILITIES: lounge, bar, brasserie, restaurant, function/conference/wedding facilities, spa (swimming pool, 11 by 6 metres, whirlpool, gym), civil wedding licence, courtyard garden (fountain, alfresco eating), unsuitable for ♿.
BACKGROUND MUSIC: none.
LOCATION: town centre, parking.
CHILDREN: all ages welcomed.
DOGS: allowed, only guide dogs in restaurant and brasserie.
CREDIT CARDS: all major cards.
PRICES: [2012] B&B £95–£127 per person, full alc £37.50, New Year package.

'Quaint and atmospheric as ever', David Elliston's 400-year-old coaching inn in the centre of the old market town is a 'great place to stay', say fans. A visitor this year was given 'an excellent welcome; our bags were carried up the quirky old staircase to our second-floor bedroom'. Older rooms have beamed walls and ceiling, antique furniture; the largest has a seating area. More modern rooms, with high ceiling and tall windows, are in the former ballroom. A small room overlooking the high street was 'very comfortable; a compact but adequate bathroom'. The bar and lounges are a popular local gathering place. There are two dining areas: *Fuggles Brasserie*, a panelled room with a hop-clad ceiling, and *Quills*, the more formal option, suited to a 'romantic dinner for two'. 'A delicious dinner in *Fuggles*; good pea and ham soup; free-range chicken, a wonderful Pimm's jelly. The service was very good; all the staff are friendly.' The lack of muzak pleased visitors in 2012. Breakfast is 'cheerfully served; a choice of fruit and cereals and a very tasty full English with good-quality sausages and bacon; lots of toast'. (*Roland Cassam*)

LEDBURY Herefordshire

Map 3:D5

VERZON HOUSE

In large grounds with views to the Malvern hills, this handsome red brick Georgian farmhouse is run as a small upmarket hotel by Peter and Audrey Marks. They refurbished throughout 'with no expense spared': the furnishings and decor are 'modern, not traditional; no sign of chintz'. Original features have been retained in the public rooms, which have cornices, an inlaid staircase, open fires. The *Mulberry* bar has brickwork, beams, leather seats; an elegant dining room overlooks the garden. Callum Keir was appointed chef in 2012: his modern menus have dishes like French onion tart, anchovy; corn-fed poussin, herbes de Provence, 'gone-wrong' roasted potatoes, peperonata. Afternoon tea, drinks and meals can be taken on a decked terrace in fine weather. The bedrooms are individually styled; one has a double-ended bath in the room; all have a fridge with water, soft drinks, apple juice and fresh milk; there is tea- and coffee-making; free Wi-Fi. A limited room-service menu is available. Breakfast has fresh fruit salad, home-made Bircher muesli, a generous full English and interesting alternatives (boiled eggs, Marmite solders; eggs Benedict, home-baked ham, toasted crumpet).

Hereford Road, Trumpet
Ledbury
HR8 2PZ

T: 01531-670381
F: 01531-670830
E: info@verzonhouse.com
W: www.verzonhouse.com

BEDROOMS: 8.
OPEN: Feb–Dec, except Mon in winter.
FACILITIES: bar, lounge, dining room, civil wedding licence, terrace, 4-acre grounds, only public areas suitable for ♿.
BACKGROUND MUSIC: 'occasionally' in bar.
LOCATION: 2 miles W of Ledbury.
CHILDREN: welcomed, no under-8s at dinner.
DOGS: only guide dogs allowed.
CREDIT CARDS: Amex, MasterCard, Visa.
PRICES: [2012] B&B £75–£102 per person, D,B&B £110–£145, full alc £45, winter breaks, Christmas/New Year/Cheltenham Festival packages, 1-night bookings rarely refused.

LEONARD STANLEY Gloucestershire

Map 3:E5

THE GREY COTTAGE

César award in 1999

'We enjoy going back to stay with Rosemary Reeves in her lovely home. She maintains high standards of personal service, showing great attention to detail.' Praise again this year for this popular small Cotswold stone guest house in pretty gardens. The 'enthusiastic welcome' includes tea and home-baked cake in the sitting room. Mrs Reeves tells us she has fitted new wardrobes in two of the three bedrooms; Room 2 has a new bathroom; all rooms have flat-screen TV, tea-/coffee-making facilities; the many extras include a sewing kit, hot-water bottles, books. 'We like Room 1 with its king-size bed, bath and walk-in shower.' Mrs Reeves cooks dinner by arrangement: 'A delicious meal, beautifully presented, with a hand-written menu; warm lettuce and ginger soup; roast rack of honey-glazed Welsh mountain lamb, steamed new potatoes, local spinach.' Breakfast, described as 'a memorable feast', has freshly squeezed orange juice, 'plenty of fruit and cereals'; do-it-yourself toast with 'proper' pats of butter; 'good cooked choices' include boiled egg with soldiers. (*Gordon Franklin, and others*)

Bath Road, Leonard Stanley
Stonehouse GL10 3LU

T: 01453-822515
E: rosemary.reeves@btopenworld.com
W: www.greycottage.ik.com

BEDROOMS: 3.

OPEN: all year except Christmas/New Year, occasional holidays.

FACILITIES: sitting room with TV, conservatory, dining room, ¼-acre garden, unsuitable for ♿.

BACKGROUND MUSIC: 'no, never!'

LOCATION: 3 miles SW of Stroud.

CHILDREN: not under 10.

DOGS: not allowed.

CREDIT CARDS: none.

PRICES: B&B £40–£55 per person, set dinner £23–£25, discount for 3-night stays.

LETCOMBE REGIS Oxfordshire

Map 2:C2

BROOK BARN

'A repeat visit is often proof of the pudding; our second stay at *Brook Barn* was just as good, just as comfortable.' A regular correspondent enjoyed a 'delightful' return in 2012 to Mark and Sarah-Jane Ashman's upmarket B&B, a stylish conversion of two ancient barns. 'It is clearly the owners' home but you are left to yourself; they are hands-on and caring.' The bedrooms are decorated in soft tones and have exposed beams; 'all mod cons; everything you could think of is available, even a box of spare reading glasses'. Four rooms have a door that opens on to a terrace; the Hayloft has a view of the stream and open countryside. There is a huge log fire in the double-height sitting room. Guests have an honesty bar, and a library. Dinner must be ordered by 4 pm; this disconcerted one late-arriving guest. An extensive carte is served at weekends, a bistro menu from Tuesday to Thursday. Breakfast has fresh fruit, toast from home-baked bread; 'excellent' sausages and bacon from a local farm. (*Matthew Caminer, and others*)

25% DISCOUNT VOUCHERS

Letcombe Regis
nr Wantage OX12 9JD

T: 01235-766502
F: 01235-766873
E: info@brookbarn.com
W: www.brookbarn.com

BEDROOMS: 5, 4 on ground floor.
OPEN: all year except 24–26 Dec, restaurant closed Mon.
FACILITIES: library, drawing room, dining room, 1½-acre garden (croquet), unsuitable for ♿.
BACKGROUND MUSIC: 'classical' in drawing room.
LOCATION: edge of village, 1½ miles SW of Wantage.
CHILDREN: not under 16.
DOGS: not allowed.
CREDIT CARDS: Amex, MasterCard, Visa.
PRICES: [2012] B&B £64–£125 per person, D,B&B £94–£155, full alc £50, New Year package, 1-night booking sometimes refused at weekends.

LICHFIELD Staffordshire

Map 2:A2

NETHERSTOWE HOUSE

'We were greeted as if we were visiting notables; every possible assistance was given with a friendly smile.' *Guide* inspectors, who arrived (anonymously) in a 'bedraggled state' at Ben Heathcote's small hotel, were 'almost overpowered by the quality of the service'. The Grade II listed half-timbered red brick building is a converted 19th-century mill. The bedrooms are in the main house ('lovely, feminine, some with king-size bed and retro roll-top bath'); eight 'chic' apartments are in a 'sympathetic' modern wing. 'Our large apartment was well furnished, tastefully decorated; lots of natural lighting from velux windows; a well-equipped bathroom.' The entrance hall/lounge has an imposing fireplace; 'pleasing' public rooms are 'elegantly' furnished and have comfortable seating areas. Chef Tim Barker's classic menu 'with a modern twist' is served in three dining rooms: 'The elegant *Ivy* room had a fin de siècle look (gold paint on the ornate plasterwork); the food and service were refined, the waiters wore white gloves; less than welcome background music.' More informal dining is in a vaulted cellar steakhouse. 'Good value,' readers agree. (*Richard and Catriona Smith, and others*)

Netherstowe Lane
Lichfield WS13 6AY

T/F: 01543-254270
E: info@netherstowehouse.com
W: www.netherstowehouse.com

BEDROOMS: 9, plus 8 serviced apartments in annexe.
OPEN: all year.
FACILITIES: 2 lounges, bar, 3 dining rooms, cellar, gymnasium, 2-acre grounds, unsuitable for ♿.
BACKGROUND MUSIC: in public rooms.
LOCATION: 2 miles N of city centre.
CHILDREN: over 12 in hotel, all ages welcomed in apartments.
DOGS: guide dogs only allowed.
CREDIT CARDS: MasterCard, Visa.
PRICES: [2012] B&B £42.50–£125 per person, set dinner menu £19.95–£24.95, full alc £30, special breaks.

LIFTON Devon

Map 1:C3

THE ARUNDELL ARMS

César award in 2006

'This really is an excellent hotel; we have resolved to go back for some fly-fishing.' A visitor this year loved Adam Fox-Edwards's West Country sporting inn. 'The staff are all so friendly.' The *Arundell Arms* is popular with fishing and shooting visitors (it has 20 miles of fishing rights on seven different rivers), but visitors without sporting interests are equally at home. Bedrooms ('very pleasant and well appointed') are decorated in country house style. Wi-Fi is available throughout. The best rooms are in a rear extension: 'Ours had a separate seating area.' The *Courthouse* bar has stone walls, bars over the windows indicating its original use. 'Delicious' pub favourites and dishes from a specials board are served here. The 'cosy' lounges have lots of seating. The dining room is a grander affair; once the village assembly room, it has high ceilings, and panels depicting classical statues. Here, the long-serving chef, Steve Pidgeon, serves modern dishes like wood mushroom consommé; mixed grill of sea fish with asparagus and salad leaves. 'Food and service were excellent.' (*Kenneth Moore, David RW Jervois*)

25% DISCOUNT VOUCHERS

Fore Street
Lifton PL16 0AA

T: 01566-784666
F: 01566-784494
E: reservations@arundellarms.co.uk
W: www.arundellarms.co.uk

BEDROOMS: 21, 4 on ground floor.
OPEN: all year, except Christmas (food only).
FACILITIES: ramp, lounge, cocktail bar, public bar, 2 dining rooms, conference/meeting rooms, games room, skittle alley, civil wedding licence, ½-acre garden, 20 miles fishing rights on River Tamar and tributaries, fishing school.
BACKGROUND MUSIC: varied in restaurant and bar.
LOCATION: 3 miles E of Launceston.
CHILDREN: all ages welcomed.
DOGS: not allowed in restaurant.
CREDIT CARDS: MasterCard, Visa.
PRICES: [2012] B&B £89.50 per person, D,B&B £122, set dinner £42.50, full alc £62.50, off-season breaks, sporting, gourmet, etc, New Year packages.

LODDISWELL Devon

Map 1:D4

HAZELWOOD HOUSE

'Distinctive and quirky', this early Victorian house has 'a perfect rural setting – absolute silence at night and wonderful views'. It is run as a guest house by Gillian Kean, Anabel Farnell-Watson and Jane Bowman, whose relaxed style won over inspectors. A reader agrees this year: 'Very refreshing; the owners are interesting people who get into conversation with visitors and are involved with the arts and charitable projects.' The decor is 'not for those who want immaculate minimalist interiors': there are bold colours throughout, antiques, much eclectic artwork (including Jane Bowman's watercolours). The informality is liked (no keys to bedroom doors). Rooms on the first floor have en suite facilities; simpler rooms with bathrooms nearby are on the second floor. 'Our large room was full of character; good bedlinen and towels, lashings of hot water.' In the dining room, chef Alex Sandu serves a daily-changing menu of 'imaginative' dishes, which might include ham hock terrine, apricot and thyme chutney; wild mushroom and asparagus risotto, shaved Parmesan. In summer, alfresco dining is available on the wisteria-laden veranda. (*Shirley King, and others*)

Loddiswell
nr Kingsbridge TQ7 4EB

T: 01548-821232
F: 01548-821318
E: info@hazelwoodhouse.com
W: www.hazelwoodhouse.com

BEDROOMS: 14, 7 with facilities en suite.

OPEN: all year.

FACILITIES: hall with piano, drawing room, study/TV room, dining room, function/conference facilities, civil wedding licence, 67-acre grounds (river, boathouse, chapel), only restaurant suitable for ♿.

BACKGROUND MUSIC: on request.

LOCATION: 2 miles N of Loddiswell.

CHILDREN: all ages welcomed.

DOGS: allowed in bedrooms, on leads in public rooms.

CREDIT CARDS: MasterCard, Visa.

PRICES: [2012] B&B £48–£115 per person, set dinner £25–£28, full alc £35, special breaks, Christmas/New Year packages.

LONGHORSLEY Northumberland

Map 4:B3

THISTLEYHAUGH FARM

César award in 2011

'This was our fifth visit: Enid's hospitality and kindness continue to amaze.' More praise this year for this farm guest house run by Enid Nelless, and set on the 720-acre organic sheep and cattle farm run by her husband, Henry. The Georgian house has many original features. The bedrooms are priced by size. 'Our room was huge and very comfortable; the small bathroom had masses of towels, all the goodies we needed, and lots of hot water.' Complimentary sherry ('a nice touch') is taken before dinner, which is served around a communal table at 7 pm (sociable guests find 'chatting to other guests adds to the enjoyment'). Mrs Nelless's daughter-in-law, Zoë, is the chef, cooking traditional dishes using seasonal produce from the farm. 'We had an excellent meal: goat's cheese roulade; salmon with the most delicious roast potatoes; crème brûlée.' The small wine list is liked: 'Good wines at good prices.' 'Our Japanese guests commented on the quality of the bedlinen and the china. Another relaxing and successful stay.' (*Shirley King, Sara Price*)

Longhorsley, nr Morpeth
NE65 8RG

T/F: 01665-570629
E: thistleyhaugh@hotmail.com
W: www.thistleyhaugh.co.uk

BEDROOMS: 5.
OPEN: all year except 20 Dec–1 Feb, dining room closed Sat eve.
FACILITIES: 2 lounges, dining room, 720-acre farm, 1-acre garden (summer house), fishing, shooting, golf, riding nearby, unsuitable for ♿.
BACKGROUND MUSIC: none.
LOCATION: 10 miles N of Morpeth, W of A697.
CHILDREN: all ages welcomed.
DOGS: not allowed (kennels nearby).
CREDIT CARDS: MasterCard, Visa.
PRICES: [2012] B&B £45–£85 per person, D,B&B from £70, 1-night bookings often refused.

LOOE Cornwall

Map 1:D3

THE BEACH HOUSE

Above Whitsand Bay and Looe Island, this white-fronted B&B is owned and run ('to the highest standard') by Rosie and David Reeve, who are 'friendly hosts'. 'We had a wonderfully relaxing holiday,' say visitors this year. Three of the five 'immaculate' bedrooms face the sea: Cawsand has bay windows with wide-reaching views; Fistral has floor-to-ceiling windows and a small balcony. Whitsand, in cream and gold, has a recently renovated shower room. Two bedrooms at the rear have access to a garden room across the hall, from which to enjoy the view. All rooms have a flat-screen TV, fridge and double glazing. The 'fantastic' breakfast has an extensive buffet (fresh fruit salad, home-made muffins, etc). Cooked dishes, ordered the evening before for an agreed time, include a choice of eggs any way; full English; alternative choices include porridge, pancakes with fruit and maple syrup, French toast, scrambled eggs with a smoked salmon muffin. Details of local restaurants are provided. The South West Coastal Path runs by the front gate. Private parking is appreciated. (*BB*)

Marine Drive, Hannafore
Looe PL13 2DH

T: 01503-262598
F: 01503-262298
E: enquiries@thebeachhouselooe.co.uk
W: www.thebeachhouselooe.co.uk

BEDROOMS: 5.
OPEN: all year except Christmas.
FACILITIES: garden room, breakfast room, terrace, ⅓-acre garden, beach opposite, unsuitable for ♿.
BACKGROUND MUSIC: classical in breakfast room.
LOCATION: ½ mile from centre.
CHILDREN: not under 16.
DOGS: not allowed.
CREDIT CARDS: MasterCard, Visa.
PRICES: [2012] B&B £40–£65 per person, 1-night bookings refused weekends, high season.

SEE ALSO SHORTLIST

LORTON Cumbria

Map 4: inset C2

NEW HOUSE FARM

In 'beautiful countryside', this 17th-century Grade II listed farmhouse is 'quite a find', says a visitor this year. It is run as an unpretentious guest house by owner Hazel Thompson, who restored period features (oak beams, flagged floors, stone fireplaces) when she renovated the house. The 'excellent' bedrooms are individually decorated; 'my bathroom was superb, with a freestanding bath and good soaps, etc. The Old Dairy has a queen-size solid oak four-poster bed; a Victorian bathroom with a slipper bath. Swinside, in the main house, has a window seat facing the Fell which supplies the spring water for the house. Whiteside, on the first floor of the main house, has a king-size brass bed. Mrs Thompson serves 'simple and conventional' evening meals with dishes like liver pâté, port jelly; pheasant casserole. 'The food is individual in style and very good.' Breakfast has cooked dishes to order, fresh grapefruit, home-made marmalade. Lunch and afternoon tea are served in the *Barn Tearooms*, a converted byre across the yard which is decorated with farming, shooting and fishing artefacts. (*Gwyn Morgan*)

Lorton
nr Cockermouth

T: 07841-159818
E: hazel@newhouse-farm.co.uk
W: www.newhouse-farm.com

BEDROOMS: 5, 1 in stable, 1 in Old Dairy.

OPEN: all year.

FACILITIES: 3 lounges, dining room, civil wedding licence, 17-acre grounds (garden, hot tub, streams, woods, field, lake and river, safe bathing, 2 miles), unsuitable for ♿.

BACKGROUND MUSIC: none.

LOCATION: 2 miles S of Lorton.

CHILDREN: not under 6.

DOGS: not allowed in public rooms.

CREDIT CARDS: Amex, MasterCard, Visa.

PRICES: B&B [2012] £60–£80 per person, D,B&B £30 added, Christmas/New Year packages, 1-night bookings sometimes refused.

LOW ROW North Yorkshire

Map 4:C3

THE PUNCHBOWL INN

On Alfred Wainwright's coast-to-coast walk, Charles and Stacy Cody's 17th-century inn in a Swaledale village has a 'relaxed and friendly atmosphere'. The owners have modernised in a fashion 'which is the opposite of chintzy; wooden floors, simple wooden tables and chairs'. The solid oak bar was created by Robert 'The Mouseman' Thompson. The hotel's design 'successfully combines an awareness of its place in history and the surroundings'. There is a residents' lounge with sofas to settle into. In the bar and two dining rooms, chef Andrew Short serves 'delicious' meals in 'British-gastropub' style; his menu might include smoked chicken, bacon and pickled red onion salad, balsamic dressing; herb-crusted salmon fillet with prawns and Bercy sauce. 'Tasty and leisurely,' said the nominator. The wine list is 'interesting and reasonably priced'. All the bedrooms, which have contemporary pieces alongside older features, have 'exquisite' views across Swaledale. 'Our beautifully decorated room had a large bed and a shower room.' Breakfast has home-made yogurt, fruit compote and 'delicious' cooked dishes. There is good walking from the door. (*SP, and others*)

Low Row
Richmond DL11 6PF

T: 01748-886233
F: 01748-886945
E: info@pbinn.co.uk
W: www.pbinn.co.uk

BEDROOMS: 11, 2 in annexe.

OPEN: all year except 25 Dec.

FACILITIES: bar, lounge area, 2 dining rooms.

BACKGROUND MUSIC: radio in public areas.

LOCATION: in village, 4 miles W of Reeth.

CHILDREN: all ages welcomed.

DOGS: not allowed.

CREDIT CARDS: MasterCard, Visa.

PRICES: [2012] B&B £54–£61.50 per person, D,B&B (min. 2 nights) £70.50–£79.50, set meals £24.50, full alc £32.50, special breaks, New Year package, 1-night bookings sometimes refused weekends.

LOWER BOCKHAMPTON Dorset

Map 1:C6

YALBURY COTTAGE

In a hamlet in peaceful countryside close to Dorchester, Jamie and Ariane Jones's conversion of four 300-year-old thatched cottages is 'small, informal and welcoming', say visitors in 2012. Another comment: 'Outstanding: small and well run with superb food and good service.' The building has a 'mishmash of corridors' leading to the bedrooms, which are decorated in simple rural style. All have views of gardens or fields. A large double room 'decorated in pastel colours had pictures on three walls'. Housekeeping is 'immaculate'. Jamie Jones is the 'talented' chef who serves 'excellent' meals in the restaurant in the oldest part of the building. It has exposed brickwork and inglenook fireplaces. The daily-changing dinner menu might include glazed scallops with Wigmore fondue; Jurassic Coast rose veal paupiette, home-made chorizo, creamed potato, red cabbage. 'Imaginative' breakfasts have 'porridge made to your liking'; fresh orange and ruby grapefruit segments; three types of fish and free-range eggs cooked any way. (*Michael Cornelius, Sue and Keith Britto, and others*)

25% DISCOUNT VOUCHERS

Lower Bockhampton
nr Dorchester DT2 8PZ

T: 01305-262382
E: enquiries@yalburycottage.com
W: www.yalburycottage.com

BEDROOMS: 8, 6 on ground floor.
OPEN: all year except Christmas/New Year.
FACILITIES: lounge, restaurant, unsuitable for ♿.
BACKGROUND MUSIC: 'easy listening' in lounge at dinner time.
LOCATION: 2 miles E of Dorchester.
CHILDREN: all ages welcomed, but not in restaurant after 8 pm.
DOGS: allowed in bedrooms, lounge.
CREDIT CARDS: MasterCard, Visa.
PRICES: [2012] B&B £47.50–£85 per person, D,B&B £80–£115, full alc £45.

LOWER FROYLE Hampshire

Map 2:D3

THE ANCHOR INN

NEW

In a prosperous village near the North Downs, this handsome old inn is part of Miller's Collection, a small group of inns in Hampshire and Berkshire. 'It is a classic English pub, and is as good as it gets for those who like this style of accommodation,' say trusted correspondents in 2012, restoring *The Anchor* to a full entry. The public rooms have low, beamed ceiling, log fire, wooden panelling, period pictures and prints, 'skilfully displayed ornaments'. Oak tables of various sizes are well spaced in the interconnecting dining areas. Kevin Chandler is the award-winning chef: 'The menu might suggest straightforward pub grub, but this fails to do justice to some skilful cooking: delicious crab cooked two ways with asparagus; perfect skate in black butter and caper sauce came with just-right steamed vegetables. Generous puddings.' The bedrooms are named after First World War writers: 'Our lovely room was spacious, with well-cared-for furniture, beautiful framed prints, distinctive antique plates, many interesting books; well lit with lamps and spot lights in the beamed ceiling.' Breakfast was 'promptly served and satisfactory'. (*Ian and Francine Walsh*)

Lower Froyle
GU34 4NA

T: 01420-23261
F: 01420-520467
E: info@anchorinnatlowerfroyle.co.uk
W: www.anchorinnatlowerfroyle.co.uk

BEDROOMS: 5.

OPEN: all year except 25 Dec.

FACILITIES: bar, lounge, dining room, courtyard garden.

BACKGROUND MUSIC: 'soft' in public areas.

LOCATION: centre of village, 4 miles NE of Alton.

CHILDREN: not under 10 in bedrooms.

DOGS: allowed.

CREDIT CARDS: all major cards.

PRICES: [2012] B&B £60–£75 per person, full alc £35, special breaks.

LOWER VOBSTER Somerset

Map 2:D1

THE VOBSTER INN

In a pretty hamlet in the rolling Somerset hills, Rafael and Peta Davila ('hard working and charming') have renovated this 17th-century stone inn with 'excellent taste'. 'Our small bedroom was comfortable and well equipped,' says a visitor this year. 'Dinner was good, with interesting choices; the service was friendly and efficient.' The bedrooms are furnished in 'cool, modern style'; the lighting is 'excellent'; 'stacks of pillows on the bed dressed in pristine white; eco-friendly toiletries in the lovely bathroom'. A fourth room was being added as the *Guide* went to press. The rustic public areas (exposed beams, fresh flowers, church candles) are 'inviting and immaculate'. Mr Davila is the chef, cooking modern European dishes like grilled field mushrooms Welsh rarebit; seared beef and saffron risotto, fried shallots. Tapas and light snacks are served in the bar. The 'excellent' breakfast is chosen the night before; eggs come from the inn's bantam and Maran hens. Children are welcomed. 'A good part of the country for walks and sightseeing; Bath is only 20 minutes' drive away.' (*Margaret Kershaw*)

25% DISCOUNT VOUCHERS

Lower Vobster
nr Radstock BA3 5RJ

T: 01373-812920
E: info@vobsterinn.co.uk
W: www.vobsterinn.co.uk

BEDROOMS: 4.
OPEN: all year, restaurant closed Sun night/Mon.
FACILITIES: bar/dining room, 4-acre garden.
BACKGROUND MUSIC: 'easy listening' in bar.
LOCATION: in village 4 miles W of Frome.
CHILDREN: all ages welcomed.
DOGS: allowed in 1 bar area.
CREDIT CARDS: Diners, MasterCard, Visa.
PRICES: [2012] B&B £34–£47.50 per person, full alc £30.

LUDLOW Shropshire

Map 3:C4

MR UNDERHILL'S

César award in 2000

In a 'wonderful setting', a conservation area by a weir on the River Teme below Ludlow Castle, Christopher and Judy Bradley have renovated their acclaimed restaurant-with-rooms. They have amalgamated several bedrooms in the main house to create two new suites, each with a separate sitting room, and a bathroom with a pool bath and a steam room. The timber-framed Shed in the garden is 'comfortable, spacious, with lovely views of the weir; a luxurious bathroom', say visitors this year. In the restaurant (also given a smart new look), Mr Bradley has a *Michelin* star for his eight-course 'market' menu (no choice until dessert, preferences discussed). 'We loved the playful food combinations; duck liver custard with sweetcorn cream and lemongrass glaze; black cherry sponge (actually a sorbet) and chocolate cake ice cream (more like a torte).' Mrs Bradley supervises the service: 'Attentive, unpretentious, with a sense of occasion but no stuffiness.' Breakfast was 'excellent: the bacon, steamed and then grilled was a revelation; a delicious brioche'. Residents are not required to dine in the restaurant. (*Euan and Tat Balmer*)

Dinham Weir
Ludlow SY8 1EH

T: 01584-874431
W: www.mr-underhills.co.uk

BEDROOMS: 4, 1 in annexe.

OPEN: all year except Christmas/New Year, 10 days June, 10 days Oct, restaurant closed Mon/Tues.

FACILITIES: small lounge, restaurant, function facilities, ½-acre courtyard, riverside garden (fishing, swimming), unsuitable for ♿.

BACKGROUND MUSIC: none.

LOCATION: below castle, on River Teme, station ½ mile, parking.

CHILDREN: not 2–8.

DOGS: not allowed.

CREDIT CARDS: MasterCard, Visa.

PRICES: B&B £112.50–£182.50 per person, set dinner £59.50–£66.50, 1-night bookings sometimes refused Sat.

SEE ALSO SHORTLIST

LYDFORD Devon

Map 1:C4

THE DARTMOOR INN

César award in 2007

On the edge of Dartmoor national park, Karen and Philip Burgess have turned an old inn into a 'welcoming and cosy' restaurant-with-rooms. The 'comfortable, clean and well-equipped' bedrooms are spacious (each has a sitting area) and are decorated in a light, contemporary style. All have large bed, antique and hand-painted furniture, radio and television; 'lots of hot water' in the 'good' bathrooms. In the restaurant (a series of interconnecting small rooms), Mr Burgess and Andrew Honey are the chefs. They cook modern British dishes, eg, baked gammon terrine, spiced pineapple chutney; pan-fried black bream, shrimp and wild garlic risotto. 'Dinner was excellent,' said a visitor this year. 'They had taken note of our dietary preferences (two vegetarians and a fish lover) and gave us plenty of choice; the ingredients were fresh and full of flavour.' The 'cosy' bar, which has an open fire, has its own menu on weekdays. An 'outstanding' breakfast has unusual cooked options, perhaps grilled hog's pudding and black pudding. A small boutique sells Swedish linen and glassware, quilts from France, jewellery and handbags by local designers. (*Jeanette Bloor*)

25% DISCOUNT VOUCHERS

Moorside
Lydford, nr Okehampton
EX20 4AY

T: 01822-820221
F: 01822-820494
E: info@dartmoorinn.co.uk
W: www.dartmoorinn.com

BEDROOMS: 3.

OPEN: all year, restaurant closed Sun evening.

FACILITIES: 2 bars, restaurant, shop, small sunken garden, unsuitable for ♿.

BACKGROUND MUSIC: none.

LOCATION: 6 miles E of Tavistock on A386 to Okehampton, train Exeter/Plymouth, parking.

CHILDREN: all ages welcomed.

DOGS: not allowed in bedrooms.

CREDIT CARDS: Amex, MasterCard, Visa.

PRICES: [2012] B&B £47.50–£60 per person, set dinner £20, full alc £45, special breaks.

LYME REGIS Dorset

Map 1:C6

THE MARINERS

NEW

In a town on the Jurassic coast which has many literary connections, this fine Georgian house, once a coaching inn, has been renovated by the owner, William Jeremy Ramsdale. 'It has been attractively decorated,' say the nominators (regular *Guide* correspondents). The house has historical resonances: it was the home of the fossil-hunting Philpott sisters, mentors to Mary Anning who made some of the most important discoveries of the age; later Beatrix Potter was inspired to write *The Tale of Little Pig Robinson* while staying at the inn. 'The bedrooms are well lit, and have ample storage space.' All rooms have tea- and coffee-making facilities; free Wi-Fi. The bar and restaurant have beamed ceiling, open fireplace. Local seafood is the speciality of the chef, Richard Reddaway, whose 'interesting' menus might include Lyme Bay scallops, celeriac purée, dressed rocket salad; pan-fried Cornish hake, spinach and potato curry, cucumber crème fraîche. The garden with a terrace overlooking a cliff has fine views of the bay. The staff were most helpful with information about the hotel and possible activities.' (*John and Theresa Stewart*)

Silver Street
Lyme Regis DT7 3HS

T: 01297-442753
E: enquiries@hotellymeregis.co.uk
W: www.hotellymeregis.co.uk

BEDROOMS: 14.
OPEN: all year.
FACILITIES: lounge, bar, restaurant, garden, unsuitable for ♿.
BACKGROUND MUSIC: in restaurant and bar.
LOCATION: central.
CHILDREN: all ages welcomed.
DOGS: allowed in bar and garden only.
CREDIT CARDS: Amex, MasterCard, Visa.
PRICES: [2012] B&B £52.50–£72.50 per person, D,B&B £77.50–£97.50, set meals £18.95–£24.95, full alc £40, Christmas/New Year packages, special breaks, 1-night bookings refused weekends.

SEE ALSO SHORTLIST

LYMINGTON Hampshire

Map 2:E2

BRITANNIA HOUSE

There are 'stunning' views over the harbour and marinas from the blue-and-yellow residents' lounge of Tobias Feilke's unusual B&B. Formed from two refurbished houses (one dating from 1865, the other modern) opposite each other in this popular riverside town. It is liked for the good value and comfort. Bedrooms in the three-storey modern quayside house are simply furnished with check fabrics, pine and painted furniture. Beaulieu, on the first floor, is comfortable and bright, with a village theme. Rooms in the older house have Berber carpets, patterned curtains, bedcovers and cushions; the spacious ground-floor Forest Suite stays cool in the summer; the hand-painted Courtyard Suite overlooks a small evergreen garden. All bedrooms have a king-size bed, anti-allergic duvet and pillows, flat-screen TV, free Wi-Fi, and beverage-making facilities. Mr Feilke cooks a good breakfast (with vegetarian options), which is served at a 'convivial' communal table in the large pine kitchen. Yachting breaks on the Solent (with a two-course meal on board) are new in 2012. The New Forest is nearby. More reports, please.

Station Street
Lymington SO41 3BA

T: 01590-672091
E: enquiries@britannia-house.com
W: www.britannia-house.com

BEDROOMS: 5.
OPEN: all year.
FACILITIES: lounge, kitchen/breakfast room, courtyard garden, unsuitable for ♿.
BACKGROUND MUSIC: none.
LOCATION: 2 mins' walk from High Street/quayside, parking.
CHILDREN: not under 8.
DOGS: not allowed.
CREDIT CARDS: MasterCard, Visa.
PRICES: B&B £37.50–£55 per person, midweek discount, Christmas/New Year packages.

LYNDHURST Hampshire

Map 2:E2

LIME WOOD

'A real treat, *Lime Wood* is worth the expense for the unashamed luxury.' Praise in 2012 for this laid-back country house hotel standing in extensive grounds in the New Forest. The 'inviting' public rooms in the Regency manor house are 'styled with wit, flair and humour, with fine period furniture and antiques, and quirky modern pieces'. 'The charming library was muzak-free.' Bedrooms are in the main house and three 'eye-catching' garden lodges. 'Our suite overlooked the garden; a plate of delicious exotic fruit, with starched napkins and cutlery, was a lovely touch. The beautiful bathroom had a heated floor, large shower and huge bath. There were brilliant bedside lights in the delightful double-aspect bedroom.' The minibar has 'complimentary water, reasonably priced drinks'; in a drawer, for sale, were bedsocks, sherbet dips and a Moleskine notebook. In the *Dining Room*, chef Luke Holder will be joined by Angela Hartnett in 2013 to present a new menu of informal dishes. All-day dining is available in the *Scullery*. A 'memorable' breakfast buffet had 'all kinds of fruit, yogurts, breads, ham on the bone (shame about the radio chit-chat)'. (*Barbara Watkinson, Nick Patton*)

Beaulieu Road
Lyndhurst SO43 7FZ

T: 02380-287177
F: 02380-287199
E: info@limewood.co.uk
W: www.limewoodhotel.com

BEDROOMS: 29, 5 on ground floor, 2 suitable for ♿, 5 in *Crescent*, 5 in *Coach House*, 5 in *Pavilion*.

OPEN: all year, *Dining Room* restaurant closed for lunch Mon.

FACILITIES: lifts, ramps, bar, 2 lounges, library, 2 restaurants, private dining rooms, civil wedding licence, spa (16-metre swimming pool), 14-acre gardens.

BACKGROUND MUSIC: in dining areas.

LOCATION: in New Forest, 12 miles SW of Southampton.

CHILDREN: all ages welcomed.

DOGS: allowed in selected bedrooms.

CREDIT CARDS: Amex, MasterCard, Visa.

PRICES: [2012] room £245–£775, set lunch £21–£25, tasting menu £75, full alc £55, special breaks, Christmas/ New Year packages, 1-night bookings sometimes refused weekends.

MALVERN WELLS Worcestershire

Map 3:D5

THE COTTAGE IN THE WOOD

César award in 1992

'As welcoming and comfortable as we remembered', the Pattin family's hotel is on a plateau on the side of the Malvern hills with 'an expansive and magnificent outlook' over the Severn valley. The late Georgian house is owned by John and Sue Pattin; their son, Dominic, is the chef; daughter Maria Taylor is the operations director. The family is 'ever present'; service is 'without exception, friendly and efficient; overall a very pleasant atmosphere', say returning visitors in 2012. In the original dower house, bedrooms are traditional and have 'a country feel'. Each of the four cosy rooms in *Beech Cottage* has its own front door; rooms at *Pinnacles*, 100 yards from the main building, are large and have the best views. Some bathrooms are shower-only. In the *Outlook* restaurant, the food 'is superb both in presentation and taste; we enjoyed corn-fed chicken gallottine of sun-blushed tomato and red onion; pan-roasted Gressingham duck breast, tarragon jus'. Breakfast is a 'fine experience'; a large selection of fresh fruit and cereals; 'thick but tender local bacon'; 'beautifully poached eggs' (*Sarah and Tony Thomas, Trevor Lockwood, and others*)

25% DISCOUNT VOUCHERS

Holywell Road
Malvern Wells
WR14 4LG

T: 01684-588860
F: 01684-560662
E: reception@cottageinthewood.co.uk
W: www.cottageinthewood.co.uk

BEDROOMS: 30, 4 in *Beech Cottage*, 70 yds, 19 (1 suitable for ♿) in *The Pinnacles*, 100 yds.

OPEN: all year.

FACILITIES: lounge, bar, restaurant, function facilities, 7-acre grounds.

BACKGROUND MUSIC: none.

LOCATION: 3 miles S of Great Malvern.

CHILDREN: all ages welcomed.

DOGS: guide dogs welcomed, other dogs on ground floor in *The Pinnacles* only.

CREDIT CARDS: Amex, MasterCard, Visa.

PRICES: [2012] B&B £49.50–£99 per person, D,B&B (min. 2 nights) £66–£126, set dinner £23.95–£42.50, special breaks, Christmas/New Year packages, 1-night bookings sometimes refused Sat.

MARAZION Cornwall

Map 1:E1

MOUNT HAVEN HOTEL & RESTAURANT

'A great base for exploring Cornwall', Mike and Orange Trevillion's hotel is in a village overlooking St Michael's Mount. It has a contemporary decor with oriental overtones. Incense burns in the lobby; there are tapestries from Jaipur, caskets from Bhutan, figurines from Nepal in the public areas. 'A good stay' was enjoyed this year. The dining room is furnished in dark reds with leather and velvet upholstery; a seating area by glass doors leading on to a terrace (with tables and chairs for alfresco meals) has the views. One visitor thought the room 'characterless'; others liked the 'cosiness on a chill evening'. The chef, James Morris, describes his cooking style as 'modern British with a twist'. Typical dishes: Cornish venison, caramelised chicory, red wine pear; loin of pork, beetroot Tatin, pork belly. Many of the bedrooms face the sea; some have a private garden terrace or balcony. 'Ours was nicely furnished, really comfortable.' Breakfast has a buffet with organic fruit, natural yogurts; cooked options include kedgeree, omelette Arnold Bennett, French toast with crispy bacon and watercress. (*SH, and others*)

25% DISCOUNT VOUCHERS

Turnpike Road
Marazion TR17 0DQ

T: 01736-710249
F: 01736-711658
E: reception@mounthaven.co.uk
W: www.mounthaven.co.uk

BEDROOMS: 18, some on ground floor.

OPEN: 10 Feb–14 Dec.

FACILITIES: lounge/bar, restaurant, healing room (holistic treatments), sun terrace, ½-acre grounds (rock/sand beaches 100 yds), unsuitable for ♿.

BACKGROUND MUSIC: bar, restaurant all day.

LOCATION: 4 miles E of Penzance, car park.

CHILDREN: all ages welcomed.

DOGS: allowed in public rooms only.

CREDIT CARDS: MasterCard, Visa.

PRICES: [2012] B&B £65–£110 per person, D,B&B £30 added, full alc from £35, 2/3-night breaks spring/autumn, min. 2 nights on bank holidays.

MARTINHOE Devon

Map 1:B4

HEDDON'S GATE HOTEL

'Somewhere special in a beautiful corner of England', Anne and Eddie Eyles's small traditional hotel is on the slopes of a wooded valley near the north Devon coast. Reached by a long private drive, it stands in more than two acres of gardens and woodland. 'As good as ever,' say visitors this year. 'The standards of food and service are being well maintained by the owners and their small team.' With antlers and leather sofas in the bar and a 'dizzying array of patterns and textures' in the dining room, the decor of the former Victorian hunting lodge is unashamedly traditional. Bedrooms vary in style: the Master Room has an 1840s half-tester bed; Servants' Quarters has 'generous' accommodation including its own sitting room. 'Anne cooks the most delicious meals, taking good local ingredients and combining them with interesting flavours,' say visitors in 2012. Breakfast has 'lots of fruit, good bread, perfectly judged eggs'. (*Stephen and Pauline Glover, John and Verna Aspinall*)

25% DISCOUNT VOUCHERS

Martinhoe, Parracombe
Barnstaple
EX31 4PZ

T: 01598-763481
E: hotel@heddonsgate.co.uk
W: www.heddonsgate.co.uk

BEDROOMS: 9.
OPEN: Mar–Oct, dining room closed midday.
FACILITIES: 2 reception halls, 2 lounges, library, bar, dining room, 2½-acre grounds, river, fishing, riding, pony trekking nearby, sea ¾ mile, unsuitable for ♿.
BACKGROUND MUSIC: none.
LOCATION: 6 miles W of Lynton.
CHILDREN: not under 12 (except in parties taking exclusive use).
DOGS: not allowed in dining room, not unattended in bedrooms.
CREDIT CARDS: MasterCard, Visa.
PRICES: [2012] B&B £45–£60 per person, D,B&B £65–£90, set dinner £35 (cheaper if booked in advance), special breaks, 1-night bookings sometimes refused.

MARTINHOE Devon

Map 1:B4

THE OLD RECTORY

NEW

Built as the rectory of the 11th-century church in an 'idyllic' hamlet in the Exmoor national park, this part-Georgian, part-Victorian house is run as a small hotel by owners Huw Rees and Sam Prosser. 'They are visible, friendly and calmly efficient,' said readers. Inspectors agreed: 'The amiable hosts have created an informal "house in the country" atmosphere; major improvements have been carried out; everything is new bar a few antiques.' Guests are asked to place their dinner order over drinks in a 'cosy' lounge or a conservatory. Huw Rees, the cook, uses local produce (vegetables from the garden) for his short menus. 'Good home cooking; I asked for the recipe of the delicious red pepper and tomato soup; we enjoyed Exmoor pork and sea bass; a copious dish of vegetables. Sadly, background music played.' There is 'no clutter' in the bedrooms: 'Our garden-facing room had a sofa and a large footstool, good hanging and storage space; a well-appointed bathroom.' There is direct access to the Coastal Path from the large 'well-maintained' garden. (*Tony and Ginny Ayers, and others*)

25% DISCOUNT VOUCHERS

Martinhoe EX31 4QT

T: 01598-763368
E: info@oldrectoryhotel.co.uk
W: www.oldrectoryhotel.co.uk

BEDROOMS: 10, 2 on ground floor, 2 in coach house.
OPEN: Mar–Nov.
FACILITIES: 2 lounges, conservatory, dining room, 3-acre grounds.
BACKGROUND MUSIC: in dining room.
LOCATION: 4 miles SW of Lynton.
CHILDREN: not under 14.
DOGS: not allowed.
CREDIT CARDS: Amex, MasterCard, Visa.
PRICES: [2012] B&B from £80 per person, D,B&B from £100, special breaks, 1-night bookings refused high season and weekends.

MASHAM North Yorkshire

Map 4:D4

SWINTON PARK

César award in 2011

'Just like visiting friends,' says a visitor this year to this 'dramatic' mock-Gothic castle in 'truly beautiful' grounds, the family home of Mark and Felicity Cunliffe-Lister. 'Such a comfortable place to be; the staff are so friendly, yet professional,' say other returning guests. Peter Llewellyn is the manager. Children of all ages are welcomed: 'Our two-and-a-halfer was given a guided tour of the dining room,' said a reporter. A new family suite has been added this year; the adult bedroom has a large bathroom, the twin a shower room. Nappies, wipes and baby powders are provided for families; decanters of spirits for adults. The 'exquisite' cooking of the chef, Simon Crannage, is praised. In 2012 he launched a 'garden produce' menu alongside his classic and tasting menus (typical dishes: estate partridge, glazed turnips; oak-smoked onion ricotta). More informal meals and a children's menu are available in the bar. There is much for children to do in the grounds: activity days, falconry displays, mountain biking, etc. Indoors are a playroom, billiards, a TV projected on to a wall. (*Lynn Marsay, Kay Hollingsworth*)

25% DISCOUNT VOUCHERS

Masham, nr Ripon
HG4 4JH

T: 01765-680900
F: 01765-680901
E: reservations@swintonpark.com
W: www.swintonpark.com

BEDROOMS: 31, 4 suitable for ♿.

OPEN: all year, restaurant closed midday Mon/Tues.

FACILITIES: lift, ramps, 3 lounges, library, bar, restaurant, banqueting hall, spa, games rooms, cinema, civil wedding licence, 200-acre grounds (many activities).

BACKGROUND MUSIC: in bar and dining room.

LOCATION: 1 mile SW of Masham.

CHILDREN: all ages welcomed.

DOGS: not allowed in public rooms, unattended in bedrooms.

CREDIT CARDS: MasterCard, Visa.

PRICES: [2012] B&B £92.50–£190 per person, D,B&B £127.50–£225, set dinner £52–£60, special breaks, Christmas/New Year packages, 1-night bookings sometimes refused Sat.

MATLOCK BATH Derbyshire

Map 3:B6

HODGKINSON'S HOTEL

Once part of a larger inn, Dianne Carrieri's 'welcoming' small hotel is a Grade II listed building (1770). It retains many original features and much of the grandeur of the Peak District spa town's heyday. The decor is 'quirky': stained glass, antiques, old prints, a stuffed fox. Most of the 'comfortable, not luxurious' bedrooms have a view over the wooded Derwent valley and craggy limestone crags. All have television, tea- and coffee-making facilities, mineral water, plus Wi-Fi. Bathrooms have a shower, except one, which has a freestanding bath. Mrs Carrieri tells us that rooms facing the busy A6 have been given double glazing this year to eliminate road noise. In the dining room, the chef, Leigh Matthews, serves a modern British menu, which might include tiger prawns wrapped in pancetta, spicy tomato jus; rack of lamb, tomato, aubergine and spinach millefeuille, thyme jus. Breakfast has a choice of fruit juices; fruit salad, porridge or a fruit smoothie; cooked dishes include a full English and a full vegetarian breakfast; kedgeree, omelettes and 'doorstopper' sandwiches. Children and pets are welcomed. More reports, please.

25% DISCOUNT VOUCHERS

150 South Parade
Matlock Bath, Matlock
DE4 3NR

T: 01629-582170
F: 01629-584891
E: enquiries@hodgkinsons-hotel.co.uk
W: www.hodgkinsons-hotel.co.uk

BEDROOMS: 8.

OPEN: all year except 24–26 Dec, restaurant closed Sun nights off-season.

FACILITIES: lounge, bar, restaurant, meeting/private dining room, 1-acre garden (opposite River Derwent, fishing, day ticket), unsuitable for ♿.

BACKGROUND MUSIC: blues/jazz/classical in restaurant.

LOCATION: central, parking for 5 cars.

CHILDREN: all ages welcomed.

DOGS: not allowed in public rooms.

CREDIT CARDS: Amex, MasterCard, Visa.

PRICES: [2012] B&B £46.50–£72.50, set dinner £29.50–£33, 2- to 3-night breaks, New Year package, 1-night bookings refused Sat May–Oct.

MAWGAN PORTH Cornwall

Map 1:D2

BEDRUTHAN STEPS HOTEL

César award in 2012

Above a golden sandy beach on a 'beautiful stretch' of the north Cornish coast, this large white hotel has welcomed families for over 40 years. It is owned and managed by sisters Emma Stratton, Deborah Wakefield and Rebecca Whittington. 'They know exactly what families need, and they have the space to provide it,' says a reporter this year. There are indoor and outdoor swimming pools; 'a wonderful array of entertainment'; playgrounds, a jungle gym for children; tennis courts; a 'real' spa for adults. The exterior of the building, much extended, shows its 1960s origins; inside all is 'delightful'. Major changes in the dining arrangements were introduced in 2012. The *Wild Café*, open from 8 am until late evening, replaces the family restaurant: it will provide meals for all ages; high tea is served here with child-friendly main courses cooked to order (parents have a complimentary hot drink and cookie). The new *Herring* restaurant has set menus specialising in seafood. The bedrooms have a 'fresh seaside decor, enough hanging space for a proper holiday'. *The Scarlet* (see next entry) is a child-free sister hotel.

Mawgan Porth
TR8 4BU

T: 01637-860860
E: stay@bedruthan.com
W: www.bedruthan.com

BEDROOMS: 101, 1 suitable for ♿.
OPEN: all year except 20–28 Dec.
FACILITIES: lift, 2 lounges, 2 bars, *Herring* restaurant, *Wild Café*, poolside snack bar, ballroom, 4 children's clubs, spa (indoor swimming pool), civil wedding licence, 5-acre grounds (heated swimming pools, tennis, playing field).
BACKGROUND MUSIC: 'relaxed' in bar and restaurants.
LOCATION: 4 miles NE of Newquay.
CHILDREN: all ages welcomed.
DOGS: allowed in some bedrooms, some public areas.
CREDIT CARDS: MasterCard, Visa.
PRICES: [2012] B&B £75–£227.50 per person, D,B&B £95–£247.50, set dinner £30–£35, full alc £45, special breaks, New Year package, 7-night bookings required in school holidays.

MAWGAN PORTH Cornwall

Map 1:D2

THE SCARLET

In a spectacular position above a horseshoe-shaped bay, this striking modern hotel is run on eco-friendly lines by sisters Emma Stratton, Deborah Wakefield and Rebecca Whittington, whose other hotel, *Bedruthan Steps* (see previous entry), is further up the hill. 'Luxurious and calm; the staff were, without exception, polite and helpful,' says a visitor this year. Each of the bedrooms has an outside space: some have a balcony, others a private courtyard terrace, all have a sea view. The bathrooms are state of the art. There are quiet sitting rooms, but background music (much of it New Age) plays in the bar and restaurant. 'Outside, all is peaceful.' Tom Hunter was appointed chef in June 2012 (we would welcome reports on his cooking). The wine list has only wines from Europe for green reasons. The spa 'lives up to its promise': 'our daily treatments were relaxed and therapeutic, the staff knowledgeable'. Breakfast, from a daily-changing menu, is 'exceptional'. 'We borrowed the hotel dog, Jasper, and took him for long walks.' 'Pricey; the eco-features are worth supporting.' (*Dawn Parker, Richard Tomalin, and others*)

25% DISCOUNT VOUCHERS

Tredragon Road
Mawgan Porth TR8 4DQ

T: 01637-861800
F: 01637-861801
E: stay@scarlethotel.co.uk
W: www.scarlethotel.co.uk

BEDROOMS: 37, 2 suitable for ♿.
OPEN: all year except Jan.
FACILITIES: lift, lobby, bar, lounge, library, restaurant, civil wedding licence, spa (indoor swimming pool, 4 by 13 metres, steam room, hammam, treatment room), natural outdoor swimming pool (40 sq metres), seaweed baths.
BACKGROUND MUSIC: all day in bar and restaurant.
LOCATION: 4 miles NE of Newquay.
CHILDREN: normally not under 16.
DOGS: not allowed in restaurant or bar, some bedrooms.
CREDIT CARDS: MasterCard, Visa.
PRICES: [2012] B&B £95–£225 per person, D,B&B £127.50–£257.50, special offers, Christmas/New Year packages, 1-night bookings generally refused Fri/Sat.

MAWNAN SMITH Cornwall

Map 1:E2

BUDOCK VEAN

'A super family-run place', Martin and Amanda Barlow's traditional hotel stands in extensive subtropical gardens on the banks of the Helford river. It attracts many returning visitors. A plethora of activities are available within the grounds: guests can tackle a nine-hole golf course ('in excellent order'), swim in a heated indoor pool, play tennis and snooker, take spa treatments. The 'excellent' menus of chef Darren Kelly were enjoyed again in 2012 in the 'pleasant' main restaurant 'presided over by the attentive Mo Roberts'. 'Good choice, reasonably priced.' Men are asked to wear a jacket and tie in the evening: 'We enjoyed the live music played at dinner; piano one evening, guitar another.' The same menu can be taken in the more informal *Country Club*: typical dishes are Cornish goat's cheese in breadcrumbs, beetroot salad; pan-seared breast of chicken, pancetta, flat mushrooms, plum tomatoes. The public rooms (four lounges, snooker room, cocktail bar, golf bar) are 'all delightful'. 'Our superior room was well equipped and had a comfortable bed.' The best rooms face the garden and the river. (*David RW Jervois*)

Helford Passage, Mawnan Smith
nr Falmouth TR11 5LG

T: 01326-252100
F: 01326-250892
E: relax@budockvean.co.uk
W: www.budockvean.co.uk

BEDROOMS: 57, 4 self-catering cottages.

OPEN: all year except 2–27 Jan.

FACILITIES: lift, ramps, 3 lounges, conservatory, 2 bars, restaurant, *Country Club*, snooker room, civil wedding licence, 65-acre grounds (covered heated swimming pool, 15 by 8 metres), health spa, 9-hole golf course, tennis.

BACKGROUND MUSIC: live in restaurant.

LOCATION: 6 miles SW of Falmouth.

CHILDREN: no under-7s in dining room after 7 pm.

DOGS: not allowed in public rooms.

CREDIT CARDS: all major cards.

PRICES: [2012] B&B £69–£159 per person, D,B&B £84–£174, set dinner £39.95, full alc £50, themed breaks, Christmas/New Year/Easter packages, 1-night bookings refused high season weekends.

MAWNAN SMITH Cornwall

Map 1:E2

MEUDON

The Pilgrim family's traditional hotel, a Victorian mansion in subtropical gardens that lead to a private beach, has many fans. 'It remains our favourite,' says a regular correspondent this year. 'The staff are efficient and friendly without being intrusive.' Five generations of the family have owned hotels in the area; Harry Pilgrim runs *Meudon* with his son, Mark; Mike Evans is the manager. The two 'comfortable' lounges have antiques, log fires and fresh flowers; one overlooks the 'wonderful' garden. The cream teas, served here, 'are by a long chalk the best we have ever had'. In the formal conservatory dining room, chef Shaun Treen uses fresh local produce for his traditional menus, eg, grilled Cornish goat's cheese, basil pesto; poached fillet of sole with leek and crab fricassée. 'The cooking is excellent.' All the bedrooms overlook the garden: 'Ours, on the first floor, had two comfortable chairs and a good bathroom.' Visitors like the extra services: turn-down in the evening, and the shoe cleaning (Wi-Fi is also available). *Meudon* is popular with older visitors in the off season. (*LM Mayer-Jones, and others*)

25% DISCOUNT VOUCHERS

Mawnan Smith
nr Falmouth TR11 5HT

T: 01326-250541
F: 01326-250543
E: wecare@meudon.co.uk
W: www.meudon.co.uk

BEDROOMS: 29, 16 on ground floor, 2 suitable for ♿, self-catering cottage.
OPEN: all year except Jan.
FACILITIES: lift, ramps, 2 lounges, bar, restaurant, 8½-acre grounds (gardens, private beach, yacht), golf, riding, windsurfing nearby.
BACKGROUND MUSIC: none.
LOCATION: 4 miles SW of Falmouth.
CHILDREN: all ages welcomed.
DOGS: allowed in bedrooms, Bridge Lounge.
CREDIT CARDS: Amex, MasterCard, Visa.
PRICES: [2012] B&B £69–£99 per person, set dinner £36, full alc £45, special breaks, Christmas package.

MEVAGISSEY Cornwall

Map 1:D2

TREVALSA COURT

Built as a holiday home in 1937, this Arts and Crafts house is now run as a 'welcoming and very comfortable' small hotel by owners Susan and John Gladwin. It stands on a cliff-top; landscaped subtropical gardens (with a 'welcoming' summer house) lead to the Coastal Path and a steep staircase to a private beach. The public rooms have oak panelling and antiques, with light tones in fabrics mixed with occasional bold colours. 'Lots of good space'; a sitting room/bar with newspapers, magazines, a laptop with free Internet access. 'Wonderfully relaxing, beautifully furnished, stunning views,' says a guest this year. Most of the bedrooms have sea views. 'Our beautifully designed room showed great thought.' 'Our spacious room had a bay window and a sofa.' In warm weather, pre-dinner drinks can be taken on a terrace. Jan Hemming is now the chef, serving 'contemporary Cornish' dishes, using local ingredients where possible, perhaps seared scallops with sea ling, spinach and dill; honey-roast Terras duck breast, swede purée and rhubarb. Breakfast has a 'healthy' buffet, and includes kippers (ordered the evening before). (*David Humphreys, JB*)

25% DISCOUNT VOUCHERS

School Hill
Mevagissey PL26 6TH

T: 01726-842468
E: stay@trevalsa-hotel.co.uk
W: www.trevalsa-hotel.co.uk

BEDROOMS: 15, 2 on ground floor.
OPEN: mid-Feb–mid-Nov, Christmas, New Year.
FACILITIES: lounge, bar, restaurant, 2½-acre garden.
BACKGROUND MUSIC: light jazz in bar and restaurant.
LOCATION: edge of village.
CHILDREN: all ages welcomed.
DOGS: by arrangement, supervised in bedrooms, not allowed in public rooms.
CREDIT CARDS: all major cards.
PRICES: [2012] B&B £60–£117.50 per person, D,B&B £25 added, set dinner £30, website offers, Christmas/New Year packages, 1-night bookings refused high season.

MIDSOMER NORTON Somerset

Map 2:D1

THE MOODY GOOSE AT THE OLD PRIORY

In a village which reflects its Victorian mining past, this handsome 12th-century priory (Grade II listed) stands in a walled garden by the church. It is run as a restaurant-with-rooms by Stephen (the chef) and Jennifer Shore. Many original features are retained: solid stone floors, beams, inglenook fireplaces and exposed brick walls. Curving flights of stairs lead to the bedrooms, which have original beams, antique furniture and heavy, iron-studded doors. 'All the staff were excellent and most welcoming,' said a visitor this year, who was less happy about the accommodation. 'Our room had a narrow four-poster bed with old-fashioned springs. There were plenty of hangers in the wardrobe, but the stone floor in the bathroom was slippery when wet; the shower head needed attention.' In the bright restaurant, Mr Shore cooks modern English dishes, perhaps risotto of Brixham scallops; pan-roasted fillet of beef, roasted salsify, shallots and garlic. Many of the herbs, fruit and vegetables come from the garden. Breakfast, taken in a 'cheerful' rear dining room, has croissants, brioches, freshly squeezed juice and various cooked dishes. More reports, please.

Church Square
Midsomer Norton
nr Bath BA3 2HX

T: 01761-416784
F: 01761-417851
E: info@theoldpriory.co.uk
W: www.theoldpriory.co.uk

BEDROOMS: 6.

OPEN: all year, except 24 Dec–2 Jan, restaurant closed Sun evening.

FACILITIES: 2 lounges, 2 dining rooms, private dining/function room, ¼-acre garden, unsuitable for ♿.

BACKGROUND MUSIC: classical in restaurants.

LOCATION: 9 miles SW of Bath.

CHILDREN: all ages welcomed.

DOGS: not allowed.

CREDIT CARDS: MasterCard, Visa.

PRICES: [2012] B&B £37.50–£70 per person, set dinner £39.50.

MILTON ABBOT Devon

Map 1:D3

HOTEL ENDSLEIGH

'Magical, tranquil, unhurried, superb.' A succinct summary this year of Olga Polizzi's luxurious country house hotel in 'a lovely setting' on the edge of Dartmoor. The early 19th-century house, built as a shooting and fishing lodge for the Duke and Duchess of Bedford, stands in gardens (designed by Humphry Repton), which run down to the River Tamar. Helen Costello is its manager. It has been restored in the spirit of the Regency period: modern country house furnishings and contemporary art alongside original panelling and Victorian artefacts. Bedrooms have antiques, original features and modern bathroom (but 'no shaving mirror'). In the candlelit dining room, chef Christopher Dyke serves a short menu of 'creative' modern dishes, perhaps ham hock, new potato and baby leek terrine, pickled cauliflower; loin of Brentor lamb, pommes dauphine, pea purée, sweetbreads, ginger French beans. Breakfast, served at table, has organic porridge; smoked salmon and eggs Benedict. *The Endsleigh* has seven rods on an eight-mile stretch of the Tamar. Olga Polizzi also owns *Tresanton*, St Mawes (see entry). (*P Torr, and others*)

Milton Abbot
nr Tavistock PL19 0PQ

T: 01822-870000
F: 01822-870578
E: mail@hotelendsleigh.com
W: www.hotelendsleigh.com

BEDROOMS: 16, 1 on ground floor, also 1 in lodge (1 mile from main house).
OPEN: all year except last 2 weeks Jan.
FACILITIES: drawing room, library, card room, bar, 2 dining rooms, civil wedding licence, terraces, 108-acre estate (fishing, ghillie available).
BACKGROUND MUSIC: occasionally, evenings only, during dinner.
LOCATION: 7 miles NW of Tavistock, train/plane Plymouth.
CHILDREN: all ages welcomed.
DOGS: not allowed in restaurant.
CREDIT CARDS: all major cards.
PRICES: B&B £90–£180 per person, set dinner £40, Christmas/New Year packages, 1-night bookings refused weekends.

MORETON-IN-MARSH Gloucestershire

Map 3:D6

THE MANOR HOUSE

On the southern edge of a historic market town, this part 16th-century mansion has been given a stylish interior by the small Cotswold Inns and Hotels group (see entry for *The Lamb Inn*, Burford). 'It is attractive and welcoming, with lovely log fires and a helpful staff,' writes a visitor this year, who was less keen on the cooking. Informal meals can be taken in the *Beagle* bar and brasserie (eg, lamb shanks, fondant potato). In the formal *Mulberry* restaurant (dark green walls, white tablecloths, a view of the 'secret garden'), chef Nick Orr prepares a carte and an eight-course tasting menu with elaborate dishes like deconstructed club sandwich (chicken ravioli, smoked bacon foam, baby gem purée); confit of belly pork, braised cheek, crisp Parma ham, morels. The bedrooms vary in size and style: 'Our lovely room had a fresh, clean bathroom.' A guest with mobility problems praised the facilities: 'Our beautiful ground-floor room had a superbly equipped bathroom.' Apple Cottage, at the back of the garden, has a sitting room, dining room, bedroom, and bathroom with double shower.

25% DISCOUNT VOUCHERS

High Street
Moreton-in-Marsh
GL56 0LJ

T: 01608-650501
F: 01608-651481
E: info@manorhousehotel.info
W: www.cotswold-inns-hotels.co.uk/manor

BEDROOMS: 35, 1 in cottage, 1 on ground floor suitable for ♿.
OPEN: all year.
FACILITIES: library, lounge, bar, brasserie, restaurant, function rooms, civil wedding licence, ½-acre garden.
BACKGROUND MUSIC: 'soft, gentle', in bar.
LOCATION: on edge of market town.
CHILDREN: all ages welcomed.
DOGS: 'well-behaved dogs on leads' allowed.
CREDIT CARDS: all major cards.
PRICES: [2012] B&B £79–£175 per person, D,B&B £39 added, set dinner £39 (*10% service charge*), special offers, Christmas/New Year packages, 1-night bookings sometimes refused Sat.

MORETON-IN-MARSH Gloucestershire

Map 3:D6

THE REDESDALE ARMS

Co-owner and manager Robert Smith 'is hands-on and genial', says a visitor this year to this traditional Cotswold inn on the market town's main street. 'The staff are pleasant and attentive.' Another comment: 'We cannot praise highly enough; the rooms are clean, comfortable and affordable.' Seven bedrooms are in the main building (those at the front have double glazing). Eleven more bedrooms have been completed in a converted stable block at the back (a short walk outdoors, umbrellas available). They have oak and granite furnishings; modern bathroom, some with a whirlpool bath. The residents' lounge has dark wood, leather seating, an open fire in a stone surround. There are original beams, old passages in the bars; the restaurant has been renovated this year. Loredan Gargalac is now the chef. His modern menu might include tiger prawns, lemongrass and chilli broth; roast loin of locally reared pork. 'Dinners were of good quality and quantity.' A visitor who was disappointed with breakfast was promised that his comments would be addressed. (*JCS Frood, Keith and Sue Ward, and others*)

25% DISCOUNT VOUCHERS

High Street
Moreton-in-Marsh
GL56 0AW

T: 01608-650308
F: 01608-651843
E: info@redesdalearms.com
W: www.redesdalearms.com

BEDROOMS: 32, 25 in annexe across courtyard, 1 suitable for ♿.
OPEN: all year.
FACILITIES: 3 lounge bars, 2 restaurants, heated open dining area.
BACKGROUND MUSIC: in all public areas.
LOCATION: town centre.
CHILDREN: all ages welcomed.
DOGS: allowed on lead in bar, not in bedrooms or restaurant.
CREDIT CARDS: MasterCard, Visa.
PRICES: [2012] B&B £39.50–£79.50 per person, D,B&B £69.50–£99.50, full alc £35, special breaks, Christmas/New Year packages, 1-night bookings refused Sat Apr–Nov.

MORPETH Northumberland

Map 4:B4

ESHOTT HALL

NEW

On an extensive estate with an arboretum and formal gardens, this wisteria-clad country house has been renovated with a mix of contemporary and modern styles by Robert and Gina Parker. Laura Brydon and Annabel Garren are the new managers. 'The service was impeccable, everything tailored to our requirements,' says a visitor this year. 'We were met at the car and immediately shown to our room.' The public areas have original features: stained glass, ornate plasterwork, a flying staircase in the hall; original fireplaces in the light lounge and the library, which is styled like a gentlemen's club. Chef Chris Wood serves classic British dishes 'with a contemporary twist', eg, rare breed ham hock, winter-spiced apple pear and chutney; Northumberland estates grouse, celeriac rösti, redcurrant and game jus. 'Our room was clean, well decorated with period furniture; a bath and separate shower in the immaculate bathroom.' Some rooms are themed: Tedsmore has echoes of a hunting lodge; Versailles has an ornately carved French bedhead. Children are welcomed (as are dogs). The hall is popular for weddings (exclusive bookings). (*Stephen Lee*)

Morpeth NE65 9EN

T: 01670-787454
F: 01670-786011
E: info@eshotthall.co.uk
W: www.eshotthall.co.uk

BEDROOMS: 11, plus 5 in *Dove Cottage* annexe.
OPEN: all year.
FACILITIES: drawing room, library, 2 dining rooms, civil wedding licence, 500-acre estate, tennis.
BACKGROUND MUSIC: in dining rooms at breakfast and dinner.
LOCATION: 6 miles N of Morpeth.
CHILDREN: all ages welcomed.
DOGS: allowed in 2 bedrooms, not in public rooms.
CREDIT CARDS: Amex, MasterCard, Visa.
PRICES: B&B £60–£90 per person, D,B&B £95–£125, full alc £43, special breaks.

MORSTON Norfolk

Map 2:A5

MORSTON HALL

César award in 2010

'Wonderful, and wonderfully expensive.' Tracy and Galton Blackiston's restaurant-with-rooms, a Jacobean flint-and-brick mansion on the north Norfolk coast, has many fans. Hotel visitors come for the host's 'superb' cooking (*Michelin* star). Dinner is an event, with guests gathering at 7.30 pm for drinks and canapés in two candlelit lounges with open fire. The no-choice four-course menu (allergies and dislikes catered for) is served at a single sitting at 8 pm. Typical dishes: spelt-battered whiting; ox tongue with garden herbs, beetroot and onion ring; Norfolk estate venison with black figs. 'The staff were charming and efficient,' says a visitor this year; a rare dissenter thought service was 'automated'; a trusted reporter said it 'runs like clockwork without being impersonal'. The bedrooms in the main building are decorated in country house style; spacious suites in a pavilion in the garden have large bed and light wood furniture. 'We had a gorgeous room with a giant bed and large bathroom. Nice touches were fresh milk and a separate radio as well as a TV.' Breakfast is 'excellent'; the kippers and haddock are home smoked. (*John Barnes, and others*)

Morston, Holt
NR25 7AA

T: 01263-741041
F: 01263-740419
E: reception@morstonhall.com
W: www.morstonhall.com

BEDROOMS: 13, 6 in garden pavilion on ground floor.
OPEN: all year except Christmas, 3 weeks Jan, restaurant closed midday.
FACILITIES: hall, lounge, sunroom, conservatory, restaurant, 3½-acre garden (pond, croquet).
BACKGROUND MUSIC: none.
LOCATION: 2 miles W of Blakeney.
CHILDREN: all ages welcomed.
DOGS: not allowed in public rooms.
CREDIT CARDS: all major cards.
PRICES: D,B&B £170–£185 per person, set dinner £65, special breaks, New Year package, 1-night bookings sometimes refused Sat.

MULLION COVE Cornwall

Map 1:E2

MULLION COVE HOTEL

In an 'idyllic' cliff-top position, on the Cornish Coastal Path and surrounded by National Trust land, this former railway hotel is owned and run by the 'hands-on' Grose family. 'We wish there were more like it,' say the nominators, who were impressed by the 'thoughtful' staff and the quality of the cooking. Most of the renovated bedrooms have sea views. 'The housekeeping is excellent': fresh fruit is renewed daily in the suites, and home-made biscuits are provided with the hospitality tray. The lounges have floor-to-ceiling windows, easy chairs and settees. In the *Atlantic View* restaurant, Lee Brooking is now the chef. His daily-changing menu might include pan-seared woodland pigeon breast; crispy fillet of sea bass and ling with tapenade. The bistro/bar was refurbished in early 2012 and reopened as the *Marconi Bar*. Snacks and light evening meals are served here, and on a terrace in warm weather. At breakfast 'the cooked selection was very good, and there is a reasonable choice of cereals, fruit, juices and yogurt'. Children of all ages are welcomed, as are dogs. (*PD and MTS*)

25% DISCOUNT VOUCHERS

Mullion
Helston TR12 7EP

T: 01326-240328
F: 01326-240998
E: enquiries@mullion-cove.co.uk
W: www.mullion-cove.co.uk

BEDROOMS: 30, some on ground floor.

OPEN: all year except 2–10 Jan.

FACILITIES: lift, 3 lounges, bar, restaurant, 3-acre garden, heated outdoor swimming pool (11 by 5½ metres).

BACKGROUND MUSIC: 'easy listening' in bar.

LOCATION: on edge of village.

CHILDREN: all ages welcomed.

DOGS: allowed in some bedrooms, 1 lounge.

CREDIT CARDS: Amex, MasterCard, Visa.

PRICES: [2012] B&B £60–£170 per person, D,B&B £75–£185, set meals £36, special breaks, Christmas/New Year packages.

NEAR SAWREY Cumbria

Map 4: inset C2

EES WYKE COUNTRY HOUSE

'Very enjoyable and comfortable, with a roaring log fire in the lounge,' say visitors to Richard and Margaret Lee's small country hotel in Beatrix Potter country. The writer rented the Georgian house as a holiday home, later purchasing nearby Hill Top, where she wrote the Peter Rabbit books. Mr Lee's 'excellent' cooking has long been recommended by *Guide* readers: his five-course daily-changing menu of modern English/French dishes might include seared scallops; duckling breast, red onion and juniper marmalade. Guests gather in the two traditionally furnished lounges at 6.30 pm to place their order for a meal served at 7.30 in the dining room with its views over the 'beautiful' grounds above Esthwaite Water. All the simple bedrooms have the views: two have a private bathroom across a landing (dressing gown provided). Breakfast has home-baked bread, freshly squeezed orange juice, and a generous buffet of cereals and fruit. Cumberland sausages and bacon from an award-winning local butcher are among the cooked dishes. (*Mrs E Talbot*)

Near Sawrey
Ambleside LA22 0JZ

T: 015394-36393
E: mail@eeswyke.co.uk
W: www.eeswyke.co.uk

BEDROOMS: 8, 1 on ground floor.
OPEN: all year.
FACILITIES: 2 lounges, restaurant, veranda, 1-acre garden, unsuitable for ♿.
BACKGROUND MUSIC: none.
LOCATION: edge of village 2½ miles SE of Hawkshead on B5286.
CHILDREN: not under 12.
DOGS: not allowed.
CREDIT CARDS: MasterCard, Visa.
PRICES: B&B £69 per person, D,B&B £104, set dinner £35, New Year package, 1-night bookings sometimes refused.

NETHER WESTCOTE Oxfordshire

Map 3:D6

THE FEATHERED NEST NEW

César award: newcomer of the year

In a quiet village on a hillside, this country pub has been 'transformed' into a smart restaurant-with-rooms by owners Tony and Amanda Timmer. 'They are friendly hosts and the food is excellent,' said readers. Inspectors agreed: 'What stood out was the outstanding service; all the staff addressed us by name; we felt it mattered to them that everything was right for us.' The renovation has been 'done with a sure touch': the bar has flagstone floors, a log fire; 'light floods into the dining rooms with its French doors opening on to a terrace and the garden'. There is a 'stunning' view of the Evenlode valley ('not a pylon in sight'). In the dining room, chef Peter Eaton serves a seasonal menu: 'The dishes might be elaborate, but every morsel was delicious.' A typical dish: sucking pig (pie, loin, head terrine, shoulder), quinoa, Calvados sauce. 'Our village-facing room was beautifully done and thoughtfully equipped; a coffee machine, fruit, chocolates and biscuits on the dressing table; decent bedside lighting; a smashing double-aspect bathroom. Everything was peaceful at night.' (*Bruce and Pat Orman, and others*)

Nether Westcote
Chipping Norton OX7 6SD

T: 01993-833030
F: 01993-833031
E: info@thefeatherednestinn.co.uk
W: www.thefeatherednestinn.co.uk

BEDROOMS: 4.

OPEN: all year except 25 Dec, restaurant closed Mon.

FACILITIES: bar, dining room, garden room, civil wedding licence, unsuitable for ♿.

BACKGROUND MUSIC: in public areas.

LOCATION: in village.

CHILDREN: all ages welcomed.

DOGS: allowed in bar only.

CREDIT CARDS: Amex, MasterCard, Visa.

PRICES: [2012] B&B £65–£125 per person, full alc £55, midweek/ weekend packages, Christmas/New Year packages, 1-night bookings refused weekends.

NETLEY MARSH Hampshire

Map 2:E2

HOTEL TERRAVINA

César award in 2009

'Welcoming hosts', Gérard and Nina Basset, run their small New Forest hotel in hands-on style. They have given the interiors of the red-brick Victorian building a contemporary look: glass panels, natural wood or slate flooring. The lounge opens on to a garden terrace. 'A lot of care has been taken in furnishing the bedrooms,' say visitors, who were 'delighted to find that we each had a bedside light that you could read by, a detail so often overlooked'. Bedrooms, decorated in neutral colours, have natural wood, state-of-the-art fittings. Many have a patio or terrace. Planning permission has been given for five new rooms. In the dining room, Neil Cooper has been promoted to head chef. He cooks modern dishes 'with a Californian influence', eg, poached hen's egg with crispy potato, wilted spinach, wild mushrooms; rabbit en croute, wholegrain mustard and cider, creamed leek, carrot purée and pickled carrots. 'It pays to get Gérard to give you a recommendation for a wine to go with the meal,' say visitors, acknowledging his award-winning skills as a sommelier. (*M and PF*)

174 Woodlands Road
Netley Marsh
nr Southampton SO40 7GL

T: 02380-293784
F: 02380-293627
E: info@hotelterravina.co.uk
W: www.hotelterravina.co.uk

BEDROOMS: 11, some on ground floor, 1 suitable for ♿.
OPEN: all year.
FACILITIES: ramp, lounge, bar, restaurant, private dining room, civil wedding licence, 1-acre grounds (heated outdoor swimming pool).
BACKGROUND MUSIC: none.
LOCATION: NW of Southampton, 2 miles W of Totton.
CHILDREN: all ages welcomed.
DOGS: not allowed.
CREDIT CARDS: Amex, MasterCard, Visa.
PRICES: B&B £77.50–£132.50 per room, full alc £60, 2-night bookings preferred at weekends (check with hotel).

NEW MILTON Hampshire

Map 2:E2

CHEWTON GLEN

'Absolutely delightful: first-class, attentive service.' Praise in 2012 for this privately owned, luxurious country house hotel (Relais & Châteaux) in extensive grounds on the edge of the New Forest. Another comment: 'The attention to detail, courteous staff and calm atmosphere make this an absolute treat.' The manager, Andrew Stembridge, has overseen significant changes. Children are now actively welcomed (family rooms, a Kids Club, swings in the trees, and special meals). The restaurant has been relaunched as *Vetiver* with a contemporary decor and a conservatory extension. Andrew Dubourg has joined as head chef working alongside Luke Matthews. They use fruit, herbs and vegetables from a newly built walled kitchen garden. 'Our scallop starter and fillet steak main course were memorable.' Six two-bedroom tree house suites on stilts in the woodland were due to open as the *Guide* went to press. Bedrooms in the main house have antiques, modern fabrics; most have a terrace, balcony or private garden. Mr Stembridge also oversees *Cliveden*, Taplow (see Shortlist), which is under the same ownership. (*Janette Wright, Sue Pepper, and others*)

Christchurch Road
New Milton BH25 6QS

T: 01425-275341
F: 01425-272310
E: reservations@chewtonglen.com
W: www.chewtonglen.com

BEDROOMS: 58, 14 on ground floor, 1 suitable for ♿.
OPEN: all year.
FACILITIES: 3 lounges, bar, restaurant, function rooms, civil wedding licence, spa, indoor 17-metre swimming pool, 130-acre grounds, outdoor 15-metre swimming pool, tennis centre, par-3 golf course.
BACKGROUND MUSIC: in public areas.
LOCATION: on S edge of New Forest national park.
CHILDREN: all ages welcomed.
DOGS: not allowed.
CREDIT CARDS: all major cards.
PRICES: [to 30 Mar 2013] room £310–£1,205, full alc £65, special breaks, Christmas/New Year packages, 1-night bookings refused weekends.

NEW ROMNEY Kent

Map 2:E5

ROMNEY BAY HOUSE

César award in 2012

Designed by Sir Clough Williams-Ellis for actress/journalist Hedda Hopper, this three-storey house stands hard by the sea in a 'wonderfully quiet spot' on the Kent coast. The owners, Clinton and Lisa Lovell, are 'very welcoming hosts', says a visitor in 2012. 'Lisa has a sure sense of detail: everything seems to have been thought through; the linen was first class,' is another comment. There are 'pastel colours, shelves with china cups, stripped pine and floral sofas', 'little books of quotations' in the lounge. A first-floor lounge has telescopes and models of sailing ships. On four evenings a week, Mr Lovell cooks a four-course dinner (no choice but ingredients are discussed in advance). It is served in a conservatory dining room: 'Our preferences were carefully observed; we enjoyed delicious local smoked fish and perfectly cooked duck breast.' The bedrooms face the sea or a links golf course. Breakfast, 'freshly prepared and delightfully served', has 'excellent home-made compotes, wonderful bacon'. The Lovells, who have added a website this year, prefer to take bookings by telephone. (*Elaine Sandell, David Leibling, and others*)

25% DISCOUNT VOUCHERS

Coast Road, Littlestone
New Romney TN28 8QY

T: 01797-364747
W: www.romneybayhousehotel.co.uk

BEDROOMS: 10.
OPEN: all year except 1 week Christmas, 1 week early Jan, dining room closed midday, Sun/Mon/Thurs evenings.
FACILITIES: 2 lounges, bar, conservatory, dining room, small function facilities, 1-acre garden, unsuitable for ♿.
BACKGROUND MUSIC: none.
LOCATION: 1½ miles from New Romney.
CHILDREN: not under 14.
DOGS: not allowed.
CREDIT CARDS: Amex, MasterCard, Visa.
PRICES: B&B £47.50–£95 per person, set menu £45, winter breaks, New Year package, 1-night advance bookings refused weekends.

NEWBIGGIN-ON-LUNE Cumbria

Map 4:C3

BROWNBER HALL

NEW

On raised ground with 'fine views of the Yorkshire Dales', this Victorian country house is run as a B&B by the 'personable' owner, Hilary Reid. 'An appealing domesticity is underpinned by professional hospitality,' says the nominator (a trusted correspondent) in 2012. The lounge has wing chairs by a wood-burning stove, an antique settle. The bedrooms, on the first floor, are reached by 'a fine staircase with wooden and rope banisters' or a lift. 'Our south-facing room had shutters and richly coloured full-length curtains; green-striped wallpaper and a green fitted carpet; a small bed with a comfortable mattress; a spotless bathroom.' Breakfast is taken at separate tables in a 'tastefully furnished' dining room: 'Prompt service from Hilary; juice, cereal and yogurt on the sideboard; local ingredients for the cooked dishes; excellent thick-cut sweet smoked bacon, perfectly done poached eggs; home-made oatmeal bread, and marmalade in a dish (hooray).' Dogs are welcomed (the number at any one time is limited). 'Our three border terriers, who slept in a box in our room, were made to feel as pampered as we were.' (*Robert Gower*)

Newbiggin-on-Lune
CA17 4NX

T/F: 015396-23208
E: enquiries@brownberhall.co.uk
W: www.brownberhall.co.uk

BEDROOMS: 10.
OPEN: all year except Christmas.
FACILITIES: lounge, dining room, terrace, garden, unsuitable for ♿.
BACKGROUND MUSIC: none.
LOCATION: outside village, 5 miles SW of Kirkby Stephen.
CHILDREN: not under 8.
DOGS: allowed.
CREDIT CARDS: MasterCard, Visa.
PRICES: [2012] B&B £35–£55 per person, 1-night bookings refused bank holiday weekends.

NEWCASTLE UPON TYNE Tyne and Wear Map 4:B4

JESMOND DENE HOUSE

César award: city hotel of the year

'An unexpected pleasure; a country house almost in the city.' 'A very good hotel; outstanding accommodation and attentive service from the young staff.' Praise comes from two sets of trusted reporters in 2012. Owned by Terry Laybourne and Peter Candler, this Arts & Crafts mansion is in a wooded suburb. Eric Kortenbach is the manager. The 'generously equipped' bedrooms, which vary in size and view, are decorated in contemporary style. 'Space is well organised; masses of storage; a super bright bathroom; excellent housekeeping.' 'Our ground-floor suite in an annexe had a supremely comfortable double bed, a sitting area with a large sofa, table and chairs; access to the garden.' In the two dining areas, the 'interesting' menus of chef Michael Penaluna have 'some unusual, well-presented' dishes, perhaps Kielder venison carpaccio, pickled plums, beetroot and horseradish cream; monkfish, north country mixed radishes, bread jus. 'A superb meal at a fair price.' At breakfast, a large buffet has freshly squeezed orange juice; fresh fruit salad, 'good bread'; 'excellent scrambled eggs'. (*Pat and Jeremy Temple, David and Kate Wooff, and others*)

Jesmond Dene Road
Newcastle upon Tyne
NE2 2EY

T: 0191-212 3000
F: 0191-212 3001
E: info@jesmonddenehouse.co.uk
W: www.jesmonddenehouse.co.uk

BEDROOMS: 40, 8 in adjacent annexe, 2 suitable for ♿.

OPEN: all year.

FACILITIES: lift, 2 lounges, cocktail bar, restaurant, conference/function facilities, civil wedding licence, 2-acre garden.

BACKGROUND MUSIC: in public areas.

LOCATION: 5 mins' drive from centre via A167.

CHILDREN: all ages welcomed.

DOGS: only guide dogs allowed.

CREDIT CARDS: all major cards.

PRICES: [2012] B&B £65–£175 per person, set dinner £28, Christmas/ New Year packages.

SEE ALSO SHORTLIST

NEWENT Gloucestershire

Map 3:D5

THREE CHOIRS VINEYARDS

In a 'beautiful' setting on the crest of a hill between Newent and Dymock, this restaurant-with-rooms on an award-winning vineyard is endorsed by readers again this year. 'Tempered by marine air from the Severn estuary', it looks down on a south-facing vine-clad valley ('in hues of yellow and orange on an autumnal day'). Eight of the bedrooms are in a single-storey building beside the restaurant. 'Our room was of reasonable size,' says a visitor this year. 'It was furnished in black-lacquered oriental style; best of all, a French door opened on a private mini-patio where we enjoyed a bottle of the vineyard's wine.' Three 'airy' rooms in a lodge among the vines have private parking. A fireplace in the restaurant creates a 'cosy' atmosphere; chef Darren Leonard's 'excellent' modern European menu might include goat's cheese soufflé, spiced beetroot chutney; seared duck breast, parsnip purée, crisp Anna potato, red wine jus. Breakfast has a large buffet and various cooked dishes. 'Even those familiar with wine-making will enjoy a tour of the vineyard.' (*Rich Weinhold, and others*)

Newent
GL18 1LS

T: 01531-890223
F: 01531 890877
E: info@threechoirs.com
W: www.three-choirs-vineyards.co.uk

BEDROOMS: 11, 3 in lodges 500 yds from restaurant, all on ground floor, 1 suitable for ♿.

OPEN: all year, except 24 Dec–5 Jan.

FACILITIES: lounge, restaurant, wine shop, 100-acre grounds.

BACKGROUND MUSIC: none.

LOCATION: 2 miles N of Newent.

CHILDREN: well-behaved children of all ages welcomed.

DOGS: in vineyards only.

CREDIT CARDS: MasterCard, Visa.

PRICES: [2012] B&B £67.50–£97.50 per person, D,B&B £102.50–£127.50 (min. 2 nights), full alc £40, wine-tasting breaks, 1-night bookings sometimes refused weekends.

NEWICK East Sussex

Map 2:E4

NEWICK PARK

'As good as ever,' says a visitor returning in 2012 to this Grade II* listed Georgian house which owners Michael and Virginia Childs run as a country house hotel; Andrew Hawkes is the manager. 'It is a beautiful place in splendid grounds; the rooms are lovely and the food is very good.' The building has been sympathetically restored; there are four large lounges ('light and spacious') with 'something for everyone'. Bedrooms vary in size; most have a big bed, Egyptian linens and large windows (some double-aspect), overlooking the estate and gardens or the South Downs. Two have a four-poster bed, and one has an eight-foot-wide bed. Each of three rooms in the *Granary*, a short walk from the main house, has a sitting room; two have French doors opening on to a patio. In the dining room chef Chris Moore's modern European menus have organic fruit and vegetables from the hotel's walled garden, and game in season from the estate. His dishes might include wild garlic soup, poached egg; roast guineafowl breast, thyme boudin, garlic creamed cabbage. 'Breakfast is fine.' (*Peter Adam*)

25% DISCOUNT VOUCHERS

Church Road
Newick BN8 4SB

T: 01825-723633
F: 01825-723969
E: bookings@newickpark.co.uk
W: www.newickpark.co.uk

BEDROOMS: 16, 3 on ground floor suitable for ♿, 3 in *Granary*.
OPEN: all year except 30 Dec–7 Jan.
FACILITIES: lounges, bar, study, library, restaurant, conference facilities, civil wedding licence, 255-acre grounds, heated outdoor swimming pool (12 by 6 metres).
BACKGROUND MUSIC: classical/jazz in public areas.
LOCATION: 2 miles S of Newick.
CHILDREN: not under 3 in restaurant.
DOGS: allowed in 4 bedrooms, not in public rooms.
CREDIT CARDS: Amex, MasterCard, Visa.
PRICES: [2012] B&B £62.50–£142.50 per person, D,B&B from £105, full alc £45, special breaks, Christmas package.

NEWLANDS Cumbria

Map 4: inset C2

SWINSIDE LODGE

In a 'lovely, secluded setting with Lake District peaks all around', Mike and Kath Bilton run their white-painted Regency house as a small hotel. It is 'strongly endorsed' by readers for the 'very high standards of service' (this year's comment). Other praise: 'They are lovely people running a welcoming hotel with a strong personal touch.' There are two 'inviting' sitting rooms. In a 'lovely' dining room the chef, Clive Imber, serves an 'outstanding' daily-changing four-course menu with dishes like sesame tiger prawns, cucumber salad; fillet of Cumbrian beef, stuffed artichoke, roast parsnips. 'Dinner was delicious; original, well balanced and beautifully presented.' The bedrooms come in three sizes; a superior room 'with glorious views' was 'nicely furnished'; a small room was 'spotless with a bed'. Evening turn-down is appreciated as are 'nice touches' like guidebooks, a sewing kit, mineral water. The 'yummy' breakfast has 'more than the full English; interesting options include local ham with poached eggs. When we had to go out on a photo shoot early, Kath gave us great bacon butties on our return.' (*JG, and others*)

Grange Road
Newlands
nr Keswick CA12 5UE

T: 017687-72948
F: 017687-73312
E: info@swinsidelodge-hotel.co.uk
W: www.swinsidelodge-hotel.co.uk

BEDROOMS: 7.
OPEN: all year except 9 Dec–1 Feb.
FACILITIES: 2 lounges, dining room, ½-acre garden, unsuitable for ♿.
BACKGROUND MUSIC: in Reception.
LOCATION: 2 miles SW of Keswick.
CHILDREN: not under 12.
DOGS: not allowed in house (dry store available).
CREDIT CARDS: MasterCard, Visa.
PRICES: [2012] D,B&B £98–£152 per person, set dinner £60, special offers.

NORTH MOLTON Devon

Map 1:B4

HEASLEY HOUSE

César award in 2010

A '*Guide* classic', this Grade II listed Georgian dower house stands in a hamlet on the fringes of Exmoor national park. It is run as a small hotel by Jan and Paul (the chef) Gambrill. 'In far from welcoming weather, Paul greeted us warmly, bringing us tea and home-made sponge in front of a roaring fire,' said visitors. 'Jan made herself known, worried that we had not been welcomed sufficiently. No concerns on that score.' Mr Gambrill cooks 'outstanding' modern European dishes on a short seasonal menu, perhaps home-cured gravadlax, honey mustard sauce; Devon Red sirloin steak, roasted cherry tomatoes, sauté potatoes. The 'excellent' wine list has a 'modest' mark-up. 'After dinner, Jan suggested we look at her well-stocked library of DVDs; we retired happily to the settee in our room.' The 'extremely comfortable' bedrooms are individually styled. 'Ours was lovely, almost a suite, and it had a spacious bathroom.' 'I fell asleep listening to an owl outside my window.' Breakfast was 'great, with freshly squeezed orange juice, good selection of cereals and yogurts, and perfectly cooked full English'. (*VF, and others*)

25% DISCOUNT VOUCHERS

Heasley Mill
North Molton EX36 3LE

T: 01598-740213
E: enquiries@heasley-house.co.uk
W: www.heasley-house.co.uk

BEDROOMS: 8.
OPEN: all year except Christmas, Feb (private parties only at New Year).
FACILITIES: lounge, bar, restaurant, ¼-acre garden, unsuitable for ♿.
BACKGROUND MUSIC: none.
LOCATION: N of N Molton.
CHILDREN: all ages welcomed.
DOGS: not allowed in restaurant.
CREDIT CARDS: MasterCard, Visa.
PRICES: B&B £75–£85 per person, set meals £26–£32.

RTH WALSHAM Norfolk

Map 2:A6

BEECHWOOD HOTEL

In a market town near the north Norfolk coast, this creeper-clad Georgian house is run as a small hotel by Lindsay Spalding and Don Birch. 'They are friendly hosts who create a great atmosphere,' say visitors returning in 2012. 'The charming young staff remembered us; service was faultless.' Other praise: 'No penalties were charged when we had to cancel due to illness: excellent food, service and ambience.' The bedrooms come in three sizes: 'Our spacious room had a huge bed with an incredibly comfortable mattress; the bathroom had a big bath and a separate power shower; the evening turn-down was impressive.' In the restaurant, chef Steven Norgate serves a short menu using ingredients sourced from within ten miles wherever possible. 'Generous portions of imaginative dishes; succulent Cromer crab was caught the same day; tasty sea bass with rösti potato, baby spinach, courgette ribbons, brown shrimp and chive velouté; a perfect combination.' Breakfasts are 'varied and fun: exotic fruit salad, dried fruits and yogurt; freshly squeezed fruit juices; especially tasty tomatoes and field mushrooms'. (*Steven Hur, Alec Frank, and others*)

25% DISCOUNT VOUCHERS

20 Cromer Road
North Walsham
NR28 0HD

T: 01692-403231
F: 01692-407284
E: info@beechwood-hotel.co.uk
W: www.beechwood-hotel.co.uk

BEDROOMS: 17, some on ground floor, 1 suitable for ♿.

OPEN: all year, except Christmas, restaurant closed midday Mon–Sat.

FACILITIES: 2 lounges, bar, restaurant, 1-acre garden (croquet).

BACKGROUND MUSIC: none.

LOCATION: near town centre.

CHILDREN: not under 10.

DOGS: allowed (3 'dog' bedrooms).

CREDIT CARDS: MasterCard, Visa.

PRICES: B&B £50–£80 per person, D,B&B £60–£95, set dinner £38, short breaks, New Year package, 1-night bookings sometimes refused Sat.

NORTHAM Devon

Map 1:B4

YEOLDON HOUSE

'A vista of gardens and a fine view of the River Torridge' greets visitors to Jennifer and Brian Steele's 18th-century gabled house which they run as a small country hotel. The decor is traditional: suitcases on the stairs, old stained glass, lots of artefacts, 'a bit over-decorated with knick-knacks'. The bedrooms vary in size and style: 'Ours, Kingsley, was a beautiful square space; windows on two sides; glistening linen, an antique dressing table. A balcony opened to a river view. The lighting was good; the small bathroom lacked storage space. We liked the personal letter of welcome.' Mr Steele's cooking is 'the important strength' in the river-facing restaurant, *Soyer's*, which is 'deservedly popular with locals'. His short menus have 'exquisitely cooked local fare (sea bass, pork belly, rack of lamb) served with old-world courtesy'. Typical dishes: ham hock, mustard and parsley terrine, apple and cider brandy chutney; chump of West Country lamb, parsnip and horseradish mash. Breakfast is 'equally sumptuous: local sausage, black pudding and so much else'. The North Devon Coastal Path passes the house. (*Canon Michael Bourdeaux, and others*)

25% DISCOUNT VOUCHERS

Durrant Lane
Northam, nr Bideford
EX39 2RL

T: 01237-474400
F: 01237-476618
E: yeoldonhouse@aol.com
W: www.yeoldonhousehotel.co.uk

BEDROOMS: 10.

OPEN: all year except 22–31 Dec, restaurant closed midday and Sun evening.

FACILITIES: lounge/bar, restaurant, civil wedding licence, 2-acre grounds, beach 5 mins' drive, unsuitable for ♿.

BACKGROUND MUSIC: classical evenings in public rooms.

LOCATION: 1 mile N of Bideford.

CHILDREN: all ages welcomed.

DOGS: allowed, but not left unattended and not in restaurant.

CREDIT CARDS: Amex, MasterCard, Visa.

PRICES: B&B £65–£90 per person, D,B&B £80–£110, set menu £35, short breaks, New Year package, 1-night bookings sometimes refused in summer.

NORTHLEACH Gloucestershire

Map 3:D6

THE WHEATSHEAF

NEW

On the main street of a small Cotswolds market town, this old coaching inn has been 'imaginatively' restored by the owners, Sam and Georgie Pearman. 'It has been executed with flair; the staff are charming, the cooking is excellent,' said *Guide* inspectors in 2012. The bar has flagstone floors, a log fire, 'locals popping in for a drink'. There is striking artwork throughout. The bedrooms come in three sizes: 'Our high-ceilinged room had a freestanding bath beneath a massive Sebastian Krüger portrait of a gunslinger; sisal carpets by the massive bed, old wooden floorboards. Useful extras were in a "have-you-forgotten" bag.' Some rooms have hangers on hooks rather than a wardrobe. In the dining room, the menu has an 'interesting' mix of dishes: 'We enjoyed a delicious twice-baked cheese soufflé; moist sea bass with chorizo, girolles and haricot beans. Background music was not oppressive.' A continental breakfast is included in the room rate: 'The orange juice was tingling fresh; the toast was home baked and thick cut; preserves were home made.' The manager, Peter Creed, 'made a point of asking us had we had enjoyed our stay'.

West End
Northleach GL54 3EZ

T: 01451-860244
E: reservations@cotswoldswheatsheaf.com
W: www.cotswoldswheatsheaf.com

BEDROOMS: 14, 3 on ground floor, 2 in annexe.
OPEN: all year.
FACILITIES: sitting room, 2 bars, dining room, 2 private dining rooms, garden.
BACKGROUND MUSIC: in public areas.
LOCATION: town centre.
CHILDREN: all ages welcomed.
DOGS: allowed in 3 bedrooms, on lead in public rooms.
CREDIT CARDS: Amex, MasterCard, Visa.
PRICES: [2012] B&B (continental) £65–£100 per person, cooked breakfast £9, full alc £40, special breaks.

NORWICH Norfolk

Map 2:B5

THE OLD RECTORY

NEW

In the Yare valley on the outskirts of Norwich, this three-storey Grade II listed Georgian rectory is the family home of Chris and Sally Entwistle and their Birman cats, Rollo and Milli. 'A very comfortable family-run hotel', it returns from the Shortlist to a full entry thanks to a positive report by regular correspondents. 'The house is spacious and the cooking is of a high standard; we would readily return.' The bedrooms in the main house have Georgian proportions; some have the original fireplace. 'Our standard room was large with an excellent bathroom with bath and separate shower. We were given a choice of blankets or duvet.' Three rooms in a converted coach house (20 yards away) have sloping beams. In the conservatory-style restaurant, which faces the walled garden, chef James Perry has a short menu of modern dishes, perhaps smooth parsnip and thyme soup; roasted marinated chicken breast, crushed new potatoes, Puy lentil and vegetable sauce. Breakfast has 'chef's own' toasted muesli; local bacon, sausages and ham, free-range eggs. In summer, it can be taken in a gazebo by the swimming pool. (*Bryan and Mary Blaxall*)

103 Yarmouth Road
Thorpe St Andrew
Norwich NR7 0HF

T: 01603-700772
F: 01603-300772
E: enquiries@oldrectorynorwich.com
W: www.oldrectorynorwich.com

BEDROOMS: 8, 3 in coach house.

OPEN: all year except Christmas/New Year, restaurant closed Sun.

FACILITIES: drawing room, conservatory, dining room, 1-acre garden, unheated swimming pool (9 by 5 metres, summer only), unsuitable for ♿.

BACKGROUND MUSIC: in drawing room, dining room.

LOCATION: 2 miles E of Norwich.

CHILDREN: all ages welcomed.

DOGS: only guide dogs allowed.

CREDIT CARDS: Amex, MasterCard, Visa.

PRICES: [2012] B&B £65–£80 per person, set dinner £30, full alc £50, 1-night bookings refused weekends (spring and summer).

SEE ALSO SHORTLIST

NOTTINGHAM Nottinghamshire

Map 2:A3

HART'S HOTEL

César award in 2007

Built on the site of Nottingham's medieval castle, Tim Hart's purpose-built hotel has striking modern lines with curved buttresses and lots of glass. In a quiet cul-de-sac, it has 'lovely views over the city'. The interiors, designed by Mr Hart's wife, Stefa, are equally striking; a brightly coloured ceiling, much art on the walls, vast windows. Most of the bedrooms are 'small but well equipped', with high ceiling, a 'masculine' decor; the best have the views. Each of six garden rooms has a private terrace. Bathrooms are modern; large bath and power shower. *Hart's* restaurant, a short distance away in the former A&E department of the local hospital, has velvet banquette seating, wood floors, well-spaced tables. The chef is now Dan Burridge: his modern British menus might include pan-fried calf's liver, bulgar wheat, smoked bacon, passionfruit and turmeric bhaji. Lighter meals are available throughout the day in the *Park Bar*. The 'excellent' cooked breakfast has 'wonderful freshly brewed coffee'. Mr Hart also owns *Hambleton Hall*, Hambleton (see entry). (*Clare Johnstone*)

25% DISCOUNT VOUCHERS

Standard Hill, Park Row
Nottingham NG1 6GN

T: 0115-988 1900
F: 0115-947 7600
E: reception@hartshotel.co.uk
W: www.hartsnottingham.co.uk

BEDROOMS: 32, 2 suitable for ♿.
OPEN: all year.
FACILITIES: lift, ramps, reception/lobby, bar, restaurant (30 yds), conference/banqueting facilities, small exercise room, civil wedding licence, small garden, private car park with CCTV.
BACKGROUND MUSIC: light jazz in bar.
LOCATION: city centre.
CHILDREN: all ages welcomed.
DOGS: not allowed in public rooms, or unattended in bedrooms.
CREDIT CARDS: Amex, MasterCard, Visa.
PRICES: [2012] room £125–£265, breakfast £9–£14, set dinner £26, full alc £45.

OBORNE Dorset

Map 1:C6

THE GRANGE AT OBORNE

In a charming hamlet near Sherborne, this 200-year-old manor house is owned and run as a traditional hotel by Karenza and Ken Mathews; it is managed by their daughter, Jennifer, and her husband, Jonathan Fletcher. 'The hotel is well furnished and the staff are most pleasant,' say visitors this year. 'Full marks', too, for the accommodation. 'Our large first-floor room overlooked the courtyard entrance; it had a good, fully tiled bathroom.' The rooms are decorated in various styles: original rooms have traditional furnishings; newer rooms a more contemporary feel. In the candlelit restaurant, which overlooks the floodlit garden, chef Nick Holt serves a seasonal menu (changing every ten days) of modern English dishes, eg, air-dried venison, kumquat jelly; poached halibut, creamy champagne sauce. The award-winning breakfast has a buffet with compotes, cereals and fruit salad; Fairtrade teas; a choice of omelettes; two types of locally smoked bacon, black pudding come with the full English. Mr and Mrs Mathews spent a year researching the visitor attractions of the area to write their detailed guide to Wessex. (*Ken and Mildred Edwards, and others*)

25% DISCOUNT VOUCHERS

Oborne, nr Sherborne
DT9 4LA

T: 01935-813463
F: 01935-817464
E: reception@thegrange.co.uk
W: www.thegrangeatoborne.co.uk

BEDROOMS: 18, 1 suitable for ♿.
OPEN: all year except 27–30 Dec.
FACILITIES: lounge, bar, restaurant, 2 function rooms, civil wedding licence, ¾-acre garden.
BACKGROUND MUSIC: 'easy listening' all day, in public rooms.
LOCATION: 2 miles NE of Sherborne by A30.
CHILDREN: all ages welcomed.
DOGS: only guide dogs allowed.
CREDIT CARDS: Amex, MasterCard, Visa.
PRICES: B&B £54.50–£82.50 per person, D,B&B £90–£111.50, set dinner £36, full alc £44.50, hibernation breaks Oct–Mar, Christmas/New Year packages, 1-night bookings sometimes refused Sat in summer.

OLD HUNSTANTON Norfolk

Map 2:A5

THE NEPTUNE

At their creeper-clad 18th-century former coaching inn, which they run as a restaurant-with-rooms, chef/patron Kevin Mangeolles and his wife, Jacki, are hands-on owners. The *Michelin*-starred chef 'opened the door as soon as we parked, and carried our bags to the bedroom', said *Guide* inspectors. 'He has no airs or graces, joining his wife to serve at table.' Pre-dinner drinks are taken in a bar/lounge area with Lloyd Loom seating, subdued lighting, slate flagstone floors. In the restaurant, tables are laid with 'lovely napery, generously proportioned, stiff white napkins'. Mr Mangeolles uses local, seasonal produce for his evolving menus which might include asparagus, sweetcorn custard, deep-fried hen's egg; lamb loin and tongue, wild mushrooms, butternut squash. The old building has 'lots of steps, narrow corridors, low doorway openings'. 'Our compact bedroom was white and fresh, in New England-style; it had a seaside theme, and pleasant fabrics.' The bathroom was 'minute'. 'Everything is served (no buffet)' at breakfast: 'divine Greek yogurt with compote, croissants as well as toast; a good selection of cooked dishes'. (*GM, and others*)

85 Old Hunstanton Road
Old Hunstanton PE36 6HZ

T: 01485-532122
E: reservations@theneptune.co.uk
W: www.theneptune.co.uk

BEDROOMS: 6, all with shower.
OPEN: all year, except 25/26 Dec, 3 weeks Jan, 2 weeks Nov, Mon.
FACILITIES: residents' lounge, bar, restaurant, unsuitable for ♿.
BACKGROUND MUSIC: jazz in bar.
LOCATION: village centre, on A149.
CHILDREN: not under 10.
DOGS: not allowed.
CREDIT CARDS: MasterCard, Visa.
PRICES: B&B £60–£90, D,B&B £105–£125, full alc £55, website offers, New Year package, 1-night bookings sometimes refused weekends.

ORFORD Suffolk

Map 2:C6

THE CROWN AND CASTLE

César award: Suffolk inn of the year

'Such service: the cheerful staff answered questions with a smile.' 'A very good example of a *Good Hotel Guide* hotel.' There is much praise in 2012 for this old red brick inn beside the castle on the square of a peaceful Suffolk village. It is owned by Ruth Watson (TV presenter), her husband, David, and Tim Sunderland, who is the partner/manager. 'The place is a joy to return to; the guest is regally pampered,' says a trusted reporter. 'The staff really seem to enjoy their work,' is another comment. Bedrooms in the main house have sea views: 'Dazzling colours and reflections; a chance to enjoy a *Peter Grimes* dawn at sea experience.' Garden rooms are 'nicely decorated and well kitted out'; each has a terrace with a view of the castle. Two new rooms in a converted outbuilding were due to open as we went to press. Mrs Watson oversees the cooking ('she explained one of the items on the menu when I asked'). 'Guineafowl with apricot couscous was divine and generous in quantity.' 'It would be hard to find a better breakfast.' (*Peter Canon, Gordon Murray, Robert Gower, John Jenkins, Pat and Jeremy Temple*)

Orford, nr Woodbridge
IP12 2LJ

T: 01394-450205
E: info@crownandcastle.co.uk
W: www.crownandcastle.co.uk

BEDROOMS: 19, 10 (all on ground floor) in garden, 1 in courtyard.
OPEN: all year.
FACILITIES: lounge/bar, restaurant, private dining room, gallery (with Wi-Fi), 1-acre garden.
BACKGROUND MUSIC: none.
LOCATION: market square.
CHILDREN: not under 8 in hotel and *Trinity* restaurant (any age at lunch).
DOGS: allowed in bar, 5 garden rooms.
CREDIT CARDS: MasterCard, Visa.
PRICES: B&B £65–£122.50 per person, D,B&B £99.50–£157.50, full alc £40, special breaks, Christmas/New Year packages, 1-night bookings refused Sat.

OSWESTRY Shropshire

Map 3:B4

PEN-Y-DYFFRYN

César award in 2003

In beautiful countryside on the Shropshire/Wales border ('only the wildlife breaks the silence'), this small country hotel is liked for its 'unfussy and relaxed' atmosphere. The owners, Miles and Audrey Hunter, serve complimentary tea to guests on arrival, before a log fire in one of the 'homely' lounges on cold days, or on the terrace which has views over the hills. In the south-facing restaurant, chef David Morris serves modern dishes, eg, wood pigeon breast tandoori, onion bhaji; black bream fillet, baby spinach, basil cream sauce. 'Dinner was superb, with a good choice and well presented,' says a visitor in 2012. Bedrooms in the coach house have a private patio opening on to the garden (good for dog owners). Even the smaller bedrooms are thought 'comfortable', but one couple felt that their bathroom needed 'some TLC'. A visitor with limited mobility appreciated a ground-floor room, which was 'quiet despite being near the lounge'. There is good walking locally and the hotel boasts that guests can 'walk in Wales, relax in England'. (*Clive Blackburn, and others*)

25% DISCOUNT VOUCHERS

Rhydycroesau
Oswestry SY10 7JD

T: 01691-653700
E: stay@peny.co.uk
W: www.peny.co.uk

BEDROOMS: 12, 4, each with patio, in coach house, 1 on ground floor.
OPEN: all year except 20 Dec–20 Jan (but open New Year).
FACILITIES: 2 lounges, bar, restaurant, 5-acre grounds (dog-walking area), unsuitable for ♿.
BACKGROUND MUSIC: light classical in evening.
LOCATION: 3 miles W of Oswestry.
CHILDREN: not under 3.
DOGS: not allowed in public rooms after 6 pm.
CREDIT CARDS: MasterCard, Visa.
PRICES: [2012] B&B £63–£90 per person, D,B&B £88–£124, set dinner £37, New Year package, 1-night bookings sometimes refused Sat.

OXFORD Oxfordshire

Map 2:C2

OLD BANK

César award in 2011

Liked for the 'cheerful atmosphere and laid-back luxury', Jeremy Mogford's modern hotel is a conversion of three old stone buildings (one a former bank) on the High Street opposite All Souls College. Mr Mogford's impressive art collection is on display throughout; large canvases (collected mainly from art college degree shows) in the busy bar/brasserie, *Quod*, which occupies the former banking hall; more than 200 Stanley Spencer pencil drawings, and modern works in the corridors and bedrooms. Town meets gown at *Quod* where tables are tightly packed and the atmosphere is buzzy; 'service is prompt and the cooking is good' says a visitor in 2012. Most of the bedrooms, 'nicely finished, and with good facilities', have views of the 'dreaming spires'. 'Our comfortable, quiet room was at the back,' said a visitor who would have liked more storage space. Another guest had a 'peaceful, spacious superior room with a marble bathroom'. The 'excellent' breakfast (not included in the room price) can be English, continental or vegetarian; 'very good bread, proper marmalade'. (*RG*)

92–94 High Street
Oxford OX1 4BJ

T: 01865-799599
E: reservations@oldbank-hotel.co.uk
W: www.oldbank-hotel.co.uk

BEDROOMS: 42, 1 suitable for ♿.
OPEN: all year.
FACILITIES: lift, residents' lounge/bar, bar/grill, dining terrace, 2 meeting/private dining rooms, small garden.
BACKGROUND MUSIC: jazz in library/bar in evenings.
LOCATION: central (windows facing High St double glazed), access to rear car park.
CHILDREN: all ages welcomed.
DOGS: not allowed.
CREDIT CARDS: Amex, MasterCard, Visa.
PRICES: [2012] room £134–£420, breakfast £14.50, full alc £35, 'last-minute rates', Christmas/New Year packages, 1-night bookings sometimes refused weekends.

SEE ALSO SHORTLIST

OXFORD Oxfordshire

Map 2:C2

OLD PARSONAGE

Behind high stone walls just outside the centre, Jeremy Mogford's popular hotel, formerly a 17th-century parsonage, is a 'wonderfully relaxing place'. The wisteria-clad building has an original (1660) iron-studded oak door; a fire is lit year round in the 'intimate, welcoming' bar/restaurant. A club-like lounge has Russian-red walls covered with prints and portraits. Alicia Storey is the new chef this year, serving a 'tempting' menu of classic dishes ('with a modern interpretation'), perhaps lobster and saffron tart; rump of lamb, piperade and goat's cheese. A 'top to bottom' make-over had begun as the *Guide* went to press. Seven new bedrooms are being added; existing rooms are being redesigned. All have air conditioning and free Wi-Fi. In warm weather, drinks and meals are served on a terrace at the front with a canvas cover. There are complimentary walking tours of the city; bicycles can be borrowed. Mr Mogford also owns *Old Bank* (see previous entry). (*Rosemary Grande, Penelope Visman*)

1 Banbury Road
Oxford OX2 6NN

T: 01865-310210
F: 01865-311262
E: reservations@oldparsonage-hotel.co.uk
W: www.oldparsonage-hotel.co.uk

BEDROOMS: 37, 10 on ground floor, 1 suitable for ♿.

OPEN: all year.

FACILITIES: lounge, bar/restaurant, civil wedding licence, terrace, roof garden, small walled garden.

BACKGROUND MUSIC: 'quiet' jazz in bar/restaurant area.

LOCATION: NE end of St Giles, some traffic noise, windows double glazed, small car park.

CHILDREN: all ages welcomed.

DOGS: allowed.

CREDIT CARDS: Amex, MasterCard, Visa.

PRICES: [2012] room £132–£295, breakfast £12.95–£14, full alc £32.25, special breaks, Christmas/New Year packages, 1-night bookings sometimes refused weekends.

SEE ALSO SHORTLIST

PANGBOURNE Berkshire

Map 2:D3

THE ELEPHANT

'Quirkiness rather than quaintness' is the motto of this informal hotel in a busy village in the Thames valley. The first of Christoph Brooke's small but growing Hillbrooke group, it has 'the qualities of a good town hotel', said a *Guide* inspector. The bar and the restaurant are popular with locals. The Victorian building has been decorated throughout in colonial style: there are rugs on wooden floors, armchairs and comfortable sofas in the public areas. The bedrooms have eccentric touches: walls with collages of postcards and photographs. Charleston, facing the garden and a church at the back, had a 'massive Indian dark wooden bed, very comfortable with good sheets and blankets; a huge wooden chest at the base'. A miniature of elderflower liqueur by the bedside 'was a nice touch'. A reader in 2012 commented again on maintenance issues and poor lighting. Chris Ayres, the chef, has a short menu of 'interesting and flavourful' dishes in *Christoph*'s restaurant, eg, Vicars Game smoked venison; poppadom-encrusted coley, Bombay potatoes. Bistro dishes can be taken in the bar. Breakfast 'was good'.

Church Road
Pangbourne
RG8 7AR

T: 01189-842244
F: 01189-767346
E: reception@elephanthotel.co.uk
W: www.elephanthotel.co.uk

BEDROOMS: 22, 8 in annexe, 4 on ground floor, 1 suitable for ♿.
OPEN: all year.
FACILITIES: bar, 2 lounges, restaurant, conference rooms, civil wedding licence, garden.
BACKGROUND MUSIC: variety.
LOCATION: in village, 6 miles NW of Reading.
CHILDREN: all ages welcomed.
DOGS: allowed in public rooms, 1 bedroom.
CREDIT CARDS: Amex, MasterCard, Visa.
PRICES: [2012] B&B from £77.50 per person, D,B&B £110, full alc £45, website offers, Christmas package.

PENZANCE Cornwall

Map 1:E1

THE ABBEY HOTEL

César award in 1985

'An antidote to blandness', this Georgian town house (painted a vivid blue) is on a narrow street that leads down to the harbour. Owned for more than 30 years by Jean (Shrimpton) Cox, it is managed by her 'charming' son, Thaddeus. The building, which dates from 1660 but was 'modernised' in 1820, has been decorated with boldness and flair. The gated entrance and lobby are in the oldest section; the corridors have scarlet walls and carpets; a 'wonderful' collection of original artwork. The magnificent 19th-century drawing room on the first floor has high ceilings, peach walls, deep velvet curtains on huge arched windows which open on to a walled garden with exotic plants, cobbled paths, many places to sit. In summer, cream teas can be taken here. The quirky bedrooms, each different, have a sometimes faded charm; two apartments are in an adjoining building with a separate entrance. Breakfast, in an oak-panelled dining room, is a leisurely affair. No evening meals in the hotel: the Cox family also owns the restaurant next door, *Untitled by Robert Wright*, which has a *Michelin* Bib Gourmand.

25% DISCOUNT VOUCHERS

Abbey Street
Penzance TR18 4AR

T: 01736-366906
E: hotel@theabbeyonline.co.uk
W: www.theabbeyonline.co.uk

BEDROOMS: 6, also 2 apartments in adjoining building.
OPEN: Mar–Jan, except Christmas.
FACILITIES: drawing room, dining room, garden, unsuitable for ♿.
BACKGROUND MUSIC: none.
LOCATION: 300 yds from centre, parking.
CHILDREN: all ages welcomed.
DOGS: not allowed in dining room.
CREDIT CARDS: Amex, MasterCard, Visa.
PRICES: [2012] B&B £50–£100 per person, midweek offers, New Year package, 1-night bookings refused bank holidays.

PENZANCE Cornwall

Map 1:E1

HOTEL PENZANCE

On a hill in a residential area with views across Mount's Bay to St Michael's Mount, Stephen and Yvonne Hill's small hotel is a conversion of two Edwardian townhouses. 'The welcome and service was unstinted and spontaneous,' says a visitor this year. 'The food was, on balance, good, but patchy.' Another comment: 'Our room was nice and the staff were helpful.' Many of the bedrooms, which have bright colours, traditional patterned bedspread, have sea views. In the restaurant, which holds monthly-changing exhibitions of work by local artists, chef Ben Reeve serves modern dishes on a seasonal menu, eg, steamed West Country mussels in a shallot, garlic and Pernod sauce; pan-fried breast of guineafowl, goat's cheese gnocchi, braised chicory. An 'interesting' wine list has a good choice by the glass. Breakfast has home-made bread, a buffet of cereals and fruit; a 'fine grill' among the cooked choices. There is a heated swimming spool in the small Mediterranean-style garden. One visitor advises drivers to take care on the road leading to the limited car parking. (*Lord Coleraine, and others*)

25% DISCOUNT VOUCHERS

Britons Hill
Penzance TR18 3AE

T: 01736-363117
F: 01736-350970
E: reception@hotelpenzance.com
W: www.hotelpenzance.com

BEDROOMS: 25, 2 on ground floor.

OPEN: all year except 2–17 Jan.

FACILITIES: ramps, 3 lounges, bar/restaurant, civil wedding licence, ½-acre garden, terrace, 15-metre swimming pool, rock beach, safe bathing nearby, civil wedding licence, unsuitable for ♿.

BACKGROUND MUSIC: in restaurant and adjacent lounge.

LOCATION: on hill, ½ mile from centre.

CHILDREN: all ages welcomed.

DOGS: not allowed in restaurant.

CREDIT CARDS: Amex (2½% *surcharge*), MasterCard, Visa.

PRICES: [2012] B&B £65–£92.50 per person, D,B&B £30 added, set dinner from £25, full alc £42, special breaks, Christmas/New Year packages.

PETERSFIELD Hampshire

Map 2:E3

JSW

Close to the centre of the busy market town, this white-painted 17th-century former coaching inn is run as a restaurant-with-rooms by Jake Watkins (whose middle name is Saul, hence the name *JSW*). He has a *Michelin* star for his modern British cooking. His philosophy is to keep his dishes simple: his menu might include smoked haddock and pea tart with a crispy egg; Dover sole, Jerusalem artichoke risotto. Five- and seven-course tasting menus have matching wines. 'The eclectic mix of wines fitted the locally sourced food perfectly; the home-made chocolates which finished the meal were irresistible,' said a returning visitor. The oak-beamed restaurant has 'plenty of space around the tables'. A bedroom overlooking the rear courtyard has been added this year. The others overlook the street. Decorated in shades of brown and cream, they have widescreen LCD TV, shower cabinet (no baths) and Wi-Fi. A continental breakfast, delivered to the bedroom, has muesli, freshly squeezed orange juice, home-made bread and preserves, pastries from the Rungis market in Paris, tea or cafetière coffee. (*R and JB, and others*)

20 Dragon Street
Petersfield GU31 4JJ

T: 01730-262030
E: jsw.restaurant@btconnect.com
W: www.jswrestaurant.com

BEDROOMS: 4.
OPEN: all year except Mon/Sun, 2 weeks Jan, Aug.
FACILITIES: restaurant, courtyard, unsuitable for ♿.
BACKGROUND MUSIC: none.
LOCATION: town centre.
CHILDREN: Over 5, not allowed at dinner Fri/Sat.
DOGS: not allowed.
CREDIT CARDS: Amex, MasterCard, Visa.
PRICES: [2012] B&B £42.50–£55 per person, D,B&B £70–£117.50, set menus £27.50–£32.50, alc £48, Christmas/New Year packages.

PETWORTH West Sussex

Map 2:E3

THE OLD RAILWAY STATION

'When can we come back?' asked a visitor in 2012 who had initial misgivings about this unusual B&B, a conversion of a disused railway station and four Pullman carriages. 'We checked in at the old ticket office window and were ushered along the platform to our carriage. Returning to the waiting room, a wonderful space with leather-buttoned sofas and chairs, we sat by the fire and enjoyed complimentary coffee and a slice of very English cake.' The atmosphere was one of 'well-organised clutter' and 'great comfort'. The owners, Gudmund Olafsson (Icelandic) and Catherine Stormont, are supported by a 'highly competent staff'. Eight bedrooms are in the carriages: 'Ours was narrow as you would expect, but comfortable, well furnished with a good bed, two antique chairs and chest of drawers. The adjustable radiator heating was good; the bathroom was surprisingly spacious, with a proper bath.' Two larger rooms are in the main building. Breakfast has a 'beautifully presented fruit salad, good juice, a cafetière of freshly ground coffee and various cooked dishes (eggs were free range).' (*Andrew and Moira Kleissner*)

Petworth GU28 0JF

T: 01798-342346
F: 01798-343066
E: info@old-station.co.uk
W: www.old-station.co.uk

BEDROOMS: 10, 8 in Pullman carriages, 1 suitable for ♿.

OPEN: all year except 24–26 Dec.

FACILITIES: lounge/bar/breakfast room, platform/terrace, 2-acre garden.

BACKGROUND MUSIC: classical/soft 1940s in waiting room.

LOCATION: 1½ miles S of Petworth.

CHILDREN: not under 10.

DOGS: not allowed.

CREDIT CARDS: Amex, MasterCard, Visa.

PRICES: B&B £46–£99 per person, special breaks, 1-night bookings refused weekends and during Goodwood events.

PICKERING North Yorkshire

Map 4:D4

THE WHITE SWAN INN

Once a coaching stop for the York to Whitby stagecoach, this old inn is in the centre of a pretty market town. It has been owned by the Buchanan family for more than a quarter of a century. Victor and Marion Buchanan are in charge; Lisa Jones (née Fraser) is the manager. The mainly local staff are 'always friendly, helpful'. The residents' lounge has an open fire, complimentary tea and coffee, an honesty bar, newspapers and magazines. In the dining room, with its terracotta walls, flagstone floor and country kitchen oak furnishings, chef Darren Clemmit describes his cooking style as 'simple goodness from Yorkshire'. His menus might include Whitby fishcakes, herbed shrimp salad; slow-cooked belly pork, braised red cabbage, mustard mash. Bread, ice cream and chutneys are home produced. 'Vintage' bedrooms in the main building, recently renovated, have a traditional style; rooms in converted stables in a courtyard are more contemporary. Breakfast has cereals, fruit, yogurts, porridge with golden syrup, free-range 'boiled eggs with soldiers', and a full Yorkshire. The family has opened a deli/café/gift shop next door to the inn.

25% DISCOUNT VOUCHERS

Market Place
Pickering YO18 7AA

T: 01751-472288
F: 01751-475554
E: welcome@white-swan.co.uk
W: www.white-swan.co.uk

BEDROOMS: 21, 9 in annexe.
OPEN: all year.
FACILITIES: ramps to ground-floor facilities, lounge, bar, club room, restaurant, private dining room, conference/meeting facilities, small terrace (alfresco meals), 1½-acre grounds.
BACKGROUND MUSIC: none.
LOCATION: central.
CHILDREN: all ages welcomed.
DOGS: allowed.
CREDIT CARDS: Amex, MasterCard, Visa.
PRICES: [2012] B&B £75–£135 per person, D,B&B £105–£165, full alc £48, Christmas/New Year packages, 1-night bookings sometimes refused weekends.

PICKHILL North Yorkshire

Map 4:C4

THE NAG'S HEAD

'We have never been disappointed, as the staff are so welcoming,' says a regular visitor to Edward and Janet Boynton's 300-year-old coaching inn on the main street of a pretty Domesday village. Another comment from a returning guest: 'The high standards continue to be maintained; another pleasurable experience.' Rooms are simply furnished, but 'perfectly adequate'; housekeeping is 'good'. Dinner orders are taken in the bar, which 'comes to life in the evening'. Guests can dine in the tap room, lounge or restaurant, which has immaculate table settings, a huge bookcase, large mirrors. The chef, Louie Miller, serves 'fantastic' traditional dishes with vegetarian choices (coeliacs are also catered for). 'The food is excellent as always; we enjoyed devilled deep-fried whitebait, divine tempura prawns, perfect fillet steak. No room for a dessert.' The bar has 'the best pint of Black Sheep bitter in Yorkshire'. The 'lovely' breakfast has an extensive buffet, 'proper butter'; cooked dishes include 'splendid haddock and poached egg'. 'Everything an English inn should be.' Ask for directions when booking; new roads in the area are not on satnav. (*Ian Malone, Barry and Jean Davis, Neil Phillips*)

25% DISCOUNT VOUCHERS

Pickhill, nr Thirsk
YO7 4JG

T: 01845-567391
F: 01845-567212
E: enquiries@nagsheadpickhill.co.uk
W: www.nagsheadpickhill.co.uk

BEDROOMS: 12, 6 in annexe, 3 on ground floor.

OPEN: all year except 25 Dec.

FACILITIES: ramps, lounge, bar, restaurant, meeting facilities, lawn (croquet).

BACKGROUND MUSIC: in lounge, bar and restaurant.

LOCATION: 5 miles SE of Leeming.

CHILDREN: all ages welcomed.

DOGS: allowed in some bedrooms.

CREDIT CARDS: MasterCard, Visa.

PRICES: [2012] B&B £60–£85 per person, themed breaks, New Year package.

PORLOCK Somerset

Map 1:B5

THE OAKS

Surrounded by lawns and oak trees in a coastal village within Exmoor national park, this gabled Edwardian house has long been run in 'hands-on' style as a small hotel by Tim and Anne Riley. 'They provide that little bit extra which makes a stay so special,' say returning visitors this year (there are many such repeat guests). 'They forget nothing, and are perfect hosts.' Luggage is 'taken to your room and you are given tea and home-made cake as a welcome'. Original features in the house 'have been jealously guarded and maintained': there are polished parquet floors in the hall, antiques, pictures, flowers, log fires. The reception rooms and all the bedrooms have views across Porlock Bay. The 'beautifully kept' bedrooms have traditional furnishings, fresh fruit, flowers, tea-making facilities and magazines. In the dining room, where tables are arranged around the panoramic windows, Mrs Riley's short four-course menu of traditional dishes might include cream of pear and watercress soup; breast of chicken, mushroom risotto, Bath Blue cheese. The cooked breakfast is 'a good start to the day'. Marmalade is home made. (*Michael and Jenifer Price*)

Porlock TA24 8ES

T: 01643-862265
F: 01643-863131
E: info@oakshotel.co.uk
W: www.oakshotel.co.uk

BEDROOMS: 8.
OPEN: Mar–Nov, Christmas/New Year.
FACILITIES: 2 lounges, bar, restaurant, 2-acre garden, pebble beach 1 mile, unsuitable for ♿.
BACKGROUND MUSIC: classical during dinner.
LOCATION: edge of village.
CHILDREN: unsuitable for children.
DOGS: not allowed.
CREDIT CARDS: MasterCard, Visa.
PRICES: D,B&B £110 per person, set menu £37.50, special breaks, Christmas/New Year packages, 1-night bookings occasionally refused.

PORT ISAAC Cornwall

Map 1:D2

PORT GAVERNE HOTEL

'A pub at heart', this unpretentious inn stands in a 'gorgeous little port' near Port Isaac. The owners, Graham and Annabelle Sylvester, 'clearly care about their guests' experience', say inspectors in 2012. 'There is a good atmosphere: lovely traditional features (wooden beams, slate floors, cosy corners); the pub was always busy with regulars and visitors.' 'We sometimes have more dogs than people in the bar,' says Mr Sylvester, who has four dogs of his own. Children are also welcomed (but not in the bar: they can take meals in a snug and other areas). Ian Brodey has been the chef for more than 30 years. Simple meals (eg, half pint of shell-on prawns) are provided in the bar. He serves a 'short, traditional' menu in the separate dining room: 'Delicious bread rolls; a good shrimp starter and lots of side dishes of vegetables with the main courses. The staff were accommodating.' A steep staircase leads to the simple bedrooms: 'Ours was traditionally furnished; the bathroom was dated; some modernising would help but the room had charm.' Breakfast has a buffet, with cooked dishes served at the table.

Port Gaverne
nr Port Isaac
PL29 3SQ

T: 01208-880244
FP: 0500 657867
F: 01208-880151
E: graham@port-gaverne-hotel.co.uk
W: www.port-gaverne-hotel.co.uk

BEDROOMS: 15.

OPEN: all year except Christmas/New Year, 2 weeks Feb.

FACILITIES: lounge, 2 bars, restaurant, beer garden, golf, fishing, surfing, sailing, riding nearby, unsuitable for ♿.

BACKGROUND MUSIC: none.

LOCATION: ½ mile N of Port Isaac.

CHILDREN: all ages welcomed.

DOGS: not allowed in restaurant.

CREDIT CARDS: MasterCard, Visa.

PRICES: B&B £50–£60 per person, set dinner £30, New Year package.

PORTSCATHO Cornwall

Map 1:E2

DRIFTWOOD HOTEL

César award in 2010

On a low cliff above Gerrans Bay on the Roseland peninsula, this small, upmarket hotel is run in hands-on style by Paul and Fiona Robinson, the 'welcoming' owners. 'The level of comfort and hospitality is second to none,' say returning visitors this year. 'Each time we have stayed, it has been in a beautiful room with excellent attention to detail.' Fiona Robinson is responsible for the interiors, which have 'the colours of the coast'; there are rugs on bare floors, driftwood table lamps and mirrors. All but one of the bedrooms have a sea view: they also have a seaside theme. Ground-floor rooms have a decked terrace. A 'quaint' cabin in the garden has two bedrooms. In the dining room, the chef, Chris Eden, was awarded a *Michelin* star in 2012 for his modern European cooking, eg, seared black bream, cauliflower, lime, vanilla and curry; venison loin, pomme purée, salsify, green peppercorns and beetroot. Children are well catered for (there is a games room). Breakfast is lavish. Steep steps lead through woodland to a beach (picnics are provided). (*Mandy Crook, and others*)

Rosevine
nr Portscatho TR2 5EW

T: 01872-580644
E: info@driftwoodhotel.co.uk
W: www.driftwoodhotel.co.uk

BEDROOMS: 15, 4 in courtyard, also 2 in Cabin (2 mins' walk).
OPEN: 3 Feb–9 Dec.
FACILITIES: 2 lounges, bar, restaurant, children's games room, 7-acre grounds (terraced gardens, private beach, safe bathing), unsuitable for ♿.
BACKGROUND MUSIC: jazz in restaurant and bar.
LOCATION: N side of Portscatho.
CHILDREN: all ages welcomed.
DOGS: not allowed.
CREDIT CARDS: Amex, MasterCard, Visa.
PRICES: [2012] B&B £95–£132.50 per person, D,B&B (off-season) £102.50–£137.50, set dinner £46, full alc £60, website offers, 1-night bookings refused weekends.

POSTBRIDGE Devon

Map 1:D4

LYDGATE HOUSE

In a 'gem of a position' within Dartmoor national park, this unassuming house is reached by a private lane near a famous clapper bridge over the River Dart. The owners, Stephen and Karen Horn, 'welcome guests, old and new, with great hospitality', says one visitor. Other praise this year: 'We were warmly welcomed with a delicious cream tea, which is clearly popular: most of the tables were taken by non-residents.' The house faces south 'with stunning views across valley and moorland'. A 'homely' lounge has a wood-burning stove, well-stocked library and small bar. Housekeeping standards are 'high' in the bedrooms, which are named after birds. 'I love the single room, House Martin: with the window open you can hear the rushing river and watch the martins flying in and out of the eaves.' In the spacious conservatory dining room, Mrs Horn 'serves generous portions of a good standard'. Her short menu of British dishes might include smoked duck and orange salad; sirloin steak, brandy and peppercorn sauce. Breakfasts are 'excellent'. 'Very good value; they deserve to do well.' (*Helen Anthony, Jean Taylor*)

25% DISCOUNT VOUCHERS

Postbridge, Dartmoor
PL20 6TJ

T: 01822-880209
E: info@lydgatehouse.co.uk
W: www.lydgatehouse.co.uk

BEDROOMS: 7, 1 on ground floor.
OPEN: all year except Jan, restaurant closed Sun/Mon.
FACILITIES: lounge/bar, snug, dining room, terrace, 36-acre grounds (moorland, paddock, river, private access for guests), fishing, swimming, unsuitable for ♿.
BACKGROUND MUSIC: none.
LOCATION: on edge of hamlet, 8 miles SW of Moretonhampstead.
CHILDREN: not under 12.
DOGS: not allowed in public rooms.
CREDIT CARDS: MasterCard, Visa.
PRICES: [2012] B&B £45–£60 per person, set dinner £27.50, full alc £42.50, Christmas/New Year packages.

PURTON Wiltshire

Map 3:E5

THE PEAR TREE AT PURTON

On the outskirts of a village between the Cotswolds and the Marlborough Downs, this extended former vicarage is run as a small hotel (Pride of Britain) by Francis and Anne Young. 'They managed our golden wedding celebration impeccably,' says a visitor this year. 'The staff were attentive and the food was excellent.' The Youngs supervised the conversion of the 16th-century sandstone building, later adding more bedrooms in an extension. The original building has a panelled library with a stone fireplace and a door opening onto the garden. In the formal dining room, spread over two conservatories, the chef, Alan Postill, serves modern English dishes, perhaps tian of crab with avocado and sweet potato; loin of lamb, Puy lentil ragout, walnut juice. The house stands in mature gardens, with wetlands, a wild-flower meadow, and a vineyard with 600 vines which produce a cuvée available in the restaurant. Bedrooms, each named after a character associated with the village, have fresh fruit and home-made shortbread. The award-winning breakfast has a 'good full English', honey from the Youngs' own hives and jams made in the village. (*Michael Baker*)

25% DISCOUNT VOUCHERS

Church End
Purton, nr Swindon SN5 4ED

T: 01793-772100
F: 01793-772369
E: stay@peartreepurton.co.uk
W: www.peartreepurton.co.uk

BEDROOMS: 17, some on ground floor.
OPEN: all year except 26 Dec.
FACILITIES: ramps, lounge/bar, library, restaurant, function/conference facilities, civil wedding licence, 7½-acre grounds (vineyard, croquet, pond, jogging route).
BACKGROUND MUSIC: none.
LOCATION: 5 miles NW of Swindon.
CHILDREN: all ages welcomed.
DOGS: not unattended in bedrooms.
CREDIT CARDS: all major cards.
PRICES: [2012] B&B £59.50–£149 per person, set dinner £35.50, full alc £55.50, special breaks, New Year package.

RADNAGE Buckinghamshire

Map 2:C3

THE THREE HORSESHOES

In a 'truly rural village' in the less populated eastern Chilterns, this mid-18th-century pub is run as a country inn and restaurant by chef/patron Simon Crawshaw. He has retained the simplicity of the old building: a low latch door, worn flagstones, blackened beams, an original inglenook fireplace. The restaurant is in a handsome south-facing extension with a wide view of the hills. With chef James Norie, Mr Crawshaw serves an 'extensive, ambitious' menu of modern British dishes, eg, sautéed calf's liver, smoked bacon, roast shallots, caramelised red onion potato purée. The wine list has a wide choice of wines by the glass; local real ales are available. The service was 'sympathetic and efficient'. The bedrooms have been 'designed with flair', given bold contemporary colours, 'furnishings chosen with taste'. 'Ingenious use of space' has been made in a suite in the eaves with a separate sitting room; it was well equipped (a generous hospitality tray, an iron and ironing board). Two rooms are in a garden annexe; each has a private terrace. Breakfast is 'delicious'. Advice is given on the excellent walking in the valley.

Horseshoe Road
Radnage
High Wycombe HP14 4EB

T: 01494-483273
E: threehorseshoe@btconnect.com
W: www.thethreehorseshoes.net

BEDROOMS: 6, 2 on ground floor in garden annexe.
OPEN: all year, restaurant closed Sun eve, Mon lunch.
FACILITIES: bar, restaurant, garden.
BACKGROUND MUSIC: in restaurant.
LOCATION: outskirts of village.
CHILDREN: all ages welcomed.
DOGS: allowed (£15 charge), not in restaurant.
CREDIT CARDS: MasterCard, Visa.
PRICES: [2012] B&B £40–£75 per person, set dinner £16–£21, full alc £45, Christmas/New Year packages.

RAMSGILL-IN-NIDDERDALE N. Yorkshire Map 4:D3

THE YORKE ARMS

César award in 2000

By the green in a village below the moors, Bill and Frances Atkins's creeper-covered 18th-century coaching inn has 'a country house party atmosphere which encourages a companionship between guests', says a visitor in 2012. Mr Atkins is the host, assisted by an 'unfailingly pleasant staff who seem to care', in the flagstoned bar and beamed dining room. His wife has a *Michelin* star for her 'brilliant' cooking: 'Her combinations of good ingredients are exciting but well balanced. We enjoyed her six-course truffle dinner; a truffled pea brûlée with asparagus, and langoustine was outstanding.' The produce comes from the Dales; herbs and vegetables are grown in a field behind the inn. Some of the well-equipped bedrooms are small: 'Ours might not have been spacious but it was comfortable; the bathroom was modern.' Four two-storey suites are in a courtyard building; a two-bedroom cottage (200 yards from the inn) has a private garden and terrace. Other comments: 'Hard to fault'; 'Good if pricey'. The Gouthwaite Reservoir bird sanctuary is nearby. (*David Hampshire, John and Haf Davies-Humphreys, and others*)

Ramsgill-in-Nidderdale
nr Harrogate HG3 5RL

T: 01423-755243
F: 01423-755330
E: enquiries@yorke-arms.co.uk
W: www.yorke-arms.co.uk

BEDROOMS: 16, 2 in *Ghyll Cottage*.
OPEN: all year, Sun dinner for residents only.
FACILITIES: ramp, lounge, bar, 2 dining rooms, function facilities, 2-acre grounds, unsuitable for ♿.
BACKGROUND MUSIC: classical in dining rooms.
LOCATION: centre of village, train from Harrogate.
CHILDREN: not under 12.
DOGS: allowed by arrangement in 1 bedroom, not in public rooms.
CREDIT CARDS: Diners, MasterCard, Visa.
PRICES: [2012] D,B&B £150–£200 per person, tasting menu £85, full alc £80, winter offers, Christmas/New Year packages.

RAVENSTONEDALE Cumbria

Map 4:C3

THE BLACK SWAN

César award: pub-with-rooms of the year
'Warm, friendly and very well run', Alan and Louise Dinnes's restored Victorian pub in a village near Kirkby Stephen is much liked by readers, not least for its 'remarkable value'. 'What a joy to find it in such exuberant form,' say returning guests this year. 'They are hands-on owners; the staff are interested in their guests.' The Dinneses have made the pub the hub of local life: its bars 'are well patronised'; they run the village shop on the ground floor. 'The bedrooms are all different: mine had a private bathroom across the passage, another small room had a splendid view to Wild Boar Fell.' Two ground-floor rooms are suitable for visitors with mobility problems; one is being given a wet room fully equipped for the disabled. Chef Kev Hillyer serves 'artisan dishes' on a seasonal menu (with daily specials). 'The choice is varied: I particularly enjoyed garlic mushrooms in a Stilton sauce; belly of lamb came with excellent vegetables and scrumptious chips. Simpler alternatives are available. Substantial breakfasts also have a daily special (eg, smoked salmon and scrambled eggs).'
(Trevor Lockwood, Ian Dewey)

25% DISCOUNT VOUCHERS

Ravenstonedale
Kirkby Stephen CA17 4NG

T/F: 015396-23204
E: enquiries@blackswanhotel.com
W: www.blackswanhotel.com

BEDROOMS: 14, 2 in ground-floor annexe, 1 suitable for ♿.
OPEN: all year.
FACILITIES: bar, lounge, 2 dining rooms, beer garden, tennis and golf in village.
BACKGROUND MUSIC: optional 'easy listening' in bar, restaurant.
LOCATION: in village 5 miles SW of Kirkby Stephen.
CHILDREN: all ages welcomed.
DOGS: allowed in 2 bedrooms, not in restaurant.
CREDIT CARDS: Amex, MasterCard, Visa.
PRICES: [2012] B&B £40–£70 per person, full alc £26, Christmas/New Year packages.

REETH North Yorkshire

Map 4:C3

THE BURGOYNE

NEW

At the top of the green of a 'beautiful' village in Herriot country, this Georgian Grade II listed country house was bought by Mo and Julia Osman in May 2011. 'She is a hands-on hostess who runs the hotel with a happy staff,' say inspectors in 2012, restoring the *Burgoyne* to the *Guide*. The two lounges, which have original features ('fancy' cornices, carved stone ceilings, fine joinery), are 'well furnished'. Dinner is a 'delight' in the dining room (green walls, white linen cloths, good crockery and glasses). Chef Paul Salonga's daily-changing menu might include mango and papaya, prawns, curried mayonnaise; guineafowl cooked in orange and sherry, cinnamon and medjool dates. 'Our exceptionally comfortable room had a super-king-size bed, a settee, writing desk, retro-style wardrobe and chest of drawers; a generous hospitality tray; sheets and blankets were provided at turn-down when we asked for them; a high standard of housekeeping.' Breakfast has 'a fresh fruit salad with a myriad of fruits, a lovely rich plain yogurt; unlimited toast; a wide choice of dishes promptly and well cooked'. Packed lunches are available on request.

On the Green, Reeth
nr Richmond DL11 6SN

T/F: 01748-884292
E: enquiries@theburgoyne.co.uk
W: www.theburgoyne.co.uk

BEDROOMS: 8, 1 on ground floor suitable for ♿.
OPEN: all year, except Christmas.
FACILITIES: ramp, 2 lounges, dining room, ½-acre garden.
BACKGROUND MUSIC: 'quietly' in evening in public rooms.
LOCATION: village centre.
CHILDREN: under-10s only by arrangement.
DOGS: allowed in bedrooms, 1 lounge.
CREDIT CARDS: MasterCard, Visa.
PRICES: [2012] B&B £64–£120 per person, D,B&B from £120, full alc £45, New Year package, winter breaks, 1-night bookings sometimes refused Sat.

RICHMOND North Yorkshire

Map 4:C3

MILLGATE HOUSE

César award in 2011

'Helpful, friendly, and passionate about their home and garden', former teachers Austin Lynch and Tim Culkin run their early Georgian house off the town's market square as a B&B. They have decorated it in idiosyncratic style: 'It's as if a blizzard of antiques, paintings and souvenirs has blown through the elegant drawing room; the end result is impressive,' said a reporter. Two of the three bedrooms overlook the award-winning walled garden: 'Our huge room had double-aspect windows with views of the castle and the rushing river below; it had comfy chairs, a bookcase of tempting titles.' Two rooms have en suite facilities (one with a massive seven-foot claw-footed bath); the third has its own private bathroom. The apartment on the lower ground floor has direct access to the garden, which is open to the public between April and October. Breakfast is 'a fantastic spread' – a buffet of fresh fruit, croissants, cereals, seeds and yogurts; hot food is cooked to order. Dogs are welcome (*Millgate*'s owners have three whippets). A set dinner is available for groups of 16 or more.

Richmond DL10 4JN

T: 01748-823571
E: oztim@millgatehouse.demon.co.uk
W: www.millgatehouse.com

BEDROOMS: 3, also self-catering facilities for 12.
OPEN: all year.
FACILITIES: hall, drawing room, dining room, ⅓-acre garden, unsuitable for ♿.
BACKGROUND MUSIC: occasional classical in hall.
LOCATION: town centre.
CHILDREN: all ages welcomed.
DOGS: not in public rooms.
CREDIT CARDS: none.
PRICES: B&B [2012] £55–£72.50 per person, Christmas/New Year packages.

RICHMOND-UPON-THAMES Surrey

Map 2:D3

BINGHAM

NEW

A conversion of two Georgian houses with a walled garden bordering the Thames, this small hotel/restaurant has been given an elegant, modern look by the owners, the Trinder family. Samantha Fitzgerald is the manager. The 'opulent' public rooms are at the back, 'making the most of a wonderful setting', say inspectors in 2012. A 'magnificent' bar/lounge has a double-height ceiling, mirrored walls, a glass chandelier, silver-leaf ceiling; drinks, afternoon tea and light meals can be taken here. In the plush dining room (heavy silk curtains, a gold fabric mural), Shay Cooper is the chef: 'We enjoyed a superb meal with distinct flavours coming through in some elaborate dishes: Cornish turbot with light shrimp and pork dumplings; roast pork and seaweed consommé; service was attentive.' Some of the bedrooms are small; the best ones face the river. 'Our compact room had a sofa at the end of the large bed; lighting was too dim for reading; a well-equipped bathroom.' Breakfast 'lived up to the standard of dinner; a lovely mango and banana smoothie; fine leaf tea, toast from home-baked bread; tasty cooked ingredients'.

61–63 Petersham Road
Richmond-upon-Thames
TW10 6UT

T: 020-8940 0902
E: info@thebingham.co.uk
W: www.thebingham.co.uk

BEDROOMS: 15.

OPEN: all year, restaurant closed Sun evening.

FACILITIES: bar, restaurant, function room, civil wedding licence, terrace, garden, unsuitable for ♿.

BACKGROUND MUSIC: in restaurant.

LOCATION: ½ mile S of centre, underground Richmond.

CHILDREN: all ages welcomed.

DOGS: not allowed.

CREDIT CARDS: all major cards.

PRICES: [2012] room £170–£285 per person, D,B&B £140–£187.50, breakfast £11–£15, set dinner £45–£65, Christmas/New Year packages, special breaks.

RIPLEY North Yorkshire

Map 4:D4

THE BOAR'S HEAD

César award in 1999

In a village 'steeped in history' on the Ripley Castle estate, this 300-year-old coaching inn has been renovated by Sir Thomas and Lady Ingilby. 'Our experience was very good indeed,' say visitors this year, who stayed in 'a dog-friendly room complete with basket and drinking bowl'. Guests whose visit overlapped with a wedding at the castle were less happy. The bedrooms, designed by Lady Ingilby, vary in size: 'We stayed in the beautiful Cayton Room overlooking the market square. It was clean and spacious, with a luxuriously large bed.' Ten rooms face a courtyard; six are in an adjacent house. The lounges have antiques, period furniture and paintings (some from the castle's attic). In the two dining rooms, locally sourced and seasonal food is served. In the formal restaurant, chef Kevin Kindland's modern menus might include black pudding potato cakes; honey-roasted pork chops with cider potato fondant and apple purée. 'The food was divine, the service warm and attentive.' Breakfast is 'first class'. Guests have free access to Ripley Castle and gardens. (*Nichola Pemberton, Gordon Mursell, and others*)

Ripley Castle Estate, Ripley
nr Harrogate HG3 3AY

T: 01423-771888
F: 01423-771509
E: reservations@boarsheadripley.co.uk
W: www.boarsheadripley.co.uk

BEDROOMS: 25, 10 in courtyard, 6 in Birchwood House adjacent, some on ground floor.
OPEN: all year.
FACILITIES: ramps, 2 lounges, bar/bistro, restaurant, civil wedding licence (in castle), 150-acre estate (deer park, lake, fishing, 20-acre garden).
BACKGROUND MUSIC: 'easy listening' in restaurant and bistro.
LOCATION: 3 miles N of Harrogate.
CHILDREN: all ages welcomed.
DOGS: allowed.
CREDIT CARDS: all major cards.
PRICES: B&B £50–£75 per person, D,B&B £75–£95, full alc £32, Christmas/New Year packages.

ROMALDKIRK Co. Durham

Map 4:C3

THE ROSE AND CROWN

César award in 2003

Beside a Saxon church opposite the green of a Teesdale village (where the stocks still stand), this 18th-century coaching inn is owned and run by Christopher and Alison Davy; Matt Scott is the manager. 'We have been staying for 12 years and it has been consistently great in all that time,' say visitors this year. 'It may be expensive, but the young manager and the staff are perfect; we cannot fault the accommodation or the food.' Mr Davy and Andrew Lee cook modern dishes with a regional influence, eg, loin of venison, potato rösti, wild mushroom jus. A brasserie menu is available in the bar, which has oak beams, old farming implements, log fires. The 'warm and comfortable' bedrooms in the main house are furnished with antiques; two have a private sitting room. The style is contemporary in five rooms in a rear courtyard, which are popular with dog owners and walkers because of the direct access to the car park. There is good walking, mountain biking, shooting and fishing in the area. (*David Ribble, and others*)

25% DISCOUNT VOUCHERS

Romaldkirk
nr Barnard Castle
DL12 9EB

T: 01833-650213
F: 01833-650828
E: hotel@rose-and-crown.co.uk
W: www.rose-and-crown.co.uk

BEDROOMS: 12, 5 in rear courtyard, some ground floor.
OPEN: all year except 24–26 Dec.
FACILITIES: residents' lounge, lounge bar, *Crown Room* (bar meals), restaurant, fishing (grouse shooting, birdwatching) nearby.
BACKGROUND MUSIC: none.
LOCATION: village centre.
CHILDREN: all ages welcomed.
DOGS: allowed in bar, not unattended in bedrooms.
CREDIT CARDS: MasterCard, Visa.
PRICES: [2012] B&B £75–£125 per person, D,B&B £110–£160, set dinner £35, winter discounts, New Year package.

ROSS-ON-WYE Herefordshire

Map 3:D5

WILTON COURT

In an 'excellent position with good views' on the banks of the River Wye, this pink stone building (part Elizabethan) is run as a restaurant-with-rooms by Helen and Roger Wynn. 'We were impressed with the welcome, and enjoyed our stay; the cost was reasonable,' say visitors this year. The building, once a magistrates' court, has many original features (wood panelling, leaded windows, uneven floors) to which the owners have added curios and objets d'art collected during their time working in hotels in the Far East. This year they have redecorated another bedroom, and replaced carpets and windows. The bedrooms, which overlook the river or the gardens, have patterned carpets and bold printed wallpaper; some have exposed beams and an original fireplace. 'Ours was well furnished but rather small for two people and two dogs.' In the 'attractive' conservatory dining room ('plenty of space between tables'), Martyn Williams is the chef. 'He produced interesting and tasty dishes, particularly for fish eaters like us', perhaps grilled stone bass, braised baby gem, broad beans, brown shrimp. 'Our dogs were made most welcome.' (*Simon Rodway*)

25% DISCOUNT VOUCHERS

Wilton Lane, Ross-on-Wye
HR9 6AQ

T: 01989-562569
F: 01989-768460
E: info@wiltoncourthotel.com
W: www.wiltoncourthotel.com

BEDROOMS: 10.
OPEN: all year except 2–15 Jan.
FACILITIES: sitting room, bar, restaurant, private dining room, conference facilities, civil wedding licence, 2-acre grounds (riverside garden, fishing), only restaurant suitable for ♿.
BACKGROUND MUSIC: classical at mealtimes in restaurant/bar.
LOCATION: ½ mile from centre.
CHILDREN: all ages welcomed.
DOGS: not allowed in restaurant.
CREDIT CARDS: Amex, MasterCard, Visa.
PRICES: [2012] B&B £67.50–£155 per person, D,B&B £92.50–£175, full alc £45, special breaks, Christmas/New Year packages, 1-night bookings refused weekends Apr–Nov.

SEE ALSO SHORTLIST

RUSHLAKE GREEN East Sussex

Map 2:E4

STONE HOUSE

25% DISCOUNT VOUCHERS

Down a long, meandering driveway, this country hotel stands in 'rambling', extensive grassland in a tranquil East Sussex village. A Tudor manor house with Georgian additions, it has been in Jane and Peter Dunn's family for more than five centuries. A visitor from the US in 2012 enjoyed 'the hospitality of the house'. Another comment: 'Peter Dunn is an attentive host who offers a warm welcome.' The house is decorated with family antiques and vintage fabrics; the spacious public rooms have log fires ('even in August'). 'Every bedroom is comfortable and different', whether in the grand Georgian wing or the Tudor section, where smaller rooms have beams and sloping ceiling. In the 'beautifully kept gardens', a walled potager and summer orchard provide vegetables, herbs and fruit for the kitchen: 'The great variety of fresh, healthy vegetables made you look forward to dinner.' Mrs Dunn's 'superb meals' might include nettle tip and wild garlic soup, rosemary croutons; roast South Down partridge, wild rice, parsnip slivers. A picnic can be provided for Glyndebourne, 20 minutes' drive away. (*Keith Irvine, JW*)

Rushlake Green
Heathfield TN21 9QJ

T: 01435-830553
F: 01435-830726
W: www.stonehousesussex.co.uk

BEDROOMS: 6, plus 2 in coach house.

OPEN: all year except 22 Dec–3 Jan, 20 Feb–20 Mar.

FACILITIES: hall, drawing room, library, dining room, billiard room, 1,000-acre estate (5½-acre garden, farm, woodland, croquet, shooting, pheasant/clay-pigeon shooting, 2 lakes, rowing, fishing), unsuitable for ♿.

BACKGROUND MUSIC: none.

LOCATION: 4 miles SE of Heathfield, by village green.

CHILDREN: not under 9.

DOGS: not allowed in public rooms.

CREDIT CARDS: MasterCard, Visa.

PRICES: B&B £74–£140 per person, set dinner from £30, weekend house parties, winter breaks, cookery courses, 1-night bookings refused Sat.

RYE East Sussex

Map 2:E5

THE GEORGE IN RYE

The owners, Alex and Katie Clarke, have added ten rooms this year in a new block in the courtyard of this 16th-century coaching inn which they have given a vibrant modern make-over. They have made 'lovely use of bright colours' in the new rooms, which have 'a pleasant view' of the back streets of the old town. The bedrooms in the main building vary considerably in size (and price). They have a mix of solid wooden furnishings, grey and beige walls, 'spot use of primary colours'. A superior room was 'good, especially the recently refurbished bathroom'. An attic room was the 'size of a shoebox, perfectly formed, with a bed that almost filled the space'. The beamed bar is popular with locals (and can be noisy). The unpretentious cooking of the chef, Andy Billings, was liked this year: his all-day menu in the *George Grill* (leather banquettes, wooden tables) might include potted shrimps, caper and fennel salad; and, from the wood charcoal oven, Romney Marsh leg of lamb, roast garlic jus. A reporter remarked on the 'cheery staff' but one couple found the service 'dozy'.

25% DISCOUNT VOUCHERS

98 High Street
Rye TN31 7JT

T: 01797-222114
F: 01797-224065
E: stay@thegeorgeinrye.com
W: www.thegeorgeinrye.com

BEDROOMS: 34, 16 in annexe.

OPEN: all year.

FACILITIES: sitting room, lounge/bar, restaurant, ballroom, civil wedding licence, terrace, courtyard garden, unsuitable for ♿.

BACKGROUND MUSIC: 'easy listening' in public rooms.

LOCATION: town centre, pay-and-display car park nearby.

CHILDREN: all ages welcomed.

DOGS: 'well-behaved' dogs allowed in bar/lounge/courtyard.

CREDIT CARDS: all major cards (*3% surcharge for Amex*).

PRICES: [2012] B&B £67.50–£147.50 per person, D,B&B £92.50–£172.50 (min. 2 nights Sun–Thurs), full alc £50, special breaks, Christmas/New Year packages, £50 supplement for 1-night bookings Sat.

SEE ALSO SHORTLIST

RYE East Sussex

Map 2:E5

JEAKE'S HOUSE

César award in 1992

'As welcoming and comfortable as ever', Jenny Hadfield's much-loved B&B is a gabled 16th-century house created from three adjoining buildings, one of which was a hospital during the Napoleonic wars. 'She ensures that everything is in good order, and that the needs of visitors are satisfied,' says a returning visitor this year. The bedrooms are reached along a warren of corridors (some are up steep staircases – luggage is always carried). Some rooms are named after the literary figures who congregated here when the house was owned by the American poet Conrad Aitken. Although wooden floors have settled, in some rooms, 'it is an uphill walk to bed'; some rooms have low beams. The bar/lounge is 'delightful'; an honesty bar is 'useful before departing for dinner' at one of Rye's many restaurants. In the galleried dining room (once a Quaker meeting house, later a Baptist chapel), breakfast has a sideboard buffet of juices and seasonal fruit dishes; the cooked options include devilled kidneys; Rye rarebit. Parking, difficult in Rye, can be arranged in a private car park (for a small charge). (*Michael Green*)

Mermaid Street
Rye TN31 7ET

T: 01797-222828
E: stay@jeakeshouse.com
W: www.jeakeshouse.com

BEDROOMS: 11.
OPEN: all year.
FACILITIES: parlour, bar/library, breakfast room, unsuitable for ♿.
BACKGROUND MUSIC: classical in breakfast room.
LOCATION: central, car park (£3 per 24 hours, advance booking needed).
CHILDREN: not under 8.
DOGS: allowed, on leads 'and always supervised'.
CREDIT CARDS: MasterCard, Visa.
PRICES: [2012] B&B £45–£64 per person, 2-night midweek breaks Nov–Mar, Christmas/New Year packages, 1-night bookings sometimes refused busy weekends.

SEE ALSO SHORTLIST

ST HILARY Cornwall

Map 1:E1

ENNYS

'This exceptionally nice place', a creeper-covered 17th-century manor house, is run as a stylish B&B by travel writer Gill Charlton. Standing in a 'lovely' garden with exotic plants, it has a secluded setting amid fields that lead to the River Hayle. 'Definitely five stars,' says a visitor in 2012. 'So much stands out: newly made scones and a pot of tea when we arrived back in the afternoon; clean linen every day; lots of fascinating artefacts around the house that Gill has brought back on her travels.' There are books on the area and original artwork in the 'delightful' large sitting room; a log fire on colder days. The bedrooms in the main house have a larger-than-average bed ('super comfortable,' said an earlier visitor). There are two spacious suites in a converted barn; each has a sitting room and kitchenette, and its own entrance. Breakfast has home-made muesli and fresh fruit salad; organic ingredients in the cooked dishes. There is much to do locally: 'excellent information in the bedroom about good places to eat, walks, drives'. Guests have use of an outdoor swimming pool. (*Virginia Lynch*)

Trewhella Lane, St Hilary
nr Penzance TR20 9BZ

T: 01736-740262
F: 01736-740055
E: ennys@ennys.co.uk
W: www.ennys.co.uk

BEDROOMS: 5, 2 in barn, 3 self-catering apartments (can be B&B off-season).

OPEN: Apr–Oct.

FACILITIES: sitting room, breakfast room, 3-acre grounds (tennis, 13-metre heated swimming pool), unsuitable for ♿.

BACKGROUND MUSIC: none.

LOCATION: 5 miles E of Penzance.

CHILDREN: not under 16.

DOGS: not allowed.

CREDIT CARDS: MasterCard, Visa.

PRICES: B&B £50–£95 per person, 1-night bookings refused high season, bank holidays.

ST IVES Cornwall

Map 1:D1

BOSKERRIS HOTEL

In a suburban setting above Carbis Bay, Jonathan and Marianne Bassett have given their small hotel (built in the 1930s) a cool, contemporary feel. 'The staff have a refreshing attitude of "how can we help?"' say inspectors in 2012. The 'immaculate' open-plan lounge has comfortable sofas; it opens on to decking with smart outdoor seating. From here, visitors enjoy 'the compelling view' of the bay. Most of the bedrooms have a sea view; all have muted colours, tea- and coffee-making facilities; a modern bathroom. One of the 'celebration' rooms has a sunken corner bath by a window, and a separate wet room with a rain shower. In a 'lovely, light' dining room, an informal Mediterranean supper (eg, carpaccio of beef, horseradish celeriac; lamb tagine, buttered couscous) is served every evening except Sunday; the wine list includes Cornish wines. Notes about local restaurants are sent with confirmation of the booking. Local trains to St Ives can be caught at the station below the hotel. A large map of Cornwall gives suggestions of places to visit.

25% DISCOUNT VOUCHERS

Boskerris Road
Carbis Bay
St Ives TR26 2NQ

T: 01736-795295
E: reservations@boskerrishotel.co.uk
W: www.boskerrishotel.co.uk

BEDROOMS: 15, 1 on ground floor.
OPEN: mid-Feb–mid-Nov, restaurant closed Sun.
FACILITIES: lounges, bar, restaurant, private dining/meeting room, decked terrace, 1½-acre garden.
BACKGROUND MUSIC: jazz/Latin.
LOCATION: 1½ miles from centre (5 mins by local train), car park.
CHILDREN: not under 7.
DOGS: not allowed.
CREDIT CARDS: MasterCard, Visa.
PRICES: [2012] B&B £57.50–£120 per person, full alc £30, 1-night bookings refused in high season, bank holidays.

SEE ALSO SHORTLIST

ST LEONARDS-ON-SEA East Sussex

Map 2:E4

HASTINGS HOUSE

On a garden square by the seafront, this white stuccoed Victorian house is run as a B&B by owner Seng Loy. 'Highly recommended,' says a visitor this year. 'The place is immaculately clean with a very modern, stylish decor. The owner helped arrange secure parking, and greeted us with a welcoming drink after our long journey.' The bedrooms have bold colours and striking designs; some have a sea view; all have large windows. Room 7, in dusty pinks and Sahara browns, can accommodate two adults and a child. Room 5 ('lovely') has black and brown leather furnishings; a view of the pier. Little touches (flowers in the room, complimentary refreshments) are appreciated. The lounge has a marble-topped bar, a widescreen TV with DVDs; the dining room, which overlooks the garden with views out to sea, has slate mats on dark wood tables, leather chairs, linen napkins. Breakfast has organic apple juice, freshly cut fruits, and cereals; cooked choices include smoked salmon and scrambled eggs; French toast. Bread comes from a local bakery. An evening meal can be arranged if requested when booking.

25% DISCOUNT VOUCHERS

9 Warrior Square
St Leonards-on-Sea TN37 6BA

T: 01424-422709
F: 01424-420592
E: info@hastingshouse.co.uk
W: www.hastingshouse.co.uk

BEDROOMS: 8.
OPEN: all year.
FACILITIES: bar/lounge, dining room, small terrace, unsuitable for ♿.
BACKGROUND MUSIC: jazz in bar/lounge.
LOCATION: seafront, 1 mile from town centre.
CHILDREN: all ages welcomed.
DOGS: allowed in public areas only.
CREDIT CARDS: Amex, MasterCard, Visa.
PRICES: B&B £49.50–£70 per person, 1-night bookings refused weekends and bank holidays.

ST LEONARDS-ON-SEA East Sussex

Map 2:E4

ZANZIBAR INTERNATIONAL HOTEL

On the seafront at the quiet, 'posh' end of Hastings, Max O'Rourke has turned this five-storey Victorian town house into a 'boutique B&B with an exceptionally good restaurant'. *Guide* inspectors in 2012 were 'greeted on the seafront by the chatty manageress, who helped with the suitcase and pointed us to the nearest free parking'. The bedrooms are named after continents and countries: 'The theming hasn't been overdone: India has modern Indian wooden furniture, big table lamps (good for reading), framed silver necklaces, an antique mirror; white floorboards and wooden floors. A vast bed; twin basins and a powerful spa bath in the bathroom.' All rooms have hospitality tray, bathrobes, TV and beach towels. The restaurant, *Pier Nine at Zanzibar*, has an 'appealing south coast Boho' feel. The chef, Ben Krikorian, serves a contemporary British menu: 'The unusual flavour combinations worked well; a melting beef carpaccio was perfectly balanced by a Stilton and tarragon mousse; a creamy anchovy vinaigrette didn't overpower the John Dory; a white chocolate cheesecake was intensely satisfying; low-volume background music.'

9 Eversfield Place
St Leonards-on-Sea
TN37 6BY

T: 01424-460109
E: info@zanzibarhotel.co.uk
W: www.zanzibarhotel.co.uk

BEDROOMS: 8, 1 on ground floor.
OPEN: all year, restaurant closed Mon.
FACILITIES: lounge, bar, restaurant, conservatory, small garden, beach across road, unsuitable for ♿.
BACKGROUND MUSIC: in bar, restaurant.
LOCATION: seafront, 650 yds W of Hastings pier, free parking vouchers issued.
CHILDREN: not under 5.
DOGS: not allowed.
CREDIT CARDS: Amex, MasterCard, Visa.
PRICES: [2012] B&B £49.50–£105 per person, full alc £30, special breaks, Christmas/New Year packages, 1-night bookings often refused Sat.

ST MARY'S Isles of Scilly

Map 1: inset C1

STAR CASTLE

César award in 2009

In a commanding position above Hugh Town, this star-shaped Tudor fortress, with additional rooms in single-storey buildings in the grounds, is owned by the Francis family; James Francis runs front-of-house with a long-serving staff. Guests are met at the harbour or airport. Bedrooms in the castle have bold colours and dark furniture in keeping with the building's age. The garden rooms are built around lawns and flowerbeds; each has a veranda. 'The view of the seascape of islands from our garden room more than compensated for the sometimes blustery walk from the main building,' say visitors this year. 'The room was smallish but had everything you need – comfortable bed, decent lighting, a tea tray.' The chef, Gareth Stafford, serves 'beautifully presented and imaginative' English/French dishes in the *Castle* restaurant, once the officers' mess, eg, roast saddle of rabbit stuffed with spinach, pine nuts and blue cheese. In summer, seafood is a speciality in the more informal *Conservatory*. At breakfast, James Francis provides a weather report, while Tim, the boatman, outlines his itinerary for the day. (*Jill and Mike Bennett, and others*)

The Garrison, St Mary's
Isles of Scilly
Cornwall TR21 0JA

T: 01720-422317
F: 01720-422343
E: info@star-castle.co.uk
W: www.star-castle.co.uk

BEDROOMS: 38, 27 in 2 garden wings.

OPEN: Feb–Dec, New Year.

FACILITIES: lounge, bar, 2 restaurants, civil wedding licence, 3-acre grounds (covered swimming pool, 12 by 3 metres, tennis), beach nearby, unsuitable for ♿.

BACKGROUND MUSIC: none.

LOCATION: ¼ mile from town centre, boat (2¾ hours)/helicopter (20 mins) from Penzance, air links.

CHILDREN: not under 5 in restaurants.

DOGS: not allowed in restaurants.

CREDIT CARDS: Amex, MasterCard, Visa.

PRICES: [2012] B&B £86–£184 per person, D,B&B £96–£194, set dinner £36.50–£42.50, short breaks, Christmas/New Year packages.

ST MAWES Cornwall

Map 1:E2

TRESANTON

César award in 2009

'A very special place', Olga Polizzi's stylish hotel spreads across a cluster of buildings (converted cottages and a former yacht club) on a hillside overlooking the Fal estuary. 'A lovely hotel with spectacular views and brilliant staff,' says a visitor this year. All the bedrooms, which are in five separate buildings (some reached by flights of stairs, 'quite a climb'), have the view; some have a private terrace. They are individually furnished with antiques and Cornish artwork. 'Ours was spacious and beautiful, with its own balcony overlooking the river.' The dining room, all white, has a Mediterranean atmosphere and a terrace on two sides where drinks and candlelit dinners are served in summer. 'The most delicious food', cooked by chef Paul Wadham, 'is great for those who like fish.' The menu might include grilled mackerel, piccalilli and crostini; John Dory with steamed mussels, crab cake and carrots. 'More frequent changes to the menu would make dinner times perfect,' says one visitor. 'It is cooked to order, so don't be in a hurry.' Children are welcomed. (*Juliet Sebag-Montefiore, Paul Ockenden*)

27 Lower Castle Road
St Mawes TR2 5DR

T: 01326-270055
F: 01326-270053
E: info@tresanton.com
W: www.tresanton.com

BEDROOMS: 31, in 5 houses.
OPEN: all year.
FACILITIES: 2 lounges, bar, restaurant, cinema, playroom, conference facilities, civil wedding licence, terrace, ¼-acre garden, by sea (shingle beach, safe bathing, 15-metre yacht), unsuitable for ♿.
BACKGROUND MUSIC: none.
LOCATION: on seafront, valet parking (car park up hill).
CHILDREN: all ages welcomed, not under 6 in restaurant in evening.
DOGS: allowed in 3 bedrooms, not in public rooms.
CREDIT CARDS: Amex, MasterCard, Visa.
PRICES: [2012] B&B £95–£275 per person, set dinner £43.50, special breaks, Christmas/New Year packages, 1-night bookings refused weekends in high season.

SALCOMBE Devon

Map 1:E4

SOUTH SANDS

'An informal atmosphere, smart yet relaxed' prevails at this wood-clad hotel 'almost on the beach with its big tides, sea tractors and views across the estuary'. It has been decked out in New England style with a battleship-grey weatherboard exterior; marine pastels in the interior. The 'no-nonsense' decor ('not designer, just contemporary good taste') impressed inspectors, as did the check-in. 'We were asked whether we wanted newspapers and a turn-down service.' Stephen Ball is now the manager. The bedrooms have pale wood, white walls, 'good storage space with free-range coat-hangers'. The best (and most expensive rooms) overlook the beach; valley rooms at the back could be noisy. The large public area has a bar, restaurant and a sea-facing terrace (no separate sitting room). In the beachside restaurant (wooden floors, low ceilings, and loud music), Stuart Downie is the chef: his menu includes 'today's local seafood', perhaps lemon sole, capers and shrimps, buttered new potatoes. Breakfast has 'a smallish buffet, decent toast, croissants, etc; fine haddock and poached egg'. Children are welcomed (special menus, babysitters), as are dogs (bowls and biscuits).

Bolt Head
Salcombe TQ8 8LL

T: 01548-859000
E: enquiries@southsands.com
W: www.southsands.com

BEDROOMS: 27, 5 beach apartments at side, 2 suitable for ♿.
OPEN: all year.
FACILITIES: bar, restaurant, civil wedding licence, terrace.
BACKGROUND MUSIC: in restaurant and bar area.
LOCATION: 1 mile S of Salcombe.
CHILDREN: all ages welcomed.
DOGS: allowed in some bedrooms.
CREDIT CARDS: Diners, MasterCard, Visa.
PRICES: B&B £75–£217.50 per person, full alc £45, special breaks, Christmas/New Year packages, 1-night bookings refused weekends in peak season.

SALCOMBE Devon

Map 1:E4

THE TIDES REACH

Owned by the Edwards family for three generations, this traditional hotel is popular with readers who like the situation (opposite South Sands beach) and the 'attentive' service. The purpose-built 1960s building might reflect its age but visitors who felt in a time warp in the entrance were enthusiastic about their 'attractively furnished' bedroom: 'You could see the sea across a large balcony without getting out of bed.' Children aged eight and over can be accommodated in two-bedroom family suites. In the restaurant, chef Finn Ibsen serves a daily-changing menu with an emphasis on fish caught locally; his 'excellent' dishes might include razor clams steamed in cider with leeks, spinach and cream; Exmoor venison steak, plum chutney, red onion 'tarte Tatin'. Lunch can be taken in a sun lounge or in the 'relaxing' garden (which has a large duck pond). Breakfast, a leisurely affair, has a daily fresh fish option. It can also be enjoyed alfresco. The 'traditions' will appeal to an older generation, said one visitor. The South Sands ferry sails from the beach to Salcombe quay. (*APM, and others*)

South Sands
Salcombe TQ8 8LJ

T: 01548-843466
F: 01548-843954
E: enquire@tidesreach.com
W: www.tidesreach.com

BEDROOMS: 32.

OPEN: Feb–Nov.

FACILITIES: lift, ramps, 3 lounges, 2 bars, restaurant, leisure centre (indoor swimming pool, 13 by 6 metres, gym, games room, beauty treatments), ½-acre grounds (pond), sandy beach 10 yds, unsuitable for ♿.

BACKGROUND MUSIC: none.

LOCATION: on Salcombe estuary, 1 mile from town.

CHILDREN: not under 8.

DOGS: allowed in some bedrooms, 1 lounge.

CREDIT CARDS: all major cards.

PRICES: [2012] B&B £63–£155 per person, D,B&B £73–£175, set dinner £34.50, special breaks, 1-night bookings sometimes refused.

SANDWICH Kent

Map 2:D5

THE SALUTATION

'Stunning, immaculate, romantic; we've run out of adjectives to describe the quality of accommodation at this impeccable B&B, the finest we've ever experienced.' *Guide* inspectors were much taken with this mansion beside the original town wall in a 'fascinating' Cinque port. Designed in 1912 by Sir Edwin Lutyens as a weekend retreat for the Farrar family, the main house remains the home of Dominic and Stephanie Parker. Guests are welcomed in three restored cottages in a large enclosed gravel courtyard (which has parking, and a tea room). *Knightrider House* has four bedrooms and three bathrooms; *Gardener's Cottage* has three bedrooms and one bathroom. Two en suite bedrooms are in the *Coach House*. Rooms without a private bathroom are usually let to groups of friends. Children of all ages are now welcomed. 'Our bedroom in *Gardener's Cottage* had a wooden sleigh bed, dressing table, sumptuous curtains; fresh flowers and mineral water. The kitchen was exceptionally well equipped.' Breakfast is taken in the 'grand' dining room of the main house. Guests have free access to the restored 'secret' gardens, which are open to the public.

25% DISCOUNT VOUCHERS

Knightrider Street
Sandwich CT13 9EW

T: 01304-619919
F: 01304-617115
E: dominic@the-salutation.com
W: www.the-salutation.com

BEDROOMS: 9, in three cottages.

OPEN: all year, except Christmas/New Year.

FACILITIES: drawing room, dining room, kitchen in *Knightrider House*, sitting room, kitchen in *Coach House*, sitting room, kitchen, terrace in *Gardener's Cottage*, 3½-acre gardens, unsuitable for ♿.

BACKGROUND MUSIC: none.

LOCATION: town centre.

CHILDREN: all ages welcomed.

DOGS: not allowed.

CREDIT CARDS: Amex, MasterCard, Visa.

PRICES: [2012] B&B £90–£107.50 per person.

SEE ALSO SHORTLIST

SCOTBY Cumbria

Map 4:B2

WILLOWBECK LODGE

'A great place to stop on the way to or from Scotland', this spacious architect-designed building near Carlisle is run by owners John and Liz McGrillis as an upmarket guest house. 'They are friendly and helpful, working hard to assist guests,' writes a visitor. In woodland, with a duck pond and weeping willows, the house is 'very modern; a wonderful galleried dining room has masses of windows allowing you to look at the stars through a powerful telescope'. They have taken 'great care with every detail', says a 2012 guest. Bedrooms are named after trees (Willow, Oak, Ash, etc), and vary in price and size. 'Our room was very nice indeed, newly decorated and furnished to a high standard, with comfortable chairs and plenty of space. The bathroom was bright and well appointed.' Mrs McGrillis cooks a fixed menu in the evenings, which might include stuffed red peppers; salmon marinated in lime juice and grilled. Phone ahead to discuss preferences. Breakfast has a 'well-stocked sideboard with compote, yogurt, cereals, etc; John cooks an excellent full English'. (*Sara Price, Patrick Wilson*)

Lambley Bank
Scotby, nr Carlisle CA4 8BX

T: 01228-513607
F: 01228-501053
E: info@willowbeck-lodge.com
W: www.willowbeck-lodge.com

BEDROOMS: 6, 2 in cottage annexe.

OPEN: all year except 20–28 Dec, restaurant closed Sun.

FACILITIES: lounge, lounge/dining room, conference/function facilities, civil wedding licence, 1½-acre garden (stream, pond), unsuitable for ♿.

BACKGROUND MUSIC: 'at owners' discretion'.

LOCATION: 2½ miles E of Carlisle.

CHILDREN: not under 12.

DOGS: not allowed.

CREDIT CARDS: MasterCard, Visa.

PRICES: [2012] B&B £55–£125 per person, set dinner £30.

SEAVIEW Isle of Wight

Map 2:E3

THE SEAVIEW

'Excellent for grandparents and grandchildren', this informal hotel with a nautical air stands above the beach in a sailing village. Dean Bailey has been promoted to manager this year. All agree the 'welcome is warm': 'A charming girl took us to our room, then lugged up our heavy suitcase; the girl who offered us turn-down was happy to come back later, most unusual.' The bedrooms vary greatly in size and style: 'We had a nice room which had lots of storage space; they put hot-water bottles in our bed, lovely and snuggly.' The public areas have 'lots of character': nautical photographs, a framed letter written from the *Titanic*. The simpler dishes are recommended in the dining rooms; meals are also available in the bars. Some visitors have issues about the speed of service and maintenance in the bedrooms. Inspectors took a broader view: 'One of the functions of the *Guide* is to lead people to nice places, and Seaview is delightful. The atmosphere at the hotel is relaxed and friendly and the spirit is generous; they prided themselves on remembering our likes and dislikes.'

High Street
Seaview PO34 5EX

T: 01983-612711
F: 01983-613729
E: reception@seaviewhotel.co.uk
W: www.seaviewhotel.co.uk

BEDROOMS: 29, 11 in annexe, 4 on ground floor, 1 suitable for ♿.

OPEN: all year except Christmas.

FACILITIES: lift, ramps, lounge, 2 bars, 2 dining rooms, treatment room, function room, patio, access to local sports club (swimming pool, gym, tennis, etc).

BACKGROUND MUSIC: occasionally in 1 bar.

LOCATION: village centre.

CHILDREN: all ages welcomed.

DOGS: allowed.

CREDIT CARDS: all major cards.

PRICES: [2012] B&B £67.50–£122.50 per person, D,B&B £97.50–£152.50, full alc £37.50, website offers, 1-night bookings refused weekends Apr–Oct.

SHAFTESBURY Dorset

Map 2:D1

LA FLEUR DE LYS

In a hilltop market town, this 'delightful' restaurant-with-rooms is a conversion of a girls' boarding school. The ivy-clad mellow stone building is run by David and Mary Griffin-Shepherd and Marc Preston. 'They are hands-on, much in evidence,' says a visitor in 2012. 'The public areas are immaculate; the staff are willing and well trained.' There is a 'welcoming' lounge/bar; pre-dinner drinks (and afternoon tea) can also be taken, in fine weather, in a pretty courtyard garden. The 'well-kept' bedrooms vary in size: 'Although our room was small, it had a wonderful bathroom with piping hot water.' Superior rooms are larger, and have a sofa and a laptop computer. 'Bedroom windows at the front are double glazed to exclude noise from the 'light' traffic. 'Good-quality cooking [by David Griffin-Shepherd and Marc Preston] at dinner and breakfast.' Their dinner menu might include lime-marinated smoked salmon with samphire; honey-roasted breast of local duck, broad beans and spring onions. Breakfast has freshly squeezed orange juice, porridge, butter and marmalade in pots; a choice of cooked dishes. Festival weeks are held. (*Anthony Bradbury, and others*)

Bleke Street
Shaftesbury SP7 8AW

T: 01747-853717
F: 01747-853130
E: info@lafleurdelys.co.uk
W: www.lafleurdelys.co.uk

BEDROOMS: 7, 1 on ground floor.

OPEN: all year, restaurant closed Sun night, midday Mon and Tues.

FACILITIES: lounge, bar, dining room, conference room, small courtyard.

BACKGROUND MUSIC: none.

LOCATION: edge of centre, car park.

CHILDREN: all ages welcomed.

DOGS: not allowed.

CREDIT CARDS: Amex, MasterCard, Visa.

PRICES: [2012] B&B £50–£85 per person, D,B&B £82.50, set meals £27–£33, full alc £45–£55, Christmas/New Year packages.

SHANKLIN Isle of Wight

Map 2:E2

RYLSTONE MANOR

'Great hosts helped by a delightful staff', Mike and Carole Hailston run their Victorian gentleman's house as a small traditional hotel. It stands in the middle of a quiet public park 'with wonderful sea views'. A visitor in 2012 found it 'delightful and comfortable, full of wonderful decorative details'. In the dining room (damask wall covering, a chandelier with matching wall lights), Mr Hailston's daily-changing short menu might include tomato and basil soup; sea bass fillet in a herb crust, Pernod and thyme jus. He tells us that following comments in the *Guide*, background music is no longer played. The green-walled lounge has heavy fabrics, books and ornaments; a Victorian-style covered patio has basket chairs, magazines to read. Each bedroom is named after an English tree. Maple, the largest, has a triangular window seat and alcove with a sofa and easy chair; Beech has a four-poster and dual-aspect windows; Cedar, with bedside cabinets in Shaker style, is the smallest. Breakfast has 'lovely sausages'; local butter is now served (not pre-packed containers). (*Diana Chrzaszcz, and others*)

25% DISCOUNT VOUCHERS

Rylstone Gardens
Popham Road, Shanklin
PO37 6RG

T/F: 01983-862806
E: rylstone.manor@btinternet.com
W: www.rylstone-manor.co.uk

BEDROOMS: 9.
OPEN: 10 Feb–20 Nov.
FACILITIES: drawing room, bar lounge, dining room, terrace, 1-acre garden in 4-acre public gardens, direct access to sand/shingle beach, unsuitable for ♿.
BACKGROUND MUSIC: none.
LOCATION: Shanklin old village.
CHILDREN: not allowed.
DOGS: not allowed.
CREDIT CARDS: MasterCard, Visa.
PRICES: [2012] B&B £67.50–£82.50 per person, D,B&B £96.50–£111.50, set menu £29–£33, website offers, 1-night bookings refused June–Aug and bank holidays (unless space permits).

SHREWSBURY Shropshire

Map 3:B4

LION AND PHEASANT NEW

'A good dining inn with simple modern rooms, in the centre of an interesting town.' Praise from trusted correspondents in 2012 brings an entry for this old inn near the English Bridge, the main Severn crossing into the town. 'The updating has retained the character while providing thoroughly modern facilities. The style is uniform throughout: white walls, rustic doors painted grey, exposed beams, solid wood furniture in natural colours; wooden floors in public areas, coir matting in the bedrooms.' A maze of corridors linked by short flights of steps connects the bars and restaurant; a 'magnificent' staircase leads to the bedrooms: 'Ours had discreet voile curtains, white cotton bedlinen and throws, smart mirrors and stylish electrical appliances; generous goodies in the shower room.' Meals can be taken in one of the bars and in the first-floor dining room (on two levels, with rectangular tables with tea lights): 'The food was excellent: good-sized scallops were interlaced with black pudding; a lovely loin of venison with juniper-infused greens; an excellent crème brûlée. Wooden floors and a low ceiling made it noisy.' (*Ian and Francine Walsh*)

50 Wyle Cop
Shrewsbury SY1 1XJ

T: 01743-770345
F: 01743-770350
E: info@lionandpheasant.co.uk
W: www.lionandpheasant.co.uk

BEDROOMS: 22.
OPEN: all year except 25 Dec.
FACILITIES: restaurant, 3 bars, function room, unsuitable for ♿.
BACKGROUND MUSIC: in public areas.
LOCATION: central, near English Bridge.
CHILDREN: all ages welcomed.
DOGS: not allowed.
CREDIT CARDS: all major cards.
PRICES: [2012] B&B £47.50–£95 per person, full alc £40, special offers, New Year package.

SEE ALSO SHORTLIST

SNETTISHAM Norfolk

Map 2:A4

THE ROSE & CROWN

'In most respects a delight,' says a visitor this year to Jeannette and Anthony Goodrich's 14th-century inn opposite the cricket pitch in a village on the Wash. Although many original features remain – low ceilings, old beams, winding passages, log fires – the bedrooms, in the original part of the building and an extension, have been given a contemporary make-over using bold candy colours. They are well equipped with tea- and coffee-making equipment, books, and a useful guide to the area written by the Goodriches. There is a separate guest lounge, or visitors can sit in one of the three dining areas, which have been refurbished this year. The cellar bar now has a dado rail with a subtle taupe colour; the garden room, popular with families, has new roman blinds and giant photographs of Norfolk beaches and boats. Jamie Clark has been promoted to head chef: he uses local suppliers for his traditional food with a modern twist, and his dishes might include Brancaster mussels in marinière sauce; sweet chilli beef stir fry, udon noodles. The Goodriches also own *The Bank House*, King's Lynn (see entry).

Old Church Road, Snettisham
nr King's Lynn
PE31 7LX

T: 01485-541382
F: 01485-543172
E: info@roseandcrownsnettisham.co.uk
W: www.roseandcrownsnettisham.co.uk

BEDROOMS: 16, 2 suitable for ♿.
OPEN: all year.
FACILITIES: ramp, garden room with guests' seating area, lounge, 3 bars, 3 dining areas, large walled garden (play galleon, barbecue, heat lamps), beaches 5 and 10 mins' drive.
BACKGROUND MUSIC: none.
LOCATION: village centre, 4 miles S of Hunstanton.
CHILDREN: all ages welcomed.
DOGS: allowed.
CREDIT CARDS: all major cards.
PRICES: [2012] B&B £45–£85 per person, D,B&B (Sun–Thurs) £67.50–£95, full alc £32.50, website breaks, Christmas/New Year packages, 1-night bookings occasionally refused bank holiday Sat (supplement charged July/Aug).

SOAR MILL COVE Devon

Map 1:E4

SOAR MILL COVE HOTEL

In 'a stunning location, with wonderful views', Keith Makepeace's family-friendly hotel stands in extensive grounds above a sandy cove in an area of outstanding natural beauty. It has many fans who admire the 'personal attention to detail by staff' and 'the immaculate housekeeping'. Popular with older guests in off-season, it is busy with families in the school holidays. 'We never impose rules, but we try to offer a range of options,' says the hotel. There is much for young people to do: small swimming pools, indoor and outdoor play areas, activity packs, rock pooling on the beach. There are high teas and family dinner times; *Castaways* coffee bar is for 'muddy paws and boots and younger guests'. In the formal *Serendipity* restaurant, chef Ian MacDonald's dinner menus might include a salad of Salcombe scallops with spicy chorizo; grilled fillet of West Country beef, celeriac purée and roasted shallots. 'A continual delight; the fish is always excellent,' says a visitor in 2012. All bedrooms have French doors opening on to a private patio. Breakfast includes fruit, cereals, croissants and a variety of cooked dishes. Walks down to Soar Mill Cove are 'wonderful'. (*Chris Smith, Margaret H Box*)

25% DISCOUNT VOUCHERS

Soar Mill Cove
nr Salcombe TQ7 3DS

T: 01548-561566
F: 01548-561223
E: info@soarmillcove.co.uk
W: www.soarmillcove.co.uk

BEDROOMS: 22, all on ground floor.
OPEN: all year, except 2–31 Jan.
FACILITIES: lounge, 2 bars, restaurant (pianist), coffee shop, indoor swimming pool (10 by 6 metres), treatment room (hairdressing, reflexology, aromatherapy, etc), civil wedding licence, 10-acre grounds (tennis, children's play area), sandy beach, 600 yds.
BACKGROUND MUSIC: piano, twice weekly.
LOCATION: 3 miles SW of Salcombe.
CHILDREN: all ages welcomed.
DOGS: well-behaved small dogs allowed, but not in public rooms other than coffee shop.
CREDIT CARDS: MasterCard, Visa.
PRICES: B&B £70–£140 per person, D,B&B £95–£155, full alc £45, Christmas/New Year packages, 1-night bookings sometimes refused.

SOMERTON Somerset

Map 1:C6

THE LYNCH COUNTRY HOUSE

NEW

In a medieval market town above the Cary valley, this Grade II listed Regency house is managed as a B&B by Mike and Chris McKenzie ('friendly hosts') for the owner, former jazz musician Roy Copeland. It returns to a full entry after positive reports. 'As good as ever, if not better,' says a returning visitor. The house 'feels like a genuine home with family photographs and memorabilia'. The largest bedrooms are on the first floor of the main building: they have high ceiling, large sash windows. One has an antique oak four-poster bed with a full canopy. Two rooms in the eaves have starlight windows; one has an extra bed and a 'campaign couch' for smaller guests, a private bathroom across the landing. Dogs are allowed in four ground-floor rooms in the coach house, which has a separate entrance. Breakfast is served in a 'bright' orangery whose tall windows overlook a lake with black swans. 'Superb: a good selection of cereals, seasonal fresh fruit and juices; the full English had both black and white pudding.' 'Good advice' is given about local eating places. (*David Humphreys, and others*)

4 Behind Berry
Somerton TA11 7PD

T: 01458-272316
F: 01458-272590
E: enquiries@thelynchcountryhouse.co.uk
W: www.thelynchcountryhouse.co.uk

BEDROOMS: 9, 4, in coach house, on ground floor.

OPEN: all year (limited opening at Christmas/New Year).

FACILITIES: breakfast room, small sitting area, 2½-acre grounds (lake), unsuitable for ♿.

BACKGROUND MUSIC: none.

LOCATION: N edge of village.

CHILDREN: all ages welcomed.

DOGS: allowed in coach house, not in public rooms.

CREDIT CARDS: Amex, MasterCard, Visa.

PRICES: B&B £40–£80 per person, 1-night bookings sometimes refused.

STAMFORD Lincolnshire

Map 2:B3

THE GEORGE

César award in 1986

Visitors this year 'loved' the atmosphere of Lawrence Hoskins's 16th-century coaching inn in the centre of the market town on the old Great North Road. It is thought 'excellent if expensive'. Forty coaches a day once stopped here: the doorways on the panelled rooms on either side of the entrance, marked 'York' and 'London', were once waiting rooms. Today they are part of a network of sitting rooms busy with locals and visitors. Afternoon tea is taken seriously with a cake trolley, scones and sandwiches; in warm weather, light meals and teas can be taken at canopied tables in a pretty courtyard. Chris Pitman doubles as manager and executive chef for the dining rooms. Men are asked to wear a jacket and tie in the *George* restaurant, which has an extensive menu of traditional dishes (with modern, international ideas), eg, baked salmon, crisp bacon, pinenuts, beurre noisette. Simpler meals are taken in the *Garden Room*. The largest bedrooms have a four-poster bed, a sitting area; modern bathroom. Other rooms vary considerably: 'Our pleasantly decorated room had a large bathroom.' (*Antony and Barbara Hill*)

71 St Martins
Stamford
PE9 2LB

T: 01780-750750
F: 01780-750701
E: reservations@georgehotelofstamford.com
W: www.georgehotelofstamford.com

BEDROOMS: 47.

OPEN: all year.

FACILITIES: ramps, 2 lounges, 2 bars, 2 restaurants, 4 private dining rooms, business centre, civil wedding licence, 2-acre grounds (courtyard, herb garden, monastery garden, croquet), only public areas suitable for ♿.

BACKGROUND MUSIC: none.

LOCATION: ½ mile from centre (front windows double glazed).

CHILDREN: all ages welcomed.

DOGS: allowed, but not unattended in bedrooms, only guide dogs in restaurants.

CREDIT CARDS: all major cards.

PRICES: [2012] B&B £75–£140 per person, full alc £60, seasonal breaks, 1-night bookings refused Sat.

SEE ALSO SHORTLIST

STANTON WICK Somerset

Map 1:B6

THE CARPENTER'S ARMS

The atmosphere is 'warm and welcoming, with a great big open fire and newspapers' at this pub-with-rooms. It has a 'surprisingly peaceful' rural setting overlooking the Chew valley south of Bristol. Converted from a row of miners' cottages, it has hanging baskets outside 'with cascades of flowers' in summer (a nice place to 'enjoy a drink before dinner'). The bedrooms are 'simple, modern': 'Our large double was well presented, with light wood furniture and a two-seater sofa. A comfy bed with quality linen; not a cobweb in sight. Fresh milk with the tea/coffee tray was a joy, but no water, alas. All was silent at night.' 'Piping hot water in our all-tiled bathroom.' In the two eating areas, chef Chris Dando serves 'generous portions' of 'honest, tasty dishes, not messed about', eg, breaded pan-roasted pork loin, fondant potato, spinach. Breakfast was 'good, with quick and efficient service'. 'Very good value,' said a regular correspondent. 'It does its job well' (an inspector's view). Guests' cars are secured in a yard at night. (*Jeanette Bloor, Ken and Mildred Edwards, and others*)

Stanton Wick, nr Pensford
BS39 4BX

T: 01761-490202
F: 01761-490763
E: carpenters@buccaneer.co.uk
W: www.the-carpenters-arms.co.uk

BEDROOMS: 12.
OPEN: all year except 25/26 Dec, 1 Jan.
FACILITIES: bar, 2 restaurants, function room, patio, unsuitable for ♿.
BACKGROUND MUSIC: none.
LOCATION: 8 miles S of Bristol, 8 miles W of Bath.
CHILDREN: all ages welcomed.
DOGS: allowed in bar only.
CREDIT CARDS: Amex, MasterCard, Visa.
PRICES: B&B £55–£80 per person, D,B&B £75–£95, full alc £34, New Year package.

STRATFORD-UPON-AVON Warwickshire Map 3:D6

CHERRY TREES

In the 'perfect position' for Stratford, south of the River Avon near a footbridge to the theatre, this architect-designed house is 'elegant, like a country retreat'. It was bought by Royd Laidlow and Tony Godel in late 2011: 'They are charming hosts,' says a visitor in 2012. Guests are greeted with tea and warm home-baked scones. There are three ground-floor bedrooms. The 'huge' Garden room is 'very comfy', with a four-poster bed, a spa shower, a seating area with a television, and a conservatory. The Art Nouveau-inspired Tiffany suite has a working fireplace, a stained-glass window and a private sitting room. The Terrace room has a king-size bed and a conservatory. All rooms have a hospitality tray (herbal teas, ground coffee) and a fridge with milk and mineral water. The landscaped garden has been redesigned and given a water feature. Free Wi-Fi. Breakfast, 'a real treat', has freshly squeezed orange juice, fruit compote and home-made granola; bread is home baked (gluten free is available on request); Drambuie cream porridge; omelettes as well as the usual cooked dishes. (*Kathleen Wilson, Mark Webster*)

Swan's Nest Lane
Stratford-upon-Avon CV37 7LS

T: 01789-292989
E: cherrytreesstratforduponavon@gmail.com
W: www.cherrytrees-stratford.co.uk

BEDROOMS: 3, all on ground floor.
OPEN: Mar–Dec.
FACILITIES: breakfast room, garden, unsuitable for ♿.
BACKGROUND MUSIC: none.
LOCATION: central, near river.
CHILDREN: not under 12.
DOGS: not allowed.
CREDIT CARDS: MasterCard, Visa.
PRICES: B&B £52.50–£62.50 per person, special offers, 1-night bookings sometimes refused.

STRATFORD-UPON-AVON Warwickshire Map 3:D6

WHITE SAILS NEW

'Highly recommended' by a reader this year, this upmarket B&B returns to a full entry in the *Guide*, now under owners Phillip Manning and Chiung-Wen Liang. We sent an inspector, who concurred with the endorsement: 'They are a lovely young couple who seem to delight in having people to stay, and want to know about one's plans for the day, and the evening at the theatre. The suburban house might not have the character expected in Stratford, but inside everything is immaculate; bedrooms are nicely styled; bathrooms are modern and spotless. Help is offered with suitcases, everything is explained, and there is lots of information.' A room facing the busy main road was 'very quiet (good double glazing) and clean; a power shower in the large bathroom'. Air conditioning units 'allow guests to control the temperature'. A bedroom with an 'enticing' conservatory has been added on the ground floor. 'Breakfast was the best I've had in 40 years: wonderful fresh fruit, home-baked bread, perfectly poached eggs on thick granary toast.' The town centre is 'quite a step away' but buses pass the door. (*Peter Reynolds, and others*)

85 Evesham Road
Stratford-upon-Avon CV37 9BE

T: 01789-550469
E: enquiries@white-sails.co.uk
W: www.white-sails.co.uk

BEDROOMS: 5, 1 on ground floor.
OPEN: all year.
FACILITIES: lounge, dining room, garden (summer house).
BACKGROUND MUSIC: none.
LOCATION: 1 mile W of centre.
CHILDREN: not under 12.
DOGS: not allowed.
CREDIT CARDS: MasterCard, Visa.
PRICES: B&B £50–£67.50 per person, 1-night bookings sometimes refused weekends.

STUCKTON Hampshire

Map 2:E2

THE THREE LIONS

Once a farmhouse, this restaurant-with-rooms has a quiet setting surrounded by fields on the northern edge of the New Forest national park. The owners, Mike and Jayne Womersley, 'friendly without being nosy', are much liked. The main building has a bar, small lounge area, intimate restaurant and conservatory. Bedrooms overlook two acres of gardens and the forest beyond; four are in a wooden single-storey chalet-style building in the grounds. Children are 'warmly' welcomed: cots and a baby-listening service are available and there is a play area in the garden (which also has a hot tub). Guests with mobility problems have praised the help they received. There are no printed menus: guests order from a portable blackboard which is taken around the bar and restaurant. Mr Womersley's cooking style is British/French, based on local produce where possible; dishes might include asparagus and wild mushrooms; trimmed loin of lamb and crispy bits. The room price includes continental breakfast; cooked dishes cost extra. Access is limited outside restaurant opening hours; guests should confirm arrival times in advance. More reports, please.

25% DISCOUNT VOUCHERS

Stuckton, nr Fordingbridge
SP6 2HF

T: 01425-652489
F: 01425-656144
E: the3lions@btinternet.com
W: www.thethreelionsrestaurant.co.uk

BEDROOMS: 7, 4 in courtyard block on ground floor.

OPEN: all year except last 2 weeks Feb, restaurant closed Sun night/Mon.

FACILITIES: ramps, conservatory, meeting/sitting room, public bar, restaurant, 2½-acre garden (sauna, whirlpool).

BACKGROUND MUSIC: on request, in bar.

LOCATION: 1 mile E of Fordingbridge.

CHILDREN: all ages welcomed.

DOGS: allowed by arrangement.

CREDIT CARDS: MasterCard, Visa.

PRICES: B&B £52.50–£105 per person, cooked breakfast £8.95, set dinner (Tue–Thurs) £26.50, full alc £50, special breaks.

STURMINSTER NEWTON Dorset

Map 2:E1

PLUMBER MANOR

César award in 1987

'As friendly as ever; the cooking keeps up to a high standard,' say visitors returning to this restaurant-with-rooms in unspoilt Dorset countryside. The family home of the Prideaux-Brunes since it was built in the 1600s, the Jacobean brick-and-stone manor house stands in 'beautiful' gardens with manicured lawns, fine harbaceous borders and a stream. The *Guide*'s founder, returning after 25 years, commented in what was, sadly, his final report: 'The family were unaffectedly welcoming; the grounds are well maintained, and the location is most attractive. The main reception room had a slightly dowdy feel.' Another visitor wrote of a 'lived-in feeling, lovely flowers everywhere.' Richard Prideaux-Brune 'runs the place with evident enthusiasm'; his wife, Alison, is 'simply everywhere'; his brother, Brian, is the chef. The bedrooms in the main house lead off a gallery hung with portraits. Larger rooms are in a converted barn around a courtyard. In the three 'relaxed' dining rooms, the daily-changing menu of English/French dishes might include guineafowl breasts, black pudding bubble and squeak. (*Hilary Rubinstein, Mary Milne-Day*)

Sturminster Newton DT10 2AF

T: 01258-472507
F: 01258-473370
E: book@plumbermanor.com
W: www.plumbermanor.com

BEDROOMS: 16, 10 on ground floor in courtyard.
OPEN: all year except Feb.
FACILITIES: lounge, bar, 3 dining rooms, gallery, 20-acre grounds (garden, tennis, croquet, stream).
BACKGROUND MUSIC: none.
LOCATION: 2 miles SW of Sturminster Newton.
CHILDREN: all ages welcomed, by prior arrangement.
DOGS: allowed in 4 bedrooms, not in public rooms.
CREDIT CARDS: MasterCard, Visa.
PRICES: [2012] B&B £75–£110 per person, set dinner £28–£35.

SWAFFHAM Norfolk

Map 2:B5

STRATTONS

César award in 2003

The interiors of this Grade II listed Palladian villa, off the square of a small market town, are 'a feast for the eye', said *Guide* inspectors. Owned by Les and Vanessa Scott, who met at art college, it is managed by their daughter, Hannah, and Dominic Hughes. 'You can see the touch of two talented souls; light hangings are amazingly creative; bronze shabby-chic walls in the entrance, lots of ornamentation; statues have fluffy wings added.' Each of the themed bedrooms 'is a work of art': Opium has a bed flanked with Doric columns; Stalls replicates the feel of the old horse block it once was; Boudoir has Parisian touches. The two Print rooms, in converted buildings in the grounds, are 'simply furnished in a restrained, modern way'. In the 'charming' *Rustic* restaurant, chef Sam Bryant looks to the surrounding area for the ingredients for his contemporary dishes. His menu might include slow-braised muntjac, gin-steamed suet. Breakfast has 'an excellent selection of cooked dishes'; the eggs come from bantams in the garden. A comprehensive environmental policy is followed.

4 Ash Close
Swaffham PE37 7NH

T: 01760-723845
F: 01760-720458
E: enquiries@strattonshotel.com
W: www.strattonshotel.com

BEDROOMS: 14, 6 in annexes, 2 on ground floor.

OPEN: all year except 1 week at Christmas.

FACILITIES: drawing room, reading room, restaurant, terrace, 1½-acre garden.

BACKGROUND MUSIC: in lounges, restaurant.

LOCATION: central, parking.

CHILDREN: all ages welcomed.

DOGS: allowed in 2 bedrooms, lounges.

CREDIT CARDS: Amex, MasterCard, Visa.

PRICES: [2012] B&B £77.50–£102.50 per person, D,B&B £106.50–£132, full alc £50, special breaks, New Year package, 1-night bookings refused weekends, bank holidays.

TALLAND-BY-LOOE Cornwall

Map 1:D3

TALLAND BAY HOTEL

NEW

'In a magical setting overlooking a secluded bay', this old manor house returns to the *Guide* under a new owner, Vanessa Rees, who has renovated throughout; Lauren Holmyard is the manager. 'It is a very well-run place,' says the nominator (a regular *Guide* correspondent). 'The food is exceptionally good. The decor is eccentric, with much modern art and furniture (if some of the ornaments might be kitsch, they are within the spirit of amusement).' The candlelit lounge has zebra-print sofas and burgundy armchairs. In the wood-panelled dining room (which has sea views and modern velvet-striped high-backed chairs), Dave Tunnicliffe's daily-changing menu of 'imaginative' dishes might include roast fillet of beef, savoury bread-and-butter pudding. A lighter brasserie menu is served in the bar at lunchtime and in the evenings. The bedrooms vary in size, aspect and decor. 'Our sea-facing room was comfortable and had an OK bathroom.' Three rooms have direct access to the garden; three cottages (one with two bedrooms) are suitable for families. Visiting pets are greeted with treats (there are two house dogs and two house cats). (*Janet Walker*)

Porthallow, nr Looe
PL13 2JB

T: 01503-272667
F: 01503-272940
E: info@tallandbayhotel.co.uk
W: www.tallandbayhotel.co.uk

BEDROOMS: 21, 6 on ground floor.
OPEN: all year.
FACILITIES: lounge, bar, restaurant, civil wedding licence, patio, 2-acre garden.
BACKGROUND MUSIC: in bar and restaurant.
LOCATION: 2½ miles SW of Looe.
CHILDREN: all ages welcomed.
DOGS: allowed.
CREDIT CARDS: MasterCard, Visa.
PRICES: [2012] B&B £57.50–£112.50 per person, D,B&B £30 added, full alc £50, special breaks, Christmas/ New Year packages.

TARRANT LAUNCESTON Dorset

Map 2:E1

LAUNCESTON FARM

On her family's working farm in the Tarrant valley, Sarah Worrall has stylishly renovated this Grade II listed Georgian farmhouse. It is a family affair: she looks after the guests; her son, Jimi, manages the organic beef herd, and her daughter, Eve, is the resident gardener and forager, providing vegetables, herbs and 'all things delicious' for the kitchen. An original 19th-century cast iron staircase leads up from the hall to the six individually styled bedrooms, which have been furnished with an eclectic mix of auction-house finds. Meadow has a six-foot bed and a shower room; Penfold has a roll-top bath in the bedroom and an en suite shower room. In the grounds is the Bothy, a self-catering cottage for two. Mrs Worrall, a trained Cordon Bleu cook, serves a two-course meal of 'hearty country fare', taken around a communal table on Monday and Friday evenings (it must be discussed at the time of booking). There are many pubs in the area. Breakfast, also communal and cooked to order, is served at a pre-arranged time in a converted cart shed. More reports, please.

25% DISCOUNT VOUCHERS

Tarrant Launceston
nr Blandford Forum DT11 8BY

T: 01258-830528
E: info@launcestonfarm.co.uk
W: www.launcestonfarm.co.uk

BEDROOMS: 6.

OPEN: all year except 19–26 Dec.

FACILITIES: 2 lounges, dining room, breakfast room, terrace, 1-acre walled garden, heated outdoor swimming pool (5 by 10 metres, summer only), unsuitable for ♿.

BACKGROUND MUSIC: classical during breakfast.

LOCATION: 5 miles NE of Blandford Forum.

CHILDREN: not under 12.

DOGS: not allowed in house.

CREDIT CARDS: MasterCard, Visa.

PRICES: B&B £40–£52.50 per person, D,B&B (Mon & Fri) £22.50 added, 1-night bookings refused weekends Easter–Sept.

TAUNTON Somerset

Map 1:C5

THE CASTLE AT TAUNTON

César award in 1987

'Each member of staff that we met during our stay was delightful,' says a visitor this year to this wisteria-covered, castellated hotel in the centre of Taunton. Once a Norman fortress, it has been run by the Chapman family for 60 years. Kit and Louise Chapman are in charge; Marc MacCloskey is their new manager in 2012. The bedrooms, reached by a fine wrought iron staircase, have been designed by Mrs Chapman. They vary in size and outlook: 'Although not huge, my single room had a good-sized desk and wardrobe; the bathroom was gleaming and exceptionally well lit, and had very good towels.' Changes to the dining options were announced as the *Guide* went to press: a new chef was being appointed, and a 'cool, informal, retro-chic' restaurant, *Castle Bow Bar and Grill*, was due to open. It will have a separate street entrance and will run alongside the 'excitingly modern' *BRAZZ* restaurant, which has 'a warm and friendly buzz'. Breakfast is self-service; there is an 'impressive array of cereals, fruit, yogurts and preserves'; a selection of dishes cooked to order. (*Trevor Lockwood*)

25% DISCOUNT VOUCHERS

Castle Green
Taunton TA1 1NF

T: 01823-272671
F: 01823-336066
E: reception@the-castle-hotel.com
W: www.the-castle-hotel.com

BEDROOMS: 44.
OPEN: all year.
FACILITIES: lift, ramps, lounge, bar, brasserie, dining room, private dining/meeting rooms, billiard room, civil wedding licence, 1-acre garden, shop.
BACKGROUND MUSIC: in bar and brasserie.
LOCATION: central.
CHILDREN: all ages welcomed.
DOGS: small 'well-behaved' dogs allowed.
CREDIT CARDS: Amex, MasterCard, Visa.
PRICES: [2012] B&B £85–£145 per person, D,B&B £99.50–£260, full alc £45, special breaks, Christmas/New Year packages.

TEFFONT EVIAS Wiltshire

Map 2:D1

HOWARD'S HOUSE

César award in 2010

In a fold in the Wiltshire hills, this mellow stone dower house with a charming hillside garden is run as a small hotel by a partnership that includes the chef, Nick Wentworth. His mother-in-law, Noële Thompson, is the 'courteous' manager. 'A delightful place', it stands close to the church in a pretty village of stone houses. The 'welcoming' lounge has sofas around a huge fireplace; exposed beams, pictures of hunting scenes (the hotel is popular with shooting parties). The 'good-size' bedrooms have pastel colours, floral curtains; some have been recently refurbished. A room overlooking the garden was 'delightful and comfortable'. A large room at the top of the house has a four-poster bed, a white sofa. Mr Wentworth uses seasonal ingredients for his modern dishes, eg, hand-dived Cornish scallops, Laverstoke Park Farm black pudding, celeriac and apple syrup; loin of Fonthill roe deer, beetroot gratin, shallot purée, juniper and port jus. 'Beautiful cooking, well matched to the season. The service was impeccable.' In warm weather, meals can be taken on a flagstone terrace in the garden. There is excellent walking in the valley. (*RP*)

25% DISCOUNT VOUCHERS

Teffont Evias
nr Salisbury SP3 5RJ

T: 01722-716392
F: 01722-716820
E: enq@howardshousehotel.co.uk
W: www.howardshousehotel.co.uk

BEDROOMS: 9.
OPEN: all year except Christmas.
FACILITIES: lounge, restaurant, 2-acre grounds (croquet), river, fishing nearby, unsuitable for ♿.
BACKGROUND MUSIC: 'easy listening', jazz.
LOCATION: 10 miles W of Salisbury.
CHILDREN: all ages welcomed.
DOGS: allowed (£11 surcharge in rooms).
CREDIT CARDS: Amex, MasterCard, Visa.
PRICES: B&B £95–£120 per person, full alc £70, winter breaks, New Year package.

TEIGNMOUTH Devon

Map 1:D5

THOMAS LUNY HOUSE

César award in 1995

Built in 1808 by marine artist Thomas Luny, when the town was favoured by Nelson's admirals and captains, this white-painted house is approached through an archway into a walled courtyard ('fairly narrow; take care'). It has long been run as an upmarket B&B by John and Alison Allan, 'charming hosts who maintain high standards'. They greet guests with complimentary afternoon tea and home-made cake. This may be taken in the 'lovely' drawing room furnished with antiques or, in summer, in the walled garden. Upstairs, there are three spacious bedrooms and one smaller, each furnished to a particular theme: Edwardian for the Clairmont, nautical for the Luny, oriental for the Chinese. All have a spare blanket chest, books, magazines, mineral water and fresh flowers. Bathrooms are 'sparkling'. The extensive breakfast has freshly squeezed orange juice, cereals, muesli, fresh fruit salad and home-made compote; a choice of cooked options. Bread is home made, as are the preserves. 'Very attractive and reasonably priced,' says a fan. 'Teignmouth is being upgraded; the countryside around is full of delights.' (*MF*)

Teign Street
Teignmouth TQ14 8EG

T: 01626-772976
E: alisonandjohn@thomas-luny-house.co.uk
W: www.thomas-luny-house.co.uk

BEDROOMS: 4.
OPEN: all year, except Christmas.
FACILITIES: 2 lounges, breakfast room, small walled garden, sea (sandy beach 5 mins' walk), unsuitable for ♿.
BACKGROUND MUSIC: none.
LOCATION: town centre.
CHILDREN: not under 12.
DOGS: not allowed.
CREDIT CARDS: MasterCard, Visa.
PRICES: [2012] B&B £40–£75 per person, 1-night bookings sometimes refused.

TEMPLE SOWERBY Cumbria

Map 4: inset C3

TEMPLE SOWERBY HOUSE

In a conservation village in the Eden valley, this Grade II listed red brick mansion is a popular country hotel run by owners Paul and Julie Evans. 'Wonderful; everything was first class; the staff were attentive and friendly, the food was delicious,' is this year's praise. Standing in two acres of walled gardens, the core of the building is a 17th-century farmhouse with a Georgian wing added. The classically styled public rooms are 'immaculate'. The bedrooms, which vary in size, are in the main building or in a coach house. Superior rooms are at the front, looking over the village green and the fells. In fine weather, drinks can be taken on the terrace before dinner in the conservatory-style restaurant, where chef Ashley Whittaker cooks contemporary dishes using seasonal, local and garden-grown produce. Typical dishes: warm crab cake, coriander salad, mango salsa; roast breast of Cumbrian chicken, crisp bacon, sautéed lettuce. Breakfast, served at table ('none of your buffet nonsense'), has 'good choice and quality'. Dogs are welcomed in the coach house rooms. (*Barbara Bilton, and others*)

25% DISCOUNT VOUCHERS

Temple Sowerby
Penrith CA10 1RZ

T: 017683-61578
F: 017683-61958
E: stay@templesowerby.com
W: www.templesowerby.com

BEDROOMS: 12, 2 on ground floor, 4 in coach house (20 yds).

OPEN: all year except 25/26 Dec.

FACILITIES: 2 lounges, bar, restaurant, conference/function facilities, civil wedding licence, 2-acre garden (croquet).

BACKGROUND MUSIC: in restaurant at night.

LOCATION: village centre.

CHILDREN: not under 12.

DOGS: by prior arrangement in 2 bedrooms, not allowed in public rooms.

CREDIT CARDS: Amex, MasterCard, Visa.

PRICES: [2012] B&B £67.50–£77.50 per person, D,B&B £80–£110, set dinner £39.50, special breaks, New Year package, 1-night bookings occasionally refused.

TETBURY Gloucestershire

Map 3:E5

CALCOT MANOR

César award in 2001

Adults and children 'co-exist happily together' at this 'civilised' Cotswold hotel. It combines a 'genuine welcome' for younger visitors with spa facilities and fine dining for their parents. Richard Ball is the managing director; his wife, Cathy, runs the spa. Older children have the run of the *Mez*, which has games consoles, computers; a cinema and an outdoor swimming pool. Little ones have an Ofsted-registered *Playzone*, which has appropriate toys and a crèche. There are two restaurants: in the *Conservatory*, chef Michael Croft serves modern dishes in a formal setting (eg, venison osso bucco, smoked pancetta, grilled onions). The informal *Gumstool Inn* 'is popular with people of all ages and buzzes with activity' (says a regular visitor this year). High teas for families are served here in the evening. Younger children have restricted access to the spa and its 'inviting' pool. Family rooms are in a converted barn beside the main house; some have a bunk bed, others a sofa bed. Five rooms can accommodate three children. *Barnsley House*, Barnsley (see entry), has the same ownership. (*Tony Kay, and others*)

nr Tetbury GL8 8YJ

T: 01666-890391
F: 01666-890394
E: reception@calcotmanor.co.uk
W: www.calcotmanor.co.uk

BEDROOMS: 35, 10 (family) in cottage, 11 around courtyard, on ground floor.
OPEN: all year.
FACILITIES: ramps, lounge, 2 bars, 2 restaurants, private dining room, cinema, crèche, civil wedding licence, 220-acre grounds (tennis, heated outdoor 8-metre swimming pool, children's play area, spa with 16-metre swimming pool).
BACKGROUND MUSIC: in restaurants.
LOCATION: 3 miles W of Tetbury.
CHILDREN: all ages welcomed.
DOGS: in courtyard bedrooms.
CREDIT CARDS: all major cards.
PRICES: [2012] B&B £130–£242.50 per person, D,B&B (min. 2 nights midweek) from £160, full alc £50, 2-day breaks, Christmas/New Year packages, 1-night bookings sometimes refused weekends.

SEE ALSO SHORTLIST

THORPE MARKET Norfolk

Map 2:A5

THE GUNTON ARMS

NEW

Art dealer Ivor Braka and his artist wife, Sarah Graham, have restored this run-down hotel in the middle of a deer park, to create a 'relaxed' restaurant/pub-with-rooms. A reader who enjoyed a 'delicious' lunch and decided to stay admired the 'high standards of food and hospitality'. Inspectors agreed: 'There is a refreshing vibrancy about the decor: stunning wallpapers, deep red rustic paintwork; an eclectic selection of artwork and unusual pieces.' The main dining room has 'the feel of a medieval banqueting hall; plain wooden tables and chairs, multi-coloured panels, oversized elk antlers (an artwork)'. The chef, Stuart Tattersall, can be seen cooking 'prodigious chunks of meat' and potatoes on an open fire. 'An excellent dinner with good steaks and fish; vegetables are charged extra.' Hotel guests have use of two lounges, 'packed with books and magazines, each with a television'. There are no TVs in the bedrooms ('to encourage people to go out and about'). 'Our large and comfortable room was pre-warmed for our arrival; good lighting, everything of the highest quality.' Breakfast has 'interesting choices'. (*Sara Price, and others*)

Cromer Road
Thorpe Market NR11 8TZ

T: 01263-832010
E: office@theguntonarms.co.uk
W: www.theguntonarms.co.uk

BEDROOMS: 8.
OPEN: all year except 25/26 Dec.
FACILITIES: 2 lounges, bar, restaurant, pantry.
BACKGROUND MUSIC: in public areas.
LOCATION: 4 miles S of Cromer.
CHILDREN: all ages welcomed.
DOGS: allowed (£10 charge).
CREDIT CARDS: all major cards.
PRICES: [2012] B&B £42.50–£75 per person, full alc £35, 1-night bookings refused weekends.

TITCHWELL Norfolk

Map 2:A5

TITCHWELL MANOR

'The friendly, helpful staff' are praised by visitors this year to the Snaith family's small hotel/restaurant, a restoration of an 1890 farmhouse near the RSPB reserve at Titchwell Marsh. 'The epitome of a family hotel', it is owned and run by Ian and Margaret Snaith; their son, Eric, is the chef. The 'impeccable' public areas have wooden floors, seaside paintings; an open fire ('kept going all day in winter') in the bar which has an informal dining area (the *Eating Rooms*). The cooking in the *Conservatory* restaurant is 'excellent and beautifully presented'. There is a brasserie-style carte, and a tasting menu with dishes like whelk paella; best end of Norfolk lamb, lamb crackling, wild garlic, hazelnut. The bedrooms vary in size: three in the main house have sea views: 'Our compact room was well organised, with plenty of drawers and proper hangers in the wardrobe.' Twelve contemporary rooms are in a single-storey building around a pretty garden. 'Scrupulously clean, every need catered for; even a hot-water bottle.' The 'very good' breakfast has a 'plentiful' buffet; 'excellent' cooked dishes. (*Sara Price, Revd Peter Cannon*)

25% DISCOUNT VOUCHERS

Titchwell, nr Brancaster
PE31 8BB

T: 01485-210221
F: 01485-210104
E: margaret@titchwellmanor.com
W: www.titchwellmanor.com

BEDROOMS: 27, 12 in herb garden, 2 suitable for ♿.
OPEN: all year.
FACILITIES: 2 lounges, bar, restaurant, civil wedding licence, ⅓-acre garden (beaches, golf nearby).
BACKGROUND MUSIC: in public rooms.
LOCATION: on coast road, 5 miles E of Hunstanton.
CHILDREN: all ages welcomed.
DOGS: not allowed in restaurant.
CREDIT CARDS: MasterCard, Visa.
PRICES: [2012] B&B £45–£125 per person, D,B&B (min. 2 nights) £70–£125, full alc £50, midweek breaks, Christmas/New Year packages, 1-night bookings sometimes refused Sat.

TITLEY Herefordshire

Map 3:C4

THE STAGG INN

César award: dining pub of the year

'There is a good feeling at *The Stagg*. It is an unpretentious village pub with excellent food and interesting bedrooms.' Confirmation this year by *Guide* inspectors of reports from readers visiting Steve and Nicola Reynolds's 'delightful' white-fronted inn. Other praise: 'A lovely place; we were shown to our room by Nicola Reynolds, who is chatty and friendly.' 'A superb meal served by the pleasant staff.' Mr Reynolds has a *Michelin* star for his modern cooking, served informally in an 'understated' dining room. The cooking is as easy-going as the surroundings; we greatly enjoyed perfectly seared scallops, cauliflower purée, cumin; good beef and moist sea bass.' The desserts are 'heavenly'. The three bedrooms above the bar have a 'comfortable bed; a spacious bathroom with good toiletries'. The three best rooms are in an old vicarage with 'lovely gardens' 300 yards away (transport is offered to those who prefer not to walk). 'Our enormous, handsome room had two armchairs; a large iron bedstead, and a freestanding claw bath.' Breakfast, taken in the pub, has 'chunky toast, home-made black pudding, meaty sausages'. (*Margaret Wall, and others*)

Titley, nr Kington
HR5 3RL

T: 01544-230221
F: 01544-231390
E: reservations@thestagg.co.uk
W: www.thestagg.co.uk

BEDROOMS: 6, 3 at *Old Vicarage* (300 yds).

OPEN: all year except Sun night/Mon, 25–27 Dec, 1–3 Jan, first 2 weeks Nov, 1 week in Feb.

FACILITIES: (*Old Vicarage*) sitting room, 1½-acre garden, (*Stagg Inn*) bar, restaurant areas, small garden, unsuitable for ♿.

BACKGROUND MUSIC: none.

LOCATION: on B4355 between Kington (3½ miles) and Presteigne.

CHILDREN: all ages welcomed.

DOGS: only allowed in pub, some pub bedrooms.

CREDIT CARDS: Amex, MasterCard, Visa.

PRICES: B&B £70–£80 per person, full alc £40, 1-night bookings sometimes refused.

ULLSWATER Cumbria

Map 4: inset C2

HOWTOWN HOTEL

César award in 1991

Without pretension or frills, this modest guest house is well suited to its isolated setting on the quieter eastern shore on Lake Ullswater. It is popular with those who prefer a simpler life: guests cannot book by email or fax; mobile phone reception is limited at best; there is no telephone, television or radio in the bedrooms. Jacquie Baldry, whose family has owned the house for more than 100 years, is in charge with her son, David. Newcomers are 'coached through the house drill' by returnees, said a recent visitor. Guests are encouraged to socialise. A gong announces breakfast at 9 am and dinner at 7 pm. A four-course meal of traditional dishes is served on six nights; a set lunch and a cold supper are provided on a Sunday. Visitors welcome the cup of tea brought to the bedroom in the morning, and a turn-down service during dinner. The simple bedrooms might 'evoke times past' but they are comfortable; most have a lake view; four have a private bathroom across the corridor. Breakfasts – and picnics for walkers – are substantial. More reports, please.

Ullswater, nr Penrith CA10 2ND

T: 01768-486514
W: www.howtown-hotel.com

BEDROOMS: 13, 4 in annexe, 4 self-catering cottages for weekly rent.
OPEN: Mar–1 Nov.
FACILITIES: 3 lounges, TV room, 2 bars, dining room, 2-acre grounds, 200 yds from lake (private foreshore, fishing), walking, sailing, climbing, riding, golf nearby, unsuitable for ♿.
BACKGROUND MUSIC: none.
LOCATION: 4 miles S of Pooley Bridge, bus from Penrith station 9 miles.
CHILDREN: all ages welcomed (no special facilities).
DOGS: not allowed in public rooms.
CREDIT CARDS: none.
PRICES: [2012] D,B&B £85 per person, set dinner £24, 1-night bookings sometimes refused.

SEE ALSO SHORTLIST

ULVERSTON Cumbria

Map 4: inset C2

THE BAY HORSE

César award in 2009

'Always a joy to visit', Robert Lyons and Lesley Wheeler's 17th-century former coaching inn has long been liked for the 'warm and homely atmosphere' and the 'serene setting'. On the shore of the Leven estuary, it faces the broad expanse of Morecambe Bay ('you can watch the racing tide'). The decor 'might seem somewhat retro but we love it', says a fan in 2012. Another comment: 'It won't appeal to everyone but to folks like us it gives comfort, good food and value for money without any pretensions.' The bedrooms are small, beds are 'very comfortable', bathrooms simple; six front rooms have French windows which open on to a terrace overlooking the estuary. Mr Lyons is the chef in the 'excellent' conservatory restaurant where the evening meal has a single sitting at 8 pm ('we will be flexible about time wherever possible,' say the owners). 'We had an extremely tender duck breast, well-hung fillet steak, lamb and apricot pie, and beef casserole.' There is also a bar menu. At breakfast, 'everything seemed to be home made or sourced locally'. (*Lynn Wildgoose, G and M Schofield, CLH*)

25% DISCOUNT VOUCHERS

Canal Foot
Ulverston
LA12 9EL

T: 01229-583972
F: 01229-580502
E: reservations@thebayhorsehotel.co.uk
W: www.thebayhorsehotel.co.uk

BEDROOMS: 9.

OPEN: all year, restaurant closed Mon midday (light bar meals available).

FACILITIES: bar lounge, restaurant, picnic area, unsuitable for ♿.

BACKGROUND MUSIC: mixed 'easy listening'.

LOCATION: 8 miles NE of Barrow-in-Furness.

CHILDREN: not under 9.

DOGS: allowed.

CREDIT CARDS: Amex, MasterCard, Visa.

PRICES: [2012] B&B £47.50–£60 per person, full alc £47.50, bargain breaks, cookery courses, Christmas package, 1-night bookings refused bank holidays.

VENTNOR Isle of Wight

Map 2:E2

THE HAMBROUGH

On a cliff-top in a Victorian resort on the sheltered side of the island, this villa has been restored as a restaurant-with-rooms by chef/patron Robert Thompson, who has a *Michelin* star for his cooking. 'The whole ethos is maintained by the young, cheerful and competent staff,' say visitors this year. Dinner, taken in a smart restaurant ('pretty Isle of Wight glass adds interest to the plain modern table setting'), is 'what we would expect of a *Michelin* star, plus a bit extra'. Locally landed fish and island meat are used for the seasonal menus, which have dishes like line-caught brill, fennel croquant, pesto and purée; loin of rose veal, bone marrow, Madeira and thyme jus. Mr Thompson's wife, Diana, supervises the service. The 'faultless' bedrooms are light and airy (six have sea views), decorated in modern neutral colours with bold wallpaper designs. Breakfast has a continental buffet; cooked dishes include 'the best-ever kippers'. Mr Thompson also runs the *Pond Café*, along the coast. And he is involved in the development of the Ventnor Winter Gardens.
(*John and Sara Leathes*)

Hambrough Road
Ventnor PO38 1SQ

T: 01983-856333
E: reservations@robert-thompson.com
W: www.robert-thompson.com

BEDROOMS: 7, plus 5-bedroom villa.
OPEN: all year, restaurant closed Sun/Mon.
FACILITIES: lounge, restaurant, civil wedding licence, small patio garden, unsuitable for ♿.
BACKGROUND MUSIC: 'relaxed, jazz' in Reception, restaurant and lounge.
LOCATION: S end of Ventnor Bay.
CHILDREN: all ages welcomed.
DOGS: not allowed.
CREDIT CARDS: MasterCard, Visa.
PRICES: B&B £85–£140 per person, tasting menu £85, full alc £65, Christmas/New Year packages.

SEE ALSO SHORTLIST

VENTNOR Isle of Wight

Map 2:E2

HILLSIDE

NEW

On a hill above the seaside town, this thatched Georgian villa has been given a 'distinct and agreeable Scandinavian feel' by the Danish owner, Gert Bach, and his English wife, Anna. The house has some unusual rules: meals must be ordered in advance; drinks are served at 6.30 pm, dinner at 7; no drinks are allowed in bedrooms; a two-night minimum stay. Any fears that 'it might be regimented' evaporate: 'The atmosphere is warm and hospitable; although guests dine separately, it is like a gathering in a private house.' A visitor in 2012 was pleased to be 'welcomed in the car park; our bags were carried to a spotless light room with a sea view; minimalist matching furniture, sparkling linen'. In the dining room, contemporary dishes with a French influence might include Brie and cranberry filo parcel; beef with bordelaise sauce. 'The cooking is of a notable standard; a well-thought-out wine list; coffee was served in the conservatory, where we were offered soft Welsh wool shawls in a cooling evening.' Meals can be taken on a terrace in warm weather.
(*Terry Carlton, and others*)

151 Mitchell Avenue
Ventnor PO38 1DR

T: 01983-852271
F: 01983-855310
E: mail@hillsideventnor.co.uk
W: www.hillsideventnor.co.uk

BEDROOMS: 11, plus 2 self-catering cottages.
OPEN: all year, restaurant closed Sun.
FACILITIES: bar, lounge, restaurant, conservatory, terrace, 5-acre garden, unsuitable for ♿.
BACKGROUND MUSIC: in public areas.
LOCATION: Top of town, at foot of St Boniface Down.
CHILDREN: not under 12.
DOGS: not allowed.
CREDIT CARDS: MasterCard, Visa.
PRICES: [2012] B&B £68–£73 per person, set meals £28, Christmas/New Year packages, min. 2-night stay.

SEE ALSO SHORTLIST

VERYAN-IN-ROSELAND Cornwall

Map 1:D2

THE NARE

César award in 2003

In large grounds above a sandy beach on the Roseland peninsula, Toby Ashworth's luxury hotel (Pride of Britain) is commended by returning visitors for the 'excellent standards that never vary'. Other praise this year: 'Everything good that has been said is justified; the staff are friendly, cheerful and highly efficient.' While it has the feel of 'a long-gone world', the *Nare* is not in a 'time warp of nostalgia'; the 'well-planned' bedrooms have 'lovely' antique furniture, state-of-the-art plumbing. Most sea-facing rooms are spacious; country-view rooms are smaller. Appreciated extra touches include a hot-water bottle in the bed, evening turn-down, no extra charge for breakfast in bed. 'My only quibble is the charge for Internet access.' There are two dining options: a daily-changing menu is served in the formal main dining room, where men are asked to wear a jacket and a tie; a 'more relaxed' menu is available in the *Quarterdeck*. 'The cuisine is superb.' Breakfast has 'a wide range of choices'. There are 'wonderful' coastal walks. 'Expensive, but by golly you get what you pay for.' (*Sylvia Keith, Stanley Salmons*)

Carne Beach
Veryan-in-Roseland
nr Truro TR2 5PF

T: 01872-501111
F: 01872-501856
E: reservations@narehotel.co.uk
W: www.narehotel.co.uk

BEDROOMS: 37, some on ground floor, 1 in adjoining cottage, 5 suitable for ♿.

OPEN: all year.

FACILITIES: lift, ramps, lounge, drawing room, sun lounge, bar, billiard room, light lunch/supper room, 2 restaurants, conservatory, indoor 10-metre swimming pool, gym, 2-acre grounds (heated 15-metre swimming pool, tennis, safe sandy beach).

BACKGROUND MUSIC: none.

LOCATION: S of Veryan, on coast.

CHILDREN: all ages welcomed.

DOGS: not allowed in public rooms.

CREDIT CARDS: Amex, MasterCard, Visa.

PRICES: [2012] B&B £135–£384 per person, set dinner £49.50, full alc £60, special breaks, Christmas/New Year packages.

WADDESDON Buckinghamshire

Map 2:C3

THE FIVE ARROWS

25% DISCOUNT VOUCHERS

Taking its name from the Rothschild family emblem of five arrows (representing the sons sent to establish banking houses across Europe), this small hotel was built to house the craftsmen working on Waddesdon Manor. Like the manor, the hotel is run by the Rothschild family trust for the National Trust; the manager is Alex McEwen. 'He is very much in charge, keeping an eye on the front desk and the restaurant,' said a trusted reporter in 2012. A reader thought the staff were 'extremely friendly and helpful'. In the 'immaculate' dining room, divided into three separate areas with well-spaced tables, chef Karl Penny serves 'interesting choices' on his modern European menu. 'We had a fine ham hock with dill dressing and pickled vegetables, and a splendid sea bream with crisp skin and moist flesh.' 'Although on a busy road, the hotel is surprisingly peaceful inside; our bedroom in the courtyard was very quiet indeed.' A small room in the main house was not liked. National Trust members qualify for a ten per cent discount on B&B rates. (*Michael Cornelius, and others*)

High Street
Waddesdon HP18 0JE

T: 01296-651727
F: 01296-655716
E: five.arrows@nationaltrust.org.uk
W: www.thefivearrows.co.uk

BEDROOMS: 11, 3, in courtyard, on ground floor.
OPEN: all year.
FACILITIES: bar, restaurant, civil wedding licence, 1-acre garden.
BACKGROUND MUSIC: none.
LOCATION: in village.
CHILDREN: all ages welcomed.
DOGS: not allowed in bedrooms.
CREDIT CARDS: Amex, MasterCard, Visa.
PRICES: [2012] B&B £52.50–£117.50 per person, D,B&B £80–£120, full alc £40–£50, special offers, New Year package.

WAREHAM Dorset

Map 2:E1

THE PRIORY

César award in 1996

'Very atmospheric, we could not have enjoyed our stay more.' Praise comes in 2012 from a regular correspondent for this 16th-century former convent in a 'lovely position' on the banks of the River Frome. Owned by Anne Turner and her brother-in-law, Stuart, it has 'much going for it; traditional in style and proposition, it delivers'. Another comment by returning visitors: 'As good as ever; the staff remembered us, and addressed us by name.' The ground-floor drawing room has access to the garden; a first-floor lounge has views across the river and meadows. Bedrooms are in the main house and in a converted boathouse. 'Our room was serviced efficiently during breakfast; it had a glorious view.' 'My small suite had a semi-private terrace by the river.' Drinks and canapés are taken in the *Cloisters Bar* or drawing room before dinner in the *Abbot's Cellar* dining room ('we prefer gentlemen to wear a jacket and tie'). Chef Stephan Guinebault's menu might include kiln-roasted and poached salmon rillettes; loin of Purbeck venison, herb mashed potatoes, fine beans. (*David Craig, Jim Grover, Nigel and Jennifer Jee*)

25% DISCOUNT VOUCHERS

Church Green
Wareham
BH20 4ND

T: 01929-551666
F: 01929-554519
E: reservations@theprioryhotel.co.uk
W: www.theprioryhotel.co.uk

BEDROOMS: 18, some on ground floor (in courtyard), 4 suites in Boathouse.
OPEN: all year.
FACILITIES: ramps, lounge, drawing room, bar, 2 dining rooms, 4-acre gardens (croquet, river frontage, moorings, fishing), unsuitable for ♿.
BACKGROUND MUSIC: pianist in drawing room Sat night.
LOCATION: town centre.
CHILDREN: not under 14.
DOGS: only guide dogs allowed.
CREDIT CARDS: all major cards.
PRICES: [2012] B&B £102.50–£182.50 per person, D,B&B £130–£210, set dinner £44.50, off-season breaks, Christmas/New Year packages, 1-night bookings sometimes refused.

WARMINSTER Wiltshire

Map 2:D1

CROCKERTON HOUSE

Endorsed again this year, this Georgian house (Grade II listed) stands in 'beautiful' gardens overlooking the Wylye valley in an area of outstanding natural beauty. The owners, Christopher and Enid Richmond, have meticulously restored the house, preserving original features in the handsome hall and lounge. Visitors are greeted with complimentary afternoon tea and home-made cake (if they arrive before 5 pm); help is given taking baggage to the spacious first-floor bedrooms. The Officer's Room has a king-size bed; a private bathroom (with bath and walk-in shower) and a separate lavatory are off the corridor. The Heytesbury Suite has double-aspect windows over the gardens; the Silk Room is at the back facing a lane leading to the old mill. Dinner, served from Monday to Thursday by arrangement, is a set menu cooked by Mrs Richmond, perhaps West Country cheese soufflé; chicken with sage stuffing; chocolate brownies. Guests may bring their own wine. Breakfast has freshly squeezed fruit juices, home-made bread and preserves, organic ingredients for cooked dishes. A red cedar tree in the garden is more than 200 years old. (*JW*)

Crockerton Green
Warminster BA12 8AY

T: 01985-216631
E: stay@crockertonhouse.co.uk
W: www.crockertonhouse.co.uk

BEDROOMS: 3, also self-catering cottage.

OPEN: all year except Christmas, dining room closed Fri–Sun.

FACILITIES: drawing room, dining room, 1½-acre garden, unsuitable for ♿.

BACKGROUND MUSIC: none.

LOCATION: 1½ miles S of Warminster.

CHILDREN: not under 12.

DOGS: not allowed.

CREDIT CARDS: MasterCard, Visa.

PRICES: [2012] B&B £39–£69 per person, set dinner £30, reduced rates for longer stays, 1-night bookings usually refused weekends, especially Apr–Oct.

WATERMILLOCK Cumbria

Map 4: inset C2

RAMPSBECK

In extensive parkland and gardens, this 18th-century whitewashed country house has spectacular views of Lake Ullswater and the Fells. The long-serving Marion Gibb is co-manager with Tracey McGeorge. 'It is relaxed and the service is great,' says a returning visitor this year. Bedrooms vary in size and aspect; most have views of the garden or lake; larger rooms have a lounge area. A small room was 'furnished to a high level'; all rooms are equipped with 'everything you could expect' (fresh fruit, mineral water, Wi-Fi access). The panelled hall has comfortable settees, a log fire in winter; the drawing room has a marble fireplace and an ornate ceiling. A lounge bar opens on to a terrace where tea and light meals are served in summer. In the candlelit dining room, chef Andrew McGeorge wins praise from vegetarian visitors: his daily-changing menu of modern dishes (with French influences) might include baked goat's cheese, red onion marmalade; roasted fillet of beef, shallot confit, celeriac fondant, Cumbrian air-dried ham. *Rampsbeck*'s motor cruiser, *Misty Lady*, can be chartered for a lake trip. (*Kate Colgrave, and others*)

Watermillock on Ullswater
nr Penrith CA11 0LP

T: 01768-486442
F: 01768-486688
E: enquiries@rampsbeck.co.uk
W: www.rampsbeck.co.uk

BEDROOMS: 19.
OPEN: all year.
FACILITIES: 2 lounges, bar, restaurant, civil wedding licence, 18-acre grounds (croquet), lake frontage (fishing, windsurfing, sailing, etc), unsuitable for ♿.
BACKGROUND MUSIC: occasionally in bar and restaurant.
LOCATION: 5½ miles SW of Penrith.
CHILDREN: young children not allowed in restaurant at night.
DOGS: allowed in 3 bedrooms, hall lounge.
CREDIT CARDS: MasterCard, Visa.
PRICES: [2012] B&B £72.50–£150 per person, D,B&B £120–£195, set dinner £54.50, special breaks, Christmas/New Year packages, 1-night bookings occasionally refused.

WELLS Somerset

Map 2:D1

STOBERRY HOUSE

'Very much a family home', this converted coach house (dating back to 1745) is run as a B&B (Wolsey Lodge) by Frances Young. The 'interesting' owner 'loves to engage with her guests', said an inspector who enjoyed the personal contact. The house stands in parkland with 'stunning views' over the cathedral to Glastonbury Tor; sheep graze in the grounds, which have a 'lovely' formal garden. The sitting room is furnished with family antiques and objects collected on Mrs Young's travels. Bedrooms, individually decorated, have a hospitality tray with biscuits and mineral water; free Wi-Fi. 'I appreciated the turn-down at night, with a bottle of soothing sleep-inducing spray left by the bed.' The studio suite has been refurbished, and the house, which hosts weddings and other functions, now has a drinks licence. Breakfast is served at separate tables in a room with sofas at one end, and a baby grand piano. 'Amazing' cooked dishes (which cost extra) include eggs Benedict, pancakes with grilled bacon and maple syrup. The continental version has 'so much to offer': home-made jams, yogurt with fruit purée.

Stoberry Park
Wells BA5 3LD

T: 01749-672906
F: 01749-674175
E: stay@stoberry-park.co.uk
W: www.stoberry-park.co.uk

BEDROOMS: 5, 1 in studio cottage.
OPEN: all year except 15 Dec–5 Jan.
FACILITIES: sitting room, breakfast room, 6½-acre grounds, unsuitable for ♿.
BACKGROUND MUSIC: none.
LOCATION: outskirts of Wells.
CHILDREN: all ages welcomed.
DOGS: not allowed.
CREDIT CARDS: Amex (*3% surcharge*), MasterCard, Visa.
PRICES: [2012] B&B (continental) £37.50–£77.50 per person, cooked breakfast £5–£10, midweek off-season rates.

WHITEWELL Lancashire

Map 4:D3

THE INN AT WHITEWELL

On the bend of a river in the Forest of Bowland, this 14th-century manor house has been owned by three generations of the Bowman family. 'We had a delightful stay,' says an American visitor this year, echoing the comments of a trusted reporter who 'wants to return'. Charles Bowman is in charge of a 'delightful' staff. The inn is furnished with antiques, artefacts, prints of hunting and fishing scenes; tartan armchairs by a log fire in the bar. The best of the individually decorated bedrooms have river views. A large room had 'antique painted headboards, blankets on the comfortable bed, a small desk, a pleasingly warm bathroom'; the 'most unusual bathroom fixtures' were admired. Service in the 'thriving' restaurant and bar is 'prompt and attentive'. Chef Jamie Cadman uses local produce for his menu in dishes like smoked Goosnargh chicken salad, beetroot relish; roast rack of Lonk lamb. The outlook from the dining room is 'quintessential English countryside: far-reaching views of hills and sheep-covered pastures'. Breakfast has freshly squeezed orange juice; home-made granola and muesli; 'proper toast; good, strong coffee'. (*Peter McNally, RG*)

Whitewell, Forest of Bowland
nr Clitheroe BB7 3AT

T: 01200-448222
F: 01200-448298
E: reception@innatwhitewell.com
W: www.innatwhitewell.com

BEDROOMS: 23, 4 (2 on ground floor) in coach house, 150 yds.

OPEN: all year.

FACILITIES: 2 bars, restaurant, boardroom, orangery, civil wedding licence, 5-acre garden, 7 miles fishing (ghillie available), unsuitable for ♿.

BACKGROUND MUSIC: none.

LOCATION: 6 miles NW of Clitheroe.

CHILDREN: all ages welcomed.

DOGS: not allowed in dining room.

CREDIT CARDS: MasterCard, Visa.

PRICES: [to March 2013] B&B £60–£120 per person, full alc £50.

WILMINGTON East Sussex

Map 2:E4

CROSSWAYS HOTEL

Long popular with Glyndebourne aficionados, this white-painted Georgian house has been run for 25 years as a restaurant-with-rooms by owners David Stott and Clive James. 'Their warmth and friendliness is the keynote,' says a returning visitor this year. 'Warmly endorsed, nothing changes,' is another comment. The bedrooms, recently redecorated in a more contemporary style, have many extra touches: 'a clothes brush in the wardrobe, a slipcase full of Penguin classics', a pint of fresh milk in the refrigerator. The food is universally admired: on the fixed-price modern English menu of four courses are dishes like hot duck sausage, red onion relish; game pie with a shortcrust pastry topping. 'Clive and David seem able to cook, serve and chat without any evidence of strain, making for lots of happy guests.' The breakfast room, 'sunny and pleasing', holds an 'astonishing collection of covered cheese dishes ("you should see the attic," say the hosts)'. The 'hugely enjoyable' breakfast has 'delicious' scrambled eggs. There is a busy main road at the end of the 'delightful' garden but windows are double glazed. (*Richard D Parish, and others*)

Lewes Road
Wilmington
BN26 5SG

T: 01323-482455
F: 01323-487811
E: stay@crosswayshotel.co.uk
W: www.crosswayshotel.co.uk

BEDROOMS: 7, also self-catering cottage.

OPEN: all year except 23 Dec–23 Jan, restaurant closed Sun/Mon evening.

FACILITIES: breakfast room, restaurant, 2-acre grounds (duck pond), unsuitable for ♿.

BACKGROUND MUSIC: quiet classical in restaurant.

LOCATION: 2 miles W of Polegate on A27.

CHILDREN: not under 12.

DOGS: not allowed.

CREDIT CARDS: Amex, MasterCard, Visa.

PRICES: B&B £72.50–£90 per person, D,B&B £99–£125, set dinner £39.

WINCHELSEA East Sussex

Map 2:E5

STRAND HOUSE

Once on the quayside below the old town (before the river silted up), these Grade II listed buildings (one 13th-century, the other Tudor) are run as a small hotel by Mary Sullivan and Hugh Davie. There are woodland gardens with paths up into the town and hidden seating areas with sea views. In the house, residents have the use of two sitting rooms: the main one has sofas and a large inglenook fireplace; a smaller room is used as a reading room, 'ideal for quiet moments'. A new bar area and breakfast buffet were created in 2012. The largest bedrooms in the main house have a four-poster, fireplace, views of the garden (but beware of low beams). Three have been redecorated this year in Flemish style (cool greys and muted colours). A modern garden cottage has two ground-floor rooms and a suite on the first floor. Dinner is available on Saturday nights in the oak-beamed dining room, or by arrangement for groups. There are good local restaurants. Breakfast has farm-pressed apple juice, scallops during the Rye Bay scallop festival. More reports, please.

25% DISCOUNT VOUCHERS

Tanyards Lane
Winchelsea TN36 4JT

T: 01797-226276
F: 01797-224806
E: info@thestrandhouse.co.uk
W: www.thestrandhouse.co.uk

BEDROOMS: 13, 1 on ground floor, 3 in adjacent cottage.

OPEN: all year except first 3 weeks Jan.

FACILITIES: Reception, 2 sitting rooms, bar, breakfast room, civil wedding/partnership licence, 1-acre garden, unsuitable for ♿.

BACKGROUND MUSIC: classical in Reception area.

LOCATION: 300 yds from centre, 2 miles SW of Rye.

CHILDREN: preferably not under 5.

DOGS: allowed in 3 bedrooms by arrangement, not in public rooms.

CREDIT CARDS: MasterCard, Visa.

PRICES: [2012] B&B £32.50–£90 per person, D,B&B £65–£122.50, set dinner £32.50, full alc £42.50, special breaks, Christmas/New Year packages, 1-night bookings refused summer weekends.

WINCHESTER Hampshire

Map 2:D2

THE WYKEHAM ARMS

25% DISCOUNT VOUCHERS

Between the college and the cathedral, this 'uniquely hospitable' 18th-century former coaching inn is managed by Jon and Monica Howard for Fullers Brewery. Originally called *The Fleur de Lys*, it was renamed after Bishop William of Wykeham, the founder of Winchester College. The association is reflected in the memorabilia displayed in the bar and restaurant (old school desks are used as dining room tables). Booking in advance for dinner is recommended. The new chef, Adam Thomason, serves classic dishes with modern influences, eg, crackling-crusted poached duck egg, pea fricassée; smoked haddock fish pie, Parmesan and oat crumble, lemon new potatoes. Bedrooms are above the pub (reached by a narrow staircase; some are small) and in a 16th-century building opposite. Some have a four-poster bed and Victorian roll-top bath; all are 'well provided', with TV, minibar and fresh milk in the fridge. The Bakehouse Suite has a mezzanine-level bedroom, separate living room and garden access. Breakfast has 'the usual buffet, well served', with fresh fruit, cereals, pastries and home-made compote; cooked dishes to order. More reports, please.

75 Kingsgate Street
Winchester SO23 9PE

T: 01962-853834
F: 01962-854411
E: wykehamarms@fullers.co.uk
W: www.wykehamarmswinchester.co.uk

BEDROOMS: 14, 7 in annexe.
OPEN: all year.
FACILITIES: 2 bars, 2 dining rooms, function room, small garden, unsuitable for ♿.
BACKGROUND MUSIC: light classical in breakfast room.
LOCATION: central.
CHILDREN: not under 12.
DOGS: allowed in bars, 2 bedrooms.
CREDIT CARDS: Amex, MasterCard, Visa.
PRICES: [2012] B&B £64.50–£72 per person, set meals £20–£35, full alc £40, Christmas/New Year packages.

WINDERMERE Cumbria

Map 4: inset C2

GILPIN HOTEL AND LAKE HOUSE

César award in 2000

'We had been there only an hour when we decided to extend our stay,' say readers of their 2012 visit to the Cunliffe family's country house hotel (Relais & Châteaux). 'Charming and helpful staff, beautiful rooms, excellent meals, and all those little touches that make a place spot-on.' The Edwardian building is run by John and Christine Cunliffe, with son Barney and his wife, Zoë. 'The staff are highly trained,' notes a *Guide* inspector: 'One is always greeted by name; Barney Cunliffe is keen to see his guests right.' Pre-dinner drinks are served in the large lounge, 'with an open fire and capacious sofas'. The individually decorated bedrooms vary in size and view. In the restaurant, the new chef, Phil Cubin, serves an 'appetising' menu, which might include fillet of beef with ox cheek, horseradish and potato purée, smoked bacon, red wine sauce. An 'excellent' breakfast is taken in the conservatory overlooking the 'immaculate' gardens: 'Freshly squeezed orange juice, beautiful scrambled eggs, sweet-cured bacon in plump rashers, good nutty coffee.' (*Harry and Annette Medcalf, Susan Raymond*)

25% DISCOUNT VOUCHERS

Crook Road
nr Windermere LA23 3NE

T: 015394-88818
F: 015394-88058
E: hotel@gilpinlodge.co.uk
W: www.gilpinlodge.co.uk

BEDROOMS: 26, 6 in orchard wing, 6 in *Lake House* (½ mile from main house).

OPEN: all year.

FACILITIES: ramps, bar, 2 lounges, 4 dining rooms, 22-acre grounds (ponds, croquet), free access to nearby country club, golf course opposite, unsuitable for ♿.

BACKGROUND MUSIC: none.

LOCATION: on B5284, 2 miles SE of Windermere.

CHILDREN: not under 7.

DOGS: not allowed (kennels at nearby farm).

CREDIT CARDS: all major cards.

PRICES: [2012] B&B £120–£250 per person, D,B&B £40 added, set dinner £52, special breaks, Christmas/New Year packages, 1-night bookings refused Sat.

SEE ALSO SHORTLIST

WINDERMERE Cumbria

Map 4: inset C2

HOLBECK GHYLL

Built as a hunting lodge for Lord Lonsdale, this Arts and Crafts house stands in large grounds which slope down to the lake. Managed by Andrew McPherson, it is owned by Stephen and Lisa Leahy, who have invested in considerable renovation. 'There is a constant programme of improvement in the house and the grounds, but it is not intrusive,' says a visitor returning in 2012. 'The service is exemplary and the food on song.' Another comment: 'The things that you expect from a hotel of this calibre are there: clean, well-appointed bedrooms, ample tea/coffee facilities and, a nice touch, a decanter of damson gin.' The rooms in a lodge and cottages in the grounds have 'superb views'. The entrance hall to the main house has stained glass, ornate fittings and wood carvings. Dinner orders are taken in two 'comfortable' lounges which overlook the lake. The chef, David McLaughlin, has a *Michelin* star for modern cooking: 'Delicious fishy starters; all meat is tender and tasty. Breakfasts are very good: with a wide choice of juices, fruits, cereals, pastries, bread.' (*ST, and others*)

25% DISCOUNT VOUCHERS

Holbeck Lane
Windermere LA23 1LU

T: 015394-32375
F: 015394-34743
E: stay@holbeckghyll.com
W: www.holbeckghyll.com

BEDROOMS: 25, 1 suitable for ♿, 6 in lodge, 5 in cottages.
OPEN: all year.
FACILITIES: ramp, 2 lounges, bar, restaurant, function facilities, civil wedding licence, small spa, 17-acre grounds (tennis, putting, croquet, jogging track).
BACKGROUND MUSIC: none.
LOCATION: 3 miles N of Windermere.
CHILDREN: not under 8 in restaurant.
DOGS: not allowed in public rooms.
CREDIT CARDS: Amex, MasterCard, Visa.
PRICES: [2012] B&B £80–£115 per person, D,B&B £145–£180, set dinner £65, Christmas/New Year packages, 1-night bookings sometimes refused Sat.

SEE ALSO SHORTLIST

WOLD NEWTON East Yorkshire

Map 4:D5

THE WOLD COTTAGE

The 'friendly welcome and excellent accommodation' are praised by visitors this year to Katrina and Derek Gray's red brick Georgian country house, formerly a city gentleman's country retreat which they run as a B&B. It stands in extensive landscaped grounds in a 'wonderful rural location' (the area was the inspiration for David Hockney's 'A Bigger Picture'). Bedrooms are spacious and individually designed; four are in the main house, two in a converted barn. A 'well-appointed' barn room was 'light and airy; lots of hot water in the bathroom'. There are also two self-catering cottages. Evening meals are served by arrangement in the dining room, which overlooks the garden. The hostess cooks traditional English dishes with vegetables from the garden. They are accompanied by a 'fairly priced' wine list. At the award-winning breakfasts, a buffet has 'masses of fresh fruit', home-made compotes, cereals; bread is home baked, preserves are also prepared in the kitchen; the sausages, bacon and black pudding come from local butchers. (*Florence and Russell Birch, and others*)

Wold Newton, nr Driffield
YO25 3HL

T/F: 01262-470696
E: katrina@woldcottage.com
W: www.woldcottage.com

BEDROOMS: 6, 2 in converted barn, 1 on ground floor.
OPEN: all year.
FACILITIES: lounge, dining room, 3-acre grounds (croquet) in 200-acre farmland.
BACKGROUND MUSIC: at mealtimes, contemporary.
LOCATION: just outside village.
CHILDREN: all ages welcomed.
DOGS: not allowed.
CREDIT CARDS: MasterCard, Visa.
PRICES: B&B £50–£75 per person, D,B&B £75–£100, full alc £40.

WOLTERTON Norfolk

Map 2:A5

THE SARACEN'S HEAD

'Almost off the map' deep in rural Norfolk, this country inn is distinctive, though history doesn't record why it was built in 1806 in the style of a Tuscan farmhouse. The owners, Tim and Janie Elwes, who formerly ran a small hotel in the French Alps, have renovated the bedrooms and bathrooms; the bar and restaurant were refurbished in early 2012. The nominator liked the combination of style and modest prices; *Guide* inspectors commented on the 'informal, laid-back accommodation'. We would welcome reports on the cooking of Mark Sayers, who has joined as chef; his seasonal menus can be taken in the 'relaxed' bar ('full of locals') and the smarter dining room. Typical dishes: button mushrooms in Binham Blue cheese sauce; baked Lowestoft cod, wilted spinach, mustard sauce. The bedrooms, decorated in modern style, have a flat-screen television, tea- and coffee-making facilities; plug-in Internet access ('as we are in the middle of nowhere, it is going to be slower than you are used to'). There are guidebooks and maps in a small upstairs sitting room. (*MB, and others*)

Wall Road
Wolterton, nr Erpingham
NR11 7LZ

T: 01263-768909
F: 01263-768993
E: info@saracenshead-norfolk.co.uk
W: www.saracenshead-norfolk.co.uk

BEDROOMS: 6.

OPEN: all year except 25–29 Dec, restaurant closed Mon (except bank holidays), Tues lunchtime except summer.

FACILITIES: lounge, bar, restaurant, courtyard, 1-acre garden, accommodation unsuitable for ♿.

BACKGROUND MUSIC: 'when suitable' in bar and dining rooms.

LOCATION: 5 miles N of Aylsham.

CHILDREN: all ages welcomed.

DOGS: not allowed in restaurant during meals.

CREDIT CARDS: MasterCard, Visa.

PRICES: B&B £50–£70 per person, D,B&B £30 added, full alc £40.

WOOLACOMBE Devon

Map 1:B4

WATERSMEET

'The position is lovely, the food is excellent, and the pleasant staff are attentive.' There is much praise this year for Amanda James's traditional hotel, on a cliff above Woolacombe Bay. 'The comfortable lounge and the dining room have excellent views stretching from Hartland Point to Lundy.' Tables are on three levels in the dining room 'ensuring every table has the view'; the chef, John Prince, uses local produce for his 'very good' modern English dishes, eg, bream, bacon and herb brioche, pesto, home-dried tomato dressing. Service is 'friendly and quick without being rushed'. 'The background music, though not intrusive, sometimes seemed inappropriate to the ambience.' All but three of the bedrooms face the sea: 'Our large room had a view of the cove, which was washed constantly by the tide.' 'Our magnificent ground-floor room had two comfortable chairs; its good bathroom had plenty of shelf space.' Light lunches are available in the bar. Breakfast has a small buffet, 'excellent' cooked dishes. 'The staff were always glad to offer advice on local places of interest.' *(RW, HJ Martin Tucker, LM Mayer Jones)*

Mortehoe
Woolacombe EX34 7EB

T: 01271-870333
F: 01271-870890
E: info@watersmeethotel.co.uk
W: www.watersmeethotel.co.uk

BEDROOMS: 29, 3 on ground floor, 1 suitable for ♿.
OPEN: all year.
FACILITIES: lift, lounge, bar, function room, civil wedding licence, terrace, ½-acre gardens, heated indoor and outdoor swimming pools, sandy beach below.
BACKGROUND MUSIC: classical/modern in restaurant.
LOCATION: by sea, 4 miles SW of Ilfracombe.
CHILDREN: all ages welcomed.
DOGS: not allowed.
CREDIT CARDS: MasterCard, Visa (*2% surcharge on credit cards*).
PRICES: [2012] B&B £51–£126 per person, D,B&B £76–£166, set dinner £36, full alc £50, midweek breaks, Christmas/New Year packages.

YARM North Yorkshire

Map 4:C4

JUDGES

Well away from the road in peaceful, wooded grounds with a stream and gardens (floodlit at night), this Victorian house (Pride of Britain) was built as a private residence and later became the residence for circuit judges. It is managed by Tim Howard ('friendly and charming') for the owners, the Downs family, who have converted the building into a hotel with sympathy and imagination. 'We loved our stay: our room was spacious but cosy, and the food was superb,' says a visitor in 2012. The chef, John Schwarz, serves 'excellent' modern dishes, perhaps 'perfectly cooked and attractively presented lobster with langoustines and crushed potatoes'. The bedrooms are furnished in keeping with the period: 'Our room had a lovely marble fireplace, two big armchairs, a large chest with cupboards and a minibar; all the usual modern equipment. The renovated bathroom was smart and well lit. A novelty was a goldfish, Finn, whom we were asked to talk to and feed.' A 'delicious' breakfast, served at table, has freshly squeezed orange juice, good unsalted butter and fresh fruits; 'plenty of cooked options from local fish to full Yorkshire'. (*Rebecca Walker, and others*)

25% DISCOUNT VOUCHERS

Kirklevington Hall
Yarm TS15 9LW

T: 01642-789000
F: 01642-782878
E: reservations@judgeshotel.co.uk
W: www.judgeshotel.co.uk

BEDROOMS: 21, some on ground floor.
OPEN: all year.
FACILITIES: ramps, lounge, bar, restaurant, private dining room, function facilities, business centre, civil wedding licence, 36-acre grounds (paths, running routes), access to local spa and sports club.
BACKGROUND MUSIC: none.
LOCATION: 1½ miles S of centre.
CHILDREN: all ages welcomed.
DOGS: only guide dogs allowed.
CREDIT CARDS: all major cards.
PRICES: [2012] B&B £65–£110 per person, D,B&B £97.50–£142.50, full alc £52, Christmas/New Year packages.

25%
DISCOUNT
VOUCHER

THE GOOD HOTEL GUIDE 2013
Use this voucher to claim a 25% discount off the normal price for bed and breakfast at hotels with a 25% DISCOUNT VOUCHERS sign at the end of the entry. **You must request a voucher discount at the time of booking and present this voucher on arrival. Further details and conditions overleaf.** Valid to 8th October 2013.

25%
DISCOUNT
VOUCHER

THE GOOD HOTEL GUIDE 2013
Use this voucher to claim a 25% discount off the normal price for bed and breakfast at hotels with a 25% DISCOUNT VOUCHERS sign at the end of the entry. **You must request a voucher discount at the time of booking and present this voucher on arrival. Further details and conditions overleaf.** Valid to 8th October 2013.

25%
DISCOUNT
VOUCHER

THE GOOD HOTEL GUIDE 2013
Use this voucher to claim a 25% discount off the normal price for bed and breakfast at hotels with a 25% DISCOUNT VOUCHERS sign at the end of the entry. **You must request a voucher discount at the time of booking and present this voucher on arrival. Further details and conditions overleaf.** Valid to 8th October 2013.

25%
DISCOUNT
VOUCHER

THE GOOD HOTEL GUIDE 2013
Use this voucher to claim a 25% discount off the normal price for bed and breakfast at hotels with a 25% DISCOUNT VOUCHERS sign at the end of the entry. **You must request a voucher discount at the time of booking and present this voucher on arrival. Further details and conditions overleaf.** Valid to 8th October 2013.

25%
DISCOUNT
VOUCHER

THE GOOD HOTEL GUIDE 2013
Use this voucher to claim a 25% discount off the normal price for bed and breakfast at hotels with a 25% DISCOUNT VOUCHERS sign at the end of the entry. **You must request a voucher discount at the time of booking and present this voucher on arrival. Further details and conditions overleaf.** Valid to 8th October 2013.

25%
DISCOUNT
VOUCHER

THE GOOD HOTEL GUIDE 2013
Use this voucher to claim a 25% discount off the normal price for bed and breakfast at hotels with a 25% DISCOUNT VOUCHERS sign at the end of the entry. **You must request a voucher discount at the time of booking and present this voucher on arrival. Further details and conditions overleaf.** Valid to 8th October 2013.

CONDITIONS

1. Hotels with a **25% DISCOUNT VOUCHERS** sign have agreed to give readers a discount of 25% off their normal bed-and-breakfast rate.
2. One voucher is good for the first night's stay only, at the discounted rate for yourself alone or for you and a partner sharing a double room.
3. Hotels may decline to accept a voucher reservation if they expect to be fully booked at the full room price.

CONDITIONS

1. Hotels with a **25% DISCOUNT VOUCHERS** sign have agreed to give readers a discount of 25% off their normal bed-and-breakfast rate.
2. One voucher is good for the first night's stay only, at the discounted rate for yourself alone or for you and a partner sharing a double room.
3. Hotels may decline to accept a voucher reservation if they expect to be fully booked at the full room price.

CONDITIONS

1. Hotels with a **25% DISCOUNT VOUCHERS** sign have agreed to give readers a discount of 25% off their normal bed-and-breakfast rate.
2. One voucher is good for the first night's stay only, at the discounted rate for yourself alone or for you and a partner sharing a double room.
3. Hotels may decline to accept a voucher reservation if they expect to be fully booked at the full room price.

CONDITIONS

1. Hotels with a **25% DISCOUNT VOUCHERS** sign have agreed to give readers a discount of 25% off their normal bed-and-breakfast rate.
2. One voucher is good for the first night's stay only, at the discounted rate for yourself alone or for you and a partner sharing a double room.
3. Hotels may decline to accept a voucher reservation if they expect to be fully booked at the full room price.

CONDITIONS

1. Hotels with a **25% DISCOUNT VOUCHERS** sign have agreed to give readers a discount of 25% off their normal bed-and-breakfast rate.
2. One voucher is good for the first night's stay only, at the discounted rate for yourself alone or for you and a partner sharing a double room.
3. Hotels may decline to accept a voucher reservation if they expect to be fully booked at the full room price.

CONDITIONS

1. Hotels with a **25% DISCOUNT VOUCHERS** sign have agreed to give readers a discount of 25% off their normal bed-and-breakfast rate.
2. One voucher is good for the first night's stay only, at the discounted rate for yourself alone or for you and a partner sharing a double room.
3. Hotels may decline to accept a voucher reservation if they expect to be fully booked at the full room price.

YORK North Yorkshire

Map 4:D4

MIDDLETHORPE HALL & SPA

'We were greeted by name,' say guests returning in 2012 to this 'faultless' red brick William and Mary country house, owned by the National Trust and managed by Lionel Chatard. Bordered by a busy road on the outskirts of the city, it stands in extensive grounds with 'beautiful' restored gardens, a lake and many specimen trees. Fruit trees in the walled gardens (guests may visit) provide the kitchens with heritage pears, peaches and greengages. 'Stylish without being staid', the public rooms have Chesterfields, gilded mirrors, antiques and historic paintings. Bedrooms are divided between the main house and an adjacent courtyard (the former stables); some have garden views. A 'delightful' courtyard suite had 'a comfortable king-size bed; relaxing lounge; excellent bathroom'. There is a smart dress code in the panelled dining room, where chef Nicholas Evans's cooking is 'delicate, tasty and innovative'. Desserts, eg, blood orange soufflé, are 'delicious'. The spa is 'an added bonus', with an 'inviting' swimming pool and 'relaxing' massages. (*Jane Bailey, and others*)

Bishopthorpe Road
York YO23 2GB

T: 01904-641241
F: 01904-620176
E: info@middlethorpe.com
W: www.middlethorpe.com

BEDROOMS: 29, 17 in courtyard, 2 in garden, 1 suitable for ♿.

OPEN: all year.

FACILITIES: drawing room, sitting rooms, library, bar, restaurant, private dining rooms, function facilities, civil wedding licence, 20-acre grounds, spa (heated indoor swimming pool, 13 by 6 metres).

BACKGROUND MUSIC: none.

LOCATION: 1½ miles S of centre, by racecourse.

CHILDREN: not under 6.

DOGS: only in garden suites, not in public rooms.

CREDIT CARDS: MasterCard, Visa.

PRICES: [2012] B&B (continental) £99.50–£239.50 per person, D,B&B from £129, set lunch £19.50–£24, gourmet menu £65, Christmas/New Year packages.

SEE ALSO SHORTLIST

ZENNOR Cornwall

Map 1:D1

THE GURNARD'S HEAD

César award in 2009

'Just how a pub should be', Charles and Edmund Inkin's laid-back inn is on the road from Zennor towards Land's End. The bar and restaurant have an informal air: wooden tables and chairs, rugs on wooden floors; strong colours, 'lots of interesting artwork'. Visitors this year found the bar busy at lunchtime: 'The bright cheerful staff were on top of everything. We enjoyed two delicious starters with home-baked soda bread, the best I've tasted outside Ireland.' Chef Bruce Rennie uses local suppliers for his modern menus which have a good selection of dishes for vegetarians (eg, beetroot risotto, sage, walnuts). More work has been done on the bedrooms this year: they have fresh flowers, a Roberts radio (no television), Welsh blankets. Some face the Atlantic, others the moors. The largest room, at the back, has double-aspect windows; a large light bathroom. Breakfast ('simple but good') has Cornish apple juice, seasonal fresh fruit; the soda bread 'makes excellent toast'; home-made preserves and marmalade; kippers and full English. The Inkin brothers also own the *Felin Fach Griffin*, Felin Fach, in Wales (see entry). (*DB*)

25% DISCOUNT VOUCHERS

Treen, nr Zennor
St Ives TR26 3DE

T: 01736-796928
E: enquiries@gurnardshead.co.uk
W: www.gurnardshead.co.uk

BEDROOMS: 7.
OPEN: all year except 24/25 Dec, 4 days in Jan.
FACILITIES: bar area, small connecting room with sofas, dining room, ½-acre garden, unsuitable for ♿.
BACKGROUND MUSIC: in bar.
LOCATION: 6½ miles SW of St Ives, on B3306.
CHILDREN: all ages welcomed.
DOGS: not allowed in dining room.
CREDIT CARDS: MasterCard, Visa.
PRICES: [2012] B&B £48.75–£80 per person, D,B&B £68.75–£110, full alc £35, midweek offers, 'Sunday sleepover' rates, 1-night bookings 'occasionally' refused.

SCOTLAND

Corrieshalloch Gorge, Highland

ACHILTIBUIE Highland

Map 5:B1

SUMMER ISLES

NEW

In a remote position reached by a single-track road north of Ullapool, this small hotel/ restaurant has spectacular views over the sea to the Summer Isles and the Hebrides. Owned by Terry and Irina Mackay, it is managed by Jody Marshall. For more than 25 years, the cooking of chef Chris Firth-Bernard has persuaded visitors to make the journey. 'It is one of our very favourites,' says a returning guest this year. 'The food gets better and better.' No choice on the five-course dinner menu (dietary requirements accommodated): 'He has a real lightness of touch, and makes the most of the wonderful local ingredients (langoustines, fish, etc). The cheese trolley is a delight and the puddings (all home made) are superb.' The hotel now has its own herd of Highland cattle and a flock of rare breed sheep. Three bedrooms are in the main house ('very comfortable'); other rooms are in cottages and converted outbuildings. They have local soaps and spring water. An attached bar is a friendly local with a 'good selection of whiskies'; informal meals are served here. Breakfast is a 'triumph'. (*Angy Kirker*)

25% DISCOUNT VOUCHERS

Achiltibuie
by Ullapool IV26 2YG

T: 01854-622282
F: 01854-622251
E: info@summerisleshotel.com
W: www.summerisleshotel.com

BEDROOMS: 13, 10 in annexe and cottages.
OPEN: Apr–Oct.
FACILITIES: sitting room, whisky snug, sun lounge, dining room, wedding facilities, 1-acre garden.
BACKGROUND MUSIC: traditional in bar.
LOCATION: 25 miles NW of Ullapool.
CHILDREN: all ages welcomed.
DOGS: not allowed in public rooms.
CREDIT CARDS: MasterCard, Visa.
PRICES: B&B £77.50–£145 per person, set dinner £58, full alc £45.

ARDUAINE Argyll and Bute

Map 5:D1

LOCH MELFORT HOTEL

'A lovely hotel in beautiful surroundings,' says a visitor this year to Calum and Rachel Ross's country hotel on Asknish Bay. 'The staff are friendly and efficient; the peace and quiet is the perfect chill-out; they have Highland cattle, ducks and hens to keep little ones interested; nice walks in the grounds.' Another comment (in 2012): 'A very good place in a peaceful setting.' The five bedrooms in the main house vary in size; 20 are in a wood-framed extension (some noise) attached to the main house by a partly open walkway. These are spacious, 'well furnished and comfortable', and each has a private terrace or balcony. There are two 'comfortable' lounges; all rooms have 'wonderful' views. Guests again enjoyed the 'excellent cooking' of chef David Bell. His four-course menu of modern Scottish dishes in the dining room might include boudin of quail stuffed with Stornoway black pudding. Puddings are 'daintily served'. Informal meals are available in the *Chartroom* bistro next to Arduaine Garden, which is owned by the National Trust for Scotland. The 'excellent' breakfast has 'whole kippers, smoked haddock with a free-range egg'. (*Andrea McLellan, Marc Wall*)

25% DISCOUNT VOUCHERS

Arduaine
By Oban PA34 4XG

T: 01852-200233
F: 01852-200214
E: reception@lochmelfort.co.uk
W: www.lochmelfort.co.uk

BEDROOMS: 25, 20 in *Cedar Wing* annexe, 10 on ground floor.
OPEN: all year except 2 weeks mid-Jan.
FACILITIES: sitting room, library, bar, restaurant, wedding facilities, 19-acre grounds (including National Trust for Scotland's Arduaine Gardens).
BACKGROUND MUSIC: modern Scottish in public areas.
LOCATION: 19 miles S of Oban.
CHILDREN: all ages welcomed, under-2s free.
DOGS: allowed in 6 bedrooms, not in public rooms.
CREDIT CARDS: MasterCard, Visa.
PRICES: [2012] B&B £72–£134 per person, D,B&B £98–£153, £30 single supplement, set meals £36.95, full alc £52.50, special breaks, Christmas/New Year packages.

AULDEARN Highland

Map 5:C2

BOATH HOUSE

César award: Scottish hotel of the year

'There is a real feeling of warmth about this wonderful small hotel.' *Guide* inspectors were impressed this year by Wendy and Don Matheson's stylishly restored Regency mansion. The manager, Jonny Ross, is 'a huge asset; he did everything while we were there; taking orders, waiting at table, taking luggage to rooms, etc.' The lounges and library are 'full of interesting pictures and sculptures'. Guests gather in a candlelit lounge for 'delicious' cocktails and canapés, before addressing *Michelin*-starred chef Charlie Lockley's 'memorable and unfussy' daily-changing menu. 'I particularly remember the sensation of roasted seeds bursting in my mouth as I ate the soup, the earthy flavour of chickweed and Puy lentils with the rabbit, the most scrumptious hot chocolate pudding.' The bedrooms are individually styled. 'Our lovely large room had a very comfortable four-poster bed, a day bed at the window, and a view overlooking the lake. The bathroom had beautiful soft towels and gowns.' A 'wonderful' breakfast has plum smoothies; 'lovely' organic porridge; duck eggs with wild mushrooms.

Auldearn
Nairn
IV12 5TE

T: 01667-454896
F: 01667-455469
E: info@boath-house.com
W: www.boath-house.com

BEDROOMS: 8, 1 in cottage (50 yds) suitable for ♿.

OPEN: all year.

FACILITIES: 2 lounges, library, orangery, restaurant, health/beauty spa, wedding facilities, 20-acre grounds (woods, gardens, meadow, streams, trout lake).

BACKGROUND MUSIC: none.

LOCATION: 1½ miles E of Nairn.

CHILDREN: all ages welcomed.

DOGS: not in public rooms.

CREDIT CARDS: MasterCard, Visa.

PRICES: B&B £115–£190 per person, D,B&B £172.50–£260, set dinner £70, midweek and winter breaks, Christmas/New Year packages.

BALLANTRAE South Ayrshire

Map 5:E1

COSSES COUNTRY HOUSE

Built as a shooting lodge (later a farm), Susan and Robin Crosthwaite's small guest house has a gold award in the Green Tourism Business Scheme. For her daily-changing menus, Susan Crosthwaite, who has written a book of local recipes, uses produce from nearby farms, and vegetables and herbs from her garden where greenhouses have solar heating and water-harvesting facilities. Her 'Scottish gourmet' meals, which are taken communally, might include Ballantrae crab with a hint of grapefruit and yogurt, strawberries and rocket; loin of Ayrshire lamb, garlic, ginger and rosemary, home-grown potatoes, spring cabbage, mangetout. Two of the bedrooms are in converted byres across the stable yard. They are traditionally furnished; each has a private sitting room (books, maps, games, local information). In the bathrooms is a walk-in shower, bath, under-floor heating. A smaller room in the house is cheaper but has no shower. There is tea and home-made cakes and scones for arriving visitors in a pretty drawing room. Breakfast has fresh fruit, home-made bread and preserves; hot dishes include shirred (baked) eggs. More reports, please.

Ballantrae
KA26 0LR

T: 01465-831363
F: 01465-831598
E: staying@cossescountryhouse.com
W: www.cossescountryhouse.com

BEDROOMS: 3, on ground floor, 2 across courtyard.
OPEN: Mar–20 Dec.
FACILITIES: drawing room, dining room, games room (table tennis, darts), 12-acre grounds.
BACKGROUND MUSIC: none.
LOCATION: 2 miles E of Ballantrae.
CHILDREN: not under 12.
DOGS: allowed by arrangement in 1 suite, not in public rooms.
CREDIT CARDS: MasterCard, Visa.
PRICES: [2012] B&B £45–£75 per person, set dinner £35, special breaks.

BALLANTRAE South Ayrshire

Map 5:E1

GLENAPP CASTLE

In 'delightful' gardens on high ground overlooking Ailsa Craig, this classic example of a 19th-century baronial castle is run as a luxurious hotel (Relais & Châteaux) by owners Graham and Fay Cowan. 'We were greeted by three staff members at the entrance,' says a visitor in 2012. 'Our luggage was taken to our room and everything was explained to us. The service was exemplary; friendly, no standing on ceremony.' Another comment: 'A perfect stay; the food was outstanding.' The castle has been furnished with fine paintings, Middle Eastern rugs, antiques. The library has floor-to-ceiling bookshelves. Guests have exclusive access to the gardens, which have a huge Victorian glasshouse, rare plants and shrubs, a walled garden and woodland walks. Adam Stokes, the 'innovative and confident' *Michelin*-starred chef, serves 'beautifully presented' dishes on a daily-changing menu which is 'interspersed with little tasters'. The large bedrooms have swagged curtains and wide bed. 'Our spacious ground-floor room (with access to the garden) had a seating area; a large bathroom had a claw-footed bath and separate shower. Tariffs are high but expectations were met.' (*ST, and others*)

25% DISCOUNT VOUCHERS

Ballantrae
KA26 0NZ

T: 01465-831212
F: 01465-831000
E: info@glenappcastle.com
W: www.glenappcastle.com

BEDROOMS: 17, 7 on ground floor.
OPEN: late Mar–2 Jan, except Christmas (though available on request).
FACILITIES: ramp, lift, drawing room, library, 2 dining rooms, wedding facilities, 36-acre gardens (tennis, croquet), fishing, golf nearby, access to spa.
BACKGROUND MUSIC: none.
LOCATION: 2 miles S of Ballantrae.
CHILDREN: no under-5s in dining room after 7 pm.
DOGS: allowed in certain bedrooms, not in public rooms.
CREDIT CARDS: Amex, MasterCard, Visa.
PRICES: [2012] B&B £177.50–£280 per person, D,B&B £207.50–£310, set dinner £65, website offers, New Year package.

BALLATER Aberdeenshire

Map 5:C3

DEESIDE HOTEL

In 'a pretty wooded garden' (where red squirrels can be seen), Gordon Waddell and Penella Price's small hotel in the Cairngorm national park is 'as good as ever', says a third-time visitor this year. She is the 'polite and helpful' host in a Victorian house that has 'welcoming' log fires in a 'small, comfortable' library and lounge (leather and tartan), and in the restaurant in winter. In summer, meals are taken in the conservatory area overlooking the walled garden which supplies herbs, vegetables and soft fruit for Mr Waddell's 'modern Scottish' cooking. 'The food is excellent; the seasonal menu has daily variations; venison and duck particularly good; desserts are especially fine; our favourite was orange pudding with whisky marmalade and orange ice cream.' There is always a vegetarian option. The bedrooms, with king-size bed, vary in size and have good storage; the hospitality trays have Deeside mineral water, herbal teas and Fairtrade hot chocolate. Breakfast includes a wide choice of cooked dishes with local bacon, eggs and sausage, tattie scones, cheese omelette. Balmoral is nearby. (*Alan and Edwina Williams, Graeme Ballantine*)

25% DISCOUNT VOUCHERS

45 Braemar Road
Ballater AB35 5RQ

T: 013397-55420
F: 0871 989 5933
E: mail@deesidehotel.co.uk
W: www.deesidehotel.co.uk

BEDROOMS: 9, 2 on ground floor.
OPEN: March–Nov.
FACILITIES: ramp, library, lounge/bar, restaurant, 1-acre garden.
BACKGROUND MUSIC: classical in bar and restaurant.
LOCATION: village outskirts.
CHILDREN: all ages welcomed.
DOGS: not allowed.
CREDIT CARDS: MasterCard, Visa.
PRICES: [2012] B&B £45–£65 per person, D,B&B £70–£90, set dinner menus £25, £30, full alc £47, 1-night bookings sometimes refused Sat.

BLAIRGOWRIE Perth and Kinross

Map 5:D2

KINLOCH HOUSE

Liked for the 'strong and appealing Scottish domestic atmosphere', the Allen family's country house hotel (Relais & Châteaux) stands on a hillside near Dunkeld. A 'graceful, upward-sweeping drive' leads to the creeper-clad, early Victorian mansion (with a modern extension). A former *Guide* hotelier this year welcomed 'the owners' attention to the comfort and well-being of their guests'. The reception rooms are 'well maintained'; the hall is oak-panelled; a portrait gallery has an ornate glass ceiling; there are 'pretty painted bird lamps, leather sofas and chairs' in the bar, 'blazing log fires' in the lounges. Many of the traditionally furnished bedrooms are spacious; 'sheets and blankets on our exceptionally comfortable bed'. One visitor would have liked a tray of tea, coffee and bottled water. Most showers are hand held. In the 'pleasant' dining room, with 'well-spaced' tables, the cooking of chef Steven MacCallum is 'of a high order'. His 'modern British' dishes might include breast of duck, chestnuts, creamed pearl barley, celeriac, a prune and apple sauce. The service is 'formal, polite'. Popular with shooting parties. (*Robert Gower, Dennis Marler, and others*)

Dunkeld Road
by Blairgowrie PH10 6SG

T: 01250-884237
F: 01250-884333
E: reception@kinlochhouse.com
W: www.kinlochhouse.com

BEDROOMS: 15, 4 on ground floor.
OPEN: all year except 12–29 Dec.
FACILITIES: ramp, 5 public rooms, private dining room, wedding facilities, 25-acre grounds.
BACKGROUND MUSIC: none.
LOCATION: 3 miles W of Blairgowrie.
CHILDREN: no under-7s in dining room at night.
DOGS: allowed by arrangement only.
CREDIT CARDS: MasterCard, Visa.
PRICES: [2012] B&B £107.50–£162.50 per person, set dinner £53, full alc £70, New Year package, 1-night bookings refused at New Year.

BROADFORD Highland

Map 5:C1

TIGH AN DOCHAIS

'Recommended without hesitation' this year by a three-time visitor, this striking contemporary house was designed by award-winning architects to make the most of the views across Broadford Bay. The owners, Neil Hope and Lesley Unwin, are 'delightful hosts, offering tea and coffee and shortbread on arrival, and serving delicious breakfasts and evening meals'. The house is entered by a bridge to the upper floor: the guest lounge has a wood-burning stove, shelves crammed with books, comfortable seating. The ground-floor bedrooms 'are spacious and well equipped, and have fantastic views across the bay'. The house is within walking distance of pubs and restaurants. Mr Hope will cook an evening meal, which must be booked in advance, when a menu can be tailored to tastes. It might include langoustine bisque; artisan cheeses and an individual baked fruit sponge. Breakfast, taken communally in the lounge, has a buffet of fruits, cereals, home-made bread and preserves, and smoked salmon; dishes cooked to order include haddock and kipper 'smoked by Ian'. Afterwards, 'walk straight on to the beach (when the tide is out)'. (*Michael Fraser*)

13 Harrapool, Broadford
Isle of Skye IV49 9AQ

T: 01471-820022
E: hopeskye@btinternet.com
W: www.skyebedbreakfast.co.uk

BEDROOMS: 3, all on ground floor.
OPEN: Apr–Nov.
FACILITIES: lounge, dining area, ½-acre garden, unsuitable for ♿.
BACKGROUND MUSIC: Celtic at breakfast.
LOCATION: 1 mile E of Broadford.
CHILDREN: all ages welcomed.
DOGS: not allowed.
CREDIT CARDS: Amex, MasterCard, Visa.
PRICES: B&B £42.50–£45 per person, set dinner £25, 1-night bookings sometimes refused.

BRODICK North Ayrshire

Map 5:E1

KILMICHAEL COUNTRY HOUSE

Thought to be the oldest house on Arran, this white-painted 17th-century mansion stands in wooded grounds with fine views of Goat Fell, the island's highest peak. It retains the atmosphere of a private house: the owners, Geoffrey Botterill and Antony Butterworth, treat visitors as 'personal guests'. They have filled the house with furniture and pictures collected on their travels. The two 'spacious, properly lit' first-floor lounges are 'good places in which to relax'; the Yellow Drawing Room has a Broadwood piano for guests to play. Five bedrooms are in the main house (one has a four-poster and a bath 'big enough for two'). Three are in neighbouring converted stables. 'Our lovely room had lots of thoughtful touches: a bone china tea set, OS map.' In the conservatory dining room, Antony Butterworth's four-course menu changes daily (no choice, preferences discussed). Typical dishes: leek, pea and asparagus tartlet; breast of pheasant en papillote, rosemary and redcurrant sauce, apples in calvados. Guests praise the flexibility shown to those with special dietary needs. 'Gluten-free bread was baked specially.' The garden is patrolled by peacocks and ducks. (*PS, and others*)

Glen Cloy, by Brodick
Isle of Arran KA27 8BY

T: 01770-302219
F: 01770-302068
E: enquiries@kilmichael.com
W: www.kilmichael.com

BEDROOMS: 8, 3 in converted stables (20 yds), 7 on ground floor, 4 self-catering cottages.
OPEN: Easter–Oct, restaurant closed Mon and Tues.
FACILITIES: 2 drawing rooms, dining room, 4½-acre grounds (burn).
BACKGROUND MUSIC: light classical during meals.
LOCATION: 1 mile SW of village.
CHILDREN: not under 12.
DOGS: not allowed in public rooms.
CREDIT CARDS: MasterCard, Visa.
PRICES: [2012] B&B £65–£102.50 per person, dinner £45, various packages, 1-night bookings sometimes refused Sat.

SEE ALSO SHORTLIST

CARRADALE Argyll and Bute

Map 5:E1

DUNVALANREE IN CARRADALE

On the outskirts of a pretty village on the Kintyre peninsula, Alan and Alyson Milstead's small hotel/restaurant is at the end of a quiet road with beaches on both sides. 'The brown and cream paintwork gives it an old-fashioned air, which is precisely its charm,' says a visitor this year. 'Alan runs the front-of-house in a likeable, amusing way.' The simple bedrooms are decorated in pale colours with modern pine furniture: 'Our room at the front had a fantastic sea view; a large and very comfortable bed; lots of extras (whisky, home-made shortbread, fresh milk for tea- and coffee-making); a generous range of toiletries in the bathroom which also had the view.' Guests gather at 7 pm in the large lounge to choose from Mrs Milstead's daily-changing menu. 'Exceptional cooking of fine ingredients beautifully presented; each evening a tiny bowl of home-made soup was a delicious amuse-bouche.' A typical 'generous' main course dish: honey-roasted duckling with spiced blueberries. 'Breakfast doesn't disappoint: each person has an individual jug of freshly squeezed juice; good thick toast; fantastic cooked dishes.' (*CLH*)

25% DISCOUNT VOUCHERS

Port Righ, Carradale
PA28 6SE

T: 01583-431226
E: book@dunvalanree.com
W: www.dunvalanree.com

BEDROOMS: 7, 1 on ground floor suitable for ♿.
OPEN: all year except Christmas.
FACILITIES: lounge, dining room, ½-acre garden.
BACKGROUND MUSIC: Scottish in dining room.
LOCATION: on edge of village 15 miles N of Campbeltown.
CHILDREN: all ages welcomed.
DOGS: allowed in bedrooms only.
CREDIT CARDS: MasterCard, Visa.
PRICES: [2012] B&B £40–£75 per person, D,B&B £60–£95, set menus £23.50–£28, full alc £45, New Year package.

COLONSAY Argyll and Bute

Map 5:D1

THE COLONSAY

'Just right for the setting; the atmosphere is relaxing and unpretentious, catering for people leading an outdoors kind of life.' Inspectors in 2012 were happy staying at Jane and Alex Howard's renovated mid-18th-century inn, on a hill above the harbour. It has 'stunning views all round'. Lorne Smith, the quietly spoken manager, 'has his finger on the pulse; the staff are welcoming and friendly'. The 'well-maintained' garden has outdoor seating areas; public rooms 'have good sofas and plenty of light; wood-burning stoves and open fires to give them a cosy feel'. The bedrooms vary in size and outlook: 'Our room was large and warm, simply furnished but comfortable.' There is locally brewed beer in the bar, which is popular with islanders. In the dining room, head chef Robert Smyth's 'simply prepared but delicious' menus include much seafood, and vegetables and herbs from the hotel's kitchen garden. 'We enjoyed haddock with butter sauce and home-made chips; lamb stew and sirloin steak with pepper sauce.' Breakfast is continental (an extra charge is made for 'tasty' cooked dishes); bread and jams are home made.

25% DISCOUNT VOUCHERS

Isle of Colonsay
PA61 7YP

T: 01951-200316
F: 01951-200353
E: hotel@colonsayestate.co.uk
W: www.colonsayestate.co.uk

BEDROOMS: 9.
OPEN: Mar–Oct, Christmas, New Year, no check-in Mon and Sat.
FACILITIES: conservatory lounge, log room, bar, restaurant, wedding facilities, accommodation unsuitable for ♿.
BACKGROUND MUSIC: 'easy listening' occasionally in bar.
LOCATION: 400 yds W of harbour.
CHILDREN: all ages welcomed.
DOGS: allowed in 2 bedrooms.
CREDIT CARDS: MasterCard, Visa.
PRICES: [2012] B&B £42.50–£72.50 per person, D,B&B £27 added, full alc £35, seasonal breaks, Christmas/New Year packages.

CONTIN Highland

Map 5:C2

COUL HOUSE

A Georgian hunting lodge in attractive wooded grounds outside a small Highland village, this country hotel is thought 'a wonderful place to stay'. The 'helpful' resident owners, Susannah and Stuart Macpherson, are 'hands-on' hosts, say visitors this year. Their manager, Chris McLeod, is 'deft and attentive'. Inspectors were greeted by name in the large hall/sitting room. The bedrooms have 'good storage, excellent bedlinen and lighting'. 'My very comfortable room had an excellent new bed; I slept like a dream. My bathroom was adequate, but maybe due for a little modernisation.' The 'lovely' public rooms are 'beautifully proportioned'. In the 'stunning' octagonal dining room, chef Garry Kenley serves a contemporary Scottish menu, perhaps crab cakes, fennel and cashew salad; duck breast, star anise, spiced potato and cauliflower croquette. 'This is seriously good food; the service was excellent, the wine list interesting.' A 'delicious' cooked breakfast, taken in a 'handsome, high-ceilinged room', is chosen from a comprehensive menu and has home-baked bread, home-made marmalade, 'good' coffee. 'There is easy access to the east and west coasts and Inverness.' (*Tony Hall, and others*)

25% DISCOUNT VOUCHERS

Contin
by Strathpeffer
IV14 9ES

T: 01997-421487
F: 01997-421945
E: stay@coulhouse.com
W: www.coulhouse.com

BEDROOMS: 20, 4 on ground floor.
OPEN: all year except Christmas.
FACILITIES: ramp, bar, lounge, restaurant, conference/wedding facilities, 8-acre garden (children's play area, 9-hole pitch and putt).
BACKGROUND MUSIC: in lounge bar and restaurant.
LOCATION: 17 miles NW of Inverness.
CHILDREN: all ages welcomed, discounts up to age 15.
DOGS: allowed except in restaurant (£5 per day, less for longer).
CREDIT CARDS: MasterCard, Visa.
PRICES: [2012] B&B £82.50–£112.50 per person, full alc £40, special breaks, New Year package.

CRINAN Argyll and Bute

Map 5:D1

CRINAN HOTEL

'In a superb position for scenery gazing', this white-painted hotel by the Crinan Canal is run 'with friendly informality and a leisurely ambience' by Nick and Frances Ryan. It has views of sea, canal locks and distant hills from the public rooms and the bedrooms. It is sometimes described as an art-gallery-with-rooms: Mrs Ryan (the artist Frances Macdonald) oversees a gallery on the top floor; original paintings and drawings are displayed throughout (some are for sale). 'Mr Ryan gave us a warm welcome and assisted us with our luggage,' says a visitor this year. 'The staff are friendly; some are Eastern European, which made for interesting conversations.' In the *Westward* restaurant ('spanking white linen and fresh flowers'), chef Gregor Bara uses local produce for his traditional French/Scottish dishes, eg, fillet of halibut, crushed potato, broccoli, beurre blanc. Meals are also served in a seafood bar (the menu includes steak and sausages), which is popular with sailors. Breakfast is served at table: 'The cooked dishes were good, in particular scrambled eggs and smoked salmon.' Children and dogs are welcomed. (*ST*)

Crinan
by Lochgilphead
PA31 8SR

T: 01546-830261
F: 01546-830292
E: reservations@crinanhotel.com
W: www.crinanhotel.com

BEDROOMS: 20.
OPEN: all year except Christmas, might close Mon/Tues Nov/Mar.
FACILITIES: lift, ramps, 2 lounges, gallery bar, seafood bar, restaurant, coffee shop, treatment room (health and beauty), wedding facilities, patio, ¼-acre garden.
BACKGROUND MUSIC: none.
LOCATION: village centre, waterfront.
CHILDREN: all ages welcomed.
DOGS: not allowed in restaurant.
CREDIT CARDS: MasterCard, Visa.
PRICES: [2012] B&B £65–£135 per person, D,B&B £105–£175, set dinner (restaurant) £45, full alc (seafood bar) £28, last-minute breaks, courses.

DERVAIG Argyll and Bute

Map 5:C1

KILLORAN HOUSE

'The gorgeous setting on a hillside' appealed to visitors to Janette and Ian McKilligan's 'immaculate' small hotel a few miles from Tobermory. The welcome from Mrs McKilligan – 'helpful and friendly, without being effusive' – was praised. 'She greeted us at the car and seized cases to carry to our room.' The white-painted house is 'substantial and new looking'; the 'handsome' sitting room, with large balcony, on the first floor, provides 'splendidly dramatic views' of the sea loch. 'Tea and very good cake were provided when we had settled.' Mr McKilligan is the chef, serving a no-choice dinner at 7.30 pm at well-spaced tables. The four courses (a two-course version is available) might include seared king scallops, minted pea purée, carrot crisps; saddle of venison with juniper and redcurrant sauce. Bedrooms, varying in size and outlook, have mostly modern pine furniture. Bathrooms, with power shower, are spacious with 'plenty of hot water and fluffy towels'. Breakfast has 'an attractive choice of cereals; stewed fruit; chunky toast'; various cooked choices, eg, pancakes and maple syrup; scrambled eggs with smoked salmon. (*SS, and others*)

25% DISCOUNT VOUCHERS

Dervaig, Isle of Mull PA75 6QR

T: 01688-400362
F: 01688-400552
E: enquiries@killoranmull.co.uk
W: www.killoranmull.co.uk

BEDROOMS: 6, 1 on ground floor suitable for ♿.
OPEN: all year except Christmas/New Year.
FACILITIES: sitting room, study, conservatory dining room, 1¾-acre gardens.
BACKGROUND MUSIC: 'easy listening' in dining room.
LOCATION: 1½ miles SW of Dervaig.
CHILDREN: not under 13.
DOGS: not allowed in public rooms.
CREDIT CARDS: MasterCard, Visa.
PRICES: [2012] B&B (min. 2 nights) £60–£90 per person, 2-course set dinner from £25, 4 courses £36, discount for returning guests.

DORNOCH Highland

Map 5:B2

2 QUAIL

In the main street of a town of mellow stone houses, noted for its small cathedral, long sandy beach and championship golf course, this Victorian house is run as a licensed B&B by Michael and Kerensa Carr. They are 'friendly and helpful; delightful hosts', as well as enthusiastic golfers. It is within walking distance of Royal Dornoch Golf Club, an outstanding 'natural' course, where *Ritz*-trained Mr Carr is executive chef. Advice is given, for non-golfing visitors, on places to eat in the town 'for a variety of budgets'. Guests are encouraged to enjoy a glass of wine or 'a wee dram' in the lounge/ library, which has floor-to-ceiling bookcases, tartan carpet. An award-winning picture framer and restorer, Mrs Carr is 'cheerful and amusing'. The three 'clean, comfortable' bedrooms are well proportioned, with traditional furnishings, wood or iron bedstead with feather duvet, power shower. Breakfast, served at an agreed time from 7 am ('for those with early tee times'), has fresh fruit, home-made yogurts and muesli, croissants; cooked dishes include kippers and smoked salmon from Golspie. More reports, please.

Castle Street
Dornoch IV25 3SN

T: 01862-811811
E: goodhotel@2quail.com
W: www.2quail.com

BEDROOMS: 3.
OPEN: all year except Christmas.
FACILITIES: lounge, dining room, unsuitable for ♿.
BACKGROUND MUSIC: none.
LOCATION: central.
CHILDREN: not under 10 except for 'babes in arms'.
DOGS: not allowed.
CREDIT CARDS: Amex, MasterCard, Visa.
PRICES: B&B £45–£55 per person.

DRUMBEG Highland

Map 5:B1

BLÀR NA LEISG AT DRUMBEG HOUSE

In secluded wooded grounds high above Eddrachillis Bay, this 'delightful' restaurant-with-rooms is run by 'perfect hosts' Anne and Eddie Strachan. 'It was like staying with your dearest friends,' say visitors this year. The 'simple, modern' public rooms are filled with contemporary, mostly Scottish art; the library is stocked with books to borrow. Bedrooms have a 'wonderfully big and comfy' bed; 'well-thought-out' bathrooms. Mrs Strachan's 'superb', leisurely dinners – 'never before 9 pm' – begin with amuse-bouche in the library. The no-choice menus (preferences discussed) might include squash gnocchi roulade, spinach, wild mushrooms; John Dory, samphire, salmon caviar butter. Inspectors 'could gladly have curled up by the fire, read to our hearts' content, listened to music, eaten delicious things, sipped fine wine and never stirred again'. Breakfast, 'served at a time to suit guests', has 'racks of home-baked bread, home-made marmalade, wonderful Caithness bacon, plentiful supplies of coffee and hot milk'. 'Altogether an unforgettable experience.' (*Kate and Malcolm MacMaster*)

Drumbeg IV27 4NW

T/F: 01571-833325
E: info@blarnaleisg.com
W: www.blarnaleisg.com

BEDROOMS: 4, plus self-catering studio.
OPEN: all year.
FACILITIES: lounge, library, day room, dining room, 4-acre grounds, unsuitable for ♿.
BACKGROUND MUSIC: live traditional music on request.
LOCATION: outskirts of village.
CHILDREN: all ages welcomed (by arrangement).
DOGS: only allowed in studio.
CREDIT CARDS: none.
PRICES: [2012] D,B&B £125–£130 per person, set meals £54, New Year package.

DUNVEGAN Highland

Map 5:C1

THE THREE CHIMNEYS AND THE HOUSE OVER-BY

César award in 2001

On the shore of Loch Dunvegan, this remote restaurant-with-rooms has been run by Shirley and Eddie Spear since 1984. 'This is a haven of comfort, the staff are incredibly warm hearted and natural, and the food is really that good,' says a visitor this year. The restaurant occupies a 120-year-old crofter's cottage; the 'comfortable, modern' bedrooms are in *The House Over-By*, next door. In the candlelit restaurant, chef Michael Smith's contemporary cooking is 'fresh, simple, not too quirky and absolutely convincing in its quality'. A typical dish: Arisaig mussel and surf clam risotto, lemon sole, fennel and spiced shellfish oil. The bedrooms have 'good views' of the sea and access to a shared garden; a telescope in the Morning Room, where an 'excellent' breakfast (home-made granola, porridge cooked to order, the house's smoked fish pâté) is served, gives close-ups of seals in the loch. 'A terrace in full sun' is ideal on warmer days; in inclement weather, 'you can spend hours in the lounge'. 'The whole operation is better than anything else on the island.' (*Christian Bartoschek and Régine Marcy, Barbara Watkinson, Angy Kirker*)

Colbost, Dunvegan
Isle of Skye IV55 8ZT

T: 01470-511258
F: 01470-511358
E: eatandstay@threechimneys.co.uk
W: www.threechimneys.co.uk

BEDROOMS: 6, all on ground floor in separate building, 1 suitable for ♿.

OPEN: all year except 30 Nov–24 Jan, restaurant closed midday Sun and midday in winter.

FACILITIES: ramps, 3 public rooms, garden on loch.

BACKGROUND MUSIC: in lounge in evenings.

LOCATION: 4 miles W of Dunvegan.

CHILDREN: no under-5s at lunch, no under-8s at dinner, tea at 5 pm.

DOGS: not allowed.

CREDIT CARDS: Amex, MasterCard, Visa.

PRICES: [2012] B&B £147.50 per person, D,B&B from £207.50, set lunch £28.50–£37, set dinner £60–£90, full alc £77.50, winter/spring offers.

DUROR Argyll and Bute

Map 5:D1

BEALACH HOUSE

César award in 2009

In a 'fabulous' location between Oban and Fort William, this small but well-planned guest house (Wolsey Lodge) is run by Jim and Hilary McFadyen, 'superb hosts'. Up a mile and a half of forestry track ('Porsche and Ferrari owners should give it a miss'), it is the only house in the glen. The lounge has a wood-burning stove, books and games, jigsaws. Bedrooms, if not large, 'had everything we needed'. Each has tea- and coffee-making with 'fresh chilled milk'; 'we were treated to a small decanter of whisky'. Bathrooms have a power shower (one also has a bath). The conservatory and patio have 'wonderful views', as do the eight-acre grounds. Guests eat together in the small dining room at dinner, and at breakfast, when dinner choices (always one vegetarian option) are made from Hilary McFadyen's daily-changing menu. 'She is a great cook' (serving dishes like halibut with a creamy prawn and Pernod sauce). Chutneys and ice creams are home made as are breads and jams; breakfasts are praised. There is 'lots to do' locally. 'Good value.' (*Esler Crawford, and others*)

Salachan Glen
Duror PA38 4BW

T: 01631-740298
E: info@bealachhouse.co.uk
W: www.bealachhouse.co.uk

BEDROOMS: 3.
OPEN: March–Oct.
FACILITIES: lounge, conservatory, dining room, 8-acre grounds, unsuitable for ♿.
BACKGROUND MUSIC: none.
LOCATION: 2 miles S of Duror, off A828.
CHILDREN: not under 14.
DOGS: not allowed.
CREDIT CARDS: MasterCard, Visa.
PRICES: B&B £50–£60 per person, set dinner £30.

EDINBANE Highland

Map 5:C1

GRESHORNISH HOUSE

'We felt like guests of friends at a grand estate.' Praise this year for Neil and Rosemary Colquhoun's country house in a 'tranquil' corner of Skye. Because of the remote position, guests are expected to stay for a minimum of two nights. There are 'gorgeous views' of a sea loch from the 'elegant' white-painted house (Georgian with Victorian additions), set in 'beautiful grounds'. The interiors are 'archetypal country house hotel', with 'squashy sofas, log fires, billiard room, candlelit dinners'. Rooms are named after Scottish islands: Rum, one of two with a four-poster, is very large, and suitable as a family room. Another room was 'graciously appointed, with very comfortable beds, kettle, snacks, books and magazines'. Luxury toiletries and 'heaps of fluffy white towels'. No reports yet of the cooking of the new chef, Glyn Musker; his traditional, seasonal four-course menus (pre-booking essential) might include scallops in sweet chilli sauce, crème fraîche, organic Glendale leaves. Lighter dinners are available by arrangement. 'We appreciated the flexibility when we were given an early breakfast to allow us to catch a ferry.'

25% DISCOUNT VOUCHERS

Edinbane, by Portree
Isle of Skye IV51 9PN

T: 01470-582266
F: 01470-582345
E: info@greshornishhouse.com
W: www.greshornishhouse.com

BEDROOMS: 6, plus 2 attic rooms if booked with a double.
OPEN: mid-Mar–Nov.
FACILITIES: drawing room, bar, billiard room, dining room, conservatory, wedding facilities, only public rooms accessible for ♿.
BACKGROUND MUSIC: none.
LOCATION: 17 miles NW of Portree.
CHILDREN: all ages welcomed.
DOGS: not allowed in public rooms, or unaccompanied in bedrooms.
CREDIT CARDS: MasterCard, Visa.
PRICES: [2012] B&B £50–£95 per person, light dinner from £30, set dinners £38 (three courses), £45 (four courses), seasonal, 4- and 7-day discounts, 1-night bookings usually refused.

EDINBURGH

Map 5:D2

ARDMOR HOUSE

NEW

Opposite Pilrig Park in Leith, Robin Jack's 'boutique-style' B&B enters the *Guide* thanks to a positive report by regular correspondents who found it 'by chance'. 'He gave us a warm welcome; the immaculate house is tastefully furnished in modern style. Our large bedroom at the front had a sofa; a good tray of tea and coffee, and chocolate bars.' All rooms have a digital radio with an iPod dock, a hairdryer; a powerful shower (no baths). 'Don't hesitate to ask' for extras like an iron, ice, etc. There are daily papers in the morning in the breakfast room, which faces the park. 'They go to some lengths to source local produce for the excellent breakfast, not the least the yogurts and fish.' A buffet has fresh fruit, home-made oatcakes, cereals and bread for do-it-yourself toasting. Cooked dishes include porridge ('for the authentic Scottish experience') and smoked bacon, potato waffles and maple syrup. Mr Jack says: 'We are gay-owned and straight-friendly, with the emphasis on friendly.' There is free on-street parking; a bus-stop outside the front door. (*Ian and Barbara Dewey*)

74 Pilrig Street
Edinburgh EH6 5AS

T/F: 0131-554 4944
E: info@ardmorhouse.com
W: www.ardmorhouse.com

BEDROOMS: 5, 1 on ground floor.
OPEN: all year.
FACILITIES: breakfast room.
BACKGROUND MUSIC: classical in breakfast room.
LOCATION: Leith, 1 mile NE of city centre.
CHILDREN: all ages welcomed.
DOGS: allowed by arrangement.
CREDIT CARDS: MasterCard, Visa.
PRICES: B&B £45–£75 per person, 1-night bookings refused at busy times.

SEE ALSO SHORTLIST

EDINBURGH

Map 5:D2

THE BONHAM

'Venerable buildings full of modern art and interesting architectural detail.' These appealed to regular *Guide* reporters who stayed this year in this 49-bedroom hotel formed from three Victorian town houses. In a quiet square not far from the west end of Princes Street, it makes a 'relaxed and pleasant base' for exploring Edinburgh. Johanne Falconer manages it for Peter Taylor's Town House Collection. 'The service is very good.' Previously used as a medical practice and student halls of residence, the buildings have been renovated in modern style. The bedrooms have strong colours, rich, textured and striped fabrics. 'Ours was spacious with a nice view, huge four-poster and quirky bath with integrated neo-Victorian shower (good fun).' Another room has oak-panelled walls and a freestanding copper bath. In the oak-panelled dining room the Breton chef, Michel Bouyer, serves a seasonal, sophisticated menu. One of his 'favourite dishes at the moment' is hand-dived scallops, crab cannelloni, a pear and caper dressing. Children are welcomed (high chairs provided in the restaurant). Free car parking is 'a bonus'.
(*Christian Bartoschek and Régine Marcy*)

35 Drumsheugh Gardens
Edinburgh EH3 7RN

T: 0131-274 7400
F: 0131-274 7405
E: reserve@thebonham.com
W: www.thebonham.com

BEDROOMS: 49, 1 suitable for ♿.
OPEN: all year.
FACILITIES: reception lounge, bar, restaurant, wedding facilities.
BACKGROUND MUSIC: in public areas all day.
LOCATION: central.
CHILDREN: all ages welcomed.
DOGS: not allowed in public rooms.
CREDIT CARDS: all major cards.
PRICES: [2012] B&B £50–£200 per person, D,B&B £72–£222, set menus £18–£22, full alc £60, special breaks, Christmas/New Year packages, 1-night bookings refused Sat.

SEE ALSO SHORTLIST

EDINBURGH

Map 5:D2

MILLERS64 NEW

Sisters Shona and Louise Clelland 'clearly take pride and pleasure' in running their small B&B in a 'beautiful' Victorian town house on a 'relatively quiet' street off Leith Walk. 'The impeccably kept house has been decorated in a clean, modern style with oriental influences reflecting their childhood in Malaysia,' say the nominators. The sisters show 'great humour and warmth while giving guests space'; simple touches like a scented candle in the hallway make it 'a place you are keen to get back to'. A front-facing bedroom was 'spacious with high ceiling, confident proportions, and bold furnishings; stunning Victorian detailing; a sofa by the bay window, lots of storage; home-made fudge and shortbread biscuits. The huge, elegant bathroom had a chandelier, modern fittings, lovely toiletries.' Breakfast is taken at a communal table in a room with sofas, newspapers and magazines. 'Louise baked something new every morning (gingerbread or scones); their mother's marmalade and jams were delicious as were the miniature pots of fruit and cereal.' There is a choice of cooked dishes, including a daily special. (*Anna and Bill Brewer*)

64 Pilrig Street
Edinburgh EH6 5AS

T: 0131-454 3666
E: reservations@millers64.com
W: www.millers64.com

BEDROOMS: 3.
OPEN: all year.
FACILITIES: dining room, patio, unsuitable for ♿.
BACKGROUND MUSIC: none.
LOCATION: Leith.
CHILDREN: not under 12.
DOGS: not allowed.
CREDIT CARDS: none.
PRICES: [2012] B&B £42.50–£80 per person, min. 3-night stay 'in busy periods'.

SEE ALSO SHORTLIST

EDNAM Scottish Borders

Map 5:E3

EDENWATER HOUSE

'Visiting *Edenwater* is like staying with friends in their very comfortable country house.' An old stone manse with a pretty garden in the Scottish Borders, this small hotel is run by owners Jacqui and Jeff Kelly. 'I particularly like the friendly reception; he looks after front-of-house and is happy to chat or not as you wish.' Guests are greeted with tea or coffee on arrival, 'which we had with Selkirk bannock in the cosy lounge in front of the log fire – lovely'. 'Spacious, elegant' bedrooms have 'everything you might need' and 'wonderful views': 'We like the attractive Church Room for its comfortable bed, large shower and outlook over the garden and beyond.' Mrs Kelly's three-course dinners in the candlelit dining room are 'superb'. 'We had an amuse-bouche of fennel soup; sea bass, pak choi and pickled vegetables; quail wrapped in pancetta, porcini mousseline, fondant potatoes. Jeff chose two bottles of wine for us, which we enjoyed.' In the morning, a 'substantial and varied breakfast' is served, with a 'good range' of different fresh fruits, cereals, yogurts and cooked dishes. (*Archie Brown, and others*)

Ednam, nr Kelso
TD5 7QL

T: 01573-224070
E: jeffnjax@hotmail.co.uk
W: www.edenwaterhouse.co.uk

BEDROOMS: 4.
OPEN: Mar–Nov.
FACILITIES: drawing room, TV room, study, dining room, wine-tasting room, 5-acre grounds, unsuitable for ♿.
BACKGROUND MUSIC: none.
LOCATION: 2 miles N of Kelso on B6461.
CHILDREN: not under 10.
DOGS: not allowed.
CREDIT CARDS: MasterCard, Visa.
PRICES: [2012] B&B £50–£55 per person, D,B&B £88.50–£93.50, set dinner £38.50, gourmet weekend breaks.

ERISKA Argyll and Bute

Map 5:D1

ISLE OF ERISKA HOTEL, SPA AND ISLAND

César award in 2007

'Expensive but right in every way,' is the view of a returning visitor to Beppo and Chay Buchanan-Smith's luxury hotel, a baronial mansion on a private island. There have been changes this year: *Eriska* has joined Relais & Châteaux, and Simon McKenzie is now the chef. 'More resort than hotel', the island has a nine-hole golf course and a driving range, a sports hall with badminton and table tennis and indoor putting, and a spa with a swimming pool. There is a rack of wellington boots by the entrance to the house, which has grand panelled lounges, log fires all year round, large comfortable sofas. In the formal dining room (jacket and tie preferred), the daily-changing dinner menu might include poached lemon sole, couscous; loin of Eriska venison, celeriac, braised cabbage, pickled pear. Light meals are served on a veranda. The bedrooms in the main house have a mix of traditional and contemporary furnishings. Modern spa suites in the grounds have a private terrace with hot tub. Badgers come most evenings to the library steps for bread and milk. (*DJ, RC*)

Benderloch, Eriska
by Oban PA37 1SD

T: 01631-720371
F: 01631-720531
E: office@eriska-hotel.co.uk
W: www.eriska-hotel.co.uk

BEDROOMS: 23, including 5 spa suites and 2 garden cottages, some on ground floor.
OPEN: all year except 3–20 Jan.
FACILITIES: ramp, 5 public rooms, leisure centre, swimming pool (17 by 6 metres), gym, sauna, treatments, wedding facilities, tennis, 350-acre grounds, 9-hole golf course.
BACKGROUND MUSIC: none.
LOCATION: 12 miles N of Oban.
CHILDREN: all ages welcomed, but no under-5s in leisure centre, and special evening meal arrangements.
DOGS: not allowed in public rooms or unattended in bedrooms.
CREDIT CARDS: Amex, MasterCard, Visa.
PRICES: [2012] B&B £172.50–£240, set dinner £47, special breaks, Christmas/New Year packages, 2-night min. stay.

FORT AUGUSTUS Highland

Map 5:C2

THE LOVAT

In the centre of an 'appealing' little town, this former Victorian station hotel is run with an eco-conscious ethos by the owner, Caroline Gregory. 'It is a comfortable, well-run place,' says a *Guide* inspector in 2012. 'The ambience is pleasing and the staff are friendly, willing.' Much is made of the green credentials: heating is from a biomass woodchip burner, all food waste is composted, guests arriving by public transport get a discount. A Victorian sitting-room/lobby has an open fire, a grand piano. The bedrooms are well furnished and comfortable, decorated in big-hotel style. 'Ours had attractive views of hills and canal; a good-sized bathroom with nice toiletries, but a captive hairdryer.' Each of six studio rooms in an annexe has a private parking space. In the 'elegant' dining room, chef Sean Kelly serves a no-choice 'Scottish creative' menu. 'He delivered five delicious courses, including tartare of sea bass and crab, roast venison and root vegetables with a piping of smoked potatoes, Dunsyre blue cheese with apple jelly.' There is also a conservatory brasserie serving simpler dishes. Breakfast is 'very good apart from the packet juice'.

25% DISCOUNT VOUCHERS

Fort Augustus
PH32 4DU

T: 0845-4501100
F: 01320-366677
E: info@thelovat.com
W: www.thelovat.com

BEDROOMS: 28, 6 in annexe, 2 suitable for ♿.

OPEN: all year, restaurant closed Sun/Mon.

FACILITIES: drawing room, dining room, brasserie, reception, bar, wedding facilities, 2-acre grounds.

BACKGROUND MUSIC: in bar.

LOCATION: in village SW of Inverness by A82.

CHILDREN: all ages welcomed.

DOGS: allowed in 1 bedroom only and bar.

CREDIT CARDS: Amex, MasterCard, Visa.

PRICES: [2012] B&B £30–£130 per person, D,B&B £55–£175, set menu £45, full alc in brasserie £38.50, off-season breaks, Christmas/New Year packages.

FORT WILLIAM Highland

Map 5:C1

THE GRANGE

In a peaceful garden with lovely views over Loch Linnhe and to the hills above Treslaig, this white-painted Victorian house with a turret has long been run as a B&B by John and Joan Campbell. They are 'wonderfully welcoming and helpful', booking restaurants and offering advice and maps for walks. Tea and home-made shortbread are served for arriving guests. There are three 'immaculate' bedrooms, each decorated individually in pale colours, with a mix of antique and modern furniture. Rob Roy, which accommodated Jessica Lange when she was making the eponymous film, has a colonial-style bed and a mirrored marble bathroom. The Garden Room has its own sitting room with chaise longue and armchairs, and a bathroom with a pedestal bath. The Turret Room has a window seat overlooking the garden and loch. Guests have always enjoyed the flowers from the garden and the complimentary 'decanter of sherry with lovely glassware'. A 'fantastically good' breakfast is ordered the evening before from an extensive menu, perhaps porridge with whisky, cream, brown sugar and honey; poached haddock; fresh fruit and yogurt. More reports, please.

Grange Road
Fort William PH33 6JF

T: 01397-705516
E: joan@thegrange-scotland.co.uk
W: www.thegrange-scotland.co.uk

BEDROOMS: 3.
OPEN: Apr–Nov.
FACILITIES: lounge, breakfast room, 1-acre garden, unsuitable for ♿.
BACKGROUND MUSIC: none.
LOCATION: edge of town.
CHILDREN: not under 16.
DOGS: not allowed.
CREDIT CARDS: none.
PRICES: [2012] B&B £58–£60 per person, 1-night bookings sometimes refused in season.

SEE ALSO SHORTLIST

FORT WILLIAM Highland

Map 5:C1

INVERLOCHY CASTLE

'I never saw a lovelier or more romantic spot.' So thought Queen Victoria in 1873, when she visited this grand baronial mansion, now a luxury hotel (Relais & Châteaux). *Guide* readers who visited this year agreed. 'The building, outside and even more inside, is impressive. The huge hall/lounge with its enormous chandeliers and painted ceiling is stunning. The staff were friendly, courteous and efficient.' Men are asked to wear a jacket and tie in the three dining rooms, which are furnished with period pieces originally given to the castle by the King of Norway. The chef, Philip Carnegie, has a *Michelin* star for his modern cooking. 'The best dinner we enjoyed in Scotland: creative but never exaggerated, inspiring, and with fine ingredients.' Typical dishes: Parmesan-crusted scallops, curried parsnip; roast guineafowl, truffle polenta, asparagus and wild garlic. Bedrooms are light and 'spacious', as are the bathrooms, which have 'classy toiletries'. 'Our suite had a wonderful view.' The setting, in the foothills of Ben Nevis, is magnificent; the 'beautifully kept' grounds and walled garden allow for 'a decent walk'. (*Christian Bartoschek and Régine Marcy*)

Torlundy
Fort William PH33 6SN

T: 01397-702177
F: 01397-702953
E: info@inverlochy.co.uk
W: www.inverlochycastlehotel.com

BEDROOMS: 17, plus 2 in Gate Lodge.
OPEN: all year.
FACILITIES: Great Hall, drawing room, dining room, wedding facilities, 600-acre estate (tennis), only restaurant suitable for ♿.
BACKGROUND MUSIC: pianist or harpist in Great Hall in evening.
LOCATION: 4 miles NE of Fort William.
CHILDREN: all ages welcomed, young children not allowed in public areas after 6 pm.
DOGS: not allowed in public rooms.
CREDIT CARDS: Amex, MasterCard, Visa.
PRICES: [2012] B&B £160–£347.50 per person, D,B&B (off-season) £190–£414.50, set dinner £67, winter offers. Christmas/New Year packages.

SEE ALSO SHORTLIST

FORTROSE Highland

Map 5:C2

THE ANDERSON

'Hospitable and helpful' American owner Jim Anderson runs this restaurant-with-rooms with his wife, Anne (the chef), in a seaside village on the Black Isle (not an island but a peninsula surrounded by water on three sides). Visitors praise his 'cheery' manner and his willingness to share his knowledge of local attractions and to provide other information and assistance. The restaurant, decorated in 'pleasing and appropriate colours', has white linen table settings. Mrs Anderson, who trained in New Orleans, serves international dishes on an extensive menu that changes daily according to what is available at market. Her dishes might include Shetland mussels in Belgian ale and Ullapool-smoked Cheddar cheese; shank of Scotch lamb, garlic mash and Fyne Sublime Stout gravy. 'A good-value meal, and fair prices on the excellent wine list.' The 'lively' *Whisky Bar* has 240 single malt whiskies (some rare); meals are sometimes served here. There are real ales in the cosy public bar (and 120 Belgian beers). The bedrooms have 'basic comforts'; good storage in the wardrobe and drawers, tea-making facilities with fresh milk. More reports, please.

Union Street
Fortrose, by Inverness IV10 8TD

T: 01381-620236
E: info@theanderson.co.uk
W: www.theanderson.co.uk

BEDROOMS: 9.
OPEN: 26 Dec–7 Nov.
FACILITIES: bar, *Whisky Bar*, dining room, beer garden, only public areas suitable for ♿.
BACKGROUND MUSIC: bar and dining room.
LOCATION: town centre.
CHILDREN: all ages welcomed.
DOGS: allowed in 2 bedrooms, bar and garden.
CREDIT CARDS: Diners, MasterCard, Visa.
PRICES: B&B £45–£55 per person, full alc £29.

GATESIDE Fife

Map 5:D2

EDENSHEAD STABLES

Set in wooded grounds leading down to the River Eden, this modern B&B is housed in a traditional pink-stone stable building, restored from a ruin by 'delightful' owners Gill and John Donald. Two of the three bedrooms have been redecorated this year and given new rugs; bathroom floors have been upgraded. All rooms are spacious (one has a four-poster bed). Guests have use of a large sitting room with French doors which open on to a patio (with colourful plant pots) and the garden. There are magazines, guidebooks and maps to the area's attractions of golf, coast and castles (the royal palace and gardens at Falkland are nearby). Guests sit together around a large table for breakfast; a speciality is smoked fish from east coast villages; soft fruit in season is from local orchards; home-made preserves. A three-course 'traditional' dinner can be cooked by arrangement for groups of four to six. There are pubs and restaurants for all pockets nearby. No visiting dogs, but the owners' Hungarian vizslas, Rosa and Zeta, are part of the picture. (*J and AK*)

Gateside, by Falkland, Cupar
KY14 7ST

T: 01337-868500
E: info@edensheadstables.com
W: www.edensheadstables.com

BEDROOMS: 3, all on ground floor.
OPEN: Mar–Nov.
FACILITIES: lounge, dining room, 3-acre grounds, unsuitable for ♿.
BACKGROUND MUSIC: none.
LOCATION: on edge of village 3 miles E of M90 Jct 8.
CHILDREN: not under 14.
DOGS: not allowed.
CREDIT CARDS: Amex, MasterCard, Visa.
PRICES: B&B £45–£60 per person, set dinner £28, 1-night bookings refused weekends June–Aug.

GLASGOW

Map 5:D2

GRASSHOPPERS

NEW

Beside Central Station, Barry Munn's conversion of the top floor of the Victorian headquarters of the Caledonian Railway Company might not match 'everyone's expectation of a *Guide* hotel', say inspectors in 2012. 'But it is incredible value and the staff – friendly, informative, willing – transform the experience.' *Grasshoppers* occupies the sixth floor of the building: entry is by a lift accessed between two nondescript shops. This opens on to a contemporary space; there are 'nice light wooden floors' throughout, contemporary art in the corridors. The bedrooms, in different shapes and sizes, have Scandinavian-style furnishings, oak floors, bright colours. 'Our room was stylish, spare and comfortable; not oppressive thanks to the high ceiling and big Victorian windows (some traffic hum); a small but well-designed shower room.' A light supper is served from Monday to Thursday in *The Kitchen*, an 'internal but surprisingly cheerful space' with a mix of small and large (shared) wooden tables. 'Excellent home-cooked food; delicious celery and Stilton soup; chicken breast with bacon and leek sauce.' A 'good' breakfast has a buffet, eggs cooked to order.

6th floor Caledonian Chambers
87 Union Street
Glasgow G1 3TA

T: 0141-222 2666
F: 0141-248 3641
E: info@grasshoppersglasgow.com
W: www.grasshoppersglasgow.com

BEDROOMS: 29.
OPEN: all year except Christmas.
FACILITIES: breakfast/supper room, unsuitable for ♿.
BACKGROUND MUSIC: none.
LOCATION: by Central station.
CHILDREN: all ages welcomed.
DOGS: only guide dogs allowed.
CREDIT CARDS: all major cards.
PRICES: [2012] B&B £42.50–£85 per person, full alc £25.

SEE ALSO SHORTLIST

GLENFINNAN Highland

Map 5:C1

GLENFINNAN HOUSE

A Victorian mansion set in 'beautiful' grounds, this 'lovely traditional hotel' stands on the shores of Loch Shiel. 'You arrive to the sound of a tumbling stream and the scent of the hotel's cheerful log fires.' The 'welcoming' public rooms are 'comfortable, traditionally furnished'; they had 'lots of space' even when the hotel was busy during an inspector's visit. Bedrooms vary in size: a comfortable double had 'plenty of storage', but a small family room was 'disappointing' and cramped. There are no keys – 'we think of this as a Highland home' – though they can be provided. One bedroom and a suite have been added this year. Chef Duncan Gibson's traditional Scottish menus – eg, Inverawe smoked salmon, home-made brown soda bread; roast venison, celeriac mash – are served in the dining room and the 'busy' bar, where 'traditional music enhanced the atmosphere'. 'The excellent children's menu has good, healthy choices.' A 'wonderful' cooked breakfast accompanies a buffet in the morning. Packed lunches may be provided for the many walks and loch cruises to be had in the area.
(*DP, and others*)

25% DISCOUNT VOUCHERS

Glenfinnan
by Fort William PH37 4LT

T: 01397-722235
F: 01397-722249
E: availability@glenfinnanhouse.com
W: www.glenfinnanhouse.com

BEDROOMS: 14.
OPEN: 21 Mar–3 Nov.
FACILITIES: ramps, drawing room, playroom, bar, restaurant, wedding facilities, 1-acre grounds, playground, unsuitable for ♿.
BACKGROUND MUSIC: Scottish in bar and restaurant.
LOCATION: 15 miles NW of Fort William.
CHILDREN: all ages welcomed.
DOGS: not in restaurant.
CREDIT CARDS: Amex, MasterCard, Visa.
PRICES: [2012] B&B £65–£105 per person, full alc £40, special breaks.

GLENFINNAN Highland

Map 5:C1

THE PRINCE'S HOUSE

NEW

In a small village at the head of Loch Shiel, this traditional white-painted coaching inn has 'much to commend it', says a visitor returning this year (upgrading *The Prince's House* from the Shortlist to a full entry). It is run in 'an informal and relaxed manner' by owners Kieron and Ina Kelly: 'She exudes friendliness, and deals with front-of-house'; he is the chef. Dinner is served in a 'spacious' bar with a vaulted pine ceiling, and more formally in the dining room. The bar has an extensive blackboard menu: 'The well-cooked dishes include a variety of soups with delicious home-baked bread; a selection of fish, steaks, chicken dishes, etc; unusual flavours in the home-made ice cream. Service is good even when under pressure.' Modern British dishes in the dining room might include loin of hill lamb, red wine-baked mushroom, parsnip fondant. The best of the traditionally furnished bedrooms are at the front: 'Our room was well appointed and comfortable.' Breakfast has freshly squeezed fruit juice, 'excellent' porridge. 'An opportunity to explore some of the most remote and beautiful areas of the Western Highlands.' (*AJ Gillingwater*)

25% DISCOUNT VOUCHERS

Glenfinnan
by Fort William PH37 4LT

T: 01397-722246
E: princeshouse@glenfinnan.co.uk
W: www.glenfinnan.co.uk

BEDROOMS: 9.
OPEN: Mar–Dec, except Christmas, restricted opening Nov/Dec, Mar, restaurant open Easter–end Sept.
FACILITIES: lounge/bar, bar, dining room, small front lawn, only bar suitable for ♿.
BACKGROUND MUSIC: classical in public areas.
LOCATION: 15 miles NW of Fort William.
CHILDREN: all ages welcomed.
DOGS: allowed in bar, some bedrooms.
CREDIT CARDS: MasterCard, Visa.
PRICES: [2012] B&B £65–£75 per person, D,B&B £95–£105, set meals £30, full alc £43, New Year package.

GRANTOWN-ON-SPEY Highland

Map 5:C2

CULDEARN HOUSE

On the edge of a picturesque market town popular with skiers at Aviemore, this 'delightful' but 'unassuming' Victorian house is 'warm and cosy'. It is run by 'charming' William Marshall and his wife, Sonia, 'a very good cook'. The setting, adjoining Anagach Woods, is 'peaceful'. A visitor liked the welcome 'with tea' in the wood-panelled lounge, which has a log fire, 'lots of armchairs and sofas' and a choice of 50 malt whiskies. 'I was given a whole lemon tart to myself.' Bedrooms, decorated individually with modern furniture and antiques, are 'charming and thoughtfully done'; most are spacious; bath/shower rooms are 'immaculate'. The four-course dinner menu changes daily and is served by candlelight. Readers have admired the 'thoughtful combinations', eg, loin of Morayshire lamb, port and plum jus. 'The food is excellent, especially the meat; plentiful vegetables.' Breakfast includes 'outstanding' warm fruit compote, 'porridge, delicious potato scones', and lots of cooked dishes. The Marshalls, who 'know the area well', will guide visitors to local attractions; fishing and, with enough notice, shooting can be arranged. (*MB, and others*)

Woodlands Terrace
Grantown-on-Spey PH26 3JU

T: 01479-872106
F: 01479-873641
E: enquiries@culdearn.com
W: www.culdearn.com

BEDROOMS: 6, 1 on ground floor.
OPEN: all year.
FACILITIES: lounge, dining room, ¾-acre garden.
BACKGROUND MUSIC: pre-dinner classical in lounge.
LOCATION: edge of town.
CHILDREN: not under 10.
DOGS: only guide dogs allowed.
CREDIT CARDS: Diners, MasterCard, Visa.
PRICES: [2012] B&B £65–£75 per person, D,B&B £100–£130, full alc £50, off-season and 4-night breaks, Christmas/New Year packages.

SEE ALSO SHORTLIST

INVERNESS Highland

Map 5:C2

TRAFFORD BANK GUEST HOUSE

Interior designer Lorraine Pun has furnished her stone-built Victorian house with a mix of antiques and contemporary pieces (some of which she designed herself). In mature gardens with sculptures and seating, it was once the home of the Bishop of Moray and Ross-shire and is a short walk from the centre. Most of the bedrooms are large; all have a hospitality tray, decanter of sherry, silent fridge, flat-screen TV, iPod docking. The Thistle Room has dramatic handmade Grand Thistle wallpaper and furnishings; the Tartan Room is more discreet in its application of its theme; it has a Victorian-style roll-top bath in the bathroom, and a separate shower. The Green Room (on a middle landing) and the larger Trafford Suite have an extra single bed for family use. Visitors have commented on the quality of the welcome and the accommodation: 'The best we have found in Inverness,' said the nominator. Breakfast, ordered the evening before, is taken in a conservatory overlooking the garden. It 'hits all the right buttons: excellent choices, served piping hot'. Free Wi-Fi is available throughout.

96 Fairfield Road
Inverness IV3 5LL

T: 01463-241414
F: 01463-241421
E: enquiries@trafffordbankguesthouse.co.uk
W: www.traffordbankguesthouse.co.uk

BEDROOMS: 5.
OPEN: all year except mid-Nov–mid-Dec.
FACILITIES: ramps, 2 lounges, conservatory, garden, unsuitable for ♿.
BACKGROUND MUSIC: none.
LOCATION: 10 mins' walk from centre.
CHILDREN: all ages welcomed.
DOGS: only guide dogs allowed.
CREDIT CARDS: MasterCard, Visa.
PRICES: B&B £45–£62.50 per person.

SEE ALSO SHORTLIST

KILBERRY Argyll and Bute

Map 5:D1

KILBERRY INN

César award in 2010

'In the middle of nowhere', Clare Johnson and David Wilson's small restaurant-with-rooms is in a hamlet on the Argyll coast. Although the 'quirky' whitewashed cottage with its red tin roof has no views, the drive down a single-track road is 'wild and magical'. He is 'a charming, witty host; service is exemplary', says a visitor in 2012. Each of the 'simple but comfortable' bedrooms, around the back in 'individual little cottages', has its own hall. 'Our room, which faced a car park, was plenty big enough; modern furnishings, a firm bed; a good-sized walk-in shower in the bathroom.' Clare Johnson has a *Michelin* Bib Gourmand for her short, seasonal menus, with the emphasis on 'seafood in summer, red meat and game in winter'. Visitors this year 'greatly enjoyed monkfish tails with a light touch of tomato sauce and Puy lentils'. 'The choices are varied, sometimes unusual; good ingredients, well cooked.' The two dining rooms (there is no lounge) are open to non-residents. They have beams, bare stone walls, paintings by local artists. There are 'fantastic walks nearby'. (*CLH, Val Ferguson*)

Kilberry, by Tarbert
PA29 6YD

T: 01880-770223
E: relax@kilberryinn.com
W: www.kilberryinn.com

BEDROOMS: 5, all on ground floor.
OPEN: Tues–Sun 15 March–end Oct, weekends only Nov and Dec, except New Year.
FACILITIES: bar/dining room, smaller dining room, small grounds.
BACKGROUND MUSIC: in larger dining room, lunch and dinner.
LOCATION: 16 miles NW of Tarbert, on B8024.
CHILDREN: no under-12s.
DOGS: only in one bedroom, not in public rooms.
CREDIT CARDS: MasterCard, Visa.
PRICES: [2012] D,B&B £97.50 per person, full alc £38, 1-night bookings sometimes refused weekends.

KILCHRENAN Argyll and Bute

Map 5:D1

ARDANAISEIG

Down a ten-mile track by Loch Awe, this late Georgian house stands in extensive wooded grounds. It is endorsed 'even more emphatically' this year by a returning visitor who was impressed by the 'exceptional kindness shown by the staff in regard to my wife's disability'. Log fires burn in the gilt-and-beige drawing room and the intimate library bar, which owner Bennie Gray, founder of Gray's Antiques Market in London, has fitted with antique furniture and works of art. Individually designed bedrooms have views on to the garden or the loch: sunny, yellow Cuaig has a bold red brass bed and a bath alcove; split-level Orchy has a small conservatory. At the bottom of the woodland garden, a former boathouse is now a modern, glass-fronted 'cottage' perched on the water. In the dining room overlooking the loch, chef Gary Goldie's much-praised Franco-Scottish cooking is 'varied, inventive and delicious'. He forages in the woods for ingredients for his dishes. 'A tomato consommé with herbs was as subtle and delicate as many a fine wine. Saddle of roe deer was tasty and tender.' There are woodland and loch-side trails for walkers and cyclists. (*Robert Chandler*)

25% DISCOUNT VOUCHERS

Kilchrenan
by Taynuilt PA35 1HE

T: 01866-833333
F: 01866-833222
E: info@ardanaiseig.com
W: www.ardanaiseig.com

BEDROOMS: 18, some on ground floor, 1 in boatshed, 1 self-catering cottage.

OPEN: all year.

FACILITIES: drawing room, library/bar, games room, restaurant, wedding facilities, 360-acre grounds on loch (open-air theatre, tennis, bathing, fishing).

BACKGROUND MUSIC: classical/jazz in restaurant during dinner.

LOCATION: 4 miles E of Kilchrenan.

CHILDREN: all ages welcomed, but no under-10s at dinner.

DOGS: not allowed in public rooms, small charge in bedrooms.

CREDIT CARDS: Amex, MasterCard, Visa.

PRICES: [2012] B&B £71–£181.50 per person, D,B&B £121–£231.50, set dinner £50, special offers, Christmas/New Year packages.

KILLIECRANKIE Perth and Kinross

Map 5:D2

KILLIECRANKIE HOTEL

César award in 2011

'We arrived in glorious sunshine and were given an equally sunny welcome inside,' say visitors this year to Henrietta Fergusson's ever-popular small hotel, a 19th-century dower house in expansive wooded grounds at the entrance to the Pass of Killiecrankie. Other praise: 'Henrietta is a dominant presence – in the best possible sense'; 'To say she is hands-on doesn't do justice to her ubiquity.' In the restaurant and 'buzzing' bar, 'talented' chef Mark Easton serves 'excellent' dinners. 'We had beautifully tender local venison with rösti; plaice with scallops was very nice indeed; a plum and ginger mousse was delicious and light.' Service is by 'efficient' young staff dressed in tartan trousers (a Scottish guest thought them 'naff not elegant', but conceded that non-Scots might consider them 'charming'). Much attention to detail in the 'comfortable' bedrooms ('lots of bathroom goodies', hot-water bottles left in the bed during turn-down). Breakfast has a 'lavish' selection of conserves but 'too-small portions of butter'. 'We had some good walks in the surrounding countryside.' 'Wonderfully relaxing.' (*Sara Price, Esler Crawford, John Gibbon, Dennis Marler*)

Killiecrankie
by Pitlochry PH16 5LG

T: 01796-473220
F: 01796-472451
E: enquiries@killiecrankiehotel.co.uk
W: www.killiecrankiehotel.co.uk

BEDROOMS: 10, 2 on ground floor.
OPEN: mid-Mar–early Jan.
FACILITIES: ramp, sitting room, bar with conservatory, dining room, breakfast conservatory, 4½-acre grounds.
BACKGROUND MUSIC: none.
LOCATION: hamlet 3 miles W of Pitlochry.
CHILDREN: all ages welcomed.
DOGS: not allowed in eating areas, some bedrooms.
CREDIT CARDS: MasterCard, Visa.
PRICES: [2012] B&B £90–£100 per person, D,B&B £115–£140, set dinner £42, special breaks, Christmas/New Year packages, 1-night bookings sometimes refused.

KILMARTIN Argyll and Bute

Map 5:D1

DUNCHRAIGAIG HOUSE

'Delightful' hosts Cameron Bruce and Lynn Jones run this 'excellent' B&B in a house set back from the road in an area with the richest concentration of prehistoric sites in Scotland. There are 350 monuments, including the standing stones close to the house, in a six-mile radius. Lynn Jones, a former teacher, has compiled a 'comprehensive' guide to the area. 'Perfect in every respect; excellent rooms, a good breakfast, welcoming hosts,' said the nominators. There are books, games and local information in the lounge and hall. Some of the bedrooms face the standing stones; others have an outlook of woodland at the back. The rooms, which have been recently decorated in 'relaxing colours', have good bedlinen and storage; a cordless kettle was appreciated. Breakfast, in a spacious dining room, can be taken communally or at individual tables. Each guest is given a fresh fruit salad; the cooked dishes (chosen the evening before) include a daily special, perhaps Loch Fyne kipper or smoked salmon with scrambled eggs. Simple suppers are served in March and April; nearby inns are recommended for eating out. (*J and DA*)

25% DISCOUNT VOUCHERS

Kilmartin Glen
Lochgilphead PA31 8RG

T: 01546-605300
E: info@dunchraigaig.co.uk
W: www.dunchraigaig.co.uk

BEDROOMS: 5.
OPEN: Mar–Nov.
FACILITIES: lounge, dining room, 1-acre garden, unsuitable for ♿.
BACKGROUND MUSIC: none.
LOCATION: 1 mile south of village, 7 miles N of Lochgilphead.
CHILDREN: not under 12.
DOGS: not allowed.
CREDIT CARDS: none.
PRICES: [2012] B&B £35–£45 per person, 1-night bookings refused bank holiday weekends.

KINGUSSIE Highland

Map 5:C2

THE CROSS AT KINGUSSIE

This converted 19th-century tweed mill stands in wooded grounds by the River Gynack, in the Cairngorms national park. Its dining room, beamed with stone walls, opens on to a terrace which overlooks the river, as do some of the bedrooms. It was run for ten years as a restaurant-with-rooms by David and Katie Young, who achieved a reputation for 'stunning, highly accomplished' food. Now, we learned as we went to press, they are moving on. *The Cross* has been bought by Derek and Celia Kitchingman, who 'intend to maintain and build upon its reputation for hospitality and food'. We'd be grateful for reports on the new regime; some of the details on the right may no longer be accurate.

Tweed Mill Brae, Ardbroilach Road
Kingussie PH21 1LB

T: 01540-661166
F: 01540-661080
E: relax@thecross.co.uk
W: www.thecross.co.uk

BEDROOMS: 8.

OPEN: early Feb–end Dec except Christmas, normally closed Sun/Mon.

FACILITIES: 2 lounges, restaurant, 4-acre grounds, only restaurant suitable for ♿.

BACKGROUND MUSIC: none.

LOCATION: 440 yds from village centre.

CHILDREN: 'generally' not under 9.

DOGS: not allowed.

CREDIT CARDS: all major cards.

PRICES: [2012] B&B £55–£145 per person, D,B&B £100–£205, set dinner £50, wildlife and gourmet breaks, New Year package.

KIRKBEAN Dumfries and Galloway

Map 5:E2

CAVENS

There is a 'homely feel (lots of family pictures)' to Angus and Jane Fordyce's white-painted manor house near Dumfries. They run it as a small country hotel. 'It passes the tests – clean, comfortable, good food and service,' says a regular correspondent this year. Mr Fordyce, the chef, has introduced a market menu alongside his short carte in the 'impressive' dining room ('antique furniture, white tablecloths, beautiful glassware, silver cutlery'). He uses vegetables from the kitchen garden for his 'tasty' dishes, perhaps pigeon breast in port wine; ling with caper sauce. 'Good value' on the short wine list. The 'lovely, light' public rooms have 'comfortable sofas and chairs', books, magazines and guidebooks. The bedrooms (some are large), which face the garden or the countryside, have tea and coffee, fruit, biscuits, boiled sweets. 'Mine had a big sofa in an alcove overlooking the garden; the small shower room was spotless.' An information pack has 'inspiring ideas for leisure activities'. Breakfast has 'well-presented local ingredients'. New this year are two self-catering cottages in the extensive grounds.
(JG, Christine Hughes)

25% DISCOUNT VOUCHERS

Kirkbean
by Dumfries DG2 8AA

T: 01387-880234
F: 01387-880467
E: enquiries@cavens.com
W: www.cavens.com

BEDROOMS: 7, 1 on ground floor, also 2 self-catering cottages.
OPEN: Mar–Nov, New Year.
FACILITIES: sitting room, dining room, wedding/meeting facilities, 20-acre grounds, unsuitable for ♿.
BACKGROUND MUSIC: none.
LOCATION: 12 miles S of Dumfries.
CHILDREN: all ages welcomed, but no cots, high chairs.
DOGS: Allowed by arrangement, not in public rooms.
CREDIT CARDS: MasterCard, Visa.
PRICES: [2012] B&B £75–£105 per person, set dinner £25, full alc £47, spring breaks, New Year package, 1-night bookings rarely refused.

KIRKCUDBRIGHT Dumfries and Galloway Map 5:E2

GLADSTONE HOUSE

An 'attractively proportioned Georgian town house'. In the centre of Kirkcudbright (pronounced Kir*coob*ree), a 'pleasant little town' with an impressive artistic heritage near the Solway Firth, it is run as a guest house by Gordon and Hilary Cowan. They are 'welcoming hosts', encouraging guests to enjoy the secluded gardens, and the fine drawing room which occupies most of the first floor. The 'cosy, comfortable' bedrooms on the top floor have sloping ceilings, with 'good views over the rooftops', especially a double room with window seat facing the High Street and the maze of gardens leading down to the River Dee. Mr Cowan is the cook, and all breads and chutneys, jams and marmalades are home made. He will prepare a three-course dinner ('English with French influence') by arrangement, maybe game terrine with chutney and oat biscuits; pan-fried sea bass on a bed of leeks and beans. No licence; bring your own wine. A recent visitor found breakfast 'more than up to standard; Gordon's cooked dishes are hard to beat'. It has a large selection of fresh and dried fruit. More reports, please.

48 High Street
Kirkcudbright DG6 4JX

T: 01557-331734
E: gladstonehouse48@btinternet.com
W: www.kirkcudbrightgladstone.com

BEDROOMS: 3.
OPEN: all year except Christmas, New Year.
FACILITIES: drawing room, dining room, ½-acre garden, unsuitable for ♿.
BACKGROUND MUSIC: none.
LOCATION: town centre.
CHILDREN: not under 12.
DOGS: not allowed.
CREDIT CARDS: MasterCard, Visa.
PRICES: [2012] B&B £39–£60, set dinner £28 (by arrangement), discount for 3 nights or longer.

KIRKCUDBRIGHT Dumfries and Galloway Map 5:E2

GLENHOLME COUNTRY HOUSE NEW

Retired diplomat Laurence Bristow-Smith and his artist wife, Jennifer, spent three years restoring this high Victorian mansion as an upmarket guest house. 'It is a civilised place with a delightful decor,' said *Guide* inspectors. 'They are adaptable hosts and serve a generous breakfast.' They have given the house 'a cultured feel': the guest sitting room is a library lined with bookshelves ('the sort of book one actually wants to read'). 'Laurence introduced himself by first name and showed us round; he brought us tea and carried our luggage to the room.' The bedrooms have been decorated in Victorian style. 'Lansdowne is a charming room in white and pale grey, with good reading lights, a pleasant surprise; a splendid shower room had a huge antique mirror.' Curzon has vintage fabrics and antique furnishings. No television; Wi-Fi is available throughout. Mr Bristow-Smith cooks a short no-choice menu by arrangement, with dishes like chicken in lime and ginger sauce. Breakfast, served until 10 am, has a small buffet of fruit and cereal, freshly squeezed orange juice, chunky toast; 'all manner of cooked dishes'.

Tongland Road
Kirkcudbright DG6 4UU

T: 01557-339422
E: info@glenholmecountryhouse.com
W: www.glenholmecountryhouse.com

BEDROOMS: 4.
OPEN: all year except Christmas/New Year.
FACILITIES: library, dining room, 1½-acre garden, unsuitable for ♿.
BACKGROUND MUSIC: music system in library and dining room at guests' discretion.
LOCATION: 1 mile N of town.
CHILDREN: not under 12.
DOGS: not allowed.
CREDIT CARDS: MasterCard, Visa.
PRICES: [2012] B&B £47.50–£80 per person, dinner £30, 1-night bookings refused high season weekends.

KYLESKU Highland

Map 5:B2

KYLESKU HOTEL

Beside a working harbour on a sea loch in the largest unspoilt wilderness in the UK, this white-painted former coaching inn is run in personal style by its owners. Tanja Lister, 'warm and energetic', is front-of-house, and Sonia Virechauveix oversees the kitchen. 'It is a setting that few hotels can equal,' said inspectors, who were impressed. 'A small volcano of words and actions, Tanja Lister went to great trouble to see that we were cared for; she brought us tea and cake in the pretty lounge and gave our Labrador a bowl of water.' There has been much renovation this year: all bathrooms have been refitted (power shower over bath), and three bedrooms redecorated; remaining work is set for late 2012. The bedrooms are not large, but 'ours had generous hanging space (free-range hangers), a comfortable bed'. Four rooms have loch views; two in the attic have private facilities. In both bar and dining room, a menu with much local shellfish, meat and game has daily-changing specials, eg, John Dory fillet, colcannon, lemongrass and dill butter.

Kylesku
IV27 4HW

T: 01971-502231
E: info@kyleskuhotel.co.uk
W: www.kyleskuhotel.co.uk

BEDROOMS: 8, 1 in annexe.
OPEN: 1 Mar–31 Oct.
FACILITIES: lounge, bar, restaurant, small garden (tables for outside eating), unsuitable for ♿.
BACKGROUND MUSIC: in bar.
LOCATION: 10 miles S of Scourie, 30 miles north of Ullapool.
CHILDREN: all ages welcomed.
DOGS: not allowed in dining room.
CREDIT CARDS: MasterCard, Visa.
PRICES: B&B [2012] £45–£72.50 per person, alc £30.

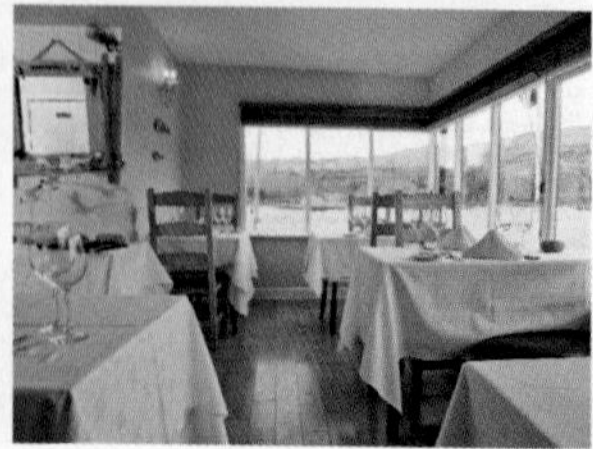

LANARK South Lanarkshire

Map 5:E2

NEW LANARK MILL HOTEL

In a 'stupendous setting', this converted Georgian cotton mill is run by the New Lanark Trust, the charity which has 'lovingly restored' an 'interesting' World Heritage Site. In a steep valley of native woodland below the Falls of Clyde, the 'impressive' building is 'beautifully decorated'. All the bedrooms have a 'superb outlook' over the river. Service from John Stirrat, the manager, and his young staff is 'discreet and helpful'. In the restaurant, Trevor McGuinness's contemporary Scottish food has been described as 'tasty and well presented'. His menu might include shin of beef with carrot purée, pomme mousseline, red wine and thyme jus. 'Perfectly pleasant' light meals are available in the bar. Breakfast has a buffet of hot dishes and cooked-to-order choices (preferred by our correspondent). The mill is popular for weddings, which can be 'disruptive' (avoid the fifth floor, say visitors, and check before booking). A quiet alternative is the self-catering two-storey *Waterhouses* in a separate building alongside. 'One could easily spend a weekend exploring the site', which has a visitors' centre and museum; excellent woodland walks. 'Very good value.' (*David Fowler, and others*)

Mill One, New Lanark Mills
Lanark ML11 9DB

T: 01555-667200
F: 01555-667222
E: hotel@newlanark.org
W: www.newlanarkmillhotel.co.uk

BEDROOMS: 38, 4 suitable for ♿.
OPEN: all year.
FACILITIES: roof garden, lounge, bar, restaurant, heated indoor swimming pool (16.5 by 4.5 metres), wedding facilities, conference centre.
BACKGROUND MUSIC: instrumental, in public areas.
LOCATION: 1 mile S of Lanark.
CHILDREN: all ages welcomed.
DOGS: only guide dogs in public rooms.
CREDIT CARDS: all major cards.
PRICES: B&B £24.50–£59.50 per person, D,B&B £49.50–£84.50, alc £32.50, special breaks, website offers, Christmas/New Year packages.

LOCHEPORT Western Isles

Map 5: inset A1

LANGASS LODGE

'Interesting hosts' Niall and Amanda Leveson Gower have been running this 'elegant' modern hotel in an isolated setting by a sea loch for twenty years. They extended the former hunting lodge giving it a sympathetic modern wing. There are 'lovely views; a sight of Skye on a good day'. 'The best stop on our tour of the Highlands and islands,' says a visitor in 2012. Rooms in the main house are smaller and cheaper; four in the hillside wing open onto the garden. 'Ours was comfortable and spacious; the bathroom was very modern.' There is 'plenty of storage, a king-size bed, wooden floors with rugs'. In the restaurant (modern conservatory extension with pitched ceiling) chef John Buchannan cooks a short, daily-changing menu with much seafood, locally shot game and home-grown herbs and vegetables. 'The food is wonderful: scallops and black pudding to start; monkfish wrapped in Parma ham; lemon tart with strawberries and prosecco cream.' Guests can also dine in the bar. Children and dogs are 'positively encouraged'. There are high chairs, a special menu, toys in the lounge. 'Complete peace and quiet.' (*Marc Wall*)

Locheport
Isle of North Uist
Western Isles HS6 5HA

T: 01876-580285
F: 01876-580385
E: langasslodge@btconnect.com
W: www.langasslodge.co.uk

BEDROOMS: 11, 1 suitable for ♿.
OPEN: all year except 24-26 Dec, 31 Dec–1 Jan.
FACILITIES: lounge, bar, restaurant, wedding facilities, 11-acre garden.
BACKGROUND MUSIC: in bar.
LOCATION: 7½ miles S of Lochmaddy.
CHILDREN: all ages welcomed.
DOGS: allowed 'everywhere', £5 charge.
CREDIT CARDS: MasterCard, Visa.
PRICES: B&B £47.50–£95 per person, alc £44.

LOCHINVER Highland

Map 5:B1

THE ALBANNACH

Britain's most northerly *Michelin*-starred restaurant, this handsome white-painted building has been run in hands-on style for more than 20 years by Lesley Crosfield and Colin Craig. They are the joint chefs who 'take no short cuts' with their 'imaginative' five-course, no-choice dinners (preferences are discussed), which are served in the conservatory restaurant. The hand-written menu might include seared hake, sauce vierge; wild chanterelle risotto; roast saddle of Highland lamb, braised lentils, baby turnip, red wine sauce. All but one of the bedrooms have the views over a deep sea loch to Suilven, the 'sugar-loaf' mountain. A four-poster double room has had a 'decor tweak' this year; 'serious reader' lights and 'quality wooden coat-hangers' have been introduced. The loft suite has a deck terrace and 'the most elegant modern bathroom'. The afternoon tea (with home-baked cakes), served to arriving guests, is now included in the price. *The Albannach* closes on Mondays 'to allow us to provide at least some of our own vegetables and herbs from the garden'; a polytunnel is planned. (*RP, and others*)

Baddidarroch
Lochinver IV27 4LP

T: 01571-844407
E: info@thealbannach.co.uk
W: www.thealbannach.co.uk

BEDROOMS: 5, 1 in byre.
OPEN: mid-Mar–early Jan, closed Mon.
FACILITIES: ramp, snug, conservatory, dining room, ½-acre garden, unsuitable for ♿.
BACKGROUND MUSIC: none.
LOCATION: ½ mile from village.
CHILDREN: not under 12.
DOGS: not allowed.
CREDIT CARDS: MasterCard, Visa.
PRICES: [2012] D,B&B £124–£220 per person, set dinner £61, off-season breaks, Christmas/New Year packages, 1-night bookings generally refused Sat in high season.

SEE ALSO SHORTLIST

LOCHRANZA North Ayrshire

Map 5:D1

APPLE LODGE

César award in 2000

Near the sea (and the Kintyre ferry) in a 'sleepy' village at the north end of Arran, this Victorian former manse is run by John and Jeannie Boyd as a 'good-value' guest house with a homely atmosphere. It has wonderful views of the surrounding hills, where red deer and eagles can be seen. Inside, the style is chintzy, with floral fabrics, teddy bears, antiques, framed embroideries, paintings and family photographs. The four bedrooms, each named after an apple variety, have home-made biscuits, original fireplace, 'ornaments, knitted toys, elaborate trimmings'. Bathrooms are 'beautifully fitted'. Apple Cottage on the ground floor is a self-contained suite with a sitting room and kitchen, and French doors on to the garden. Mrs Boyd, 'a first-class all-rounder', serves a three-course, no-choice dinner menu (not Tuesdays, or in July and August) at 7 pm, with dishes discussed beforehand. It might include roast leg of lamb, garlic, coriander and rosemary, a redcurrant, orange and port sauce. No licence; bring your own wine. Breakfasts are 'hearty', with a choice of omelettes, smoked haddock; 'good porridge'. (*O and DW, J and DA*)

Lochranza
Isle of Arran KA27 8HJ

T/F: 01770-830229
W: www.a1tourism.com/uk/applelodge2.html

BEDROOMS: 4, 1 on ground floor.
OPEN: all year except Christmas/New Year, dining room closed midday, for dinner Tues and July/Aug.
FACILITIES: lounge, dining room, ¼-acre garden, unsuitable for ♿.
BACKGROUND MUSIC: none.
LOCATION: outside village on N side of island.
CHILDREN: not allowed.
DOGS: not allowed.
CREDIT CARDS: none.
PRICES: [2012] B&B £39–£54 per person, set dinner £25, usually min. 3-night booking.

MUIR OF ORD Highland

Map 5:C2

THE DOWER HOUSE

César award in 2008

'Like a miniature treasure chest', this pretty, single-storey Georgian cottage-orné is run as a small guest house by Robyn Aitchison and his wife, Mena. 'She is charming and hard-working; he is an excellent cook,' says a regular correspondent this year. The house stands in a 'large, beautiful, wooded garden' bordered by two rivers. Warm colours, antiques, Persian rugs and flowery fabrics and wallpapers give it a 'much-loved feel'. The lounge has an open fire, a baby grand, a self-service cupboard of malt whiskies. All the bedrooms face the garden. Some are small but all have a large bed and a well-equipped bathroom. A suite has Edwardian fittings and a Victorian bath. Mr Aitchison uses local produce and home-grown herbs and vegetables for his no-choice menu (discussed in advance). It might include darn of salmon with sorrel butter; medallions of pork with grain mustard and tarragon. Generous breakfasts have fresh fruit salad, free-range eggs, heather honey. The whisky trail, golf and walking are all nearby. Children are welcomed: the garden has swings and a tree house. 'I would go back.' (*Esler Crawford*)

Highfield
Muir of Ord IV6 7XN

T/F: 01463-870090
E: info@thedowerhouse.co.uk
W: www.thedowerhouse.co.uk

BEDROOMS: 4, all on ground floor.
OPEN: all year except Christmas Day.
FACILITIES: lounge, dining room, TV room with Internet access, wedding facilities, 4½-acre grounds, unsuitable for ♿.
BACKGROUND MUSIC: none.
LOCATION: 14 miles NW of Inverness.
CHILDREN: no under-5s at dinner (high tea at 5).
DOGS: not allowed in public rooms.
CREDIT CARDS: MasterCard, Visa.
PRICES: [2012] B&B £60–£75 per person, set dinner £38.

MUTHILL Perth and Kinross

Map 5:D2

BARLEY BREE

The exterior of this 18th-century coaching inn might be 'rather sombre', but 'the welcome is warm and the cooking is excellent'. Praise from a trusted reporter this year for this restaurant-with-rooms run by French chef Fabrice Bouteloup and his wife, Alison, in a conservation village. 'Recommended for anyone who enjoys really good food,' is another comment. In the candlelit restaurant, popular with locals, the host cooks modern French dishes 'with a twist'. 'He is a wonderful chef who uses almost entirely local ingredients. There is nothing nouvelle about the portion sizes; rare roast beef, thinly carved, melted in the mouth.' Service by mainly local staff and a 'communicative' manager was 'prompt'. A 'warm, domestic' guest lounge has sofas, and doubles as an overflow dining room. The bedrooms are decorated in 'classic contemporary' style. 'Our corner room had windows on two sides and was light and airy; it had a large sofa and plenty of storage; the bathroom was fine but lacked goodies.' Breakfast has freshly baked croissants, pains au chocolat and 'delicious' porridge. Children are welcomed. (*Robert Gower, Sara Price*)

6 Willoughby Street
Muthill PH5 2AB

T: 01764-681451
E: info@barleybree.com
W: www.barleybree.com

BEDROOMS: 6.

OPEN: all year except Christmas, one week Feb and Oct, restaurant closed Mon/Tues.

FACILITIES: lounge, restaurant, small terrace, unsuitable for ♿.

BACKGROUND MUSIC: classical in lounge.

LOCATION: village centre.

CHILDREN: all ages welcomed.

DOGS: only guide dogs allowed.

CREDIT CARDS: Diners, MasterCard, Visa.

PRICES: [2012] B&B £52.50–£70 per person, full alc £45, discount for 2 or more nights, walking and golf breaks.

NEWTON STEWART Dumfries and Galloway Map 5:E1

KIRROUGHTREE HOUSE

César award in 2003

'The overwhelming feature of this hotel is the friendliness of the staff.' Praise from a regular correspondent this year is echoed by others for this 'elegant', part-Georgian, part-Victorian mansion, set in 'wild, breathtaking countryside'. The 'wonderful kindness' extends to the cleaners who were quick to assist a disabled guest. Jim Stirling is the long-serving manager for the small McMillan group. 'He creates a jolly atmosphere with the warmth of his personality and humour.' 'A porter appeared before we were out of the car, to take our cases.' The hall and the drawing room, which have 'rich oak panelling', are 'places to relax'. Each of the traditionally decorated bedrooms has a separate sitting area, a decanter of sherry, fruit, biscuits, a 'well-lit dressing table'. A deluxe turret room has its own sitting room with 'spectacular' views. A spacious ground-floor room with shower for the disabled was liked. In the high-ceilinged dining room, Matt McWhir's daily-changing menu has dishes like guineafowl with rösti, flageolet bean cassoulet, peas and thyme sauce. Meals feel 'like a special occasion'. (*Alec Frank, Fiona Lorimer*)

Newton Stewart DG8 6AN

T: 01671-402141
F: 01671-402425
E: info@kirroughtreehouse.co.uk
W: www.kirroughtreehouse.co.uk

BEDROOMS: 17.

OPEN: mid-Feb–2 Jan.

FACILITIES: lift, 2 lounges, 2 dining rooms, 8-acre grounds (gardens, tennis, croquet, pitch and putt).

BACKGROUND MUSIC: none.

LOCATION: 1½ miles NE of Newton Stewart.

CHILDREN: not under 10.

DOGS: allowed in lower ground-floor bedrooms only, not in public rooms.

CREDIT CARDS: Amex, MasterCard, Visa.

PRICES: [2012] B&B £95–£130 per person, set dinner £35, discount for 3 or more nights, Christmas/New Year packages, 1-night bookings refused Christmas/New Year.

OBAN Argyll and Bute

Map 5:D1

THE MANOR HOUSE

Once the dower house of the Duke of Argyll's Oban estate, this Georgian stone mansion on the south shore of the bay is run as a small hotel/restaurant by owners Leslie and Margaret Crane. Gregor MacKinnon, the manager, 'looked after everyone in an efficient but laid-back manner', say inspectors in 2012. The 'pristine' public areas are 'cosy' (wrote a reader). Decorated in Scottish country house style (rich colours, tartan), 'they are comfortable and well furnished, with interesting books and pictures'. In the dining room, there are 'nicely set tables with crisp white table linen, fresh flowers and candles'. Head chef Shaun Squire's 'excellent' menu changes daily. 'Cheese soufflé and scallops were well received; perfectly cooked steaks and delicious rösti; interesting Scottish cheeses. The manager oversaw the attentive service. The classical background music was very quiet.' Bedrooms are 'prettily decorated'; each has a tea tray, fresh fruit and chocolates, Wi-Fi. 'Our small room had lovely views; the bathroom had an efficient shower; everything was very clean.' Breakfast has a mixed buffet and table service 'with plenty of choice'. (*Alan Ross, and others*)

Gallanach Road
Oban PA34 4LS

T: 01631-562087
F: 01631-563053
E: info@manorhouseoban.com
W: www.manorhouseoban.com

BEDROOMS: 11, 1 on ground floor.
OPEN: all year except 25/26 Dec.
FACILITIES: 2 lounges, bar, restaurant, wedding facilities, 1½-acre grounds, unsuitable for ♿.
BACKGROUND MUSIC: traditional in bar and dining room.
LOCATION: ½ mile from centre.
CHILDREN: not under 12.
DOGS: by arrangement, not allowed in public rooms.
CREDIT CARDS: all major cards.
PRICES: [2012] B&B £57.50–£112.50 per person, D,B&B £92.50–£147.50, set dinner £39, off-season breaks, New Year package.

SEE ALSO SHORTLIST

PEAT INN Fife

Map 5:D3

THE PEAT INN

In a hamlet in undulating countryside near St Andrews, this whitewashed former coaching inn is now a restaurant-with-rooms which is 'deservedly popular, and a sought-after focus for foodies'. The 'attractive', white-walled restaurant is run by owner/chef Geoffrey Smeddle and his wife, Katherine. A 'well-lit' lounge has 'a cheerful log fire and comfortable chairs'. In the candlelit restaurant, Mr Smeddle has a *Michelin* star for his 'imaginative' cooking of seasonal 'modern Scottish/French' dishes, eg, winter salad of pink candy-striped beetroot, goat's curd cheese, walnut brittle, pomegranates; maple-glazed duck breast, wilted wild garlic, quince purée. A *Guide* inspector found the food 'appetising and colourfully presented'. The bedrooms are in an adjoining building (umbrellas provided for the short walk); seven are split-level, with a gallery sitting room which has a table for breakfast. A large room was 'pleasingly warm and had a good selection of magazines; there were thick, comfortable bathrobes in the well-appointed bathroom'. Breakfast, brought to the room and 'beautifully laid out by efficient ladies', had 'wonderful home-made granola, a perfectly soft-boiled egg.'

Peat Inn, by St Andrews
KY15 5LH

T: 01334-840206
F: 01334-840530
E: stay@thepeatinn.co.uk
W: www.thepeatinn.co.uk

BEDROOMS: 8 suites, all on ground floor in annexe, 7 split level.
OPEN: all year except Christmas and 2 weeks Jan, restaurant closed Sun/Mon.
FACILITIES: ramp, lounge, restaurant, ½-acre garden.
BACKGROUND MUSIC: none.
LOCATION: 6 miles SW of St Andrews.
CHILDREN: all ages welcomed.
DOGS: only guide dogs allowed.
CREDIT CARDS: Amex, MasterCard, Visa.
PRICES: [2012] B&B £92.50–£97.50 per person, D,B&B (Tues/Wed) £147.50, set lunch £19, set dinner £40, full alc £75, special breaks, New Year package.

PITLOCHRY Perth and Kinross

Map 5:D2

CRAIGATIN HOUSE AND COURTYARD

'A lovely homely feeling' has been established by Martin and Andrea Anderson in the B&B they have created within a Victorian house in wooded grounds close to the centre of Pitlochry. 'We were made to feel welcome from the moment we arrived,' says a visitor this year. The Andersons are 'charming', the house is 'warm and inviting', and the lounge and dining room, in a striking Scandinavian-style wood, exposed-stone and glass extension, were thought 'fabulous'. The decor is modern ('city chic in a rural setting' is what the owners aspire to create) in the 'spotless' bedrooms; half are in the main house, half in a courtyard of converted stables behind. 'Excellent towels and good toiletries.' All rooms have a hospitality tray with mineral water, tea and coffee, and local biscuits. Breakfast is 'delicious'. 'We had a divine omelette Arnold Bennett, rich, indulgent and satisfying.' There is also whisky porridge, fresh fruit, fruit compote; hot dishes include apple pancake with banana, sultanas and honey. Distilleries, walking, golf and the Festival Theatre are all nearby. (*Elizabeth McVey, and others*)

25% DISCOUNT VOUCHERS

165 Atholl Road
Pitlochry PH16 5QL

T: 01796-472478
E: enquiries@craigatinhouse.co.uk
W: www.craigatinhouse.co.uk

BEDROOMS: 14, 7 in courtyard, 2 on ground floor, 1 suitable for ♿.
OPEN: all year except Christmas.
FACILITIES: lounge, 2 dining rooms, 2-acre garden.
BACKGROUND MUSIC: soft jazz.
LOCATION: central.
CHILDREN: not under 13.
DOGS: not allowed.
CREDIT CARDS: MasterCard, Visa.
PRICES: B&B £38.50–£57.50 per person (single prices by arrangement), New Year package, 1-night bookings refused Sat.

SEE ALSO SHORTLIST

PITLOCHRY Perth and Kinross

Map 5:D2

DALSHIAN HOUSE

'A lovely stay from start to finish' was enjoyed by visitors this year to Martin and Heather Walls's B&B. The 18th-century building stands on the outskirts of the Victorian resort town. 'Comfortable in a small country house style', it has 'lots of fine touches'. The spacious rooms are decorated with 'a hint of shabby chic', in a mix of traditional furnishings and more contemporary colours. There are hairdryers, self-controlled heating and Wi-Fi in the bedrooms. Children are welcomed: there are two family rooms on the top floor. 'The afternoon tea with home baking was exceptional.' Breakfast, described as 'a delight', is served at well-spaced tables. Poached apple and sultanas and nutmeg, compote of berries with cinnamon, Earl Grey-infused figs feature in an extensive buffet. As well as full Scottish, cooked options might include poached haddock, free-range egg, hollandaise. There are unusual home-made breads and preserves. The lounge has a wood-burning stove, sofas and armchairs in neutral colours. There are sitting areas in the garden; red squirrels and interesting birdlife in the woodland. The theatre is nearby. (*Alasdair and Ruth McDonald, and others*)

Old Perth Road
Pitlochry PH16 5TD

T: 01796-472173
E: dalshian@btconnect.com
W: www.dalshian.co.uk

BEDROOMS: 7.
OPEN: all year except Christmas.
FACILITIES: lounge, dining room, 1-acre garden, unsuitable for ♿.
BACKGROUND MUSIC: none.
LOCATION: 1 mile S of centre.
CHILDREN: all ages welcomed.
DOGS: allowed by arrangement, not in public rooms.
CREDIT CARDS: MasterCard, Visa.
PRICES: [2012] B&B £35–£40 per person, winter offers.

SEE ALSO SHORTLIST

PITLOCHRY Perth and Kinross

Map 5:D2

THE GREEN PARK

NEW

On the banks of Loch Faskally, this traditional hotel is run by the McMenemie family (John and Mary, their son, Alistair, and his wife, Diane). It is upgraded from the Shortlist to a full entry after enthusiastic reports from regular *Guide* readers. 'The family works tirelessly to keep the premises pristine, and has extended the facilities without allowing modernity to prejudice the elegance and charm.' 'The best accommodation we have found for anyone with a mobility problem.' There are two lifts and 16 ground-floor bedrooms (one has a fully equipped disabled bathroom). Guests (many are returnees) 'tend towards the mature', say the family. 'The little extras are special': complimentary tea and cakes in the lounge; 'a glass or two' of sherry before dinner; a ready supply of books, magazines and newspapers. 'They remembered that we preferred extra pillows and liked streaky bacon at breakfast.' In the dining room, chef Chris Tamblin serves a daily-changing menu of traditional British/French dishes, eg, salmon, sole and pistachio nut terrine; fillet of pork with a thyme mousse. Early meals are provided for theatre-goers. (*Oonagh and Bill Morrison, Dr Gillian Todd*)

25% DISCOUNT VOUCHERS

Clunie Bridge Road
Pitlochry PH16 5JY

T: 01796-473248
F: 01796-473520
E: bookings@thegreenpark.co.uk
W: www.thegreenpark.co.uk

BEDROOMS: 51, 16 on ground floor, 1 suitable for ♿.
OPEN: all year except Christmas.
FACILITIES: 2 lifts, 3 lounges, library, bar, restaurant, 3-acre garden.
BACKGROUND MUSIC: none.
LOCATION: western edge of town.
CHILDREN: all ages welcomed.
DOGS: allowed, not in public rooms.
CREDIT CARDS: MasterCard, Visa.
PRICES: [2012] B&B £68–£80 per person, D,B&B £79–£103, full alc £30, activity breaks, New Year package.

SEE ALSO SHORTLIST

PORT APPIN Argyll and Bute

Map 5:D1

THE AIRDS HOTEL

With good views of Loch Linnhe, this low-slung former ferry inn is now a 'very comfortable' small luxury hotel (Relais & Châteaux). It is run by the owners, Shaun (the manager) and Jenny McKivragan. The decor blends traditional Scottish and boutique hotel: redecorated hallways 'have a great fresh look'; two large lounges have 'comfy seating', log fires, books and magazines. 'Our bright bedroom was pleasantly furnished with two easy chairs; very hot water in the good-sized bathroom; good toiletries and a decanter of Whisky Mac were appreciated.' Light lunches (until 1.45 pm) and afternoon tea are served, and dinner orders taken, in the lounges or a 'light and airy' conservatory. The atmosphere in the dining room is 'formal' with 'attentive' service from mainly East European staff. Meals cooked by the new chef, Robert MacPherson, are 'even better than before': enjoyed this year were 'seafood starters, cod tapenade and tasty lamb'. Breakfast, served at the table, has freshly squeezed fruit juice, a large choice of breads, croissants, cereals and fruit salad; 'cooked dishes were good'.
(ST, Mrs J Brown, and others)

Port Appin PA38 4DF

T: 01631-730236
F: 01631-730535
E: airds@airds-hotel.com
W: www.airds-hotel.com

BEDROOMS: 11, 2 on ground floor, also self-catering cottage.
OPEN: all year except 2 days a week Nov, Dec, Jan.
FACILITIES: 2 lounges, conservatory, snug bar, restaurant, wedding facilities, ¾-acre garden (croquet, putting), unsuitable for ♿.
BACKGROUND MUSIC: none.
LOCATION: 25 miles N of Oban.
CHILDREN: all ages welcomed, but no under-9s in dining room after 7.30 (high tea at 6.30).
DOGS: allowed by prior agreement; not in public rooms.
CREDIT CARDS: Amex, MasterCard, Visa.
PRICES: [2012] D,B&B £135–£240 per person, off-season breaks, Christmas/ New Year and gourmet packages.

PORTPATRICK Dumfries and Galloway

Map 5:E1

KNOCKINAAM LODGE

Sheltered on three sides by a horseshoe of wooded hills, Sian and David Ibbotson's hotel is a former hunting lodge in 'lovely, large grounds' stretching down to a private beach on the Irish Sea. 'There is much to recommend: a wonderful, secluded position, and caring, well-trained staff,' say inspectors this year. Filled with 'comfy' sofas, stag's heads and paintings of pastoral scenes, the 'welcoming public rooms' have 'a country house feel'. Bedrooms vary in size and aspect: a 'pokey', west-facing attic room was 'overheated' in sunny weather; an attractive large first-floor room had a 'huge bathroom' with a window overlooking the pond and gardens. Turn-down takes place while guests dine. In the candlelit dining room, chef Tony Pierce has a *Michelin* star for his modern Scottish tasting menus ('small portions', perhaps of Galloway lamb loin, shallot purée, haggis beignet). 'We had excellent soup – cauliflower with truffle one night, an apple concoction the next – and exquisite puddings.' The breakfast menu includes 'plenty for those who don't want a cooked affair: good kippers, delicious poached fruit, but boring toast'.

25% DISCOUNT VOUCHERS

Portpatrick
DG9 9AD

T: 01776-810471
F: 01776-810435
E: reservations@knockinaamlodge.com
W: www.knockinaamlodge.com

BEDROOMS: 10.

OPEN: all year.

FACILITIES: 2 lounges, 1 bar, restaurant, wedding facilities, 30-acre grounds, only restaurant suitable for ♿.

BACKGROUND MUSIC: classical in restaurant.

LOCATION: 3 miles S of Portpatrick.

CHILDREN: no under-12s in dining room after 7 pm (high tea at 6).

DOGS: allowed in some bedrooms, not in public rooms.

CREDIT CARDS: Amex, MasterCard, Visa.

PRICES: [2012] D,B&B £137.50–£220 per person, set lunch £40, set dinner £58, special offers, midweek breaks, Christmas/New Year packages, 1-night bookings sometimes refused.

PORTREE Highland

Map 5:C1

VIEWFIELD HOUSE

César award in 1993

'We felt like a Scottish king,' says a continental visitor this year to this 'baronial pile' on the outskirts of Portree. It is 'a very comfortable place with a nice atmosphere; perfect for discovering Skye'. The house has been the home of Hugh Macdonald's family for two centuries, and it is liked for the 'faded grandeur', and 'absence of hotel-type notices'. The public rooms have family pictures, Persian rugs, log fires, stags' antlers and relics of the family's colonial service. Mr Macdonald might join guests for a drink and a chat in the evening. Supper is available by arrangement (check when you book). 'Our huge bedroom had four windows overlooking the gardens and bay,' is an earlier comment. A tiny tower room has 'a fabulous view'. There is television in the morning room, but not in the bedrooms: 'We want guests to enjoy the public rooms, the whole point of staying in a house like this,' says Mr Macdonald. Wi-Fi Internet is available throughout. A generous breakfast is presented in the large dining room. Children and dogs are welcomed. (*Maarten Louwen, and others*)

Viewfield Road
Portree
Isle of Skye IV51 9EU

T: 01478-612217
F: 01478-613517
E: info@viewfieldhouse.com
W: www.viewfieldhouse.com

BEDROOMS: 11, 1, on ground floor, suitable for ♿.
OPEN: Apr–Oct.
FACILITIES: ramp, drawing room, morning/TV room, dining room, 20-acre grounds (croquet, swings).
BACKGROUND MUSIC: none.
LOCATION: S side of Portree.
CHILDREN: all ages welcomed.
DOGS: not allowed in public rooms except with permission of other guests (except guide dogs).
CREDIT CARDS: MasterCard, Visa.
PRICES: [2012] B&B £58–£70 per person, set dinner £20, alc £30, discount for stays of 3 days or more, 1-night group bookings sometimes refused.

SEE ALSO SHORTLIST

ST OLA Orkney Islands

Map 5:A3

FOVERAN

With 'wonderful views over Scapa Flow', this simple, single-storey building is run as a restaurant-with-rooms by the Doull family. While the unassuming building might not catch the eye, the welcome more than compensates, say recent visitors. Pre-dinner drinks are served, and dinner orders taken, by a fire in the lounge. The 'large, light and airy' restaurant (bookings advised) faces the water. Mr Doull 'showcases local produce' in his menus, which might include pan-seared Orkney scallops, roasted tomato and basil butter; slow-roasted North Ronaldsay mutton with a Scapa special ale and mature island Cheddar sauce. A post-meal Highland coffee provided by the barman with 'a very generous measure' came with home-made Orkney tablet. The service, by 'a splendid team of youngsters', is 'relaxed but professional'. Binoculars are provided on the window tables. The bedrooms, furnished in modern pale wood, look inland and may be small but are well equipped and 'comfortable'. Breakfast is thought 'excellent'. Guests can walk to the beach. There are 'abundant wildlife and fascinating archaeological sites' nearby. (*SB, and others*)

St Ola
Kirkwall KW15 1SF

T: 01856-872389
F: 01856-876430
W: www.foveranhotel.co.uk

BEDROOMS: 8, all on ground floor.
OPEN: mid-Apr–early Oct, by arrangement at other times, only restaurant Christmas/New Year, restaurant closed Sun evening end Sept–early June.
FACILITIES: lounge, restaurant, 12-acre grounds (private rock beach).
BACKGROUND MUSIC: Scottish, in evening, in restaurant.
LOCATION: 3 miles SW of Kirkwall.
CHILDREN: all ages welcomed.
DOGS: not allowed.
CREDIT CARDS: MasterCard, Visa.
PRICES: [2012] B&B £55–£78 per person, D,B&B £80–£103, full alc £137.50, 1-night bookings sometimes refused.

SCARISTA Western Isles

Map 5:B1

SCARISTA HOUSE

César award in 2012

'A wondrous shelter from an inevitable storm', this 'elegant' white-painted Georgian manse (*pictured on front cover*) is run as a small hotel by the owners, Tim and Patricia Martin. 'The combination of food, setting, comfort and welcome make it a special place,' said *Guide* inspectors, who enjoyed the sociable atmosphere. On the western edge of Harris, *Scarista* faces a three-mile sandy beach. It is 'beautifully furnished'; rugs on wooden floors, comfortable sofas, open fires; books and good art in the downstairs library and the first-floor drawing room. Patricia Martin's dinners are taken in two adjoining areas ('if you're lucky, you can eat with a glorious sunset streaming through the windows'). Her 'simple but perfectly executed' menu (no choice, but tastes discussed) might include Stornoway-landed halibut, Champagne and chive sauce, garden vegetables. Three bedrooms are in a single-storey outbuilding to the rear: 'Ours had a light-filled sitting room; a large bed, a well-appointed bathroom.' The 'delicious' breakfast has freshly squeezed orange juice; local sausages, black and white pudding in the cooked plate.

Scarista
Isle of Harris HS3 3HX

T: 01859-550238
F: 01859-550277
E: timandpatricia@scaristahouse.com
W: www.scaristahouse.com

BEDROOMS: 6, 3 in annexe.
OPEN: Mar–Dec, except Christmas.
FACILITIES: drawing room, library, dining room, 1-acre garden, unsuitable for ♿.
BACKGROUND MUSIC: none.
LOCATION: 15 miles SW of Tarbert.
CHILDREN: all ages welcomed.
DOGS: by arrangement in bedrooms, library.
CREDIT CARDS: MasterCard, Visa.
PRICES: [2012] B&B £105–£117.50 per person, set meals £43–£50.

SKIRLING Scottish Borders

Map 5:E2

SKIRLING HOUSE

César award in 2004

In a 'superb setting' by a tranquil village green, 'warm and welcoming' hosts Isobel and Bob Hunter run a small guest house at their 1908 Arts and Crafts home. 'They are warm and welcoming hosts in a fascinating house,' says a visitor in 2012. Another comment: 'Everything was excellent; the food is brilliant, the ambience relaxed,' says a visitor this year. The sunny drawing room has a 16th-century carved Florentine ceiling; throughout the house, Mrs Hunter's collection of contemporary, largely Scottish art is 'worth an examination'. Well-equipped bedrooms have garden views, books, 'comfortable bed and good linen'. 'Well-fitted' bathrooms (now all newly remodelled) have 'excellent organic soaps and plenty of towels'. Dinner, taken in the conservatory or, in winter, by the log fire in the dining room, is a 'carefully paced affair'. 'Outstanding home cooking: excellent soup, main courses cooked to perfection; a delicious lemon tart.' 'Breakfast is an event': home-made preserves, home-baked bread, drop scones, freshly squeezed juices, eggs from the Hunters' hens, a daily-changing cooked special. (*David Fowler, Val Ferguson*)

25% DISCOUNT VOUCHERS

Skirling, by Biggar ML12 6HD

T: 01899-860274
F: 01899-860255
E: enquiry@skirlinghouse.com
W: www.skirlinghouse.com

BEDROOMS: 5, plus 1 single available if let with a double, 1 on ground floor suitable for ♿.

OPEN: Mar–Dec, except 1 week in Nov.

FACILITIES: ramps, 4 public rooms, 5-acre garden (tennis, croquet) in 100-acre estate with woodland.

BACKGROUND MUSIC: none.

LOCATION: 2 miles E of Biggar, by village green.

CHILDREN: all ages welcomed.

DOGS: allowed by arrangement, not in public rooms or unattended in bedrooms.

CREDIT CARDS: MasterCard, Visa.

PRICES: [2012] B&B £60–£72.50 per person, set dinner £35.

SLEAT Highland

Map 5:C1

TORAVAIG HOUSE

In a beautiful setting on the coast road near the Armadale ferry, this white-painted hotel is owned by Anne Gracie and Kenneth Gunn, who renovated it from a near ruin. 'They gave us a good welcome,' say visitors. 'The staff were very pleasant.' The bedrooms, some small, have rich fabrics and wallpapers, white bedlinen; hillside or sea views. They are colour-themed and named after Hebridean islands. Eriskay, in olive and gold, has a wooden sleigh bed. Colonsay, in nutmeg and copper, has a sea-facing sitting/dining area. The drawing room has a marble fireplace, log fire, grand piano, comfortable seating. We would welcome reports on new chef Chris Coombe's cooking. His 'modern Scottish' menus have elaborate dishes like pistachio- and herb-crusted turbot, black pudding, red kale, cauliflower, caper and tomato vinaigrette. One guest this year found the service slow. From April to September, trips can be taken on a 42-foot yacht belonging to Mr Gunn, who used to be a professional sea captain. Guests can get married on it. *Duisdale House*, Sleat, nearby (see Shortlist), is under the same ownership.

25% DISCOUNT VOUCHERS

Knock Bay, Sleat
Isle of Skye
IV44 8RE

T: 01471-820200
F: 01471-833231
E: info@skyehotel.co.uk
W: www.skyehotel.co.uk

BEDROOMS: 9.

OPEN: all year.

FACILITIES: lounge, dining room, wedding facilities, 2-acre grounds, unsuitable for ♿.

BACKGROUND MUSIC: none.

LOCATION: 7 miles S of Broadford.

CHILDREN: all ages welcomed.

DOGS: not allowed.

CREDIT CARDS: MasterCard, Visa.

PRICES: [2012] B&B £74.50–£120 per person, D,B&B £95–£165, set dinner £48, seasonal and midweek offers, Christmas/New Year packages.

SEE ALSO SHORTLIST

STRATHYRE Perth and Kinross

Map 5:D2

CREAGAN HOUSE

NEW

On the side of a sheltered valley at the head of Loch Lubnaig, this 17th-century farmhouse is run as a restaurant-with-rooms by owners Gordon (the chef) and Cherry Gunn. It returns to a full *Guide* entry after several warm reports. 'We were given an attentive, personal welcome,' says a trusted reporter. 'Mrs Gunn likes to get to know her guests, and says many come back as friends.' Other praise: 'A delight; attention to detail shines through the house.' Mr Gunn's cooking, served and 'lovingly described' by his wife in a baronial dining hall with a high ceiling and a vast fireplace, is the 'focal point'. He 'takes great pride in everything he presents', using local produce (vegetables from his own polytunnel) for his modern dishes, perhaps breast of grouse boudin; lamb cutlets, pattie of leg with mint and ginger. 'A fantastic cheese plate.' 'Our good-sized bedroom was newly decorated; it had a four-poster bed upholstered in hand-embroidered satin; china dogs and teddy bear cushions.' It is in a 'beautiful' part of the country though 'there might be some road noise in the morning'. (*ANR, Mrs W Montague*)

25% DISCOUNT VOUCHERS

Strathyre FK18 8ND

T: 01877-384638
F: 01877-384319
E: eatandstay@creaganhouse.co.uk
W: www.creaganhouse.co.uk

BEDROOMS: 5, 1 on ground floor.
OPEN: all year except Christmas, 16 Jan–7 Mar, 7–22 Nov, closed Wed/Thurs.
FACILITIES: lounge, restaurant, private dining room, 1-acre grounds.
BACKGROUND MUSIC: none.
LOCATION: ¼ mile N of village.
CHILDREN: all ages welcomed.
DOGS: not allowed in public rooms.
CREDIT CARDS: MasterCard, Visa.
PRICES: B&B £65–£95 per person, D,B&B £97.50–£127.50, set meals £32.50, New Year package.

SEE ALSO SHORTLIST

STRONTIAN Highland

Map 5:C1

KILCAMB LODGE

Inspectors were 'greeted warmly' in 2012 at Sally and David Ruthven-Fox's luxury hotel. Their 18th-century stone lodge stands in ancient woodland on the shores of Loch Sunart on the remote Ardnamurchan peninsula. The manager, Anne Goh, 'is friendly and thoroughly observant, anticipating your needs at all times'. The 'warm and homely' public rooms have 'tasteful decoration, comfortable furniture, lovely pictures throughout'. The bedrooms, all of which overlook the loch, have tartan throws and carpets. 'Ours had a large and exceptionally comfortable bed; the bathroom had a large bath and good-quality toiletries; everything scrupulously clean.' Pre-dinner drinks and canapés are taken in the lounge with its open fire. In the 'pleasant' candlelit dining room, which has white linens and fresh flowers on the tables, chef Gary Phillips serves local fish, shellfish and game on his daily-changing menus. 'All of it was delicious, particularly the wild mushroom risotto and the beetroot velouté; helpings were small.' Breakfast is 'first rate', with 'delicious' home-made muesli, 'lovely porridge and good-quality cooked breakfasts'.

25% DISCOUNT VOUCHERS

Strontian
PH36 4HY

T: 01967-402257
F: 01967-402041
E: enquiries@kilcamblodge.co.uk
W: www.kilcamblodge.co.uk

BEDROOMS: 10.

OPEN: Feb–New Year, closed Mon and Tues in Feb and March.

FACILITIES: drawing room, lounge bar, dining room, wedding facilities, 22-acre grounds, unsuitable for ♿.

BACKGROUND MUSIC: jazz/classical/guitar in dining room.

LOCATION: edge of village.

CHILDREN: not under 10.

DOGS: not allowed in public rooms.

CREDIT CARDS: MasterCard, Visa.

PRICES: [2012] D,B&B £124–£184.50 per person, full alc £60, off-season breaks, Christmas/New Year packages.

TARBERT Western Isles

Map 5:B1

CEOL NA MARA

Set above a rocky tidal loch, minutes from the ferry terminal, this old stone house was renovated by John and Marlene Mitchell, the 'friendly and hard-working' hosts. There are 'lovely views from all windows, and rooms equipped as well as any hotel'. 'This was the find of our holiday,' said the nominators. The large guest lounge is 'full of books and family treasures'. There are lounges on each of the upper floors, including a sun lounge with far-reaching views, and a decked terrace overlooking Loch Kindebig. A 'large, comfortable' bedroom had a flat-screen TV, silent fridge, 'good' storage; an 'excellent' bathroom with a shower. Breakfast has the 'most generous choice ever', with a large selection of cooked choices: 'The porridge has to be sampled; home-made breads and yogurt; a wide selection of fish and fruit.' The cooked dishes include 'Ceol na Mara cairn' (black pudding, potato scone, bacon, with a poached egg). There is no evening meal offered, but the Mitchells recommend the *Pierhouse* restaurant at the nearby *Hotel Hebrides* (see next entry). More reports, please.

7 Direcleit, Tarbert
Isle of Harris HS3 3DP

T: 01859-502464
F: 01859-575707
E: midgie@madasafish.com
W: www.ceolnamara.com

BEDROOMS: 4.
OPEN: all year.
FACILITIES: 2 lounges, sun lounge, dining room, unsuitable for ♿.
BACKGROUND MUSIC: soft Highland/Celtic at breakfast.
LOCATION: ½ mile S of Tarbert.
CHILDREN: all ages welcomed.
DOGS: not allowed.
CREDIT CARDS: Diners, MasterCard, Visa (*3% surcharge*).
PRICES: B&B £40–£50 per person.

TARBERT Western Isles

Map 5:B1

HOTEL HEBRIDES

By the pier in a small ferry port, this modern, slightly boxy-looking hotel is run by owners Angus and Chirsty Macleod. Inside, it has been given an 'adroit and stylish' make-over, with original paintings of the Hebrides by Willie Fulton, a local artist, in public rooms and bedrooms. The *Mote* bar, 'a lively, sociable place in the evening', is the hub of village life, serving bar food year round. The *Pierhouse* restaurant (open April to September) is 'light and airy'. No reports yet of new chef Chris Martin, who continues the 'Scottish high-end bistro' style of food, eg, Stornoway cod, roasted vegetables, chorizo and tomato jus. The bedrooms, which vary in size, are furnished in contemporary, 'boutique-hotel' style. 'Ours,' say inspectors, 'had an excellent shower room with generous toiletries, and dressing gowns.' Rooms above the bar may be noisy till it closes. Breakfast has packaged orange juice, 'delicious porridge'. Well placed for touring the Western Isles, the hotel is near the white sandy beach at Luskentyre Bay; boat trips can be taken to St Kilda (weather permitting) and other islands. Fishing, walking and wildlife nearby.

Pier Road
Tarbert
Isle of Harris HS3 3DG

T: 01859-502364
F: 01859-502578
E: stay@hotel-hebrides.com
W: www.hotel-hebrides.com

BEDROOMS: 21.

OPEN: all year, *Pierhouse* restaurant closed Oct–Mar.

FACILITIES: bar, restaurant, unsuitable for ♿.

BACKGROUND MUSIC: in bar and restaurant.

LOCATION: opposite pier.

CHILDREN: all ages welcomed.

DOGS: not allowed.

CREDIT CARDS: Diners, MasterCard, Visa.

PRICES: [2012] B&B £55–£80 per person, full alc £40, special breaks, Christmas/New Year packages.

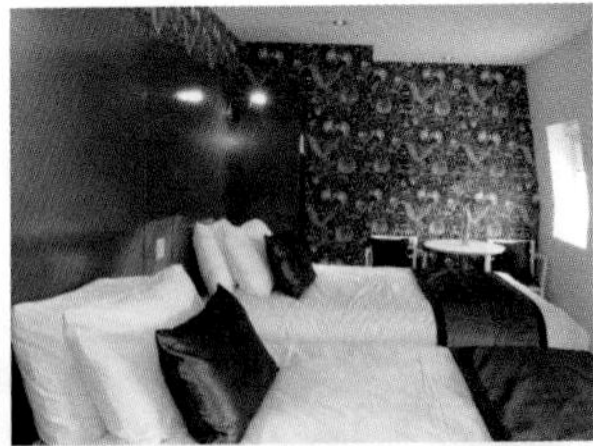

THORNHILL Dumfries and Galloway

Map 5:E2

TRIGONY HOUSE

In a 'lovely setting of garden and woodland', this distinguished Edwardian shooting lodge is run as a small country hotel by owners Adam and Jan Moore. She is a 'chatty and helpful' hostess, say inspectors in 2012. The light wood-panelled hall has an elegant staircase with a viewing balcony halfway up. The public rooms are 'cosy' with roaring fires, board games, period furniture. Traditionally furnished bedrooms vary in size; some have lovely views. 'Our large room had a conservatory sitting room, big bed, well-equipped bathroom (power shower).' The wood-floored dining room overlooks the pretty garden with a terrace for alfresco eating. Mr Moore, the chef, takes his inspiration from Elizabeth David, using much home-grown and organic produce. 'Dinner was delicious. We had pigeon breast on light, tasty haggis; venison two ways; profiteroles with crunchy praline filling, good local cheeses.' There are simpler dishes on the bar menu. Breakfast is, 'if anything, over-generous'. Good walking and fishing nearby. *Trigony* is 'extremely' dog-friendly, 'though your pooch may have to take second place to the doe-eyed resident Labrador, Rosie'. (*Helen Pank, and others*)

25% DISCOUNT VOUCHERS

Closeburn
Thornhill DG3 5EZ

T: 01848-331211
E: info@trigonyhotel.co.uk
W: www.countryhousehotelscotland.com

BEDROOMS: 9, 1 on ground floor.
OPEN: all year except 25–27 Dec.
FACILITIES: lounge, bar, dining room, wedding facilities, 4½-acre grounds.
BACKGROUND MUSIC: jazz in bar in evening.
LOCATION: 1 mile S of Thornhill.
CHILDREN: all ages welcomed.
DOGS: not allowed in dining room.
CREDIT CARDS: Amex, MasterCard, Visa.
PRICES: B&B £52.50–£130 per person, D,B&B £82.50–£160, full alc £38.50, special breaks and courses, New Year package, 1-night bookings refused Sat except last-minute.

TIRORAN Argyll and Bute

Map 5:D1

TIRORAN HOUSE

'Visitors this year were welcomed with grace and enthusiasm' at Laurence and Katie Mackay's Victorian hunting lodge in 'beautiful' gardens on the shores of Loch Scridain. 'A friendly chap full of good advice', Mr Mackay 'introduced us to the other arrivals'; all guests are received with tea and home-made cakes. The two 'tastefully decorated' lounges have log fire, books and local guides; guests are invited to have pre-dinner drinks here. In the candlelit dining room and vine-covered conservatory, Mrs Mackay, a *Cordon Bleu* chef, cooks a daily-changing short menu, with local fish, meat and game, and vegetables and fruit from the hotel's garden and orchard. Her 'imaginative' dishes might include island venison and Scottish pork terrine, warm home-made sultana bread, garden apple chutney; fillet of sea bass on buttered asparagus spears. The bedrooms vary in size and style: 'Our large room was very comfortable, with a large armchair and a chaise longue, a king-size bed, a desk and a chair.' The 'appetizing' breakfast buffet has home-made muesli and granola; cooked options include smoked haddock and kippers. (*Dr Gillian Todd, Charles Grant, Barbara Watkinson*)

Tiroran, Isle of Mull
PA69 6ES

T: 01681-705232
F: 01681-705240
E: info@tiroran.com
W: www.tiroran.com

BEDROOMS: 10, 2 on ground floor, 3 in annexe.
OPEN: 20 Mar–20 Nov.
FACILITIES: 2 sitting rooms, dining room, conservatory, 17½-acre grounds, beach with mooring.
BACKGROUND MUSIC: low-volume at dinner 'if suitable'.
LOCATION: N side of Loch Scridain.
CHILDREN: all ages welcomed.
DOGS: allowed in 3 bedrooms, not in public rooms.
CREDIT CARDS: MasterCard, Visa.
PRICES: [2012] B&B £67.50–£99.50 per person, dinner £45.

TOBERMORY Argyll and Bute

Map 5:D1

HIGHLAND COTTAGE

Above the harbour of the main village in Mull (noted for its colourfully painted houses), this purpose-built small hotel is run by 'hands-on' owners David and Josephine Currie. Visitors like the 'personal service' and the lack of stuffiness. The Curries rebuilt a semi-derelict cottage to their own design; it is a short steep walk from the main street. Upstairs, the sitting room, which has views across Tobermory Bay, has a writing desk, magazines and an honesty bar. 'Cosy' bedrooms are decorated in dark wood furnishings and rich fabrics; they have flat-screen television with Freeview, digital radio, DVD- and CD-player, an iPod dock, and a hospitality tray with tea- and coffee-making kit and confectionery. Two have a fully dressed four-poster bed. Bathrooms have a full-size bath with overhead shower. Booking is essential in the dining room, where Mrs Currie uses island produce for her three-course menus which have been simplified for 2012 (and reduced in price). Her dishes might include Croig crab cakes, mixed leaves, chilli caper sauce; pan-fried sea bass fillet, braised leeks, sauté potatoes and tomato, olive and caper butter. More reports, please.

25% DISCOUNT VOUCHERS

Tobermory
Isle of Mull PA75 6PD

T: 01688-302030
E: davidandjo@highlandcottage.co.uk
W: www.highlandcottage.co.uk

BEDROOMS: 6, 1 on ground floor.
OPEN: 30 Mar–24 Oct.
FACILITIES: 2 lounges, restaurant.
BACKGROUND MUSIC: in 1 lounge, restaurant.
LOCATION: village centre.
CHILDREN: not under 10.
DOGS: not allowed in public rooms.
CREDIT CARDS: Diners, MasterCard.
PRICES: [2012] B&B £67.50–£82.50 per person, dinner £39.50, special breaks, 1-night bookings refused Sat.

SEE ALSO SHORTLIST

TORRIDON Highland

Map 5:C1

THE TORRIDON

'A wonderful welcome from delightful staff' was received by a visitor this year to this grand loch-side former shooting lodge on the 'wildly beautiful' west coast. It is run as a 'romantic' luxury hotel (Pride of Britain) by owners Rohaise and Daniel Rose-Bristow. Decorative plaster ceilings and panelling give the public rooms a sense of 'Victorian grandeur'. There are big open fireplaces and leather sofas. The 'especially well-equipped' bedrooms vary in size; many are spacious. 'Our lovely room had modern fittings and a most comfortable bed.' New this year is the 1887 Suite, which has a Victorian theme with contemporary touches. In the restaurant, the chef, Jason 'Bruno' Birkbeck, serves a five-course seasonal menu of Scottish dishes 'with French influence', eg, butternut squash velouté, Parmesan espuma; guineafowl breast, with rösti, lentil and Ventrèche bacon casserole. An informal alternative is offered at the neighbouring *Torridon Inn*. Breakfasts are 'leisurely and substantial'. The many activities on the large estate include mountain biking, archery, kayaking, dawn and sunset guided walks. 'Worth the price for special occasions.' (*PNA Hayes*)

Annat, by Achnasheen
IV22 2EY

T: 01445-791242
F: 01445-712253
E: info@thetorridon.com
W: www.thetorridon.com

BEDROOMS: 18, 1, on ground floor, suitable for ♿, 1 suite in adjacent cottage.

OPEN: all year except Jan, Mon–Wed Nov–Mar.

FACILITIES: ramp, lift, drawing room, library, whisky bar, dining room, wedding facilities.

BACKGROUND MUSIC: classical at night in dining room.

LOCATION: 10 miles SW of Kinlochewe.

CHILDREN: no under-10s in dining room in evening (high tea provided).

DOGS: in cottage only.

CREDIT CARDS: Amex, MasterCard, Visa.

PRICES: [2012] B&B £110–£227.50 per person, set dinner £50, special breaks, Christmas/New Year and web packages.

ULLAPOOL Highland

Map 5:B2

THE CEILIDH PLACE

A lively gathering place in a Highland fishing village, this characterful destination is at once bookshop, arts centre, café/bar and small hotel. It is 'a vast, rambling affair, full of side rooms and alcoves, and beautifully furnished', said a visitor. Actor Robert Urquhart opened a small café out of a boatshed here in 1970, with visions of it becoming 'a place for eating, meeting, talking and singing'; today, owned by his widow, Jean Urquhart (Effie MacKenzie is the manager), it remains faithful to those roots. While some visitors find the accommodation lacking, others love the place for its spirit. The atmosphere is 'warm and welcoming', the simple bedrooms – each with a small library selected by a Scottish author – are 'perfectly adequate'. The Clubhouse across the road has more basic bunk-bedded rooms. A guest lounge has an honesty bar and a pantry with free tea and coffee. In the café, chef Scott Morrison's 'Scottish eclectic' menu might include locally smoked haddock, rocket mash; stalker's pie. Public rooms act as a gallery for local artists, while a small concert room hosts plays, music and literary events and discussions.

25% DISCOUNT VOUCHERS

12–14 West Argyle Street
Ullapool IV26 2TY

T: 01854-612103
F: 01854-613773
E: stay@theceilidhplace.com
W: www.theceilidhplace.com

BEDROOMS: 13, 10 with facilities en suite, plus 11 in Clubhouse across road.

OPEN: all year except 2 weeks mid-Jan.

FACILITIES: bar, parlour, café/bistro, restaurant, bookshop, conference/function/wedding facilities, 2-acre garden, only public areas suitable for ♿.

BACKGROUND MUSIC: classical/jazz/blues/traditional in public areas.

LOCATION: village centre, large car park.

CHILDREN: all ages welcomed.

DOGS: not allowed in public rooms.

CREDIT CARDS: MasterCard, Visa.

PRICES: B&B £50–£79 per person, full alc £40, special breaks, Christmas/New Year packages.

SEE ALSO SHORTLIST

WALKERBURN Scottish Borders

Map 5:E2

WINDLESTRAW LODGE

Above the River Tweed, this 'stunning' pink Edwardian house is run as a small hotel by the 'friendly and professional' owners, Alan and Julie Reid. They have restored many of the original features of the house, which was built in 1906 by a Borders mill owner for his Austrian bride. There is decorative wood panelling and, in a separate section, a two-foot-deep plaster frieze, in the dining room, where Alan Reid uses local meat and seafood for his much-praised daily-changing menu. Typical dishes: seared monkfish, sea bream and prawns, pancetta and pea shoots; rack of lamb, redcurrant, rosemary and claret sauce. 'Exceptionally yummy' puddings. The open-plan public rooms have family photographs and objets d'art, open fires; six distinct sitting areas. The bedrooms are 'smart, comfortable'. The McIntosh room, once the master bedroom, has sumptuous fabrics, a brass bed; an Edwardian bathtub in the bathroom. Breakfast has an extensive choice: perhaps prunes, apricots and berries in Earl Grey syrup; Mull Cheddar cheese omlette among the cooked options. Fishing and golf can be arranged, and there is good walking. (*VF*)

Galashiels Road
Tweed Valley
Walkerburn EH43 6AA

T: 01896-870636
E: reception@windlestraw.co.uk
W: www.windlestraw.co.uk

BEDROOMS: 6, all on first floor.

OPEN: all year except Jan, Christmas/New Year.

FACILITIES: bar lounge, sun lounge, drawing room, dining room, 1-acre grounds, unsuitable for ♿.

BACKGROUND MUSIC: none.

LOCATION: outskirts of village, 2 miles E of Innerleithen.

CHILDREN: not under 12 at dinner (high tea 5–6 pm).

DOGS: not allowed in some public rooms.

CREDIT CARDS: MasterCard, Visa.

PRICES: [2012] B&B £55–£100 per person, D,B&B £110–£145, set dinner £45, 2-night midweek and last-minute breaks.

www.goodhotelguide.com

WALES

Solva, Pembrokeshire

ABERAERON Ceredigion

Map 3:C2

HARBOURMASTER HOTEL

César award in 2005

'Friendly and relaxed' owners, Glyn and Menna Heulyn, and their staff make this handsome small hotel 'a happy, buzzy place', say fans this year. The 'comfortable and well-equipped' bedrooms, in three historic buildings on the harbour, are singled out for praise. 'Our favourite, Gwalia, has muted sea colours spiced with scarlet Welsh blankets. No cushions! No knick-knacks! No frills! Why can't more hotels be like this?' It is 'good to watch the candy colours of Aberaeron in the fading light'. Fresh local produce – Welsh cheese, locally landed fish, bread baked on the premises – predominate in chef Kelly Thomas's cooking in the restaurant and the 'chic' bar. 'The food is delicious in that straightforward British way of superb ingredients cooked just so, with the right imaginative touches: a tamarind chutney with crab cakes, a tarragon Béarnaise with Welsh beef on the bone. It's the kind of food you yearn for.' 'Super' breakfasts have fresh croissants and unusual juices: apple and cherry, pear and raspberry. 'There's little to fault about this lovely, and very Welsh, hotel.' (*Lynn Wildgoose, Frances Thomas, Peter Adam*)

Pen Cei, Aberaeron
SA46 0BT

T: 01545-570755
F: 01545-570762
E: info@harbour-master.com
W: www.harbour-master.com

BEDROOMS: 13, 2 in cottage, 1 suitable for ♿.

OPEN: all year except 25 Dec.

FACILITIES: bar, restaurant, pebble beach (safe bathing nearby).

BACKGROUND MUSIC: 'modern, relaxed'.

LOCATION: central, on harbour.

CHILDREN: under-5s in cottage only.

DOGS: not allowed.

CREDIT CARDS: MasterCard, Visa.

PRICES: [2012] B&B £55–£125 per person, D,B&B £80–£150, set dinner £25–£30, Sunday lunch £18–£23, special breaks, 1-night bookings refused weekends.

ABERDYFI Gwynedd

Map 3:C3

TREFEDDIAN HOTEL

In a 'stunning location' in Snowdonia national park, this traditional hotel has been owned and run by the Cave family for more than a century. 'The decor is tasteful rather than modern, but that adds to the classic charm of the place,' said a visitor in 2012. Another comment: 'The attitude of the approachable staff rubs off on guests; there is often merry laughter in the lift.' Bedrooms are 'spotless', with good storage space; beds are 'very comfortable'. Sea-facing rooms overlook 'a magnificent sweep of Cardigan Bay'. Traditional dishes are served in the formal dining room, where 'the freedom from background music is a blessing'. 'The meal was a revelation, the quality of ingredients superb and cooked by a creative chef [Tracey Sheen] who knows her craft.' 'Plenty of seating areas with a view' in the bar where a 'decent' lunch was enjoyed. 'The cooked breakfasts are first class, and set you up for the day – no lunch required.' In the off season, 'most of the guests are golden oldies like us'. During school holidays, *Trefeddian* is popular with families for the games room, play area and early dinners for children. (*Jayne Whitfield, Ken and Mildred Edwards, Jelly Williams*)

Tywyn Road
Aberdyfi LL35 0SB

T: 01654-767213
F: 01654-767777
E: info@trefwales.com
W: www.trefwales.com

BEDROOMS: 59.
OPEN: all year except 9 Dec–13 Jan.
FACILITIES: lift, 3 lounges, bar lounge, restaurant, fitness centre, indoor swimming pool (6 by 12 metres), beauty salon, 15-acre grounds (tennis, putting green).
BACKGROUND MUSIC: none.
LOCATION: ½ mile N of village.
CHILDREN: all ages welcomed.
DOGS: allowed in 1 lounge, some bedrooms.
CREDIT CARDS: MasterCard, Visa.
PRICES: [2012] B&B £45–£65 per person, D,B&B £67–£93, set dinner £29.50, special breaks, 1-night bookings sometimes refused.

ABERGAVENNY Monmouthshire

Map 3:D4

THE ANGEL HOTEL

A busy coaching inn in the early 19th century, this Georgian building has been restored by the Griffiths family, who run it as a busy town hotel. The restaurant and the award-winning afternoon teas are popular with locals. Many of the bedrooms and public areas were recently refurbished; a lift was added. The rooms have cream walls, quality furnishings, a cashmere throw on the bed; there are 'neat, modern' bathrooms. Visitors sensitive to noise may prefer rooms overlooking the courtyard rather than the street. In the restaurant, chef Mark Turton's menus follow the seasons, with ingredients from local suppliers. The 'good, unfussy' modern European dishes might include hot croustade of confit duck, sautéed apple, wild mushroom sauce; seared scallops, gnocchi, chorizo, red pepper sauce. Younger guests can choose from a sophisticated children's menu (eg, salmon fillet, new potatoes). Two cottages, each with its own outdoor space, are available for larger parties or guests seeking more privacy. The family co-owns the nearby *Walnut Tree* restaurant (*Michelin* star) with chef Shaun Hill; the *Angel* can organise gourmet breaks. 'Thoroughly recommended.' (*TB, and others*)

15 Cross Street
Abergavenny NP7 5EN

T: 01873-857121
F: 01873-858059
E: mail@angelabergavenny.com
W: www.angelabergavenny.com

BEDROOMS: 33, 2 in adjacent mews, plus 2 cottages.

OPEN: all year except 25 Dec; no guest rooms 24–30 Dec.

FACILITIES: ramps, lift, lounge, bar, restaurant, private function rooms, civil wedding licence, courtyard.

BACKGROUND MUSIC: occasionally in the ballroom.

LOCATION: town centre.

CHILDREN: all ages welcomed.

DOGS: not allowed in restaurant (£10 charge).

CREDIT CARDS: Amex, MasterCard, Visa.

PRICES: [2012] B&B £55.50–£89 per person, D,B&B £83.50–£133, full alc £35, special breaks, Christmas/New Year packages.

ABERSOCH Gwynedd

Map 3:B2

PORTH TOCYN HOTEL

César award in 1984

The views across Cardigan Bay and Snowdonia are 'stupendous' at this family hotel which has been created organically over 60 years from a group of lead miners' cottages. It is run in individual style by the owners, Nick and Louise Fletcher-Brewer. 'His friendly voice and welcome were instantly recognisable,' say visitors returning after 30 years. Another enthusiast found it 'as good as ever' this year. There is a 'laid-back, homely feel', with traditional furnishings, books, 'interesting knick-knacks'. Most of the bedrooms have a sea view; many have been upgraded ('ours was tastefully refurbished'); they have country antiques, watercolours and prints. Children have a dedicated snug and games in a conservatory. Younger children take high tea at 5.30 pm in the children's room, and 'simple suppers' have been introduced for families seeking flexible dining. An age limit of six is imposed in the restaurant at dinner, where Louise Fletcher-Brewer and Al Manzin serve modern dishes, perhaps loin of venison, mini venison pie, baked fig, chocolate jus. The Welsh Coastal Footpath skirts the grounds. (*Chris and Ann Chater, CLVP Evans*)

25% DISCOUNT VOUCHERS

Bwlch Tocyn
Abersoch LL53 7BU

T: 01758-713303
F: 01758-713538
E: bookings@porthtocyn.fsnet.co.uk
W: www.porthtocynhotel.co.uk

BEDROOMS: 17, 3 on ground floor.
OPEN: week before Easter–end Oct.
FACILITIES: ramp, sitting rooms, children's rooms, cocktail bar, dining room, 25-acre grounds (swimming pool, 10 by 6 metres, heated May–end Sept, tennis), telephone to discuss disabled access.
BACKGROUND MUSIC: none.
LOCATION: 2 miles outside village.
CHILDREN: no tiny children at dinner.
DOGS: by arrangement, not allowed in public rooms.
CREDIT CARDS: MasterCard, Visa.
PRICES: [2012] B&B (continental) £50–£90 per person, cooked breakfast £7, set dinner £36.25–£43.50, off-season, golf, walking and mid-week breaks, 1-night bookings occasionally refused.

ABERYSTWYTH Ceredigion

Map 3:C3

GWESTY CYMRU

On Aberystwyth's Victorian seafront promenade, this white-painted listed house, in a multi-coloured pastel terrace, is run as a restaurant-with-rooms by owners Huw and Beth Roberts. They have converted it with sympathy and flair, in sleek, modern style using Welsh slate and oak. Rooms vary in size, but all have a walk-in shower, bathrobes and slippers. A room at the top has old beams and a sofa that converts to an additional bed for children. 'Our ground-floor room at the back (booked because of mobility problems) was small, but it was spotlessly clean and comfortable,' said a visitor this year. Pawel Banaszynski ('Polish, with a Welsh soul', says Mr Roberts) is the chef. There is praise for his 'innovative take on local Welsh ingredients' on seasonal menus. 'Portions were generous, and lamb and duck both excellent. The young staff were efficient and friendly.' Breakfast has freshly squeezed orange juice; 'the addition of Welsh laver bread to the full cooked was an interesting novelty'. The owners promise 'spectacular sunset views' from the restaurant's sea-facing terrace. (*Alison Askins, and others*)

19 Marine Terrace
Aberystwyth SY23 2AZ

T: 01970-612252
F: 01970-623348
E: info@gwestycymru.co.uk
W: www.gwestycymru.co.uk

BEDROOMS: 8, 2 on ground floor.
OPEN: all year except Christmas/New Year, restaurant closed for lunch Tues.
FACILITIES: bar, restaurant, terrace, secure parking (book in advance), unsuitable for ♿.
BACKGROUND MUSIC: in reception and restaurant.
LOCATION: central, on seafront.
CHILDREN: not under 5.
DOGS: only guide dogs allowed.
CREDIT CARDS: MasterCard, Visa.
PRICES: B&B £43.50–£77.50 per person, £10 supplement for twin beds, full alc £37.50.

BALA Gwynedd

Map 3:B3

BRYNIAU GOLAU

Visitors consistently speak of the warm welcome – and home-made cakes and scones – which they receive from owners Katrina Le Saux and Peter Cottee at this hillside Victorian home overlooking Bala Lake in Snowdonia national park. From the terrace and garden nooks, guests can watch 'breathtaking' sunsets over the Arenig Mountains, or, on chillier evenings, gather on sofas in front of the log fire in the sitting room. The house has been refurbished this year: the large Berwyn bedroom, with its antique four-poster bed, has been redecorated, as have the dining room and guest cloakroom. Work has begun on a guest car park. On Friday and Sunday nights, Mr Cottee cooks a three-course dinner, by arrangement (special diets can be catered for); the menu might include prosciutto, blue cheese, sweet red peppers; pan-fried halibut, aubergine compote. Breakfast, at a long table in a room with a grand piano, has award-winning home-made marmalade and *Bryniau Golau* honey from the house's own bees. Bala, a 14th-century market town, is reachable by foot; walks also take visitors through countryside and along the lake. More reports, please.

25% DISCOUNT VOUCHERS

Llangower, Bala
LL23 7BT

T: 01678-521782
E: katrinalesaux@hotmail.co.uk
W: www.bryniau-golau.co.uk

BEDROOMS: 3.
OPEN: Mar–end Oct.
FACILITIES: sitting room, dining room, ½-acre garden, unsuitable for ♿.
BACKGROUND MUSIC: none.
LOCATION: 2 miles SE of Bala.
CHILDREN: not under 12.
DOGS: not allowed.
CREDIT CARDS: MasterCard, Visa.
PRICES: [2012] B&B £45–£65 per person, dinner £27.50, 1-night bookings refused weekends and peak times.

BARMOUTH Gwynedd

Map 3:B3

LLWYNDU FARMHOUSE

On a hillside overlooking Cardigan Bay, this restored 16th-century farmhouse (Grade II listed) is run as a small hotel/restaurant by Peter and Paula Thompson. 'They are warm and engaging hosts; it is a delightful place to relax and unwind,' say visitors in 2012. 'The personal touches (like Welsh cakes and a pot of tea when we arrived) make all the difference.' The history of the 'lovely old house' is reflected in the bedrooms: a walk-in cupboard in what was once a latrine, a sink fitted to a door. Three rooms, in an adjacent converted granary, have high ceilings with exposed beams of pitch pine; these are good for a family. Mr Thompson uses local produce for his meals, which are taken in a candlelit restaurant with an inglenook fireplace. Typical dishes: smoked fish chowder; chicken layered with leeks and blue cheese, tarragon sauce. 'Great food and a good wine list at sensible prices.' A visitor appreciated the vegetarian choice at breakfast (Glamorgan cutlet, scrambled eggs, laver bread). The house is 'convenient for the town, yet far enough away to maintain peace and quiet'. (*PJ, and others*)

Llanaber
Barmouth LL42 1RR

T: 01341-280144
E: intouch@llwyndu-farmhouse.co.uk
W: www.llwyndu-farmhouse.co.uk

BEDROOMS: 6, 3 in granary, 1 on ground floor.
OPEN: all year except 25/26 Dec, restaurant closed Sun evening.
FACILITIES: lounge, restaurant, 4-acre garden, unsuitable for ♿.
BACKGROUND MUSIC: occasionally 'depending on the guests'.
LOCATION: 2 miles N of Barmouth.
CHILDREN: all ages welcomed.
DOGS: allowed in some bedrooms, not in public rooms.
CREDIT CARDS: MasterCard, Visa.
PRICES: B&B £45–£53 per person, D,B&B £74–£82, set meals £24.50–£28, full alc £47.50, special breaks, New Year package.

BEAUMARIS Isle of Anglesey

Map 3:A3

YE OLDE BULLS HEAD

'Excellent; charming and helpful staff,' say visitors this year to this five-centuries-old inn in a busy ferry port, which has been owned for the last 25 years by David Robertson (the manager) and Keith Rothwell. There are two dining options. In the *Loft* restaurant, chef Hefin Roberts uses locally sourced produce for his daily-changing menus of modern dishes, perhaps seared king scallop, curried mussels, crisp crab fritter; fillet of Welsh beef, salt beef and potato hash, carrots and swede. 'The food was so good we dined there twice.' Simpler bistro-style dishes are served in the brasserie. The accommodation is in two buildings. Rooms in the inn, named after characters in Dickens's novels, are decorated in country cottage style; several have original roof timbers. Thirteen rooms are 100 yards from the *Bulls Head*, in *The Townhouse*, a contemporary conversion of a Grade II listed building dating back to 1550. These are decorated in modern style with bright colours. 'Bathroom and bed were first class.' The 'very good' breakfast has a continental buffet and a large choice of cooked dishes. (*RSC Abel Smith, Robert and Shirley Lyne*)

Castle Street
Beaumaris, Isle of Anglesey
LL58 8AP

T: 01248-810329
F: 01248-811294
E: info@bullsheadinn.co.uk
W: www.bullsheadinn.co.uk

BEDROOMS: 26, 2 on ground floor, 1 in courtyard, 13 in *The Townhouse* adjacent, 1 suitable for ♿.
OPEN: all year, except 25/26 Dec, 1 Jan, *Loft* restaurant closed lunch, Sun/Mon nights.
FACILITIES: lift (in *Townhouse*), lounge, bar, brasserie, restaurant, sea 200 yds, only brasserie and *Townhouse* suitable for ♿.
BACKGROUND MUSIC: 'chill-out', jazz in brasserie.
LOCATION: central.
CHILDREN: no under-7s in restaurant or bedroom suites.
DOGS: only assistance dogs allowed.
CREDIT CARDS: Amex, MasterCard, Visa.
PRICES: [2012] B&B £52.50–£77.50 per person, set dinner (restaurant) £42.50, full alc £57, special breaks.

BRECHFA Carmarthenshire

Map 3:D2

TŶ MAWR

César award in 2011

'Rare perfection was delivered at this charming country house.' High praise this year from *Guide* readers for this 'comfy and welcoming hotel', owned and managed by Annabel and Stephen Thomas. In a peaceful village location by a bubbling stream on the edge of the Brechfa forest, the 16th-century building has thick exposed stone walls, old fireplaces and beams. Rooms are 'comfortable', with simple pine furnishings. 'Ours was vast, with an extended sitting area, huge sofa, coffee table, large flat-screen TV.' Stephen Thomas cooks a daily-changing menu of seasonal dishes using local ingredients. 'We were particularly impressed with the interesting canapés: three different varieties each evening. We enjoyed a shellfish soup of intense flavour, beef stroganoff that melted in the mouth and an orange and pomegranate panna cotta'. Annabel Thomas is responsible for the often-praised puddings. The cooked breakfast has 'good sausages and home-made bread', free-range eggs; honey and preserves come from a nearby farm. 'Excellent value for money'. (*Janet and Dennis Allom, John and Haf Davies-Humphreys*)

Brechfa SA32 7RA

T: 01267-202332
E: info@wales-country-hotel.co.uk
W: www.wales-country-hotel.co.uk

BEDROOMS: 6, 2 on ground floor.
OPEN: all year.
FACILITIES: sitting room, bar, breakfast room, restaurant, 1-acre grounds, unsuitable for ♿.
BACKGROUND MUSIC: classical in restaurant.
LOCATION: village centre.
CHILDREN: not under 12.
DOGS: not allowed in breakfast room, restaurant.
CREDIT CARDS: Amex, MasterCard, Visa.
PRICES: [2012] B&B £56.50–£64 per person, D,B&B £77.50–£85, set meals £24–£29, full alc £37, seasonal breaks, Christmas/New Year packages.

BRECON Powys

Map 3:D3

CANTRE SELYF

Liked for its peaceful setting and well-kept walled garden, this 'pleasant' B&B is run by owners Helen and Nigel Roberts, in an interesting market town in the Brecon Beacons. 'Everything is just as good as before,' say visitors this year, returning for the Brecon Baroque Festival. The 'intriguing'17th-century town house has many original features: moulded ceilings, elegant fireplaces and oak beams. Bedrooms are reached via an old wooden staircase ('all the creaks and squeaks are authentic,' the Robertses say); all have a 'comfortable' brass bed. The rooms vary in size: Einon is a large twin/king room overlooking the patio; Tewdos is a compact double with polished dark-wood floorboards. The cosy sitting room has a log-burning fireplace, books and board games; in warm weather, guests also sit in the 'delightful' garden. With fresh fruit, yogurt and home-made scones and bread, breakfast is thought 'good'; cooked dishes: smoked salmon, scrambled eggs and soda bread. Special diets can be catered for. The hosts will recommend nearby 'slow food' restaurants for dinner. Off-street parking, 'essential in Brecon', is available. (*Jill and Mike Bennett*)

5 Lion Street
Brecon LD3 7AU

T: 01874-622904
F: 01874 625951
E: enquiries@cantreselyf.co.uk
W: www.cantreselyf.co.uk

BEDROOMS: 3.
OPEN: closed Dec/Jan.
FACILITIES: sitting room, dining room, 1-acre walled garden, unsuitable for ♿.
BACKGROUND MUSIC: none.
LOCATION: central.
CHILDREN: all ages welcomed.
DOGS: not allowed.
CREDIT CARDS: MasterCard, Visa.
PRICES: [2012] B&B £40–£60 per person, midweek breaks.

BROAD HAVEN Pembrokeshire

Map 3:D1

THE DRUIDSTONE

'We are a house that's open, not a hotel,' says Jane Bell, who runs her Victorian stone buildings in family-friendly style with her husband, Rod, and son, Angus. 'One of my favourite secret places, it is beautiful, charming, restful and artistic,' a visitor said this year. Another comment (in 2012): 'The place and the style don't change; many of the staff are long serving. There is investment: we could see new windows, and the clearing of land for growing vegetables. To be sure, it doesn't suit everyone; shabby chic is a good description, or perhaps homely and welcoming.' Not all visitors like the simple accommodation and informality. 'It might be a tad expensive, but the upside is the feeling of freedom, the space to wander or just sit, and the sense that the staff really do want to look after your needs.' Five bedrooms have en suite facilities; six share three bathrooms. In the restaurant and bar, chef Angus Bell serves 'imaginative world' meals: eg, Burmese chicken and bamboo curry. The farmhouse kitchen hosts children's suppers, and private dinners. (*MM, and others*)

nr Broad Haven
Haverfordwest SA62 3NE

T: 01437-781221
E: enquiries@druidstone.co.uk
W: www.druidstone.co.uk

BEDROOMS: 11, also 5 holiday cottages.

OPEN: all year.

FACILITIES: sitting room, TV room, bar (occasional live music), farmhouse kitchen, restaurant, small conference/function facilities, civil wedding licence, 22-acre grounds, sandy beach, safe bathing 200 yds.

BACKGROUND MUSIC: in bar and on feast nights.

LOCATION: 7 miles W of Haverfordwest.

CHILDREN: all ages welcomed.

DOGS: not allowed in restaurant.

CREDIT CARDS: Amex, MasterCard, Visa.

PRICES: [2012] B&B £40–£90 per person, full alc £35, courses, conferences, 1-night bookings refused Sat.

CAERNARFON Gwynedd

Map 3:A2

PLAS DINAS COUNTRY HOUSE

Standing in large grounds of trees and greenery, this guest house, run by owners Andy and Julian Banner-Price, celebrates its past as the once-upon-a-time country home of the Armstrong-Jones family. The Grade II listed gentleman's residence, which won a 2012 Visit Wales gold award, is 'elegant but by no means stuffy', its owners are 'amiable', 'witty' and 'keen to share their home'. After drinks on the terrace (in warm weather), guests may dine, by arrangement, in the gun room, which has a 400-year-old fireplace and a host of royal memorabilia. The large drawing room, with its open fire and 'comfy sofas', is ideal for tea and 'delicious home-made chocolate brownies'. The spacious, individually styled bedrooms overlook the vast garden to open countryside or the Menai Strait; they have original antiques alongside modern facilities (an iPod video dock). Andy Banner-Price's 'excellent' dinners of traditional recipes updated with a pinch of contemporary twists might include fish pie with a Welsh cheesy mash; a gooseberry and apple crumble tart. Two self-catering cottages in the grounds can host larger parties. (*AA*)

25% DISCOUNT VOUCHERS

Bontnewydd
Caernarfon LL54 7YF

T: 01286-830214
E: info@plasdinas.co.uk
W: www.plasdinas.co.uk

BEDROOMS: 9, 1 on ground floor.
OPEN: all year except Christmas/New Year, restaurant closed Sun/Mon.
FACILITIES: drawing room, dining room, gun room, civil wedding licence, 15-acre grounds.
BACKGROUND MUSIC: in dining room.
LOCATION: 2 miles S of Caernarfon.
CHILDREN: not under 12.
DOGS: small dogs welcomed (£10 charge).
CREDIT CARDS: Amex, MasterCard, Visa.
PRICES: [2012] B&B £64.50–£137.50 per person, D,B&B £90.50–£167.50, set dinner £26–£30, full alc £40, special breaks.

CAPEL GARMON Conwy

Map 3:A3

TAN-Y-FOEL COUNTRY GUEST HOUSE

The 'fantastic views' and 'excellent and imaginative cooking' stand out at this rural guest house run by owners Janet and Peter Pitman and their daughter, Kelly. 'Peter is a helpful, friendly front-of-house man who gave us a choice of rooms.' Individually styled bedrooms in the 16th-century stone house look out on to the expansive Snowdonia mountain range or the Conwy valley; two – the Oriental Lily and the Hayloft – have a private entrance. A 30-yard-long greenhouse in the garden grows the leafy greens, Purple Dragon carrots, golden beetroot and loganberries used in the restaurant, where dinner, a single sitting, is served at 7.30 pm. Mrs Pitman uses local, organic produce for her daily-changing short menu (two choices for each course); visitors this year enjoyed 'high-class' dishes: a Pant-Ysgawn goat's cheese and thyme soufflé, a plate of Welsh pork loin, braised shoulder and slow-roasted belly, and a vanilla panna cotta with an apricot brandy purée. Vegetarians and others on special diets are not catered for. A copious, cooked-to-order breakfast is served between 8 and 9 am. (*Gordon Franklin*)

Capel Garmon
nr Betws-y-Coed LL26 0RE

T: 01690-710507
E: enquiries@tyfhotel.co.uk
W: www.tyfhotel.co.uk

BEDROOMS: 6, 1 on ground floor, 2 in annexe.
OPEN: Feb–Nov, restaurant closed Sun/Mon.
FACILITIES: sitting room, breakfast room, dining room, 6-acre grounds, unsuitable for ♿.
BACKGROUND MUSIC: none.
LOCATION: 2 miles N of Betws-y-Coed.
CHILDREN: not under 12.
DOGS: not allowed.
CREDIT CARDS: MasterCard, Visa.
PRICES: B&B £60–£120 per person, D,B&B £110–£170, set dinner £50, special offers, 1-night bookings refused weekends.

CRICKHOWELL Powys

Map 3:D4

GLANGRWYNEY COURT

In expansive parkland with 'splendid' walled gardens, this 'immaculate' Georgian Grade II listed family home is run as a 'very pleasant' country B&B by 'friendly' hosts Christina and Warwick Jackson. Renovations after a fire in early 2011 are complete, and the barn, for special functions, is again hosting weddings and other celebrations. 'Everything was top-notch: there was a wonderful ambience,' says a visitor this year. In the main house, the 'beautifully furnished' period bedrooms have a view of the gardens; they have antiques, fine fabrics; several have a coronet over the bed. One room has a Victorian roll-top bath in the en suite bathroom, while another, the largest, has a bay window overlooking the lily pond. In summer, guests enjoy drinks on the patio; in cooler months, a log fire burns in the sitting room. Evening meals – short simple menus of dishes like salmon rillettes; chicken in white wine – can be provided, by arrangement, for small groups. This year, the Jacksons have added a lodge to the collection of self-catering cottages in the grounds. (*Charles Grant, Philip Hanna*)

Glangrwyney, Crickhowell
NP8 1ES

T: 01873-811288
F: 01873-810317
E: info@glancourt.co.uk
W: www.glancourt.co.uk

BEDROOMS: 9, 1 on ground floor, in courtyard.
OPEN: all year.
FACILITIES: sitting room, library/honesty bar, dining room, civil wedding licence, 4-acre garden (croquet, boules, tennis) in 33-acre parkland, unsuitable for ♿.
BACKGROUND MUSIC: on request.
LOCATION: 2 miles SE of Crickhowell, off A40.
CHILDREN: all ages welcomed.
DOGS: allowed in cottages only.
CREDIT CARDS: MasterCard, Visa.
PRICES: [2012] B&B £60–£67.50 per person, D,B&B £82–£92.50, set dinner £22–£25, special breaks, off-season discounts, occasional Christmas package, 1-night bookings sometimes refused in summer months.

SEE ALSO SHORTLIST

CRICKHOWELL Powys

Map 3:D4

GLIFFAES

César award in 2009

'A lovely family-run hotel in a wonderful setting', this handsome 19th-century property (*pictured on page 4*) stands in wooded grounds on the banks of the River Usk. The 'very hands-on' owners, Susie and James Suter, are the third generation of her family to run the hotel since 1948. 'The staff couldn't have been more helpful or tolerant with our three young children,' say visitors this year. There is 'nothing formal or starchy', from the abundant cream teas taken on the broad stone terrace to the tandem bike that guests may borrow to head into the Brecon Beacons. Four of the 'beautifully furnished' bedrooms have a balcony overlooking the river; several have a sofa bed (suitable for children sharing). 'Eat local, eat fresh' is the motto of chef Karl Cheetham, whose menu of British dishes with a French influence might include chicken and wild mushroom terrine; rack of local lamb, black pudding galette. There are good walks from the door, including a tree trail through the grounds, showcasing native and exotic specimen trees. Fishing courses are held on the hotel's private stretch of the river. (*M and JP, and others*)

Crickhowell
NP8 1RH

T: 01874-730371
F: 01874-730463
E: calls@gliffaeshotel.com
W: www.gliffaeshotel.com

BEDROOMS: 23, 4 in annexe, 1 on ground floor.
OPEN: all year except Jan, restaurant closed lunch (except Sun).
FACILITIES: ramp, 2 sitting rooms, conservatory, bar, dining room, civil wedding licence, 33-acre garden (tennis, croquet, fishing).
BACKGROUND MUSIC: in bar in evening.
LOCATION: 3 miles W of Crickhowell.
CHILDREN: all ages welcomed, £14 to share parents' room.
DOGS: not allowed indoors.
CREDIT CARDS: all major cards.
PRICES: [2012] B&B £54–£127.50 per person, D,B&B £94–£167.50, fishing courses, special breaks, website deals, Christmas/New Year packages, 1-night bookings refused weekends.

SEE ALSO SHORTLIST

DOLFOR Powys

Map 3:C4

THE OLD VICARAGE

With 'glorious' views over the Montgomeryshire countryside, this former Victorian vicarage is run as an intimate guest house by 'affable' owners Tim and Helen Withers. 'The place strikes a balance not often found between high standards, professionalism and exquisite taste, and a homely, welcoming and relaxing ambience,' said a visitor this year. 'The beds are excellent – just like being at home – and the pillows perfect; a slate floor in the glamorous bathroom.' Tea with Welsh cakes and cherry cakes is given to guests in the afternoon. Vegetables come from the garden and 'everything is locally sourced and/or organic' for the host's no-choice menus: 'Superb, unfussy, but cooked with panache; the tender lamb in orange and laver bread sauce was as good as it's ever going to be; first-rate lemon and raspberry posset.' The owners' Jack Russells 'have the run of the place but we were happy to see them'. Bike hire and an electric car charging point are available; guests who leave their car at home receive a ten per cent discount. (*Sara Hollowell*)

25% DISCOUNT VOUCHERS

Dolfor, nr Newtown
SY16 4BN

T: 01686-629051
E: tim@theoldvicaragedolfor.co.uk
W: www.theoldvicaragedolfor.co.uk

BEDROOMS: 4.
OPEN: all year except Christmas/New Year.
FACILITIES: drawing room, dining room, 2-acre garden, unsuitable for ♿.
BACKGROUND MUSIC: none.
LOCATION: 3 miles S of Newtown.
CHILDREN: not under 12.
DOGS: not allowed.
CREDIT CARDS: Amex, MasterCard, Visa.
PRICES: [2012] B&B £47.50–£75 per person, D,B&B £77.50–£105, set dinner £30–£35, special breaks.

DOLYDD Gwynedd

Map 3:A2

Y GOEDEN EIRIN

César award in 2008

In a hamlet on the edge of the Snowdonia national park, with views of mountain and sea, John and Eluned Rowlands run their renovated farm buildings as an informal guest house (the name means 'the plum tree'). 'What a treat. They represent the epitome of good hotel-keeping,' said the *Guide*'s founding editor. The house is filled with good modern British art and Welsh books (the host is emeritus professor of Welsh at the University of Wales). 'They are fascinating about devolution, and are seriously green, but not in any oppressive way.' There are just three rooms, two in an annexe 'with an Arts and Crafts feel'. 'Good-sized bathrooms' and under-floor heating. 'Everything about our room showed care and attention to the needs of the guest.' Most dishes are Aga-cooked by John Rowlands, using mostly organic local or home-grown ingredients, 'wholesome with the occasional exotic touch', eg, green chicken Thai curry with jasmine rice; pork in cider and honey with pears. 'Excellent' breakfasts have freshly squeezed orange juice, home-made bread and preserves, a choice of cooked dishes. (*HR, and others*)

25% DISCOUNT VOUCHERS

Dolydd, Caernarfon
LL54 7EF

T: 01286-830942
E: john_rowlands@tiscali.co.uk
W: www.ygoedeneirin.co.uk

BEDROOMS: 3, 2 in annexe.
OPEN: all year except Christmas/New Year, dining room occasionally closed.
FACILITIES: dining room (occasional live piano music), lounge by arrangement, Wi-Fi access, 20-acre pastureland, unsuitable for ♿.
BACKGROUND MUSIC: none.
LOCATION: 3 miles S of Caernarfon.
CHILDREN: not under 12.
DOGS: not allowed.
CREDIT CARDS: none, cash or cheque payment requested on arrival.
PRICES: B&B £40–£70 per person, set dinner £28, full alc £42, 1-night bookings sometimes refused weekends.

EGLWYSFACH Powys

Map 3:C3

YNYSHIR HALL

César award in 1997

In January 2012, Joan and Rob Reen bought back this small luxury hotel from the administrators of the von Essen group (they had sold it in 2006 but she had remained 'very much in charge'). They tell us they have made a 'fresh start': the exterior and many of the public rooms have been redecorated; the studio wing has been remodelled to create a single large suite; two new garden suites were being completed as the *Guide* went to press. 'The lovely large grounds where you can roam at will and the proximity to the RSPB reserve are the strongest points,' say inspectors, who noted that 'investment was needed'. Paul Croasdale, who has been appointed chef, serves modern dishes on a short carte and a tasting menu. 'The usual modern paraphernalia of (delicious) canapés, amuse bouche; small portions and long waits between courses; sea bass on vegetables (otherwise scarce) was the best dish; an identical menu on the second night; muzak was also a surprise.' The bedrooms, named after famous artists and decorated in keeping, have vibrant colour ('fun if sometimes opulent').

25% DISCOUNT VOUCHERS

Eglwysfach
nr Machynlleth SY20 8TA

T: 01654-781209
F: 01654-781366
E: info@ynyshirhall.co.uk
W: www.ynyshirhall.co.uk

BEDROOMS: 9, 2 in studio annexe, 1 on ground floor.
OPEN: all year.
FACILITIES: drawing room, bar lounge, breakfast room, restaurant, civil wedding licence, 14-acre gardens in 1000-acre bird reserve.
BACKGROUND MUSIC: classical in bar, restaurant.
LOCATION: 6 miles SW of Machynlleth.
CHILDREN: not under 9 in evening in restaurant.
DOGS: allowed in some bedrooms, not in public rooms.
CREDIT CARDS: Amex, MasterCard, Visa.
PRICES: [2012] B&B £137.50–£202.50 per person, D,B&B £210–£275, set meals £72.50–£90, Christmas/New Year packages, 1-night bookings refused weekends, bank holidays.

FELIN FACH Powys

Map 3:D4

THE FELIN FACH GRIFFIN

César award: Welsh inn of the year

'An extraordinary haven in a storm for a family depressed by a week's exceptionally damp camping holiday.' This old inn on the road between the Brecon Beacons and the Black Mountains is managed by Julie Bell for brothers Charles and Edmund Inkin. 'I cannot sing its praises enough,' said a visitor this year. 'They dried our wet stuff in the boiler room, fed our four-year-old beans on toast and strawberry ice cream in the bar; added fish and chips to the menu for the older boys; re-laid our table with candles and dessert for two after we'd put the offspring to bed.' Two of the simple 'but well-designed' bedrooms have been redecorated and given a new bathroom this year. All have a Roberts radio, fresh flowers. The inn's organic kitchen garden provides chef Ross Bruce with ingredients for his modern menus (dishes like monkfish fricassée, roasted new potatoes, crème fraîche). 'Breakfast with a dog at our toes and Aga toast on the table sent us off in an entirely cheerful frame of mind.' The brothers also own *The Gurnard's Head*, Zennor (see entry) and manage *The Old Coastguard*, Mousehole (see Shortlist). (*Sophie Harrowes*)

25% DISCOUNT VOUCHERS

Felin Fach, nr Brecon
LD3 0UB

T: 01874-620111
E: enquiries@felinfachgriffin.co.uk
W: www.felinfachgriffin.co.uk

BEDROOMS: 7.

OPEN: All year except 24/25 Dec.

FACILITIES: bar area, dining room, breakfast room, private dining room, ½-acre garden (stream, kitchen garden), only bar/dining room suitable for ♿.

BACKGROUND MUSIC: Radio 4 at breakfast, 'carefully considered music at other times'.

LOCATION: 4½ miles NE of Brecon, in village on A470.

CHILDREN: all ages welcomed.

DOGS: allowed in bedrooms, at some tables in bar.

CREDIT CARDS: MasterCard, Visa.

PRICES: [2012] B&B £57.50–£80 per person, D,B&B £82.50–£105, set meals £21.50–£27, full alc £38.50, special breaks, 1-night bookings occasionally refused.

FISHGUARD Pembrokeshire

Map 3:D1

THE MANOR TOWN HOUSE

In the centre of a historic harbour town, this Grade II listed Georgian house has 'wonderful views' over the working port and across the water to Dinas Head. The B&B is run by 'friendly' owners Helen and Chris Sheldon, whose home-made Welsh cakes, cream teas and 'excellent' breakfasts – taken, in good weather, on a terrace facing the sea – garner unreserved praise. Beside a buffet selection of cereals, fruit and yogurt, a full Welsh breakfast (with traditional laver bread, when available) is offered, as is a separate waffle menu – Mrs Sheldon's speciality. 'Warm, accommodating' bedrooms, each individually styled, have antique furniture and an original fireplace; reception rooms and three bedrooms were refurbished this year. Housekeeping is 'impeccable'. Bicycles are available for hire, to explore the Pembrokeshire countryside; walkers appreciate the Coastal Path accessed via the woods below the property's garden. There is no parking on the busy road; guests may use a public car park five minutes' walk away. Popular with passengers taking the ferries to Ireland. (*Curt Walton, and others*)

11 Main Street
Fishguard SA65 9HG

T: 01348-873260
E: enquiries@manortownhouse.com
W: www.manortownhouse.com

BEDROOMS: 6.
OPEN: all year except Christmas.
FACILITIES: 2 lounges, breakfast room, small walled garden, unsuitable for ♿.
BACKGROUND MUSIC: classical at breakfast.
LOCATION: central.
CHILDREN: all ages welcomed.
DOGS: not allowed.
CREDIT CARDS: MasterCard, Visa.
PRICES: [2012] B&B £40–£60 per person, 1-night bookings refused weekends high season.

GLYNARTHEN Ceredigion

Map 3:D2

PENBONTBREN

César award in 2012

An 'oasis' in the Carmarthenshire countryside, this former farmhouse has been converted (via a spell as a rural hotel) into five 'well-appointed and beautifully furnished' suites. The owners, Richard Morgan-Price and Huw Thomas, 'are charming hosts', says a visitor this year. 'The enormous rooms wouldn't look out of place in a five-star hotel,' wrote a reporter. Each has a sitting room and private terrace; one, with a separate single bedroom and a wet room, is suitable for families and wheelchair-users. 'Our suite was as comprehensively satisfactory as any we have come across,' was the judgment of the *Guide*'s founder. Larger parties can stay in a four-bedroom self-catering cottage with a big farmhouse kitchen. Cooked to order and served on 'crisp white linen' in a converted barn, 'the breakfasts are varied, generous and delicious', 'a gourmet extravaganza', with meats and smoked fish from the neighbouring village of Rhydlewis, and eggs from the B&B's own hens. There are 'excellent' nearby eateries. 'You'll not want for anything, not even a gin and tonic.' (*Paul Scott, Anne James, Jennifer Reynolds, HR, and others*)

25% DISCOUNT VOUCHERS

Glynarthen
Llandysul SA44 6PE

T: 01239-810248
F: 01239-811129
E: contact@penbontbren.com
W: www.penbontbren.com

BEDROOMS: 5 in annexe, 3 on ground floor, 1 suitable for ♿.
OPEN: all year except Christmas.
FACILITIES: breakfast room, 32-acre grounds.
BACKGROUND MUSIC: none.
LOCATION: 5 miles N of Newcastle Emlyn.
CHILDREN: all ages welcomed.
DOGS: not allowed in breakfast room, most bedrooms.
CREDIT CARDS: MasterCard, Visa.
PRICES: [to May 2013] B&B £47.50–£70 per person, special breaks, 1-night bookings sometimes refused peak weekends.

KNIGHTON Powys

Map 3:C4

MILEBROOK HOUSE

'A very friendly place with no stuffiness', this 'quintessential country hotel' in the Welsh Marches has been run by resident owners Beryl and Rodney Marsden for more than 40 years. 'Old world in the best sense, like staying with friends in the country,' says a visitor in 2012. 'Mrs Marsden has an abundance of energy: she greets arrivals, sees guests off, operates the bar and takes orders for dinner.' In the bar and restaurant, chef Amy Lewis serves a modern British menu, including 'well-prepared' daily specials, perhaps duck breast, chestnut potato rösti, parsnip and vanilla purée. 'Breakfast is good.' 'Local produce is much in evidence'; a kitchen garden and the house's fruit trees provide most of the vegetables and fruit used in the meals. Beyond these working gardens, from croquet lawn to paddock and wildlife pond, the grounds around this 18th-century dower house invite exploration. Rear bedrooms are particularly quiet (the road at the front is busy); a visitor found his 'spacious and comfortable', with 'lovely views'. There are excellent walks to be had in the area, including the 1,200-year-old Offa's Dyke Path along the Welsh/English border. (*AJ Gillingwater, Penelope Visman*)

25% DISCOUNT VOUCHERS

Milebrook
Knighton
Powys LD7 1LT

T: 01547-528632
F: 01547-529490
E: hotel@milebrookhouse.co.uk
W: www.milebrookhouse.co.uk

BEDROOMS: 10, 2 on ground floor.

OPEN: late Jan–Dec, restaurant closed Mon lunch.

FACILITIES: lounge, bar, 2 dining rooms, 3½-acre grounds on river (terraces, pond, croquet, fishing).

BACKGROUND MUSIC: classical in bar and restaurant.

LOCATION: on A4113, 2 miles E of Knighton.

CHILDREN: not under 8.

DOGS: not allowed.

CREDIT CARDS: MasterCard, Visa.

PRICES: [2012] B&B £60.50–£66.50 per person, D,B&B £92.50, set lunch £15.95, full alc £50, short breaks, Christmas/New Year packages.

LLANARMON DYFFRYN CEIRIOG Denbighshire Map 3:B4

THE HAND AT LLANARMON

In 'outstandingly beautiful' surroundings in the Ceiriog valley, this 500-year-old drovers' inn welcomes travellers 'while playing a vital role in the community'. The owners, Martin and Gaynor De Luchi, 'have created a laid-back country hotel that is a pleasant place to relax in', say returning visitors. Bedrooms in the original farmhouse, and in converted stables and barns, are decorated in muted heritage shades. There are clean, white-tiled bathrooms. A ground-floor room has been fully adapted for wheelchair-users; disabled visitors have found access 'excellent'. 'The bar is often busy with locals enjoying their meals.' Here, and in the restaurant with its wood-burning stove, chef Grant Mulholland 'continues to expand his repertoire of straightforward dishes using good local ingredients'. Daily specials might include Cheddar cheese brûlée, basil jam, home-made bread; honey-roasted confit duck, glazed apples, chilli and garlic gravy. 'Local staff are friendly, helpful and obviously happy in their work.' A residents' lounge is a quiet space to sit; guests may also enjoy a drink on the pretty flowered terrace. The De Luchis tell us that *The Hand* is no longer for sale. (*Richard and Jean Green*)

25% DISCOUNT VOUCHERS

Llanarmon Dyffryn Ceiriog
Ceiriog Valley
LL20 7LD

T: 01691-600666
F: 01691-600262
E: reception@thehandhotel.co.uk
W: www.thehandhotel.co.uk

BEDROOMS: 13, 4 on ground floor, 1 suitable for ♿.

OPEN: all year, accommodation closed at Christmas.

FACILITIES: ramp, lounge, bar, restaurant, games/TV room, civil wedding licence, terrace, ¾-acre grounds.

BACKGROUND MUSIC: none.

LOCATION: 10 miles W of Oswestry.

CHILDREN: all ages welcomed.

DOGS: not allowed in some bedrooms.

CREDIT CARDS: MasterCard, Visa.

PRICES: [2012] B&B £45–£65 per person, set lunch £14.50–£18, full alc £35, midweek breaks, New Year package, 1-night bookings refused mid-Jul–end Aug.

LLANDRILLO Denbighshire

Map 3:B4

TYDDYN LLAN

César award in 2006

In well-maintained grounds facing the Berwyn Mountains, this Georgian country house is run as a restaurant-with-rooms by Bryan (the chef) and Susan Webb. 'Dinner was excellent, and I doubt that better food can be had anywhere else in North Wales,' said a visitor this year. The service is well paced in the two candlelit dining rooms. 'The hostess is charming and the food is very good,' said a visitor in 2012. Mr Webb's *Michelin*-starred restaurant showcases Welsh food; typical dishes are home-cured bresaola of Welsh Black beef, rocket, Parmesan; wild bass, laver bread butter sauce. 'The dining room staff were lovely,' commented a visitor, who wrote of a casual welcome. The Webbs have been busy redecorating: the exterior has been repainted and several bedrooms refitted. The rooms are individually styled: some have antique beds, one has a Victorian roll-top bath. 'Our bedroom at the top was tiny though well-appointed.' All have bathrobes and slippers, tea/coffee-making facilities. 'Breakfast was delicious.' Gastronomically inclined guests may spend a day observing and working with the team in the kitchen. (*GH, Jane Savery*)

25% DISCOUNT VOUCHERS

Llandrillo
nr Corwen LL21 0ST

T: 01490-440264
F: 01490-440414
E: mail@tyddynllan.co.uk
W: www.tyddynllan.co.uk

BEDROOMS: 13, 1, on ground floor, suitable for ♿.
OPEN: all year, restaurant closed for lunch Mon–Thurs.
FACILITIES: ramp, 2 lounges, bar, 2 dining rooms, civil wedding licence, 3-acre garden.
BACKGROUND MUSIC: none.
LOCATION: 5 miles SW of Corwen.
CHILDREN: all ages welcomed.
DOGS: not allowed in public rooms.
CREDIT CARDS: MasterCard, Visa.
PRICES: B&B £60–£95 per person, D,B&B £55–£75 added, full alc £70, 2-night D,B&B rates, special offers, Christmas/New Year packages.

LLANDUDNO Conwy

Map 3:A3

BODYSGALLEN HALL AND SPA

César award in 1988

'Beautifully situated', and providing 'great old-fashioned luxury', this Grade I listed 17th-century mansion (Pride of Britain) with a medieval tower has long been a *Guide* favourite. It has views of Conwy Castle and Snowdonia, woodland walks, a knot garden and follies. It is owned by the National Trust, and run by Historic House Hotels. Half the bedrooms are in the main hall, where the best are 'large and elegant'; the style is traditional and chintzy. Others, suitable for families (no children under six), are in cottage suites dotted around the extensive parkland. Michael Cheetham, who has been promoted to head chef (he was sous-chef to both his predecessors), maintains the modern style with dishes like citrus-spiced pollack, lemon gel, fennel two ways, whipped anise. There is alternative dining in the *1620 Bistro*. A smart casual dress code (no T-shirts, trainers or shorts) is applied in the restaurant. The atmospheric public rooms have oak panelling, splendid fireplaces, mullioned windows; they are filled with antiques and portraits. Various treatments are offered in the spa, which has a large swimming pool, sauna and gym.

Llandudno LL30 1RS

T: 01492-584466
F: 01492-582519
E: info@bodysgallen.com
W: www.bodysgallen.com

BEDROOMS: 31, 16 in cottages, 1 suitable for ♿.

OPEN: all year, restaurant closed Mon.

FACILITIES: hall, drawing room, library, bar, dining room, bistro, civil wedding licence, 220-acre park (gardens, tennis, croquet), spa (16-metre swimming pool).

BACKGROUND MUSIC: none.

LOCATION: 2 miles S of Llandudno.

CHILDREN: no children under 6 in hotel, under 8 in spa.

DOGS: allowed in some cottages.

CREDIT CARDS: Amex, MasterCard, Visa.

PRICES: B&B (continental) £84.50–£212.50 per person, D,B&B £132.50–£245, cooked breakfast £7.50, special breaks, Christmas/New Year packages, 1-night bookings sometimes refused.

SEE ALSO SHORTLIST

LLANDUDNO Conwy

Map 3:A3

ST TUDNO HOTEL

César award in 1987

A Grade II listed building opposite the Victorian pier and gardens in this seaside town, this traditional hotel has been run by Martin Bland for 40 years. Visitors like the intimate welcome they receive: very much a presence, Mr Bland 'makes a point of chatting to everyone', saying goodbye personally to all guests. A fan said: 'We couldn't have been looked after better.' In the Italianate *Terrace* restaurant, with its chandeliers and mural of Lake Como, chef Andrew Foster serves 'delicious dinners with a good choice'. His 'excellent' modern classics include Anglesey scallops, slow-cooked belly pork, apples, crackling; poached monkfish, Carmarthenshire ham, red pepper, polenta. The brightly decorated bedrooms come with a hospitality tray bearing home-made biscuits, and fresh milk in the fridge. Sea-view rooms are particularly sought after: 'We love the Rhoda Suite with its panoramic view.' Public rooms have patterned wallpaper and swagged drapery; the hotel's award-winning afternoon tea – with buttered Welsh cakes and bara brith – is served in the bar lounge with a view across Llandudno Bay. (*MS, BE*)

25% DISCOUNT VOUCHERS

North Parade, Promenade
Llandudno LL30 2LP

T: 01492-874411
F: 01492-860407
E: sttudnohotel@btinternet.com
W: www.st-tudno.co.uk

BEDROOMS: 18.
OPEN: all year.
FACILITIES: lift, three lounges, restaurant, indoor heated swimming pool (8 by 4 metres), civil wedding licence, patio, 'secret garden', unsuitable for ♿.
BACKGROUND MUSIC: occasionally when quiet.
LOCATION: on promenade opposite pier, parking.
CHILDREN: all ages welcomed, under-5s have early supper.
DOGS: by arrangement (£10 per night), only in coffee lounge, not unattended in bedrooms.
CREDIT CARDS: all major cards.
PRICES: B&B £49–£110 per person, D,B&B £79–£140, full alc (dinner) £48, special breaks, Christmas/New Year packages.

SEE ALSO SHORTLIST

LLANGAMMARCH WELLS Powys

Map 3:D3

THE LAKE

César award in 1992

A 19th-century hunting and fishing lodge in 'peaceful' surroundings by the River Irfon, this half-timbered building is today a country house and spa retreat offering 'good walks' through woodland and in the countryside. 'The welcoming, friendly staff are highly efficient, the rooms fabulously comfortable,' says one visitor (a *Guide* hotelier) this year. Bedrooms in the main house are decorated in country house style with rich fabrics and wallpaper; suites in the lodge have a more contemporary decor and an open-plan sitting room. The lounges, with antiques and paintings, have lots of seating on large sofas and armchairs; but a visitor commented on a 'tired' decor. The restaurant serves a daily-changing menu of modern Celtic dishes, eg, ham hock, spring pea and broad bean salad; pavé of sewin, Provençal vegetables, chicory and tomato syrup. There is 'good selection of wines at sensible prices'. Service at mealtimes 'can be slow, making it awkward for small children'. A guest visiting over the holidays found 'Christmas celebrations muted, which we liked'. 'The walk around the lake and down the river is wonderful.' (*SK, Annabel Thomas*)

25% DISCOUNT VOUCHERS

Llangammarch Wells
LD4 4BS

T: 01591-620202
F: 01591-620457
E: info@lakecountryhouse.co.uk
W: www.lakecountryhouse.co.uk

BEDROOMS: 31, 12 suites in adjacent lodge, 7 on ground floor, 1 suitable for ♿.

OPEN: all year.

FACILITIES: ramps, 3 lounges, orangery, restaurant, spa (20-metre swimming pool), civil wedding licence, 50-acre grounds (tennis).

BACKGROUND MUSIC: none.

LOCATION: 8 miles SW of Builth Wells.

CHILDREN: all ages welcomed.

DOGS: allowed.

CREDIT CARDS: all major cards.

PRICES: [2012] B&B £97.50–£122.50 per person, D,B&B £122.50–£155, set dinner £38.50, special breaks on website, Christmas/New Year packages.

LLANIDLOES Powys

Map 3:C3

LLOYDS

25% DISCOUNT VOUCHERS

In a medieval market town on the River Severn, Tom Lines and Roy Hayter have run their B&B for 20 years. Regular winter closures allow them to keep things fresh; in 2012, one bedroom was repapered and painted, the restaurant floor sanded and revarnished, the pictures rearranged and rehung. 'Hands-on' owners Mr Lines and Mr Hayter are particularly known – among returning guests and local residents – for their convivial dinners (booking required). Leisurely evenings of eclectic five-course menus are 'more an event than a meal'; typical dishes might be tomato tarte Tatin, parsnip crisps; slow-cooked leg of lamb, sweetcorn and spring onion fritters, Parmesan-crumbed courgette. Mr Hayter, who cooks, is sensitive to diners with food allergies or intolerances. 'Our guests don't usually retire until after 11 pm, and frequently later,' they advise. The bedrooms, up a steep flight of narrow stairs, are traditionally furnished, with a well-fitted bathroom. One room has a roll-top bath and a small balcony with a view to the hills beyond; another, with a connecting small single room, can be converted into family accommodation.
(S and PG, and others)

6 Cambrian Place
Llanidloes SY18 6BX

T: 01686-412284
E: lloyds@dircon.co.uk
W: www.lloydshotel.co.uk

BEDROOMS: 7.
OPEN: mid-Mar–early Jan, closed Christmas/New Year.
FACILITIES: sitting room, dining room, unsuitable for ♿.
BACKGROUND MUSIC: none.
LOCATION: near the town centre.
CHILDREN: all ages welcomed.
DOGS: not allowed.
CREDIT CARDS: MasterCard, Visa.
PRICES: [2012] B&B £40–£66 per person, D,B&B £82–£108, set dinner £42, special breaks.

LLANWRTYD WELLS Powys

Map 3:D3

CARLTON RIVERSIDE

César award in 1998

In an old spa town at the foot of the Cambrian Mountains, this restaurant-with-rooms has long been run by Mary Ann and Alan Gilchrist, 'warm, welcoming hosts'. The stone house, said to be the second oldest in town, has an 'attractive position' by a bridge on the River Irfon; 'the countryside close by is a draw'. Mrs Gilchrist's cooking 'deserves a special mention': served in the 'simple but elegant' dining room, her dinners might include a goat's cheese and apple soufflé; sweet soy and chilli slow-roast pork belly. Simpler meals (pizzas, burgers, etc) can be taken in the basement bar (though not on Mondays). A small L-shaped lounge has large windows, 'comfortable' seating, a bar and library. The bedrooms vary in size and aspect: the Chapel Room has a dressing table and bedside cabinets with Venetian glass; the Bridge Room overlooks the river; the Oriental Room, 'with no view to speak of', has chinoiserie lacquer furnishings, and a sitting area. The 'satisfactory' breakfasts include 'very good scrambled eggs'. Special diets can be catered for by arrangement. (*JM, and others*)

25% DISCOUNT VOUCHERS

Irfon Crescent
Llanwrtyd Wells LD5 4ST

T: 01591-610248
E: info@carltonriverside.com
W: www.carltonriverside.com

BEDROOMS: 5.
OPEN: all year except 23–28 Dec, restaurant closed Sun.
FACILITIES: Reception, bar/lounge, restaurant, unsuitable for ♿.
BACKGROUND MUSIC: classical piano in lounge.
LOCATION: town centre, no private parking.
CHILDREN: all ages welcomed.
DOGS: not allowed in public rooms.
CREDIT CARDS: MasterCard, Visa.
PRICES: [2012] B&B £37.50–£50 per person, D,B&B £49.50–£70, set meals £21.50–£43.50, full alc £52, gourmet breaks, 1-night bookings sometimes refused Sat, bank holidays.

SEE ALSO SHORTLIST

NANT GWYNANT Gwynedd

Map 3:A3

PEN-Y-GWRYD HOTEL

César award in 1995

'Time has stood wonderfully still in this unique and historic climbing hotel.' Once used by Sir Edmund Hillary and Tenzing Norgay as the training base for their 1953 Everest expedition, this 19th-century mountain farmhouse at the foot of Snowdon – 'no neighbours,' the owners say – has been in the Pullee family for three generations. 'The welcome and service are second to none. The Pullees have performed a remarkable conjuring trick keeping the old with the new.' There is neither TV nor radio; nor locks on the bedroom doors. Just five of the simple rooms have an en suite bathroom. There is nonetheless plenty of hot water: 'Returning after a day on the hills, a hot soak in a Victorian tub awaits in the genuine Victorian bathrooms.' A gong announces dinner at 7.30, when guests choose from two main courses on chef Lene Jensen's 'wholesome' menus, perhaps lamb cutlets, red onion and port reduction, or chicken, bacon and mushroom pie. Hearty breakfasts (porridge; kippers; a full Welsh) and packed lunches send guests off into the hills. 'A rare delight.' (*Jane Horovitch*)

Nant Gwynant
LL55 4NT

T: 01286-870211
E: escape@pyg.co.uk
W: www.pyg.co.uk

BEDROOMS: 16, 1 on ground floor, garden suite in annexe.
OPEN: Mar–Nov, New Year.
FACILITIES: lounge, bar, games room, dining room, chapel, 1-acre grounds (natural unheated 60-metre swimming pool, sauna).
BACKGROUND MUSIC: none.
LOCATION: between Beddgelert and Capel Curig.
CHILDREN: all ages welcomed.
DOGS: allowed.
CREDIT CARDS: MasterCard, Visa.
PRICES: [2012] B&B £42–£52 per person, set dinner £25–£30, full alc £40, 1-night bookings refused weekends.

NARBERTH Pembrokeshire

Map 3:D2

THE GROVE

NEW

In a hollow facing the Preseli hills, this 'imposing' 18th-century mansion has been rescued from dereliction by owners Neil Kedward and Zoë Agar, who have turned it into an intimate hotel. They run it in 'a relaxed but attentive way', says a regular contributor, upgrading *The Grove* from the Shortlist to a full entry. 'Many of the staff are local as is much of the produce.' The bedrooms are in the main house, a coach house and a 15th-century longhouse next to the main building. 'Our spacious room in the main house overlooked the beautiful formal garden and rolling countryside.' In the restaurant, Duncan Barham is the chef: 'We enjoyed some delicious meals: ceviche of local sea bass, pickled clams, wild garlic dressing; sirloin of Welsh beef, onion mousse, peas and asparagus.' Breakfast, in a garden room, has 'wonderful softly smoked kippers'. 'Not everything is perfect; some housekeeping blips only proved that this is a hotel run by humans like the rest of us.' Eight additional bedrooms were being added as the *Guide* went to press. (*David Birnie*)

Molleston
Narberth SA67 8BX

T: 01834-860915
F: 01834-861000
E: info@thegrove-narberth.co.uk
W: www.thegrove-narberth.co.uk

BEDROOMS: 12, 2 in coach house (1 on ground floor), 4 in longhouse, plus 4 self-catering cottages.

OPEN: all year.

FACILITIES: lounge, library, restaurant, breakfast room, civil wedding licence, 20-acre grounds.

BACKGROUND MUSIC: in lounge and restaurant.

LOCATION: 1 mile S of village.

CHILDREN: all ages welcomed.

DOGS: not allowed.

CREDIT CARDS: Amex, MasterCard, Visa.

PRICES: [2012] B&B £75–£145 per person, D,B&B £120–£190, set menus £45, full alc £54, special breaks, Christmas/New Year packages, 1-night bookings refused Sat.

NEWPORT Pembrokeshire

Map 3:D1

CNAPAN

Three generations of the Lloyd and Cooper families – 'lovely, caring owners' – have run this restaurant-with-rooms since 1984. These days, Michael and Judith Cooper have been joined by their son, Oliver, to welcome visitors to the listed Georgian town house, which is the family home. 'Mike and Judy are delightful hosts and very well informed about the locality,' says a visitor this year. 'Comfortable' bedrooms, decorated with knick-knacks, pictures and borrowable books, vary in size: a 'substantial' room was praised this year; a 'compact' room with a 'minute' shower was less liked. Guests who prefer a bath have access to a shared bathroom. No complaints about the 'high-quality' cooking: Mrs Cooper's 'splendid dinners' – with dishes like citrus home-cured salmon, celeriac remoulade; pork tenderloin, fennel and lemon rub, Calvados crème fraîche – are roundly praised. Breakfast brings home-made muesli, cinnamon-stewed prunes, local honey and bacon. 'One of the friendliest places we have ever stayed in.' Sadly, Eluned Lloyd died in 2011: 'She will be much missed.' (*Andrew Laugharne, Margaret Kershaw, David Lowde*)

East Street, Newport
nr Fishguard SA42 0SY

T: 01239-820575
F: 01239-820878
E: enquiry@cnapan.co.uk
W: www.cnapan.co.uk

BEDROOMS: 5, plus a self-catering cottage.
OPEN: Mar–Dec, closed Christmas, restaurant closed Tues.
FACILITIES: lounge, bar, restaurant, small garden, unsuitable for ♿.
BACKGROUND MUSIC: jazz/Latin in evenings in dining room.
LOCATION: town centre.
CHILDREN: all ages welcomed (£10 for B&B in family room).
DOGS: only guide dogs allowed.
CREDIT CARDS: MasterCard, Visa.
PRICES: [2012] B&B £45 per person, D,B&B £70–£75, dinner £25–£30, full alc £45, 1-night bookings sometimes refused during peak season and on Saturdays.

SEE ALSO SHORTLIST

NEWPORT Pembrokeshire

Map 3:D1

LLYS MEDDYG

There is 'a special atmosphere' at this restaurant-with-rooms run by owners Ed and Lou Sykes in a restored Georgian coaching inn. Brightly decorated bedrooms have hand-spun Welsh blankets, art by local artists, and fresh milk in the fridge; many have views toward Carn Ingli. A 'spacious' attic room is 'a place you could enjoy spending time in'. Larger parties or guests seeking more privacy may prefer Room on the Hill, a newly converted barn three miles away from the main house, 'where your only neighbours are the sheep and wildlife'. In the restaurant and informal bar, head chef James Oakley's menu focuses on local ingredients, typically home-smoked salmon, wild sorrel, pennywort, beetroot; roast rump Preseli lamb, ratatouille, wild garlic. (A half-day foraging course has guests scouring the countryside for their dinner.) The kitchen garden is open for meals in the summer months and is child-friendly, with toddler bikes and garden games. Breakfast – 'great fuel for a day's walking' – includes freshly squeezed orange juice, fresh fruit pancakes and 'first-class' smoked haddock. More reports, please.

25% DISCOUNT VOUCHERS

East Street, Newport
nr Fishguard SA42 0SY

T: 01239-820008
E: info@llysmeddyg.com
W: www.llysmeddyg.com

BEDROOMS: 8, 1 on ground floor, 3 in annexe, plus a cottage.

OPEN: all year, restaurant closed Sun/Mon Nov–May.

FACILITIES: bar, restaurant, sitting room, civil wedding licence, garden.

BACKGROUND MUSIC: in bar and restaurant.

LOCATION: central.

CHILDREN: all ages welcomed.

DOGS: allowed in 3 bedrooms, cellar bar.

CREDIT CARDS: MasterCard, Visa.

PRICES: [2012] B&B £50–£90 per person, D,B&B £80–£120, set dinner £29.50–£35, full alc £40, website offers, 1-night bookings sometimes refused weekends.

SEE ALSO SHORTLIST

PENMYNYDD Isle of Anglesey

Map 3:A3

NEUADD LWYD

César award in 2010

Standing amid fields and farmland, this 'lovely' grey-stoned Victorian rectory is run as a guest house by owners Susannah and Peter Woods. 'It was lovely to meet them again,' said a returning visitor. 'The standard of everything is first class.' The handsome bedrooms have views of the gardens, the Anglesey countryside and Snowdonia beyond. Owain has a king-size antique French bed and a pair of duck-egg-blue armchairs. Siasper is a compact twin-bed room lit by the morning sun. Pre-dinner canapés are served in the drawing room or, in summer months, on the terrace. 'You cannot fault Susannah's set menu of fantastic cooking.' A graduate of Ballymaloe cookery school in Ireland, she uses local produce for her daily-changing four-course dinners; typical dishes are Snowdonia wild mushroom and Madeira risotto; fillet of wild Menai sea bass, tarragon beurre blanc. At breakfast, there are home-made breads, preserves and granola; Llandudno oak-smoked salmon; locally cured bacon. A table by the French windows has unbeatable views of the mountains; on balmy evenings, guests are encouraged to dine alfresco. (*Gordon Franklin*)

Penmynydd
nr Llanfairpwllgwyngyll
Isle of Anglesey LL61 5BX

T/F: 01248-715005
E: post@neuaddlwyd.co.uk
W: www.neuaddlwyd.co.uk

BEDROOMS: 4.
OPEN: 23 Jan–30 Nov, closed Sun/Mon/Tues except bank holidays.
FACILITIES: drawing room, lounge, dining room, 6-acre grounds, only dining room suitable for ♿.
BACKGROUND MUSIC: none.
LOCATION: 3 miles W of Menai Bridge.
CHILDREN: not under 16.
DOGS: only guide dogs allowed.
CREDIT CARDS: MasterCard, Visa.
PRICES: B&B £75–£180 per person, D,B&B £95–£200, set dinner £42, see website for midweek rates.

PENTREFOELAS Denbighshire

Map 3:A3

HAFOD ELWY HALL

The 'peace and quiet' of this working farm 'far from anywhere' in the bare Denbighshire mountains 'should be a magnet for those tired of city life', said a trusted reporter. Down a country track, the farm and house are run on green lines by Roger and Wendy Charles-Warner, who welcome B&B guests and provide country-style evening meals. They are 'always attentive' hosts, and have won awards for their sustainability: there is a wind turbine, carbon-neutral stoves, a biomass boiler. The low, grey farmhouse is 'characterful', with 'an Edwardian feel'. There are slate floors, a bread oven, old wells and 'lots of odd knick-knackery'. Two bedrooms have a four-poster bed (one has an Edwardian bathroom with an antique cast iron bath, separate shower and Thunderbox lavatory). The third suite has a double and a single bedroom sharing a bathroom. In the dining room, guests sit together to enjoy Mrs Charles-Warner's 'authentic' cooking, eg, chicken with cream cheese, pistachio, peppercorns. No licence; bring your own wine. Breakfast has eggs 'from our own hens', sausages and bacon from the farm's 'happy free-range animals'. More reports, please.

Hiraethog, nr Pentrefoelas
LL16 5SP

T: 01690-770345
F: 01690-770266
E: enquiries@hafodelwyhall.co.uk
W: www.hafodelwyhall.co.uk

BEDROOMS: 3, 1 on ground floor suitable for ♿.
OPEN: all year.
FACILITIES: lounge, sun room, gun room, dining room, 60-acre grounds (private fishing).
BACKGROUND MUSIC: none.
LOCATION: 12 miles SE of Betws-y-Coed, 11 miles SW of Denbigh, 6½ miles N of Pentrefoelas off A543.
CHILDREN: not under 16.
DOGS: allowed in sun room and lounge 'if clean and well behaved', not in bedrooms.
CREDIT CARDS: MasterCard, Visa.
PRICES: B&B £37.50–£80 per person, set dinner £20, Christmas package, telephone discounts, 1-night bookings refused high-season weekends.

PORTMEIRION Gwynedd

Map 3:B3

HOTEL PORTMEIRION

César award in 1990

In a 'fabulous' setting in sprawling woodlands on a Snowdonia peninsula, this 'quirky' resort, created in 1926 by Sir Clough Williams-Ellis, now welcomes 250,000 visitors a year (many just for the day). 'It is one of the best tourist attractions in Wales,' said a visitor (a *Guide* hotelier) in 2012. Overnight guests can stay in the main hotel, with its 'beautiful views overlooking the estuary'; the Victorian mansion, *Castell Deudraeth*; or rooms and suites in buildings around the estate (choose carefully: some rooms may attract the curious eyes of day visitors). The village, a juxtaposition of styles and structures which 'would be hideous anywhere else but look as though they belong here', is a designated Conservation Area. Several of the village rooms have been renovated this year. Diversions are plenty: woodland trails, coastal walks, garden visits, organic spa treatments. The staff are 'friendly, helpful and professional'. In the hotel's main dining room, new chef Steven Rowlands serves 'generally good' modern Welsh dishes eg, canon of beef, truffle potato, confit tomatoes. 'Breakfast was very good.' (*Annabel Thomas*)

Minffordd
Penrhyndeudraeth LL48 6ER

T: 01766-770000
E: gwesty@portmeirion-village.com
W: www.portmeirion-village.com

BEDROOMS: 14 in hotel, some on ground floor, 1 suitable for ♿, 11 in *Castell Deudraeth*, 28 in village.

OPEN: all year.

FACILITIES: hall, lift, 3 lounges, bar, restaurant, brasserie in *Castell*, children's supper room, function room, beauty salon, civil wedding licence, 170-acre grounds (garden), heated swimming pool (8 by 15 metres, May–Sept).

BACKGROUND MUSIC: harpist Fri and Sat nights, Sun lunch.

LOCATION: 2 miles SE of Porthmadog.

CHILDREN: all ages welcomed.

DOGS: only guide dogs allowed.

CREDIT CARDS: Amex, MasterCard, Visa.

PRICES: [2012] B&B £54.50–£109.50 per person, D,B&B £69.50–£119.50, set meals £38, full alc £69, Christmas/New Year packages, 1-night bookings sometimes refused weekends.

PWLLHELI Gwynedd

Map 3:B2

THE OLD RECTORY

NEW

In a large 'cared-for' garden, this 'handsome' former Georgian rectory stands near the church of a village in the 'beautiful' Lleyn peninsula. It is run as a B&B by new owners Gary and Lindsay Ashcroft: 'They clearly love the place and what they are doing,' says a trusted reporter in 2012, restoring *The Old Rectory* to the *Guide*. 'They wanted to make the house their own and have completed a successful refurbishment; everything from the furniture, to the pictures, to the pretty cups on the tea tray in the bedroom has been chosen with care.' All the bedrooms have views of the grounds: 'Ours was not large but was cosy, with a built-in wardrobe, a dressing table and an armchair. It had a light, airy feel; pristine white bedlinen, an immaculate bathroom.' Breakfast, at a communal table in a dining room which catches the morning sun, has help-yourself juices, cereals and yogurts: 'Highly recommended are the creamy porridge and the full Welsh, which has bacon cured by a butcher just down the road.' The Ashcrofts recommend local restaurants: 'We were late and he gave us a lift'. Dogs are welcomed; they stay in a 'classy, well-built and sheltered kennel'. (*Sarah Thomas, Jane Forshaw*)

25% DISCOUNT VOUCHERS

Boduan
nr Pwllheli LL53 6DT

T: 01758-721519
E: theashcrofts@theoldrectory.net
W: www.theoldrectory.net

BEDROOMS: 3, also self-catering cottage.
OPEN: all year except Christmas.
FACILITIES: drawing room, dining room, 3½-acre grounds, walking, riding, sailing.
BACKGROUND MUSIC: none.
LOCATION: 4 miles NW of Pwllheli.
CHILDREN: all ages welcomed.
DOGS: not allowed in house (kennel and run available).
CREDIT CARDS: MasterCard, Visa.
PRICES: [2012] B&B £45–£90 per person, seasonal offers, 1-night bookings refused high season and bank holidays.

PWLLHELI Gwynedd

Map 3:B2

PLAS BODEGROES

César award in 1992

Up an avenue of 200-year-old beeches, this restaurant-with-rooms in a Georgian manor house on the remote Lleyn peninsula has been run by Chris and Gunna Chown for more than 25 years. 'Outstanding, in an exceptionally attractive garden; we were impressed with the food and service,' says a visitor in 2012. 'Helpful and caring staff' and 'excellent, imaginative cooking' make it a favourite of readers. Gunna Chown supervises the service in the L-shaped dining room, which has a polished wooden floor, modern Welsh paintings, 'perfect' lighting. Mr Chown and Hugh Bracegirdle are the chefs serving 'beautifully presented' classically based dishes. A visitor this year enjoyed paupiette of skate with crab mousse, stir-fried oriental vegetables; trio of Lleyn pork, roast root vegetables, sage sauce. A recently refurbished private dining room leads on to the courtyard for drinks and canapés. There is an 'excellent selection' at breakfast. The Scandinavian-style bedrooms, which overlook the tranquil gardens, are decorated in grey, blue and fawn; the Chowns have added a walk-in wet room in one bathroom. (*Peter Hutchinson, Gordon Franklin*)

Nefyn Road
Pwllheli LL53 5TH

T: 01758-612363
F: 01758-701247
E: gunna@bodegroes.co.uk
W: www.bodegroes.co.uk

BEDROOMS: 10, 2 in courtyard annexe.
OPEN: Mar–Nov, closed Sun and Mon except bank holidays.
FACILITIES: lounge, bar, breakfast room, restaurant, 5-acre grounds, unsuitable for ♿.
BACKGROUND MUSIC: 'occasionally' in restaurant.
LOCATION: 1 mile W of Pwllheli.
CHILDREN: all ages welcomed.
DOGS: not allowed in public rooms, 1 bedroom.
CREDIT CARDS: MasterCard, Visa.
PRICES: [2012] B&B £65–£90 per person, D,B&B from £97.50, set dinner £45, midweek breaks, 1-night bookings sometimes refused.

REYNOLDSTON Swansea

Map 3:E2

FAIRYHILL

Near the magnificent beaches of the Gower coast, this 18th-century Georgian mansion is run as a small country hotel by its owners, Andrew Hetherington and Paul Davies; Audrey McMillan is the manager. Its smartly dressed young staff are 'friendly, attentive'. It stands in extensive grounds with lawns, woodland, a stream, and a lake where wild ducks roam. There are log fires in the public rooms; the modern background music in the restaurant is less liked. A kitchen garden provides fresh vegetables and herbs for the modern British menus of Neil Hollis, perhaps wild garlic risotto, Parmesan crisp; loin of Welsh lamb, braised leeks, spring vegetables. Meals can be taken on a terrace in warmer weather. The individually styled bedrooms (some are small) are 'well equipped' (with all the latest technology); their fruit bowls replenished daily. 'Immaculate' housekeeping includes evening turn-down. Breakfast has a comprehensive buffet, as well as the usual cooked options. Jams are home made; 'proper bread' is supplied for toasting. Holistic therapy treatments (aromatherapy, Indian head massages, etc) can be booked in advance. (*EL, EMH*)

Reynoldston, Gower
nr Swansea SA3 1BS

T: 01792-390139
F: 01792-391358
E: postbox@fairyhill.net
W: www.fairyhill.net

BEDROOMS: 8.
OPEN: all year except 24–26 Dec, first 3 weeks in Jan.
FACILITIES: lounge, bar, 3 dining rooms, meeting room, civil wedding licence, spa treatment room, 24-acre grounds, unsuitable for ♿.
BACKGROUND MUSIC: jazz/classical/pop in lounge, bar, dining room at mealtimes.
LOCATION: 11 miles W of Swansea.
CHILDREN: not under 8.
DOGS: not in public rooms.
CREDIT CARDS: MasterCard, Visa.
PRICES: [2012] B&B £90–£140 per person, D,B&B £125–£175, set lunch £20–£25, set dinner £35–£45, full alc £64.50, special breaks, New Year package, 1-night bookings refused Sat.

ST DAVID'S Pembrokeshire

Map 3:D1

CRUG-GLAS

'A very happy stay at *Crug-Glas*; the owner and staff are charming.' Praise this year from a regular correspondent for Perkin and Janet Evans's restaurant-with-rooms, a Georgian house on their working farm near the coast. Bedrooms vary in size: 'We had the suite on the top floor, which was huge and comfortable and had a modern bathroom.' Earlier visitors thought this room was 'as big as a London flat'. One room has a four-poster bed; a smaller room has a pair of inlaid French twin beds, which can be turned into a double. Pre-dinner drinks are taken from a well-stocked honesty bar in the lounge, which has antiques, paintings, games and books. Guests are asked to order their dinner choices in advance from Mrs Evans's menus, which are put out in late afternoon on the hall table. 'The cooking is superb: we had the best lamb anywhere, sea bass, duck breast – all first class.' 'Just let us know what time you would like breakfast,' says Mrs Evans; this 'excellent' meal has 'lots of fresh fruit' and local cheeses; 'hearty' cooked dishes. (*Peter Adam*)

25% DISCOUNT VOUCHERS

nr Abereiddy, St David's
Haverfordwest SA62 6XX

T: 01348-831302
E: janet@crugglas.plus.com
W: www.crug-glas.co.uk

BEDROOMS: 7, 2 in coach house, 1 on ground floor.
OPEN: all year except 23–27 Dec.
FACILITIES: drawing room, dining room, civil wedding licence, 1-acre garden on 600-acre farm.
BACKGROUND MUSIC: classical in restaurant.
LOCATION: 3½ miles NE of St David's.
CHILDREN: not under 12.
DOGS: not allowed.
CREDIT CARDS: Amex, MasterCard, Visa.
PRICES: [2012] B&B £57.50–£85 per person, full alc £40, special breaks, New Year package.

SEE ALSO SHORTLIST

SKENFRITH Monmouthshire

Map 3:D4

THE BELL AT SKENFRITH

'We give the staff one hundred per cent for courtesy, cheerfulness and effectiveness: when there were problems, they were dealt with with genuine concern.' Praise in 2012 from regular *Guide* correspondents for Janet and William Hutchings's white-painted 17th-century coaching inn by a humpbacked stone bridge across the River Monnow. In the bar are flagstone floors, an inglenook fireplace, comfortable seating. 'The elegant dining room is well run by a motivated staff.' The inn's organic kitchen garden supplies vegetables, herbs, salads and soft fruits for the modern menus. A new chef was being appointed as we went to press. The bedrooms have been given a modern look: all have a hospitality tray with freshly ground coffee, fresh milk and home-made shortbread. 'Our room, with a beautiful view of the garden and hills at the back, had an extremely comfortable bed, quality linen; the spotless bathroom had recently been renovated. Unfortunately, the lighting was dim and ill-directed.' Children are welcomed (and have their own menu). There are good circular walks from the front door. (*Caroline and Richard Faircliff*)

25% DISCOUNT VOUCHERS

Skenfrith NP7 8UH

T: 01600-750235
F: 01600-750525
E: enquiries@skenfrith.co.uk
W: www.skenfrith.co.uk

BEDROOMS: 11.

OPEN: all year except 2 weeks end Jan/early Feb, also Tues Nov–Mar (not Christmas fortnight).

FACILITIES: open sitting area, bar, restaurant, private dining room, 1-acre grounds, only restaurant suitable for ♿.

BACKGROUND MUSIC: none.

LOCATION: 9 miles W of Ross-on-Wye.

CHILDREN: all ages welcomed, no under-8s in restaurant in the evening.

DOGS: not unattended in bedrooms, not allowed in restaurant.

CREDIT CARDS: MasterCard, Visa.

PRICES: [2012] B&B £55–£110 per person, D,B&B £75–£120, full alc £38, midweek breaks, Christmas/New Year packages, 1-night bookings refused Sat, bank holidays.

TALSARNAU Gwynedd

Map 3:B3

MAES-Y-NEUADD

César award in 2003

In 'a wonderful, peaceful location' between Mount Snowdon and the sea, this 14th-century manor house stands in extensive grounds with meadows and woodland. A 'laid-back place with a great atmosphere', it is run as a small hotel by Lynn Jackson and her brother-in-law, Peter Payne. The public areas, which have 'lots of good space', have oak beams, an inglenook fireplace, antique and modern furniture. The bedrooms vary considerably in size and style ('15 rooms, 15 different designs,' say the owners): two are as old as the original building; some have 16th-century beams; Georgian rooms have a high ceiling. Guests appreciate the bottle of home-made sloe gin in their room: 'Blissful!' John Owen Jones is the chef, serving 'a fusion of modern Welsh, traditional English and classic French' dishes, perhaps guineafowl and pheasant croquette, orange and toasted sesame salad; loin of venison, lentil casserole, chocolate jus. Children may order from their own menu at an early supper. Breakfast and afternoon tea are taken in a conservatory, or on the terrace. (*GH*)

25% DISCOUNT VOUCHERS

Talsarnau LL47 6YA

T: 01766-780200
F: 01766-780211
E: maes@neuadd.com
W: www.neuadd.com

BEDROOMS: 15, 4 in coach house, 3 on ground floor.
OPEN: all year.
FACILITIES: lift, ramps, lounge, bar, conservatory, family dining room, main dining room, civil wedding licence, terrace, 85-acre grounds.
BACKGROUND MUSIC: traditional music during special breaks.
LOCATION: 3 miles NE of Harlech.
CHILDREN: all ages welcomed but no under-8s in main dining room at night.
DOGS: allowed in 2 bedrooms only.
CREDIT CARDS: MasterCard, Visa.
PRICES: [2012] B&B £52–£106, D,B&B £91–£146, set dinner £30–£39.75, full alc £48, special breaks, New Year package.

TYWYN Gwynedd

Map 3:B3

DOLFFANOG FAWR

NEW

By water meadows at the head of Lake Talyllyn, this restored 17th-century farmhouse is run as a small guest house by the owners Alex Yorke and Lorraine Hinkins. 'They are friendly and professional; we could not find fault,' say the nominators (regular *Guide* correspondents). The bedrooms overlook the lake and Cader Idris. 'Ours was small, but quiet and well appointed; good lighting and storage, comfortable beds; a sparkling new bathroom with a large bath and shower.' Tea is given on arrival in a lounge with plenty of reading matter, guidebooks, etc. 'Alex likes to chat before dinner, giving advice on walking and climbing routes.' A three-course no-choice dinner is served communally. 'We had been asked about our likes and dislikes: we particularly enjoyed twice-baked goat's cheese soufflé; rack of Welsh lamb (extra cutlets left on the table to help yourself); a proper sticky toffee pudding. A vegetarian was well looked after.' There are 'no rules' in the information folder in the room. An 'extremely generous' breakfast has 'beautifully prepared fresh fruits; home-made bread; a good selection of cooked dishes'. (*Dennis and Janet Allom*)

Talyllyn
Tywyn LL36 9AJ

T: 01654-761247
E: info@dolffanogfawr.co.uk
W: www.dolffanogfawr.co.uk

BEDROOMS: 4.

OPEN: Mar–Oct, dining room closed Sun/Mon except bank holidays.

FACILITIES: lounge, dining room, 1-acre garden, unsuitable for ♿.

BACKGROUND MUSIC: varied.

LOCATION: by lake 10 miles E of Tywyn.

CHILDREN: not under 7.

DOGS: allowed in bedrooms and lounge.

CREDIT CARDS: MasterCard, Visa.

PRICES: [2012] B&B £48 per person, set menu £25, 4-night deals, 1-night bookings sometimes refused.

USK Monmouthshire

Map 3:E4

THREE SALMONS HOTEL

'Friendly, helpful' staff at this 'decent small town hotel' give it 'all those qualities which one expects but seldom finds'. The 300-year-old inn stands in the centre of a lovely little market town, and is also at the centre of town life (weddings and conferences are held). The public rooms and kitchen and many of the bedrooms have been recently refurbished; rooms are 'of a reasonable size and have good storage space'. In the 'pleasant' restaurant and informal bar, chef/co-owner James Bumpass serves traditional and modern British dishes 'of an unexpectedly high quality', such as carpaccio of Welsh beef, pickled mushrooms; pan-fried monkfish, crushed new potatoes, pak choi, curried mussel sauce. Ingredients are locally sourced as far as possible. Meats, fish and other produce come from nearby Cwmbran, Cardiff and Abergavenny; the hotel's own kitchen garden provides other greens. Real ales and ciders from the local area appear on the drinks list. Walks from the front door follow country lanes and river banks into the Monmouthshire countryside. Fishing breaks can be arranged. (*MW*)

Bridge Street
Usk NP15 1RY

T: 01291-672133
E: general@threesalmons.co.uk
W: www.threesalmons.co.uk

BEDROOMS: 24, 14 in annexe.
OPEN: all year.
FACILITIES: 2 bars, restaurant, 2 function rooms, civil wedding licence, small garden.
BACKGROUND MUSIC: during meals in public areas.
LOCATION: town centre.
CHILDREN: all ages welcomed.
DOGS: allowed in 3 bedrooms.
CREDIT CARDS: Amex, MasterCard, Visa.
PRICES: [2012] B&B £45–£57.50 per person, D,B&B £87.50, full alc £35–£40, fishing breaks, New Year package.

CHANNEL ISLANDS

Island of Sark

HERM

Map 1: inset D6

THE WHITE HOUSE

César award in 1987

The setting is the 'greatest attraction' of the only hotel on this 'beautiful car-free island which you can walk around comfortably in half a day'. Siôn Dobson Jones is the manager; 'all the staff are friendly and efficient'. The island has cliffs, beaches, a little harbour, an inn and a 10th-century chapel; guests arrive by ferry (a tractor transports luggage from the quay). Refurbishment of the bedrooms continues; visitors this year who found their bedroom 'utilitarian' liked the modern bathroom. There is no television, clock or telephone in the rooms ('they don't seem appropriate on Herm'). Some rooms are in cottages in the grounds. Children are welcomed: high teas, family suites with a second bedroom, baby listening. In the formal conservatory restaurant (jacket and tie required for men), chef Nigel Waylen's daily-changing menus might include chilled poached salmon, cucumber noodles; honey-roast breast of duck, roasted sweet potato, red wine jus. No background music. There are no dress or age restrictions in the *Ship Inn* brasserie. Much to do: tennis, croquet, a solar-heated swimming pool.

25% DISCOUNT VOUCHERS

Herm, via Guernsey GY1 3HR

T: 01481-750075
F: 01481-710066
E: hotel@herm.com
W: www.herm.com

BEDROOMS: 40, 18 in cottages, some on ground floor.

OPEN: 27 Mar–6 Oct.

FACILITIES: 3 lounges, 2 bars, 2 restaurants, conference room, 1-acre garden (tennis, croquet, 7-metre solar-heated swimming pool), beach 200 yds, Herm unsuitable for ♿.

BACKGROUND MUSIC: none.

LOCATION: by harbour, air/sea to Guernsey, then ferry from Guernsey (20 mins).

CHILDREN: all ages welcomed.

DOGS: allowed in 1 room, not allowed in public rooms.

CREDIT CARDS: MasterCard, Visa.

PRICES: B&B £100–£150 per person, set dinner £27.95, see website for special offers.

ST BRELADE Jersey

Map 1: inset E6

THE ATLANTIC HOTEL

The exterior of this upmarket hotel suggests its 1960s heritage; the interiors are altogether more glamorous, with all-white reception rooms giving a timeless feel. Built by Henry Burke (opening in 1970), it is now run by his son, Patrick; Liz Ballinger was appointed manager in March 2012. In extensive landscaped grounds, it has a prominent headland position with 'fabulous views' of the five-mile beach at St Ouen's Bay. The public areas have terracotta flagstones, a wrought iron staircase, urns, fountains, antiques and bespoke furniture. In the blue, white and beige *Ocean* restaurant, chef Mark Jordan has a *Michelin* star for his modern British cooking with dishes like bouillabaisse of roasted Jersey sea fish and shellfish, with aïoli; roast loin of roe deer, butternut squash purée, mushroom tortellini. Bedrooms are decorated in 'understated' colours and have a balcony with views over the ocean or La Moye golf course; there are 'opulent' marble bathrooms. Guests have free access to a leisure centre. Children are welcomed (no extra charge for under-12s sharing their parents' room): they have their own menu. More reports, please.

Le Mont de la Pulente
St Brelade JE3 8HE

T: 01534-744101
F: 01534-744102
E: info@theatlantichotel.com
W: www.theatlantichotel.com

BEDROOMS: 50, some on ground floor.
OPEN: 3 Feb–2 Jan.
FACILITIES: lift, lounge, library, cocktail bar, restaurant, private dining room, fitness centre (swimming pool, sauna), wedding facilities, 6-acre garden (tennis, indoor and outdoor heated swimming pools, 10 by 5 metres), unsuitable for ♿.
BACKGROUND MUSIC: in restaurant.
LOCATION: 5 miles W of St Helier.
CHILDREN: all ages welcomed.
DOGS: not allowed.
CREDIT CARDS: all major cards.
PRICES: [2012] B&B £80–£280 per person, D,B&B £135–£335, set meal £55, full alc £77.50, special breaks, off-season rates, Christmas/New Year packages.

SEE ALSO SHORTLIST

ST SAVIOUR Jersey

Map 1: inset E6

LONGUEVILLE MANOR

In 'delightful, immaculate' gardens by a lovely wooded valley, this extended 14th-century manor house is Jersey's most sumptuous hotel (Relais & Châteaux). Owned by the Lewis family for more than 60 years, it is run by Malcolm Lewis, his wife, Patricia, and her brother-in-law, Pedro Bento. Visitors commend the 'friendly, helpful staff'. Patricia Lewis oversees the design, working 'by instinct' to provide 'a homely feel', mixing the contemporary with the classic in the bar area, drawing room, snug and reception. The spacious bedrooms have fresh flowers, bowls of fruit, home-made shortbread; each of the ground-floor rooms has a private patio. A standard room had 'a sitting area with soft chairs, good hanging and storage space; two basins, a bath and a separate shower in the bathroom'. There are two dining areas; the panelled *Oak Room* and the less formal *Garden Room*. The chef, Andrew Baird, serves a modern menu which might include baked cheese soufflé; grilled seafood 'choucroute', saffron potatoes, lobster sauce. Breakfast has a 'beautifully presented' buffet, a comprehensive choice of cooked dishes, home-made jam and honey. (*J and MB*)

Longueville Road
St Saviour JE2 7WF

T: 01534-725501
F: 01534-731613
E: info@longuevillemanor.com
W: www.longuevillemanor.com

BEDROOMS: 31, 8 on ground floor, 2 in cottage.
OPEN: all year.
FACILITIES: lift, ramp, 2 lounges, cocktail bar, 2 dining rooms, function/conference/wedding facilities, 15-acre grounds (croquet, tennis, heated swimming pool, woodland), sea 1 mile.
BACKGROUND MUSIC: in restaurant.
LOCATION: 1½ miles E of St Helier.
CHILDREN: all ages welcomed.
DOGS: not allowed.
CREDIT CARDS: all major cards.
PRICES: [2012] B&B £125–£325 per person, D,B&B £160–£360, set dinner £57.50, full alc £80, special breaks, Christmas/New Year packages.

SARK

Map 1: inset E6

LA SABLONNERIE

A pony and trap conveys visitors from the ferry to Elizabeth Perrée's whitewashed 16th-century former farmhouse on this small car-free island. She is 'a force of nature' who welcomes many returning visitors by name. 'It remains wonderful,' says one. 'The memories linger; the hydrangeas, the views,' says an American guest. 'A slice of paradise,' is a comment in 2012. The 'glories' are the large gardens, with benches for alfresco drinks, and the walks from the door. The beamed interior has low ceilings, a log fire in the bar, comfortable chairs and settees. The bedrooms vary greatly: most are in small buildings in the garden. 'We always stay in the lovely room over the bar, excellent views and not noisy,' is this year's comment. There are candles, formal place settings, elegant white china in the dining room (and no background music). Chef Colin Day's daily-changing menu has dishes like terrine of monkfish and salmon; caramelised Barbary duck breast with sarladaise potatoes, green peppercorn, sage jus. There is also a short menu devoted to lobsters. In the summer meals can be taken in the garden. (*John Barnes, Dick Beers, Rachel McLoughlin*)

Little Sark
Sark, via Guernsey GY10 1SD

T: 01481-832061
F: 01481-832408
E: reservations@sablonneriesark.com
W: www.lasablonnerie.com

BEDROOMS: 22, also accommodation in nearby cottages.
OPEN: Easter–Oct.
FACILITIES: 3 lounges, 2 bars, restaurant, wedding facilities, 1-acre garden (tea garden/bar, croquet), Sark unsuitable for ♿.
BACKGROUND MUSIC: classical/piano in bar.
LOCATION: S part of island, boat from Guernsey (hotel will meet).
CHILDREN: all ages welcomed.
DOGS: allowed at hotel's discretion, but not in public rooms.
CREDIT CARDS: MasterCard, Visa.
PRICES: B&B £40–£97.50 per person, D,B&B £69.50–£145, set meal £29.50, full alc £45.50 (*excluding 10% service charge*).

SEE ALSO SHORTLIST

IRELAND

Giant's Causeway, Co. Antrim

BAGENALSTOWN Co. Carlow

Map 6:C6

LORUM OLD RECTORY

'Our visit to this beautiful home in a gorgeous country setting was the highlight of our trip.' American visitors this year were delighted by Bobbie Smith's Victorian former rectory, her family's home for three generations. 'She is a lovely hostess, and treated us so well.' The house has rich Victorian colours, prints on the walls, comfortable sofas and open fires. The 'spacious' bedrooms have large bed, 'good linen and bathroom items; an extensive collection of books'. All have views across fields where horses graze, to the Blackstairs Mountains. Guests take pre- and after-dinner drinks (and afternoon tea if they wish) in the large drawing room, which has a fire burning wood or turf. The 'delicious' five-course dinners are taken communally around a large mahogany table in a room lit by candles, and with a large black marble fireplace. Bobbie Smith 'is a superb chef': a typical meal might include melon and avocado; sweet potato soup; buttermilk sorbet; 'perfect' rack of lamb; white chocolate tart. The 'wonderful' breakfasts have much fresh fruit; 'enormous, freshly cooked dishes'. (*Patricia Fahey Turner, and others*)

25% DISCOUNT VOUCHERS

Kilgreaney, Bagenalstown

T: 00 353 59-977 5282
F: 00 353 59-977 5455
E: bobbie@lorum.com
W: www.lorum.com

BEDROOMS: 4.
OPEN: Mar–Nov.
FACILITIES: drawing room, study, dining room, wedding facilities, 1-acre garden (croquet), unsuitable for ♿.
BACKGROUND MUSIC: none.
LOCATION: 4 miles S of Bagenalstown.
CHILDREN: welcomed by arrangement.
DOGS: allowed by arrangement.
CREDIT CARDS: MasterCard, Visa.
PRICES: B&B €75–€95 per person, set dinner €45, 10% discount for stays of more than 3 nights.

BALLINGARRY Co. Limerick

Map 6:D5

THE MUSTARD SEED AT ECHO LODGE

A former convent, this Victorian lodge, in extensive grounds near the small, pretty village of Adare, is run as a restaurant-with-rooms by the owner Daniel Mullane; Breda O'Kelly is the manager. The building has been filled with objets d'art, prints and photographs from around the world; the decor is 'quirky and amusing': green walls in the living room (where guests are given tea and cake); blue in the restaurant. Bedrooms are decorated in a mix of period and contemporary styles (dark wood antiques, modern wallpapers and fabrics) and are well equipped, 'everything to hand', fresh flowers. The largest rooms in the main house have dual-aspect windows with country views. In the restaurant, Angel Pirev serves a seasonal four-course menu, which might include smoked salmon, an apple and kohlrabi remoulade, tempura of prawns and lemon oils; pan-seared Skeaghanore duck breast, confit gizzards, savoy cabbage spring roll, wild nettle purée and orange glaze. Dogs are welcomed: a ground-floor room has direct access to the garden. Many outdoor activities are available in the surroundings hills and pastureland. More reports, please.

Ballingarry

T: 00 353 69-68508
F: 00 353 69-68511
E: mustard@indigo.ie
W: www.mustardseed.ie

BEDROOMS: 15, 1 on ground floor suitable for ♿.
OPEN: all year except 23–25 Dec, mid-Jan–mid-Feb, restaurant closed Mon/Tues off-season.
FACILITIES: lounge, library, dining room, wedding facilities, 12-acre grounds.
BACKGROUND MUSIC: in restaurant.
LOCATION: in village, 18 miles SW of Limerick.
CHILDREN: all ages welcomed.
DOGS: not allowed in public rooms.
CREDIT CARDS: Amex, MasterCard, Visa.
PRICES: [2012] B&B €65–€165 per person, D,B&B €99–€170, set dinner €60.

BALLYCASTLE Co. Mayo

Map 6:B4

STELLA MARIS

In a beautiful setting on Mayo's rugged north-west coast, this white-painted building dominates Bunatrahir Bay as befits a former coastguard fortress. It was painstakingly converted into a hotel by the owners, Frances Kelly, a Mayo-born, US-trained chef, and her American husband, Terence McSweeney. All but two of the bedrooms (each named after a golf course, as Mr McSweeney is a keen golfer and sportswriter) look out to the Atlantic Ocean. 'Mine was small and simply furnished; decorated in tones of blue. The superbly comfortable bed had crisp white linen; free-range hangers in an alcove, two upright chairs and a window overlooking the bay; the small bathroom was dated.' There is a 'lovely bar', with separate seating spaces, a fireplace, golf memorabilia. A conservatory, which runs the length of the building, has a 'hotchpotch of chairs, sofas and tables; books and magazines'. 'Frances Kelly's superb cooking is reason enough to visit,' says a *Guide* inspector in 2012. 'I enjoyed a delicious salad of tomatoes and cucumber; monkfish in a rosemary-infused ham crust was divine; superb home-made bread; service was friendly if uneven.' Breakfast is served at table.

Ballycastle

T: 00 353 96-43322
F: 00 353 96-43965
E: info@stellamarisireland.com
W: www.stellamarisireland.com

BEDROOMS: 11, 1, on ground floor, suitable for ♿.
OPEN: 1 May–1 Oct, restaurant closed to non-residents on Mon.
FACILITIES: ramps, lounge, bar, restaurant, conservatory, wedding facilities, 3-acre grounds (golf), sea/freshwater fishing, sandy beach nearby.
BACKGROUND MUSIC: in public rooms.
LOCATION: 1½ miles W of Ballycastle.
CHILDREN: all ages welcomed (by arrangement).
DOGS: not allowed.
CREDIT CARDS: Diners, MasterCard, Visa.
PRICES: [2012] B&B €96–€120 per person, D,B&B €125–€165, full alc €55.

BALLYLICKEY Co. Cork

Map 6:D4

SEAVIEW HOUSE

25% DISCOUNT VOUCHERS

'Ten out of ten,' is awarded by visitors this year to Kathleen O'Sullivan's white-painted extended Victorian building overlooking Bantry Bay. 'In every sense excellent. The room, cleanliness, staff and food were all of an exceptionally high standard.' The 'comfortable, well-run house' is packed with 'good-quality Victorian furniture and miscellany'. The bedrooms are in the main building and in an extension: all are large (the family rooms are vast), with 'ample storage' and modern bathroom. Front rooms overlook the bay, others face the 'meticulously tended' garden. Dinner is served in an 'attractive', light-filled conservatory restaurant, which is open to non-residents. The chef, Eleanor O'Donovan, serves country house dishes in 'generous portions'; her extensive menu might include Bantry Bay crab, West Cork lamb or locally caught fish; potatoes might be offered 'four ways (roast, boiled, mashed, chipped) in a single meal'. After-dinner drinks are taken in the lounge before an open fire, and tea is served in the garden in warm weather. Breakfast has a large buffet; cooked dishes include 'delicious lamb's liver and kidneys'. (*Peter and Penny Bull, and others*)

Ballylickey, Bantry Bay

T: 00 353 27-50073
F: 00 353 27-51555
E: info@seaviewhousehotel.com
W: www.seaviewhousehotel.com

BEDROOMS: 25, 2, on ground floor, suitable for ♿.
OPEN: mid-Mar–mid-Nov.
FACILITIES: bar, library, 2 lounges, restaurant/conservatory, wedding facilities, 3-acre grounds on waterfront (fishing, boating), riding, golf nearby.
BACKGROUND MUSIC: none.
LOCATION: 3 miles N of Bantry.
CHILDREN: all ages welcomed, special menus and babysitting available.
DOGS: not allowed in public rooms.
CREDIT CARDS: Amex, MasterCard, Visa.
PRICES: [2012] B&B €70–€120 per person, D,B&B €95–€120, set dinner €45, special breaks.

BANGOR Co. Down

Map 6:B6

CAIRN BAY LODGE

'Small extra touches made this stand out from the crowd,' says a visitor this year to Chris and Jenny Mullen's 'homely' guest house overlooking Ballyholme beach. 'A tea tray with fresh milk, home-made cake and gluten- and dairy-free products was immediately provided on request,' says another guest. The seaside villa was built in 1914 for a Belfast city councillor whose son was honorary surgeon to the Queen; its balconies were, it is said, built in anticipation of a royal visit that never happened. The house has oak panelling, Dutch fireplaces and stained-glass windows. Two double bedrooms have been added this year; each room is individually styled with 'imagination and taste; lots of interesting artwork'. Rooms at the front have the sea view. Mr Mullen's 'fantastic' breakfasts have unusual choices (eg, duck eggs with Vegemite soda-bread soldiers; grilled halloumi; poached eggs and sautéed spinach) alongside the traditional Ulster fry. There is a small gift shop; Mrs Mullen, a beauty therapist, offers treatments in her salon. The restaurants at Bangor marina are a 20-minute walk away. (*Pauline Quilty, Ian and Jan Gilchrist*)

25% DISCOUNT VOUCHERS

278 Seacliff Road
Ballyholme, Bangor
BT20 5HS

T: 028-9146 7636
F: 028-9145 7728
E: info@cairnbaylodge.com
W: www.cairnbaylodge.com

BEDROOMS: 7, plus 2 self-catering villas each sleeping 8.
OPEN: all year.
FACILITIES: 2 lounges, dining room, beauty salon, small shop, ½-acre garden, unsuitable for ♿.
BACKGROUND MUSIC: in dining room during breakfast.
LOCATION: ¼ mile E of centre.
CHILDREN: all ages welcomed.
DOGS: not allowed.
CREDIT CARDS: MasterCard, Visa.
PRICES: [2012] B&B £35–£45 per person, special breaks, 1-night bookings refused weekends in high season.

CAPPOQUIN Co. Waterford

Map 6:D5

RICHMOND HOUSE

On the outskirts of a 'pleasant, old-fashioned' town, this grand country house (built for the Earl of Cork in 1704) is run by Paul and Claire Deevy as a small hotel and restaurant. The 'solid, high-ceilinged house' is furnished with antiques; hunting and fishing trophies abound. Mrs Deevy has a 'relaxed front-of-house style', assisted by pleasant local women, in the dining room, 'a succession of small spaces with an intimate feel' (only drawback 'relentless' background music). 'Paul Deevy is a fine cook; his menus have new options daily of generous portions of local meat and fish, with vegetables, salads and herbs from the garden. We particularly enjoyed perfect deep-fried squid with tartare sauce; rump of lamb, with Puy lentils, mint jelly, a rosemary and garlic jus.' The bedrooms, which vary in size, are decorated in country house style. 'Our first-floor bedroom had a large bed with blankets; the bathroom was small.' Breakfast has 'lots of fresh fruit, muffins straight out of the oven; excellent ingredients in the cooked dishes'. Mr Deevy's mother, Jean, is on hand to give advice about sightseeing. (*AW*)

Cappoquin

T: 00 353 58-54278
F: 00 353 58-54988
E: info@richmondhouse.net
W: www.richmondhouse.net

BEDROOMS: 10.

OPEN: 15 Jan–23 Dec, restaurant normally closed Sun/Mon except July and Aug.

FACILITIES: lounge, restaurant, 12-acre grounds, fishing, golf, pony trekking nearby, unsuitable for ♿.

BACKGROUND MUSIC: 'easy listening' in restaurant.

LOCATION: ½ mile E of Cappoquin.

CHILDREN: all ages welcomed.

DOGS: not allowed.

CREDIT CARDS: all major cards.

PRICES: [2012] B&B €60–€75 per person, D,B&B €95–€150, set dinner €33–€55, special breaks.

CARAGH LAKE Co. Kerry

Map 6:D4

CARRIG COUNTRY HOUSE

On the wooded shores of a lake, this ochre-painted Victorian house stands in 'lovely gardens' with a waterfall and a well-manicured lawn; in May it is 'ablaze with azaleas and rhododendrons'. Frank and Mary Slattery run it as a country hotel in personal style; guests are welcomed on first-name terms; the staff are 'caring and kind'. Turf fires burn in the drawing room where soft background music plays; guests can sit in a quieter lounge, a snug and a library. Free Wi-Fi. Amuse-bouche are served, while dinner orders are taken, in the drawing room; the 'excellent' meal is taken in a dining room (William Morris green leaf paper) with a lake view. Typical dishes: seared tiger prawns, soy-glazed garlic and ginger; rack of Kerry lamb, flageolet bean mash, salsify and shallot purée. The best bedrooms face the lake: 'Our spacious room had big windows; matching dark wood furniture; flowered wallpaper and fabrics; no television (which we like).' At an 'excellent' breakfast, a non-cooked-dish eater welcomed a buffet table 'laden with compotes, cereals, yogurts and jams'; cooked choices include smoked haddock and poached egg.

25% DISCOUNT VOUCHERS

Caragh Lake
Killorglin

T: 00 353 66-976 9100
E: info@carrighouse.com
W: www.carrighouse.com

BEDROOMS: 17, some on ground floor.

OPEN: Mar–Nov, restaurant open only at weekends Mar/Apr, 6 nights a week May–Sept.

FACILITIES: 2 lounges, snug, library, TV room, dining room, wedding facilities, 4-acre garden on lake.

BACKGROUND MUSIC: classical in lounge and restaurant.

LOCATION: 22 miles W of Killarney.

CHILDREN: not under 8 (except infants under 12 months).

DOGS: not allowed in house.

CREDIT CARDS: Diners, MasterCard, Visa.

PRICES: [2012] B&B €75–€240 per person, set dinner €43.50, full alc €55, special breaks.

CASHEL BAY Co. Galway

Map 6:C4

CASHEL HOUSE

In rambling gardens at the head of a sheltered bay, this mid-19th-century mansion has been run as a country house hotel for more than 40 years by the McEvilly family. Kay McEvilly is the ever-present matriarch; she can be found in the front office, in the dining room at lunch and dinner, and in the garden in the afternoon. Her 'considerable energy' belies the relaxed nature of the house ('a what's-the-hurry sort of place,' says one visitor). The decor has changed little over the years: a 'warm and cosy' take on traditional country house style. In the conservatory restaurant, which faces the garden, John O'Toole serves Irish country house dishes, perhaps a parcel of quail and smoked duck, brandy sauce; seared sea trout, almond sauce. Fruit, vegetables and herbs come from the hotel's gardens. On Saturday mornings, Mr O'Toole holds cookery demonstrations for guests. The best bedrooms at the front have sea views (across the trees); rooms at the side of the house overlook the garden. Writer Ciaran Burke leads seasonal garden courses; there is good walking and fishing in the area.

25% DISCOUNT VOUCHERS

Cashel Bay

T: 00 353 95-31001
F: 00 353 95-31077
E: res@cashel-house-hotel.com
W: www.cashel-house-hotel.com

BEDROOMS: 30.

OPEN: all year except Jan.

FACILITIES: ramps, 2 lounges, bar, library, dining room/conservatory, wedding facilities, 50-acre grounds (tennis, riding, small private beach).

BACKGROUND MUSIC: harpist plays occasionally at dinner.

LOCATION: 42 miles NW of Galway.

CHILDREN: all ages welcomed.

DOGS: not allowed in public rooms.

CREDIT CARDS: Amex, MasterCard, Visa.

PRICES: [2012] (*10% service charge added*) B&B €75–€150 per person, early bird dinner €32, set dinner €58, winter breaks, Christmas/New Year packages.

CASTLEHILL Co. Mayo

Map 6:B4

ENNISCOE HOUSE

25% DISCOUNT VOUCHERS

'Excellent: welcoming hosts, lovely house and fine food. What the *Guide* is all about.' An endorsement this year from a trusted correspondent for this large Georgian manor overlooking Lough Conn. The estate has been in ownership of one family since the 1650s; today it is run by Susan Kellett and her son, Donald John ('everyone calls me DJ'). Walls are covered in family portraits, and memorabilia abounds. 'It is like being invited into someone's grand home,' said inspectors. The three rooms at the front, which overlook the lough, are reached by an elliptical staircase; other staircases and corridors lead to the other rooms, which have parkland views. Many are spacious, bathrooms less so. Pre- and after-dinner drinks are taken in the impressive drawing room. The set menu, which changes daily, explains where meat and fish are sourced; vegetables come from the hotel's organic garden. Typical dishes: warm salad of black pudding and apple; roasted partridge with green grapes. There is a restored Victorian pleasure garden in the grounds. Fisherfolk can rent a rod for brown trout, spring salmon and grilse in season. (*Esler Crawford, and others*)

Castlehill, Ballina

T: 00 353 96-31112
F: 00 353 96-31773
E: mail@enniscoe.com
W: www.enniscoe.com

BEDROOMS: 6, plus self-catering units behind house.
OPEN: Apr–Oct, groups only at New Year.
FACILITIES: 2 sitting rooms, dining room, wedding facilities, 150-acre estate (garden, tea room, farm, heritage centre, conference centre, forge, fishing), unsuitable for ♿.
BACKGROUND MUSIC: none.
LOCATION: 2 miles S of Crossmolina.
CHILDREN: all ages welcomed.
DOGS: not allowed in public rooms, some bedrooms.
CREDIT CARDS: MasterCard, Visa.
PRICES: B&B €98–€130 per person, D,B&B €146–€178, set dinner €50, 10% discount for 3 nights or more, New Year package.

CASTLELYONS Co. Cork

Map 6:D5

BALLYVOLANE HOUSE

César award in 2009

A grand country house built in 1728 for a Lord Chief Justice of Ireland, later enlarged in the Italianate style, this is the family home of Justin and Jenny Green. They welcome guests in informal style (on first-name terms; no room keys), fostering a house party atmosphere. The house is furnished with family heirlooms, antique sofas and chairs, a baby grand piano, large portraits and pictures. Dinner is a 'grand affair'. Generally taken communally at a mahogany table liberally dressed with silver (candelabras, cruets, cutlery). Teena Mahon uses Cork produce (with vegetables and herbs from the walled garden tended by Justin's father, Jeremy). Dishes might include asparagus with hollandaise sauce; slow-roast belly of pork with apple and cider sauce. The bedrooms, off a corridor that runs the length of the house, have 'lovely furnishings', large comfortable bed; some bathrooms have a freestanding roll-top bath. An unrushed breakfast is served until noon. Children are welcomed: there are woods to explore, a tree house, pigs to feed, donkeys to pet. The entire house can be booked for a wedding party in a rustic barn. Excellent fishing is available.

Castlelyons, Fermoy

T: 00 353 25-36349
F: 00 353 25-36781
E: info@ballyvolanehouse.ie
W: www.ballyvolanehouse.ie

BEDROOMS: 6.
OPEN: 4 Jan–23 Dec, closed Mon–Wed in winter.
FACILITIES: hall, drawing room, honesty bar, dining room, wedding facilities, 80-acre grounds (15-acre garden, croquet, 3 trout lakes), unsuitable for ♿.
BACKGROUND MUSIC: yes.
LOCATION: 22 miles NE of Cork.
CHILDREN: all ages welcomed.
DOGS: allowed.
CREDIT CARDS: MasterCard, Visa.
PRICES: B&B €95–€125 per person, set dinner €60, fishing school, monthly supper club, special breaks.

CLIFDEN Co. Galway

Map 6:C4

THE QUAY HOUSE

César award in 2003

On the waterfront of a small town on the Connemara coast, Paddy and Julia Foyle's quirky B&B has long been liked by *Guide* readers for the warmth of the welcome and their 'friendly professionalism'. Spread across three buildings on the small tidal harbour (one of them the former harbour master's house), it has a 'lovable eccentricity'. Some bedrooms have open fire and four-poster bed; 12 overlook the harbour, two have garden views. Individually decorated, they have tea- and coffee-making facilities. Some are themed; the Napoleon Bonaparte Room has artefacts relating to the emperor, the African Room has animal skins, horns and hooves; the Mirror Room has a large antique mirror behind the bed. All bathrooms have large tub and shower; six of the studios have a kitchenette. The public rooms are furnished with gilt-framed family photos, 'wonderful' original Irish artwork and antiques. Breakfast 'is to die for', with home-made compotes, smoked salmon and even oysters in season; cooked options include devilled kidneys. The Foyles will recommend restaurants in the town, perhaps *Foyles* ('yes, a relation'). (*JM, and others*)

Beach Road
Clifden

T: 00 353 95-21369
F: 00 353 95-21608
E: res@thequayhouse.com
W: www.thequayhouse.com

BEDROOMS: 14, 2 on ground floor, 1 suitable for ♿, 7 studios (6 with kitchenette) in annexe.
OPEN: end Mar–end Oct.
FACILITIES: 2 sitting rooms, breakfast conservatory, ½-acre garden, fishing, sailing, golf, riding nearby.
BACKGROUND MUSIC: none.
LOCATION: harbour, 8 mins' walk from centre.
CHILDREN: all ages welcomed.
DOGS: not allowed.
CREDIT CARDS: MasterCard, Visa.
PRICES: B&B €60–€90 per person, special breaks.

CLIFDEN Co. Galway

Map 6:C4

SEA MIST HOUSE

NEW

On a quiet street off the town square, Sheila Griffin has restored her 19th-century town house throughout, and she runs it as a B&B. 'It is beautifully maintained and good value; we plan to return,' says the nominator. The bedrooms vary in size (and are priced accordingly). 'Our light and airy room was decorated in relaxing colours, with patterns only in the heavy curtains, matching bedhead and window-seat cushion; good-quality bedlinen; plenty of lighting; a table with tea tray and bottle of drinking water; everything worked in the bathroom.' The house has lots of pictures: 'something for everyone from landscapes to modern art'. A sofa and bookcase on a landing form a mini-library. Guests can bring their own wine to the lounge, which has large sofas, armchairs and a TV (none in the bedrooms). Breakfast is taken in a conservatory overlooking the garden. 'A selection of juices, cereals, bowls of fresh and stewed fruit; a wide choice of hot dishes (chosen the night before); butter, jams and marmalade on each table; brown soda bread on the buffet. (*Jeanette Bloor*)

Seaview
Clifden

T: 00 353 95-21441
E: sheila@seamisthouse.com
W: www.seamisthouse.com

BEDROOMS: 4.
OPEN: Mar–Nov.
FACILITIES: 2 sitting rooms, conservatory dining room, ¾-acre garden, unsuitable for ♿.
BACKGROUND MUSIC: none.
LOCATION: central.
CHILDREN: not under 4.
DOGS: not allowed.
CREDIT CARDS: Amex, MasterCard, Visa.
PRICES: B&B €40–€55 per person.

CLONES Co. Monaghan

Map 6:B6

HILTON PARK

'It was like staying in a friend's rather grand country house, lived in and not caring for modern ways.' A *Guide* inspector was 'sad to leave' this imposing mansion which has been the home of the Madden family since 1734. Fred and Joanna (of the ninth generation) welcome guests in house-party style; he is helped in the kitchen by his mother, Lucy, who also looks after the gardens. His father, Johnny, 'entertains guests with stories (some tall, all fascinating) about the family and the house'. 'I was met by a family friend who brought me a gin and tonic in the beguiling drawing room (lots of lived-in sofas and chairs, ancient electrics). In a dining room that 'a Ruritanian monarch would be proud of', dinner has a 'tasty' no-choice menu (dislikes discussed). 'Home-made bread was nutty and delicious; an exquisite wild garlic soup; a huge fillet steak, cooked to perfection, on spinach from the garden and with mini roast potatoes; portions were generous.' The principal bedrooms have a four-poster bed ('so high, I almost needed a stepladder'), eight-foot sash windows and antique bath.

Clones

T: 00 353 47-56007
F: 00 353 47-56033
E: mail@hiltonpark.ie
W: www.hiltonpark.ie

BEDROOMS: 6.
OPEN: Mar–Sept, groups only Oct–Mar.
FACILITIES: drawing room, sitting room, TV room, breakfast room, dining room, 400-acre grounds (3 lakes, golf course, croquet), unsuitable for ♿.
BACKGROUND MUSIC: none.
LOCATION: 3 miles S of Clones.
CHILDREN: not under 8.
DOGS: not allowed in bedrooms, public areas.
CREDIT CARDS: MasterCard, Visa.
PRICES: [2012] B&B €80–€135 per person, set dinner €55, special breaks.

COBH Co. Cork

Map 6:D5

KNOCKEVEN HOUSE

A short walk from the harbour which was the *Titanic*'s final departure point on her ill-fated maiden voyage, this elegant 1840 house is run as a 'very comfortable' B&B by John and Pamela Mulhaire. It stands in large gardens which have an abundance of camellias, azaleas and magnolias (this coastline is warmed by the Gulf Stream). Mrs Mulhaire likes to welcome guests with afternoon tea in the drawing room, taken with her home-baked scones. The spacious bedrooms are individually decorated with rich colours and patterns; one has long silk curtains and matching throws. Visitors commend the powerful showers in the bathrooms. Breakfast is taken at a mahogany table in the light and airy dining room; it has a buffet with freshly squeezed orange juice, home-made muesli, fresh fruit and rhubarb compote; bread and scones are home made; full Irish includes black and white pudding. The Mulhaires, who have a wealth of knowledge on the area, will advise on places to dine. An Aga-cooked evening meal can be provided if arranged in advance. The town's museum has a small but affecting *Titanic* exhibition.

Rushbrooke
Cobh

T: 00 353 21-481 1778
F: 00 353 21-481 1719
E: info@knockevenhouse.com
W: www.knockevenhouse.com

BEDROOMS: 4.
OPEN: all year except 16–26 Dec.
FACILITIES: lounge, drawing room, dining room, 2-acre garden, unsuitable for ♿.
BACKGROUND MUSIC: classical music sometimes in lounge.
LOCATION: 1 mile W of centre.
CHILDREN: all ages welcomed.
DOGS: not allowed.
CREDIT CARDS: MasterCard, Visa.
PRICES: B&B €45–€55 per person, D,B&B €80, New Year package.

CONG Co. Mayo

Map 6:C4

BALLYWARREN HOUSE

'From the moment we stepped through the door we knew we'd made the right decision,' says an American visitor in 2012 to David and Diane Skelton's family home, built in Georgian style on the edge of Connemara. 'They greeted us warmly and gave us afternoon tea.' Bedrooms are brightly painted: 'Our large room had wonderful views; an excellent bed and good linen; the modern, bright bathroom was spotless, with lots of hot water.' Dinner is served in 'a lovely room' overlooking the garden. 'Diane is a top chef, asking us in advance what we might like; David is the perfect host.' The dinners, 'cooked without pretension', might include dressed Donegal crab salad, Irish whiskey sauce; roast guineafowl, apricot and Madeira sauce. Coffee can be taken in front of the fire in the 'cosy drawing room'. A generous breakfast has home-made bread, cereals and fresh fruit: 'excellent' coffee; a wide choice of cooked dishes. Eggs come from hens that roam the garden. 'David kindly provided goat's milk for my lactose-intolerant husband.' The Connemara national park is nearby. (*Carole Loftin*)

Cross, Cong

T/F: 00 353 9495-46989
E: ballywarrenhouse@gmail.com
W: www.ballywarrenhouse.com

BEDROOMS: 3.
OPEN: all year.
FACILITIES: reception hall, sitting room, 2 dining rooms, 1-acre garden in 6-acre grounds (lake, fishing nearby), unsuitable for ♿.
BACKGROUND MUSIC: none.
LOCATION: 2 miles E of Cong.
CHILDREN: not under 14, except babies.
DOGS: not allowed in house.
CREDIT CARDS: Amex, MasterCard, Visa.
PRICES: B&B €62–€80 per person, set dinner €45.

SEE ALSO SHORTLIST

DUBLIN

Map 6:C6

ARIEL HOUSE

NEW

'Wonderful: it has a personal feel that is often missing in city hotels.' Retired hoteliers were impressed in 2012 by the McKeown family's hotel, a conversion of Victorian town houses close to Dublin's dramatic glass and steel Aviva rugby stadium. Deirdre McDonald is the 'hands-on' manager. The family have renovated the buildings, retaining original fireplaces, cornices and stained-glass windows. A 'gracious' room in the main house had 'a high ceiling, appropriate Georgian period furniture; a beautiful four-poster bed and a large and airy bathroom'. Standard rooms in a simpler style are in a modern wing overlooking the garden. Breakfast is taken until 10 am (later at weekends) in a 'bright' split-level conservatory dining room. 'The food was freshly cooked, and served by a pleasant, well-groomed staff (a supervisor kept a discreet eye on proceedings).' There are fruits and cereals, farmhouse cheeses, and 'today's home-baking' on a buffet. The cooked choices include herby scrambled eggs with crispy bacon and a pancake stack. 'A perfect *Guide* choice: this is the standard we would be happy to achieve.' (*Ken and Cathleen Buggy*)

50–54 Lansdowne Road
Ballsbridge, Dublin 4

T: 00 353 1-668 5512
F: 00 353 1-668 5845
E: reservations@ariel-house.net
W: www.ariel-house.net

BEDROOMS: 37, 8 in garden mews.
OPEN: all year except 22 Dec–3 Jan.
FACILITIES: Drawing room, dining room, garden.
BACKGROUND MUSIC: classical.
LOCATION: Ballsbridge.
CHILDREN: all ages welcomed.
DOGS: only guide dogs allowed.
CREDIT CARDS: Amex, MasterCard, Visa.
PRICES: [2012] B&B €39.50–€99 per person, seasonal packages.

SEE ALSO SHORTLIST

DUNFANAGHY Co. Donegal

Map 6:A5

THE MILL

'An unexpected delight', this former 19th-century flax mill on the outskirts of a small resort town is run as an unpretentious restaurant-with-rooms by Susan Alcorn and her husband, Derek. She is the granddaughter of Frank Egginton, celebrated watercolour artist, whose work is displayed throughout. She welcomes guests, who are asked to arrive after 4 pm, with 'pleasing informality'. A 'vivacious' host, she supervises front-of-house, taking orders in the conservatory, overlooking the lake, and the drawing room, which has an open fire on cooler evenings. The restaurant, on two levels with large tables and plenty of space, is popular with non-residents (booking is advisable). Mr Alcorn, the chef, serves an 'imaginative' modern Irish menu using local produce: his 'delicious' dishes might include warm Irish rabbit salad, sautéed new potatoes; seared Cranford scallops, lentil and coriander dhal. The modest bedrooms are individually decorated. A 'nice corner room was simple but functional'. Breakfast is 'equally good': an 'above-average' buffet has yogurts, fruit, carrageen milk mousse; 'lovely home-made breads and preserves'; 'excellent' eggs and bacon with potato bread. (*CJ*)

Figart
Dunfanaghy

T/F: 00 353 74-913 6985
E: themillrestaurant@oceanfree.net
W: www.themillrestaurant.com

BEDROOMS: 6.
OPEN: mid-Mar–mid-Dec, weekends only off-season, restaurant closed Mon.
FACILITIES: sitting room, conservatory, restaurant, 1-acre grounds (lake, beach ½ mile), only restaurant suitable for ♿.
BACKGROUND MUSIC: in lounge and restaurant.
LOCATION: at Figart, ½ mile W of Dunfanaghy.
CHILDREN: all ages welcomed.
DOGS: not allowed.
CREDIT CARDS: Amex, MasterCard, Visa.
PRICES: B&B €48–€60 per person, set dinner €41.

DUNGARVAN Co. Waterford

Map 6:D5

THE TANNERY RESTAURANT & TOWNHOUSE

More a restaurant than a hotel, this converted leather warehouse, in a small seaside town at the mouth of the River Colligan, is a magnet for Irish food lovers. Chef/patron Paul Flynn, a well-known television cook, and his wife, Máire (who runs front-of-house), added bedrooms in two buildings 'around the corner'. The cooking is excellent and the rooms are 'cool and stylish', said a recent visitor (a *Guide* hotelier). Mr Flynn can be seen cooking in an open kitchen on the ground floor of the two-level restaurant. His modern menus might include Gubbeen white pudding with chorizo, coco bean stew and soft egg; slow-cooked pork belly, fennel, lemon, tuna mayonnaise and broad beans. There is a three-course 'easy evening' menu and evening tapas from Tuesday to Friday. Children are welcomed. Bedrooms in the *Townhouse* are white, with splashes of vivid colour; all have television, 'comfortable beds and a good shower room'. There are no public rooms; guests take breakfast in their bedroom: fresh milk, juice and yogurt are in a small fridge; a bag with fresh bread and pastries is hung on the door.

10 Quay Street
Dungarvan

T: 00 353 58-45420
E: info@tannery.ie
W: www.tannery.ie

BEDROOMS: 14, 2 on ground floor.

OPEN: all year except Christmas, 2 weeks in Jan, restaurant closed Sun evening, Mon.

FACILITIES: restaurant, private dining room.

BACKGROUND MUSIC: light jazz.

LOCATION: town centre.

CHILDREN: all ages welcomed.

DOGS: not allowed.

CREDIT CARDS: Amex, MasterCard, Visa.

PRICES: [2012] B&B €55–€65 per person, 'easy evening' menu €30, full alc €75, special breaks.

ENNISCORTHY Co. Wexford

Map 6:D6

BALLINKEELE HOUSE

César award in 2012

'A wonderful house in a wonderful setting', this distinguished Georgian manor was built for the Maher family in 1840. It remains the family home to which visitors are welcomed by Margaret Maher and her daughter, Mary. 'Such a warm greeting; we were looked after extremely well,' says a visitor in 2012. A reporter agreed: 'This is a cracker: it's blessed with big bedrooms, big windows and a magnificent dining room.' The family has retained the period glamour of the Italianate mansion: the entrance has porticoes of Wicklow granite; the hall has two impressive Corinthian columns; a floating staircase leads to the first-floor bedrooms. They have original antique furniture, period details; all have a view of the parkland (with lakes and woods) and the well-maintained gardens. 'Standards of housekeeping and cleanliness were high in our large room.' In the candlelit dining room, Mrs Maher's Irish country house menu might include smoked salmon salad; roast lamb, minted peas. Meals are taken communally: 'The success of this depends on how much everyone contributes; in such august surroundings, everyone raised their game.'

Ballymurn
Enniscorthy

T: 00 353 53-913 8105
E: info@ballinkeele.ie
W: www.ballinkeele.ie

BEDROOMS: 5.
OPEN: 1 Mar–10 Nov.
FACILITIES: 2 drawing rooms, dining room, 6-acre gardens in 350-acre estate, lakes, ponds, unsuitable for ♿.
BACKGROUND MUSIC: none.
LOCATION: 6 miles SE of Enniscorthy.
CHILDREN: not under 16.
DOGS: not allowed.
CREDIT CARDS: MasterCard, Visa.
PRICES: B&B €75–€130 per person, D,B&B €120–€175, full alc €63, special offers.

ENNISCORTHY Co. Wexford

Map 6:D6

SALVILLE HOUSE

César award: Irish country house of the year

'Still terrific; excellent housekeeping and amazing food; such style and value.' There is much praise this year for Gordon and Jane Parker's Victorian country house in large grounds on a quiet hilltop. The three spacious bedrooms in the main house have views over the River Slaney. 'Ours was extremely well equipped; a wardrobe, dressing table, tea/coffee-making kit,' says a 2012 visitor. 'The furniture was old and solid in keeping with the house; the bathroom was well fitted and had thick towels.' Two other rooms are in a self-contained apartment. The drawing room has 'fascinating artwork and Malaysian memorabilia; family photographs suggest a lifetime of memories'. Mr Parker is the cook, using locally caught fish for his dishes served in a 'lovely' dining room: 'We enjoyed bruschetta and the best vegetable tempura we have ever had, followed by a vegetarian version of Malaysian laksa, served with a curry puff.' Breakfast has 'poached plums, leaf tea, interesting cheese, nice preserves, home-made sourdough bread'. A handy base for the Wexford opera festival and the Rosslare ferries.
(*Dr Catherine Fraher, Jeanette Bloor*)

Salville
Enniscorthy

T/F: 00 353 53-923 5252
E: info@salvillehouse.com
W: www.salvillehouse.com

BEDROOMS: 5, 2 in apartment at rear.
OPEN: all year except Christmas.
FACILITIES: drawing room, dining room, 3-acre grounds ('rough' tennis, badminton, croquet), golf nearby, beach, bird sanctuary 10 miles, unsuitable for ♿.
BACKGROUND MUSIC: none.
LOCATION: 2 miles S of town.
CHILDREN: all ages welcomed.
DOGS: allowed by arrangement, but not in public rooms.
CREDIT CARDS: none.
PRICES: B&B €55–€65 per person, set dinner €40, New Year package.

GOREY Co. Wexford

Map 6:D6

MARLFIELD HOUSE

NEW

Once the Irish residence of the earls of Courtown, the Bowe family's fine Regency mansion is run by sisters Margaret and Laura Bowe as a sophisticated country house hotel (Relais & Châteaux). It returns to a full entry after a positive report this year: 'The building, fixtures and fittings are beautiful; the staff are exceptionally friendly.' Antiques and pictures abound: a grand marble hall, a lounge with an open fire, spectacular flower displays. The best bedrooms have antiques, dramatic wallpaper and curtains, marble bathroom. A large ground-floor room has French windows opening on to the lovely grounds. In the 'most attractive' dining room (frescoes, a domed conservatory), service is formal. Ruadhan Furlong, the chef, cooks 'excellent' classical dishes, eg, confit duck and prune terrine, crab apple jelly; seared monkfish, pomme purée, pancetta, garden chive velouté. Fruit, vegetables and herbs come from the kitchen garden. The house stands in woodlands; there is a wildfowl reserve, a lake with ducks, geese and black swans. Children are welcomed; under-eights have their own high tea menu. (*Peter and Penny Bull*)

Courtown Road
Gorey

T: 00 353 53-942 1124
F: 00 353 53-942 1572
E: info@marlfieldhouse.ie
W: www.marlfieldhouse.com

BEDROOMS: 19, 8 on ground floor.
OPEN: Mar–Dec except Christmas, restaurant closed Mon/Tues in Mar/Apr, Oct–Dec.
FACILITIES: reception hall, drawing room, library/bar, restaurant with conservatory, wedding facilities, 36-acre grounds (gardens, tennis, croquet, wildfowl reserve, lake).
BACKGROUND MUSIC: classical in library.
LOCATION: 1 mile E of Gorey.
CHILDREN: no under-8s at dinner, high tea provided, babysitting available.
DOGS: not allowed in public rooms.
CREDIT CARDS: all major cards.
PRICES: B&B €75–€300 per person, D,B&B €140–€360, set dinner €64, special breaks, 1-night bookings sometimes refused Sat.

SEE ALSO SHORTLIST

HOLYWOOD Co. Down

Map 6:B6

RAYANNE HOUSE

'An individualistic place', this Victorian merchant's mansion stands in large 'smart' gardens above a small dormitory town on the Belfast Lough. It is run as a guest house by Conor and Bernadette McClelland, who have extended and renovated throughout. 'They clearly adore Art Deco and have made the house a tribute to this; not like a museum, just charming,' said a *Guide* inspector returning after several years. There are sweeping staircases, display cabinets, lots of ornaments. Conor McClelland has won awards for his 'amazing' breakfasts. Guests order the evening before from a comprehensive menu (a choice of five fruit juices, five starters plus cereals, and 11 cooked choices). Guests might opt for pomegranate juice; prune soufflée on a purée of fresh green figs; crock-baked Irish ham and eggs, Italian tomato sauce. Evening meals are served by arrangement. A 'huge' bedroom on the top floor has a small balcony with 'stunning views' across to the Antrim hills; an enormous walk-in wardrobe; 'every little thing you could think of among the extras'. A ground-floor room is equipped for disabled visitors.

60 Demesne Road
Holywood BT18 9EX

T/F: 028-9042 5859
E: info@rayannehouse.com
W: www.rayannehouse.com

BEDROOMS: 11, 1, on ground floor, suitable for ♿.
OPEN: all year.
FACILITIES: 2 lounges, dining room, conference facilities, 1-acre grounds.
BACKGROUND MUSIC: light jazz in dining room.
LOCATION: ½ mile from town centre, 6 miles E of Belfast.
CHILDREN: all ages welcomed.
DOGS: not allowed.
CREDIT CARDS: Amex, MasterCard, Visa.
PRICES: [2012] B&B £57.50–£95 per person, set meals £47, full alc £67.

INIS MEÁIN Co. Galway

Map 6:C4

INIS MEÁIN RESTAURANT AND SUITES

Returning islander Ruairí de Blacam is the owner/chef of this striking stone-and-glass restaurant-with-rooms; his wife, Marie Thérèse, looks after the front-of-house. It is a 'very special place', said a visitor. Inis Meáin is the middle of the three Aran Islands, off the windswept Galway coast; its rough-hewn landscape of terraced limestone is unique in Europe. The first language of most islanders is Gaelic. The interior of the building has rough stone walls and ceilings, given splashes of colour by alpaca throws from the island's knitwear factory. The five suites have wooden floors, modern wooden furnishings. Each has a large bed, a living area, an outside sitting area, and a continuous 10-metre-long window (the largest suite has a 15-metre-long, dual-aspect window). Bicycles, fishing rods and swimming towels are provided. In the contemporary dining room, Ruairí de Blacam cooks 'superb' meals based mainly on local fish and shellfish, perhaps smoked salmon with capers and herbs; roast monkfish, garden spinach, grain mustard sauce. A breakfast tray is delivered to the suite, with scones, soda bread, eggs, salamis, fresh fruit, etc.

Inis Meáin, Aran Islands
Galway

T: 00 353 86-826 6026
E: post@inismeain.com
W: www.inismeain.com

BEDROOMS: 5.
OPEN: Apr–Sep, hotel and restaurant closed Sun–Tues.
FACILITIES: restaurant, 3-acre grounds, unsuitable for ♿.
BACKGROUND MUSIC: Irish music in evening.
LOCATION: on island, 15 miles off Galway coast (45-minute ferry from Ros a' Mhíl, flights from Connemara airport).
CHILDREN: all ages welcomed.
DOGS: not allowed.
CREDIT CARDS: MasterCard, Visa.
PRICES: B&B €118.50–€200 per person, full alc €60, min. stay 2 nights.

KENMARE Co. Kerry

Map 6:D4

SHELBURNE LODGE

'A great place' (according to a returning visitor in 2012), Tom and Maura Foley's handsome 18th-century farmhouse has long been popular with *Guide* readers for the welcome, the ambience and the 'magnificent' breakfasts. Another comment (from a trusted correspondent): 'The house is full of the personality of the owners; everyone is a friend from the moment they arrive.' A family member is invariably on hand to greet visitors, providing home-made cake and tea in an elegant drawing room, which has good seating, an open fire. In extensive grounds on the edge of the town, the house is furnished with flair: striking colours, plants and flowers, antiques, modern art. Wi-Fi is free. The bedrooms are divided between the house and a coach house (especially good for families). Mr Foley presides at breakfast: orange juice is freshly squeezed; starters include fresh fruit and natural yogurt; bread is home baked; don't miss the fish of the day. Kenmare has many eating places but guests might be tempted by the Foleys' own popular bar/restaurant, *Packie's*; Maura Foley's sister runs *The Purple Heather* bistro. (*Esler Crawford, Eithne Scallan*)

Cork Road
Kenmare

T: 00 353 64-664 1013
F: 00 353 64-664 2135
E: shelburnekenmare@eircom.net
W: www.shelburnelodge.com

BEDROOMS: 8, 2 in coach house, 1 on ground floor.
OPEN: mid-Mar–mid-Nov.
FACILITIES: drawing room, library, lounge in annexe, breakfast room, 3-acre garden (tennis), golf adjacent, unsuitable for ♿.
BACKGROUND MUSIC: none.
LOCATION: on R569 to Cork, ⅓ mile E of centre.
CHILDREN: all ages welcomed.
DOGS: not allowed.
CREDIT CARDS: MasterCard, Visa.
PRICES: B&B €50–€95 per person.

SEE ALSO SHORTLIST

KENMARE Co. Kerry

Map 6:D4

VIRGINIA'S GUESTHOUSE

'The welcome from our hosts was warm,' says a visitor this year to Neil and Noreen Harrington's unpretentious guest house above a restaurant in this small town. On the eastern edge of the Ring of Kerry, Kenmare is a popular base for overnight visitors. The 'engaging' Harringtons supply earplugs for guests staying in front rooms, where street noise can be an issue. The simple but cheerful bedrooms are well equipped; bathrooms are 'spotless', and have power shower and fluffy towels. 'Our room was large and airy, with an enormous bed.' Tea- and coffee-making is available for guests in a sitting room. An 'excellent' breakfast, ordered the evening before, has a seasonal menu which might include rhubarb and rosemary compote, 'porridge as good as any I tasted in Ireland'; freshly squeezed orange juice or Neil's 'zingy' juice cocktail (orange, cranberry and ginger). Banana pancakes with maple syrup are among an extensive choice of cooked dishes. Bread and preserves are home made. Kenmare has many good eating places (*Mulcahy's* is below *Virginia's*), and traditional Irish music is played in the pubs. (*Valerie Durkan*)

36 Henry Street
Kenmare

T: 00 353 86-372 0625
E: virginias@eircom.net
W: www.virginias-kenmare.com

BEDROOMS: 8.
OPEN: all year except 24–26 Dec.
FACILITIES: library, breakfast room, unsuitable for ♿.
BACKGROUND MUSIC: classical, in breakfast room.
LOCATION: central.
CHILDREN: not under 12.
DOGS: not allowed.
CREDIT CARDS: MasterCard, Visa.
PRICES: B&B €32.50–€45 per person, 3-night off-season breaks, 1-night bookings refused bank holidays.

SEE ALSO SHORTLIST

KILMALLOCK Co. Limerick

Map 6:D5

FLEMINGSTOWN HOUSE

César award in 2005

An 'aura of relaxed informality and comfort' draws visitors back to Imelda Sheedy-King's guest house, an 18th-century building on a working dairy farm at the base of the Ballyhoura Mountains. Her family have been farming in the Golden Vale (an area of outstanding beauty where three counties meet) for five generations; visitors can watch the milking of the cows. The 'wonderful' hostess shows an 'impeccable attention to detail', say visitors. 'Full marks on all counts.' The bedrooms have king-size bed, antique furnishings. 'Spotlessly clean' bathrooms have power shower and fluffy towels. Mrs Sheedy-King cooks dinner by arrangement: it is served in a room with large stained-glass windows; her seasonal fare might include cucumber soup; chicken with mustard and crème fraîche. Guests are asked to bring their own wine. There is a nearby pub with food for nights when she is not cooking. An 'incomparable' breakfast has a buffet with freshly squeezed orange juice, fresh fruits and yogurts, home-made breads, jams and cakes; cooked options include Dingle Bay kippers with a honey and lemon sauce. (*LA*)

Kilmallock

T: 00 353 63-98093
F: 00 353 63-98546
E: info@flemingstown.com
W: www.flemingstown.com

BEDROOMS: 5, 1 self-catering lodge.
OPEN: Mar–Oct.
FACILITIES: lounge, dining room, 1-acre garden in 100-acre farm (golf, riding, fishing, cycling nearby), unsuitable for ♿.
BACKGROUND MUSIC: none.
LOCATION: 2 miles SE of Kilmallock.
CHILDREN: not under 16.
DOGS: upon request.
CREDIT CARDS: MasterCard, Visa.
PRICES: B&B €50–€60 per person, set dinner €40, special rates for stays of more than 1 night.

LETTERFRACK Co. Galway

Map 6:C4

ROSLEAGUE MANOR

César award in 2010

'Happily endorsed' this year by a first-time visitor, this Georgian manor house is run in 'effortless' style by owners Mark Foyle and his father, Edmund. A guest who has been visiting for 30 years commends the 'informal atmosphere: we watched two groups arrive looking frazzled, departing a few days later cheerful and refreshed'. The pink-painted house stands on the shores of Ballinakill Bay, a quiet sea lough in Connemara. Bedrooms range 'from large to enormous': a room at the front of the house has 'one of the biggest Victorian bathtubs we have ever seen'. The 'elegant' lounges have 'copious flower arrangements' and open fires burning turf and logs (one quibble: 'the chairs might need restuffing'). Emmanuel Neu, the chef, cooks highly praised French country house dishes: 'We particularly enjoyed boned quail with a salad of leaves from the garden, and Cleggan crab claws with a lightly curried mayonnaise; portions are well judged.' Breakfast has freshly squeezed orange juice, 'genuinely fresh' fruit salad, rhubarb from the garden, and home-baked scones and brown bread; hot dishes cooked to order. (*Colin Adams, AW*)

Letterfrack

T: 00 353 95-41101
F: 00 353 95-41168
E: info@rosleague.com
W: www.rosleague.com

BEDROOMS: 20, 2 on ground floor.
OPEN: mid-Mar–mid-Nov.
FACILITIES: 2 drawing rooms, conservatory/bar, dining room, wedding facilities, 25-acre grounds (tennis), unsuitable for ♿.
BACKGROUND MUSIC: none.
LOCATION: 7 miles NE of Clifden.
CHILDREN: all ages welcomed.
DOGS: 'well-behaved dogs' allowed in public rooms, with own bedding in bedrooms.
CREDIT CARDS: MasterCard, Visa.
PRICES: [2012] B&B €75–€125 per person, D,B&B €95–€135, set dinner €46, 1-night bookings refused bank holiday Sat.

LIMERICK Co. Limerick

Map 6:D5

NO. 1 PERY SQUARE

NEW

In a terrace regarded as one of the finest examples of late Georgian architecture in Ireland, this conversion of two town houses is run as a small hotel by Patricia Roberts. It gains a full entry following reports from regular correspondents. 'One of the nicest places in Ireland; the food is streets ahead of most,' says a fellow *Guide* hotelier. 'Outstanding; we were looked after with genuine care,' is another comment. The four most spacious bedrooms and a suite are on the top floors; other rooms are more compact: 'Ours was small but well furnished, with an enormous bed; the bathroom was almost as big as the bedroom; no tea-making facilities but the lads who greeted us were quick to bring complimentary tea; they told us to ring any time we needed more.' Afternoon tea can be taken in an elegant drawing room with an original marble fireplace. In *Brasserie One*, the chef, Alan Burns, cooks dishes with a 'strong French influence', eg, halibut, basil-crushed potatoes, aubergine caviar, sauce vierge. 'The menu is innovative, the cooking sensitive.' (*Johnny Madden, Valerie Durkan*)

Georgian Quarter
1 Pery Square
Limerick

T: 00 353 61-402402
F: 00 353 61-313060
E: info@oneperysquare.com
W: www.oneperysquare.com

BEDROOMS: 20, 2 suitable for ♿.
OPEN: all year except 24–29 Dec, restaurant closed Mon.
FACILITIES: lounge, drawing room, bar, restaurant, private dining room, wedding facilities, terrace, basement spa.
BACKGROUND MUSIC: 'easy listening' in public areas.
LOCATION: central.
CHILDREN: all ages welcomed.
DOGS: not allowed.
CREDIT CARDS: all major cards.
PRICES: B&B €67.50–€125 per person, D,B&B €30 added, set menus €20–€25, full alc €50, New Year package, special breaks.

LISDOONVARNA Co. Clare

Map 6:C4

SHEEDY'S

'It has all the modern comforts while retaining some pleasantly old-fashioned touches,' says a visitor to John and Martina Sheedy's small hotel/restaurant on the edge of the Burren. 'Beds have blankets, tea is made with leaves, and breakfast is buffet free.' Another comment (in 2012): 'An excellent small hotel with a warm welcome.' The house has been in the family since the mid-1700s, and run as a hotel since 1935. Mr Sheedy is the chef, while his wife looks after front-of-house; 'Martina runs it so well; she is a constant presence, leading by example and putting the needs of her guests first.' The bar and library 'are cosy but a little dark'; the lighter reception area has a turf fire and large windows overlooking the garden. 'Our large bedroom had a sitting area; the bathroom was impressive; twin basins, bath, separate walk-in shower, abundant white towels.' Mr Sheedy serves an à la carte menu in the dining room, simpler dishes in the bar. 'All very good: excellent crispy duck with spiced pears; hake with spinach and red pepper sauce. Portions are generous.' Breakfast 'is a particular strength', with 'some unusual and imaginative options'. (*AW, Florence and Russell Birch*)

Lisdoonvarna

T: 00 353 65-707 4026
F: 00 353 65-707 4555
E: info@sheedys.com
W: www.sheedys.com

BEDROOMS: 11, some on ground floor, 1 suitable for ♿.
OPEN: Apr–early Oct.
FACILITIES: ramp, sitting room/library, sun lounge, bar, restaurant, ¼-acre garden (rose garden).
BACKGROUND MUSIC: light jazz at dinner.
LOCATION: 20 miles SW of Galway.
CHILDREN: all ages welcomed.
DOGS: not allowed.
CREDIT CARDS: Amex, MasterCard, Visa.
PRICES: [2012] B&B €50–€90 per person, D,B&B €95–€125, full alc €65, special breaks, 1-night bookings refused Sept weekends.

MAGHERALIN Co. Armagh

Map 6:B6

NEWFORGE HOUSE

'Excellent in every way.' Owned by the 'helpful' John and Louise Mather, this 'beautiful' Georgian country house stands in well-kept grounds on the edge of a small village. It is 'strongly recommended' by readers this year. 'I was given such a warm welcome by John; my stepdaughters, who joined me for dinner, fell in love with the house when they came through the front door.' The Mathers, the sixth generation to live here, have converted it sympathetically. The sitting room and dining room have open log fires, good-quality fabrics, antiques, decent paintings. The spacious bedrooms are individually designed. Hannah, 'arguably our most romantic room', has a four-poster bed; floor-to-ceiling windows in both bedroom and bathroom. The Waddle Room has a canopy bed draped in toile. All rooms are supplied with fresh milk for tea- and coffee-making. 'Good food', too. Dinner is served in a light room overlooking the garden: the host's seasonal menus might include wild boar, juniper and thyme sauce. 'The local beef was fantastic.' The 'delicious' breakfast has eggs from the owners' hens; breads are home-made. (*RSC Abel Smith, Stewart Martin*)

25% DISCOUNT VOUCHERS

58 Newforge Road
Magheralin
Craigavon BT67 0QL

T: 028-9261 1255
F: 028-9261 2823
E: enquiries@newforgehouse.com
W: www.newforgehouse.com

BEDROOMS: 6.
OPEN: all year except 21 Dec–mid-Jan.
FACILITIES: drawing room, dining room, civil wedding licence, 4-acre gardens (vegetable garden, orchard), unsuitable for ♿.
BACKGROUND MUSIC: mixed in dining room.
LOCATION: edge of village, 3 miles E of Craigavon.
CHILDREN: not under 10 (except for under-1s).
DOGS: not allowed.
CREDIT CARDS: Diners, MasterCard, Visa.
PRICES: [2012] B&B £60–£85 per person, D,B&B £98–£148, set dinner £38, special breaks.

MILLSTREET Co. Waterford

Map 6:D5

THE CASTLE COUNTRY HOUSE

Guests are invited 'to experience a slice of life' on Emmet and Joan Nugent's working dairy farm which is run as a B&B, serving evening meals by arrangement. Visitors can watch milking in the dairy (the enthusiastic can lend a hand if they choose). The accommodation on the farm is in the restored wing of an older fortified tower house (16th century), built to protect livestock. The spacious bedrooms are individually decorated in vibrant colours; they have period furniture, large bed with crisp linen; tea- and coffee-making facilities are supplied. All rooms overlook the gardens which run down to the River Finisk, where anglers can fish for trout; reels and rods are provided. In the dining room, Mrs Nugent serves a set evening meal, with produce that comes mostly from the farm (perhaps locally caught salmon with vegetables). There is an open fire in the sitting room. Breakfast has a buffet of home-grown fruit, cereals, home-baked breads; cooked dishes on offer include a traditional Irish fry; grilled bananas wrapped in bacon. This is the closest to Dungarvan of three villages called Millstreet. More reports, please.

Millstreet
Cappagh

T: 00 353 58-68049
F: 00 353 58-68099
E: castle@castlecountryhouse.com
W: www.castlecountryhouse.com

BEDROOMS: 5.
OPEN: May–Oct.
FACILITIES: sitting room, dining room, 32-acre garden on 170-acre farm, unsuitable for ♿.
BACKGROUND MUSIC: none.
LOCATION: 10 miles NW of Dungarvan towards Cappoquin.
CHILDREN: all ages welcomed.
DOGS: not allowed in house.
CREDIT CARDS: MasterCard, Visa.
PRICES: B&B €40–€60 per person, set dinner €25, 3-night breaks.

MOUNTRATH Co. Laois

Map 6:C5

ROUNDWOOD HOUSE

César award in 1990

'So relaxing; the welcome couldn't be more genuine.' Praise in 2012 for Paddy and Hannah Flynn's Palladian villa in pastures and woods in the rural Irish Midlands. The hosts continue the task begun by her parents of restoring this heritage building. 'It is a house and home, not an immaculate hotel; excellent value,' says a trusted reporter. Spacious bedrooms in the main house have original features: 'Our spotless room had emerald-green walls, crisp white paintwork and bedlinen.' Four smaller rooms in the Yellow House (an even older building) face a walled garden. Paddy Flynn cooks a five-course no-choice dinner five nights a week (a shorter supper on other evenings). 'The food is delicious and plentiful; we enjoyed a superb broccoli and cashew nut soup; dauphinoise potatoes were decorated with wild garlic; the home-made ice cream is lovely. Paddy and Hannah joined us for coffee in the lounge; we talked long into the night.' Breakfast has a generous sideboard with cereals, fruit salads, etc; home-baked bread and scones; 'superb mushrooms on toast with blue cheese'. (*Jeanette Bloor*)

Mountrath

T: 00 353 57-873 2120
F: 00 353 57-873 2711
E: info@roundwoodhouse.com
W: www.roundwoodhouse.com

BEDROOMS: 10, 4 in garden building.
OPEN: all year except Christmas.
FACILITIES: drawing room, study/library, dining room, playroom, table tennis room, wedding facilities, 20-acre grounds (garden, woodland), golf, walking, river fishing nearby, unsuitable for ♿.
BACKGROUND MUSIC: none.
LOCATION: 3 miles N of village.
CHILDREN: all ages welcomed.
DOGS: not allowed indoors.
CREDIT CARDS: all major cards.
PRICES: [2012] B&B €60–€85 per person, supper €35 (Sun/Mon), set dinner (Tues–Sat) €50, special breaks.

MULTYFARNHAM Co. Westmeath

Map 6:C5

MORNINGTON HOUSE

'We thoroughly enjoyed our stay; the host served the best dinner we had during our entire visit to Ireland,' say American visitors this year to Warwick and Ann O'Hara's 'intimate' country house. 'Ann is a great cook and Warwick is a gracious host.' His family have lived here since 1858: 'We enjoyed our conversations with him and were impressed with his knowledge of the property.' The house, in extensive grounds (with 'spectacular walled gardens'), is reached by a long winding driveway. A *Guide* inspector was warmly welcomed. 'The elegant drawing room has good antiques, lots of light from large windows, and an interesting mix of paintings.' The bedrooms, which vary in size, have good linens, and fluffy towels in the bathroom. Meals are served communally in the dining room: Mrs O'Hara's country house dishes, locally sourced (fruit and vegetables from the gardens), might include Guinness stew. Breakfast has freshly squeezed juice, yogurt, muesli, home-made nut bread and 'the most perfectly cooked rhubarb I've ever tasted'; hot food is cooked to order by Mr O'Hara. (*Frank and Andrea Russo, and others*)

25% DISCOUNT VOUCHERS

Multyfarnham

T: 00 353 44-937 2191
F: 00 353 44-937 2338
E: stay@mornington.ie
W: www.mornington.ie

BEDROOMS: 4.
OPEN: Apr–Oct.
FACILITIES: drawing room, dining room, 5-acre garden, 50-acre grounds (croquet, bicycle hire), unsuitable for ♿.
BACKGROUND MUSIC: none.
LOCATION: 9 miles NW of Mullingar.
CHILDREN: all ages welcomed.
DOGS: not allowed in house.
CREDIT CARDS: all major cards.
PRICES: B&B €75 per person, D,B&B €120, set dinner €45, 3-night breaks.

NEWPORT Co. Mayo

Map 6:B4

NEWPORT HOUSE

Behind deceptively unimposing gates, this Georgian country house hotel has been owned by Kieran Thompson since 1985. It stands on the estuary of the River Newport, for which it owns extensive fishing rights. The long-serving manager is Catherine Flynn: 'She is the heart and soul of the place,' says an inspector in 2012. 'She gives a warm welcome, help with bags, and explains the layout. She is chatty but knows when to leave guests alone.' The public rooms are traditionally decorated; an entrance vestibule leads to two drawing rooms ('high ceilings, comfy seating, bookcases and open fires'). A grand staircase leads to a Regency drawing room, which overlooks the park. Eleven bedrooms are in the main house; five in converted courtyard houses are good for families, anglers and dog owners. 'They are slightly faded; my room, which had three windows, was decorated in muted tones; a wonderfully comfortable bed; a turquoise suite in the bathroom.' The chef, John Gavin, serves 'a meticulously presented five-course meal of traditional dishes (many creamy sauces); fish was cooked to perfection. All the local staff try hard to please.'

25% DISCOUNT VOUCHERS

Newport

T: 00 353 98-41222
F: 00 353 98-41613
E: info@newporthouse.ie
W: www.newporthouse.ie

BEDROOMS: 16, 5 in courtyard, 2 on ground floor.
OPEN: 20 Mar–31 Oct.
FACILITIES: sitting room, bar, dining room, restaurant, billiard/TV room, table-tennis room, 15-acre grounds (walled garden, private fishing on River Newport), unsuitable for ♿.
BACKGROUND MUSIC: none.
LOCATION: in village 7 miles N of Westport.
CHILDREN: all ages welcomed.
DOGS: allowed in courtyard bedrooms, not in public rooms.
CREDIT CARDS: Amex, MasterCard, Visa.
PRICES: [2012] B&B €105–€152 per person, D,B&B €170–€217, set dinner €65, full alc €56, special breaks on website.

OUGHTERARD Co. Galway

Map 6:C4

CURRAREVAGH HOUSE

César award in 1992

'An absolute delight', a returning visitor's praise for this early Victorian manor house which has been run as a hotel by the Hodgson family since 1890. Henry Hodgson is assisted front-of-house by his mother, June; his wife, Lucy, is the chef. 'We run it as a private country house without pretension,' they say; there are no keys to the bedroom doors. 'Lucy's cooking is seriously good,' writes a guest. The four-course no-choice meal is 'visually stunning, intensely flavoured, with inventive combinations; we enjoyed crab, squid and superb risotto; duck confit and breast; stuffed lamb'. Meat is brought round on a silver tray ('you can take as much as you want') and second helpings are offered. The bedrooms are individually decorated; there are large beds with sheets and blankets, fresh flowers; views of Lough Corrib or Benlevy Mountain. Afternoon tea, with home-made scones, sponge and sandwiches, is served in the drawing room. Breakfast has home-made soda bread, croissants, marmalade and muesli; local sausages, bacon and black and white pudding. *Currarevagh* has its own boats and ghillies on Lough Corrib. (*Richard Parish, Gareth Pearce*)

25% DISCOUNT VOUCHERS

Oughterard

T: 00 353 91-552312
F: 00 353 91-552731
E: info@currarevagh.com
W: www.currarevagh.com

BEDROOMS: 12.
OPEN: 28 Mar–28 Oct.
FACILITIES: sitting room/hall, drawing room, library/bar with TV, dining room, 180-acre grounds (lake, fishing, ghillies available, boating, swimming, tennis, croquet), golf, riding nearby, unsuitable for ♿.
BACKGROUND MUSIC: none.
LOCATION: 4 miles NW of Oughterard.
CHILDREN: all ages welcomed.
DOGS: allowed.
CREDIT CARDS: MasterCard, Visa.
PRICES: B&B €75–€85 per person, D,B&B €110–€130, set dinner €45.

OUGHTERARD Co. Galway

Map 6:C4

ROSS LAKE HOUSE

'Everything is first class' at Henry and Elaine Reid's fine Georgian house, once the home of local landed gentry. Set among rambling woods and rolling lawns in untamed Connemara countryside, it is a 'homely, friendly' hotel, say guests. The Reids are 'excellent hosts': 'All that we needed was provided without hesitation.' There is plenty of good seating in the elegant drawing rooms. The spacious bedrooms, some with four-poster, are light and airy. The larger rooms have a sitting area. Pre-dinner drinks are taken in the library before guests move to the softly lit dining room. Mrs Reid is the chef, serving a daily-changing menu of traditional dishes, locally sourced from farm and lake, or in season the day's catch from the Atlantic. Her menus might include oak-smoked salmon with capers and red onion; roast rack of Connemara lamb, red wine and rosemary jus. 'Hearty fresh produce from the region prepared in an exquisite way and accompanied by Henry's great wine list.' There are extensive walks within the grounds as well as a tennis court; good golfing and fishing nearby. (*HGRT, PO'R*)

Rosscahill
Oughterard

T: 00 353 91-550109
F: 00 353 91-550184
E: rosslake@iol.ie
W: www.rosslakehotel.com

BEDROOMS: 13.
OPEN: 15 Mar–30 Oct.
FACILITIES: drawing room, library bar, restaurant, 7-acre grounds (tennis), unsuitable for ♿.
BACKGROUND MUSIC: classical in bar and restaurant.
LOCATION: 14 miles NW of Galway city.
CHILDREN: all ages welcomed.
DOGS: not allowed.
CREDIT CARDS: Amex, MasterCard, Visa.
PRICES: [2012] B&B €60–€92 per person, D,B&B €103–€135, set dinner €43, full alc €53.

RATHMULLAN Co. Donegal

Map 6:B5

RATHMULLAN HOUSE

'It is difficult to think of any hotel in Ireland which is more comfortable than *Rathmullan House*.' Praise from a visitor returning this year to the Wheeler family's Georgian mansion above a beach on Lough Swilly (a sea inlet). Brothers Mark (the manager) and William, with their wives, Mary and Yvonne, are the second generation of the family to run the hotel. The house is elegantly decorated throughout, with chandeliers, ornate plasterwork and comfortable sofas in the public areas. Bedrooms in the main house are traditional in style, some with four-poster. Rooms in the extension are more airy and have a contemporary feel; ground-floor rooms have doors that lead to an outside sitting area and the well-kept gardens. Pre-dinner drinks are served in the drawing rooms: there are two menus to choose from in the *Weeping Elm* restaurant, which has views over the lough; simpler fare is served in *Batt's Bar* and the *Cellar Bar*. The chef, Kelan McMichael, an advocate of the Slow Food movement, serves locally sourced meat and fish, and vegetables from the hotel's kitchen garden. (*EC*)

Rathmullan

T: 00 353 74-915 8188
F: 00 353 74-915 8200
E: info@rathmullanhouse.com
W: www.rathmullanhouse.com

BEDROOMS: 32, some on ground floor, 2 suitable for ♿.

OPEN: 3 Feb–6 Jan except Christmas, midweek Nov, Dec.

FACILITIES: ramps, 4 sitting rooms, library, TV room, cellar bar/bistro, restaurant, 15-metre indoor swimming pool, wedding facilities, 7-acre grounds (tennis, croquet).

BACKGROUND MUSIC: none.

LOCATION: ½ mile N of village.

CHILDREN: all ages welcomed.

DOGS: allowed in some bedrooms, but not in public rooms.

CREDIT CARDS: Amex, MasterCard, Visa.

PRICES: B&B €70–€110 per person, D,B&B €110–€150, set dinner €40–€50, full alc €70, special breaks, New Year package, 1-night bookings refused bank holiday Sat.

SEE ALSO SHORTLIST

RIVERSTOWN Co. Sligo

Map 6:B5

COOPERSHILL

César award in 1987

The O'Hara family have lived in *Coopershill*, a magnificent 1774 house, for eight generations; Simon O'Hara is the current custodian; his partner, Christina McCauley, is the *Ballymaloe*-trained chef. His parents now live in a stone house in the grounds. A long drive leads to the imposing Palladian building, which stands on a large estate and deer farm. Bedrooms (some with four-poster/canopy bed) are spacious and individually decorated; each has a modern en suite bathroom (some are windowless). A room at the top of the staircase had 'a wonderful view of greenery and distant hills; a large four-poster bed, divinely soft to slip into'. Dinner is taken at separate tables in the 'gracious' dining room ('adorned with family pictures, art, and ornaments'). The 'wonderful' meal might include modern Irish dishes like smoked venison (from the estate), raspberry vinaigrette; rack of lamb, wild garlic and basil pesto. 'You will get more from a stay if you are willing to be a house guest and mix,' is an inspector's advice. *Coopershill* is 'proud of its green philosophy'; rainfall is captured, electricity comes from renewable sources.

25% DISCOUNT VOUCHERS

Riverstown

T: 00 353 71-916 5108
E: ohara@coopershill.com
W: www.coopershill.com

BEDROOMS: 8.
OPEN: Apr–Oct, off-season house parties by arrangement.
FACILITIES: 2 halls, drawing room, dining room, snooker room, wedding facilities, 500-acre estate (garden, tennis, croquet, woods, farmland, river with trout fishing), unsuitable for ♿.
BACKGROUND MUSIC: none.
LOCATION: 11 miles SE of Sligo.
CHILDREN: by arrangement.
DOGS: by arrangement.
CREDIT CARDS: MasterCard, Visa.
PRICES: B&B €99–€122 per person, D,B&B (2 nights min.) €148–€171, set dinner €49.

SCHULL Co. Cork

Map 6:D4

GROVE HOUSE

NEW

Overlooking the harbour of a coastal village popular with the yachting fraternity, this interesting place was built as a hotel in 1880. Today it is run as an informal guest house by Katrina Runske and her son, Nico (the chef). 'Excellent: the Swedish owner is charming; the house has a well-used feel, with a fair share of clutter,' says the nominator (a trusted reporter). Katrina Runske maintains the artistic associations of the house (George Bernard Shaw and Jack B Yeats signed the original guest list): she teaches the piano (there's a grand piano in the sitting room) and hosts 'musical gigs'; work by local artists is displayed in the bar (and is for sale). Period features have been retained in the nicely proportioned rooms; spacious bedrooms have a pitch pine floor and are found 'comfortable'. In the dining room (with a conservatory attached), Nico Runske uses local produce for his menus, which have a Swedish influence; typical dishes: Macka Lisa (lumpfish roe, mayonnaise, eggs, onion on toast); chicken wrapped in bacon, stuffed with Gubbeen cheese. 'Great pride' is taken in the wine list. 'Excellent value.' (*Esler Crawford*)

Colla Road
Schull

T: 00 353 28-28067
F: 00 353 28-28069
E: info@grovehouseschull.com
W: www.grovehouseschull.com

BEDROOMS: 5.
OPEN: all year.
FACILITIES: bar, sitting room, dining room, wedding facilities, terrace, 1-acre garden, only dining room suitable for ♿.
BACKGROUND MUSIC: classical at breakfast.
LOCATION: outskirts of village.
CHILDREN: all ages welcomed.
DOGS: allowed in bedrooms.
CREDIT CARDS: all major cards.
PRICES: B&B €35–€45 per person, D,B&B €50–€65, set dinner €23, full alc €45.

SHANAGARRY Co. Cork

Map 6:D5

BALLYMALOE HOUSE

César award in 1984

'*Ballymaloe* remains as lovely as ever; a genuine country house hotel without pretension, and a true family affair.' Praise from inspectors returning this year to the Allen family's renowned ivy-covered Georgian mansion. Readers visiting in 2012 agree: 'we love the timeless feel; you are made to feel so secure and comfortable.' Founded by Myrtle Allen more than 40 years ago, the hotel/restaurant is managed by her daughter-in-law, Hazel; another daughter-in-law, Darina, runs the famous cookery school. 'Myrtle came to chat during dinner and was much in evidence at other times. We love the cultured atmosphere: books scattered around, interesting paintings and sculpture; no muzak, no little notes.' The mood in the dining rooms is 'cheerful, lots of chat and laughter'. The 'delicious' food is prepared by chef Jason Fahey: 'We had turbot with chopped scallops in an exquisite sauce; a lovely dish of stuffed marrow.' Bedrooms vary in size and view: 'Ours was cosy, two deep armchairs, a large wardrobe, good lighting, blankets and sheets on the bed; smallish but good bathroom.' Breakfast is a leisurely affair. (*Diane and David Skelton*)

25% DISCOUNT VOUCHERS

Shanagarry

T: 00 353 21-465 2531
F: 00 353 21-465 2021
E: res@ballymaloe.ie
W: www.ballymaloe.ie

BEDROOMS: 29, 7 in adjacent building, 4 on ground floor, 5 self-catering cottages.

OPEN: all year except 25/26 Dec, 3 weeks in Jan.

FACILITIES: drawing room, 2 small sitting rooms, conservatory, 7 dining rooms, wedding and conference facilities, 6-acre gardens, 400-acre grounds (tennis, swimming pool, 10 by 4 metres), cookery school nearby.

BACKGROUND MUSIC: none.

LOCATION: 20 miles E of Cork.

CHILDREN: all ages welcomed.

DOGS: allowed in courtyard rooms, not in house.

CREDIT CARDS: Amex, MasterCard, Visa.

PRICES: B&B €85–€130 per person, D,B&B €155–€200, set dinner €70, special breaks, New Year package.

WATERFORD Co. Waterford

Map 6:D5

FOXMOUNT COUNTRY HOUSE

On a working dairy farm, David and Margaret Kent's 'elegant' creeper-covered 17th-century house is reached by a long drive. The 'wonderful hosts run it as a B&B'. The homely, 'well-decorated' bedrooms, which face the gardens, have fresh fruit; good towels in the bathroom. Tea and home-made cakes are served in the traditionally decorated drawing room; a fire is lit in the evening, when guests may bring their own drinks before eating out in local restaurants (recommendations are given). Eight purpose-built kennels have been added; visiting dogs are promised the 'same service that their owners enjoy', including a twice-daily walk (bed and bowl €10 a night). Mrs Kent has won awards for her breakfasts; she turns to the garden for the ingredients of compotes and preserves; bread is home baked. Porridge might have raisins soaked in Irish whiskey. Free-range eggs are cooked to order. In the extensive grounds is a two-acre garden with manicured lawns, mature trees and a profusion of azaleas and rhododendrons. These come from Mount Congreve, one of a number of nearby gardens open to the public. More reports, please.

Passage East Road
Waterford

T: 00 353 51-874308
F: 00 353 51-854906
E: info@foxmountcountryhouse.com
W: www.foxmountcountryhouse.com

BEDROOMS: 4.
OPEN: Apr–Oct.
FACILITIES: sitting room, dining room, 2-acre gardens in 200-acre grounds, unsuitable for ♿.
BACKGROUND MUSIC: none.
LOCATION: 3 miles SW of Waterford.
CHILDREN: all ages welcomed.
DOGS: not allowed in house, kennels in grounds.
CREDIT CARDS: MasterCard, Visa.
PRICES: B&B €55–€65 per person.

SHORTLIST

The Shortlist complements our main section by including potential but untested new entries and appropriate places in areas where we have limited choice. It also has some hotels that have been full entries in the *Guide*, but have not attracted feedback from our readers.

Cley Windmill, Cley-next-the-Sea

LONDON

Map 2:D4
Avo Hotel, 82 Dalston Lane, Hackney, E8 3AH. Tel 020-3490 5061, www.avohotel.com. In Dalston, this friendly, eco-conscious hotel, run by Narendra Kotecha, has the added lure of a chocolate 'laboratory' on site (Wed–Sun; shop and chocolate-inspired drinks and brunches). The modern but snug black, white and purple bedrooms have iPod docking stations, memory foam mattresses, dressing gowns. Swish bathrooms. Sitting area. Complimentary DVDs; library; use of pay-as-you-go mobile phones. Occasional background music. Wi-Fi. Children welcomed. 6 bedrooms. B&B (continental) £79–£109. (Overground: Dalston Junction)

B+B Belgravia, 64–66 Ebury Street, SW1W 9QD. Tel 020-7259 8570, www.bb-belgravia.com. 'What a surprise. It was as nice a small hotel as we have ever stayed in.' In an elegant Grade II listed Georgian town house, managed by Arek Rapala, the decoration is clean-lined, contemporary and 'excellent'. 'A great deal for a London hotel.' Lounge (fireplace, complimentary tea/coffee/hot chocolate and biscuits, DVDs, library), open-plan kitchen/breakfast room (organic breakfasts), small garden. Free Wi-Fi and bicycles. No background music. Children and dogs welcomed. 17 bedrooms (2 family; 1 suitable for ♿), plus 9 studios close by. B&B £72.50–£99 per person. (Underground: Victoria)

base2stay, 25 Courtfield Gardens, SW5 0PG. Tel 020-7244 2255, www.base2stay.com. Part of a small hotel group whose goal is no-frills 'affordable luxury' (see also Liverpool), this pillared, white stucco town house has flexible accommodation decorated in a simple, modern style. It is managed by Sandra Anido. There is no restaurant or bar, but every room has a mini-kitchen, with a microwave and fridge. Guests receive discounts in shops in the Kensington/Earls Court area. An eco-friendly ethos is followed. Reception lobby (background music). Wi-Fi, music library, games. Children welcomed. 67 bedrooms (some with bunk beds; 1 suitable for ♿): £127–£220. (Underground: Earls Court, Gloucester Road)

Bermondsey Square Hotel, Bermondsey Square, Tower Bridge Road, SE1 3UN. Tel 020-7378 2450, www.bermondseysquarehotel.co.uk. In an increasingly vibrant area, well located for Borough Market, the South Bank, and galleries, restaurants and shops, this contemporary hotel has a 1970s flamboyance. Colourful bedrooms have Apple iMacs, and wet rooms with a drench shower; one suite, Lucy, has a private roof terrace and an 8-person hot tub. The newly opened *Gregg's Table* (Gregg Wallace's latest venture) has 'good, honest food' and alfresco dining. Background music. Business facilities. Lift. Wi-Fi. Children and dogs welcomed (boutique dog beds). 80 bedrooms (5 suites; some suitable for ♿): from £170. (Underground: Bermondsey, Tower Hill)

Charlotte Street Hotel, 15–17 Charlotte Street, W1T 1RJ. Tel 020-7806 2000, www.charlottestreethotel.com. A 'Bloomsbury Set' theme underlies the styling of this luxury hotel just north of Soho, which has original work by artists such as Vanessa Bell, Duncan Grant and Roger Fry. It is part of Tim and Kit Kemp's Firmdale group; Anna Jackson is the manager. Bedrooms are individually designed; bathrooms are solid granite, most with a walk-in shower and double basins. Drawing room, library, *Oscar* bar, open-plan restaurant (run by chef Rachel Hitchcock). 3 private dining/meeting rooms, 75-seat screening room, gym. No background music. Children welcomed. 52 bedrooms: £230–£1,050 (*excluding VAT*). Breakfast £18–£20. (Underground: Goodge Street, Tottenham Court Road)

CORINTHIA HOTEL LONDON, Whitehall Place, SW1A 2BD. Tel 020-7930 8181, www.corinthia.com. 'You are transported to a world where everything is beyond reproach.' Near Trafalgar Square, in the former home of the Ministry of Defence, this hotel was lavishly redesigned in April 2012 in classical contemporary style. Part of the Corinthia Hotels collection, it is managed by Matthew Dixon. Grand public areas are vast and light, with decorative pillars and stunning chandeliers. Spacious, elegant bedrooms have parquet flooring, and a TV in the marble bathroom. The spa takes up four floors. Lounge, bar, 2 restaurants: *The Northall* (British cuisine) and *Massimo Restaurant and Oyster Bar*, specialising in seafood. Courtyard. Gym; spa (sauna, hammam, steam room; beauty treatments). Background music in some areas. Civil wedding licence/function facilities. Wi-Fi. Children welcomed. 294 bedrooms and suites: from £407. Breakfast £26–£31. (Underground: Charing Cross)

COUNTY HALL PREMIER INN, Belvedere Road, SE1 7PB. Tel 0871-527 8648, www.premierinn.com. In the old County Hall building beside the London Eye, this busy hotel (owned by Whitbread) is just across the river from the Houses of Parliament and many tourist attractions. With comfortable, simply furnished rooms (and double-glazed windows), it is good value for money. Ed Pyke is the operations manager. Self-service check-in. Lobby, bar, *Thyme* restaurant; lift. Conference facilities. Background music. Children welcomed. 314 bedrooms (some suitable for ♿): from £189. Meal deal (dinner and breakfast) £22 per person. (Underground: Waterloo)

DORSET SQUARE HOTEL, 39–40 Dorset Square, Marylebone, NW1 6QN. Tel 020-7723 7874, www.firmdalehotels.com. Kit and Tim Kemp recently reacquired and reopened this Regency town house – the first in their Firmdale Hotels portfolio – on a private garden square in Marylebone. It has been enlivened by Kit Kemp's signature interiors: bold colours, exciting textiles, bespoke and original pieces. It is managed by Eva Mount. The contemporary, English-style bedrooms have a marble bathroom, and come equipped with an iPod docking station; many overlook the leafy square. The plush drawing room has an open fireplace. Drawing room, bar, *The Potting Shed* brasserie. No background music. Room service. DVD library. 38 bedrooms: £150–£330. (Underground: Marylebone)

DUKES HOTEL, 35 St James's Place, SW1A 1NY. Tel 020-7491 4840, www.dukeshotel.com. In a peaceful courtyard, this discreet town house hotel has a mix of contemporary and traditional furnishing and artwork, up-to-date technology and glamorous bathrooms. It is owned by the Dubai-based Seven Tides group; Debrah Dhugga is the manager. A 'Cigar and Cognac Garden' and 'PJ Champagne Lounge' are recent additions. Drawing room (afternoon tea), bar, conservatory, *Thirty Six* restaurant (classic British food with a modern twist; Nigel Mendham is the new chef); 24-hour room service; health club; courtyard garden. Background music. Wi-Fi. Children welcomed. 90 bedrooms: £318–£485. Breakfast £16–£24, dinner £60–£85. (Underground: Green Park)

THE EGERTON HOUSE HOTEL, 17–19 Egerton Terrace, SW3 2BX. Tel 020-7589 2412, www.egertonhousehotel.com. Well placed for the museums and Knightsbridge shopping, this luxury town house hotel (Red Carnation group) is managed by Rosslee Wagenaar. Rooms are sumptuously decorated and well equipped (iPod docking station, flat-screen TV, etc). Guests have use of a gym and pool at a local club. Drawing room, bar (classical background music), breakfast room. 24-hour butler service. Lift. Wi-Fi. Children welcomed. Valet parking. 30 bedrooms (some on ground floor): £384–£468. Breakfast £17–£24.50, dinner £60. (Underground: Knightsbridge, South Kensington)

41, 41 Buckingham Palace Road, SW1W 0PS. Tel 020-7300 0041, www.41hotel.com. Overlooking the Royal Mews at Buckingham Palace, this discreet luxury hotel has the atmosphere of a London club. It is on the fifth floor of its sister hotel, *The Rubens* (both are part of the Red Carnation Hotel Collection). A black-and-white theme prevails, offset by mahogany panelling and polished brass. The lounge has leather seating, a fireplace and a glass roof. Bedrooms are equipped with state-of-the-art technology; bathrooms are ultra chic. From 8.30 pm, guests are invited to 'plunder the pantry' and help themselves to complimentary snacks and light bites. The ratio of staff to guests is high; Frederic Dallot is the manager. Room, and butler service. Background music. Wi-Fi. Business facilities. Complimentary pass to nearby fitness club (swimming pool, sauna, spa). Children and dogs welcomed. 30 bedrooms and suites: £322–£499. Breakfast £19.50–£25. (Underground: Victoria)

FOX & ANCHOR, 115 Charterhouse Street, EC1M 6AA. Tel 020-7250 1300, www.foxandanchor.com. With Smithfield market directly across the street, there is a wide selection of eating and shopping options on the doorstep of this renovated Victorian pub-with-rooms (part of the Malmaison group). The bustling interior has plenty of original features (mahogany doors, etched glass, heavy brass), cosy snugs. Bedrooms have a king-size bed, surround-sound hi-fi, a claw-footed bath and a drench shower. Real ales and more than 40 varieties of whisky are available to accompany the traditional British food. Scott Malaugh is manager. Dining room, 3 snugs, bar. Background music. Some late-night/early-morning street noise. 6 bedrooms: £95–£275 (*excluding VAT*). Breakfast £8.95, dinner £25. (Underground: Barbican)

The Halkin, 5 Halkin Street, SW1X 7DJ. Tel 020-7333 1000, www.halkin.como.bz. A minimalist, sophisticated blend of Asian and Italian design on a quiet Belgravia side street, this hotel belongs to the COMO group. Bedrooms have a king-size bed and a marble bathroom; a touch-screen console controls lighting, temperature and the doorbell, and connects guests with guest services and the butler. Australian chef David Thompson serves Thai food in nahm restaurant; the bar serves snacks and afternoon tea. Background music in bar and restaurant. Guests have access to the Shambhala Urban Escape spa in sister hotel *Metropolitan* on Park Lane. Bar, restaurant. Gym (trainer and yoga teacher available). Wi-Fi. Children welcomed. 41 bedrooms: £260–£972. (Underground: Hyde Park Corner)

Haymarket Hotel, 1 Suffolk Place, SW1Y 4HX. Tel 020-7470 4000, www.haymarkethotel.com. In the heart of the theatre district, three John Nash-designed buildings have been 'beautifully decorated' in bold, contemporary style by Kit Kemp of Firmdale Hotels. There is plenty to make young guests feel welcome in this family-friendly hotel, managed by Lisa Brooklyn: DVDs and popcorn, books, Nintendo Wii, etc. Lift, drawing room, library, bar, *Brumus* restaurant; background music. Civil wedding licence. 'Stunning' indoor swimming pool, gym. 50 bedrooms: £250–£2,500. (Underground: Green Park, Piccadilly)

High Road House, 162–170 Chiswick High Road, W4 1PR. Tel 020-8742 1717, house.highroadhouse.co.uk. Owned by the Soho House group, this hotel/private members' club is decorated in retro-modern style. Food is served all day in the brasserie (some outdoor seating) and bar. Minimalist bedrooms come in 'tiny', 'small' or 'playroom' size; all have a king-size bed. There are various areas open to members and guests: the Games Room has red leather sofas, TV, table football, pool table, board games; the Playground has low-level seating and a large screen for watching TV and films; the Playpen has comfortable seating and a bar. Kristen Cronin is the manager. Background music. Wi-Fi. 14 bedrooms: £155–£195. English breakfast from £11. (Underground: Turnham Green)

Hotel 55, 55 Hanger Lane, W5 3HL. Tel 020-8991 4450, www.hotel55-london.com. A chic, contemporary interior hides behind the Edwardian facade of this hotel in the west London suburbs. It has been fully restored by the Tohani family, and has bespoke modern furniture and original artwork; a decked walkway leads to the landscaped garden. Bedrooms are compact; garden rooms are quietest. The hotel is managed by Tiberius Tordavescu. 24-hour lounge bar (background music), *Momo* restaurant. Wi-Fi. Children welcomed. 30 mins from Heathrow and central London by tube. Limited free parking. 26 bedrooms (some suitable for ♿). B&B (continental) £85–£129 per person. Dinner from £35. (Underground: North Ealing)

The Hoxton, 81 Great Eastern Street, EC2A 3HU. Tel 020-7550 1000, www.hoxtonhotels.com. In the centre of hip Hoxton, this 'urban lodge' holds a £1-a-room sale online every three months. Mirroring the booking policies of budget airlines, the price of the remaining rooms increases as availability decreases. 'Intensely stylish', the industrial interior (bare brick walls, polished concrete, leather sofas) is 'curiously comforting'. Three bedrooms have been decorated by renowned designers; others, 'well equipped', are done in milk and dark chocolate colours. A Pret a Manger Lite breakfast is included in the room rate. Alternatively, in the 'very buzzy' *Hoxton Grill* brasserie and bar, the food is 'simply excellent'. Lounge (background music) and outdoor space (interior courtyard); lift. Meeting rooms; shop. Wi-Fi. Children welcomed. 205 rooms. B&B £189. (Underground: Old Street)

H10 London Waterloo, 284–302 Waterloo Road, SE1 8RQ. Tel 020-7928 4062, www.hotelh10londonwaterloo.com. 'Standards are high' at this good-value Spanish chain hotel in a purpose-built 11-storey block with a contemporary interior. Sleek, compact bedrooms have feature wallpaper and large windows. 'The cooking was excellent; starters were particularly outstanding. There was a breakfast buffet of considerable size.' It is on a busy road, south of Waterloo station (some traffic noise). Lounge, bar, *Three O Two* restaurant; leisure centre (gym, sauna, hydromassage shower; treatments); meeting rooms. Wi-Fi. 177 bedrooms: £159–£309. Breakfast £16, dinner £30. (Underground: Waterloo)

Indigo, 16 London Street, W2 1HL. Tel 020-7706 4444, www.hipaddington.com. Nine adjoining Georgian houses form the exterior of this trendy hotel (part of the InterContinental Hotels Group), managed by Denise Kelton. It is three minutes' walk from Paddington station and the London–Heathrow Express. Inside are wood floors, striking colours and photographic murals of interesting local architecture. Lounge/lobby, bar, brasserie, terrace. Background music. Fitness studio. Wi-Fi. Children welcomed. 64 bedrooms (some with private balcony or terrace; 2 suitable for ♿): £99–£185. Breakfast from £10.95, dinner £30. (Underground: Paddington)
25% DISCOUNT VOUCHERS

Knightsbridge Hotel, 10 Beaufort Gardens, SW3 1PT. Tel 020-7584 6300, www.knightsbridgehotel.com. Near the shops, this white-pillared town house hotel stands in a peaceful, tree-lined cul-de-sac. It is managed by Fiona Milne for the Firmdale group. Decorated with flair and colour, it has an intimate feel: cosy sitting areas have 20th-century British art, open fires. Bathrooms are done in granite and oak. Afternoon tea is also available to non-residents. Drawing room, library, bar. Room-service meals. No background music. Wi-Fi. 44 bedrooms (*excluding VAT*): £195–£675. Breakfast £19. (Underground: Knightsbridge)

The Main House, 6 Colville Road, Notting Hill, W11 2BP. Tel 020-7221 9691, www.themainhouse.co.uk. On a quiet street off Portobello Road, Caroline Main's stylish Victorian town house B&B is the antithesis of a large chain hotel. In this 'elegant home from home', each suite occupies an entire floor and has period features, antique furnishings, modern technology, and an airy, uncluttered look. No background music. Guests may borrow a mobile phone and DVDs. There are special rates for day membership at Lambton Place health club; a smart deli and an artisan baker are nearby. Roof terrace. Wi-Fi. Children welcomed. 4 bedrooms: from £55 per person (excluding breakfast; no single-night bookings). (Underground: Notting Hill Gate)

The Orange, 37 Pimlico Road, SW1W 8NE. Tel 020-7881 9844, www.theorange.co.uk. Renovated in chic rustic style, this old public house, with buzzing restaurant above and bedrooms on the second floor up narrow stairs, is in an impressive white-painted building dating back to 1846. It is owned by the Cubitt House group (see also *The Grazing Goat*, Marble Arch, London, main entry). Rooms (some compact) have limewash paint, king-size beds, marble bathrooms; iPod docking station. 'We were impressed by the attention to detail.' Bar, dining room. Traditional and fish dishes, as well as 'very good' pizzas from a wood-fired oven. Background music (soul, jazz). Wi-Fi. Children welcomed. 4 bedrooms: £195–£225. Breakfast £3–£12. (Underground: Sloane Square, Victoria)

The Rookery, 12 Peter's Lane, Cowcross Street, EC1M 6DS. Tel 020-7336 0931, www.rookeryhotel.com. Three Georgian houses, once at the centre of the lawless slum after which the hotel is named, have been painstakingly restored to create this small luxury hotel. From the Rook's Nest Suite on the top floor, there are views of St Paul's Cathedral and the Old Bailey. Public rooms and bedrooms have period features; even the bathroom fittings are antique. Peter McKay and Douglas Blain (who also own *Hazlitt's*, Soho, London, see main entry) are the owners. Drawing room, library, conservatory; courtyard garden; meeting rooms. No restaurant, but a limited room-service menu is available. No background music. Children welcomed. 33 bedrooms: £225–£299. (Underground: Farringdon, Barbican)

St James's Hotel and Club, 7–8 Park Place, SW1A 1LS. Tel 020-7316 1600, www.stjameshotelandclub.com. This opulent town house hotel, managed by Henrik Muehle (for the Althoff Hotel & Gourmet Collection), is in a quiet cul-de-sac. It has chandeliers; furnishings and decorations of silk, velvet and cashmere; restful bedrooms (some have their own balcony); and a dramatic dining room. Original artwork includes a collection of portraits from the 1920s to the 1950s. Lounge, bar, *William's* bar and bistro, *Seven Park Place* (*Michelin* star; under the direction of chef William Drabble; closed Sun, Mon). Background music. 4 meeting rooms. Wi-Fi. Children welcomed. 60 bedrooms (10 suites; 2 on ground floor): £250–£485; suites from £440. Breakfast £16–£22. (Underground: Green Park)

St John Hotel, 1 Leicester Street, WC2H 7BL. Tel 020-3301 8069, www.stjohnhotellondon.com. Trevor Gulliver and chef Fergus Henderson (the team behind the renowned *St John*

Bar and Restaurant, Smithfield) have transformed the famous *Manzi's* restaurant into a white, minimalist restaurant-with-rooms. Bedrooms have bright green floors and sparkling bathrooms; they come as Mini Grand, Urban Hut or Post-Supper (smaller, these latter rooms 'remove the need for a taxi home after supper'). The Long Room at the top of the building can be extended to include three bedrooms and a large living area. Tom Harris and sous-chef Jon Rotheram cater for breakfast, lunch and dinner, along with elevenses and 'Little Bun Moments' in the afternoon. No background music. Bar, restaurant. 15 bedrooms (1, on ground floor, suitable for ♿): £240–£420. Breakfast from £18. (Underground: Leicester Square, Piccadilly Circus)

ST PANCRAS RENAISSANCE LONDON HOTEL, Euston Road, NW1 2AR. Tel 020-7841 3540, www.marriott.co.uk. Beautifully renovated, Sir Gilbert Scott's glamorous Victorian-Gothic railway hotel retains spectacular architectural and decorative features and fittings in the public areas. Most bedrooms are in a modern extension and have a contemporary decor; 38 rooms in the original structure have period fittings. Marcus Wareing is the chef for the *Gilbert Scott* bar and restaurant, where the cooking style is inspired by old recipes and English culinary heritage. Lounge, meeting rooms, spa (treatments; barber), health club (pool, gym). Background music in lobby and restaurant. Wi-Fi. Parking (£50 per day). Pets allowed by arrangement. 245 bedrooms and suites: £355–£795. (Underground: King's Cross St Pancras)

THE SANCTUARY HOUSE, 33 Tothill Street, SW1H 9LA. Tel 020-7799 4044, www.fullershotels.com. In a 'first-class' location near Westminster Abbey and the Houses of Parliament, there are good-value rooms above a popular pub (part of Fuller's Hotels and Inns), updated from a traditional Victorian ale-and-pie house. Bedrooms are 'very comfortable', with modern bathrooms; some have a four-poster bed. Sol Yepes is the manager. Bar, restaurant. Background music. Lift. Room service. Wi-Fi. Children welcomed. 34 bedrooms: £45–£137.50 per person (some suitable for ♿). Breakfast £9.25–£12.90. (Underground: St James's Park)

THE SLOANE SQUARE, 7–12 Sloane Square, SW1W 8EG. Tel 020-7896 9988, www.sloanesquarehotel.co.uk. On a fashionable South Kensington square, this newly opened 'very pleasant' hotel is managed by Richard Mackie, with 'nice, helpful staff'. Snug rooms decorated in light, modern colours are 'brilliantly fitted out; not an inch of space wasted'. Smart fixtures include a flat-screen TV with sports channels, a DVD-player, an iPod docking station and a PlayStation console. In the restaurant, chef Simon Henbery's seasonal, modern European dishes are 'good brasserie standard, pleasantly served'. Tapas-style food is available in the bar. *Chelsea brasserie* (background music), bar. Lift. Wi-Fi. Free national calls. Parking (charge). Children welcomed. 102 bedrooms: £165 per person. Breakfast from £16. (Underground: Sloane Square)

THE SOHO HOTEL, 4 Richmond Mews, off Dean Street, W1D 3DH. Tel 020-7559 3000, www.sohohotel.com. A glamorous hotel with funky touches, this Firmdale property sits in a quiet side street in the heart of Soho. Carrie Wicks is the manager. Bedrooms are spacious, with a luxurious bathroom. Families are welcomed (children's menu, books, Sony PlayStation, Nintendo Wii, DVDs and popcorn). Drawing room, library, bar, *Refuel* restaurant, 4 private dining rooms; background music. Gym. 2 screening rooms; DVD library. Lift. Civil wedding licence. Children welcomed. 91 bedrooms and suites (some suitable for ♿; excluding VAT): £295–£2,250. Also 4 apartments. Breakfast £20. (Underground: Leicester Square)

SYDNEY HOUSE CHELSEA, 9–11 Sydney Street, SW3 6PU. Tel 020-7376 7711, www.sydneyhousechelsea.com. This Georgian town house (part of Brownsword Hotels' Baby ABode collection), on seven floors, has a sleek interior and every modern comfort. Rooms are bright and spacious, with up-to-date technology. The Room at the Top has a 'romantic' private roof garden. Drawing room, bar, restaurant (open to non-residents for breakfast), room service (light snacks); roof terrace; boardroom. Background music in lobby. Wi-Fi. Children welcomed. 21 bedrooms: £125–£280. Breakfast from £6. (Underground: South Kensington)

TEN MANCHESTER STREET, Marylebone, W1U 4DG. Tel 020-7317 5900, www.tenmanchesterstreethotel.com. 'You are definitely comfortable here.' This discreet, designer-furnished hotel, in a red brick Edwardian town house (part of Bespoke Hotels Ltd), is in a residential area just off Marylebone High Street. Most rooms are small, but quiet; four open on to an outdoor terrace with seating, music and heaters. A set menu for lunch and dinner and an all-day snack menu are available in the cosy, L-shaped *Ten Lounge Bar*. For cigar smokers, there is a humidor and large cigar menu, and an all-weather smoking terrace. 'Service is attentive and helpful overall.' The manager is Stefano Lodi. Lounge/bar (background music). Wi-Fi. 24-hour room service; chauffeur service on request. 45 bedrooms (9 suites): £152–£400. Breakfast £15.95–£17.95. (Underground: Bond Street)

THREADNEEDLES, 5 Threadneedle Street, EC2R 8AY. Tel 020-7657 8080, www.theetoncollection.com. In the City, close to the Bank of England, this hotel was converted from a Victorian banking hall. It has an impressive stained-glass dome over the reception lounge, marble floors, walnut panelling and ornate pillars. Five new bedrooms were being built as the *Guide* went to press. Modern rooms have contemporary art on the walls; bathrooms have a limestone bath. The hotel is part of the Eton Collection; Brian Tapson is the new manager. Background music. Bar, *Bonds* restaurant (French cuisine and tapas; Stephen Smith has taken over as chef; closed at weekends). Lift. 3 meeting rooms; conference facilities. Wi-Fi. 74 bedrooms (some suitable for ♿): £417–£702. Breakfast £22.95. (Underground: Bank)

TOWN HALL HOTEL & APARTMENTS, Patriot Square, E2 9NF. Tel 020-7871 0460, www.townhallhotel.com. Hotelier

Peng Loh has brought this imposing Grade II listed Edwardian building, formerly Bethnal Green's town hall, back to life. Marie Baxter is the manager. Marble pillars, a green stone lobby and a vast council chamber have been restored; Art Deco features have been accentuated, and contemporary design added. Bedrooms are stark, in wood and white, with vintage pieces. Many have a mini-kitchen. Downstairs, *Viajante* restaurant is run by Portuguese chef Nuno Mendes, who has a *Michelin* star for his experimental fusion food. Bar, 2 restaurants. Background music. Civil wedding licence/function facilities. Lift. Wi-Fi. Indoor pool, gym (open 6 am to midnight). Children welcomed. 98 bedrooms and studios (with kitchen): £192–£245. Breakfast from £15. (Underground: Bethnal Green)

ENGLAND

ALDEBURGH Suffolk
Map 2:C6
OCEAN HOUSE, 25 Crag Path, IP15 5BS. Tel 01728-452094, www.oceanhousealdeburgh.co.uk. On the seafront, with bay windows that almost hang over the town's shingle beach, Juliet and Phil Brereton's restored Victorian house makes a homely B&B. It is simply decorated with period furniture. The suite on the second floor has a sitting room with stove, baby grand piano, and sea views in all directions. A 'good choice' is available at the communal breakfast, including vegetarian options; marmalade, bread and spicy scones are all home made. Dining room (open fire, no background music). Bikes may be borrowed; table tennis. 3 bedrooms. B&B £50–£62.50 per person.
25% DISCOUNT VOUCHERS

WHITE LION, Market Cross Place, IP15 5BJ. Tel 01728-452720, www.whitelion.co.uk. On the beachfront and close to town, this recently refurbished hotel has 'the delights of the location' and 'stylishly reconfigured public rooms and spaces'. It is owned by TA Hotel Collection, a small group of Suffolk hotels. Bedrooms have an ocean and beach freshness; many face the sea. A contemporary all-day brasserie, run by head chef Jason Shaw, serves 'back-to-basics' food using local produce. 'Excellent' breakfasts. Background music. Bar, brasserie; private dining room. Wi-Fi. Children and dogs welcomed. 38 bedrooms (14 are sea-facing). B&B £68–£210 per person.

ALFRISTON East Sussex
Map 2:E4
DEANS PLACE, Seaford Road, BN26 5TW. Tel 01323-870248, www.deansplacehotel.co.uk. Michael Clinch's country hotel, evolved from a large farm estate, sits at the foot of the South Downs national park. In a beautiful setting close to the River Cuckmere, it is perfect walking country, and convenient for Glyndebourne: picnic hampers can be arranged. Graeme Coles manages, with 'helpful, friendly and efficient' staff. 'We had a really good stay, and would return.' Lounge, bar, *Harcourts* restaurant (chef Stuart Dunley's modern British food is 'excellent'; background music). 3-acre garden, terrace, putting lawn, heated outdoor swimming pool (May–Sept). Meeting/conference rooms. Civil

wedding licence. Parking. Wi-Fi. Children and dogs welcomed. 10 miles from town centre. 36 bedrooms (some with four-poster; 1 suitable for ♿). B&B £57.50–£92.50 per person; D,B&B £87.50–£122.50.
25% DISCOUNT VOUCHERS

Wingrove House, High Street, BN26 5TD. Tel 01323-870276, www.wingrovehousealfriston.com. Nick Denyer's restaurant-with-rooms is in a 19th-century colonial-style house with a veranda and terrace for alfresco dining. The colonial clubhouse theme extends into the public areas with leather seating, wall antlers and a wood-burning stove. The dining room and bedrooms have stylish furnishings, seagrass flooring and bespoke chandeliers. Ian Graham is the manager. Modern European cooking features locally reared meat and game, and fish and organic produce sourced from nearby suppliers. Background music. Lounge/bar, brasserie (closed Mon–Fri lunchtime). Wi-Fi. Children welcomed. 5 bedrooms (2 with access to balcony). B&B £42.50–£90 per person. Dinner from £30.

ALNWICK Northumberland
Map 4:A4
The Old School, Newton on the Moor, NE65 9JY. Tel 01665-575767, www.theoldschool.eu. In south-facing gardens surrounded by woodland, Kath and Malcolm Downes's stylish B&B is in an 18th-century stone property in a conservation village. The bedrooms have contemporary colours, modern fittings. Impressive choice at breakfast, using Northumberland ingredients. Sitting room, dining room (classical background music). ½-acre garden. Wi-Fi (most of house). Parking. 4 bedrooms (1 ground-floor business suite). B&B £45–£50 per person. Closed Dec.

AMBLESIDE Cumbria
Map 4: inset C2
Nanny Brow, LA22 9NF. Tel 015394-33232, www.nannybrow.co.uk. 'A most attractive view.' Up a steep, winding drive, Sue and Peter Robinson's Arts and Crafts house stands on a crag above Brathay valley and has direct access to the fells. Maintaining many original features, the Robinsons refurbished the interior in 2011 to provide guest house accommodation with large rooms, modern fabrics and antiques; eco-efficient improvements include a biomass boiler, insulation and thermal blackout blinds. Light two-course suppers may be ordered in advance (not available on Fri, Sat eve). Lakeland breakfasts. Lounge, bar, dining room. Background music. Wi-Fi. Parking. 6 acres of formal garden and woodlands; 1½ miles W of town. Resident dog and cat. 8 bedrooms (some on ground floor). B&B £60–£145 per person.
25% DISCOUNT VOUCHERS

ARNSIDE Cumbria
Map 4: inset C2
Number 43, The Promenade, LA5 0AA. Tel 01524-762761, www.no43.org.uk. From the front terrace of this contemporary B&B on the promenade, guests may enjoy wonderful vistas, birdwatch or catch sight of the tidal bore wave that sweeps into the estuary twice a day. The secluded terrace at the back has a working Victorian fireplace for barbecues on summer evenings. Owner Lesley

Hornsby has given her house, one in a row of Victorian hillside villas, a light, airy, coastal look. Bathrooms have underfloor heating, robes and a magnifying mirror. Traditional Cumbrian breakfasts; home-baked muffins. Light suppers Nov–Mar, by arrangement. Lounge (books, magazines, CDs), dining room (honesty bar); garden; front and rear terrace. Wi-Fi. Children over 5 allowed. 6 bedrooms (some with estuary views). B&B £60–£160 per person.

ARUNDEL West Sussex
Map 2:E3
BURPHAM COUNTRY HOUSE, The Street, BN18 9RJ. Tel 01903-882160, www.burphamcountryhouse.com. Within the South Downs national park, this cream-painted 18th-century building – formerly a hunting lodge, then a rectory – is run as a small country hotel by owners Stephen and Jackie Penticost. It is in an 'idyllically remote', peaceful village, 3 miles NE of Arundel. 'We had a comfortable stay.' Steve, 'a mine of information who genuinely enjoys his guests', cooks modern French brasserie food using local or garden produce, and serves it in the elegant Georgian dining room or the airy conservatory. 2 lounges, restaurant (open to non-residents, background music); garden (free-range chickens). Children allowed (in ground-floor room); dogs by arrangement. Resident cat, Lucy. 9 bedrooms. B&B £35–£70 per person. Dinner £40. Closed Jan.

BAMPTON Devon
Map 1:C5
THE BARK HOUSE, Oakfordbridge, EX16 9HZ. Tel 01398-351236, www.thebarkhouse.co.uk. In the Exe valley near Exmoor national park, this wisteria-clad cottage was built to store bark for use in the tanning process. It is now a guest house with comfortable rooms. Owners Melanie McKnight and Martin French welcome guests with afternoon tea and home-made cake by an open fire in the cosy lounge. 'Generous', freshly prepared dinners use local ingredients; Sunday lunches are also available for non-residents. By busy road, 6 miles S of Dulverton. Lounge, dining room (Celtic background music). Garden. Wi-Fi. Children and dogs welcomed. Parking. 6 bedrooms. B&B £45–£60 per person. Dinner (2 courses; Tues–Sat) £22.

BARNSLEY Gloucestershire
Map 3:E6
THE VILLAGE PUB, Barnsley, GL7 5EF. Tel 01285-740421, www.thevillagepub.co.uk. In a pretty Cotswold village, this classic pub-with-rooms, managed by Michele Mella, is under the same ownership as *Calcot Manor*, Tetbury, and *Barnsley House*, up the street (see main entries). The sophisticated, country-style bedrooms have a separate entrance from the pub; some have exposed beams and a four-poster bed. In the welcoming dining room – with beams, wooden and stone floors, and fresh flowers, chef Graham Grafton serves contemporary cuisine, much of it locally sourced or from *Barnsley House*'s kitchen garden. Guests may take afternoon tea at *Barnsley House* and tour its gardens or, for a fee, use the hotel's spa and private cinema. English farmhouse breakfasts. 6 bedrooms. B&B £62.50–£160 per person. Dinner £40.

BATH Somerset
Map 2:D1

Aquae Sulis, 174–176 Newbridge Road, BA1 3LE. Tel 01225-420061, www.aquaesulishotel.co.uk. A short bus ride from the centre, or a pleasant 30-minute stroll along the river, David and Jane Carnegie's traditional guest house is in an Edwardian house in the suburbs. It has an informal ambience and simply furnished bedrooms with a modern bathroom. There is an evening snack menu. French and Spanish are spoken. Lounge bar, dining room, computer lounge; patio/garden. Wi-Fi; iPod docking stations. Background music. Courtesy car to and from Bath Spa railway and bus station. Parking and unrestricted parking on road. Children welcomed; dogs by arrangement. 14 bedrooms (1 large one in annexe). B&B £35–£99 per person.

Brindleys, 14 Pulteney Gardens, BA2 4HG. Tel 01225-310444, www.brindleysbath.co.uk. 'We did like it here.' There is an elegant French-style interior in this family-owned Victorian villa, which has white-painted furniture, pretty fabrics and fresh flowers in light-filled rooms. Owned by Michael and Sarah Jones, it is run as a B&B with great enthusiasm by James Grundy and his wife, Anel. In a quiet residential area south of the city (ten-minute walk to the centre), it has 'very nice' bedrooms (some are small). Breakfast is taken in a 'smart' room overlooking the 'attractive' front garden. Lounge, breakfast room ('easy listening' background music); small garden. Wi-Fi. Complimentary on-street parking permits supplied. 6 bedrooms. B&B £55–£110 per person. 2-night min. stay at weekends preferred.

Dorian House, 1 Upper Oldfield Park, BA2 3JX. Tel 01225-426336, www.dorianhouse.co.uk. Imbued with a musical ambience, this B&B in a Victorian stone house is owned by 'friendly, chatty' Tim (a cellist) and Kathryn Hugh. It is on a steep incline, and has 'fabulous' views over the city. Restful bedrooms, named after musicians, have views over the Royal Crescent or gardens. The black-and-white tiled foyer has a huge stained-glass window, original and unusual modern art, and framed music scores on the walls. Robert and Lize Briers are the managers. Lounge (with an open fire), breakfast room/music library; classical background music. Wi-Fi. 'Immaculate, vertiginous' small garden. A ten-minute downhill walk to the centre (plenty of buses come back up the hill). Parking. Children welcomed. 13 bedrooms (1 on ground floor). B&B £40–£78 per person.

Dukes Hotel, Great Pulteney Street, BA2 4DN. Tel 01225-787960, www.dukesbath.co.uk. Near the city centre, this sandstone town house has period furnishing, fine fabrics, prints and portraits. It is owned by Alan Brookes and Michael Bokenham; Tina Paradise is the manager. Bedrooms are elegantly furnished and have richly coloured walls. Lounge, bar, *Cavendish* restaurant in basement (Roland Hughes is the new chef; background music). Patio garden with pond and fountain (alfresco dining). Wi-Fi. Parking permits can be reserved. Children welcomed. 17 bedrooms (1 on ground floor). B&B £60.50–£192 per person. Dinner from £45.

The Halcyon, 2–3 South Parade, BA2 4AA. Tel 01225-444100, www.thehalcyon.com. Close to the station and the Roman Baths, this Grade I listed Georgian building is a contemporary hotel managed by Hector Main. Chic bedrooms are small, with vividly coloured headboards, covers and cushions; those higher up are quietest. An atmospheric, low-lit vaulted cellar, done in grey and burnt orange with leather chesterfields, old panelling and modern artwork, houses the large cocktail bar, lounge and dining area (noisy at night). Bicycles are provided, along with recommendations for places to eat and drink in, and to explore. Organic breakfasts. Lounge, café/*Circo* bar (light meals, snacks served Wed–Sun; background music). Small courtyard. Wi-Fi. Secure reserved parking nearby. Children welcomed. 21 bedrooms, plus 4 self-catering studio apartments. B&B £49.50–£188 per person.

Harington's Hotel, 8–10 Queen Street, BA1 1HE. Tel 01225-461728, www.haringtonshotel.co.uk. On a quiet, cobbled Georgian side street in the centre, Melissa and Peter O'Sullivan's small contemporary hotel (managed by Julian Mather) is just over 300 yards from the Roman Baths. Jewel-toned bedspreads and cushions provide colour in otherwise neutral bedrooms. All-day snacks are served in the café/bar; staff are happy to advise on local restaurants. Lounge, café/bar (background music). Small courtyard. Wi-Fi. Secure reserved parking nearby (£11 for 24 hrs). Children welcomed. 13 bedrooms, plus 2 self-catering apartments. B&B £44–£79 per person.

The Kennard, 11 Henrietta Street, BA2 6LL. Tel 01225-310472, www.kennard.co.uk. 'Excellent in every respect.' Mary and Giovanni Baiano are the 'very welcoming and helpful' owners of this conveniently situated town house B&B (built in 1794) just over Pulteney Bridge. The interior is ornate, with a touch of Italian flamboyance on the landings (there are 6 flights of stairs). The small Georgian-style garden is inspired by Jane Austen. 'Superlative breakfast.' No background music. 2 sitting areas, breakfast room; courtyard. Children over 8 allowed. Drivers are given a free parking permit. 12 bedrooms (2 on ground floor; 2 share a bathroom). B&B £55–£80 per person.

Paradise House, 86–88 Holloway, BA2 4PX. Tel 01225-317723, www.paradise-house.co.uk. In a walled landscaped garden, with panoramic views over the city (a ten-minute walk downhill), this listed Georgian house with a Victorian extension has been elegantly refurbished by owners David and Annie Lanz; Nicci and Russell Clarke are the managers. Bedrooms are equipped with a modern entertainment system; some have a four-poster bed. Drawing room, breakfast room. Classical background music. Wi-Fi. Parking for 6 cars. Children welcomed. 11 bedrooms (4 on ground floor, 2 in annexe). B&B £35–£95 per person.

Three Abbey Green, 3 Abbey Green, BA1 1NW. Tel 01225-428558, www.threeabbeygreen.com. In a Grade II listed town house on a quiet square in the heart of Bath, this 'very comfortable, friendly' B&B is run by mother and daughter Sue Wright and Nici Jones, who provide visitors with much information about the city. Handsome bedrooms retain original features such as wood panelling, fireplaces, antiques. There is 'a good choice of breakfast, all freshly cooked and served promptly'. Dining room (background radio). Close to the Abbey, Roman Baths and Pump Rooms. Wi-Fi (computer available). Children welcomed. 7 bedrooms (2 family suites). B&B £46–£180 per person. 2-night min. stay at weekends.

BELFORD Northumberland
Map 4:A3
WAREN HOUSE, Waren Mill, NE70 7EE. Tel 01668-214581, www.warenhousehotel.co.uk. 'We loved the house, the tranquil surroundings, our comfortable and spacious room.' Six miles from Bamburgh, Anita and Peter Laverack's Georgian country house is 'in a lovely spot' with views of Holy Island, and it overlooks the natural bird sanctuary of Budle Bay. Head chef Steve Owens's 'beautifully cooked and presented' modern Northumberland dishes are 'superb'. Steve's wife, Lynne, manages the hotel. Drawing room, *Grays* restaurant (open to non-residents). No background music. Wi-Fi. Formal garden in 6-acre grounds; secure parking. Dogs welcomed. 15 bedrooms (3 suites; 4 rooms in courtyard; 2 suitable for ♿). B&B £75–£140 per person.

BELPER Derbyshire
Map 2:A2
DANNAH FARM, Bowmans Lane, Shottle, DE56 2DR. Tel 01773-550273, www.dannah.co.uk. Set on a ridge above the Ecclesbourne valley, Joan and Martin Slack's Derbyshire Dales country B&B is part of a working farm. Many bedrooms have a spa bath; a Leisure Cabin (available for exclusive use) houses a Finnish sauna, double steam shower and outdoor hot tub. Farmhouse cooked breakfasts; supper platters available. 2 sitting rooms, dining room; meeting room. No background music. Wi-Fi. Large walled garden; arbour. Medieval moat. Parking. Children welcomed. 8 bedrooms (4 in courtyard; 3 on ground floor). B&B £75–£140 per person.

BERWICK East Sussex
Map 2:E4
THE ENGLISH WINE CENTRE & CUCKMERE BARNS, Alfriston Road, BN26 5QS. Tel 01323-870164, www.englishwine.co.uk. 'A thoroughly enjoyable stay in a unique setting.' Dedicated to the promotion of English wines, owners Christine and Colin Munday have given this enterprise, in landscaped gardens on the South Downs, a new lease of life. Guests find 'smart and comfortable' accommodation, with original art, in the converted *Green Oak Barn*; the small restaurant in the neighbouring *Flint Barn* has 'a short, but interesting' seasonal menu, and unusual wines by the glass. Mark Goodwin is chef. Wine lovers can explore the 140 varieties of English wine on sale in the shop; 'staff are knowledgeable and helpful'. Bar/lounge, restaurant (no background music). Garden with water features. Tutored wine tastings; vineyard tours. Wi-Fi. Civil wedding licence. 5 bedrooms. B&B £67.50–£135 per person. Dinner £35.

BEXHILL-ON-SEA East Sussex
Map 2:E4
COAST, 58 Sea Road, TN40 1JP. Tel 01424-225260, www.coastbexhill.co.uk.

Linda and Chris Wain's B&B is in an Edwardian villa a few minutes' walk from the seafront, local shops and restaurants. Recently refurbished rooms (Teal, Crimson, Sage) are 'practical, modern, bright and clean'; breakfasts are 'nicely presented' and have lots of choice (vegetarian options available). Breakfast room. No background music. Children over 5 allowed. 3 bedrooms. B&B £35–£45 per person.

BIBURY Gloucestershire
Map 3:E6
Bibury Court, GL7 5NT. Tel 01285-740337, www.biburycourt.com. In a 'magical setting' in a village by the River Coln near Cirencester, this Jacobean mansion has been renovated by new owner John Lister (of Shipton Mill organic flour). Reception is a discreet modern desk in an alcove in the 'wonderful' old hall (polished stone floors); there is a massive high-ceilinged lounge, a bar with 1920s panelling. Dining is in an informal conservatory or a 'luxurious' dining room: chef Adam Montgomery serves 'sophisticated dishes with rich flavours'. Background music in public areas. Civil wedding licence. Children welcomed. 18 bedrooms. B&B £75–£212.50 per person. Dinner from £42.

The Swan, GL7 5NW. Tel 01285-740695, www.cotswold-inns-hotels.co.uk. On the banks of the River Coln in a lovely village, this 17th-century former coaching inn (part of the small Cotswold Inns and Hotels group) has been refurbished in modern English country house style by owners Pamela and Michael Horton. The 14-acre grounds produce the mineral-rich, natural spring water (bottled at the source) provided in the bedrooms. Traditional dishes are available in the bar; the more formal *Gallery* restaurant has a European-style table d'hôte dinner menu. 'Gentle' background music. Lounge, bar, restaurant. Lift. Garden. Civil wedding licence; function facilities. Wi-Fi (charge). Children welcomed. Trout fishing can be arranged. 22 bedrooms (4 in garden cottages, 1 with hot tub). B&B £85–£185 per person. Dinner £35.
25% DISCOUNT VOUCHERS

BIRKENHEAD Merseyside
Map 4:E2
The RiverHill Hotel, Talbot Road, Oxton, CH43 2HJ. Tel 0151-653 3773, www.theriverhill.co.uk. Nick and Michele Burn's small hotel on the Wirral peninsula is in a residential area, set back from the road in landscaped gardens. The staff are 'friendly, welcoming'; traditionally furnished bedrooms are large, with plenty of storage space. 'Good' breakfasts have a well-stocked buffet and dishes cooked to a 'high standard'. The Birkenhead tunnel and the Woodside ferry to Liverpool are five minutes' drive away. Lounge, bar, *Bay Tree* restaurant (modern English food cooked by Claire Lara; open to non-residents; background music). Civil wedding licence; business facilities. Wi-Fi. Parking. Children welcomed. 15 bedrooms. B&B £45–£69.50 per person. Dinner from £35.

BISHOP'S TACHBROOK Warwickshire
Map 2:B2
Mallory Court, Harbury Lane, CV33 9QB. Tel 01926-330214, www.mallory.co.uk. 'Elegant and calm: a

stalwart of the English country house hotel genre.' This manor house in ten-acre grounds was built in the early 1900s, and seamlessly extended to provide extra accommodation, meeting facilities and a 'bright, modern' brasserie. It belongs to the Eden Hotel Collection and is a member of Relais & Châteaux; Sarah Baker is the long-serving manager. The 'beautiful' garden, arranged in six distinct areas, has a formal Old English rose garden; a pond garden with its original stone paths, mature trees and shrubs; herbaceous borders; manicured lawns; and a kitchen garden, where a range of herbs, vegetables and soft fruits are grown year-round for use in the restaurants. 2 lounges, brasserie, restaurant ('excellent cooking; fish dishes are particularly good'; Simon Haigh is chef). Background music. Terrace (alfresco snacks). Civil wedding licence; function facilities. 31 bedrooms (11 in new wing). B&B £77.50–£350 per person. Dinner £30–£60.

BLACKBURN Lancashire
Map 4:D3

MILLSTONE AT MELLOR, Church Lane, Mellor, BB2 7JR. Tel 01254-813333, www.millstonehotel.co.uk. In the Ribble valley, this stone-built former coaching inn (part of Thwaites Inns of Character) has award-winning food and comfortable, country-style bedrooms. Chef/patron Anson Bolton cooks a wide-ranging selection of seasonal Lancashire dishes, served in the informal, newly refurbished dining areas. Breakfasts are hearty. Residents' lounge (log fire), bar, restaurant; background radio at breakfast. Parking. Children welcomed. 23 bedrooms (6 in courtyard; 2 suitable for ♿). B&B from £45 per person; D,B&B from £75.

STANLEY HOUSE, Mellor, BB2 7NP. Tel 01254-769200, www.stanleyhouse.co.uk. In 'marvellous surroundings', the Walker family's Grade II listed 17th-century manor house is in an elevated position at the end of a long drive. It was brought back from dereliction and given glamorous bedrooms with rich fabrics and glitzy touches. Philip Wharton is the manager. The adjoining, sympathetically converted barn houses the reception area, with its large inglenook fireplace and wood-burning stove, and two restaurants (one for formal dining). Lounge, *Grill on the Hill* restaurant (Andrew Parker is chef; closed Mon), *Mr Fred's* bar and lounge. Background music. Extensive grounds. Civil wedding licence; function facilities. Wi-Fi. Parking. Children welcomed. 12 bedrooms (some suitable for ♿; a further 18 are planned). B&B £92.50–£205 per person.

BLACKPOOL Lancashire
Map 4:D2

NUMBER ONE ST LUKE'S, 1 St Luke's Road, South Shore, FY4 2EL. Tel 01253-343901, www.numberoneblackpool.com. In the residential South Shore area, this B&B in a detached 1930s Art Deco house combines elegant, period-style furniture with state-of-the-art design and gadgetry, including large plasma TV screens, DVD- and CD-players, spa baths and remote lighting. It is run by Mark and Claire Smith, who also own *Number One South Beach* on the promenade (see below).

Conservatory; garden (hot tub); putting green. Background music. Wi-Fi. Parking. Children over 3 allowed. 3 bedrooms. B&B £50–£110 per person.

Number One South Beach, 4 Harrowside West, FY4 1NW. Tel 01253-343900, www.numberonesouthbeach.com. Janet and Graham Oxley, with Claire and Mark Smith (see *Number One St Luke's*, above), own this low-carbon-footprint boutique hotel, with sea views over South Beach Promenade. It has a welcoming atmosphere and a lively modern interior. Bedrooms are thoughtfully equipped and some have a four-poster bed, balcony and whirlpool bath. Lounge, bar, restaurant; background music; pool table; meeting/conference facilities. Lift. Garden with putting green. Parking. 14 bedrooms (disabled facilities). B&B from £65 per person. Dinner £30.

Raffles Hotel & Tea Room, 73–77 Hornby Road, FY1 4QJ. Tel 01253-294713, www.raffleshotelblackpool.co.uk. A colourful display of flowers enlivens the bay-fronted windows of Ian Balmforth (chef) and Graham Poole's small, traditionally furnished hotel with English tea rooms (closed Mon). Home-made cakes and light snacks are served at teatime; good-value three-course set dinners are also available. Close to the shops, the Winter Gardens and the promenade. Lounge, bar, breakfast room, tea rooms; classical background music. Wi-Fi. Parking. Children welcomed; dogs by arrangement. 17 bedrooms, plus 4 apartment suites. B&B £36–£40 per person. Dinner from £9.95.

BORROWDALE Cumbria
Map 4: inset C2

Leathes Head Hotel, CA12 5UY. Tel 017687-77247, www.leatheshead.co.uk. 'The perfect place to relax; we had a very happy stay here.' This country hotel in an Edwardian house has 'magnificent' views across the valley and easy access to Keswick. Proprietors Ian Burke and Jane McGuinnes are upgrading the classic decoration; the hotel remains popular with regular guests. Jamie Adamson and Jane Cleary are the 'enthusiastic, helpful, caring' managers. Long-serving chef David Jackson 'is still producing good food'; his six-choice menu, which changes every six weeks, includes a daily special. Lounge, bar, restaurant. Background music. Dogs allowed in some rooms (£7.50 per day charge). 11 bedrooms. B&B £60–£74 per person; D,B&B £88–£94. Closed end Dec–Feb.
25% DISCOUNT VOUCHERS

Seatoller House, Keswick, CA12 5XN. Tel 017687-77218, www.seatollerhouse.co.uk. Ramblers and walkers have been staying at this unpretentious guest house at the head of the unspoilt Borrowdale valley for more than a century. Owned by a private company, it is newly managed by Nigel and Trish Dixon. There is a homely atmosphere, with oak panelling, creaky floorboards, cosy chairs and cushioned window seats. Guests may help themselves to hot drinks at a tea bar. Bedrooms are 'unexpectedly spacious, though the door lintels are low'. A gong summons guests to dinner, when a daily-changing, no-choice menu is taken communally at two large oak tables. No background music or TVs. Sitting room, library, dining room; drying room. 1-acre grounds. Children over 2, and dogs allowed. 10 bedrooms (2 on ground floor, 1 in garden bungalow). B&B £48–£58 per person; D,B&B £60–£70. Closed Dec–Mar.

BOSCASTLE Cornwall
Map 1:C3
The Bottreaux, PL35 0BG. Tel 01840-250231, www.boscastlecornwall.co.uk. At the top of the village, this 'delightful' guest house, in a 200-year-old white building, has 'well-appointed and reasonably priced' bedrooms. A short walk away is the Elizabethan harbour and Coastal Path. Service is cheerful and 'friendly' under the management of Heather Graham. The bar has plenty of character, with beams and a slate floor. Lounge, bar, breakfast room (background music); private parties and functions catered for by arrangement. Wi-Fi. Parking. 8 bedrooms. B&B £27–£55 per person. Closed Nov–Jan.

BOURNEMOUTH Dorset
Map 2:E2
Urban Beach, 23 Argyll Road, BH5 1EB. Tel 01202-301509, www.urbanbeachhotel.co.uk. Close to Boscombe beach, this small, relaxed, contemporary hotel is run by 'laid-back' owner Mark Cribb, with manager Chris Warwick. The individually decorated rooms have luxury bedding and toiletries, and are equipped with a plasma TV and DVD-player. The bar has a large cocktail list; the bistro serves local produce and home-baked bread. Hotel guests have priority booking at *Urban Reef*, the sister restaurant on the beach. Bar, bistro; background music (live guitar music every Thurs eve); seating deck. Wi-Fi. DVD library. Wellies, umbrellas provided. Complimentary use of local gym. Children welcomed. 12 bedrooms. B&B £48.50–£72 per person. Dinner from £35.

BOWNESS-ON-WINDERMERE Cumbria
Map 4: inset C2
Lindeth Howe, Lindeth Drive, Longtail Hill, LA23 3JF. Tel 015394-45759, www.lindeth-howe.co.uk. Beatrix Potter spent family holidays in this traditional country house; it was here that she completed *The Tale of Timmy Tiptoes* and *The Tale of Pigling Bland*. In magnificent countryside overlooking the lake, the hotel is just a mile from the village. 'A good place that does not disappoint.' The restaurant is run by award-winning chef Marc Guibert and has a comprehensive wine list. Alison Magee Barker is the manager. Lounge, library (high tea), bar, restaurant. Background music. Sun terrace; swimming pool, sauna, fitness room. 6-acre grounds. Wi-Fi. Children welcomed (no under-7s in the restaurant at night; children's high tea, babysitting available). 34 bedrooms (some on ground floor). B&B £85–£180 per person; D,B&B £121–£216.
25% DISCOUNT VOUCHERS

BRADFORD-ON-AVON Wiltshire
Map 2:D1
Swan Hotel, 1 Church Street, BA15 1LN. Tel 01225-868686, www.theswanbradford.co.uk. Beside a 14th-century bridge, this quirky old coaching inn, in a black-and-white Grade II listed building, recently underwent a change of ownership and is now run by James

Sullivan-Tailyour. It has a modern interior with muted colours, wooden floors, leather furniture. English home-cooked fare is served in the restaurant, around the fire or on the terrace. Snug, cellar bar (live music on Thurs eve), restaurant; patio. Background jazz. Wi-Fi. Function facilities. Parking. Children welcomed. 12 bedrooms. B&B £55–£90 per person. Dinner £20–£40.

BRANSCOMBE Devon
Map 1: C5
The Mason's Arms, EX12 3DJ. Tel 01297-680300, www.masonsarms.co.uk. 'A lovely, relaxing place in a sleepy village.' This creeper-covered 14th-century inn has some country-style accommodation in the original building, but most rooms are in hillside cottages with views over the valley or out to sea. John McKitterick, the manager/chef, serves 'excellent food' using locally grown, reared or caught produce; lobster and crab are landed on Branscombe beach. Lounge, restaurant, bar, garden with outdoor seating. No background music. Children, and dogs (in some cottages) welcomed. Near a small pebble beach. 21 bedrooms (14 in cottages). B&B £35 per person. Dinner £35.

BRIDPORT Dorset
Map 1:C6
The Bull Hotel, 34 East Street, DT6 3LF. Tel 01308-422878, www.thebullhotel.co.uk. Along with the eclectically styled bedrooms, an informal café, bar and 'excellent' restaurant (Mattias Larsson is the new chef) are to be found within this Grade II listed former coaching inn in the centre of town. Owners Nikki and Richard Cooper, along with 'young, very friendly and helpful' staff, offer a welcoming atmosphere to families. A popular venue for locals. 2 bars (background music), restaurant, *The Stable* cider house; ballroom; private dining room; sunny courtyard. Civil wedding licence; function facilities. Children welcomed. 19 bedrooms (3 accessed via courtyard). B&B £42.50–£97.50 per person; D,B&B £77.50–£132.50.
25% DISCOUNT VOUCHERS

BRIGHTON East Sussex
Map 2:E4
Fivehotel, 5 New Steine, BN2 1PB. Tel 01273-686547, www.fivehotel.com. Caroline and Simon Heath's Georgian town house hotel in a lovely Regency square is moments away from the beach and pier, and a short walk to the shops and restaurants. Bedrooms are bright and modern; organic, locally sourced Sussex breakfasts are served communally in a bay-windowed room looking out to sea. 2 public rooms. No background music. DVD library. Wi-Fi. Children over 5 allowed. 10 bedrooms (some with sea views). B&B £40–£80 per person.

Kemp Townhouse, 21 Atlingworth Street, BN2 1PL. Tel 01273-681400, www.kemptownhousebrighton.com. Paul Lantsbury is the new owner of this elegant B&B in a white Regency-style town house on a quiet street just off the seafront. Sleek, modern bedrooms (some compact) have a wet room; most have views of the city or the sea. Breakfast brings pancakes, bagels, eggs cooked in many ways. Lounge, breakfast room (background music). 9 bedrooms. B&B £47.50–£95 per person.

Paskins, 18–19 Charlotte Street, BN2 1AG. Tel 01273-601203, www.paskins.co.uk. Occupying two Grade II listed, 19th-century houses, Susan and Roger Marlowe's environmentally friendly B&B in a conservation area is 'just up from the seafront and right at the heart of Brighton's most interesting quarter, Kemptown'. 'Amazing' organic, locally sourced breakfasts, served in the Art Deco breakfast room, cater well for vegetarian and vegan guests. Bedrooms are small. Lounge, dining room. No background music. Sandwich room-service menu. Wi-Fi. Children welcomed. 19 bedrooms (some with sea views). B&B £45–£75 per person.
25% DISCOUNT VOUCHERS

BROADSTAIRS Kent
Map 2:D6
Royal Albion Hotel, 6–12 Albion Street, CT10 1AN. Tel 01843-868071, www.albionbroadstairs.co.uk. In a prime position overlooking the beach and Viking Bay, this Georgian hotel is owned by brewers Shepherd Neame, and managed by Shane and Marie Godwin. Fronting the hotel, *Ballard's* coffee lounge looks out over the historic town; at the sea-facing rear, guests may dine alfresco on the popular terrace and landscaped Mediterranean garden. A one-time favourite of Charles Dickens, the hotel is a focal point of the town's annual Dickens celebrations. It also serves as a music venue in the annual Broadstairs Folk Festival. Coffee lounge, bar, restaurant (seafood specialities; sea views). Garden; terrace. Parking permits available. 21 bedrooms. B&B £58–£79 per person.

BUCKFASTLEIGH Devon
Map 1:D4
Kilbury Manor, Colston Road, TQ11 0LN. Tel 01364-644079, www.kilburymanor.co.uk. The four-acre grounds of Julia and Martin Blundell's renovated 17th-century longhouse overlook the River Dart; the couple have their own island a short walk down the fields. Hospitable hosts, the Blundells offer advice on local places to eat. Rooms are 'tastefully furnished'; breakfast has 'interesting' choices. The garden and courtyard are peaceful places in which to sit. One mile from town; the South Devon Railway is close by. Breakfast room (wood-burning stove). No background music. Wi-Fi. Bicycle and canoe storage. Resident dogs, Dillon and Buster. 4 bedrooms (2 in converted stone barn; plus one 1-bedroom cottage). B&B £37.50–£50 per person.

BUCKHORN WESTON Dorset
Map 2:D1
The Stapleton Arms, Church Hill, SP8 5HS. Tel 01963-370396, www.thestapletonarms.com. In a village on the fringes of Blackmore Vale, this old coaching inn, owned by Rupert and Victoria Reeves and managed by Ashley Rowley, is now a stylish, modern pub-with-rooms with an informal atmosphere. Bedrooms have the latest technology and a state-of-the-art bathroom. Downstairs, there are comfy sofas, old wooden tables and open fires; wellies for walkers. Mark Chambers's menus are varied and inventive; the bar has a detailed list of British ciders and apple juices. Bar, dining room; terrace, garden. No background music. Wi-Fi. Children welcomed. 4 bedrooms. B&B £36–£60 per person. Dinner £35.

BUDLEIGH SALTERTON Devon
Map 1:D5
ROSEHILL ROOMS AND COOKERY, 30 West Hill, EX9 6BU. Tel 01395-444031, www.rosehillroomsandcookery.co.uk. Willi and Sharon Rehbock run wide-ranging cookery classes (using both an Aga and range cooker) at their Grade II listed Victorian house close to the beach, Coastal Path and town. A large veranda overlooks the garden, with distant views to the sea. Light, spacious rooms have sofas, bathrobes and home-made cakes or biscuits. Dining room, kitchen. Wi-Fi. 4 bedrooms. B&B £45–£55 per person (2-night min. stay).

BUNGAY Suffolk
Map 2:B6
EARSHAM PARK FARM, Old Railway Road, Earsham, NR35 2AQ. Tel 01986-892180, www.earsham-parkfarm.co.uk. On a 600-acre working arable farm, Bobbie and Simon Watchorn's elegant but homely Victorian farmhouse is set among well-tended gardens. Country-style bedrooms have antique furniture and views over the fields and the Waveney valley. Breakfast – including sausages and bacon from the farm's free-range pigs; home-made breads and jam; local free-range eggs – is served around a communal table. Lounge, dining room. No background music. Garden. Farm walks; birdwatching. Parking. Two miles from Bungay. Children, dogs and horses (by prior arrangement) welcomed. 4 bedrooms. B&B £50–£70 per person.

BURFORD Oxfordshire
Map 2:C2
BAY TREE HOTEL, Sheep Street, OX18 4LW. Tel 01993-822791, www.cotswold-inns-hotels.co.uk. 'A lovely old building' with blue wisteria climbing up its honey-coloured limestone facade, this hotel has been welcoming visitors for more than 400 years. Part of the small Cotswold Inns and Hotels group (see main entry for the nearby *Lamb Inn*), it is managed by Quinton Fisher. 'Everything is tip-top.' The hotel has a galleried staircase, oak-panelled rooms, an inglenook fireplace, tapestries and flagstone floors. Library, *Woolsack* bar (background music), award-winning restaurant (Brian Andrews is chef), patio (alfresco dining). Walled garden; croquet. Civil wedding licence; function facilities. Children welcomed. 21 bedrooms (2 on ground floor in outbuilding). B&B £85–£130 per person. Dinner from £31.95.

BURNHAM MARKET Norfolk
Map 2:A5
THE HOSTE ARMS, The Green, PE31 8HD. Tel 01328-738777, www.hostearms.co.uk. A country-house feel predominates at this popular hotel and restaurant. It occupies a 17th-century coaching inn at the centre of a charming village, close to beaches, bird sanctuaries and a golf course. Brendan and Bee Hopkins became the new owners in spring 2012; Emma Tagg and Andrew McPherson remain as managers. 'Beautifully furnished and spacious' rooms have a sense of glamour. There are six dining areas, where morning coffee, light lunches and afternoon tea are served. The upstairs dining room is reached by an open iron-work spiral staircase. Chef Aaron Smith cooks 'delicious' food on 'the biggest Aga in the world', specially commissioned for the hotel. Lounge, bar, restaurant, conservatory (background music);

garden. Spa. 34 bedrooms (some in the courtyard wing, 12 yards from main hotel). B&B £63–£125 per person. Dinner £30.

BURY ST EDMUNDS Suffolk
Map 2:B5

The Angel Hotel, 3 Angel Hill, IP33 1LT. Tel 01284-714000, www.theangel.co.uk. This historic, ivy-covered coaching inn (where Charles Dickens stayed, and to which he refers in *The Pickwick Papers*) is in a prime square opposite the Abbey Gardens and cathedral. It has been run by the Gough family since 1973; Lynn Cowan is the manager. Six bedrooms were recently added. The contemporary interior has leather sofas, vintage furnishings and modern art; the restaurant, serving bistro food 'cooked well', is popular with locals. Lounge (log fire), bar, restaurant (Simon Barker is chef); background music. Function facilities. Children welcomed; dogs by arrangement (£5 charge). 80 bedrooms (some on ground floor). B&B £62.50–£150 per person. Dinner £40.

Oak Farm Barn, Moat Lane, Rougham, IP30 9JU. Tel 01359-270014, www.oakfarmbarn.co.uk. 'Great welcome with tea and cake, charming hosts and faultless accommodation.' On the edge of Rougham village, Rachel and Ray Balmer's 19th-century timber-framed barn has solid oak doors, an open-plan oak staircase and landing walkway, and original oak beams. B&B accommodation is in quaint, cottage-style bedrooms; public rooms have full-length windows. Farmhouse breakfasts. Lounge, seating area overlooking patio. Background music. Garden with outdoor seating. Wi-Fi. Parking. 3 bedrooms (2 on ground floor; 1 suitable for ♿). B&B £37.50–£55 per person.
25% DISCOUNT VOUCHERS

Ounce House, Northgate Street, IP33 1HP. Tel 01284-761779, www.ouncehouse.co.uk. Within walking distance of shops, restaurants and tourist sites, Simon and Jenny Pott's B&B is in a spacious Victorian merchant's house in a residential street. The Pottses have furnished it traditionally with antiques and period furniture, photographs and ornaments. Drawing room (honesty bar), snug/bar/library, dining room. Communal breakfasts. No background music. Wi-Fi. Parking. Children welcomed. 5 bedrooms (quietest 2 face the ¾-acre walled garden). B&B £85–£95 per person.

BUXTON Derbyshire
Map 3:A6

Grendon, Bishops Lane, SK17 6UN. Tel 01298-78831, www.grendonguesthouse.co.uk. On a quiet country lane near the town, this B&B is run by hospitable owners Hilary and Colin Parker. Spacious bedrooms have king-size beds (some four-poster), DVD-players and Peak District views. A log fire, newspapers and board games can be enjoyed in the comfortable sitting room. The extensive breakfast menu includes fruit compotes, pancakes and omelettes, home-made bread, marmalade muesli and other specialities. Dinner by arrangement (BYO bottle). Lounge, breakfast room; terrace. No background music. DVD library. 1-acre garden. Parking (garage for bikes). Wi-Fi. 5 bedrooms. B&B £35–£50 per person.

Hartington Hall, Hall Bank, SK17 0AT. Tel 01298-84223, www.yha.org.uk/hostel/hartington. Occupying a handsome old manor house (1611) on the edge of Dovedale, with mullioned windows, oak panelling and log fires, this upmarket youth hostel is run by the YHA. The good-value accommodation is basic, and spread over three buildings: the main house, the coach house and the barn. Mark Wallis is the manager. Lounge, bar, restaurant (home-cooked traditional English fare, local ingredients); background music. Games room; self-catering kitchen; drying room; meeting rooms. Extensive grounds: beer garden, adventure playground, pet area. Civil wedding licence. Children and dogs welcomed. 35 bedrooms (19 en suite; 10 in barn annexe, 5 in coach house; 1 suitable for ♿). B&B £31 per person.

CAMBRIDGE Cambridgeshire
Map 2:B4
Hotel Felix, Whitehouse Lane, Huntingdon Road, CB3 0LX. Tel 01223-277977, www.hotelfelix.co.uk. In extensive landscaped gardens on the edge of the city, this late Victorian yellow brick mansion (with modern extensions) has a contemporary interior. Shara Ross is the manager. Tom Stewart serves modern Mediterranean dishes in the restaurant overlooking the terrace and garden. Small lounge, bar, *Graffiti* restaurant; conservatory; background music. Civil wedding licence; function facilities. 4-acre garden, terrace, gazebo. Parking. Children welcomed. 52 bedrooms (4 suitable for ♿). B&B (continental) £65–£160 per person (full English breakfast £7.99 supplement); D,B&B £105–£165 including a full English breakfast.
25% DISCOUNT VOUCHERS

Hotel du Vin Cambridge, 15–19 Trumpington Street, CB2 1QA. Tel 01223-227330, www.hotelduvin.com. A modern conversion of five town houses dating, in parts, to medieval times, this 'rambling' Hotel du Vin has retained many quirky architectural features. It has exposed brickwork, reconditioned fireplaces, an upstairs lounge, and a vaulted cellar with a bar, sitting areas and a wine shop, 'all very charming'. In the informal bistro, Jonathan Dean serves 'home-grown and local' dishes. Staff are 'very obliging'. Library, bar, bistro, wine-tasting room; terrace. Background music. Wi-Fi. Civil wedding licence; function facilities. Children welcomed. 41 bedrooms (some on ground floor): £95–£270. Breakfast £12.95–£14.50, dinner from £34.

The Varsity Hotel & Spa, Thompson's Lane, off Bridge Street, CB5 8AQ. Tel 01223-306030, www.thevarsityhotel.co.uk. Overlooking the river near Magdalene Bridge, this newly built, minimalist hotel has panoramic views over the city's landmarks from its rooftop terrace. Named after Oxbridge colleges, the loft-style rooms have floor-to-ceiling windows, an LCD TV, a DVD library and an iPod docking station. Some bathrooms are small. Roberto Pintus is the manager. *The River Bar* Steakhouse and Grill, set on two levels in a restored 17th-century warehouse on the quayside, is just next door (background music). Roof terrace; *Glassworks* health club and spa (spa bath overlooking the River Cam); lift; gym. Civil wedding licence; conference facilities. Wi-Fi. Paid parking nearby. Children welcomed. 48 bedrooms (3 suitable for ♿). B&B (continental) £80–£180 per person; D,B&B £102.50–£199.50.

CANTERBURY Kent
Map 2:D5
MAGNOLIA HOUSE, 36 St Dunstan's Terrace, CT2 8AX. Tel 01227-765121, www.magnoliahousecanterbury.co.uk. In a peaceful conservation area close to the historic centre and cathedral, this elegant Georgian guest house is run with great attention to detail by Isobelle Leggett. Well-equipped bedrooms have complimentary wine, and fresh milk for coffee and tea. Dinner is served by arrangement in winter (Nov–Feb); no licence, bring your own bottle. Sitting room, dining room (background music). Walled garden. Wi-Fi. Parking. Children over 12 welcomed. 6 bedrooms (some four-poster beds). B&B £50–£63 per person. Dinner £35.

CHADDESLEY CORBETT
Worcestershire
Map 3:C5
BROCKENCOTE HALL, DY10 4PY. Tel 01562-777876, www.brockencotehall.com. 'A very elegant hotel.' Part of the Eden Collection, Sir Peter Rigby's small group of luxury hotels, this Victorian building has been remodelled in the style of a French château, and stands in 'lovely' parkland with a 'serene' lake and grazing sheep. Dean Gunston is the manager. Refurbished bedrooms, in country house style, are large and comfortable, and have a spacious bathroom. In the oak-panelled restaurant, chef Adam Brown serves 'terrific' dinners: 'Balance, timing, combination – nothing could be faulted.' Bar, lounge, restaurant, 2 private dining rooms. Background music (light jazz). 72-acre grounds; 3 miles SE of Kidderminster. Children welcomed. 21 bedrooms (some suitable for ♿). B&B £70–£150 per person; D,B&B (2-night min.) £105–£180.
25% DISCOUNT VOUCHERS

CHAGFORD Devon
Map 1:C4
MILL END HOTEL, Sandy Park, TQ13 8JN. Tel 01647-432282, www.millendhotel.com. Once a 15th-century corn mill, this white-painted longhouse within Dartmoor national park is today a small hotel owned and run by Sue and Peter Davies. There are plans to use the original 18-foot waterwheel to generate power for the hotel. Rooms are in traditional country house style, some with a private patio. Wayne Pearson's 'excellent' British dishes include Devon beef, local game, and fish sourced from around the Devon coast. The hotel sits by a bridge on the River Teign; there are river path walks to Fingle Bridge and Castle Drogo. Packed lunches available. 3 lounges, bar, restaurant, 15-acre grounds (river, fishing, bathing). Background music (classical in the hall and one lounge). Wi-Fi. Children (under-12s not allowed in restaurant in evening; high teas) and dogs welcomed. 15 bedrooms (3 on ground floor). B&B £45–£105 per person. Dinner £38–£42.

CHARMOUTH Dorset
Map 1:C6

The Abbots House, The Street, DT6 6QF. Tel 01297-560339, www.abbotshouse.co.uk. Sheila and Nick Gilbey have carefully updated their small, comfortable B&B, a house with medieval origins. There are state-of-the-art fittings alongside oak-panelled walls, ornate beamed ceilings and flagstone floors. Bathrooms have a double-ended bath and flat-screen TV. 'The attention to detail was amazing.' Dinner is no longer served, but Mrs Gilbey's home-cooked breakfasts are 'a delight'; her home-made jams and marmalade, and home-baked bread, are available for purchase. Close to the centre, and a five-minute walk from the beach. Lounge, garden room, garden (model railway). Background music. Children not accommodated. 3 bedrooms (plus 1-bedroom self-contained cottage in the garden). B&B £60–£70 per person (2-night min.). Closed Dec–Feb.

CHATTON Northumberland
Map 4:A3

Chatton Park House, Alnwick, NE66 5RA. Tel 01668-215507, www.chattonpark.com. Paul and Michelle Mattinson's B&B 'exceeded our expectations'. It is in an imposing Georgian house on a four-acre estate on the edge of Northumberland national park. Warmly welcoming, the Mattinsons are happy to recommend local restaurants and can provide packed lunches and a luggage drop-off and pick-up service for walkers and cyclists. Well-equipped bedrooms, named after local towns or villages, are furnished in period style. 'Breakfasts are of the highest quality – quite superlative.' 'Huge' sitting room, cosy bar, breakfast room; occasional classical background music. Garden; grass tennis courts (Apr–Oct). Wi-Fi; weak mobile phone signal. 4 bedrooms (plus 2-bedroom self-catering stone lodge with private garden). B&B £65–£95 per person. Closed Jan.

CHELTENHAM Gloucestershire
Map 3:D5

Beaumont House, 56 Shurdington Road, GL53 0JE. Tel 01242-223311, www.bhhotel.co.uk. 'We loved the finer touches.' One mile out of the city, Fan and Alan Bishop's modernised, cream-painted B&B in large gardens was originally built for a wealthy Victorian merchant. Two bedrooms (Out of Asia and Out of Africa) are themed and have a whirlpool bath. Complimentary tea, coffee and biscuits and an honesty bar are available in the large lounge; there is a limited room-service menu in the evenings (Mon–Thurs). Breakfast is taken in the dining room overlooking the flower garden; breakfast in bed can be arranged. Lounge, conservatory, dining room (background music/local radio). Wi-Fi. Parking. Children welcomed. 16 bedrooms. B&B £42.50–£125.50 per person.

The Cheltenham Townhouse, 12–14 Pittville Lawn, GL52 2BD. Tel 01242-221922, www.cheltenhamtownhouse.com. Adam and Jayne Lillywhite's peaceful B&B has an elegant, contemporary interior within a grand Regency building. The leafy location is a short walk from the Pittville Pump Room, and convenient for the racecourse. The Lillywhites are happy to recommend local restaurants and places to visit. Lounge (honesty bar; help-yourself fruit bowl), breakfast room (background music); DVDs; sun deck. Lift. Wi-Fi. Parking. Children welcomed. 26 bedrooms (including 4 self-contained apartments). B&B £35–£95 per person.

Hanover House, 65 St George's Road, GL50 3DU. Tel 01242-541297, www.hanoverhouse.org. 'Charming' hosts Veronica McIntosh-Ritchie and her husband, James, run this B&B (Wolsey Lodges) in their elegant Italianate home. 'Beautiful and full of interesting objects', it has a 'splendidly varied selection of books'. Bedrooms are comfortable; organic breakfasts are taken at a communal table (classical background music). It is close to the centre; helpful advice is offered on local restaurants and places to visit. Drawing room (open fire in winter), breakfast room. Wi-Fi. 3 bedrooms. B&B £50–£70 per person.
25% DISCOUNT VOUCHERS

Hotel du Vin Cheltenham, Parabola Road, GL50 3AQ. Tel 01242-588450, www.hotelduvin.com. In the chic Montpellier district, this converted early Victorian villa has an impressive white-painted facade, and a showpiece spiral staircase and wine-glass chandelier within. It is managed by Giles Hammond with 'young, helpful' staff. Rooms are stylish and well equipped ('big, comfy beds'; 'dim lighting'). There is 'excellent' food at breakfast, but 'indifferent' coffee. Bistro, 2 bars (*Champagne* and *Grain and Grape*), courtyard (alfresco dining); cigar shack. Background music. Spa treatment rooms. Civil wedding licence; function facilities. Wi-Fi. Children and dogs welcomed. 49 bedrooms: £135–£320. Breakfast £12.50–£14.50, dinner from £35.

Thirty Two, 32 Imperial Square, GL50 1QZ. Tel 01242-771110, www.thirtytwoltd.com. On a beautiful Georgian square overlooking Imperial Gardens, designers Jonathan Sellwood and Jonathan Parkin have created a stunning contemporary B&B in their Regency town house. Decorated with flair, it is also a showcase for their interior design business and shop, which sells lighting, furniture, accessories, scents and fragrances. There are many thoughtful touches, such as fruitcake at teatime, atmospheric candle lighting and an honesty bar. Drawing room (soft background music), breakfast room. Parking. 4 bedrooms: £77.50–£145 per person. Breakfast £8.50–£11.50.

CHESTER Cheshire
Map 3:A4

The Chester Grosvenor, Eastgate, CH1 1LT. Tel 01244-324024, www.chestergrosvenor.com. In the historic centre, near the cathedral, Roman walls and Eastgate clock, this Grade II listed luxury hotel with a black-and-white timbered facade has good views over Chester. It is owned by the Duke of Westminster and managed by Jonathan Slater. Well-equipped bedrooms have elegant, traditional furnishing. Besides the casual *Brasserie*, the *Michelin*-starred restaurant, *Simon Radley at The Chester Grosvenor*, is 'an experience not to be missed'. A Rococo concession in the hotel holds chocolate tastings and hosts a mini-steam train chugging its way through 15 chocolate stations. Drawing room, *Arkle* bar, 2 restaurants. Background music. Civil wedding licence; function facilities. Spa (crystal steam room, herb sauna, themed shower, ice fountain; 5 treatment rooms). Children welcomed (interconnecting family rooms). 80 bedrooms and suites. B&B from £115 per person (*excluding VAT*). Dinner £50–£100.

Green Bough Hotel, 60 Hoole Road, CH2 3NL. Tel 01244-326241, www.greenbough.co.uk. 'Efficient, friendly and comfortable', this popular hotel, owned by Janice and Philip Martin, is managed by Laura Currie. Occupying two Victorian town houses (on a busy road), it has a rooftop garden and water feature, and traditionally furnished bedrooms. 'The food was superb, and service impeccable' in the *Olive Tree* restaurant, where chef Neil Griffiths showcases regional produce. Mr Martin's cookery school, Cheshire Cooks, has one- and two-day courses in Tarporley, about 15 miles away. Lounge, bar, restaurant. Background music (classical, jazz). Function/conference facilities. Off-street parking. Children over 12 welcomed. 15 bedrooms (8 in lodge, linked by feature bridge; some suitable for ♿). B&B £87.50–£172.50 per person; D,B&B from £97.50.

Manderley, 17 Victoria Crescent, Queens Park, CH4 7AX. Tel 01244-675426, www.manderleychester.co.uk. Close to the River Dee and the Meadows, Karen and Richard Harris's B&B is in a brick house with sunny patios at the front and back. Bedrooms, decorated in neutral tones, are neat and modern; one has views of the river. Breakfast has plenty of choice (dietary requirements catered for). Ten mins' walk (across the pedestrian suspension bridge) to the city centre. Lounge, garden room, breakfast room; patios; garden. No background music. Wi-Fi. Off-street parking. Children over 12 welcomed. 3 bedrooms: £35–£60.

CHEWTON MENDIP Somerset
Map 2:D1

The Post House, Bathway, BA3 4NS. Tel 01761-241704, www.theposthouse bandb.co.uk. 'Excellent hostess' Karen Price has 'beautifully' renovated this Grade II listed former post office and village bakery. Rustic French-style rooms have lime-washed walls and white-painted furniture. Breakfast is 'delicious'. *The Old Bakery* ('a luxurious space') is equipped for self-catering, and has a stone fireplace and its own secluded courtyard. The lovely Mendip village is 5 miles N of Wells. Sitting room, dining room (no background music); Mediterranean-style courtyard; small garden. Wi-Fi. Parking. Children welcomed. Resident dog, Monty. 2 bedrooms (plus 1 self-catering cottage). B&B £40–£60 per person.

25% DISCOUNT VOUCHERS

CHICHESTER West Sussex
Map 2:E3

Crouchers, Birdham Road, PO20 7EH. Tel 01243-784995, www.crouchers countryhotel.com. Close to the harbour and West Wittering beach, this hotel and restaurant (spread over three separate buildings) has been refurbished by South African owner Lloyd van Rooyen in sleek, modern rustic style. In the restaurant, overlooking green fields, chef Nick Markey creates dishes from local ingredients; organic wines are available. 3 miles S of the town centre. Lounge, bar, restaurant (classical background music; open to non-residents); courtyard; 2-acre garden. Wi-Fi. Civil wedding licence; function facilities. Children welcomed. 28 bedrooms (25 in coach house, barn and stables; 10 with patios; 2 suitable for ♿). B&B £61.50–£82.50 per person; D,B&B £85–£105.

George Bell House, 4 Canon Lane, PO19 1PX. Tel 01243-813586, www.chichestercathedral.org.uk. Within the cathedral grounds, this former archdeaconry hosts visiting clergy and provides tranquil accommodation for B&B guests. The house, built in the late 1800s and named for George Bell, bishop of Chichester between 1929 and 1958, is a 'centre for vocation, education and reconciliation'. Bob Harper is the manager. The bedrooms and bathrooms are spacious. A full English breakfast is available in the dining room (no background music). Civil wedding licence; function facilities. Walled garden. Limited parking. Children welcomed. 8 bedrooms (1 single suitable for ♿): £49.50–£120. Breakfast £8.90, dinner (for groups of 6 or more) £30.

CHIDDINGFOLD Surrey

Map 2:D3

The Crown Inn, The Green, Petworth Road, GU8 4TX. Tel 01428-682255, www.thecrownchiddingfold.com. On the edge of the village green, this cream-painted 14th-century inn is 'everyone's idea of an English country pub'. There are dark oak beams, sloping floors, 'passageways a bit like a rabbit warren', and stained-glass windows. It is owned by Daniel and Hannah Hall; Robert Dekkers is the manager. 2 bars (*Crown* and *Half Crown* with open fire), 'superb' oak-panelled restaurant (background music/radio); terrace for alfresco dining; private dining room. Children welcomed. 8 bedrooms (front ones hear traffic). B&B £65–£200 per person. Dinner £25.

25% DISCOUNT VOUCHERS

CHRISTCHURCH Dorset

Map 2:E2

Captain's Club Hotel, Wick Ferry, Wick Lane, BH23 1HU. Tel 01202-475111, www.captainsclubhotel.com. On Christchurch Quay, this modern metal and glass spa hotel 'with character' has a stylish interior and 'delightful' panoramic views over the harbour. It is owned by Robert Wilson and Timothy Lloyd. Guests may hire the hotel's luxury motor yacht, *Nauti Girl*, for river or sea cruises; the hotel can also arrange rides around the bay or canoe trips downriver. The open-plan ground floor opens onto a large riverside terrace. Lounge, bar, *Tides* restaurant (Andrew Gault serves dishes with a French and Asian influence; alfresco dining); function facilities. Background music. Spa (pool, sauna; treatments). Lift. Wi-Fi. Parking. Children welcomed. 29 bedrooms (12 suites with kitchen and living area; 2 suitable for ♿). B&B from £109.50 per person. Dinner £28.

Christchurch Harbour Hotel, 95 Mudeford, BH23 3NT. Tel 01202-483434, www.christchurch-harbour-hotel.co.uk. Following a sympathetic restoration and extension, this hotel overlooking the quay now has a luxury spa and a modern, waterside restaurant, *The Jetty*, headed by *Michelin*-starred chef Alex Aitken. (The property was formerly the *Avonmouth Hotel*; under its new name, it is now part of the small, privately owned Harbour Hotels group.) The recent works also included a new wing for extra accommodation, and a refurbished conservatory. 2 restaurants (*The Jetty* and *The Harbour Restaurant*), terrace (alfresco dining). Cinema room (Nintendo Wii); spa (sauna, steam room, salt grotto, hydrotherapy pool). Wi-Fi. Civil wedding licence; function facilities. Children welcomed. 60 bedrooms. B&B £65–£115 per person.

The Kings Arms, 18 Castle Street, BH23 1DT. Tel 01202-588933, www.thekings-christchurch.co.uk. Overlooking a bowling green and the ruins of an ancient castle, this Georgian hotel with a 'lovely' facade has elegant, modern rooms and 'friendly, helpful' staff. It is part of the Harbour Hotels group, and sister to the *Christchurch Harbour Hotel* (see above); Adam Terpening is the general manager. In the restaurant, chef Alex Aitken uses a Josper grill to give a distinctive charcoal flavour to his seasonal suppers. The bowling green is open for public use on weekdays between 10.30 am and 4 pm; guests are welcome to join the Monday-night gatherings of the decades-old Christchurch Bowling Club. Lounge, bar, restaurant; sun terrace (alfresco dining). Background music. Lift. Wi-Fi. Civil wedding licence; function facilities. Children welcomed. 20 bedrooms. B&B £95–£145 per person; D,B&B £125–£195 (2-night min. stay on Sat).

CLEARWELL Gloucestershire
Map 3:D4
Tudor Farmhouse, GL16 8JS. Tel 01594-833046, www.tudorfarmhousehotel.co.uk. Within a quiet village in the Royal Forest of Dean and close to Clearwell Castle, this converted farm has 'delightful views' and a 'lovely' cottage garden. Parts of the hotel, owned by Hari and Colin Fell, date back to the 13th century; period details include a spiral staircase, huge oak beams and an inglenook fireplace. 'The decor, staff and ambience were very pleasing.' Bedrooms are spread out across the main house, converted barn and cider house. Dinner, cooked by chef Blaine Reed, is 'very good'; local suppliers are listed on the menu. Wild food foraging trips can be arranged. 2 lounges, restaurant (background music in evenings). 14-acre grounds. Wi-Fi. Parking. Children and dogs welcomed. 23 bedrooms (some with a four-poster bed and spa bath). B&B £45–£97.50 per person; D,B&B £75–£125 per person.
25% DISCOUNT VOUCHERS

CLEY-NEXT-THE-SEA Norfolk
Map 2:A5
Cley Windmill, The Quay, NR25 7RP. Tel 01263-740209, www.cleywindmill.co.uk. Standing peacefully among the reed beds, this 18th-century grinding mill has been turned into a small B&B (*pictured on p. 507*). It is owned by Dr Julian Godlee and managed by Charlotte Martin and Simon Whatling. The top-floor Wheel Room, accessed via a steep ladder, has fantastic views. The 'comfortable' circular sitting room at the base of the mill has an open fire and

a beamed ceiling. A daily-changing three-course menu devised by award-winning chef Emma Weddeburn is served in the candlelit dining room in the original granary (background jazz). Sitting room, restaurant (open to non-residents); garden. Civil wedding licence. Children welcomed in some rooms (early suppers by arrangement). 9 bedrooms (3 in converted boathouse and granary). B&B £44.50–£89.50 per person. Dinner £32.50 (£27.50 if booked at same time as room).

COLCHESTER Essex
Map 2:C5
PRESTED HALL, Feering, CO5 9EE. Tel 01376-573300, www.prested.co.uk. In extensive parkland down a long, tree-shaded drive, this part-moated manor house has 15th-century origins and Art Nouveau decoration. Owned by Mike Carter, it is managed by Karen Herbert. A large organic kitchen garden supplies chef Mark Joyce with much of the fruit and vegetables. Wood-panelled rooms have a fireplace; some overlook the water. Reception room, drawing room/library, restaurant, bistro, private dining rooms. Background music. Adjacent health club (gym; indoor pool; sauna, steam room; beauty and holistic treatments). 75-acre grounds: 3 lawn tennis courts; 2 real tennis courts; nature trail. Wi-Fi. Civil wedding licence. Function facilities in *The Orangery* or *Garden Room*. Children welcomed. 10 bedrooms (plus 2-bed attic suite; 6 serviced 1- and 2-bedroom apartments in health club building; 1-bed luxury retreat near the orchard, *The Dingle*). B&B £60–£100 per person; D,B&B £85–£125.
25% DISCOUNT VOUCHERS

COLN ST ALDWYNS
Gloucestershire
Map 3:E6
THE NEW INN, GL7 5AN. Tel 01285-750651, www.new-inn.co.uk. In the centre of a pretty Cotswold village, this creeper-clad 16th-century former coaching inn has been sympathetically renovated by the Hillbrooke Hotels Group (see also *The Elephant*, Pangbourne). The manager is Stuart Hodges. Traditional features (flagstone floors and oak beams) have been retained. In the bedrooms, bold, modern colours – lime green or red walls, purple curtains – coexist with beams and stone mullion windows. All have views over the village, terrace or meadow. The bar has black leather sofas. In the relaxed dining areas, chef Darren Bartlett serves a mainly British menu. Popular with walkers; 8 miles E of Cirencester. Bar, restaurant; terrace; garden. Background music. Wi-Fi. Children, and dogs (in 1 room), welcomed. 14 bedrooms (1 on ground floor, 6 in the Dovecote annexe). B&B £65–£95 per person; D,B&B £95–£125.
25% DISCOUNT VOUCHERS

COVENTRY Warwickshire
Map 2:B2
BARNACLE HALL, Shilton Lane, Shilton, CV7 9LH. Tel 02476-612629, www.barnaclehall.co.uk. Rose Grindal's small B&B is in a Grade II listed 16th-century farmhouse with an 18th-century limestone facade. It has oak beams, polished wood, an inglenook fireplace, and large, comfortable bedrooms furnished in period style. Sitting room, dining room. No background music. Garden, patio. In a rural location 5 miles NE of the city centre. Children

welcomed. 3 bedrooms (1 with private bathroom). B&B £35–£50 per person.

CRAYKE North Yorkshire
Map 4:D4

THE DURHAM OX, Westway, YO61 4TE. Tel 01347-821506, www.thedurhamox.com. A smart new all-weather garden room for dining (the *Burns Bar*) has been added to Mike and Sasha Ibbotson's characterful 300-year-old pub-with-rooms, which has stunning views over the Vale of York. The style is traditional, with exposed beams, carved wood panelling, an inglenook fireplace, and a fire in the wood-burning stove in winter. Food is unpretentious; chef Matthew Meek specialises in Crayke game, local meats, fresh fish and seafood dishes. 3 bars, restaurant; private dining room. Background music. Function facilities. Convenient for Park and Ride in to York. Children and dogs welcomed. 5 bedrooms (1 suite, accessed from external stairs; others in converted farm cottages; 2 on ground floor). B&B £50–£75 per person. Dinner £28.

CROSTHWAITE Cumbria
Map 4: insert C2

THE PUNCH BOWL INN, Lyth Valley, Kendal, LA8 8HR. Tel 01539-568237, www.the-punchbowl.co.uk. In a picturesque valley, this popular 300-year-old inn beside a handsome church also doubles as the village post office. It is owned by Richard Rose. Modern British menus devised by chef Scott Fairweather are served in the busy traditional bar, or in the airy, 'well-appointed' L-shaped dining room with polished floorboards and leather chairs. 'The food was very good.' Beamed bedrooms have the latest fittings and 'a very comfortable bed'. 2 bars, restaurant (background jazz); 2 terraces. Parking. Civil wedding licence; conference facilities. Children welcomed. 9 bedrooms. B&B £47.50–£152.50 per person; D,B&B £80–£185.

DARLINGTON Co. Durham
Map 4:C4

HEADLAM HALL, nr Gainford, DL2 3HA. Tel 01325-730238, www.headlamhall.co.uk. In rolling countryside near Darlington, the Robinson family's handsome 17th-century country house has a Jacobean hall, stone walls, huge fireplaces and traditional furnishing, and a golf course. Meals are served in an intimate panelled dining room, the airy *Orangery*, and the spa brasserie. Private dining is also available. 3 lounges, drawing room, bar, restaurant (classical/jazz background music). Lift. Spa (outdoor hydrotherapy pool, sauna, gym; treatment rooms). Terraces. 4-acre walled garden: lake, ornamental canal; tennis, 9-hole golf course, croquet. Children and dogs welcomed. 40 bedrooms (6 in mews, 9 in coach house, 7 in spa; 2 suitable for ♿). B&B £60–£100 per person; D,B&B £89–£130.

DARTMOUTH Devon
Map 1:D4

BROWNS HOTEL, 27–29 Victoria Road, TQ6 9RT. Tel 01803-832572, www.brownshoteldartmouth.co.uk. On a side street, within easy reach of the waterfront, Clare and James Brown's contemporary hotel (managed by Robin Tozer) is in a 200-year-old town house. Bedrooms are brightly decorated in a 'fun' style; the atmosphere is informal. There are squashy sofas and an open fire in the ground-floor bar; in the restaurant, Jamie Smith cooks Mediterranean-inspired dishes using home-smoked food from Devon producers. Lounge, bar (tapas dishes on Fri eve), restaurant (closed Mon eve). Modern/jazz background music. Parking permits supplied. Children welcomed. 10 bedrooms. B&B £47.50–£110 per person. Dinner from £45. **25% DISCOUNT VOUCHERS**

STOKE LODGE, Cinders Lane, Stoke Fleming, TQ6 0RA. Tel 01803-770523, www.stokelodge.co.uk. There is plenty for guests to do at Christine and Steven Mayer's extended country hotel, which dates back to the 17th century. Furnished traditionally, the hotel has a cosy, relaxing atmosphere. Staff are 'very helpful and friendly'. 2 lounges, bar, *Garden* restaurant (Paul Howard is the chef; background music); terrace; games room (table tennis), snooker room; indoor swimming pool (sauna, whirlpool). 3-acre grounds (outdoor heated swimming pool; duck pond); tennis; giant chess. In a coastal location, 2 miles W of Stoke Fleming. Children and dogs (the latter not in public rooms) welcomed. 25 bedrooms. B&B £49.50–£75.50 per person; D,B&B £73.50–£99. **25% DISCOUNT VOUCHERS**

STRETE BARTON HOUSE, Totnes Road, Strete, TQ6 0RU. Tel 01803-770364, www.stretebarton.co.uk. From the terrace of Stuart Lister and Kevin Hooper's 16th-century manor house, guests can enjoy tea and home-made cake while taking in the panoramic views across Start Bay from Start Point lighthouse to the mouth of the River Dart. The interior is contemporary, with an eastern flavour; bedrooms have silks, Buddha carvings and bold prints. Seasonal fruit and local farm yogurts are served at breakfast. Close to the South West Coast Path, 5 miles SW of Dartmouth. Sitting room, breakfast room (classical/'easy listening' background music); garden. In-room massages/spa treatments, by arrangement. Wi-Fi. Children over 8 welcomed. 6 bedrooms (1 in cottage; dogs allowed). B&B £52.50–£97.50 per person.

DERBY Derbyshire
Map 2:A2

CATHEDRAL QUARTER HOTEL, 16 St Mary's Gate, DE1 3JR. Tel 01332-546080, www.cathedralquarterhotel.com. Near the cathedral, this hotel in Grade II listed buildings (former council offices, a bank vault and a police station) has interesting features such as a Scaglioli marble staircase, ornate ceilings, stained-glass windows and oak panelling. Bedrooms are modern. Part of the Finesse Collection, the hotel is managed by Ben Orton. Lounge, *Bar Sixteen*, *Opulence* restaurant (chef Dean Crews cooks modern British dishes); background music. Civil wedding licence; small conference facilities. Spa (treatments; sauna, steam room). Wi-Fi. 38 bedrooms (some with cathedral views; 2 suitable for ♿). B&B £55–£190 per person. Dinner from £40.

DITTISHAM Devon
Map 1:D4

FINGALS, Old Coombe, Dartmouth, TQ6 0JA. Tel 01803-722398, www.fingals.co.uk. Staying at Richard and Sheila Johnston's extended old farmhouse near Dartmouth is 'rather like being at a country house party: very relaxed, with a slight air of chaos'. Public rooms have inglenook fireplaces and oak beams. Dinner is generally served at a long table in the oak-panelled dining room, but can be taken at separate tables in a smaller room. 'Excellent, traditional' food is locally sourced. Lounge, TV room, 2 dining rooms, honesty bar, library. Background music. Indoor heated pool with partly removable roof, spa bath, sauna; orangery, summer house; grass tennis court, croquet lawn; games room; art gallery. Children welcomed. Resident dogs. 11 bedrooms (2 family suites in separate buildings beside a stream). B&B £45–£105 per person; D,B&B £67.50–£135. Closed Feb–mid-Mar.

DOVER Kent
Map 2:D5

Loddington House, 14 East Cliff, CT16 1LX. Tel 01304-201947, www.loddingtonhousehotel.co.uk. Kathy Cupper and her son, Robert, welcome guests at their elegant Grade II listed Regency house, which has views over the harbour and the White Cliffs. The comfortable bedrooms are traditionally furnished in gold and cream. Close to the ferry port (200 yds), cruise terminals (5 minutes) and Channel Tunnel rail link (15 minutes). Lounge (balcony with sea view), dining room. No background music. Small garden. 6 bedrooms (en suite or private facilities). B&B £30–£55 per person. Dinner (by arrangement, Oct–May) £25.

Wallett's Court, Westcliffe, St Margaret's-at-Cliffe, CT15 6EW. Tel 01304-852424, www.wallettscourthotelspa.com. 'We enjoyed our stay: a building of great character, an excellent dinner and a very comfy bed.' Opposite the Norman church in a pretty hamlet ten minutes from the port, there is 'attractive' accommodation in the Oakley family's Jacobean white-painted manor house and the surrounding Kentish hay barns; there are also extensive leisure facilities in the seven-acre landscaped gardens. Rooms are decorated in country house style; some have a four-poster bed. Lounge, bar, library, conservatory, restaurant (David Hoseason is chef; background music); 12-metre indoor pool with Endless Pools swim trainer and hydrotherapy massage, sauna, steam room, fitness studio, indoor hot tub, treatment cabins, relaxation room; tennis courts, croquet lawn, boules court; sun terraces. Civil wedding licence; function facilities. Wi-Fi. Children welcomed (baby-listening devices; high teas). 17 bedrooms plus 2 tipis in grounds. B&B from £47.50 per person. Dinner from £35.

DRIFFIELD East Yorkshire
Map 4:D5

Kilham Hall, Driffield Road, YO25 4SP. Tel 01262-420466, www.kilhamhall co.uk. 'A delightful place.' Staying at Joanne Long and David Berry's elegant home in the Yorkshire Wolds is 'sheer luxury'. Guests are welcomed with tea and home-made scones on arrival; in the evenings, the hosts offer a glass of chilled white wine. Bedrooms are romantic, with silk and velvet fabrics; bathrooms have a whirlpool bath and under-floor heating. Sledmere has its own entrance, a separate dressing room, and a spiral staircase leading to a decadently furnished bedroom with a

Juliet balcony. Aga-cooked breakfasts are hearty, with an 'enormous' choice: home-made bread, jams and marmalade. Picnic hampers available. Drawing room, dining room (background music), conservatory. In-room spa treatments. Wi-Fi. 1½-acre wildlife-friendly garden: outdoor heated pool (May–mid-Sept), all-weather tennis court, croquet. 3 bedrooms. B&B £65–£85 per person. Closed Nov–early Feb.

DULVERTON Somerset
Map 1:B5
THREE ACRES COUNTRY HOUSE, Brushford, TA22 9AR. Tel 01398-323730, www.threeacrescountryhouse.co.uk. Overlooking a peaceful village on the edge of Exmoor, Julie and Edward Christian's hillside hideaway is in mature grounds with lovely views. Bedrooms are thoughtfully equipped with a large bed, a fridge, a silent-tick alarm clock. Wholesome breakfasts have a daily special, and home-made fruit compotes using berries from the garden. Light suppers (soups, pâtés, sandwiches, puddings) can be arranged. Picnic hampers available. Bar, sitting room with open fire, dining room; sun terrace. No background music. Wi-Fi. 2 miles S of Dulverton. Country pursuits arranged. Children welcomed. The house is also available for exclusive use. 6 bedrooms (1 on ground floor). B&B £45–£75 per person.
25% DISCOUNT VOUCHERS

DUNWICH Suffolk
Map 2:B6
THE SHIP AT DUNWICH, St James Street, IP17 3DT. Tel 01728-648219, www.shipatdunwich.co.uk. 'Unspoilt and unpretentious. We enjoyed our stay here.' Moments from the beach, and opposite a bird sanctuary and nature reserve, this old inn is in a peaceful village that was once the capital of East Anglia, before the sea took its toll. Owned by Agellus Hotels, it is managed by Matthew Goodwin. With its original stone and wood floors, the 'spick-and-span, warren-like' interior is full of character. 'Good' and 'Best' bedrooms are 'crisp, though space can be rather tight'; some are accessed via an outside staircase. Chef Matthew Last's dinners (large portions) are 'good': 'The fishwas wonderfully fresh – the chips just right.' Bar, dining room, conservatory, courtyard; large garden. No background music. Children and dogs welcomed. 15 bedrooms (4 on ground floor in converted stables; 1 suitable for ♿). B&B £47.50–£62.50. Dinner £23.

DURHAM Co. Durham
Map 4:B4
CATHEDRAL VIEW, 212 Gilesgate, DH1 1QN. Tel 0191-386 9566, www.cathedralview.co.uk. With breathtaking views of the cathedral, Jim and Karen Garfitt's Georgian merchant's house has newly refurbished bathrooms and a new residents' lounge. Their B&B ('very clean with good decoration and fittings') has rooms with a choice of pillows and complimentary use of a netbook (with access to a printer). There is home-baked bread and an extensive choice at a 'very good' breakfast, where 'ingredients have been chosen with care'. No background music. Lounge. Garden, with seating. Ten mins' walk to cathedral; near a main road. Wi-Fi. Parking (permits supplied). 5 bedrooms. B&B £42.50–£70.

Gadds Townhouse, 34 Old Elvet, DH1 3HN. Tel 0191-384 1037, www.gaddstownhouse.com. Owners Deborah and Nigel Gadd have renamed their Grade II listed Georgian house (formerly *The Fallen Angel*) and revamped some of the themed bedrooms with lavish fabrics and wall coverings. Edwardian Express is inspired by a first-class railway carriage; The Cruise, with its portholes and curved wall, by a luxury liner. Some rooms have views of the cathedral, castle or river. Grilled meats and fish are a speciality in the opulent restaurant. 'The food is fine; a good city-centre hotel.' A small terrace overlooks the river. Cocktail bar, restaurant (jazz/classical background music). Lift. Children welcomed. 11 bedrooms (1 suitable for ♿). B&B £45–£110. Dinner £45.

EASTBOURNE East Sussex
Map 2:E4

Belle Tout Lighthouse, Beachy Head, BN20 0AE. Tel 01323-423185, www.belletout.co.uk. On Beachy Head, this restored Victorian lighthouse has been turned into a B&B. 'It is a lovely, unusual place for a romantic getaway.' There are 'fantastic' views of the English Channel across the South Downs and stunning sea views towards Seven Sisters. Themed bedrooms (Old England, Captain's Cabin, New England) have a snug bathroom; Keeper's Loft is round and small with a ladder leading to a double loft bed. The lantern room at the top has window seating and a telescope. Lounge, breakfast room, kitchen. No background music. Treatments. Garden (fish pond). 6 bedrooms. B&B £69–£115.50 per person. 2-night min. stay preferred.

Grand Hotel, King Edwards Parade, BN21 4EQ. Tel 01323-412345, www.grandeastbourne.com. 'The whole atmosphere here is lovely.' An imposing white edifice, this grand Victorian hotel on the seafront is 'an excellent example of its type'. Around the corner are the cliffs of Beachy Head, where Debussy completed *La Mer* in 1905. It is managed by Jonathan Webley. Rooms are 'sumptuous'; 'I can find no fault of any sort with this wonderful hotel.' Traditions are maintained: a monthly teatime Palm Court quartet ('an event worth going to'); a live band at weekends. Children welcomed (Junior Crew club, family dining, crèche). 2 lounges, bar, *Mirabelle* (closed Sun, Mon) and *Garden* restaurants (both with background music). Civil wedding licence; conference/function facilities. Health spa; heated indoor and outdoor swimming pools; 2-acre garden: putting, etc. Parking. 152 bedrooms (many with sea view; 1 suitable for ♿). B&B £77.50–£99.50 per person; D,B&B £109–£134.

Ocklynge Manor, Mill Road, BN21 2PG. Tel 01323-734121, www.ocklyngemanor.co.uk. Built on the site of a monastery, this magnificent pink Georgian mansion is one of Eastbourne's oldest houses, and was once home to illustrator Mabel Lucie Attwell. It is owned by Wendy and David Dugdill, whose beautiful ¾-acre walled garden (with well, 18th-century gazebo and 150-year-old manna ash) is part of the National Gardens Scheme open day. Comfortable country-style bedrooms overlook the grounds. Organic breakfasts (home-made bread and marmalade). 1 mile from seafront. No background music. Garden. DVD-players. Wi-Fi. Parking. 3 bedrooms. B&B £45–£60 per person (min. 2-night stay at weekends).

EVERSHOT Dorset
Map 1:C6
The Acorn Inn, 28 Fore Street, DT2 0JW. Tel 01935-83228, www.acorn-inn.co.uk. In a pretty Dorset village, believed to have featured in Thomas Hardy's novels, this 16th-century stone inn is run in a relaxed way by Jack Mackenzie, who cooks, and his wife, Alexandra Armstrong-Wilson. Like *Summer Lodge* (see main entry) across the street, the inn is part of the Red Carnation Hotels group; guests can use the hotel's spa swimming pool, sauna and gym (£15 charge), and book treatments there. The inn has beams, oak panelling, stone floors and log fires. Bedrooms are traditional with quirky touches; one bar has a skittle alley. Lounge, 2 bars, restaurant with sitting area; patio. Occasional background music. Wi-Fi in public areas. Parking. 10 miles NW of Dorchester. Children and dogs welcomed. 10 bedrooms. B&B £49.50–£149 per person; D,B&B £84.50–£179.

EXETER Devon
Map 1:C5
ABode, Cathedral Yard, EX1 1HD. Tel 01392-319955, www.abodehotels.co.uk. Well situated next to the cathedral, this 'excellent' hotel – the first in the ABode group started by Andrew Brownsword and Exeter-born chef Michael Caines – is in the historic *Royal Clarence Hotel*. Modern rooms (Comfortable, Desirable, Enviable and Fabulous) have a super-king bed, complimentary regional tuck box, velour bathrobes and slippers, and views of the cathedral. Guests have a range of eating options: informal meals in the café/bar, fine dining in the restaurant, or pub grub at the *Well House Tavern* next door. 2 cafés, bar, restaurant, deli. Lift. Fitness centre. Background music. Civil wedding licence; function facilities. Wi-Fi. 53 bedrooms. B&B from £65 per person.

FALMOUTH Cornwall
Map 1:E2
The Greenbank, Harbourside, TR11 2SR. Tel 01326-312440, www.greenbank-hotel.co.uk. There are 'fantastic' sea or river views from this smart, modern hotel overlooking the Fal estuary. Rooms are 'light, bright' with large windows. Paul Goodwin is the manager. Chef Fiona Were, a keen forager, specialises in seafood and seasonal Cornish produce at the *Harbourside* restaurant. Lounge, bar, restaurant (background music); terrace; function suite. 1½-acre gardens. Civil wedding licence; conference facilities. Wi-Fi. Parking. Children welcomed. 60 bedrooms (some suitable for ♿). B&B £72.50–£129 per person. Dinner £35.

The Rosemary, 22 Gyllyngvase Terrace, TR11 4DL. Tel 01326-314669, www.therosemary.co.uk. New owners, Lynda and Malcolm Cook, who took over in February 2012, give guests 'a very warm welcome'. 'They are charming and breakfast is superb.' The white-walled Edwardian house is in an 'excellent' location, a short walk from the town centre and a two-minute stroll to the beach. The B&B is quiet and has a view of the sea from the large drawing room and most of the bedrooms. Bar, lounge, dining room (no background music); south-facing garden, sun deck. Children and dogs (the latter not in high season) welcomed. Wi-Fi. 10 bedrooms (two 2-bedroom suites, ideal for families). B&B £38.50–£52.50 per person. Closed Nov–Feb.

FOLKESTONE Kent
Map 2:E5

The Relish, 4 Augusta Gardens, CT20 2RR. Tel 01303-850952, www.hotelrelish.co.uk. Close to the town centre, Sarah and Chris van Dyke's grand, cream-painted 1850s merchant's house has direct access to private, four-acre Augusta Gardens. A relaxed B&B, it is furnished in a clean-lined, contemporary style. Guests are welcomed with a glass of wine or beer on arrival; complimentary coffee, tea and home-made cake are available throughout the day. Lounge (with open fire), breakfast room (Radio 2 played). Small terrace. Wi-Fi. Parking. Children welcomed. 10 bedrooms. B&B £47.50–£135 per person.

FROGGATT EDGE Derbyshire
Map 3:A6

The Chequers Inn, Hope Valley, S32 3ZJ. Tel 01433-630231, www.chequers-froggatt.com. In 'a lovely area for walks straight from the hotel', this Grade II listed 16th-century inn on the edge of Froggatt village is owned by Jonathan and Joanne Tindall, and managed by Debbie Robinson. Graham Mitchell cooks pub-style food with European flourishes, served in two eating areas or alfresco in the elevated garden. Restaurant, garden. 'Discreet classical' background music. Overlooks a busy road. Children welcomed. 6 bedrooms. Wi-Fi. B&B £47.50–£115. Dinner from £30.

FROME Somerset
Map 2:D1

The Archangel, 1 King Street, BA11 1BH. Tel 01373-456111, www.archangelfrome.com. Renovated in a quirky rustic style, this gastropub-with-rooms is in an ancient coaching inn and stables (with 18th-century additions) by the marketplace. It is now managed by Lisa Penny for Cirrus Inns. Bedrooms, in dynamic purples, chocolates and blacks, have a golden bedstead, polished metal bath, inventive copper taps; eye-catching wall murals of Renaissance angels 'steal the show'. The restaurant has a private dining area, The Cube, a suspended glass room seating 12 around a single table. Head chef Derek Hamlen cooks imaginative dishes from West Country produce; dinner and breakfast are both 'very good'. Sitting room, bar, restaurant; small functions in the Naval Room and Library. Background music. Walled garden (tapas; alfresco dining). Limited parking. 6 bedrooms. B&B £62.50–£90 per person. Dinner from £35.

The Place to Stay, Knoll Hill Farm, BA11 5DP. Tel 01373-836266, www.theplacetostayuk.com. Gary and Alison Gamblin welcome B&B visitors to their Georgian farmhouse, which is surrounded by grazing sheep in beautiful countryside. Modern bedrooms, in the house and in converted barns accessed via a central courtyard, have a rustic character, with exposed beams, stone and brickwork. Mr Gamblin's West Country breakfasts (including vegetarian options) are served in a conservatory with soaring rafters and lovely views over the Longleat estate. Mrs Gamblin is a professional masseuse; 'romantic' and massage pampering packages are available. 11 miles from Bath. Sitting room, breakfast room (classical background music); outdoor seating. Wi-Fi. Parking. Children welcomed. 9 bedrooms (7 in outbuildings). B&B £39.50–£149 per person.

GATWICK West Sussex
Map 2:D4

LANGSHOTT MANOR, Ladbroke Road, Langshott, Horley, RH6 9LN. Tel 01293-786680, www.langshottmanor.com. 'We booked the Full English package and got the Great British! An unforgettable stay.' This Elizabethan timber-framed luxury hotel close to Gatwick airport combines exposed beams, oak panels and feature fireplaces with modern facilities and individually designed bedrooms. Staff 'pamper with friendliness'. Phil Dixon serves 'excellent' modern European/French food in the *Mulberry* restaurant; tasting menus include a vegetarian option. Gregory Broad is the manager. 2 lounges (background music), bar, restaurant, terrace. Civil wedding licence; conference facilities. 3-acre garden; medieval moat. Wi-Fi. Children welcomed. 22 bedrooms (7 in main house, some with four-poster bed; 15 across garden). B&B £95–£260 per person. Dinner from £45.

GILSLAND Cumbria
Map 4: B3

WILLOWFORD FARM, CA8 7AA. Tel 01697-747962, www.willowford.co.uk. One of the longest unbroken stretches of Hadrian's Wall, with the remains of a bridge and two turrets, is on the doorstep of Liam McNulty and Lauren Harrison's 100-acre working farm. The B&B is on the National Trail between Gilsland village and Birdoswald Roman Fort. A milking parlour, cart house and grain store have been converted into simple, energy-efficient bedrooms with exposed wooden beams, slate floors and antique furniture; bathrooms have under-floor heating and handmade organic soaps. Pre-booked three-course evening meals are accompanied by local Geltsdale ale, or wines from small, family-run vineyards. Packed lunches available. Lounge, dining room. No background music. Children welcomed (family rooms); dogs by arrangement. 5 bedrooms (all on ground floor). B&B £37.50–£60 per person. Dinner £18. Closed Dec–Mar.

GRANGE-OVER-SANDS Cumbria
Map 4: inset C2

CLARE HOUSE, Park Road, LA11 7HQ. Tel 015395-33026, www.clarehousehotel.co.uk. 'Another splendid break.' Returning guests cite the 'outstanding' views over Morecambe Bay, and the 'good combination of comfy – even homely – bedrooms, great welcome and excellent food' at the Read family's traditional Victorian hotel, now in its 43rd season. In the dining room, chefs Andrew Read and Mark Johnston serve light lunches and five-course dinners, also available to non-residents. 2 lounges, dining room. No background music. ½-acre grounds. Mile-long promenade at bottom of garden (bowling greens, tennis courts, putting green; easy access to Ornamental Gardens). Parking. Children welcomed.

18 bedrooms (1 on ground floor suitable for ♿). B&B £66–£72 per person; D,B&B £86–£92. Closed mid-Dec–end Mar.
25% DISCOUNT VOUCHERS

GRASMERE Cumbria
Map 4: inset C2
Moss Grove, LA22 9SW. Tel 015394-35251, www.mossgrove.com. Every detail at Susan Lowe's refurbished Victorian house, in a 'very pretty' Lakeland village near Ambleside, has been carefully considered to achieve sustainability 'without loss of style or luxury'. Natural materials (glass, sheep's wool) were used for the renovation. Bedrooms are decorated with natural ink wallpapers, organic paints and reclaimed-timber furniture; bathrooms are large, with under-floor heating and a spa bath. Mediterranean buffet breakfasts are made from organic, Fairtrade and local produce. Lounge, kitchen. No background music. Wi-Fi. Parking. Children and dogs welcomed. 11 bedrooms (2 on ground floor). B&B £57–£129.50 per person.

White Moss House, Rydal Water, LA22 9SE. Tel 015394-35295, www.whitemoss.com. At the northern end of Rydal Water, Sue and Peter Dixon offer cosy B&B accommodation in their grey stone creeper-clad house, once the home of William Wordsworth's family. Mr Dixon occasionally cooks for house parties and 'dinner club' weekends (five-course gourmet menus). 'The food is truly exceptional.' The homely, oak-panelled lounge has comfy sofas, a wood-burning fire, flowers, books, games and a piano. Packed lunches available. No background music. Lounge, dining room; 1-acre garden/woodland (lake views); outdoor seating on a flowery terrace. Fishing permits. Free membership at local leisure club. Wi-Fi. Parking. Children welcomed. 5 bedrooms. B&B £49–£69 per person. Closed Dec–Mar.

GRASSINGTON North Yorkshire
Map 4:D3
Grassington House, 5 The Square, nr Skipton, BD23 5AQ. Tel 01756-752406, www.grassingtonhousehotel.co.uk. Owner/chef John Rudden gives cookery demonstrations at his hotel on the Dales Way trail, which he runs with his wife, Sue. The brown-grey limestone Georgian house, which Mrs Rudden has refurbished in opulent, contemporary fashion, overlooks a cobbled square. Traditional favourites and seasonal food are served in the smart restaurant or fireside bar, or on the terrace. 'Very enjoyable.' Pork enthusiasts will appreciate products made from the Ruddens's own hand-reared rare breed Oxford Sandy and Black pigs. 'We were pleased with it in every way.' Lounge, bar, *No.5* restaurant. Background music. Tracking and foraging days in the Dales. Civil wedding licence; function facilities. Parking. 9 bedrooms. B&B £50–£60 per person; D,B&B £82–£105.

GREAT LANGDALE Cumbria
Map 4: inset C2
The Old Dungeon Ghyll, LA22 9JY. Tel 015394-37272, www.odg.co.uk. Children, walkers, cyclists and dogs are all welcomed at this extended house in the Great Langdale valley. A popular place for fell walkers and climbers for more than 300 years, it is run by Jane and Neil Walmsley for the National Trust. There are comfortable rooms,

open fires; no television. Lounge, residents' bar, dining room, public *Hikers' Bar* (old cow stalls); live music on first Wed of every month. No background music. Drying room. 1-acre garden. 12 bedrooms (6 with private facilities). B&B £50–£58 per person; D,B&B £70–£80.

GURNARD Isle of Wight
Map 2:E2

The Little Gloster, 31 Marsh Road, PO31 8JQ. Tel 01983-200299, www.thelittlegloster.com. In a low-built, angled building by the water's edge, chef Ben Cooke runs his informal restaurant-with-rooms with Holly Siddons, and support from family members; his Danish grandmother ensures that the minimalist restaurant is supplied with fresh flowers. Blue-and-white rooms have a nautical simplicity; two have wonderful sea views, binoculars supplied. Mr Cooke's uncomplicated dishes focus on fresh local food and have a Scandinavian influence. Bar, restaurant (closed Mon). Garden; croquet lawn. Function facilities. Five mins' drive from Cowes. 3 bedrooms. B&B £45–£100 per person. Dinner £35.

HALIFAX West Yorkshire
Map 4:D3

Shibden Mill Inn, Shibden Mill Fold, HX3 7UL. Tel 01422-365840, www.shibdenmillinn.com. 'A very attractive building in a lovely streamside setting.' Simon and Caitlin Heaton's renovated 17th-century country inn in the Shibden valley has oak beams, rafters, sloping ceilings and traditional furnishing. Glen Pearson is the manager. The 'bustling' bar is popular with locals and visitors (ales include Shibden Mill's own brew); chef Darren Parkinson's modern dishes, sourced from local growers and suppliers, are displayed on blackboard menus. Two miles NE of Halifax. Bar, restaurant; private dining room; patio (alfresco dining). Background music. Small conference facilities. Wi-Fi. Parking. Children welcomed. 11 bedrooms. B&B £52.50–£140 per person; D,B&B £85–£114.

HARROGATE North Yorkshire
Map 4:D4

The Bijou, 17 Ripon Road, HG1 2JL. Tel 01423-567974, www.thebijou.co.uk. Convenient for the town centre, Stephen and Gill Watson's B&B in a Victorian villa is 'stylish, with good facilities and nice touches'. There are original wooden and tiled floors, a wood-burning stove, and contemporary furnishing and artwork. The coach house behind the main building is ideal for families. Lounge (afternoon teas; honesty bar; computer), breakfast room. Background music. Small front garden. Wi-Fi. Parking. Children welcomed. 10 bedrooms (2 in coach house; 1 on ground floor). B&B £34.50–£69 per person.

Rudding Park, Follifoot, HG3 1JH. Tel 01423-871350, www.ruddingpark.com. Standing in extensive mature parkland originally laid out by landscape designer Humphry Repton, this Grade I listed Regency mansion is now a luxury spa and golf hotel with an 18-hole golf course. Owned by Simon Mackaness and his family, it is managed by Nuno César de Sá. Attractive bedrooms are in two wings. In the *Clocktower* restaurant, head chef Eddie Gray designs seasonal menus around locally sourced ingredients. Yorkshire breakfasts; complimentary newspapers. 2½ miles S of town. Bar, restaurant, conservatory. Cinema. Spa (treatment and steam rooms); gym; off-road driving, falconry. Civil wedding licence; conference facilities. Wi-Fi. Children welcomed. 90 bedrooms (8 suites, 4 spa rooms, 1 family; 3 suitable for ♿; plus 5 self-catering luxury lodges). B&B £66.50–£392 per person; D,B&B from £89.50.

HARTINGTON Derbyshire
Map 2:A2
Charles Cotton Hotel, Market Place, SK17 0AL. Tel 01298-84229, www.charlescotton.co.uk. 'A relaxing stay. There are lots of lovely walks and places to visit in the area.' In a delightful village in the Peak District national park, this renovated stone-built 17th-century coaching inn is run by 'cheerful, helpful' staff and hands-on owners Judy Dyer and Alan Shanks. The food is 'good', with some adventurous combinations. Chef Dave Thompson strives to use local, organic, GM-free produce. Lounge, bar, restaurant. Background music; live music on Fri and Sat nights. Wi-Fi. Children, and dogs (£10 per night; in some rooms only), welcomed. Fishing packages, including accommodation and luxury lunch hamper, can be arranged. 17 bedrooms (in house and converted stables; 3 on ground floor). B&B £37.50–£55. Dinner from £28.

HAWORTH West Yorkshire
Map 4:D3
Ashmount Country House, Mytholmes Lane, BD22 8EZ. Tel 01535-645726, www.ashmounthaworth.co.uk. Surrounded by stunning landscapes, Ray and Gill Capeling's stone-built guest house was once the home of Dr Amos Ingham, physician to the Brontë sisters. It is managed by Wayne and Claire Saud. Bedrooms are romantic; some have a private patio and hot tub; sauna cabin and whirlpool bath; music and 'mood lighting'. Chef Danny Ife cooks traditional food with a twist. Yorkshire breakfasts. Lounge, morning room, 2 dining rooms. Soft background music. Mature ¾-acre garden; a short stroll from the Brontë Parsonage Museum. Picnics available. Civil wedding licence; function facilities. Wi-Fi. Ample private parking. No children under 10. 12 bedrooms (4 in former chauffeur and gardener's cottage, across the street). B&B £47.50–£122.50 per person; D,B&B £80–£157.50.
25% DISCOUNT VOUCHERS

HAY-ON-WYE Herefordshire
Map 3:D4
Tinto House, 13 Broad Street, HR3 5DB. Tel 01497-821556, www.tinto-house.co.uk. By the clock tower in the town centre, this listed Georgian house, owned by artist John Clare and his wife, Karen, has a large secluded rear garden bounded by the River Wye. The B&B is handsomely furnished, with books, original paintings, drawings and wooden sculptures. The converted stable block contains an art gallery; there are sculpture exhibitions in the garden. Dining room, library. No background music. 1-acre garden. Children welcomed. 4 bedrooms. B&B £42.50–£80 per person.

HELMSLEY North Yorkshire
Map 4:C4
No54, 54 Bondgate, YO62 5EZ. Tel 01439-771533, www.no54.co.uk.

Formed from two cottages in a York stone terrace half a mile from the market square, Lizzie Would's small B&B has well-equipped bedrooms set around a sunny courtyard. The main building has flagstone floors and real fires. Breakfast, served at a communal table, includes muffins and kedgeree. Sitting room. No background music. Garden. Near the North York Moors national park; picnics available. 3 bedrooms in courtyard. B&B £45–£55 per person.

HENFIELD West Sussex
Map 2:E3
SUSSEX PRAIRIES AT MORLANDS FARM, Wheatsheaf Road, BN5 9AT. Tel 01273-495902, www.sussexprairies.co.uk. Owners Paul McBride (a trained horticulturalist) and his wife, Pauline, have planted perennials and grasses to create a 'stunning' prairie-style garden, in which sits this small B&B. Guests are encouraged to roam among the 550 plant varieties in the grounds, which are surrounded by mature oak trees. In 'truly luxurious' modern farmhouse style, the bedrooms are furnished with 'treasures' the couple have collected on their travels. Breakfast has home-made yogurt, sausages and bacon from home-reared pedigree rare breed pigs, fruit and vegetables from the farm (vegetarians catered for). Breakfast room. Pre-booked guided tours for non-residents; farm nursery. 3 bedrooms. B&B £52.50–£123 per person.

HEREFORD Herefordshire
Map 3:D4
CASTLE HOUSE, Castle Street, HR1 2NW. Tel 01432-356321, www.castlehse.co.uk. David Watkins's city-centre hotel sits in terraced gardens leading down to the old castle moat, only yards away from Hereford Cathedral. The main accommodation is in two converted Grade II listed houses. A new addition a few steps away, *Number 25*, has a further eight luxury bedrooms and is available for exclusive use. Dinner is served in the restaurant and the informal *Castle Bistro*, both of which are supplied with beef from the owner's pedigree Hereford herd and produce from his farm; Claire Nicholls is the chef. Michelle Marriott-Lodge manages. Lounge, *Bertie's* bar, restaurant, bistro; light jazz/classical background music. Lift. Garden, terrace (alfresco dining). Parking. Children welcomed. 24 bedrooms. B&B £95–£130 per person; D,B&B from £150.
25% DISCOUNT VOUCHERS

HEXHAM Northumberland
Map 4:B3
BARRASFORD ARMS, Barrasford, NE48 4AA. Tel 01434-681237, www.barrasfordarms.co.uk. 'A good bolthole.' In a small village in the North Tyne valley, this stone-built 1870s country pub-with-rooms is a magnet for locals and visitors, attracted by hand-drawn real ales and the cooking of chef/patron Tony Binks, whose traditional English dishes have a French twist. A relaxed, welcoming place, it has 'a high standard of comfort, without any unnecessary flourishes'. It regularly hosts quoits tournaments, hunt meets, darts finals and vegetable competitions. Bedrooms are smart and understated. Bar, 2 dining rooms; private dining. Wi-Fi. Parking. Children welcomed. 7 bedrooms. B&B £43.50–£67. Dinner from £25.

Battlesteads Hotel & Restaurant, Wark-on-Tyne, NE48 3LS. Tel 01434-230209, www.battlesteads.com. Dee and Richard Slade have won eco awards for their sustainably run extended farmstead with 18th-century origins close to Northumberland national park. There are organic toiletries, an electric car-charging socket, and a carbon-neutral heating and hot water system. Polytunnels supply the fruit, vegetables and herbs for chef Eddie Shilton's modern British food. Bedrooms are spacious and modern. Conservatory dining room; secret walled garden. Civil wedding licence; function facilities. Wi-Fi. Children, and dogs (by arrangement; resident cat), welcomed. 17 bedrooms (2 suitable for ♿). B&B £52.50–£67.50 per person; D,B&B £75–£90.
25% DISCOUNT VOUCHERS

The Hermitage, Swinburne, NE48 4DG. Tel 01434-681248, email katie.stewart@themeet.co.uk. 'A delight', Katie and Simon Stewart's solid, stone-built house, three miles from Hadrian's Wall, is approached through a grand arch and up a long drive. The Stewarts are welcoming owners, who create a 'true country house atmosphere'. Drawing rooms, breakfast room; 4-acre grounds: terrace, tennis. No background music. Children over 7 welcomed. Resident dogs. 7 miles N of Corbridge. Ask for directions. 3 bedrooms. B&B £45 per person. Closed Nov–Mar.

HOARWITHY Herefordshire
Map 3:D4

Aspen House, HR2 6QP. Tel 01432-840353, www.aspenhouse.net. There is good walking from the front door (maps and drying facilities provided) of Sally Dean and Rob Elliott's environmentally friendly B&B. The 18th-century red sandstone farmhouse is in a tranquil Wye valley village, four miles from Ross-on-Wye. The hosts are enthusiastic about 'real' food and run Real Food Discovery weekends. Breakfasts are organic, using scrupulously sourced eggs, bacon from rare breed pigs, and home-made bread and muesli. Lounge (opening onto a decked area overlooking the ½-acre garden). No background music. 3 bedrooms (plus self-catering cottage). B&B £39–£55 per person.

HOLMFIRTH West Yorkshire
Map 4:E3

Sunnybank, 78 Upperthong Lane, HD9 3BQ. Tel 01484-684857, www.sunnybankguesthouse.co.uk. 'Warm welcome, lovely room, tasty food.' In a Victorian gentleman's hillside residence, which has 'stunning' views over the Derwent valley, this homely guest house is run by Jason and Rachel Salter. Breakfasts are 'first class', served in the oak-panelled dining room (open fire in winter; no background music). Mr Salter cooks a three-course dinner (modern English with an Italian influence) by arrangement. Lounge. Wi-Fi. 2-acre wooded garden. ¼ mile from centre. 5 bedrooms (2 on ground floor). B&B £40–£55 per person. Dinner £25 (BYO wine).

HOPE Derbyshire
Map 3:A6

Losehill House, Losehill Lane, Edale Road, S33 6AF. Tel 01433-621219, www.losehillhouse.co.uk. 'I have rarely been happier than when seated in

their outdoor hot tub watching the amazing view, even in winter.' Paul and Kathryn Roden's secluded spa hotel is on a hillside in the Peak District national park. It has panoramic views over the Hope valley. The solid, white-painted house 'exudes style' with comfortable, modern furnishing. Drawing room, bar, *Orangery* restaurant ('excellent' modern British food from chef Darren Goodwin); lift. Background music in evenings. 1-acre garden; terrace. Indoor swimming pool; hot tub; treatment rooms. Civil wedding licence; function/conference facilities. Footpath access to Peak District national park. Wi-Fi. Children, and dogs (in 2 rooms), welcomed. 21 bedrooms (dressing gowns and slippers supplied; 4 with external entrance). B&B £85–£180 per person. Dinner £35–£45.
25% DISCOUNT VOUCHERS

HUDDERSFIELD West Yorkshire
Map 4:E3
The Three Acres Inn & Restaurant, Roydhouse, Shelley, HD8 8LR. Tel 01484-602606, www.3acres.com. Neil Truelove and Brian Orme's characterful old roadside drovers' inn has a smart, popular restaurant and traditional bar. Chef Jason Littlewood serves modern British regional food. In Pennine countryside, it is five miles from the town centre (busy morning traffic). Bar, 2 dining rooms; background music. Small function/ private dining facilities. Terraced garden; decked dining terrace. Wi-Fi. Children welcomed. 20 bedrooms (1 suitable for ♿; 6 in adjacent cottages). B&B £62.50–£82.50 per person. Dinner from £39.95.

HULL East Yorkshire
Map 4:D5
Willerby Manor, Well Lane, Willerby, HU10 6ER. Tel 01482-652616, www.bw-willerbymanor.co.uk. Four miles outside the city, this Best Western hotel sits in three acres of landscaped gardens, with good leisure facilities. It is run by Alex Townend. Bedrooms are furnished in traditional style. The contemporary *Figs Brasserie* (head chef Ben Olley cooks a varied menu) has been renovated and extended; there is now a heated outdoor area for alfresco dining. Background music. Health club (swimming pool, sauna, steam room, gym, beauty room); crèche. Civil wedding licence; extensive business/ function facilities. Garden. 4 miles W of centre. Dogs welcomed (£10 per night; in some rooms only). Parking. 51 bedrooms (1 suitable for ♿). B&B £65–£98 per person; D,B&B £85–£118.

HUNGERFORD Berkshire
Map 2:D2
The Bear, 41 Charnham Street, RG17 0EL. Tel 01488-682512, www.thebearhotelhungerford.co.uk. Said to be one of the oldest coaching inns in England, with a long history of royal visitors, this small, contemporary hotel is run by Colin Heaney. Rooms (some with low beams and creaky floorboards) are spread between the original building, the courtyard beside the River Dunn, and *Bear Island House*, which overlooks the hotel's own island. Guests dine on chef Phil Wild's seasonal menus in the brasserie, bar and courtyard, and on the riverside terrace. 2 lounges, bar. Background music (classical, jazz). Civil wedding licence; function facilities. Wi-Fi. Dogs welcomed, by arrangement. 39

bedrooms (some on ground floor). B&B £64–£81.25; D,B&B £95.50–£113.25.

ILMINGTON Warwickshire
Map 3:D6

The Howard Arms, Lower Green, nr Stratford-upon-Avon, CV36 4LT. Tel 01608-682226, www.howardarms.com. 'Fantastic, with impeccable service.' This 400-year-old Cotswold stone inn stands on a pretty village green. There are arched windows, flagstone floors, a mix of old furniture, and cheering log fires. Bedrooms have a country house look, and modern technology. Emma O'Connell is the new manager. The busy restaurant has comforting dishes, using produce from local suppliers. Snug, bar, dining room ('easy listening' background music); patio/garden. Wi-Fi. Parking. Children welcomed. 8 bedrooms (5 through separate door under covered walkway). B&B £45–£145 per person. Dinner from £28.

ILSINGTON Devon
Map 1:D4

Ilsington Country House, nr Newton Abbot, TQ13 9RR. Tel 01364-661452, www.ilsington.co.uk. 'Everyone was cheerful and had a sense of fun.' The Hassell family's dog-friendly hotel stands in ten-acre grounds by heather-clad hills in Dartmoor national park. The imposing white-painted building has a traditional decor; inside, there is plenty of seating in the public rooms. Chef Mike O'Donnell serves a modern menu in the green-carpeted dining room. Background music. An 'excellent' leisure centre has a swimming pool, spa, sauna and well-equipped gym. Lounge, bar, restaurant, *Blue Tiger Inn* pub, library, conservatory; leisure complex. Lift. Civil wedding licence; conference facilities. Wi-Fi. Children, and dogs (in ground-floor rooms; £8 per night), welcomed. 25 bedrooms (8 on ground floor). B&B £47.50–£105 per person. Dinner £36.
25% DISCOUNT VOUCHERS

IRONBRIDGE Shropshire
Map 2:A1

The Library House, Severn Bank, TF8 7AN. Tel 01952-432299, www.libraryhouse.com. 'Immensely thoughtful and welcoming', owner Lizzie Steel offers guests a complimentary drink upon arrival at her 'beautifully decorated' Grade II listed Georgian guest house overlooking the River Severn. It is in a peaceful little courtyard, a short distance from the famous bridge. The house retains original shelving from its days as a village library. Bedrooms have a flat-screen TV with DVD-player, bathrobes and real coffee. A 'superb' breakfast has 'some quite unusual choices, all immaculately served'. Sitting room, dining room. No background music. Resident terrier, Fizz. Wi-Fi. Courtyard garden. Parking passes supplied for local car parks. Restaurants nearby. 4 bedrooms (1 with private terrace). B&B £50–£75 per person.

KESWICK Cumbria
Map 4: insert C2

Dalegarth House, Portinscale, CA12 5RQ. Tel 017687-72817, www.dalegarth-house.co.uk. New owners Craig and Clare Dalton took over this guest house in a traditional Edwardian home early in 2012. In an 'idyllic' situation above Derwentwater, it has fell and lake views. Bedrooms are simply furnished and comfortable. Mrs Dalton uses regional food ('a taste of the Lakes') for her home-cooked dinners, served at 7 pm. Cumbrian breakfasts. In a village 1 mile from Keswick. Background radio at breakfast; classical/'easy listening' music at dinner. Lounge, bar, restaurant. Garden. Parking. 10 bedrooms (2 in annexe). B&B £42.50 per person; D,B&B £62.70.

Lyzzick Hall, Underskiddaw, CA12 4PY. Tel 017687-72277, www.lyzzickhall.co.uk. Surrounded by breathtaking scenery of the Borrowdale valley and Catbells, the Fernandez and Lake families' hotel is on the lower slopes of Skiddaw. Most rooms have views towards the Lakeland fells. Local suppliers are used in the restaurant, where traditional and contemporary British cuisine is served; wine is mainly from the Iberian peninsula. 2 lounges, bar, restaurant. Background music. Indoor pool, sauna, whirlpool bath. 4-acre landscaped grounds. Wi-Fi. Children welcomed. 31 bedrooms (1 on ground floor). B&B £69–£110 per person; D,B&B £89–£130.

KINGHAM Oxfordshire
Map 3:D6

The Kingham Plough, The Green, nr Chipping Norton, OX7 6YD. Tel 01608-658327, www.thekinghamplough.co.uk. Noted for its 'inventive and flavourful food', this pub-with-rooms opposite the green in a 'charming' Cotswolds village is owned by chef Emily Lampson (a former sous-chef at *The Fat Duck*) and her husband, Miles. The restaurant, in a restored barn, has a daily-changing menu using seasonal and local produce. It prides itself on 'making practically everything and wasting little'. 4 miles SW of Chipping Norton. Bar, restaurant (background music); terrace, garden. Wi-Fi. Children, and dogs (annexe only; £10), welcomed. 7 bedrooms (3 in annexe). B&B £45–£105 per person. Dinner £30.

KINGSBRIDGE Devon
Map 1:D4

Thurlestone Hotel, Thurlestone, TQ7 3NN. Tel 01548-560382, www.thurlestone.co.uk. 'We all came away feeling we had been spoilt.' Run by the Grose family, who have owned it since 1896, this large, family-friendly hotel is in 19-acre subtropical grounds close to the sea and sandy beaches. Julie Baugh is manager. The spa, newly refurbished, has an indoor pool, laconium, steam room, fitness studio, speciality showers and beauty treatment rooms. Lounges, bar, *Margaret Amelia* restaurant (open to non-residents; Hugh Miller cooks); lift. Outdoor *Rock Pool* eating area (teas, lunches, snacks, dinners); terrace (alfresco dining); *The Village Inn* 16th-century pub. Spa; outdoor heated swimming pool (May–Sept); tennis, squash, badminton, croquet, 9-hole golf course; children's club in school holidays. No background music. Civil wedding licence; function facilities. Wi-Fi. Children, and dogs (in some rooms only; £8 per night charge), welcomed. 4 miles SW of Kingsbridge. 66 bedrooms (2 suitable for ♿; some with balcony, sea views). B&B £75–£220 per person. Dinner from £38.50.

KIRKBY STEPHEN Cumbria
Map 4:C3

A Corner of Eden, Low Stennerskeugh, Ravenstonedale, CA17 4LL. Tel 015396-23370, www.acornerofeden.co.uk. Debbie Temple and Richard Greaves have done a 'wonderful' job restoring their 'unusual' Grade II listed Georgian farmhouse in an 'utterly peaceful situation, with beautiful scenery'. Bedrooms, decorated in period style with vintage and antique furniture, share a bathroom and a shower room (bathrobes supplied). A butler's pantry stocks complimentary bread, jams, chutney and cakes (all home made), fresh fruit, tea, coffee, juices and an honesty bar. The lounge has a log fire, books and CDs. 'We enjoyed breakfast in the wood-panelled dining room', with eggs from the hosts' free-range chickens. Dinner is available for house parties of eight (£34 per person), by arrangement. No background music. Lounge, dining room, pantry; 5-acre grounds. No TV or phone in rooms. Wi-Fi. Dogs welcomed (charge). 4 bedrooms. B&B £60 per person.

KNUTSFORD Cheshire
Map 4:E3

Belle Epoque, 60 King Street, WA16 6DT. Tel 01565-633060, www.thebelleepoque.com. Period features abound in this lavishly decorated restaurant-with-rooms: a Venetian glass mosaic floor, marble pillars, Art Nouveau fireplaces. In the centre of town, it has been owned by the Mooney family for over 35 years; Richard Walker is the manager. Bedrooms and bathrooms have a more contemporary feel and overlook the Mediterranean roof garden and walled courtyard. In the restaurant, chef Gareth Chappell serves classic French cuisine using local produce (farmers and suppliers are credited on the menu). Bar, restaurant (closed Sun), private dining rooms. Background jazz. Roof garden (alfresco dining); walled terrace. Civil wedding licence; function facilities. Wi-Fi. Parking. 7 bedrooms. B&B £57.50–£95 per person. Dinner £50.

LANCASTER Lancashire
Map 4:D2

The Ashton, Well House, Wyresdale Road, LA1 3JJ. Tel 01524-68460, www.theashtonlancaster.com. In large grounds near Williamson Park, on the outskirts of the city, former TV and film set designer James Gray's sandstone Georgian house has stylish bedrooms and indulgent bathrooms. There is tea and home-made cake in the afternoon; simple meals ('food for friends') are served in the evening, by arrangement. Breakfast, served until 10 am, has eggs from the free-range hens that roam the garden. Lounge, dining room (occasional background music). Wi-Fi. Parking. Children welcomed (no under-8s on Sat eve). 5 bedrooms (1 on ground floor; some overlook the garden and park). B&B £62.50–£115 per person. Dinner £24.95.

LAVENHAM Suffolk
Map 2:C5

The Swan, High Street, CO10 9QA. Tel 01787-247477, www.theswanat lavenham.co.uk. In the centre of a medieval village, this hotel, refurbished by TA Hotel Collection, occupies three timber-framed 15th-century buildings. It is managed by Ingo Wiangke. Bedrooms are furnished in country house style. Guests have a range of dining options: the snug bar, filled with Air Force memorabilia; the bright, modern brasserie, whose large windows face the garden; and the impressive medieval dining room, with its high, timbered ceiling and minstrels' gallery. Lounge, bar, brasserie, *Gallery* restaurant (Justin Kett cooks classic British dishes using locally sourced ingredients). Occasional background music. Garden. Civil wedding licence; function facilities. Wi-Fi. Children and dogs welcomed. 45 bedrooms. B&B £97.50–£280 per person; D,B&B from £122.50.

LEEDS West Yorkshire
Map 4:D4
42 THE CALLS, 42 The Calls, LS2 7EW. Tel 0113-244 0099, www.42thecalls.co.uk. Overlooking the River Aire (fishing rods supplied), this contemporary hotel, a short walk from the train station, has been imaginatively converted from an 18th-century corn mill. Original mill mechanisms have been conserved; beamed ceilings and exposed girders and brickwork are offset by contemporary art. It is managed by Belinda Dawson for JJW Hotels. A hearty breakfast has kippers, duck eggs, artisan breads. Lounge, bar, breakfast room (radio at breakfast); room service. Lift. Conference facilities. *Brasserie Forty 4* next door (closed Sun). Wi-Fi. Street noise at night. Children and dogs welcomed. 41 bedrooms (1 suitable for ♿): £95–£395. Breakfast £11.74–£14.95; dinner £35.

LEEK Staffordshire
Map 2:A2
THE THREE HORSESHOES, Buxton Road, Blackshaw Moor, ST13 8TW. Tel 01538-300296, www.3shoesinn.co.uk. 'Personable and pleasant local staff; everything runs like oiled silk.' On the edge of the Peak District national park, the Kirk family's old stone inn sits beneath the gritstone outcrops of the Roaches. They have extended to provide 'excellent' bedrooms with solid oak furniture, a pristine bathroom, modern prints. The contemporary brasserie has an open kitchen, serving modern British food with a Thai influence; the bar and popular carvery in the original part of the inn retain period charm with beamed ceilings and dark oak tables. Background music. Bar, 2 restaurants, patio, garden. Lift. Civil wedding licence; conference facilities. Beauty treatments. Wi-Fi. Parking. Children welcomed (outdoor play area). 2 miles outside the town. 26 bedrooms. B&B £42.50–£113 per person; D,B&B from £62.50.

LEICESTER Leicestershire
Map 2:B3
THE BELMONT, De Montfort Street, LE1 7GR. Tel 0116-252 9602, www.belmonthotel.co.uk. 'A quality town hotel, without the eye-watering prices.' On leafy New Walk, within easy reach of the city, this traditional hotel, formed from a row of Victorian residences, has been owned by the Bowie family for four generations. 'I loved the location.' Spacious bedrooms are modern and 'stylish'. Seasonal English and continental cuisine, cooked by Alex Ballard, is served in an L-shaped dining room with high ceilings, smart curtains, chandeliers and 'impeccably set' tables. Bar, *Cherry's* restaurant, conservatory. Lift. Background music. Civil wedding licence; function facilities. Wi-Fi (free for first 2 hours). Parking. Children

and small pets welcomed. 75 bedrooms (3 family rooms). B&B £39.50–£79 per person. Dinner from £20.50.

Hotel Maiyango, 13–21 St Nicholas Place, LE1 4LD. Tel 0116-251 8898, www.maiyango.com. On the edge of the city centre, this chic hotel, owned by Aatin Anadkat, has panoramic views of the town from its rooftop terrace. A 150-year-old former shoe factory, it has bespoke wood furnishings, rich fabrics and commissioned artwork. In the restaurant, chef Phillip Sharpe's seasonal menus focus on food from local suppliers. The casual *Maiyango Kitchen Deli* around the corner serves 'convenience restaurant food' (available to take away). Bar, cocktail lounge, restaurant; terrace. Background music in lobby/reception area. Function facilities. Cooking and cocktail classes. 14 bedrooms. B&B £45–£115 per person; D,B&B £72.50–£138.
25% DISCOUNT VOUCHERS

LEWDOWN Devon
Map 1:C3

Lewtrenchard Manor, nr Okehampton, EX20 4PN. Tel 01566-783222, www.lewtrenchard.co.uk. James and Sue Murray have repurchased this Jacobean stone manor house, the ancestral home of the Revd Sabine Baring-Gould, who wrote 'Onward Christian Soldiers'. He restyled the house as a Victorian-Elizabethan fantasy, giving it ornate ceilings, stained-glass windows, ornamental carving. It stands in extensive, peaceful parkland, with streams and ponds, fountains and statuary. John Hooker is the new chef. Lounge, bar, 2 restaurants (open to non-residents; background music), ballroom. Wi-Fi. In-room beauty treatments. Fishing, clay-pigeon shooting; falconry and owl flying can be arranged. Children and dogs welcomed. 14 bedrooms (4 in courtyard annexe; bridal suite in 2-storey folly; 1 suitable for ♿). B&B £77.50–£135 per person; D,B&B £122.50–£180.

LEWES East Sussex
Map 2:E4

Berkeley House, 2 Albion Street, BN7 2ND. Tel 01273-476057, www.berkeleyhouselewes.co.uk. 'Cordial' owners and experienced hosts Roy Patten and Steve Johnson have been offering B&B accommodation at their Georgian town house for more than 20 years. It is in a central location; a south-facing roof terrace has views over the town. The hosts are helpful with information for Glyndebourne (taxis ordered, etc). 'Cosy' lounge, dining room. No background music. Wi-Fi. Off-street parking (£5 per day). Children over 8 welcomed. 3 bedrooms (1 might hear traffic). B&B £40–£75 per person.
25% DISCOUNT VOUCHERS

LINCOLN Lincolnshire
Map 4:E5

The Castle, Westgate, LN1 3AS. Tel 01522-538801, www.castlehotel.net. In a 'splendid' position close to the cathedral and castle, this recently refurbished Grade II listed house has 'smart, slightly angular' bedrooms decorated in dove greys, taupes and mauves, with original artwork; most have views of the castle walls or the cathedral. The hotel is owned by Paul Catlow and Saera Ahmad. There is a 'charming' panelled restaurant, where chef Mark Cheseldine's innovative European cuisine is served. 'We had an excellent meal, elegantly presented.' 2 small lounges, bar (a popular local), *Reform* restaurant (evenings only; background music). Massage and beauty treatments. Wedding/function facilities. Wi-Fi. Parking. Children welcomed. 18 bedrooms (some in attic, some in courtyard; 1 suitable for ♿); plus 1 apartment). B&B £55–£110 per person; D,B&B £85–£135.

LIVERPOOL Merseyside
Map 4:E2

BASE2STAY LIVERPOOL, 29 Seel Street, L1 4AU. Tel 0151-705 2626, www.base2stay.com. 'Just what was needed.' In the RopeWalks area, this 'practical and efficient hotel' (sister to *base2stay*, London – see Shortlist) is a converted 1850s print works. The lounge has black leather chairs; exposed brick walls displaying bright, modern art; and books on John Lennon and Yoko Ono. The black-and-white bedrooms range from large singles to double-height gallery studios; all have a mini-kitchen with a microwave, fridge and sink, plus HDTV, music and games. There is no bar or dining room, but breakfast boxes (£6) can be ordered in advance. Background music. Meeting room. Lift. Vending machines. Wi-Fi. Parking discounts. Children welcomed. 106 bedrooms (some suitable for ♿): £49–£149.

HARD DAYS NIGHT, Central Buildings, North John Street, L2 6RR. Tel 0151-236 1964, www.harddaysnighthotel.com. In a grand, Grade II listed building fronted with marble columns, this Beatles-inspired hotel is decorated with original artwork and photographs of the Fab Four. Modern rooms are individually designed, with a monsoon shower in the bathroom. The hotel is managed by Michael Dewey for the Classic British Hotels Group. Lounge (live music on Fri and Sat nights), *Bar Four* cocktail bar, brasserie, *Blakes* restaurant (open to non-residents; closed Sun, Mon; Paul Feery is chef); art gallery. Background music. Civil wedding licence; function facilities. Wi-Fi. Beatles tours can be arranged. 110 bedrooms: £120–£195; D,B&B £135–£225 per person.

HOPE STREET HOTEL, 40 Hope Street, L1 9DA. Tel 0151-709 3000, www.hopestreethotel.co.uk. 'A real find.' Opposite the Philharmonic Hall, this striking, modern hotel is spread across two buildings: a 19th-century carriage works in the style of a Venetian palazzo, and an adjacent conversion, whose sixth-floor conference facilities have 'fantastic' views over the city. 'Very pleasant and tastefully decorated', the hotel is owned and managed by David Brewitt. Minimalist bedrooms in both buildings have wooden floors, under-floor heating and cherry wood furniture. In *The London Carriage Works* restaurant, chef Paul Askew cooks modern international dishes. 'We enjoyed everything enormously.' Reading room, bar, restaurant; lift; gym, treatment rooms. Parking nearby (£10 charge). Civil wedding licence; function facilities. Children, and dogs (£30 charge), welcomed. 89 bedrooms (some suitable for ♿). B&B £54.50–£105 per person; penthouse £670; D,B&B £74.50–£115.

LOOE Cornwall
Map 1:D3
BARCLAY HOUSE, St Martins Road, PL13 1LP. Tel 01503-262929, www.barclayhouse.co.uk. From its hillside position on the outskirts of a small fishing port, this white-painted Victorian villa has 'superb' views over the East Looe river. Graham Brooks is the manager; 'everyone is very kind'. Head chef Joe Sardari's 'modern coastal' cooking, featuring plenty of local fish, is 'superb'. Mornings, there are 'excellent' full Cornish breakfasts. The Brooks family also owns two other restaurants: *Trawlers on the Quay* (Jono Hancock is chef) and *The Plough* in Duloe, nearby. Sitting room, bar, restaurant (background jazz; radio at breakfast, closed Sun); terrace (alfresco dining); gym, sauna, outdoor heated swimming pool. 6-acre gardens and woodland paths. Civil wedding licence. Children welcomed. 12 bedrooms (1 suitable for ♿), plus 8 self-catering cottages. B&B £57.50–£97.50 per person; D,B&B £87.50–£127.50.
25% DISCOUNT VOUCHERS

TRELASKE HOTEL & RESTAURANT, Polperro Road, PL13 2JS. Tel 01503-262159, www.trelaske.co.uk. 'Good food, good facilities, and clean, spacious rooms made this a very enjoyable stay.' Hazel Billington and Ross Lewin's hotel is in a peaceful location, with 'excellent' views over the gardens and moorland beyond. Bedrooms have a balcony or patio. 'Friendly and always smiling', Ms Billington is a welcoming host; Mr Lewin uses fruit, vegetables and herbs from the hotel's own polytunnels for his award-winning, seasonal modern British cooking. In 4-acre grounds, 2 miles outside town. 2 lounges, library, bar/conservatory (background music); terrace (summer barbecues). Wedding/function facilities. Wi-Fi. Children welcomed (no under-4s in restaurant). 7 bedrooms (4 in building adjacent to main house; dogs allowed in 2 bedrooms, £6.50 per night). B&B £49–£53.50 per person; D,B&B £69.50–£82.50. Closed early Nov–Feb.

LOWER SWELL Somerset
Map 1:C6
LANGFORD FIVEHEAD, TA3 6PH. Tel 01460-281159, www.langfordfivehead.co.uk. Peter Steggall and Orlando Murrin have created 'a wonderfully peaceful retreat' at their meticulously restored Grade II* listed Elizabethan manor house, in the Somerset Levels. The bedrooms are furnished with antiques; some have a four-poster bed. On Friday and Saturday evenings, Mr Murrin cooks a 'delicious' set dinner of seasonal fare, served communally. Background music (classical/jazz, before dinner). Drawing room (piano), lounge, library, TV room, dining room, back porch (tea, coffee, snacks, honesty bar); courtyard. 7-acre garden: Victorian greenhouse, knot garden, small lake; tennis court, croquet lawn. Wi-Fi (guest PC). Children welcomed. 6 bedrooms (plus 3-bed cottage). B&B £65–£300 per person. Dinner £59. Closed Jan.

LUDLOW Shropshire
Map 3:C4
FISHMORE HALL, Fishmore Road, SY8 3DP. Tel 01584-875148, www.fishmorehall.co.uk. In 'a great location' outside the town, with panoramic views over countryside, this symmetrical white Regency house is run as a hotel by

owner/manager Laura Penman. Simple, stylish bedrooms have a wide bed and home-made biscuits. In the restaurant, chef David Jaram serves a Shropshire tasting menu. Sitting room, bar, brasserie, *Forelles* restaurant/conservatory (background music). Garden, terrace. Function facilities. Civil wedding licence arrangement with Ludlow Castle. 'Foodie' cooking and shopping packages. In-room massages and beauty treatments can be arranged. Wi-Fi. Children, and dogs (£30 charge), welcomed. 15 bedrooms (1 suitable for ♿). B&B £75–£125 per person; D,B&B £122.50–£172.50.
25% DISCOUNT VOUCHERS

LUPTON Cumbria
Map 4: insert C2
THE PLOUGH, Cow Brow, LA6 1PJ. Tel 015395-67700, www.theploughatlupton.co.uk. In a hamlet near Kirkby Lonsdale, this 18th-century coaching inn has been given a modern make-over by Richard Rose, who also owns *The Punch Bowl Inn* at Crosthwaite (see above). Abi Lloyd manages both inns. 'The sense of quality is tangible; the open bar and lounge are rich in quality restored antique furniture. It is an attractive (and dog-friendly) place to eat and stay.' The restaurant has small plates to share ('generous crisp whitebait; inviting honey-coated courgette fritters') and blackboard specials ('beautifully cooked haunch of venison'). The five bedrooms have soft colours, modern bathrooms. Bar, lounge, restaurant, terrace, garden. Background music in public areas. Civil wedding licence. Children and dogs welcomed. 5 bedrooms. B&B £57.50–£97.50 per person. Dinner from £35.

LYME REGIS Dorset
Map 1:C6
1 LYME TOWNHOUSE, 1 Pound Street, DT7 3HZ. Tel 01297-442499, www.1lymetownhouse.co.uk. Terrie and Brian Covington's contemporary B&B occupies a three-storey Georgian town house on a hill above Lyme Bay, within easy reach of the town and harbour. Experienced hosts, the Covingtons have worked for nearly 30 years in the hospitality industry. Bedrooms have feature wallpaper, a hospitality tray, a quirky metalwork bed; some have views towards the sea. A daily-changing breakfast hamper (fresh juice, yogurt, fruits, home-made pastries) is delivered to the room each morning. No background music. Paid parking up the street. 7 bedrooms. B&B £47.50–£100 per person.

LYNMOUTH Devon
Map 1:B4
SHELLEY'S, 8 Watersmeet Road, EX35 6EP. Tel 01598-753219, www.shelleyshotel.co.uk. Steeped in romantic history, this 18th-century house overlooks the ancient smugglers' harbour of Lynmouth. Percy Bysshe Shelley brought his 16-year-old bride, Harriet, here for their honeymoon in the summer of 1812, when it was a more humble cottage. Today it is run as a B&B by Jane Becker and Richard Briden. The airy bedrooms have views over Lynmouth Bay and the surrounding countryside, and the house is well situated for the many local attractions. Lounge, bar, conservatory breakfast room. No background music. Wi-Fi. 11 bedrooms (1 on ground floor). B&B £39.50–£59.50 per person. Closed Nov–Easter.

LYNTON Devon
Map 1:B4
Lynton Cottage Hotel, North Walk, EX35 6ED. Tel 01598-752342, www.lynton-cottage.co.uk. 'I cannot recommend this hotel highly enough.' With 'breathtaking' views of Lynmouth, the sea and the coastline to South Wales, David Mowlem and Heather Biancardi's small hotel stands high on a cliff-top on North Walk, part of the North Devon Coastal Path. 'Immaculate' bedrooms are furnished traditionally; some have a four-poster bed and roll-top bath. Chef Paul Ruttledge's classic European cooking is 'superb, the presentation excellent'. Lounge, bar, restaurant (background music); terrace; 2½-acre garden. Beauty treatments and holistic therapies. Parking. Children and dogs welcomed. 16 bedrooms (1 on ground floor; some with sea-view balcony). B&B £45–£82 per person. Dinner £40. Closed mid-Dec–mid-Jan.

LYTHAM Lancashire
Map 4:D2
The Rooms, 35 Church Road, FY8 5LL. Tel 01253-736000, www.theroomslytham.com. Jackie and Andy Baker's sophisticated, centrally located B&B is near the memorial gardens. Bedrooms have a king-size bed and modern technology (flat-screen TV, DVD-player, DAB radio, iPod docking station); bathrooms and wet rooms come with under-floor heating and bathrobes. Award-winning breakfasts, served in the walled garden if the weather permits, have a wide choice (English, Italian, Scottish; smoked haddock fishcake, eggs Arlington, vegetarian crepes); champagne at weekends. Breakfast room (background TV). No background music. Wi-Fi. Children welcomed. 5 bedrooms (plus 2-bed serviced apartment). B&B £62.50–£125 per person.

MANCHESTER
Map 4:E3
Didsbury House, Didsbury Park, Didsbury Village, M20 5LJ. Tel 0161-448 2200, www.didsburyhouse.co.uk. In a Grade II listed Victorian villa in a leafy suburb, this chic hotel retains original architectural features, such as the imposing stained-glass window over the staircase. Managed by Andrew Hughes, it is part of the Eclectic Hotel Collection (see *Eleven Didsbury Park*, below). The contemporary interior has playful touches (trompe l'oeil wallpaper, splashes of colour); the ambience is both intimate and 'friendly'. Bedrooms are decorated in subtle colour schemes; some have a freestanding roll-top bath in the room or a Victorian-style shower. Lounge, bar, breakfast room; meeting room; spa; gym; walled terrace with water feature. Wi-Fi (charge). 'Chill-out' background music. Exclusive use for weddings/functions. Children welcomed. 27 bedrooms: £72–£260. Breakfast £13.50–£15.50.

Eleven Didsbury Park, 11 Didsbury Park, Didsbury Village, M20 5LH. Tel 0161-448 7711, www.elevendidsburypark.com. Eamonn and Sally O'Loughlin own this small, peacefully located Victorian villa (part of their Eclectic Hotel Collection). Decorated in soft colours, the modern bedrooms vary in size (some are compact); one large room has a private canopied terrace with an outdoor cast-iron bathtub.

Convenient for both the airport (ten minutes' drive) and the centre. 2 lounge/bars (background music all day), veranda. Gym; treatment room. Conference facilities. Large walled garden. Parking. Children and dogs welcomed. 20 bedrooms (1, on ground floor, suitable for ♿): £150–£264. Breakfast £13.50–£15.50.

Velvet, 2 Canal Street, M1 3HE. Tel 0161-236 9003, www.velvetmanchester.com. Within easy reach of the city centre and the railway station, this quirky hotel has a lively bar and decadently furnished bedrooms. Stylish, modern bathrooms have bathrobes and slippers, steam-free mirrors, automatic lighting; some have a double bath and walk-in shower. In the restaurant. an all-day menu has British comfort food, pizzas and snacks. Bar (DJs on Fri and Sat nights; noise may affect some rooms), restaurant (alfresco dining on front terrace; background music). Wi-Fi. Discounted car park. 19 bedrooms: £54.50–£209. Breakfast £9.50–£13.50, dinner from £16.90.

MARCHAM Oxfordshire
Map 2:C2
B&B Rafters, Abingdon Road, OX13 6NU. Tel 01865-391298, www.bnb-rafters.co.uk. Warm hosts Sigrid and Arne Grawert run this good-value B&B in their half-timbered house on the edge of a village near Abingdon. Bedrooms are decorated in neutral colours, with feature wallpaper and colourful cushions and bedspreads; they have fresh flowers, a DVD-player, DAB radio, iPod docking station and speakers. 'Delicious' breakfasts have organic ingredients, home-baked bread, home-made jams and marmalade; whisky porridge is a speciality. Lounge, breakfast room; garden. No background music. Wi-Fi. Parking. Children welcomed. 4 bedrooms. B&B £47.50–£60 per person.

MARGATE Kent
Map 2:D5
The Reading Rooms, 31 Hawley Square, CT9 1PH. Tel 01843-225166, www.thereadingroomsmargate.co.uk. Close to the beach and the Turner Contemporary arts gallery, Louise Oldfield and Liam Nabb's unconventional town house B&B is on a fine Georgian square. Each bedroom takes up an entire floor and has been painstakingly renovated in 'dilapidated grandeur', with intricate plasterwork revealed, distressed walls, wooden floors and carefully chosen antiques. Spacious bathrooms are 'stunning – the size of a bedroom'; they have a cast iron roll-top bath, walk-in shower and luxury toiletries. Breakfast from an extensive choice is brought to the room. No background music. 3 bedrooms. B&B £75–£180 per person.

MATLOCK Derbyshire
Map 3:A6
Manor Farm, Dethick, DE4 5GG. Tel 01629-534302, www.manorfarmdethick.co.uk. On an attractive, 'user-friendly' farm in beautiful countryside, Gilly and Simon Groom are the 'welcoming and friendly' hosts at this 'excellent' B&B in a Grade II* listed stone house with historic associations (it was once the home of 'conspirator' Sir Anthony Babington). Country-style bedrooms have beams, old stonework or buttresses and corbels; the 'best' are in the hayloft.

Sustainable values are practised; organic breakfasts are served on a large refectory table in the original Tudor kitchen. Sitting rooms (TV, games), breakfast room. No background music. Drying facilities. Wi-Fi. Parking; bike/motorcycle storage. 2½ miles east of Matlock; collection from railway/bus station can be arranged. Children over 6 allowed. 5 bedrooms (1 with shared bathroom; 1 suitable for ♿). B&B £40–£70 per person.

MELTON MOWBRAY Leicestershire
Map 2:A3
SYSONBY KNOLL, Asfordby Road, LE13 0HP. Tel 01664-563563, www.sysonby.com. In 'attractive' landscaped grounds reaching to the River Eye, this red brick Edwardian home was extended to form a hotel and restaurant. It has been in the same family since 1965; Jenny and Gavin Howling are the owners. Vicky Wilkin is the manager. Most rooms are spacious and traditionally furnished. In the restaurant, with fine views over the river, 'the quality, execution and presentation' of chef Susan Meakin's cooking is 'first rate'. Good walks. Complimentary fishing for guests (tackle available to borrow). Lounge, bar, restaurant. Background music. 4½-acre gardens and meadow. Wi-Fi. Parking. Children and dogs welcomed (resident dog). 30 bedrooms (some on ground floor; some in neighbouring annexe; ramp). B&B £49–£106 per person. Dinner £22.50–£38.

MIDHURST West Sussex
Map 2:E3
THE ANGEL, North Street, GU29 9DN. Tel 01730-812421, www.theangelmidhurst.co.uk. In the South Downs national park, this former coaching inn on the high street of a Georgian town has been refurbished. Country house-style bedrooms have bold colours and fabrics; some have retained traditional features such as 17th-century oak beams and a Victorian fireplace. Richard Macadam is the manager. In *Bentley's* restaurant (open to non-residents), chef Richard Cook's fixed-price menus feature traditional English dishes. Lounge, bar, café, restaurant (closed Sun and Mon eves); courtyard. Background music. Wi-Fi. Parking. Civil wedding licence; function facilities. Children, and dogs (in 4 rooms), welcomed. 15 bedrooms (4 in cottage; 1 suitable for ♿). B&B £65–£150 per person; D,B&B £80–£175.
25% DISCOUNT VOUCHERS

MILLOM Cumbria
Map 4: inset C2
BROADGATE HOUSE, Broadgate, Thwaites, LA18 5JZ. Tel 01229-716295, www.broadgate-house.co.uk. With panoramic views across the Dudden estuary, this traditional Georgian house has been in the Lewthwaite family for almost 200 years. It has been decorated in period style by owner Diana Lewthwaite. The two-acre grounds are designed as a series of 'garden rooms', with a walled garden, terraces, a croquet lawn and an 'oasis' with a palm tree. Drawing room, cosy sitting room (wood-burning stove), dining room (food is locally sourced), breakfast room. No background music. 3 miles W of Broughton-in-Furness. 5 bedrooms (private bathroom with throne loo, freestanding bath). B&B £45–£55 per person. Dinner £30. Closed Dec–Mar.

MONKTON COMBE Somerset
Map 2:D1
Wheelwrights Arms, Church Lane, BA2 7HB. Tel 01225-722287, www.wheelwrightsarms.co.uk. Rolling countryside surrounds this pretty village on the outskirts of Bath, where David Munn's 18th-century country inn and former carpenter's workshop is run as an informal restaurant-with-rooms. (A history of the building's past is available.) Bedrooms are simply decorated with wood furnishings; one has a sloping ceiling and its own entrance to the garden. Chef James Hooper's frequently changing menus have interesting choices. Tickets can be arranged for Bath Rugby home games. Bar, restaurant. Background music (optional). Outdoor seating (alfresco dining). Wi-Fi. Parking (narrow entrance). Children welcomed. 7 bedrooms (in renovated building opposite; some suitable for ♿). B&B £67.50–£85 per person. Dinner £32.

MOUSEHOLE Cornwall
Map 1:E1
The Old Coastguard, The Parade, TR19 6PR. Tel 01736-731222, www.oldcoastguardhotel.co.uk. Charles and Edmund Inkin (owners of *The Gurnard's Head*, Zennor, and *The Felin Fach Griffin*, Felin Fach, Wales – see main entries) run this seaside hotel and restaurant for its new owner. Kay Bolt is the manager. They have renovated throughout: the downstairs area has been opened up to include a reception area, a dining space and a lower lounge that overlooks a subtropical garden. 'Spectacular' paintings by a local artist help create 'a characterful venue'. Bedrooms are snug, shabby-chic and well supplied with books; most overlook the bay, with views to St Clement's Isle. Simple brasserie food is served at the *Upper Deck* or *Sun Deck* eating areas, the terrace or the bar (background music). Wi-Fi. Children and dogs welcomed. 14 bedrooms. B&B £32.50–£57.50 per person. Dinner £30.

MULLION Cornwall
Map 1:E2
Polurrian Bay Hotel, Helston, TR12 7EN. Tel 01326-240421, www.polurrianhotel.com. Back in the hands of Nigel Chapman, a proponent of family-friendly hotels, this imposing white Edwardian house stands on cliffs on the Lizard peninsula. Part of Luxury Family Hotels, it has been given a subtle name change and a modern make-over; a new extension has a glass-fronted sitting area with 'amazing' views of the coastline. 'Glorious sunsets.' There are 12 acres of landscaped gardens, a sandy bay below, and plenty to occupy children and adults: indoor and seasonal outdoor pools, a hot tub, gym and spa (treatments); tennis courts, a sports field; a movie theatre; an adventure playground and more. 2 sitting rooms, dining room (background music); terrace. The Den (children 3 months–8 years old); The Blue Room (older children; video games, pool, table football). Civil wedding licence; function facilities. Wi-Fi. Children (baby equipment), and dogs (£10 per night charge), welcomed. 41 bedrooms (some on ground floor). B&B £62.50–£174.50 per person.

NEWBY BRIDGE Cumbria
Map 4: inset C2
The Swan Hotel & Spa, LA12 8NB. Tel 015395-31681, www.swanhotel.com. The Bardsley family refashioned the

interior of their whitewashed 17th-century former coaching inn to give a modern look while retaining many of the original features. It is family-friendly, with indulgent spa facilities for grown-ups. The hotel stands by a five-arch bridge on the banks of the River Leven, on the southern tip of Lake Windermere, and is popular with boating visitors. It is managed by Sarah Gibbs. Bedrooms have pretty floral wallpaper. Sitting room, library (children's games and books), bar; *River Room* restaurant, breakfast room; terrace. Background music. Spa (treatments), indoor pool, hot tub, sauna, steam room; gym. Civil wedding licence; function facilities. Wi-Fi. Parking. Children welcomed (complimentary milk and biscuits before bedtime; adventure playground; nature trail). 51 bedrooms. B&B £59.50–£105 per person. Dinner £30.

NEWCASTLE UPON TYNE Tyne and Wear
Map 4:B4
HOTEL DU VIN, Allan House, City Road, NE1 2BE. Tel 0191-229 2200, www.hotelduvin.com. Newcastle's Millennium Bridge and the Quayside can be viewed from this hotel (part of the Hotel du Vin group). On the banks of the River Tyne, the hotel has been 'attractively' converted from an imposing red brick building, the former home of the Tyne Tees Steam Shipping Company. Background music. Bistro (Ross Bootland is chef; food is 'good'), *Bubble* bar, 2 private dining rooms; courtyard (alfresco dining). Humidor. Civil wedding licence; function facilities. Parking. 42 bedrooms: £180–£310. Breakfast from £11.95; dinner £35.

THE TOWNHOUSE, 1 West Avenue, Gosforth, NE3 4ES. Tel 0191-285 6812, www.thetownhousehotel.co.uk. 'A real discovery.' Cathy Knox and Sheila Armstrong have created 'an oasis of civilisation' at their elegant Victorian town house, in a leafy suburb a short metro ride from the city centre. Their B&B has sumptuous bedrooms and luxurious bathrooms decorated 'with flair'. A café with a frequently changing blackboard menu has 'straightforward' home-cooked food; breakfasts are 'generous and varied'. 'Friendly, helpful, competent staff.' Background music. Breakfast room (morning TV), café (afternoon teas with home-made scones and cakes; open until 6 pm; 4 pm on Sun). Wi-Fi. Parking permits provided. Children welcomed. 10 bedrooms. B&B £47.50–£140 per person. Dinner £12.95–£18.95.

NEWQUAY Cornwall
Map 1:D2
THE HEADLAND HOTEL, Fistral Beach, TR7 1EW. Tel 01637-872211, www.headlandhotel.co.uk. On a jutting headland at the western end of Fistral beach, this red brick Victorian hotel (part of Best Loved Hotels) has been owned and managed by the Armstrong family for three decades. They recently added a veranda and terrace, sauna and steam room; further spa facilities are planned. Bedrooms are traditional with contemporary touches. Lounges, bar, 2 restaurants (1 for alfresco dining; Jan Wilhelm is chef). No background music. 10-acre grounds. Table tennis; 2 heated swimming pools (indoor and outdoor); croquet; 3 tennis courts; putting, boules; on-site surf school. Civil wedding licence; conference/event

facilities. Children welcomed (bunk beds, entertainment, etc). Dogs welcomed (£15 per night). 96 bedrooms (12 suites; 1 room suitable for ♿; plus 40 self-catering cottages in the grounds). B&B £79–£200 per person; D,B&B £89–£220.
25% DISCOUNT VOUCHERS

NORWICH Norfolk
Map 2:B5
By Appointment, 25–29 St George's Street, NR3 1AB. Tel 01603-630730, www.byappointmentnorwich.co.uk. Spread across a labyrinth of rooms in three 15th-century merchants' dwellings, Robert Culyer's quirky restaurant-with-rooms is filled with 'an eclectic collection of bits and bobs', some available for purchase. The bedrooms, reached by winding staircases, are also 'filled with treasures' (glove and collar boxes, antique suitcases, pictures and curios). There are two huge chandeliers and a coal fire in Queen Consort. Chef Mark Elvin's dishes have a continental bias, with 'good intensity of flavour'. In the atmospheric dining room, Mr Culyer presides over dinner 'like an impresario', reciting the menus ('the operatic background music seems entirely appropriate'). Breakfast, ordered the evening before, 'is very proper, beautifully presented'. 2 lounges, restaurant, small courtyard; 'tight' parking. 6 bedrooms. B&B £55–£90 per person. Dinner £47.40.

Norfolk Mead, Church Loke, Coltishall, NR12 7DN. Tel 01603-737531, www.norfolkmead.co.uk. In a 'near-perfect' location on the edge of the Norfolk Broads, Jill and Don Fleming's Georgian merchant's house has an air of 'faded grandeur'. 'We had an excellent room with balcony, overlooking the River Bure.' It is managed by Sharon Hardy. Chef Mark Sayers sources seasonal Norfolk fare; traditional Sunday lunches. 'The food was good.' Lounge, bar, restaurant; background music. Private dining. 8-acre grounds: walled garden, unheated swimming pool; fishing lake; off-river mooring. Civil wedding licence; conference facilities. 7 miles NE of Norwich. Children welcomed. 13 bedrooms (2 beamed ones in cottage suite; some with a four-poster bed). B&B £50–£95 per person; D,B&B £75–£160.
25% DISCOUNT VOUCHERS

38 St Giles, 38 St Giles Street, NR2 1LL. Tel 01603-662944, www.38stgiles.co.uk. Two Georgian town houses have been combined to create Jeanette and William Cheeseman's city centre B&B. Elegant hallways, landings and bedrooms display local artists' paintings, and there is complimentary home-made cake in the rooms on arrival. Breakfast has locally sourced eggs, meat and honey on the comb, and home-made bread, jams and marmalades. Breakfast room. No background music. Wi-Fi. Parking by arrangement. Children welcomed. 7 bedrooms (1 on ground floor). B&B £60–£100 per person.

OAKHILL Somerset
Map 2:D1
The Oakhill Inn, Fosse Road, nr Radstock, BA3 5HU. Tel 01749-840442, www.theoakhillinn.com. Charlie and Amanda Digney's unpretentious pub-with-rooms is in a pretty village three miles north of Shepton Mallet. Its modest interior is painted in strong

colours; there is comfortable seating and a fire in the snug. Head chef Neil Creese sources locally produced organic and free-range meat and poultry for his freshly prepared dishes; seafood is delivered daily from the Cornish coast. Breakfast has Gloucester Old Spot sausages and bacon, eggs from free-range hens, local apple juice, and home-made jam and marmalade.
2 bars, restaurant; garden. Low-level background music. Wi-Fi. Parking. Children welcomed. 5 bedrooms. B&B £45–£77.50 per person.

OTTERBURN Northumberland
Map 4:A3
THE OTTERBURN TOWER, NE19 1NS. Tel 01830-520620, www.otterburntower.com. 'Everything continues to function efficiently.' In extensive woodland close to the Northumberland national park, this fortified country house has 'magnificent' views. Inside are stained-glass windows and a Florentine marble fireplace; one bedroom suite is in the old library. Angus Benson-Blair is the manager. In the smart, oak-panelled restaurant, Thomas Arendt's cooking is admired. A converted carriage house and stables house the family-friendly *Tower Inn and Stable Bar*, which serves hearty British dishes and local ales. Newcastle is 30 minutes' drive away.
2 drawing rooms, breakfast room, *Oak Room* restaurant, *Tower Inn and Stable Bar* (alfresco eating); classical background music; function facilities; 32-acre grounds; lake; private stretch of River Rede (fishing). Civil wedding licence. Children and dogs welcomed. 18 bedrooms (1 suitable for ♿). B&B £70–£90 per person; D,B&B £90–£110.

OXFORD Oxfordshire
Map 2:C2
THE BELL, 11 Oxford Road, Hampton Poyle, OX5 2QD. Tel 01865-376242, www.thebelloxford.co.uk. In an 18th-century building, this roadside village pub has cosy snugs, flagstone floors, beams, leather seating and a large log fire. Bedrooms, decorated in neutral tones, have pale wood furniture. George Dailey is the manager. In the restaurant (open kitchen, wood-burning oven), chef Nick Anderson serves pizzas, grilled fish and shellfish, and locally sourced meats. 2 bars (background music), library, restaurant; terrace. Wedding facilities. Wi-Fi. 4 miles N of Oxford. Parking. Children and dogs welcomed. 9 bedrooms (some on ground floor; 1 suitable for ♿). B&B £42.50–£70 per person. Dinner £30 approx. Packages available at Christmas and New Year.
25% DISCOUNT VOUCHERS

BURLINGTON HOUSE, 374 Banbury Road, OX2 7PP. Tel 01865-513513, www.burlington-hotel-oxford.co.uk. In leafy Summertown, this handsome Victorian merchant's house has been sympathetically modernised to form a 'cheerfully' decorated B&B with striking wallpapers, coordinating fabrics and triple-glazed windows in the bedrooms. It is 'extremely' efficiently managed by Nes Saini. Breakfasts feature 'excellent' home-baked brown bread and home-made granola. There is a frequent bus service into the centre; bus-stop nearby. Sitting room, breakfast room. Small Japanese garden. No background music. Wi-Fi. Parking (limited). 12 bedrooms (2 in courtyard). B&B £46–£76.50 per person.

MACDONALD RANDOLPH HOTEL, Beaumont Street, OX1 2LN. Tel 0844 879 9132, www.macdonaldhotels.co.uk/randolph. Managed by Michael Grange and part of the Macdonald Hotels group, this well-positioned grand hotel stands opposite the Ashmolean Museum. The *Morse Bar* was frequented by the fictional inspector of the popular television series. Public rooms are impressive; some bedrooms are small. Chef Tom Birks cooks contemporary British dishes in the elegant, baronial-style restaurant; afternoon tea is served in the drawing room (pianist on Sat). Wood-panelled bar, restaurant, drawing room. Background music. Spa (steam rooms, saunas, plunge pool); gym. Civil wedding licence; conference facilities. Children and dogs welcomed. 151 bedrooms (1 suitable for ♿). B&B £87–£180 per person; D,B&B £112–£205.

MALMAISON, Oxford Castle, 3 New Road, OX1 1AY. Tel 01865-268400, www.malmaison.com. An imaginative, modern renovation by Malmaison Hotels has retained the iron staircases, metal walkways and (reversed) spy-hole doors of this former Victorian castle jail. In the A-Wing, the original prison cell block, smartly decorated bedrooms have 'moody' lighting. A split-level suite in the former governor's house has a private screening room and a four-poster bed. The candlelit brasserie below ground serves classic British dishes. 2 bars, brasserie, 2 private dining rooms, gym; outside seating. Ramps. Background music. Civil wedding licence; function facilities. Wi-Fi. Limited parking (£20 charge). Children welcomed. 94 bedrooms (16 in *House of Correction*, some in *Governor's House*; 3 suitable for ♿): £160–£310. Breakfast £12.50–£14.50.

PENRITH Cumbria
Map 4: inset C2

WESTMORLAND HOTEL, nr Orton, CA10 3SB. Tel 01539-624351, www.westmorlandhotel.com. 'Highly recommended as a stop-over, or as a base for touring that side of the Lakes.' Surrounded by open fell – 'so quiet and peaceful' – this secluded hotel is at the locally owned Tebay Motorway Services off the M6, between junctions 38 and 39. Inside the modern building, contemporary design blends with traditional materials; bedrooms have locally made organic toiletries. Martin Richardson is the manager. The restaurant serves 'well-cooked' rustic British dishes, particularly beef and lamb from its own farm, less than a mile away. 'A real find.' Lounge, bar (log fires), dining room. No background music. Wi-Fi. Civil wedding licence; function/conference facilities. Children and dogs welcomed. 51 bedrooms (some family rooms; 1 suitable for ♿). B&B £55–£90 per person; D,B&B £77–£112.
25% DISCOUNT VOUCHERS

PRESTON Lancashire
Map 4:D2

BARTON GRANGE HOTEL, 746–768 Garstang Road, Barton, PR3 5AA. Tel 01772-862551, www.bartongrangehotel.co.uk. Built in 1900 as a country residence for a local cotton mill owner, this now much-expanded, modernised hotel has been run by the Topping family for more than 60 years. Ian Topping is now in charge, with a 'highly competent and charming' staff. 'The utilitarian bedrooms have plenty of storage.' The contemporary, award-winning *Walled Garden* bistro and wine bar serves local, seasonal produce. A few minutes' drive from the M6. Lounge, bistro/wine bar. Background music. Leisure centre (indoor pool, sauna; gym). Pool/bar billiards. Walled garden. Private dining. Civil wedding licence; conference facilities. Wi-Fi. 51 bedrooms (some in cottage in the grounds). B&B £45–£120 per person.

ROCK Cornwall
Map 1:D2
ST ENODOC, nr Wadebridge, PL27 6LA. Tel 01208-863394, www.enodoc-hotel.co.uk. Close to a sandy beach and the ferry point to Padstow, this bright, colourful hotel is 'really liked'. It is managed by Kate Simms. Families are welcomed; there is a separate playroom for young guests. Chef Nathan Outlaw runs the restaurants: the informal *Nathan Outlaw Seafood & Grill*, which serves food all day, and *Restaurant Nathan Outlaw* (two *Michelin* stars), whose eight-course tasting menu features local seafood. Ideal for walking, cycling and water sports. Lounge (background radio), library, bar, gallery, 2 restaurants; playroom (table tennis, table football, board games); billiard room; sauna, heated outdoor swimming pool (May–Sept). Terrace; ½-acre garden. 20 bedrooms (4 family suites). B&B £77.50–£260 per person; D,B&B from £92.50. Closed end Dec–Jan.
25% DISCOUNT VOUCHERS

ROECLIFFE North Yorkshire
Map 4:D4
THE CROWN INN, Boroughbridge, YO51 9LY. Tel 01423-322300, www.crowninnroecliffe.com. Facing the village green, this green-painted 16th-century coaching inn has flagstone floors, oak beams and crackling log fires. It is owned by the Mainey family; Karl Mainey is the manager. Country-style bedrooms are decorated in soft tones; bathrooms have a freestanding bath. Chef Darryn Asher cooks an extensive menu of modern British food. Eight miles from Ripon and within easy reach of the Yorkshire Dales and North York Moors national parks. Bar, restaurant (background music), 2 dining areas. Garden. Civil wedding licence. Function facilities in converted medieval cow barn. Children welcomed. Further bedrooms and a cookery school are planned. 4 bedrooms. B&B £55–£120 per person (including complimentary newspaper); D,B&B £75–£170.

ROSS-ON-WYE Herefordshire
Map 3:D5
THE HILL HOUSE, Howle Hill, HR9 5ST. Tel 01989-562033, www.thehowlinghillhouse.com. Quirky and full of character, Duncan and Alex Stayton's 17th-century home is in four acres of private woodlands with spectacular views of the Forest of Dean and the Wye valley. It is run in a laid-back manner: guests are invited to sip champagne in the seven-seater outdoor hot tub, relax in the oak-lined bar, and write on the Wisdom and Poetry wall. Rooms are traditional, with Gothic elements; Old Mrs Thomas's Room has a Japanese bathtub for up-to-the-neck bathing. Aga-cooked organic suppers. Packed lunch/evening meal by arrangement. Vegetarians are catered for. Morning room, lounge, bar (background music: morning Radio 4), restaurant; hot tub; sauna (£4–£6);

cinema (DVD film library). Garden. Children welcomed. Resident cats. 5 bedrooms. B&B £25–£35 per person. Supper £10–£15.

ROWSLEY Derbyshire
Map 3:A6

The Peacock at Rowsley, Bakewell Road, DE4 2EB. Tel 01629-733518, www.thepeacockatrowsley.co.uk. 'Generally a very enjoyable and comfortable stay.' This charming old inn by a bridge is owned by Lord Edward Manners of Haddon Hall and was once the dower house. It is managed by Ian and Jenni MacKenzie. 'The level of service and attention from the staff was excellent.' There are mullioned windows, leaded lights, log fires in stone fireplaces; soft furnishings in the 'cosy' bar have been updated in apple green and purple velvets. The quietest bedrooms overlook the gardens that run down to the River Derwent; those that face the busy road have double glazing. Dan Smith cooks ambitious modern dishes. Breakfasts are 'superb'. No background music. Lounge, bar, dining room (live classical guitar on Fri). Civil wedding licence. Conference rooms. ½-acre garden on river (fishing Apr–Oct). 16 bedrooms. B&B (continental) £77.50–£129 per person; D,B&B £107.50–£159. Cooked breakfast £7.25.
25% DISCOUNT VOUCHERS

RYE East Sussex
Map 2:E5

The Hope Anchor, Watchbell St, TN31 7HA. Tel 01797-222216, www.thehopeanchor.co.uk. In a 'lovely location' on a grassy square at the end of a cobbled street, this white-painted, family-owned hotel has 18th-century origins and literary connections (EF Benson; Malcolm Saville). It has 'appealing' country-style bedrooms and 'above-average' food. Chef Kevin Sawyer serves fresh fish, meat and produce from the area in the spacious, modern dining room, with views over the marshes. Lounge, bar (snack menu), dining room. Background music. Room service. Wedding facilities. Wi-Fi. Children (cots, baby-listening devices, high chairs) and dogs welcomed. 16 bedrooms (1 in roof annexe; 2 apartments; cottage). B&B £47.50–£190 per person; D,B&B £49.50–£220.

The Ship Inn, The Strand, TN31 7DB. Tel 01797-222233, www.theshipinnrye.co.uk. Karen Northcote owns this cosy inn with seaside-themed bedrooms, originally a warehouse to store smugglers' contraband in the 16th century. Uneven wooden floors and exposed beams (some low) are matched with amusing retro decoration. There is bread from an artisan baker at breakfast; lunch and dinners focus on seasonal local ingredients with much of the fish from Rye Bay. Close to Rye Harbour Nature Reserve and Camber Sands. Bar, restaurant upstairs; terrace. Background music. Children and dogs welcomed. 10 bedrooms. B&B £45–£50 per person. Dinner £29.

ST AGNES Cornwall
Map 1:D2

Rose in Vale, Mithian, TR5 0QD. Tel 01872-552202, www.rose-in-vale-hotel.co.uk. 'Comfortable, in a restful, attractive and convenient situation', this Georgian manor house is run as a traditional country hotel by James and Sara Evans. Bedrooms and hallways

have recently been refreshed. On the edge of a village on the north Cornish coast, it is in a peaceful wooded valley (home to badgers, buzzards, woodpeckers and herons). Chef Colin Hankins cooks modern dishes using Cornish produce. 'A constant delight to eat his food.' Drawing room, bar, *Valley* restaurant (classical background music; resident pianist Sat night); lift; function facilities. 10-acre grounds with outdoor pool (rebuilt in 2011, 'a tremendous asset to the hotel'); ponds. Dogs welcomed, by arrangement. 23 bedrooms (2 in annexe; 2 suitable for ♿). B&B £55–£125 per person; D,B&B £80–£150.
25% DISCOUNT VOUCHERS

ST IVES Cornwall
Map 1:D1

Blue Hayes, Trelyon Avenue, TR26 2AD. Tel 01736-797129, www.bluehayes.co.uk. High up on Porthminster Point, this immaculate small hotel in a 1920s house is owned by Malcolm Herring. From the white balustraded terrace, there are stunning views of the harbour and bay below; a gate from the small garden leads directly to the beach (five minutes) or to the harbour (ten minutes). Serene bedrooms have sea views; some have a balcony, roof terrace or patio. 2 lounges, bar, dining room (light Mediterranean-style suppers prepared by Nicola Martin); terrace. No background music. Civil wedding licence; small function facilities. Parking. Children over 10 allowed. 6 bedrooms. B&B £85–£120 per person. Supper £15–£28. Open Mar–Oct.

No. 1 St Ives, 1 Fern Glen, TR26 1QP. Tel 01736-799047, www.no1stives.co.uk. On a hill, within walking distance of the town and the Tate gallery, friendly hosts Anna Bray and Simon Talbot run this small B&B in their stone-built house. Renovation continues. Well-equipped bedrooms have hot drinks and biscuits (replenished daily), an iPod docking station, TV with Freeview and DVD/CD-player; two have distant ocean views towards Godrevy Lighthouse. There is an extensive choice at breakfast, using locally sourced food. Sitting room, dining room (background jazz). Small garden; a terrace is new. Wi-Fi. Parking. Children over 7 allowed. 4 bedrooms. B&B £35–£62.50 per person.

Primrose Valley Hotel, Porthminster Beach, TR26 2ED. Tel 01736-794939, www.primroseonline.co.uk. Close to Porthminster beach, this 'attractive' seaside villa is in a terrace of Edwardian houses near a little railway viaduct. (It is accessed via a steep, narrow road.) Owners Sue and Andrew Biss and Rose Clegg run the small hotel on environmentally friendly lines; a discount of £5 per night is offered if parking is not required. Bedrooms, some with sea views, are snug; a couple have a balcony or private terrace. Light snacks (from Cornish suppliers) are served in a smart, modern open-plan area. Lounge, café/bar, breakfast room; small terrace overlooking sea. Background music. Therapy room (beauty and body treatments). Parking. Children over 8 accepted. 9 bedrooms. B&B £50–£170 per person. Closed Jan.

St Ives Harbour Hotel, The Terrace, TR26 2BN. Tel 01736-795221, www.stives-harbour-hotel.co.uk. Renovation continues at this renamed hotel (formerly *The Porthminster*) in a grand Victorian building overlooking the bay and Godrevy Lighthouse. It is now managed by Jason Parry for Harbour Hotels. Self-catering accommodation has been built in the grounds. In the *Harbour* restaurant, Daniel Dennis serves modern British fare. 'The fish was very well cooked and well timed; breakfast was uneven.' Lounge, bar, cocktail bar, 2 restaurants (alfresco dining). Lift. Background music. Spa; heated indoor swimming pool; tennis. Function/business facilities; civil wedding licence. Wi-Fi. Children and dogs welcomed. 46 bedrooms (some family; some with balcony; 1 suitable for ♿). B&B £57.50–£147.50 per person; D,B&B £72.50–£162.50.

SALISBURY Wiltshire
Map 2:D2
LEENA'S GUEST HOUSE, 50 Castle Road, SP1 3RL. Tel 01722-335419, leenas@btinternet.com. Friendly and welcoming, Leena and Malcolm Street, and their son, Gary, have run this pretty Edwardian guest house for many years. Between them they speak several languages. Just a short riverside walk from the city centre and cathedral, the guest house is 'very good', providing an 'excellent' breakfast (full English, freshly squeezed orange juice) and a 'good room'. Lounge, breakfast room. No background music. Garden. Wi-Fi. Parking. Children welcomed. 6 bedrooms (1 on ground floor). B&B £34–£51 per person.

QUIDHAMPTON MILL, Netherhampton Road, SP2 9BB. Tel 01722-741171, www.quidhamptonmill.co.uk. Overlooking water meadows and the River Wylye, Lesa and Martin Drewett's welcoming B&B is in a modern, dark clapboard building, which has a light, New Hampshire-style interior. Guests are welcomed with tea and scones or lemonade in the beautiful garden; the Drewetts have much helpful information about the area. Clean, crisp bedrooms are in a separate building. Home-made breakfasts include fresh fruit salad, pancakes and muffins. Picnic hampers available; dinner by arrangement. A classic Jaguar can be hired for trips. On the A3094; 10 mins' drive to Salisbury. No background music. Wi-Fi (iPad for guests). Parking. Children welcomed. 3 bedrooms. B&B from £42.50 per person. Dinner £20–£25.

SPIRE HOUSE, 84 Exeter Street, SP1 2SE. Tel 01722-339213, www.salisbury-bedandbreakfast.com. Close to the cathedral, this 18th-century Grade II listed town house is run as a small B&B. Owners Lois and John Faulkner provide helpful advice on local sites and places to eat. Of the four comfortable bedrooms, two overlook the quiet walled garden. Breakfast has healthy eating options and traditional dishes. Breakfast room. No background music. Garden. Parking opposite. 4 bedrooms. B&B £37.50–£70 per person. Closed late Dec–Feb.

SANDWICH Kent
Map 2:D5
THE BELL HOTEL, The Quay, CT13 9EF. Tel 01304-613388, www.bellhotelsandwich.co.uk. Occupying a 'beautifully restored' 19th-century listed building, this hotel overlooks the Quay, Barbican Gate and Toll Bridge. Acquired by Shepherd Neame in

September 2011; Matt Collins remains as manager. Lounge, 2 bars, *The Old Dining Room* restaurant (Ricardo Isolini is the new chef). Background music. Sun terrace. Civil wedding licence. Wi-Fi. Limited parking. Children and dogs welcomed. 37 bedrooms. B&B £42.50–£55 per person; D,B&B £60–£88. **25% DISCOUNT VOUCHERS**

SAWLEY Lancashire
Map 4:D3

THE SPREAD EAGLE INN, nr Clitheroe, BB7 4NH. Tel 01200-441202, www.spreadeaglesawley.co.uk. In a beautiful setting beside the River Ribble and opposite the ruins of a 12th-century Cistercian abbey, this stone-built pub-with-rooms belongs to Individual Inns. Managed by Kate Peill, it has been smartly updated and painted in modern colours while retaining original features such as beamed ceilings and flagstone floors. Bedrooms are 'comfortable'; guests help themselves to milk and water from a communal fridge/freezer in the corridor. Chef Greg Barnes gives pub classics a sophisticated slant in the informal eating areas, which have wooden tables, settles and mismatched seating. Bar, dining room. Background music. Wedding/function facilities. Wi-Fi. Parking. Children welcomed. 7 bedrooms. B&B £67.50–£90 per person.

SCARBOROUGH North Yorkshire
Map 4:C5

PHOENIX COURT, 8–9 Rutland Terrace, YO12 7JB. Tel 01723-501150, www.hotel-phoenix.co.uk. Alison and Bryan Edwards's Victorian guest house overlooks North Bay and the beach. Guests are welcomed with home-made fudge in their room on arrival. Breakfasts have locally sourced produce, including Whitby kippers (part of the 'deliciously Yorkshire' breakfast scheme). Lounge, bar area, dining room (background music). Packed lunches; drying facilities for walkers. 10 mins' walk from the town centre. Wi-Fi. Parking. Children welcomed. 14 bedrooms (9 with sea views, 1 on ground floor). B&B £25–£40 per person. **25% DISCOUNT VOUCHERS**

SEAHOUSES Northumberland
Map 4:A4

ST CUTHBERT'S HOUSE, 192 Main Street, North Sunderland, NE68 7UB. Tel 01665-720456, www.stcuthbertshouse.com. 'An impressive restoration, in keeping with the character of the old building.' Musicians Jill and Jeff Sutheran run their B&B in this converted Presbyterian church (built in 1810). The former sanctuary has become a guest lounge; the original pulpit, a balcony viewing area. A communion table and old pillars have all been preserved. The Sutherans live in the former manse, next door. Traditional, 'rather stylish' Northumbrian breakfasts include honey from the hosts' own beehives. On a quiet road, 1 mile inland from the village. Lounge, breakfast room (occasional instrumental background music). Small garden. Small function facilities. Limited parking. 6 bedrooms (1 suitable for ♿). B&B £45–£85 per person.

SHEFFIELD South Yorkshire
Map 4:E4

LEOPOLD HOTEL, 2 Leopold Street, Leopold Square, S1 2GZ. Tel 08450-780067, www.leopoldhotelsheffield.com. Close to City Hall, this quirkily converted luxury hotel (part of Small Luxury Hotels of the World) was once a boys' grammar and technical school. It retains some of the memorabilia of its past: sombre colours, panelled walls, arched doorways, old school photos and ranks of coat pegs. Michael Skehan is the manager. Good-value bedrooms have a well-appointed bathroom. Breakfast is available until 10.30 am at weekends. Lounge bar (afternoon teas, bar snacks), dining room; terrace; 24-hour room service; private dining rooms. Background music. Civil wedding licence; conference/function facilities. Wi-Fi. Parking discounts in public car park nearby. Children welcomed. 90 bedrooms (6 suitable for ♿): £84–£95. Breakfast £7.95–£8.95.

SHERBORNE Somerset
Map 2:E1

The Queens Arms, Corton Denham, DT9 4LR. Tel 01963-220317, www.thequeensarms.com. Popular with locals, Jeanette and Gordon Reid's 18th-century inn is at the heart of a little Dorset/Somerset border village. Downstairs are flagstone floors, comfortable seating and a huge fireplace. Wholesome British food, cooked by James Cole, is locally sourced. Smart, colourful bedrooms overlook rolling countryside, and have a roll-top bath. Breakfast, served communally, features eggs and bacon from the village. Bar (local ales and Somerset ciders), restaurant; private dining room; meeting room. Terrace, garden. Wi-Fi. Parking. Children, and dogs (in 1 room only), welcomed. 3 miles N of Sherborne; a free shuttle service to and from the station is available for guests. 8 bedrooms (1 on ground floor; 3 in separate buildings close by). B&B £40–£85 per person; D,B&B £70–£110.
25% DISCOUNT VOUCHERS

SHREWSBURY Shropshire
Map 3:B4

Chatford House, Bayston Hill, Chatford, SY3 0AY. Tel 01743-718301, www.chatfordhouse.co.uk. B&B guests may explore the pretty garden and orchard, or visit the hens, ducks, geese, sheep and cattle at Christine and Rupert Farmer's smallholding. Five miles south of Shrewsbury, it is within walking distance of Lyth Hill and close to the Shropshire Way. The handsome 18th-century Grade II listed farmhouse has cottage-style bedrooms. Aga-cooked breakfasts include eggs from the house's free-range poultry, and jams and compotes made from orchard fruit. Tea and home-made cakes on arrival; damson gin. Sitting room, breakfast room (open fire; background piano, CDs). Garden; orchard. Children welcomed. 3 bedrooms. B&B £35–£45 per person.
25% DISCOUNT VOUCHERS (stays of 3 nights or more)

The Golden Cross Hotel, 14 Princess Street, SY1 1LP. Tel 01743-362507, www.goldencrosshotel.co.uk. Local records reveal that this building in the historic town centre has served as an inn since 1428. It has been owned and managed for the last ten years by Gareth and Theresa Reece; they have added contemporary comforts to its medieval structure. Bedrooms have antique furnishings and a flat-screen TV; one has a four-poster bed. The restaurant serves an eclectic variety of Anglo/French dishes; lighter meals are available in the bar. Guests may eat alfresco in the ancient Golden Cross passage that runs alongside the hotel. Shropshire breakfasts. Restaurant, lounge bar (background music); function room. Children welcomed. Wi-Fi. Metered street parking (free from 6 pm and on Sundays) or long-term car park nearby. 4 bedrooms (1 suite suitable for a family). B&B £37.50–£125. Dinner from £30.

GROVE FARM HOUSE, Condover, SY5 7BH. Tel 01743-718544, www.grovefarmhouse.com. Guests appreciate the lovely views and charming rooms at Liz Farrow's small B&B in a handsome, three-storey Georgian house, peacefully situated five miles south of the town. There are considerate touches, such as home-made biscuits and a selection of local maps and guides. The hosts will make recommendations for local restaurants. Walks can be taken around the farm or through beautiful parkland and wooded areas. Breakfast has award-winning, locally produced meat, eggs from home-reared chickens, and home-made blueberry muffins. Afternoon tea is available, by arrangement. Lounge, dining room. No background music. 1½-acre garden. Children welcomed. 4 bedrooms (plus 2-bed self-catering cottage). B&B £45–£65 per person.

THE INN AT GRINSHILL, High Street, Grinshill, SY4 3BL. Tel 01939-220410, www.theinnatgrinshill.co.uk. In the lee of Grinshill hill, this Grade II listed Georgian building has a restaurant and plain, elegant bedrooms. It is owned by 'excellent hosts' Victoria and Kevin Brazier; Adam Turner is the manager. Food ranges from bar suppers to 'delicious' gourmet dinners under the supervision of chef Chris Condé. 7 miles N of Shrewsbury. 2 bars (*The Elephant and Castle* and *Bubbles*), restaurant (closed Sun, Mon eves; background music). Rose garden with fountain. Function facilities. Wi-Fi. 6 bedrooms. B&B £40–£90 per person. Dinner £35.50. **25% DISCOUNT VOUCHERS** (Nov–Mar for guests who dine in)

THE SILVERTON, 9–10 Frankwell, SY3 8JY. Tel 01743-248000, www.thesilverton.co.uk. Just across the Welsh Bridge, and an easy walk to the riverside and town centre, this modern restaurant-with-rooms, owned and managed by Doug Blackmore, is in a former dairy. 'Everyone we met seemed concerned with our comfort.' The cream, brown and green bedrooms are named after Shropshire hills; rooms at the back are quietest. Chef Michael Jordan cooks contemporary British food, and sources ingredients from local suppliers for breakfasts, lazy lunches, afternoon teas and dinner. Bar, restaurant; lift; terrace. Background music. Wi-Fi. Parking. Children welcomed. 7 bedrooms (1 suitable for ♿). B&B £42.50–£125 per person; D,B&B £72.50–£155.
25% DISCOUNT VOUCHERS

SIDLESHAM West Sussex
Map 2:E3

THE CRAB & LOBSTER, Mill Lane, PO20 7NB. Tel 01243-641233, www.crab-lobster.co.uk. 'An old favourite', this 350-year-old inn on the edge of the Pagham Harbour nature reserve is in an area of outstanding natural beauty and special scientific interest. (Binoculars and a telescope are provided in some deluxe bedrooms.) The inn has been renovated in spare, modern style by structural engineer-turned-hotelier Sam Bakose and his wife, Janet. Malcolm Goble's 'high-standard' cooking has an emphasis on fish, crab and lobster. Bar, restaurant (background jazz); terrace; garden. Wi-Fi. Children welcomed. 6 bedrooms (2 in adjoining cottage). B&B £70–£115 per person. Dinner £23.50–£50.

SIDMOUTH Devon
Map 1:D5
HOTEL RIVIERA, The Esplanade, EX10 8AY. Tel 01395-515201, www.hotelriviera.co.uk. On the seafront overlooking Lyme Bay, this traditional hotel in a fine Regency terrace has been run by the Wharton family for more than 35 years, with 'kind, helpful' staff. Chef Matthew Weaver serves English dishes and local seafood in the smart dining room (also open to non-residents). Lounge, cocktail bar (live piano music), restaurant; ballroom; terrace. Lift. 2 minutes from the town centre. Golf nearby; pheasant and duck shooting can be arranged. Wi-Fi. Children and dogs welcomed. 26 bedrooms (some suitable for ♿; many with sea views). B&B £112–£177 per person; D,B&B £125–£194.

VICTORIA HOTEL, The Esplanade, EX10 8RY. Tel 01395-512651, www.victoriahotel.co.uk. In 'delightful, colourful' gardens overlooking the bay, this large traditional hotel is popular with families. It is managed by Matthew Raistrick for the Brend group. Most of the elegantly furnished rooms are south facing; many have a balcony. Men are asked to wear a jacket and tie for di[illegible] in the *Jubilee* restaurant (the new che[illegible] Stuart White). Background music. Sun lounge, lounge bar; outdoor and indoor swimming pools; tennis court, snooker, putting. Spa. Lift. Gift shop. 'Superb' entertainment. Wi-Fi. Parking. Children welcomed. 61 bedrooms (3 poolside suites): £115.50–£336. D,B&B from £157.50.

SISSINGHURST Kent
Map 2:D5
SISSINGHURST CASTLE FARMHOUSE, nr Cranbrook, TN17 2AB. Tel 01580-720992, www.sissinghurstcastlefarmhouse.com. Near the entrance to Sissinghurst Castle Garden, Sue and Frazer Thompson's B&B has been painstakingly restored by the National Trust. Modern bedrooms (digital TV, radio, iPod docking stations) have stunning views across the grounds; some have sight of the Elizabethan Tower. Tea and cakes are offered on arrival. Guests have access to the estate grounds. No background music. Sitting room, dining room. Lift. Meeting room; small functions. Wi-Fi. Resident dog. 7 bedrooms (easy access). B&B £62.50–£170 per person (2-night min. stay on Fri and Sat, May–Sept).

SNETTERTON Norfolk
Map 2:B5
HOLLY HOUSE, Snetterton South End, Diss, NR16 2LG. Tel 01953-498051, www.hollyhouse-guesthouse.co.uk. 'Quite outstanding in both comfort and facilities.' This 'lovely' 300-year-old thatched cottage, painted pink, is the restored family home of Laurel and Jeff Stonell. It stands amid open fields in farmland 18 miles west of Norwich.

The Stonells are welcoming owners, and Laurel, an 'excellent' cook, serves a three-course menu with plenty of choice, by arrangement. The breakfast is equally 'good'. 'A rather special place.' Drawing room (log fires), dining room. No background music. Parking. Resident dogs. 3 bedrooms (1 on ground floor). B&B £45–£55 per person. Dinner £32.

SOUTHAMPTON Hampshire
Map 2:E2

WHITE STAR TAVERN, 28 Oxford Street, SO14 3DJ. Tel 02380-821990, www.whitestartavern.co.uk. More than a century old, this former seafarers' hotel takes its name from the famous shipping line. Inside, original features have been retained, including a unique stairwell, wood panelling and brass chandeliers; bedrooms (located on 'decks' and named after famous ships) are contemporary in style. Marc Wilson is the manager. Conveniently situated for the city's shops and restaurants, ferries to the Isle of Wight, and visits to the New Forest, it is also within easy access of the airport. Restaurant and bar; alfresco dining; lounge; roof terrace. Background music. Function facilities. Wi-Fi. 13 bedrooms (plus 3-bed serviced apartment): £95–£155. Breakfast £3.50–£10, dinner £30.

SOUTHPORT Merseyside
Map 4:E2

THE VINCENT, 98 Lord Street, PR8 1JR. Tel 01704-883800, www.thevincenthotel.com. On a fashionable boulevard near the train station, this stylish hotel has a lively bar and restaurant. Developed by local restaurateur Paul Adams, the hotel, a former cinema, has a contemporary glass facade with state-of-the-art features. Alan Richmond is the manager. Rooms (Residences, Suites, Corner Suites, Penthouse) are decorated in restful tones. *V Café & Sushi Bar* (outdoor seating; Andrew Carter is the chef), members' bar; background music. Spa; gym; beauty treatments. Civil wedding licence; function facilities. Valet parking. Wi-Fi. Children welcomed. 60 bedrooms (3 suitable for ♿). B&B £46.50–£103 per person. Dinner £27.

SOUTHWOLD Suffolk
Map 2:B6

THE SWAN, Market Place, IP18 6EG. Tel 01502-722186, www.adnams.co.uk. 'A delight.' On the bustling market square, this 300-year-old building with 'consistently high standards' is managed by Martin Edwards for Adnams brewery. 'An excellent meal again' from chef Rory Whelan. Breakfasts 'deserve a special mention', too. Drawing room, bar, reading room, restaurant; private dining room. Lift. Garden. Civil wedding licence; function facilities. No background music. Beauty and natural healing treatments. Parking. Beach 200 yds. Children, and dogs (in Lighthouse rooms, which have their own patio), welcomed. 42 bedrooms (some in annexe in garden; 1 suitable for ♿). B&B £75–£142.50 per person; D,B&B £80–£147.50.

25% DISCOUNT VOUCHERS

STAMFORD Lincolnshire
Map 2:B3

THE BULL AND SWAN AT BURGHLEY, St Martins, PE9 2LJ. Tel 01780-766412, www.thebullandswan.co.uk. An ancient stone building once used as a staging post for coaches on the Great North Road, this travellers' inn has been quirkily updated and is managed by Ben Larter for Hillbrooke Hotels. Bedrooms are furnished with carved dark wood, crisp linen and smart fabrics; one room has a freestanding bath. The town is easily accessible; Burghley House can be reached via a cross-country walk. Chef Phil Kent serves British bistro food using produce from local suppliers. Bar, *Bedlam* restaurant. Background music. Courtyard garden. Parking. Children, and dogs (in 1 room), welcomed. 7 bedrooms. B&B £45–£100 per person; D,B&B from £70.

STOWMARKET Suffolk
Map 2:C5
BAYS FARM, Earl Stonham, IP14 5HU. Tel 01449-711286, www.baysfarmsuffolk.co.uk. In a peaceful, rural situation, this 'attractive, tastefully modernised' mid-17th-century farmhouse is run as a B&B by Stephanie Challinor. She has given it a Victorian interior. 'Charming' bedrooms have a large bed, lots of little extras (fresh flowers, coffee machine, DVD-player), and views of the gardens. The new Hayloft suite is in a separate, converted building with a private balcony. The four-acre grounds (included in the National Gardens Scheme) have an orchard, a wildflower garden, and vegetable and fruit gardens; guests may take a cup of tea in the pavilion, which has its own heating, lighting and iPod docking station. Drawing room; beamed dining room. Background music. Garden. Wi-Fi. 3 bedrooms. B&B £42–£50 per person.

SWINBROOK Oxfordshire
Map 3:D6
THE SWAN INN, nr Burford, OX18 4DY. Tel 01993-823339, www.theswanswinbrook.co.uk. In an idyllic setting by a bridge over the River Windrush, this typically English village pub is leased by Nicola and Archie Orr-Ewing (who own the *King's Head*, Bledington, see main entry) from the Devonshire estate. They pay homage to the famous Mitford sisters (who were brought up nearby) with large family photographs displayed in the bar and restaurant. It is smartly decorated in contemporary country style; Nick Jeremik is the manager. Chef Richard Burkert's seasonal, local food (French, with a modern edge) is served in the oak-framed conservatory overlooking the garden, and alfresco, while rare breed ducks and bantams roam free. Bar (real ale, local beers and lagers), 2 dining areas, conservatory. Occasional background music. Garden, orchard. Children welcomed. 6 bedrooms (in a converted barn behind the pub; 2 with separate entrance). B&B £60–£90 per person. Dinner £40–£50. 2-night min. stay at weekends.
25% DISCOUNT VOUCHERS

SWINDON Wiltshire
Map 2:C2
CHISELDON HOUSE, New Road, Chiseldon, SN4 0NE. Tel 01793-741010, www.chiseldonhousehotel.co.uk. Set within large grounds in the Marlborough Downs, this listed Georgian country house (newly managed by Sue Higgs) is in a tranquil village well located for easy access to the M4. Several bedrooms have a balcony overlooking the garden. Bar, drawing

room (afternoon tea), *Orangery* restaurant (Robert Harwood cooks modern European food); terrace; 3-acre gardens. 'Mellow' background jazz. Civil wedding licence; conference facilities. Wi-Fi. Children welcomed (some restrictions in restaurant). 21 bedrooms. B&B £57.50–£95 per person; D,B&B £77.50–£115.

25% DISCOUNT VOUCHERS

TAPLOW Berkshire
Map 2:D3

CLIVEDEN HOUSE, SL6 0JF. Tel 01628-668561, www.clivedenhouse.co.uk. Above the Thames in National Trust grounds, this magnificent stately home with a colourful history (including John Profumo's first meeting with Christine Keeler) was acquired in 2011 by the owners of *Chewton Glen*, New Milton (see main entry). Sue Williams, formerly of *The Bath Priory*, has been appointed general manager. There are ornate public rooms with interesting artworks; bedrooms (some have a fireplace or terrace) are decorated with antiques. Lounge, library, south-facing *Terrace* restaurant, private dining rooms. *Pavilion Spa* (outdoor and indoor pool, hot tubs, steam rooms, sauna; treatments; sun terrace). Families welcomed (interconnecting bedrooms). Dogs welcomed (doggie treats, basket, information on walks; dog-sitting and walking service). 38 bedrooms (plus Spring Cottage): £210–£565. Dinner £60–£75.

TELFORD Shropshire
Map 2:A1

CHURCH FARM GUEST HOUSE, Wrockwardine Village, TF6 5DG. Tel 01952-251927, www.churchfarm-shropshire.co.uk. 'A perfect base for exploring the county.' In a pretty village three miles west of Telford, cyclists and walkers are welcomed at Melanie and Martin Board's 'charming and relaxed' B&B. The sympathetically renovated Georgian farmhouse has exposed beams, open fires and comfortable rooms. Mr Board is renowned locally for his 'amazing' regional British cooking. 'Breakfasts were first class, as were the evening meals.' Lounge, *Basil's* restaurant (weekdays; open to non-residents); drying room; garden. No background music. Wi-Fi. Cookery courses. BYO wine. Children welcomed (toys, DVDs, books; outdoor games). Dogs welcomed in 1 annexe room. Resident dog, Basil. 5 bedrooms. B&B £35–£55 per person; D,B&B £57.50–£69.50.

25% DISCOUNT VOUCHERS

TETBURY Gloucestershire
Map 3:E5

OAK HOUSE NO.1, The Chipping, GL8 8EU. Tel 01666-505741, www.oakhouseno1.com. Interior designer and art collector Gary Kennedy's Georgian house in the centre of town is a visual feast of rich fabrics, designer furniture, antiques and artefacts collected during his travels. Elegantly furnished bedrooms and suites come with home-baked cakes and scones, and a gift; bathrooms are contemporary and luxurious. Sitting room, dining room. Background music (jazz). Walled garden (afternoon tea). Luxury picnic hampers. Beauty treatments. Wellingtons supplied for walkers who want to explore the countryside. Babies, and children over 11, accepted. 4 bedrooms. B&B £82.50–£137.50 per person.

THURNHAM Kent
Map 2:D4
THURNHAM KEEP, Castle Hill, ME14 3LE. Tel 01622-734149, www.thurnhamkeep.co.uk. Owner Amanda Lane grew up in this 'very impressive', atmospheric Edwardian house on top of a hill in large grounds, with views over the Weald of Kent. 'We had a warm welcome with home-made scones and tea.' 'Beautiful' rooms are traditionally furnished; two have a huge original Edwardian bath. Breakfast, taken communally, has home-made jams, honey from the house's own hives, and eggs from the resident free-range hens. Supper available, by arrangement. Oak-panelled sitting room (wood-burning stove), conservatory, dining room, terrace (alfresco breakfasts); snooker room (in the old chapel). Background music (weekend eve only; 'easy listening'/classical/jazz). 7-acre terraced garden: heated outdoor swimming pool (June–early Sept); pond; kitchen garden, dovecote; summer house; tennis, croquet. Wi-Fi. Parking. 3 bedrooms. B&B £65–£160 per person.

TISBURY Wiltshire
Map 2:D1
THE BECKFORD ARMS, Fonthill Gifford, SP3 6PX. Tel 01747-870385, www.beckfordarms.com. In parkland on the Fonthill estate, this country pub-with-rooms has been renovated throughout (after a fire) by owners Dan Brod and Charlie Luxton (formerly of the Soho House group). Cocktails and snacks are served in the bar; chef Pravin Nayar uses local ingredients for his seasonal menus in the restaurant (alfresco dining on the terrace). Residents' sitting room (newspapers, magazines, DVD-projector). Light background jazz. Private dining room; function facilities. 1-acre garden: hammocks, boules. In-room massages, by arrangement. Children, and dogs (1 room only), welcomed. Wi-Fi. Two lodges (each with a sitting room) have been added in the grounds (hamper provided for breakfast). 9 bedrooms (1 family suite). B&B £47.50–£60 per person. Dinner £30.

THE COMPASSES INN, Lower Chicksgrove, SP3 6NB. Tel 01722-714318, www.thecompassesinn.com. In an area of outstanding natural beauty, Susie and Alan Stoneham's thatched 14th-century inn provides a splendid base for good walking and visits to local attractions such as Longleat, Stonehenge and Wilton House. Guests reach their simple, light rooms through a separate entrance. Blackboard menus have interesting 'pub grub' choices from chef Dave Cousin. All vegetables are from a local farm; there is an extensive wine list. Bar, dining room. Garden. No background music. Small function facilities. Children (baby monitor, babysitting, baby food) and dogs welcomed. 4 bedrooms (plus 2-bed cottage). B&B £42.50–£65 per person. Dinner from £30.
25% **DISCOUNT VOUCHERS**

TOTNES Devon
Map 1:D4
ROYAL SEVEN STARS, The Plains, TQ9 5DD. Tel 01803-862125, www.royalsevenstars.co.uk. Anne and Nigel Way blend old-world charm with a bright, modern interior in this 17th-century coaching inn, which retains its imposing original facade. Margaret Stone is the manager. The hotel is a

popular events venue; its restaurant and bars are patronised by local residents. Light bar meals are available all day; brasserie food is served in the evening. Lounge, 2 bars (background music; log fires in winter); *TQ9* brasserie and grill; champagne bar; terrace (alfresco dining); balcony. Civil wedding licence; business facilities. Wi-Fi. Parking. Children welcomed. 21 bedrooms (quietest at back). B&B £59.50–£115 per person. Dinner £30 approx.

TRESCO Isles of Scilly
Map 1: inset C1
The New Inn, TR24 0QG. Tel 01720-422849, www.tresco.co.uk. Near the beach and harbour, the sole pub on Robert Dorrien-Smith's private, car-free island is a hub of the community and stays open all year round. It is managed by Robin Lawson. Decorated with nautical memorabilia, the informal bars and restaurant are popular with visitors to the timeshare cottages on the island; music, beer and cider festivals are held. New chef Alex Smith's cooking uses local fish and Tresco beef. Residents' lounge, 2 bars (background music), pavilion, restaurant, patio (alfresco eating); garden. Outdoor heated swimming pool. Children welcomed. 16 bedrooms (some with terrace, some with sea views). B&B £55–£120 per person. Dinner £32.

TROUTBECK Cumbria
Map 4: inset C2
Broadoaks, Bridge Lane, LA23 1LA. Tel 015394-45566, www.broadoaks countryhouse.co.uk. A sweeping drive through extensive grounds leads to Tracey Robinson's 19th-century house built of traditional stone and slate. Richly decorated bedrooms are named after Lake District trees; new garden suites near the river are colonial in style. Andrea Carter is the manager. Chef Gareth Owen's Cumbrian cuisine is adventurous. Music room (vintage Bechstein piano; log fire), bar, *Oaks* restaurant. Background music. 7-acre grounds; stream. Civil wedding licence. Free membership at spa nearby. 19 bedrooms (some ground-floor rooms; 5 in coach house; 3 detached garden suites, 5 mins' walk from house). Children, and dogs (in some rooms), welcomed. Resident cockapoo, Molly. B&B £50–£130 per person; D,B&B £75–£160.
25% DISCOUNT VOUCHERS

TUNBRIDGE WELLS Kent
Map 2:D4
Hotel du Vin Tunbridge Wells, 13 Crescent Road, TN1 2LY. Tel 01892-526455, www.hotelduvin.com. With views over Calverley Park and its own vineyard, this branch of the du Vin chain occupies an 18th-century Grade II listed mansion managed by Simon Maguire. In the bistro (European dining; Daniel McGarey is chef), the menu details some of the kitchen's local suppliers; service is 'very friendly'. Some bedrooms overlook the park. Bathrooms have a drench shower, deep bath. Bar, bistro, private dining room; tea lounge. Function facilities. No background music. 1-acre garden: terrace (alfresco dining); vineyard; boules. Close to the station. Wi-Fi (free for 30 mins). Limited parking. Children and dogs welcomed. 34 bedrooms. B&B £120–£400; D,B&B £160.

Smart and Simple, 54–57 London Road, TN1 1DS. Tel 0845-402 5744, www.smartandsimple.co.uk. William

Inglis's hotel is 'good, straightforward and excellent value'. Five minutes from the centre of town, the hotel, in an Edwardian terraced house, faces a green. The interior is modern, with simply furnished bedrooms that have views over a secluded garden or the town common. Tapas dishes are served in the conservatory or on the terrace. Lounge, bar, conservatory; 3 meeting rooms; small gym (£5 fee). Garden (lots of steps down). Background music. Wi-Fi. Small car park. 40 bedrooms (2 family rooms; some suitable for ♿). Children welcomed. B&B (continental) £32.50–£70 per person.

TWO BRIDGES Devon
Map 1:D4

Prince Hall Hotel, Yelverton, PL20 6SA. Tel 01822-890403, www.princehall.co.uk. 'In the heart of Dartmoor, with stunning scenery and a wonderful atmosphere', this cream-painted country house (built 1787) is owned and managed by Fi and Chris Daly, whose attention and consideration 'set them apart'. It is approached down an avenue of ancient beech trees. Inside, comfortable reception rooms have crackling fires; bedrooms are 'sumptuous'. In the light and airy dining room, imaginative menus change daily, showcasing seasonal and local produce. 2 sitting rooms, bar, dining room; classical background music in early evening. 5-acre grounds. Dogs welcomed. 8 bedrooms. B&B £50–£95 per person; D,B&B £75–£135.

ULLSWATER Cumbria
Map 4: insert C2

Inn on the Lake, Glenridding, Penrith, CA11 0PE. Tel 01768-482444, www.lakedistricthotels.net. At the foot of the Helvellyn range, in extensive grounds that sweep down to the shores of Lake Ullswater, this 'excellent' hotel enjoys a spectacular location. It is ably managed by Gary Wilson and staff, who are 'universally smart, efficient, courteous and friendly'. There are 'fabulous' lake and mountain views from the public rooms and the 'richly furnished' bedrooms (six with four-poster bed). In the newly refurbished *Lake View* restaurant, chef Fraser Souta achieves 'excellence, night after night'. The *Ramblers Bar* in the grounds has traditional pub food, local real ales, hot drinks, and a plasma TV for sports programmes. Lounge, bar, restaurant, terrace (alfresco dining); gym, spa bath, sauna; 15-acre grounds: pitch and putt, croquet, 9-hole golf course; children's outdoor play area. Civil wedding licence; conference facilities. Background music. 47 bedrooms. B&B £85–£137 per person; D,B&B £114–£167.

UPPINGHAM Rutland
Map 2:B3

Lake Isle, 16 High Street East, LE15 9PZ. Tel 01572-822951, www.lakeisle.co.uk. Richard and Janine Burton run a 'nicely buzzing' restaurant-with-rooms in their 18th-century town house on the high street. Traditional bedrooms have a modern bathroom, some with a whirlpool bath. An extensive list of 160 different wines from 11 countries accompanies the 'very good' cooking of chef Stuart Mead. Lounge, bar, restaurant (booking recommended; closed Mon lunch, Sun dinner); occasional background music. Courtyard. Small function/business facilities. Wi-Fi. Limited parking.

Children welcomed. 12 bedrooms (plus 2 cottages). B&B £40–£67.50 per person; D,B&B £67.50–£97.50.

VENTNOR Isle of Wight
Map 2:E2
THE ROYAL HOTEL, Belgrave Road, PO38 1JJ. Tel 01983-852186, www.royalhoteliow.co.uk. In a Victorian coastal town, this traditional seaside hotel has plenty of 'olde-worlde charm'. It is owned by William Bailey, and managed by Philip Wilson and Paul Taylor. Bedrooms are decorated in country house style, with silks, rich velvets and toile de Jouy fabrics. In the elegant restaurant, chef Alan Staley's cooking is 'good, although rich'. Lounge, bar with terrace, *Appuldurcombe* restaurant, *Riviera* terrace (alfresco dining); conservatory; lift to some rooms. Background music; resident pianist during peak season weekends. Civil wedding licence; function rooms. 2-acre subtropical grounds: heated outdoor swimming pool (Apr–Sept), children's play area. In-room massages and beauty treatments. A five-minute walk to the seafront, with a sandy beach nearby (hilly walk). Picnic hampers available. Parking. Children welcomed (baby-listening facilities; children's high tea). Dogs welcomed (charge). 53 bedrooms (1 suitable for ♿). B&B £87.50–£137.50 per person; D,B&B £127.50–£177.50. Closed 2 weeks in Jan.

WALLINGTON Northumberland
Map 4:B3
SHIELDHALL, Morpeth, NE61 4AQ. Tel 01830-540387, www.shieldhallguesthouse.co.uk. Overlooking the National Trust's Wallington estate, this stone house sits in ten acres of gardens and parkland (with a stream, woodland and a natural meadow), and was once owned by the family of Capability Brown. It is now run as a B&B by owners Stephen and Celia Gay, who converted the farmstead and decorated it with antiques and original art. Daughter Sarah manages. Celia serves traditional Aga-cooked meals, using home-grown vegetables and fresh eggs from her own hens; dinner is served by arrangement. Handcrafted furniture was made by Stephen and his sons. Library, dining room. No background music. 4 bedrooms (all on ground floor, opening onto a central courtyard). B&B £48–£68 per person. Dinner £28. Closed Dec–Jan.

WARTLING East Sussex
Map 2:E4
WARTLING PLACE, Herstmonceux, nr Hailsham, BN27 1RY. Tel 01323-832590, www.wartlingplace.co.uk. On the edge of the Pevensey Levels nature reserve, Rowena and Barry Gittoes's B&B is in a Grade II listed former rectory. It has large windows overlooking the landscaped gardens, comfortable seating in the large lounge, tasteful furnishings, and interesting prints and pictures on the walls. Copious breakfasts are served at a long mahogany table or can be taken in the room. An evening meal or late supper is available, by arrangement. No background music. Lounge, dining room (honesty bar, CD-player). 3-acre garden. Wi-Fi. Parking. Children welcomed; dogs allowed in cottage suite. 4 bedrooms (plus 2-bedroom self-catering cottage). B&B £62.50–£82.50 per person.

WEDMORE Somerset
Map 1:B6

THE SWAN, Cheddar Road, BS28 4EQ. Tel 01934-710337, www.theswanwedmore.com. 'Bandbox fresh, inside and out', this bustling village pub-with-rooms, in an 18th-century beer house, has recently been renovated by the Draco Pub Company. Chic rooms, in soft neutrals and slate greys, have quirky light fittings and the latest gadgetry. Duncan Zvonek-Little is the 'practised and assured' manager. 'Vibrant, unfussy food' using Somerset produce is cooked by Tom Blake and Josie Cargeeg (both from the *River Cottage*); there are home-baked bread and home-cured bacon, a wood-fired oven and a barbecue. Bar (wood-burning stove), restaurant (closed Sun eve). Function facilities. Background music (jazz, world music). Terrace; garden. Wi-Fi. Parking. Children welcomed. 6 bedrooms. B&B £42.50–£85 per person. Dinner from £28.

WEST HOATHLY West Sussex
Map 2:E4

THE CAT INN, Queen's Square, RH19 4PP. Tel 01342-810369, www.catinn.co.uk. 'We thoroughly enjoyed our stay.' Opposite the church, in a pretty hilltop village in the Sussex Weald, this 16th-century inn has 'a well-deserved reputation for good food'. It is run by the 'very helpful' proprietor, Andrew Russell, with his 'superb' staff. Simply furnished bedrooms have a king-size bed and pretty fabrics. The cosy bar (real ales, 'excellent' wine list) has lots of nooks and crannies, and a huge inglenook fireplace. In the dining room, Max Leonard's pub dishes reflect the changing seasons (restaurant closed Sun eve). Bar, 2 dining areas; small terrace. No background music. Wi-Fi. Children over 7 allowed. 4 bedrooms. B&B £55–£80 per person.
25% DISCOUNT VOUCHERS

WESTON-SUPER-MARE Somerset
Map 1:B6

BEACHLANDS HOTEL, 17 Uphill Road North, BS23 4NG. Tel 01934-621401, www.beachlandshotel.com. Overlooking sand dunes and an 18-hole golf course, this recently refurbished hotel, owned by Charles and Beverly Porter, stands at the southern end of Weston Bay, convenient for the beach. It is managed by Stuart Merrick. It has a traditional interior; some bedrooms have a veranda opening on to the secluded garden. Chef Matt Price's four-course, daily-changing menus are served in the dining room overlooking the garden. 3 lounges, bar, restaurant; background music. 10-metre indoor swimming pool, sauna. Garden. Civil wedding licence; function/conference facilities. Wi-Fi. Parking. Children welcomed (baby-listening service, children's high tea; swimming lessons by arrangement). 20 bedrooms (some on ground floor; some family rooms; 1 suitable for ♿). B&B £47.50–£102 per person; D,B&B £61–£145 (2 night min. stay).

CHURCH HOUSE, 27 Kewstoke Road, BS22 9YD. Tel 01934-633185, www.churchhousekewstoke.co.uk. 'A very good stay.' Formerly the residence of Kewstoke vicars, this Georgian house by the village church is run as a B&B by Jane and Tony Chapman. There are stunning views over Kewstoke and

Sand Bay in one direction, and of the Bristol Channel and South Wales in the other. Bedrooms are elegantly furnished in rattan, Provençal or classic style. Breakfast includes eggs from the house's own hens, and Gloucester Old Spot sausages. 2½ miles from Weston-super-Mare. Lounge, conservatory, breakfast room. Small garden. Wi-Fi. Dogs welcomed. 5 bedrooms. B&B £42.50–£65 per person.

WHITBY North Yorkshire
Map 4:C5

DUNSLEY HALL, Dunsley, YO21 3TL. Tel 01947-893437, www.dunsleyhall.com. Once the home of a Victorian shipping magnate, this magnificent mansion near Whitby is now a traditional hotel owned by Walter Ward. Gordon Ward is the manager. Original features such as oak panelling and period memorabilia have been retained. The coat of arms of the Pyman family, the original owners, adorns the inglenook fireplace, and the family's seafaring connections are celebrated in an unusual stained-glass window. Smartly decorated rooms have splendid views of the grounds, surrounding countryside or North Yorkshire coastline. In the restaurant, new chef Dave Quinn cooks Mediterranean dishes with an emphasis on local produce and seafood. 2 lounges, *Oak Room* restaurant, *Pyman* bar (background music). Civil wedding licence; function facilities. 5-acre gardens, putting, croquet, tennis. Hotel's working farm nearby; sea 1 mile. Parking. 26 bedrooms (8 in new wing; 1 suitable for ♿; plus 3-bedroom cottage). B&B £70–£130 per person; D,B&B £92.50–£125 (2-night min. stay).

WHITSTABLE Kent
Map 2:D5

THE FRONT ROOMS, 9 Tower Parade, CT5 2BJ. Tel 01227-282132, www.thefrontrooms.co.uk. Julie Thorne and Tom Sutherland run a contemporary photography gallery and B&B in their terraced house in this seaside town. Painted in heritage whites, the airy rooms have a Victorian cast iron double bed and complimentary minibar. A continental breakfast (special diets catered for) is taken in *The Front View* gallery; there is a log fire in winter. Guests in Room 3 may have breakfast on the balcony. Books, magazines, DVDs and board games are available to borrow. The hosts are happy to make recommendations for restaurants, walks and places to visit. Lounge/breakfast room/gallery. Wi-Fi. Bicycles for hire. 3 bedrooms (2 share a bathroom). B&B £55–£140 per person (2-night min. stay at weekends).

WIGMORE Herefordshire
Map 3:C4

PEAR TREE FARM, HR6 9UR. Tel 01568-770140, www.peartree-farm.co.uk. Jill Fieldhouse and Steve Dawson's 17th-century stone-built farmhouse B&B lies on the edge of a small village with castle ruins, near Ludlow. Characterful bedrooms have books and linen sheets; bathrooms have candles, bath oils and fluffy bathrobes. Dinner is served on Friday and Saturday evenings by arrangement (home-cooked country food, using local and free-range produce; home-made organic bread; carefully chosen wines). Guests may bring their own wine (£6 corkage per bottle). An early-morning tea or coffee tray is delivered to the room. Good walks from the doorstep. Sitting room with log fire, dining room. No background music. 2-acre garden. 2 resident dogs, 1 cat. 3 bedrooms (1 on ground floor). B&B (2-night min. stay) £52.50 per person; D,B&B £90. Closed Jan–Apr, except for house parties.

WILMSLOW Cheshire
Map 4:E3
KINGSLEY LODGE, 10 Hough Lane, SK9 2LQ. Tel 01625-441794, www.kingsleylodge.com. Jeremy Levy and Cliff Thomson's tranquil B&B is in a 1950s Arts and Crafts house decorated with contemporary flair. Impeccable bedrooms have antiques and original art, fresh flowers and scented candles. The house sits in large landscaped gardens with a formal parterre, a pine wood, ponds, and a seating deck with a water cascade. Lounge, breakfast room; patio. In a residential area; close to Manchester airport. Wi-Fi. Parking. 6 bedrooms. B&B from £100 per person.

WINDERMERE Cumbria
Map 4: inset C2
CEDAR MANOR, Ambleside Road, LA23 1AX. Tel 015394-43192, www.cedarmanor.co.uk. Named after the 200-year-old cedar tree in the walled gardens, Caroline and Jonathan Kaye's 19th-century hotel is within easy walking distance of Lake Windermere. Bedrooms are individually decorated; some have original arched windows, others a canopy or four-poster bed. A recently refurbished suite in the coach house has locally handcrafted furniture, a lounge with a Juliet balcony, and a full entertainment system. The restaurant focuses on locally sourced ingredients and produce; menus include a list of local suppliers. Lounge, dining room (light background music during meals). Children welcomed. 10 bedrooms (1 suite in coach house). B&B £60–£110 per person; D,B&B £99.50–£149.50.
25% DISCOUNT VOUCHERS

1 PARK ROAD, 1 Park Road, LA23 2AW. Tel 015394-42107, www.1parkroad.com. 'A great base for exploring the lakes', this small guest house, formerly a gentleman's residence, retains its stained-glass windows and staircase. In a quiet area close to the centre of town and a short walk from the lake, it is owned and run with consideration by Mary and Philip Burton. Bedrooms have a DVD/CD-player and iPod docking station, a cafetière and fresh milk; the family room has a travel cot, books, crayons and pencils. There are home-made marmalade and jams, and locally sourced Lake District produce at breakfast. Lounge (grand piano), dining room (dinner Fri and Sat, and 'often' during the week). Background music ('a key point of life here') at dinner, sometimes at breakfast. Picnic hampers/rucksacks available. Children and 'well-behaved' dogs welcomed. Resident dog, Maggie. Wi-Fi. Parking. 6 bedrooms. B&B £38–£64 per person; D,B&B £65–£75.
25% DISCOUNT VOUCHERS

WOODBRIDGE Suffolk
Map 2:C5
THE CROWN, The Thoroughfare, IP12 1AD. Tel 01394-384242, www.thecrownatwoodbridge.co.uk. In the centre of this thriving market town by the River Deben, this white-painted 16th-century coaching inn has been redesigned with Nantucket overtones.

A popular drop-in place for locals, it is run by chef/patron Stephen David for the TA Hotel Collection, the Suffolk hoteliers. The stylish glass-roofed bar is decorated in black granite and seasoned oak; a wooden sailing skiff is suspended from the ceiling. Crisp, light bedrooms are outfitted in neutral tones and shades of grey. Modern lighting is 'excellent throughout'. Mr David's brasserie-style cooking (modern European/global; fixed-price dinners available) is served in all the eating areas: two informal dining rooms, the communal table in the bar, on sofas in front of the fire. Prosecco is available on draught alongside Suffolk brews. Background music; monthly jazz evenings. Bar, restaurant; courtyard garden. Private dining. Wi-Fi. Parking. 10 bedrooms. B&B £62.50–£110 per person. Dinner £18.50–£23.50.

WOODSTOCK Oxfordshire
Map 2:C2
THE FEATHERS, 16–20 Market Street, OX20 1SX. Tel 01993-812291, www.feathers.co.uk. 'We greatly enjoyed our stay – the bedrooms were comfortable, the food excellent, and, above all, the service impeccable.' In a peaceful Cotswolds village near Blenheim Palace, colourful accents and bold wallpaper enliven the traditional features of this town house hotel occupying a row of buildings dating in part back to the 17th century. It was, at various points in its history, a sanatorium, a draper's, a butcher's and a number of cottages. Luc Morel is the manager. In the wood-panelled dining room, chef Kevin Barrett's English dishes are 'rich and robust in winter, light and fresh in summer'. Breakfasts are 'excellent'. Study, *Courtyard* gin bar (over 100 varieties), restaurant. Jazz/classical background music. Function facilities. Picnic hampers. Wi-Fi. Children welcomed. 21 bedrooms (5 in adjacent town house; 1 suitable for ♿; 1 suite has private steam room). B&B £84.50–£159 per person. Dinner £65.
25% DISCOUNT VOUCHERS

WORCESTER Worcestershire
Map 3:C5
THE MANOR COACH HOUSE, Hindlip Lane, Hindlip, WR3 8SJ. Tel 01905-456457, www.manorcoachhouse.co.uk. In a semi-rural location two miles out of the city centre, Terry and Sylvia Smith's fine 1780s house sits in attractive gardens. Simply furnished bedrooms are in a renovated outbuilding next to the main house. Lots of thoughtful extras are included (fresh flowers, umbrellas, etc); one room has kitchenette facilities. Breakfast room. 1-acre garden. No background music. Wi-Fi. Parking. Children welcomed, by arrangement. 5 bedrooms (private courtyard; 1 suitable for ♿). B&B £40–£55.

WROXTON Oxfordshire
Map 2:C2
WROXTON HOUSE HOTEL, Silver Street, OX15 6QB. Tel 01295-730777, www.bw-wroxtonhousehotel.co.uk. 'A real find' on the periphery of a picturesque village, this 'exquisite' thatched-roof manor house, dating back to 1649, is run as a Best Western hotel by the Smith family. It has many original features (inglenook fireplace, original oak beams) and characterful, well-equipped bedrooms. 3 miles W of Banbury. 2 lounges (background music in one), bar, *1649* restaurant (chef Steve

Mason-Tocker cooks modern British food); terrace. 2 private function rooms. Civil wedding licence. Wi-Fi. Parking. Children welcomed. 32 bedrooms (7 on ground floor; 3 in adjoining cottage). B&B £49.50–£158 per person. Dinner £26–£31.
25% **DISCOUNT VOUCHERS**

WYE Kent
Map 2:D5
The Wife of Bath, 4 Upper Bridge Street, TN25 5AF. Tel 01233-812232, www.thewifeofbath.com. Mark Rankin and Caylee Unsworth run this friendly restaurant-with-rooms (part of Hopping Mad Management) in a stylish Victorian house on the edge of the village. Modern bedrooms are decorated in neutral tones with splashes of colour; one has a four-poster bed. Chef Robert Hymers's traditional but imaginative cuisine, featuring local and seasonal produce, is 'excellent'; the 'pleasant' dining room is popular with locals. Whole roasted joints carved at the table are a Sunday lunch speciality. Breakfast has village eggs, local Kentish apple juice, home-made granola. Lounge, restaurant (closed Sun eve, Mon, Tues lunch). No background music. Parking. Children welcomed. 5 bedrooms (2 in garden annexe that can be used as a cottage for a family). B&B £47.50–£75.00 per person. Dinner £50 approx. Closed 2 weeks in early Jan.
25% **DISCOUNT VOUCHERS**

YORK North Yorkshire
Map 4:D4
Bar Convent, 17 Blossom Street, YO24 1AQ. Tel 01904-643238, www.bar-convent.org.uk. 'Unlike any hotel in which I have stayed.' This conveniently located Grade I listed Georgian building (1760) houses England's oldest active convent. It has a rich history; notable features include a 'magnificent' glass-roofed entrance hall, an impressive library that contains a wide range of books alongside antiquarian religious texts, an 18th-century domed chapel, and its own museum. Nuns run the guest house, 'ably assisted' by an 'efficient' housekeeping staff under the management of James Foster. 'The care, thought and personal attention received could not have been bettered.' Simple rooms are furnished with 'wickedly' comfortable beds. 2 lounges (both with TV), communal self-catering facilities; games room; licensed café (closed Sun and bank hols); meeting rooms; shop. Facilities for functions and Catholic weddings. Lift. No background music. ½-acre garden. Wi-Fi. Paid parking across the road. Children welcomed. 18 bedrooms (2 recently refurbished singles; 5 with en suite bathrooms; some suitable for ♿). B&B (continental) £35–£70 per person ('good-value' cooked breakfast £4.50). 3-course dinner from £15. Closed 22 Dec–20 Jan.

The Bloomsbury, 127 Clifton, YO30 6BL. Tel 01904-634031, www.bloomsburyhotel.co.uk. Close to Clifton Green, Stephen and Tricia Townsley's B&B occupies a recently refurbished Victorian house. Traditionally decorated bedrooms are elegant and quiet. Guests can reach York city centre via a scenic river walk. Breakfasts have fresh local produce and home-made preserves. Sitting room, dining room (optional background music); terrace. Flowery

courtyard. Wi-Fi. Parking. Children welcomed. 6 bedrooms. B&B £35–£65 per person.
25% DISCOUNT VOUCHERS

DEAN COURT, Duncombe Place, YO1 7EF. Tel 01904-625082, www.deancourt-york.co.uk. In a 'stunning' location, this Best Western hotel faces York Minster. It has comfortable, traditionally decorated rooms, and 'friendly, helpful' staff. New chef Paul Laidlaw's menus are strong on local and seasonal produce, and are served in the 'attractive' dining room, with 'some splendid views' outside. 2 lounges, bar, *D.C.H.* restaurant (closed for lunch Mon–Fri), *The Court* café/bistro. Background music. Civil wedding licence; conference facilities. Wi-Fi. Children welcomed. 37 bedrooms (3 suitable for ♿). B&B £47.50–£122.50 per person; D,B&B £65–£150 (2-night min. stay).
25% DISCOUNT VOUCHERS

THE GRANGE, 1 Clifton, YO30 6AA. Tel 01904-644744, www.grangehotel.co.uk. 'The service is brilliant.' Just outside the city walls, Jeremy and Vivien Cassell's Grade II listed Regency town house has classically furnished bedrooms and two contemporary restaurants – *The Ivy Brasserie* and the informal *New York Grill* – open to non-residents. It is managed by George Briffa; Jonathan Elvin has recently joined as chef. Yorkshire breakfasts are 'very good, with a wide variety'. 'The staff were all very pleasant and professional.' Ramps. Lounge, 2 bars, brasserie (closed Sun eve); *New York Grill* (dinners only; available for private hire). Background music. Civil wedding licence; function facilities. Wi-Fi. Parking on busy road. Children and dogs welcomed. 36 bedrooms (some on ground floor). B&B £70–£121 per person; D,B&B £100–£150.
25% DISCOUNT VOUCHERS

HOTEL DU VIN YORK, 89 The Mount, YO24 1AX. Tel 01904-557350, www.hotelduvin.com. Once an orphanage, this 19th-century Grade II listed building is now an elegant hotel, part of the du Vin chain. David Macdonald is the manager. 'Very conveniently sited', it is in a tranquil area just beyond the south side of the city walls. 'We had a huge, comfy bed and an excellent, efficient bathroom.' Malcolm Storey is the chef in the bistro, where staff are 'very attentive and highly eager'. Bistro, bar; terrace, courtyard (alfresco dining); private dining rooms. Background music. Civil wedding licence; function facilities. 3-acre grounds. Limited parking. 44 bedrooms (some suitable for ♿). B&B £75–£210 per person; D,B&B £125–£250.

SCOTLAND

ABERDEEN
Map 5:C3

ATHOLL HOTEL, 54 King's Gate, AB15 4YN. Tel 01224-323505, www.atholl-aberdeen.co.uk. In the west of the city, this privately owned baronial-style hotel is popular with locals who pop in for drinks and snacks. Owned by a partnership, it is managed by Wendy Murray. The modern interior has lots of wood and touches of tartan fabrics. Traditional Scottish fare is cooked by Scott Craig. Lounge, bar, restaurant, patio. Wedding/function facilities.

Wi-Fi. Parking. Children welcomed. 34 bedrooms (some suitable for ♿). B&B £42.50–£145 per person. Dinner £25.

Malmaison, 49–53 Queens Road, AB15 4YP. Tel 01224-327370, www.malmaison.com. West of the centre, this branch of the Malmaison chain has the frontage of a traditional Scottish building, and a large extension on the back ('with all the latest creature comforts and services'). It is managed by Josie Simcox. 'We loved the big, buzzy brasserie' in an 'impressive' full-height atrium. Bar, restaurant, terrace (alfresco dining); gym, spa (treatments). Wedding/function facilities. Limited parking. Children and dogs welcomed. 79 bedrooms (some suitable for ♿): £99–£249. Breakfast £12.50–£14.50.

ABERFELDY Perth and Kinross Map 5:D2

Fortingall Hotel, PH15 2NQ. Tel 01887-830367, www.fortingall.com. At the entrance to Glen Lyon and close to Loch Tay, this small Victorian country hotel, managed by Gavin McGilp, is at the centre of an Arts and Crafts conservation village. The Fortingall Yew, the United Kingdom's most ancient tree, stands in the churchyard next to the hotel. Bedrooms are decorated in muted tones, with splashes of colour provided by the tartans and tweeds of the local estates. Walking, cycling, climbing, fishing and shooting are all on the doorstep or nearby. Live folk music evenings are held in the *Ewe* bar on Fridays. Seven miles W of town. Lounge, library, bar, restaurant (2 dining rooms; background music; open to non-residents), garden. Wedding/function facilities. Parking. Children and dogs welcomed. 1 bedrooms: £100–£125; D,B&B £135–£160.

AUCHENCAIRN Dumfries and Galloway Map 5:E2

Balcary Bay, Shore Road, Castle Douglas, DG7 1QZ. Tel 01556-640217, www.balcary-bay-hotel.co.uk. 'A place of perfect peace', this remote, traditional hotel has secret underground passages (used by 17th-century smugglers to hide contraband) and 'great views' across to Heston Island. The 'super-efficient' resident proprietor, Graeme Lamb, and his staff provide 'attentive and polite service'. Craig McWilliam's 'delectable' dishes are Scottish with a modern European influence. 2 lounges, restaurant, bar, conservatory. No background music. 3½-acre garden. Children welcomed. 20 bedrooms (3 on ground floor, with patio). B&B £78–£85 per person; D,B&B £97–£109 (min. 2-night stay). Closed Dec–Feb.
25% DISCOUNT VOUCHERS

BALLYGRANT Argyll and Bute Map 5:D1

Kilmeny Country House, Isle of Islay, PA45 7QW. Tel 01496-840668, www.kilmeny.co.uk. 'Scottish hospitality at its very best.' Margaret Rozga's white-painted 19th-century house is on a working farm with 'spectacular views' over the surrounding countryside. It has a 'warm and homely feel'; guests are welcomed 'with tea and cakes, and a friendly chat'. The 'exceptionally high-quality' dinners (Tues and Thurs only; BYO wine) include drinks and canapés before, and petits fours afterwards. A new

…ng system has … room, sun room, … nd music. On the … miles from the ferry ter… … Askaig. Children over 6 welcome… … edrooms (2 on ground floor, with walk-in shower). B&B £60–£75 per person; D,B&B £95–£110. Closed Nov–Mar.

BALQUHIDDER Stirling
Map 5:D2

MONACHYLE MHOR, Lochearnhead, FK19 8PQ. Tel 01877-384622, www.mhor.net. Siblings Tom, Dick and Melanie Lewis run their restaurant-with-rooms in converted 18th-century stone farm buildings in a 'remote, beautiful' setting four miles along a glen in the Trossachs national park. No tartan in the decor (overseen by Melanie Lewis, an artist), which has a mix of contemporary and antique furnishings. Tom Lewis, the chef, cooks modern dishes on a short set menu: 'Wonderful food: small courses, lots of extras, strong flavours.' Sitting room, bar, conservatory restaurant (background music), wedding facilities, garden. Children welcomed, dogs allowed (in 2 bedrooms). 14 bedrooms (some are small; 'elegantly minimalist'). B&B £92.50–£132.50 per person (only available Mon–Thurs), D,B&B £142.50–£182.50, set dinner £50.

BOWMORE Argyll and Bute
Map 5:D1

HARBOUR INN AND RESTAURANT, The Square, Isle of Islay, PA43 7JR. Tel 01496-810330, www.harbour-inn.com. From the conservatory of this old whitewashed inn, there are stunning views across Loch Indaal towards Jura. The inn was recently completely refurbished by owners Neil and Carol Scott. Upstairs are comfortable bedrooms, and a cosy lounge with books and games. Sandra Stevenson's cooking focuses on seafood, using local, seasonal produce. Conservatory lounge (Hebridean afternoon tea), bar, restaurant (background music), terrace, small garden. Complimentary use of nearby leisure centre with pool and spa. Birdwatching tours arranged. Wi-Fi. Children over 10 welcomed. 7 bedrooms (plus 4 rooms in *The Inns Over-by*, a 'pebble's throw' from the main building). B&B £67.50–£82.50 per person; D,B&B £105–£120.

BRODICK North Ayrshire
Map 5:E1

AUCHRANNIE HOUSE HOTEL, Isle of Arran, KA27 8BZ. Tel 01770-302234, www.auchrannie.co.uk. Owned by the Johnston family since 1988, this island enterprise in 'lovely' landscaped gardens has expanded into a large resort with two leisure clubs. Rooms in the original house (built in 1869) have 'lovely, quiet places to sit in, with big, comfy sofas, roaring log fires, beautiful antiques'. 'Fab views up Glencloy; it was well worth getting up early to watch a stunning sunrise.' A complimentary bus service operates between the resort and the ferry terminal. Bar, 3 restaurants, spa (indoor pool, steam room, spa bath; gym). Wi-Fi (in public areas). Parking. Children (indoor *Play Barn*) and dogs welcomed. 28 bedrooms (plus accommodation in the contemporary spa resort; also 30 self-catering lodges). B&B £84.50–£199 per person; D,B&B £20 added.

BRUICHLADDICH Argyll and Bute Map 5:D1

LOCH GORM HOUSE, Isle of Islay, PA49 7UN. Tel 01496-850139, www.lochgormhouse.com. A 'most comfortable' guest house, this B&B has been renovated by owner and 'excellent' hostess Fiona Doyle. 'It is furnished beautifully with designer fabrics; sea views from most rooms.' Ms Doyle is an accomplished florist; magnificent flower arrangements abound. 'Everything is perfect' at a generous breakfast. Evening meals are served by arrangement. Sitting room, dining room (no background music). Drying facilities. Dogs by arrangement. 3 bedrooms. B&B £62.50–£140 per person. Dinner £35.

CASTLEBAY Western Isles Map 5: inset A1

CASTLEBAY HOTEL, Isle of Barra, HS9 5XD. Tel 01871-810223, www.castlebayhotel.com. On the most southerly inhabited island in the Outer Hebrides, this 'excellent' small hotel stands above the village and has panoramic views of Castlebay, the harbour and Vatersay beyond. Owned by Terry Mackay and managed by John Campbell, it has a friendly, relaxed ambience. 'Good food and a spacious, well-equipped room with sea views.' Easy to reach by ferry from Oban. Lounge, bar, restaurant (Slawek Pilarski specialises in seafood), conservatory/sun porch; background music. ¼-acre garden. Wi-Fi. Children and dogs welcomed. 15 bedrooms (1 suitable for ♿). B&B £49–£165 per person; D,B&B £74–£195.

CRAIGARD HOTEL, Isle of Barra, HS9 5XD. Tel 01871-810200, www.craigardhotel.co.uk. Overlooking the bay, Julian Capewell's small, white-painted hotel on a hillside has 'breathtaking views' over Castlebay to Kisimul Castle, Vatersay and the islands beyond. Home-cooked food (specialities are cockles, scallops and fresh fish) is served in the popular restaurant. Lounge, 2 bars (pool table), restaurant, terrace (panoramic views). Background TV/radio. Beach airport 6 miles; town and ferry terminal close by. Parking. Children welcomed (not in public bar). 7 bedrooms. B&B £50–£60 per person. Dinner £24.

CHIRNSIDE Scottish Borders Map 5:E3

CHIRNSIDE HALL HOTEL, nr Duns, TD11 3LD. Tel 01890-818219, www.chirnsidehallhotel.com. With 'inspiring' views over fields to the Cheviot hills, this distinctive late Georgian mansion has been restored by hands-on owners Tessa and Christian Korsten. They run it as a small hotel with 'charming' staff. Spacious lounges are 'elegantly' furnished, with open fires in the evening. In the handsome dining room, daily-changing menus specialise in game and local ingredients. *Chirnside Hall* is busy with sporting parties in the winter; quieter breaks can be enjoyed in summer. The sea, with a sand and rock beach, is 15 mins' drive away. 2 lounges, dining room, private dining room, billiard room, fitness room, library/conference room. Background music ('easy listening', classical). Wedding facilities. Children welcomed. 10 bedrooms. B&B £80–£90 per person; D,B&B £105–£110.

CRIANLARICH Perth and Kinross Map 5:D2

EWICH HOUSE, Strathfillan, FK20 8RU. Tel 01838-300300, www.ewich.co.uk. In within Loch Lomond national park, Deb ... Richards run this B&B in ... house dating to 1811. The sitting room has a log fire and tartan blankets; guests may help themselves to drinks from the bar. Simply furnished bedrooms have comfortable beds, iPod docks, fresh milk for tea and coffee. Filling breakfasts include a hearty vegetarian option; packed lunches ('chunky doorstep sandwiches') may be provided. Dinners, for groups, by arrangement. Lounge (honesty bar, books, board games, DVDs, CDs, Sky TV, PlayStation 2), dining room, 6-acre grounds. No background music. Wi-Fi. Children welcomed. 6 bedrooms. B&B £36–£40 per person. Closed Christmas, Jan.

DALKEITH Midlothian
Map 5:D2

The Sun Inn, Lothianbridge, EH22 4TR. Tel 0131-663 2456, www.thesuninnedinburgh.co.uk. In five acres of wooded grounds, this gastropub-with-rooms, a former coaching inn, lies close to the banks of the River Esk. (Edinburgh city centre is a 20-minute drive away.) Bedrooms, decorated with striking wallpaper and locally crafted furniture, have DVDs, a Roberts radio, and home-made biscuits; public areas have exposed stone walls and log fires. In the award-winning restaurant, chef Ian Minto champions local producers and brewers. Restaurant, bar, courtyard, garden. Modern background music in restaurant. Parking. 5 bedrooms (1 suite with copper bath). B&B £42.50–£75 per person. Closed 26 Dec and 1 Jan.

DUNDEE
Map 5:D3

Apex City Quay Hotel & Spa, 1 West Victoria Dock Road, DD1 3JP. Tel 01382-202404, www.apexhotels.co.uk. With 'stunning' views over the River Tay, this modern five-storey hotel sits on the waterfront in the quay development, within easy reach of the city centre. Bedrooms are smartly decorated; the sleek bar/brasserie has dark woods and curved booths. There is a thorough kit available for babies and young children (bottle warmers, sterilisers, baby food on kids' menu; toy box, board games, treasure hunt). Bar/brasserie, spa (gym, sauna, hot tubs; treatments); background music throughout. Conference/events centre; wedding/function facilities. Wi-Fi; complimentary local calls; newspaper. Parking. 151 bedrooms: from £75. Dinner from £21.50.

Duntrune House, Duntrune, DD4 0PJ. Tel 01382-350239, www.duntrunehouse.co.uk. In a historic manor house (1826) surrounded by extensive garden and woodland, Olwyn and Barrie Jack run this peaceful B&B. The lovingly restored home has antiques, a stone staircase and, on colder evenings, a log fire in the sitting room. Breakfast, taken communally at a large table, includes fruit in season grown on the grounds. Family history enthusiasts, the Jacks will help guests trace their ancestry in the local area. Sitting room, dining room. 8-acre garden. No background music. Wi-Fi. Parking. Children welcomed. 4 bedrooms (1 on ground floor; all with garden view), plus a self-catering flat. B&B £45–£50 per person. Closed Nov–Mar.

DURNESS Highland
Map 5:B2

Mackay's Rooms & Restaurant, IV27 4PN. Tel 01971-511202, www.visitmackays.com. Part of a group of properties including a cottage, a cabin, a bunkhouse and two self-catering crofts, this hotel – in a flint-walled structure built 150 years ago as a home for the current owners' great grandfather – is owned and run by Fiona and Robbie Mackay. Stylish bedrooms have pre-loaded iPods, modern bathrooms and a mix of hand-made and vintage furniture. The restaurant has a daily-changing menu showcasing local produce. Packed lunches can be provided. Snug, restaurant (background music); garden. Wi-Fi. Parking. Children welcomed; dogs by arrangement. 7 bedrooms. B&B £55–£65 per person. Dinner £15–£25. Closed Nov–Easter.

EDINBURGH
Map 5:D2

Glenora Guest House, 14 Rosebery Crescent, EH12 5JY. Tel 0131-337 1186, www.glenorahotel.co.uk. Minutes from the city centre, Fiona Rasmusen's understated, modern B&B occupies a Victorian town house. Wendy Phillips is the manager. The lounge overlooks the garden and a newly planted apple tree. Upstairs bedrooms are 'lovely', but a guest found that basement rooms lack the same comforts. Organic breakfasts have freshly baked scones and hot dishes cooked to order. Lounge, breakfast room (background radio). Wi-Fi. Children welcomed. 11 bedrooms (2 in basement). B&B £42.50–£95 per person.

The Howard, 34 Great King Street, EH3 6QH. Tel 0131-557 3500, www.thehoward.com. 'We were pampered.' Butlers bring complimentary loose-leaf teas and warm milk to guests' rooms on request, at this luxury hotel (part of The Edinburgh Collection) occupying three Georgian town houses on a central New Town street. Bedrooms are decorated in warm colours and rich fabrics; some have a roll-top bath or spa bath. Aperitifs and nightcaps are served in the curved-walled drawing room. 'Service is exemplary.' Restaurant (background music), drawing room; small garden. Wi-Fi. Parking. Wedding/conference facilities. 18 bedrooms (5 suites). B&B £70–£180 per person. Dinner £55–£85.

94DR, 94 Dalkeith Road, EH16 5AF. Tel 0131-662 9265, www.94dr.com. Enthusiastic owners Paul Lightfoot and John MacEwan's innovative B&B is in a Victorian town house ten minutes by bus from the centre. Decorated in muted greys with splashes of colour, bedrooms (Couture, Bespoke or Tailored) have panoramic views of Salisbury Crags and Arthur's Seat, or over the walled gardens towards the Pentland hills. Imaginative breakfasts use local, organic produce. Complimentary bicycles are available to borrow. Lounge, breakfast room (classical/jazz/'easy listening' background music). Wi-Fi. Children welcomed (books, DVDs, games, Xbox). Resident labradoodle, Molli. 6 bedrooms. B&B £40–£75 per person.

One Royal Circus, EH3 6TL. Tel 0131-625 6669, www.oneroyalcircus.com. 'Another world.' Susan and Mike Gordon's handsomely decorated B&B occupies a discreet Georgian town house

on a World Heritage-listed crescent. Public areas are furnished with antique and modern pieces and vintage posters; the Grade A listed salon retains its original 1820s ceiling frescos. Large bedrooms have floor-to-ceiling windows (the best rooms overlook the private gardens). Guests are encouraged to help themselves in the kitchen or at the curving, retro bar in the lounge. Kitchen/breakfast room, lounge, drawing room (baby grand piano), pool room (with Bonzini Babyfoot table), gym, key access to private gardens. Wi-Fi. Wedding facilities. Children welcomed (books, games, babysitting by arrangement). 5 bedrooms, plus a 1-bedroom apartment. B&B £69–£129 per person.
25% DISCOUNT VOUCHERS

PRESTONFIELD, Priestfield Road, EH16 5UT. Tel 0131-225 7800, www.prestonfield.com. Surrounded by 20 acres of private grounds by the Royal Holyrood Park, James Thomson's extravagant and seductive 17th-century hotel is decadently luxurious. Bedrooms have parkland views, state-of-the-art technology and a bottle of champagne on arrival; staff wear black kilts. Visitors to *Rhubarb* restaurant (John McMahon is chef) called it 'an orgy for the eyes and senses; excellent food'. Mr Thomson also owns *The Witchery by the Castle*, Edinburgh (see below). Restaurant, 2 drawing rooms, salon, whisky bar, 4 private dining rooms; background music. Terraces, 'Gothic' tea house. Lift. Wi-Fi. Parking. Wedding/function facilities. Children and dogs welcomed. 23 bedrooms (1 suitable for ♿). B&B £147.50–£295 per person; D,B&B £177.50.

THE SCOTSMAN, 20 North Bridge, EH1 1TR. Tel 0131-556 5565, www.thescotsmanhotel.co.uk. Occupying the former offices of the *Scotsman* newspaper, this luxury hotel has preserved many original features of the 1905 building, including oak panelling, ornate ceilings and an impressive Italian marble staircase. 'Service is given the highest priority.' Well-equipped bedrooms have Scottish shortbread, an Edinburgh Monopoly board game and a complimentary shoe-shine service; some superior rooms have ornamental fireplaces or a roll-top bath in a turret. Family rooms are available; children receive a welcome pack. Drawing room, breakfast room, bar/brasserie; lift, ramps; cinema; health spa (16-metre swimming pool, sauna, gym, treatment rooms; juice bar, café). Background music. Wedding/conference facilities. Wi-Fi. 69 bedrooms (2 suitable for ♿). B&B £122.50–£245 per person.

SOUTHSIDE GUEST HOUSE, 8 Newington Road, EH9 1QS. Tel 0131-668 4422, www.southsideguesthouse.co.uk. Within walking distance of restaurants, pubs and theatres, Franco and Lynne Galgani's 'friendly' B&B occupies a Victorian terraced house near the Meadows and Holyrood Park. Colourful bedrooms have seating room; one, with a four-poster bed, also has a fireplace and its own terrace. Breakfast has vegetarian options, a daily speciality, Buck's Fizz. Breakfast room (light classical background music). Wi-Fi. Limited parking. Children over 8 allowed. 8 bedrooms. B&B £40–£90 per person.
25% DISCOUNT VOUCHERS

Tigerlily, 125 George Street, EH2 4JN. Tel 0131-225 5005, www.tigerlilyedinburgh.co.uk. Organic fruit and fresh flowers welcome guests in their bedroom at this stylish hotel occupying a Georgian town house on a street popular for shopping and nights out. Meals are served in glass-ceilinged courtyards (guests seeking more privacy can choose a beaded-curtained booth); in the buzzing bar, a cocktail trolley comes round. 2 bars, restaurant; lift. Wi-Fi. Interactive cocktail demonstrations; cupcake-decorating courses. Children welcomed. 33 bedrooms (some smoking). B&B £82.50–£212.50 per person; D,B&B £137.50–£250.

23 Mayfield, 23 Mayfield Gardens, EH9 2BX. Tel 0131-667 5806, www.23mayfield.co.uk. Guests appreciate the 'superb value, considerable comfort, meticulous attention to detail and excellent breakfast' at Ross Birnie's handsomely furnished Victorian guest house. Rooms, decorated in period style with solid dark wood furniture and heavy drapes, are equipped with the latest technology (iPod dock, digital radio, LCD TV); 'very well done' bathrooms have sea kelp toiletries. Drawing room/library, breakfast room; garden (patio; hot tub). Background music. 1 mile from the centre. Free mountain bike hire. Wi-Fi. Parking. Children welcomed (Nintendo Wii, Xbox). 9 bedrooms. B&B £50–£85 per person.

21212, 3 Royal Terrace, EH7 5AB. Tel 0845 22 21212, www.21212restaurant.co.uk. In this restored town house, a Grade A listed building at the end of a Georgian terrace, Katie O'Brien and Paul Kitching's restaurant-with-rooms is 'practical for exploring the city'. The glamorous drawing room has oversized windows and textured walls; on the upper floors, large, individually decorated bedrooms have ample seating areas, and views of the rear gardens or the city. In the restaurant, Mr Kitching has a *Michelin* star for his modern French menus. Drawing room, restaurant (closed Sun, Mon), private dining rooms. Wi-Fi. Children over 5 allowed. 4 bedrooms. B&B £87.50–£162.50 per person. Dinner £68.

The Witchery by the Castle, Castlehill, EH1 2NF. Tel 0131-225 5613, www.thewitchery.com. Decorated with flamboyance throughout, this restaurant-with-suites is in a collection of neighbouring buildings just below the castle. It was created by Scottish restaurateur-hotelier James Thomson (see *Prestonfield*, above); Jacquie Sutherland and Steven Hall are the managers. Indulgent, Gothic-style accommodation is in two 16th- and 17th-century buildings overlooking the Royal Mile. A bottle of champagne, breakfast hamper and newspaper are included in the room rate. 2 restaurants: *The Witchery* and *The Secret Garden* (Douglas Roberts is the chef; background music); terrace. 8 suites. B&B £162.50–£175 per person. Dinner £33.

ELGIN Moray
Map 5:C2

Mansion House Hotel & Country Club, The Haugh, IV30 1AW. Tel 01343-548811, www.mansionhousehotel.co.uk. Along the Grampian Highland whisky trail, this 19th-century baronial mansion sits in large grounds on the banks of the River Lossie. Rooms are decorated in country house style, with tufted armchairs and a fireplace in the lounge, and sleigh beds or four-posters in recently refurbished bedrooms. Head chefs Barry Milne and Craig Kenyon serve traditional Scottish dishes in the restaurant. Piano lounge, bar, restaurant, bistro. Background music. Leisure club (indoor swimming pool, sauna, steam room; treatments; gym, snooker room). Wedding/function facilities. Parking. 23 bedrooms (some interconnecting). B&B £77–£101.25 per person; D,B&B £100.50–£123. Closed Christmas.

FORT WILLIAM Highland
Map 5:C1

THE LIME TREE, The Old Manse, Achintore Road, PH33 6RQ. Tel 01397 701806, www.limetreefortwilliam.co.uk. Near the town centre, this old manse has been 'imaginatively' converted into an 'excellent' small hotel, restaurant and art gallery. The owner, David Wilson, is an 'exciting' artist; his work is displayed in the hotel as well as the gallery. 'The staff are exceptionally friendly, showing an interest and giving advice on the area.' John Wilson is the chef: 'Outstanding cooking with unusual but successful combinations of flavours.' 2 lounges, map room ('books and guides to help guests plan their journeys'); garden with seating area. Background music in the evenings. Children welcomed; dogs allowed (£5 charge). 9 bedrooms (in main house and extension). B&B £40–£60 per person. Dinner £27.95–£29.95 added. Closed Christmas.

GIGHA Argyll and Bute
Map 5:D1

GIGHA HOTEL, Isle of Gigha, PA41 7AA. Tel 01583-505254, www.gigha.org.uk. Guests, locals and visiting yachtsmen gather in the bar of this small, friendly hotel on a community-owned island. Spacious bedrooms are simply decorated; some have views of Ardminish Bay. The dining room serves prawns, clams and lobsters freshly caught by local fishermen. Lounge, bar (occasional background music), restaurant; garden (alfresco eating). Wedding/function facilities. 12 bedrooms, plus 9 self-catering cottages. B&B £40–£50 per person; D,B&B £60–£70. Closed Christmas.

GLASGOW
Map 5:D2

THE BELHAVEN, 15 Belhaven Terrace, G12 0TG. Tel 0141-339 3222, www.belhavenhotel.com. David Kerr's colourful town house hotel is near the Botanic Gardens in the bustling West End. Some rooms have views of the gardens; others can be compact. The Great Western Road is close by; some traffic noise. Dining room/bar (light meals; background music). Terrace. Wi-Fi (charge). Parking. Children welcomed. 16 bedrooms. B&B £27.50–£48.50 per person.

BLYTHSWOOD SQUARE HOTEL, 11 Blythswood Square, G2 4AD. Tel 0141-248 8888, www.townhousecompany.com. 'A comfortable and glamorous place to stay.' The former clubhouse of the Royal Scottish Automobile Club, this Victorian building is today a sleek, modern hotel (part of the Town House Collection).

Thoughtfully decorated bedrooms – 'contemporary, rich and stylish' – have a marble bathroom; some superior rooms are large enough to serve as a family room. There are champagne afternoon teas in the salon overlooking the garden square, a good children's menu in the dining room. 'Great' breakfasts (lavish buffet; all hot dishes cooked to order). Salon, 3 bars, restaurant, private screening room; spa (2 relaxation pools, treatment rooms, rasul mud chamber, relaxing lounge, café). Wi-Fi. Children welcomed. 100 bedrooms (some suitable for ♿): £120–£285. Breakfast £12.50–£16.50.

15GLASGOW, 15 Woodside Place, G3 7QL. Tel 0141-332 1263, www.15glasgow.com. Warm, welcoming hosts Shane and Laura McKenzie run their modern B&B, decorated in cool shades of silver, grey and caramel, out of a restored Victorian town house a short walk from the city centre. Spacious, comfortable bedrooms have tall windows, high ceilings and mood lighting; Tunnock's teacakes are a welcome gesture. Breakfast is brought to the room at an arranged time. The University of Glasgow and museums are close by. Lounge (classical radio background music); garden. Parking. Wi-Fi. Children welcomed. 5 bedrooms. B&B £50–£85 (min. 3-night stay for advance bookings). Closed Christmas and New Year.

GLENDEVON Perth and Kinross Map 5:D2

THE TORMAUKIN HOTEL, FK14 7JY. Tel 01259-781252, www.tormaukinhotel.co.uk. With beamed rooms, wood floors and open fires, this 18th-century inn in the Perthshire countryside is run as a comfortable small hotel by Dave and Lesley Morby. Head chefs Martin Cowan and David Macaskill's menu specialises in locally reared beef and lamb, and locally sourced fish and game. The breakfast room and lounge have been refurbished this year. Lounge, bar, restaurant, conservatory; terrace. Background music. Wi-Fi. Parking. Children welcomed; dogs by arrangement. 11 bedrooms (some on ground floor; 4 in stables block). B&B £35–£50 per person. Dinner £30. Closed Christmas.

GRANDTULLY Perth and Kinross Map 5:D2

THE INN ON THE TAY, PH9 0PL. Tel 01887-840760, www.theinnonthetay.co.uk. The bar and restaurant of this inn are popular for watching the canoeists and rafters negotiate the Grandtully rapids. On a bend of the roaring River Tay, this stone-built house has been refurbished in contemporary style by owners Geoff Wilson and Josie Pirie. New chef Gavin Thompson cooks locally sourced food from midday onwards. Bar (pool table), restaurant; deck. Background music (quiet classical). Wi-Fi. Parking. Wedding facilities. Children welcomed; dogs by arrangement. 6 bedrooms (3 with river views). B&B £50–£70 per person. Dinner £25. Closed early Jan.

GRANTOWN-ON-SPEY Highland Map 5:C2

THE DULAIG, Seafield Avenue, PH26 3JF. Tel 01479-872065, www.thedulaig.com. Furnished with Arts and Crafts antiques, Carol and Gordon Bulloch's environmentally friendly B&B

is in an Edwardian house in a rural position, a few minutes' walk from town. 'Attention to detail was superb and there were lots of little touches.' Freshly baked offerings are left daily by the 'cake fairy' in the elegant bedrooms. The extensive breakfast menu has a Scottish flavour, using home-grown produce and eggs from the Bullochs' flock of Black Rock free-range hens. Drawing room, dining room (quiet, contemporary Scottish background music), veranda; secluded garden (wildlife pond, summer house). Wi-Fi (computer available). Parking (garage for motorbikes and cycles). 3 bedrooms. B&B £70–£110 per person.

GULLANE East Lothian
Map 5:D3
GREYWALLS, Muirfield, EH31 2EG. Tel 01620-842144, www.greywalls.co.uk. A paradise for golfers, this elegant, crescent-shaped stone house, designed by Sir Edwin Lutyens, overlooks the eighteenth hole of Muirfield golf course. The interiors remain faithful to the Edwardian period. Chef Derek Johnstone cooks classical French dishes at *Chez Roux* restaurant, which is open to non-residents. Bar/lounge, drawing room, library, dining room; walled garden (tennis courts, croquet lawn, putting green). Wedding/function facilities. Children welcomed. 23 bedrooms (some in cottage nearby). B&B £130–£300 per person. Dinner £29.50–£55.
25% DISCOUNT VOUCHERS

INVERKEILOR Angus
Map 5:D3
GORDON'S RESTAURANT WITH ROOMS, Main Street, by Arbroath, DD11 5RN. Tel 01241-830364, www.gordonsrestaurant.co.uk. Equidistant between Montrose and Arbroath, this family enterprise in a brightly painted 1800s terraced house has been running for over 25 years. The interiors have exposed stone, stained-glass windows and a wood-burning stove. 'First-rate cooking' by Gordon and Garry Watson. Maria Watson is front-of-house. Modern Scottish dishes might include twice-baked Tobermory Cheddar soufflé, poached monkfish with ginger spiced lentils. Bedrooms are 'comfortably equipped'. No background music. Garden. Parking. 5 bedrooms (1 in courtyard). B&B £55–£85 per person. Dinner £48.

INVERNESS Highland
Map 5:C2
MOYNESS HOUSE, 6 Bruce Gardens, IV3 5EN. Tel 01463-233836, www.moyness.co.uk. Jenny and Richard Jones run this comfortable B&B in the former home of Scottish Renaissance author Neil M Gunn (whose works have given the bedrooms their names). Set in its own grounds, the restored Victorian villa is within walking distance of the city centre. Sitting room, dining room; ⅓-acre garden. Wi-Fi. Parking. Children over 5 accepted. 6 bedrooms. B&B £35–£52.50 per person. Closed Christmas.

ROCPOOL RESERVE, 14 Culduthel Road, IV2 4AG. Tel 01463-240089, www.rocpool.com. Part of the same hotel group as *Inverlochy Castle*, Fort William (see main entry), and with an Albert Roux restaurant, this luxury hotel in the centre of Inverness has views of the River Ness and the

Cairngorms. Bedrooms have a large bed, flat-screen TV and DVD-player; some rooms have a balcony. The new manager is Niki Gillies. Lounge, cocktail bar, *Chez Roux* restaurant (Ian Simpson is chef; closed Mon, Tues). Background music. In-room massage and treatments available on request. Wedding/conference facilities. Parking. Children welcomed (Xbox, board games; quad biking, go-carting, archery and riding can be arranged). 11 bedrooms. B&B £92.50–£197.50 per person; D,B&B £125–£230.

IONA Argyll and Bute
Map 5:D1

ARGYLL HOTEL, PA76 6SJ. Tel 01681-700334, www.argyllhoteliona.co.uk. Once a modest croft house, this family-run hotel and restaurant overlooking the Sound of Iona has been welcoming visitors for nearly 150 years. New owners Wendy and Rob MacManaway and Katie and Dafydd Russon took over this year. There are fires in the lounge and dining room, books in the public areas, and organic soaps in the bathrooms. Seasonal, organic meals are made by Pam Brunton on the 1920s Aga; the home-made scones, shortbreads and Amoretto biscuits are much praised. 3 lounges, television room, dining room; organic kitchen garden. No TV and phone in rooms. Children and dogs welcomed. 16 bedrooms (1 suite). B&B £64–£94.50 per person. Dinner £45. Closed Nov–Feb.

KELSO Scottish Borders
Map 5:E3

THE CROSS KEYS, 36–37 The Square, TD5 7HL. Tel 01573-223303, www.cross-keys-hotel.co.uk. On a cobbled square in a historic Borders town, this former coaching inn is run as a hotel by the Becattelli family – 'delightful' hosts. Bedrooms vary in size and shape; interconnecting family rooms, with a shared bathroom, are available. The restaurant serves 'hearty' modern Scottish and continental dishes. Popular with groups. Lounge, *No. 36* bar, restaurant, ballroom. Lift. Background music. Wi-Fi. Wedding/function/conference facilities. Children welcomed. 26 bedrooms. B&B £40–£72.50 per person; D,B&B £52.50–£90. Closed Christmas, first 2 weeks Jan.

KILLIN Perth and Kinross
Map 5:D2

ARDEONAIG HOTEL, South Loch Tay Side, FK21 8SU. Tel 01567-820400, www.ardeonaighotel.co.uk. Guests praise the stunning views, helpful staff and exceptional cooking at this small hotel, once a drovers' inn, on a single-track road surrounded by farmland. Euan Snowie is the new owner; former sommelier James Payne is the manager. Bedrooms are decorated in muted natural tones; some have views towards Loch Tay and Ben Lawers. In the grounds are cottage suites and round, heather-roofed shieling lodges with large beds and freestanding baths. Ross Miller, the chef, serves tasting menus (a creative vegetarian menu is admired). Lounge, restaurant (closed Mon, Tues), bar/snug, library, terrace, wine cellar, gardens. Background music. Wedding/function facilities. Children welcomed; dogs by arrangement. 17 bedrooms (5 shieling lodges, 2 cottage suites). B&B £60–£137.50 per person; D,B&B £100–£180.

KINCLAVEN Perth and Kinross
Map 5:D2
Ballathie House, Stanley, nr Perth, PH41 4QN. Tel 01250-883268, www.ballathiehousehotel.com. On the west bank of the River Tay, this 'impressive' 19th-century house with turrets and pointed roofs has long been associated with salmon fishing. It is owned by the Mulligan family; Wolfgang Spenke is the new manager. There are 'monster' fishing trophies in display cabinets on the walls of the public rooms; the 'grand' drawing room and morning room have 'plenty of comfortable seating'; in the dining room the food is 'of a high standard; small portions of modern dishes'. No background music. 53 bedrooms (16 in riverside building, 12 in lodge). B&B £95–£170 per person. Dinner £55.

KIRKWALL Orkney Islands
Map 5:A3
Albert Hotel, Mounthoolie Lane, KW15 1JZ. Tel 01856-876000, www.alberthotel.co.uk. 'A comfortable place to retire to at the end of a busy day.' Modern bedrooms and Scottish breakfasts attract guests to this hotel within walking distance of the cathedral, museum, harbour and bus station. Room 201 has a spacious bathroom, long bath, and an oversized heated towel rail, 'very necessary in Orkney and much appreciated'. The restaurant has a strong emphasis on local produce; the *Bothy* bar, decorated with old photos and memorabilia, has a real fire and live traditional music. Lounge, bar, restaurant. Lift. Wi-Fi. Wedding/function facilities. Children welcomed. Parking.18 bedrooms. B&B £50–£90 per person. Dinner £20. Closed Christmas and New Year.

LOCHINVER Highland
Map 5:B1
Inver Lodge, Iolaire Road, IV27 4LU. Tel 01571-844496, www.inverlodge.com. 'Lovely, well-equipped' bedrooms in this purpose-built hotel, on a hillside overlooking a quiet fishing village, have large beds and easy chairs from which to appreciate the views. Public areas are decorated in warm colours; the foyer lounge has an open fire and picture windows. Bathrooms have been refurbished this year. Mornings, breakfast porridge may be served with a dram of whisky. Lounge, bar, restaurant, snooker table; sauna; ½-acre grounds (salmon and trout fishing). No background music. Wi-Fi. Children and dogs welcomed. 21 bedrooms (some on ground floor). B&B £107.50–£240 per person; D,B&B £145–£275. Closed Nov–Mar.
25% DISCOUNT VOUCHERS

LOCKERBIE Dumfries and Galloway
Map 5:E2
The Dryfesdale, Dryfebridge, DG11 2SF. Tel 01576-202427, www.dryfesdalehotel.co.uk. Surrounded by acres of elevated parkland, this Best Western hotel, owned by Glen Wright, occupies an 18th-century manse. Bedrooms have home-made shortbread, and views of the hotel grounds and surrounding countryside; garden suites also have French windows opening onto a private patio. Lounge, bar (130 malt whiskies), restaurant; 5-acre grounds. Wedding/function/conference facilities. Background music. Children welcomed; dogs by arrangement. 29 bedrooms (some in garden suites, some suitable for

♿). B&B £59–£89 per person; D,B&B £95–£119. Closed Christmas.
25% DISCOUNT VOUCHERS

MELROSE Scottish Borders
Map 5:E3
BURT'S, Market Square, TD6 9PL. Tel 01896-822285, www.burtshotel.co.uk. In a pretty market town on the banks of the River Tweed, this hotel, in a listed 18th-century building, attracts anglers and other outdoorsy guests keen on the many rural pastimes – walking, cycling, stalking, game shooting – available on the doorstep. The restaurant specialises in local game and fish; the bar has a dedicated whisky menu. Bedrooms (some may be compact) are decorated with tartan cushions and blankets. 2 lounges, bistro bar, restaurant; ¼-acre garden. Parking. Wedding/function facilities. Wi-Fi. Children welcomed (no under-8s in restaurant). Dogs by arrangement. 20 bedrooms (some recently refurbished). B&B £66.50–£72 per person. Dinner £36. Closed Boxing Day, early Jan.

THE TOWNHOUSE, Market Square, TD6 9PQ. Tel 01896-822645, www.thetownhousemelrose.co.uk. The sleek, modern sister to the Henderson family's other venture, *Burt's*, this small hotel sits just across the square. Individually designed bedrooms have dramatic bedheads and striking wallpaper; a family room is available. Trevor Williams's modern Scottish menus in the brasserie and the more formal restaurant have been praised. Brasserie (background music), restaurant, conservatory, patio; ramps. Wi-Fi. Wedding/function facilities. Children welcomed. 11 bedrooms. B&B £62–£90 per person. Dinner £34.50. Closed Christmas, mid-Jan.

MOFFAT Dumfries and Galloway
Map 5:E2
HARTFELL HOUSE & LIMETREE RESTAURANT, Hartfell Crescent, DG10 9AL. Tel 01683-220153, www.hartfellhouse.co.uk. In a rural setting overlooking the surrounding hills, this Victorian home, built of local stone, is run as a guest house and restaurant by Robert Ash. Traditionally decorated rooms retain some of the home's original features, including ornate cornices and woodwork. The restaurant, where chef Matt Seddon serves modern British dishes, is popular with locals. There is home-baked bread at breakfast. Lounge, dining room (classical background music); garden. Wi-Fi. Parking. Children welcomed. 7 bedrooms. B&B £30–£45 per person; D,B&B £50–£70. Closed 14–25 October, Christmas. Restaurant closed Sun dinner and Mon.

NORTH BERWICK East Lothian
Map 5:D3
THE GLEBE HOUSE, 4 Law Road, EH39 4PL. Tel 01620-892608/Mobile 07973 965814, www.glebehouse-nb.co.uk. Overlooking the historic seaside town, this award-winning B&B is the family home of Gwen and Jake Scott. The Georgian manse has period features, antiques and a sizeable collection of Staffordshire china. Hearty Scottish breakfasts are taken communally around a large mahogany table. The beach is a two-minute walk away. Drawing room, sitting room, dining room, 2-acre secluded garden. Parking. Children welcomed. 3 bedrooms. B&B £60–£85 per person.

OBAN Argyll and Bute
Map 5:D1

ALT NA CRAIG HOUSE, Glenmore Road, PA34 4PG. Tel 01631-564524, www.guesthouseinoban.com. Welcoming owners Sandy and Ina MacArthur run this B&B in their turreted Victorian home. In an elevated position, the house has stunning seascape views across Oban Bay to the isles of Mull, Kerrera and Lismore. The comfortable bedrooms are equipped with Freeview TV and an iPod dock. Scottish fare at breakfast includes Loch Fyne kippers, and cheese and herb drop scones topped with home-made tomato sauce. 10 mins' walk into town. Breakfast room. 3-acre wooded grounds. 6 bedrooms. B&B £72.50–£120 per person.

LERAGS HOUSE, Lerags, PA34 4SE. Tel 01631-563381, www.leragshouse.com. A 100-year-old magnolia tree stands in the stone courtyard in front of this Georgian guest house run by new owners Nicola and Richard Fowler. Simple, tastefully decorated bedrooms look out over the mature garden or towards Loch Feochan. Mr Fowler's three-course set dinners (special diets catered for) focus on local produce. Good birdwatching in the grounds; walks from the door. Lounge, dining room (background music); 2-acre grounds. Wedding facilities. Children over 12 welcomed. 6 bedrooms. B&B £65–£75 per person; D,B&B from £85.

PEEBLES Scottish Borders
Map 5:E2

CRINGLETIE HOUSE, off Edinburgh Road, EH45 8PL. Tel 01721-725750, www.cringletie.com. Log fires burn in the lounge and library of this hotel, a turreted, pink stone Victorian baronial mansion set in extensive grounds. Individually decorated bedrooms have views of the hills beyond; junior suites also have a decanter of Tweeddale Blend whisky. In-room spa and beauty treatments are available (glitter tattoos for children). Patrick Bardoulet is the new chef; his tasting menus are served in the restaurant, with a frescoed ceiling. 2 sitting rooms, library, bar, restaurant (background music) Lift. 28-acre grounds: walled garden, woodland walks; outdoor chess, pétanque. Wedding/conference facilities. Wi-Fi. Children and dogs welcomed. 13 bedrooms (1 suitable for ♿). B&B £49.50–£97.50 per person. Dinner £82.50–£130.50. Closed 24 Nov–7 Dec.

PERTH Perth and Kinross
Map 5:D2

THE PARKLANDS, 2 St Leonard's Bank, PH2 8EB. Tel 01738-622451, www.theparklandshotel.com. Overlooking South Inch Park, this hotel in a Victorian stone-built house has been updated with a stylish contemporary interior and some Scottish flourishes by owners Penny and Scott Edwards. Bedrooms are modern and well equipped. Lounge, bar, bistro, *63@Parklands* fine-dining restaurant, private dining room; light background music. Terrace, garden leading to park. Wedding/function facilities. Wi-Fi. Parking. Dogs welcomed. 15 bedrooms. B&B £52.50–£89.50 per person; D,B&B £59.50–£97.50.
25% DISCOUNT VOUCHERS

SUNBANK HOUSE, 50 Dundee Road, PH2 7BA. Tel 01738-624882, www.sunbankhouse.com. Set in large gardens overlooking the River Tay and the city of Perth, this traditionally furnished Victorian house, a short walk from the city centre, is owned by welcoming hosts Georgina and Remo Zane. The hotel has undergone extensive refurbishment this year. Lounge/bar, restaurant (light background music). Wi-Fi. Parking. Wedding/function facilities. Children welcomed. 9 bedrooms (some on ground floor; 2 suitable for ♿). B&B £45–£79 per person; D,B&B £70–£99.

PITLOCHRY Perth and Kinross
Map 5:D2
EAST HAUGH HOUSE, by Pitlochry, PH16 5TE. Tel 01796-473121, www.easthaugh.co.uk. There are fresh flowers in the charming bedrooms of this modern sporting hotel, a turreted stone house owned by the McGown family for nearly 25 years. Rooms are decorated with tartan blankets, oil paintings, and toile de Jouy wallpaper and bedlinen; a log fire burns in the lounge. Chef/proprietor Neil McGown's menus feature fish and game in season (often caught by Mr McGown himself). 'There is something magical about *East Haugh*.' Lounge, bar, restaurant (background jazz), patio; ramps. 1½-acre grounds; river beat. Wedding/business facilities. Parking. Children welcomed; dogs by arrangement. 13 bedrooms (2 suitable for ♿, 5 in a converted 'bothy' beside the hotel), plus 2 self-catering cottages. B&B £69–£119 per person; D,B&B £119–£169. Closed Christmas.

PINE TREES, Strathview Terrace, PH16 5QR. Tel 01796-472121, www.pinetreeshotel.co.uk. 'Very comfortable, with excellent food.' Valerie and Robert Kerr's majestic Victorian mansion is set in peaceful woodland (deer, red squirrels), within walking distance of the town. 'Comfortably furnished' public areas have cosy seating areas, half-panelled walls and open log fires. 'We thoroughly enjoyed our stay.' 2 lounges (Wi-Fi), bar, restaurant (Cristian Cojocaru's cooking has a Scottish influence), 7-acre grounds. No background music. ¼ mile N of town. 20 bedrooms (2 with four-poster bed). Dogs welcomed. B&B £52–£68 per person; D,B&B £72–£88.

TORRDARACH HOUSE, Golf Course Road, PH16 5AU. Tel 01796-472136, www.torrdarach.co.uk. A stream runs through the wooded grounds of Louise and Struan Lothian's raspberry-red house (built in 1901), where red squirrels and roe deer can be glimpsed. 'The views over the gardens and the Perthshire Highlands are astounding.' The Lothians have refurbished their 'charming' B&B with luxury touches and original art. Bedrooms are thoughtfully equipped; breakfast is 'absolutely delightful'. Sitting room, breakfast room; comprehensive bar service. Mature woodland-style garden. No background music. Wi-Fi. Parking, bicycle storage. Children welcomed. 6 bedrooms (1 in 'bothy' behind the house). B&B £42.50–£75 per person. Closed Dec–Mar.
25% DISCOUNT VOUCHERS

PORTREE Highland
Map 5:C1
CUILLIN HILLS HOTEL, Isle of Skye, IV51 9QU. Tel 01478-612003, www.cuillinhills-hotel-skye.co.uk. In 15

acres of mature grounds, this Victorian hunting lodge has superb views over Portree Bay and the Cuillin Mountain range. Three superior bedrooms have been added this year; more upgrades are under way. There is an open fire in the striking scarlet-and-copper drawing room, and more than 130 malt whiskies are served in the bar. Charming Portree town is a ten-minute walk away. Drawing room, restaurant (inside an art gallery), brasserie, bar; background music. Wi-Fi. Parking. Wedding facilities. Children welcomed; dogs by arrangement. 29 bedrooms (3 on ground floor; 7 in annexe; disabled access). B&B £105–£155 per person; D,B&B £140–£190.

ST ANDREWS Fife
Map 5:D3

RUFFLETS, Strathkinness Low Road, KY16 9TX. Tel 01334-472594, www.rufflets.co.uk. A mix of antiques and contemporary pieces decorates the 'beautifully furnished' rooms in this 1920s turreted mansion. Originally built for the widow of a Dundee jute baron, this creeper-covered hotel is owned by Ann Murray-Smith and managed by Stephen Owen. 'The welcoming drawing room and lounge had roaring fires; the elegant dining room served a wide choice of food.' Good offers available. Drawing room, library, music room bar, restaurant (background music); 10-acre gardens. Wedding/function facilities. Wi-Fi. Children and dogs welcomed. 24 bedrooms (3 in *Gatehouse*; 2 in *Lodge*; 1 suitable for ♿), plus 3 self-catering cottages. B&B £107.50–£335 per person; D,B&B £132.50–£360.

SCOURIE Highland
Map 5:B2

EDDRACHILLES HOTEL, Badcall Bay, IV27 4TH. Tel 01971-502080, www.eddrachilles.com. In 'stunning' grounds at the head of Badcall Bay, this hotel, in an 18th-century manse, has gardens down to the shore. Isabelle and Richard Flannery are the 'helpful' owners. 'Well-equipped' bedrooms are traditionally furnished. In the new conservatory restaurant, the menu features fresh seafood from the bay. A smokehouse in the grounds provides the restaurant with smoked fish and meats. Reception, breakfast room, restaurant (extensive wine list), bar (over 100 single malt whiskies); classical background music. 4-acre garden. Parking. Wi-Fi. Children welcomed (high tea for under-6s). 11 bedrooms. B&B £52–£55 per person; D,B&B £70–£73. Closed Nov–Mar.

SKEABOST BRIDGE Highland
Map 5:C1

THE SPOONS, 75 Aird Bernisdale, Isle of Skye, IV51 9NU. Tel 01470-532217, www.thespoonsonskye.com. Lavish breakfasts at this whitewashed B&B include home-baked bread, home-made granola, locally smoked fish and freshly laid eggs from the house's own hens. Marie and Ian Lewis have decorated their luxury B&B, on a working croft overlooking Loch Snizort, in muted earth tones; bedrooms have cashmere and sheepskin throws, Nespresso machines. Afternoon tea has home-baked treats. Good walks from the door. Sitting room (wood-burning stove), dining room, 8-acre grounds. Wi-Fi. Children over 10 welcomed. 3 bedrooms (1 on ground floor). B&B £70–£80 per person. Closed Christmas.

SLEAT Highland
Map 5:C1
DUISDALE HOUSE, Isle of Skye, IV43 8QW. Tel 01471-833 202, www.duisdale.com. Anne Gracie and Ken Gunn, who also own nearby *Toravaig House* (see main entry), run this small hotel in a Victorian building in extensive gardens and woodland. Bedrooms and public areas are styled in rich colours and bold prints; some rooms have views over the Sound of Sleat to the mountains of mainland Scotland. Between April and September, guests are invited on sailing trips on board the hotel's yacht. Breakfast has local eggs, smoked fish, loose leaf-teas. Lounge, bar, restaurant, conservatory; 35-acre grounds (10-person garden hot tub). Wedding facilities. Children welcomed. 18 bedrooms (1 garden suite suitable for ♿). B&B £69.50–£169 per person; D,B&B £85–£194.
25% **DISCOUNT VOUCHERS**

SPEAN BRIDGE Highland
Map 5:C2
SMIDDY HOUSE, Roy Bridge Road, PH34 4EU. Tel 01397-712335, www.smiddyhouse.com. 'Immaculate and beautifully decorated', this restaurant-with-rooms is run by co-owners Robert Bryson and Glen Russell (the chef). It is in a village with a station on the scenic West Highland railway. A fine afternoon tea is served in the garden room (booking essential); Scottish breakfasts. Golf, mountain bike trails nearby. Garden room, *Russell's* restaurant (closed Mon, Tues Dec–Mar). Low-volume instrumental music. Wi-Fi. Parking. Children welcomed; dogs by arrangement. 4 bedrooms (plus self-catering accommodation in adjacent building, *The Old Smiddy*). B&B £42.50–£62.50 per person; D,B&B £67.50–£82.50.

STRACHUR Argyll and Bute
Map 5:D1
THE CREGGANS INN, PA27 8BX. Tel 01369-860279, www.creggans-inn.co.uk. On the shores of Loch Fyne, this white-painted inn, run by Gill and Archie MacLellan, has a 'fantastic location'. Simply decorated, pretty bedrooms have garden or loch views; the lounge has books and binoculars to borrow, and a handsome rocking horse for younger guests. Two moorings are available to guests arriving by boat. 2 lounges, bar/bistro ('easy listening' background music), restaurant; 2-acre garden. Wi-Fi. Wedding/function facilities. Children and dogs welcomed. Resident dog, Hector. 14 bedrooms. B&B £50–£110 per person; D,B&B £80–£140.

STRATHYRE Perth and Kinross
Map 5:D2
AIRLIE HOUSE, Main Street, nr Callendar, FK18 8NA. Tel 01877-384247, www.airliehouse.co.uk. Bedrooms have a comfortable bed and fresh milk at this B&B run by Jacquie and Ray Hill. Amid countryside and hills, the early 1900s Scottish villa is in the Trossachs and Breadalbane area of Scotland's first national park; the Rob Roy Way is nearby. Sitting room (log fires in winter), dining room, drying room. Background music. Parking. Children welcomed; 'well-behaved' dogs by arrangement. Resident dog, Poppy. 4 bedrooms (3 with views; 1 wheelchair friendly). B&B £30–£40 per person.

TAYNUILT Argyll and Bute
Map 5:D1

ROINEABHAL COUNTRY HOUSE, Kilchrenan, PA35 1HD. Tel 01866-833207, www.roineabhal.com. In the wild glens of Argyll close to Loch Awe, this small country guest house is run by Roger and Maria Soep. It is well placed for visits to Inveraray, Glencoe, Fort William and Kintyre; from the nearby port of Oban, ferries offer transport to Skye, Mull, Iona and the outer islands. Tea and cake are offered on arrival; breakfast includes Hunza apricots, locally smoked kippers and home-made toasted seed loaf. Lounge, dining room (dinner by arrangement), covered veranda; 2-acre garden. Afternoon teas. Children and pets welcomed. 18 miles E of Oban. 3 bedrooms (1 on ground floor suitable for ♿). B&B £50 per person. Closed Nov and Dec.

THURSO Highland
Map 5:B2

FORSS HOUSE HOTEL, Forss, by Thurso, KW14 7XY. Tel 01847-861201, www.forsshousehotel.co.uk. Country pursuits such as stalking, fishing, riding and falconry can be organised at this grand old Georgian mansion standing in 20 acres of woodland. It sits below a waterfall on the River Forss – 'there's a lovely walk down the side of the river to the sea'. Anne Mackenzie is the welcoming manager. Local produce such as Caithness lamb and Mey beef are used in new chef Gary Stevenson's modern Scottish dishes in the elegant restaurant, which is open to non-residents. Entrance lounge/conservatory (log fire), restaurant; background music (classical). Local golf, whitewater rides, mountain biking; beauty treatments. Wedding/function facilities. Children welcomed. 14 bedrooms (2 in *Fishing Lodge*, 4 in *River House*). B&B £82.50–£115 per person. Dinner £40.
25% DISCOUNT VOUCHERS

TOBERMORY Argyll and Bute
Map 5:D1

THE TOBERMORY HOTEL, Main Street, PA75 6NT. Tel 01688-302091, www.thetobermoryhotel.com. Guests like the breakfasts (home-made granola, local smoked fish) at this small hotel in a row of colourful converted fishermen's cottages on a working harbour. Some visitors have found the simply furnished bedrooms compact; others appreciate their authenticity and views (some have window seats for gazing over the bay). Packed lunches may include home-made brownies tied with a tartan ribbon. 2 lounges, bar, restaurant (closed Mon). Background music. Landscape photography workshops. Wedding/conference facilities. Children and dogs welcomed. 16 bedrooms (most with sea view; 1 suitable for ♿). B&B £39–£64 per person. Closed Nov–Mar.
25% DISCOUNT VOUCHERS

TONGUE Highland
Map 5:B2

THE TONGUE HOTEL, IV27 4XD. Tel 01847-611206, www.tonguehotel.co.uk. A Victorian sporting lodge in a sleepy coastal village beneath Ben Loyal, this small hotel, owned and run by Lorraine and David Hook, is decorated with paintings and antique furniture. Bedrooms have complimentary sherry, fruits and sweets; many also have original details such as fireplaces and marble washstands. The restaurant serves 'good substantial Scottish fare';

breakfast has home-made compotes, granola and muesli, and porridge with cream and heather honey. Bar, restaurant; therapy room. Wedding facilities. Children welcomed. 19 bedrooms. B&B £45–£130 per person; D,B&B £72–£185. Closed Dec–Feb (only private parties in winter).

UIG Western Isles
Map 5:B1
AUBERGE CARNISH, 5 Carnish, HS2 9EX. Tel 01851-672459, www.aubergecarnish.co.uk. A bright turquoise door marks this purpose-built beachside guest house and restaurant run by Jo-Ann and Richard Leparoux on a working croft perched above Uig Sands. Decorated in natural shades, bedrooms have views of the beach and the water. In the restaurant, also open to non-residents, Mr Leparoux's 'Franco-Hebridean' menus change with the seasons to highlight local ingredients. Breakfast has home-baked bread and home-made marmalade; guests may take their morning coffee on the decked terrace. Dining room, lounge (jazz/'easy listening' background music), patio. 4 bedrooms (1 suitable for ♿). B&B £65–£85 per person; D,B&B £98–£108. Closed Dec–Jan.

ULLAPOOL Highland
Map 5:B2
RIVERVIEW, 2 Castle Terrace, IV26 2XD. Tel 01854-612019, www.riverviewullapool.co.uk. Guests find chocolates on their pillow in Nadine Farquhar's modern B&B, in a quiet residential area in this fishing village. There are DVDs and board games in the lounge; breakfast (vegetarians catered for) is a hearty affair served at a time to suit each guest. Pubs and restaurants are a short walk away. Open-plan lounge/dining room/library. Complimentary use of leisure centre with pool. Wi-Fi. 3 bedrooms. B&B £35 per person. Closed Nov–Jan and for Loopallu (Sept).

THE SHEILING, Garve Road, IV26 2SX. Tel 01854-612947, www.thesheilingullapool.co.uk. 'Friendly' owners Lesley and Iain MacDonald run this comfortable B&B beside Loch Broom. 'Spacious' bedrooms have complimentary sherry; two have loch views. Breakfast, served in a bright room overlooking the loch and the mountains beyond, has local sausages and praiseworthy smoked haddock. The town centre is a ten-minute walk away; five minutes to the ferry for the Hebrides. Sitting room, dining room; Sportsman's Lodge (guest laundry, drying room, sauna, shower, motorcycle store). 1-acre garden, patio, fishing permits. Wi-Fi (computer available). Parking. Children welcomed. 6 bedrooms (2 on ground floor). B&B £34–£42 per person. Closed Christmas.

WALES

ABERGELE Conwy
Map 3:A3
THE KINMEL ARMS, St George, LL22 9BP. Tel 01745-832207, www.thekinmelarms.co.uk. 'A delightful hideaway.' Lynn and Tim Watson's Victorian inn (built in neo-Elizabethan style) lies in the Elwy valley, on the edge of the Kinmel estate. It is run in a 'modern, relaxed' way, with 'excellent' lunch and dining facilities at its heart. Lofty rooms have

an oak or maple super-king-size bed, paintings inspired by the North Wales landscape, a balcony or patio, and a luxurious limestone bathroom. A continental breakfast is served in the room. In the evenings, the busy restaurant has 'superb' à la carte menus devised by Gwyn Roberts; lunches are informal, brasserie-style. There are real ales and a wood-burning stove in the bar. Bar, restaurant. Wi-Fi. Parking. 4 bedrooms. B&B £67.50–£87.50 per person. Dinner from £35. Closed Sun, Mon.

CARDIFF Cardiff
Map 3:E4
HOTEL ONE HUNDRED, 100 Newport Road, CF24 1DG. Tel 07916-888423, www.hotelonehundred.com. 'Perfect for short stays in Cardiff.' Abi and Charlie Prothero's small budget hotel is in a renovated 1890s town house, a walkable distance from the city centre. There are shops, pubs and good eating places just around the corner. It has a fine staircase and stained-glass window, and a large, light and airy lounge with an honesty bar. Bedrooms have a bespoke, locally made bed, feature wallpaper, flat-screen TV and DVD-player; ornate mirrors hang over original Victorian fireplaces. The breakfast is 'excellent – never was my money better spent'. Breakfast room (background music), lounge; decked terrace. Wi-Fi. Limited on-site parking. Children welcomed. 7 bedrooms (1 on ground floor). B&B (continental) £25–£60 per person. Cooked breakfast £5.

JOLYON'S AT NO. 10, 10 Cathedral Road, CF11 9LJ. Tel 029-2009 1900, www.jolyons10.com. Opposite the Millennium Centre, Jolyon Joseph has converted this Georgian seamen's lodge into a small hotel. It is liked for the youthful, 'laid-back vibe', and hint of eccentricity. The manager is Rhian Jones. Bedrooms are decorated in contemporary colours and have an eclectic mix of furnishings. A first-floor room at the front has an antique carved wooden bed with a matching armoire; a spa bath in the bathroom. In the basement, the busy *Cwtch Mawr* (Welsh for a cuddle or a hug) is a popular local venue for its 'Dishy Bits' menu (cured meats, flatbreads, stuffed mushrooms, etc) and the extensive range of pizzas from a wood-burning oven. Breakfast is served here until 10 am (later at weekends). Lounge, bar (occasional live music), terrace. Background music. Conference/ function facilities. Wi-Fi. Parking. 7 bedrooms (1 on ground floor). B&B £44.50–£77 per person.

COLWYN BAY Conwy
Map 3:A3
ELLINGHAM HOUSE, 1 Woodland Park West, LL29 7DR. Tel 01492-533345, www.ellinghamhouse.com. In a leafy conservation area, this late Victorian villa has been elegantly furnished by 'welcoming' owners Ian Davies and Chris Jennings, whose attention to detail is praised. Bedrooms have a DVD-player, bathrobes and well-styled bathrooms; most are light and spacious. Lounge (DVD library). No background music. Wi-Fi. It is a short walk to the sea and town. Parking. Children welcomed; dogs by arrangement (£5 per night). 5 bedrooms (1 with separate shower room). B&B £37.50–£80 per person.

CONWY Conwy
Map 3:A3
Castle Hotel, High Street, LL32 8DB. Tel 01492-582800, www.castlewales.co.uk. Much photographed for its notable granite and Ruabon brick facade, this coaching inn was merged from two hostelries (parts dating back to the 1400s), on the site of a Cistercian abbey. It is now a hotel run by the Lavin family. Public rooms are furnished with antiques and paintings by Victorian artist John Dawson-Watson. Bedrooms vary in size; some have castle views. In the restaurant, chefs Andrew Nelson and Graham Tinsley use produce from artisan suppliers to create dishes that have 'a taste of Wales'. Bar, lounge, *Dawsons* restaurant. Background music. Courtyard garden (alfresco dining). Wi-Fi. Children, and dogs (charge), welcomed. 28 bedrooms (1 with 16th-century four-poster bed; some on ground floor). B&B £65–£270 per person. Dinner £30–£40.
25% DISCOUNT VOUCHERS

COWBRIDGE Vale of Glamorgan
Map 3:E3
The Bear, 63 High Street, CF71 7AF. Tel 01446-774814, www.bearhotel.com. 'A popular place', this quaint coaching inn dating back to the 12th century is in a pretty market town. Bedrooms are 'bright and airy'; some have a beamed ceiling, four-poster bed or chandelier. Chef Richard Bowles's daily blackboard specials are served in *Cellars* restaurant, with its stone-vaulted ceiling, in *Teddies Grill* bar, in the lounge by a fire, and alfresco in the courtyard. Breakfast, lunch and light snacks are available for non-residents. 'The hotel staff were very helpful and very friendly.' Background music. Lounge, 2 bars, restaurant. Civil wedding licence; conference facilities. Wi-Fi. Parking. 33 bedrooms (plus 1- and 2-bedroom apartments a short walk away). B&B £51–£82 per person.

CRICKHOWELL Powys
Map 3:D4
The Manor, Brecon Road, NP8 1SE. Tel 01873-810212, www.manorhotel.co.uk. With an 'excellent' location in the Brecon Beacons national park, this white-painted 18th-century manor house was the birthplace of Sir George Everest, the mountaineer who gave his name to the world's highest peak. Owners Glyn and Jess Bridgeman and Sean Gerrard run it as a 'very comfortable' hotel, with Catherine Smith as manager. The 'high-quality nouvelle cuisine' of chefs Merion Davis and Razvan Ralea makes use of locally reared organic meat and poultry from the family farm. Lounge, bar, bistro (background music; radio at breakfast). Leisure suite (indoor swimming pool, sauna, steam room, whirlpool; gym). Civil wedding licence; conference facilities. ¼ mile from town. Children and dogs welcomed. 23 bedrooms. B&B £40–£100 per person; D,B&B £70–£92.50.

DOLGELLAU Gwynedd
Map 3:B3
Ffynnon, Brynffynnon, Love Lane, LL40 1RR. Tel 01341-421774, www.ffynnontownhouse.com. In a small market town in the Snowdonia national park, Debra Harris and Steven Holt have sympathetically restored a Victorian rectory to create this relaxing guest house. It has period features such

as an Adam fireplace and stained-glass windows; the stylish modern bedrooms have a walk-in drench shower or spa bath, flat-screen TV, DVD-player and iPod docking station. Lounge, library, dining room, butler's pantry (honesty bar; room-service menu). Background music (classical, jazz, 'easy listening'). ½-acre garden: patio, hot tub, outdoor play area. Small function facilities. Wi-Fi. Parking. Children welcomed (high tea, baby-listening). Steps and level changes. 6 bedrooms. B&B £72.50–£130 per person.

EGLWYSWRW Pembrokeshire
Map 3:D2

AEL Y BRYN, SA41 3UL. Tel 01239-891411, www.aelybrynpembrokeshire.co.uk. 'Most enjoyable.' Between Newport and Cardigan, Robert Smith and Arwel Hughes offer 'warm hospitality and every comfort' at their spacious home in a rural setting, with magnificent views of the Preseli hills. Complimentary tea is given on arrival; breakfast is served at a time to suit guests. A 'delicious' set two- or three-course dinner is cooked by the owners (by arrangement) and served in the wood-beamed dining room. The house is close to the Coastal Path; walkers and cyclists are welcomed (secure storage; drying facilities). Background music ('easy listening', classical). Library, music room, dining room, conservatory; inner courtyard with seating and fountains. Garden with wildlife pond, stream, water features; giant chessboard; bowls court; seating. Wi-Fi. Parking. 4 bedrooms (all on ground floor, some steps; wheelchair platform lift available). B&B £44–£50 per person. Dinner £21–£25 (BYO bottle).

ERWOOD Powys
Map 3:D4

TRERICKET MILL, LD2 3TQ. Tel 01982-560312, www.trericket.co.uk. In a 'charming' old corn mill (Grade II listed) beside the River Wye, this B&B is run in an environmentally considerate way by 'friendly, easy' owners Nicky and Alistair Legge. Original machinery has been retained; there are grain bins, gear wheels, chutes and shafts in the dining room. All food is home cooked, vegetarian and organic. Guests can bring their own wine. 'Quite a breakfast.' Two 'comfortable' bedrooms, accessed by a wooden spiral staircase, have an original fireplace, beamed ceiling and handcrafted bed; another has a veranda overlooking fields. Lounge (wood-burning stove; lots of games to borrow), dining room. No background music. Wi-Fi. 9 miles SE of Builth Wells. Children welcomed. 3 bedrooms (plus small bunkroom, 1 self-catering 'eco cabin' and a riverside campsite). B&B £33–£75 per person. Dinner £15–£18.75.

HARLECH Gwynedd
Map 3:B3

CASTLE COTTAGE, Y Llech, LL46 2YL.Tel 01766-780479, www.castlecottageharlech.co.uk. A recent visitor could not fault the 'atmosphere and sheer enjoyment' Glyn and Jacqueline Roberts have created at their personally run restaurant-with-rooms near the castle. In this 17th-century inn, old beams and oak flooring are combined with modern leather seating and contemporary Welsh art. Bedrooms have colourful headboards and cushions. A champion of local producers, Mr Roberts cooks seasonal dishes, including

a daily special. Canapés are served in the bar before dinner. Lounge bar, restaurant. Wi-Fi (in bar and lounge). Children welcomed (early dinners). 7 bedrooms (4 in annexe; 2 on ground floor). B&B £65–£125 per person; D,B&B £100–£160. Closed 3 weeks in Nov.
25% DISCOUNT VOUCHERS

LAMPETER Ceredigion
Map 3:D3

The Falcondale, Falcondale Drive, SA48 7RX. Tel 01570-422910, www.thefalcondale.co.uk. In a 'great' setting within 14 acres of lawns and woodland, Chris and Lisa Hutton, and their 'outstanding' staff, have created a relaxed, unpretentious experience at this country hotel. The Italianate Grade II listed mansion has views over the Teifi valley. 'Excellent' bedrooms vary in size and are traditionally furnished. 'Really terrific' modern British food is prepared by Mike Green and Andy Beaumont, with an emphasis on local produce. 1 mile N of Lampeter. Background music. 2 lounges, bar, restaurant; lift to some floors; terrace. Civil wedding licence. Function facilities. Wi-Fi. Dogs welcomed (£10 charge; dog training breaks). Resident dogs, Pudgeley and Major. 19 bedrooms. B&B £75–£99 per person. Dinner £105–£139.
25% DISCOUNT VOUCHERS

Tŷ Mawr Mansion, Cilcennin, SA48 8DB. Tel 01570-470033, www.tymawrmansion.co.uk. Restored Georgian features have been combined with luxury modern touches and high-tech gadgetry (including a 27-seat cinema) in this Grade II listed country house owned by Catherine and Martin McAlpine. The hotel is in the Aeron valley, four miles from Cardigan Bay and the picturesque village of Aberaeron; there is good walking, cycling and fishing, and plenty of local attractions. New chef Geraint Morgan sources most of the restaurant's produce from within a ten-mile radius of the hotel. 3 lounges, restaurant; cinema. 'Easy listening' background music. Ramps. 12-acre mature grounds. Wi-Fi. 9 bedrooms (3 suites, 1 on ground floor in annexe). B&B £65–£120 per person; D,B&B £95–£169 per person.

LLANDDEINIOLEN Gwynedd
Map 3:A3

Ty'n Rhos, Seion, LL55 3AE. Tel 01248-670489, www.tynrhos.co.uk. Experienced hoteliers Stephen and Hilary Murphy took over this farmstead hotel surrounded by rolling Snowdonia countryside in late 2011. They have transformed the bedrooms, named after wildflowers. A new suite has been created in an annexe, furnished in oak, and with its own private courtyard garden; there is also a new reception and bar area. The large conservatory has views to Anglesey. In the restaurant, where patio doors open on to the garden, Mr Murphy's menus use local ingredients, and vegetables and herbs from the garden. Background radio, CDs. Lounge (wood-burning fire; board games), *Garden View* restaurant (open to non-residents), conservatory. 50-acre grounds: croquet; 2 lakes; fishing. Civil wedding licence; function facilities. 4 miles from Bangor and Caernarfon. Wi-Fi. Children welcomed; dogs by arrangement. 17 bedrooms (8 in 2 annexes; 1 family suite). B&B £40–£100 per person. Dinner £26.50–£38.50.
25% DISCOUNT VOUCHERS

LLANDEILO Carmarthenshire
Map 3:D3

Fronlas, 7 Thomas Street, SA19 6LB. Tel 01558-824733, www.fronlas.com. On a quiet street close to the centre, Eva and Owain Huw have modernised their Edwardian town house with a 'striking' interior, using bold wallpapers and cosseting fabrics, while following environmentally friendly practices (organic mattresses and bedding; solar-assisted hot water and under-floor heating; composting and recycling). Guests arriving by train receive a complimentary box of chocolates from the town's chocolatier. Rooms are 'comfortable and well kept'; the sitting room has furniture by a local Welsh designer, wood-burning stove and honesty bar. The organic breakfast has locally sourced ingredients. Lounge, breakfast room (background music). Garden. Children over 3 welcomed. Wi-Fi. 4 bedrooms (2 with views of Tywi valley towards the Brecon Beacons). B&B £35–£100 per person.

LLANDUDNO Conwy
Map 3:A3

Escape, 48 Church Walks, LL30 2HL. Tel 01492-877776, www.escapebandb.co.uk. The traditional white stucco frontage of this Victorian villa hides a surprisingly hip urban interior. Owners Sam Nayar and Gaenor Loftus have fused contemporary and retro furnishing and fabrics with existing oak panelling, stained glass and period fireplaces to create a stylish B&B. Nicholas Perkins is the manager. One bedroom has a copper roll-top bath. Up-to-date technology includes flat-screen TVs, Blu-ray Disk-players, and iPod docking stations; guests can borrow from a DVD library. Lounge, breakfast room. 'Chilled' background music. Honesty bar. Wi-Fi. Children over 10 accepted. 9 bedrooms. B&B £44.50–£70 per person.

Osborne House, The Promenade, 17 North Parade, LL30 2LP. Tel 01492-860330, www.osbornehouse.co.uk. 'Sumptuous luxury. Our favourite hotel.' Decorated throughout with Victorian grandeur, this small hotel is furnished with antiques and fine paintings. Bedroom suites have a canopied bed, a marble bathroom and a sitting room with fireplace. It is run by Elizabeth Maddocks with Elyse and Michael Waddy (who cooks brasserie-style food). Sitting room, bar, café/bistro. Background music. Wi-Fi. Parking. 6 suites (sea views; gas fire). B&B £67.50–£87.50 per person; D,B&B £77.50–£102.50.

LLANDWROG Gwynedd
Map 3:A2

Rhiwafallen, nr Caernarfon, LL54 5SW. Tel 01286-830172, www.rhiwafallen.co.uk. In extensive grounds, Kate and Rob John's small restaurant-with-rooms is in a traditional granite farmhouse with distant views of the beautiful Lleyn peninsula. The interior has been given a contemporary design in neutral tones, interspersed with rich fabrics and contemporary art. Bedrooms have bespoke oak furnishing, oak flooring, a king-size bed, and a tuck box full of local sweet and savoury treats. DVDs and CDs may be borrowed. Mr John serves a seasonal three-course menu. Welsh breakfasts (home-made bread and jams). Lounge, restaurant (closed Sun night, Mon), conservatory;

2-acre grounds. 6 miles S of Caernarfon. 3 bedrooms (1 on ground floor). B&B £50–£150 per person. Dinner £35–£45.

LLANDYRNOG Denbighshire
Map 3:A4
PENTRE MAWR, LL16 4LA. Tel 01824-790732, www.pentremawrcountryhouse.co.uk. 'I want to sing the praises of *Pentre Mawr*.' Luxury canvas safari lodges in the grounds of Graham and Bre Carrington-Sykes's farmstead have a super-king-size bed, hot tub and terrace. In the main house, a 400-year-old family home, the country house style bedrooms have traditional furnishings and a four-poster bed. Next door are two cottage suites, each with an outdoor hot tub on a private terrace. 2 sitting rooms, café, restaurant ('amazing' food; pianola/classical background music). 1-acre walled garden; solar-heated saltwater swimming pool; 190 acres of meadow, park, woodland; river with fishing rights. 11 bedrooms (2 suites in cottage; 6 lodges (2-night bookings). B&B £75–£115 per person; D,B&B £100–£140.

LLANGOLLEN Denbighshire
Map 3:B4
GALES, 18 Bridge Street, LL20 8PF. Tel 01978-860089, www.galesofllangollen.co.uk. In one of the oldest streets in Llangollen, this 18th-century building has an informal wood-panelled wine bar and restaurant at its centre, as well as 'rustic but absolutely charming' accommodation, and a wine and gift shop. It is run by wine buff Richard Gale and his family. New chef Daniel Gaskin's simple home-cooked menus change daily. Eight of the bedrooms are above the wine bar; others are in a much older timber-framed building opposite. Bar/restaurant (extensive wine list; closed Sun). Background music. Conference facilities. Children welcomed. 15 bedrooms (1 suitable for ♿). B&B (continental) £35–£55 per person. Cooked breakfast £5; dinner £30.

LLANWRTYD WELLS Powys
Map 3:D3
LASSWADE COUNTRY HOUSE, Station Road, LD5 4RW. Tel 01591-610515, www.lasswadehotel.co.uk. There are outstanding views of the Cambrian mountains, Mynydd Epynt and the Brecon Beacons from all the bedrooms of Roger and Emma Stevens's traditional Edwardian house on the outskirts of the UK's smallest town. 'My wife and I were impressed.' The friendly owners follow a green agenda; Mr Stevens uses mainly organic ingredients from local farms for his 'excellent' dinners. Special diets are catered for. Drawing room (log fire), restaurant; conservatory; function room. No background music. Garden; kennels. Parking. Children (no under-8s in restaurant), and dogs (kennels provided), welcomed. 8 bedrooms. B&B £35–£65 per person. Dinner £34.
25% DISCOUNT VOUCHERS

MACHYNLLETH Gwynedd
Map 3:C3
TŶ DERW, Dinas Mawddwy, SY20 9LR. Tel 01650-531318, www.tyderw.co.uk. 'Not a sound from anywhere – just mountains and a small brook.' In a 'lovely, peaceful valley' on the edge of the Snowdonia national park, this 'delightful' white-painted house was taken over in April 2012 by new owners Richard and Jackie Bradley. There is no

Wi-Fi, and phone reception is patchy. The sitting room has DVD- and CD-players, books, games, guides and hiking maps. A pre-booked dinner of locally sourced food, which often includes Welsh lamb and home-made ice cream, is served communally (available Wed–Sat). On other nights, simple suppers (home-made soups, pâtés and sandwiches) are available. Packed lunches. Sitting room, dining room. Garden; patio. Parking; secure bike storage. Children welcomed. 4 bedrooms (1 on ground floor). B&B £41–£50 per person. Dinner £27.

MUMBLES Swansea
Map 3:E3
Patricks with Rooms, 638 Mumbles Road, SA3 4EA. Tel 01792-360199, www.patrickswithrooms.com. Two husband-and-wife teams (Catherine and Patrick Walsh, Sally and Dean Fuller) own and manage this family-friendly restaurant-with-rooms five miles southwest of Swansea. Menus offer seasonal, locally sourced produce (Mr Walsh and Mr Fuller are the chefs; breakfast, lunch, afternoon tea and dinner are all available). Colourful bedrooms have sea views. Lounge/bar, restaurant. Background music. Gym. Greenhouse. Civil wedding licence; meeting room. Wi-Fi. Children welcomed (cots, high chairs, baby monitors, DVDs, playground across the road). 16 bedrooms. B&B £57.50–£155 per person; D,B&B £92.50–£185 per person.

NEWPORT Pembrokeshire
Map 3:D1
Y Garth, Cae Tabor, Dinas Cross, SA42 0XR. Tel 01348-811777, www.bedandbreakfast-pembrokeshire.co.uk. In the village of Dinas Cross, midway between Newport and Fishguard, Joyce Evans's B&B is decorated with rich fabrics and bold contemporary wallpapers. Rooms have distant views of the sea or of open countryside; bathrooms have a monsoon shower (bathrobes supplied). A wide selection at breakfast focuses on local Pembrokeshire produce. The coast is within easy walking distance. Convenient for the ferry to Rosslare. Lounge, dining room. Garden; patio with outdoor seating. Wi-Fi. Parking; secure bicycle storage. 3 bedrooms. B&B £40–£100 per person.

NEWTOWN Powys
Map 3:C4
The Forest Country Guest House, Gilfach Lane, Kerry, SY16 4DW. Tel 01686-621821, www.bedandbreakfastnewtown.co.uk. In a tranquil spot in the Vale of Kerry, Paul and Michelle Martin, along with their children and assorted pets, live in this white-painted Victorian country house, which they run as a family-friendly B&B. An environmentally friendly enterprise, the house has solar panels for heating water, and photovoltaic cells for generating electricity. Rooms have views of the surrounding countryside or the large garden. Breakfast, made from locally sourced, organic produce, usually includes eggs from the Martins' hens. The B&B is a five-minute drive from Newtown (train and bus stations), and well located for exploring the Marches area of Mid Wales. Drawing room, dining room; kitchenette; games room (pool, table football, table tennis). DVDs; toy box. No background music. 4-acre garden; play area with forest fort;

tennis. Wi-Fi. 3 miles SE of Newtown (train and bus stations). Children and dogs (kennels £5 per night) welcomed; stabling available. Resident spaniel, Libby. 5 bedrooms (plus 4 holiday cottages in outbuildings). B&B £37.50–£75 per person.

PONTDOLGOCH Powys
Map 3:C3
THE TALKHOUSE, Caersws, SY17 5JE. Tel 01686-688919, www.talkhouse.co.uk. 'Pleasant, welcoming' hosts Jacqueline and Stephen Garratt run this low-roofed, whitewashed 17th-century coaching inn (formerly *The Mytton Arms* pub). There are beams, low doorways and a log fire in the bar; in the restaurant, French windows open on to the garden. Mr Garratt's varied menus make use of local ingredients (restaurant closed Mon, Tues). Guests may take morning coffee or tea in their homely room before heading downstairs for a cooked breakfast. Sitting room, bar, 2 dining rooms; ⅓-acre garden with gazebo for alfresco dining. Background music ('easy listening'). 5 miles W of Newtown. 3 bedrooms. B&B £62.50–£70 per person. Dinner £35.

RUTHIN Denbighshire
Map 3:A4
MANORHAUS, Well Street, LL15 1AH. Tel 01824-704830, www.manorhaus.com. 'A most interesting and unusual place to stay.' Christopher Frost and Gavin Harris's boutique hotel/art gallery is housed within a Grade II listed Georgian building off the main square. The restaurant and lounge serve as a gallery space to display the work of contemporary Welsh artists; each 'visually stylish' bedroom has an artistic influence. In the wood-panelled dining room, Gavin Porter serves dishes based on locally sourced and sustainable produce. Lounge, bar, restaurant, library. Jazz/world background music. Cinema; fitness room, sauna, steam room; seminar/meeting facilities. Wi-Fi. Parking nearby. 8 bedrooms. B&B £92.50–£122.50 per person; D,B&B £110–£150.

ST DAVID'S Pembrokeshire
Map 3:D1
OLD CROSS HOTEL, Cross Square, SA62 6SP. Tel 01437-720387, www.oldcrosshotel.co.uk. Run by Julie and Alex Babis with 'very friendly' staff, this 'excellent' small hotel occupies a traditional stone-built house in the centre. It is close to the cathedral and within walking distance of the Coastal Path. Bedrooms are simply furnished, comfortable and well equipped. 'Excellent food.' 2 lounges, bar (popular with locals; TV for sports events; background radio), restaurant; garden (alfresco meals in summer). Small function facilities. Wi-Fi (£5 per day). Parking. Children, and dogs (£6.50 per night charge; resident dog), welcomed. 16 bedrooms. B&B £40–£69 per person; D,B&B £72.50–£94.

CHANNEL ISLANDS

KINGS MILLS Guernsey
Map 1: inset D5
FLEUR DU JARDIN, Grand Moulins, Castel, GY5 7JT. Tel 01481-257996, www.fleurdujardin.com. In a pleasant village setting on the west of the island, Ian and Amanda Walker's restaurant-with-rooms is run by Sandra Le Scanff and friendly staff. Bleached timber walls, simply furnished bedrooms and

sandstone bathrooms give the place an airy seaside feel. It is a 20-minute bus ride into town; 20 minutes' walk to the beach. Bar, restaurant (Andy Clarke cooks gastropub food with seasonal and local ingredients); background music. Health suite (beauty treatments, relaxation rooms). 2-acre garden: heated swimming pool, sunny terrace. Children welcomed. 19 bedrooms (2 garden suites; rooms at the back are quieter). B&B £46–£70 per person; D,B&B £67.50–£91.50.
25% DISCOUNT VOUCHERS

ST BRELADE Jersey
Map 1: inset E6
ST BRELADE'S BAY HOTEL, La Route de la Baie, JE3 8EF. Tel 01534-746141, www.stbreladesbayhotel.com. On Jersey's loveliest bay, this large, white hotel opposite a 'beautiful' beach stands in lush subtropical gardens. It is owned by David Whelan (who also owns Wigan Athletic football club); Tony Jones is the manager. It has been recently refurbished in traditional style; a new health club has been added, with an indoor swimming pool and spa. There are excellent facilities for children, including a play area and their own swimming pool. Franz Hacker remains as chef; his menus showcase the plentiful local supply of fresh seafood and vegetables. The *Petit Port Café* has less formal alfresco dining. Breakfast has 'a wide choice of cooked dishes'. Lounge, cocktail bar (background music), café, *The Bay* restaurant. Games room, snooker room; toddlers' room. Function room. Sun lounge; outdoor pool. Lift. Civil wedding licence; function facilities. Children welcomed (cots, high chairs, high tea). 77 bedrooms. B&B £70–£284 per person. Dinner from £45.

ST MARTIN Guernsey
Map 1: inset E5
BELLA LUCE HOTEL, La Fosse, GY4 6EB. Tel 01481-238764, www.bellalucehotel.com. A new spa has been added to this luxurious manor house with 12th-century origins, in the south of the island. The hotel is owned by Luke Wheadon; Michael McBride is the manager. Bedrooms (some small) have a colonial feel. Overlooking a courtyard garden, the smart, rustic restaurant has candles and roaring log fires at night. Local seafood, home-grown ingredients and herbs are used in Malcolm Meiers's dishes. Lounge, bar, *Garden* restaurant, *Lucifer's* cellar (extensive wine list; background music). Garden (alfresco dining); courtyard. Swimming pool (heated in summer), spa, treatment rooms. Civil wedding licence; function facilities. 2 miles to St Peter Port; rock beach 5 mins' walk. Wi-Fi. Parking. Children welcomed. 25 bedrooms (2 on ground floor; some family). B&B £109–£198 per person. Dinner from £45. Closed Jan.

ST PETER PORT Guernsey
Map 1: inset E5
THE CLUBHOUSE @ LA COLLINETTE, St Jacques, GY1 1SN. Tel 01481-710331, www.lacollinette.com. Colourful window boxes adorn the front of this family-friendly hotel close to the seafront and centre. The picturesque harbour nearby has access to the surrounding islands (and tax-free shopping). The hotel has been run by the Chambers family for almost 50 years. Rooms are bright and modern;

lounges open on to the lawns, pool terrace or balcony. A small museum is housed in a former German naval signals bunker. Bar, restaurant (brasserie menu; seafood and local produce); background music. DVD library; conference facilities. Garden; heated swimming pool; gym; massage. Wi-Fi. Children welcomed (teddy bear gift; children's pool; play area). 30 bedrooms (plus 15 self-catering cottages and apartments). B&B £55–£108 per person. Dinner from £20.

La Frégate, Beauregard Lane, Les Cotils, GY1 1UT. Tel 01481-724624, www.lafregatehotel.com. High above the town, this 18th-century manor house has 'fantastic' views over the harbour, the neighbouring islands and, on a clear day, the coast of France. Simon Dufty is the manager. The bar and restaurant have been refurbished recently. Chef Neil Maginnis uses local fish and home-grown vegetables and herbs. Lounge, bar, restaurant; terrace; *The Boardroom* and *The Orangery* (function/conference facilities). Background music. Terraced garden. 2 mins' walk from centre. Wi-Fi. Children welcomed. 22 bedrooms (all with sea views; some with balcony). B&B £90–£210 per person. Dinner £33.50–£47.50.

SARK
Map 1: inset E6

Hotel Petit Champ, via Guernsey, GY10 1SF. Tel 01481-832046, www.hotelpetitchamp.co.uk. Spectacular sunset views can be enjoyed from this late Victorian, low granite building on the west coast. Part of the Sark Island Hotels group, it was completely refurbished recently. Carl Cowell is the new manager. Bedrooms have views of the sea and neighbouring islands; four have a balcony. Served in a formal dining room, chef Adrian Graham's five-course menus make the most of local produce, from fish and seafood to lamb and vegetables. Guests may use the facilities at any of the partner hotels, including the Red Room snooker club at *Aval du Creux*. 3 sun lounges, library, TV room; bar, restaurant (classical background music; alfresco dining). 15 mins' walk from the village. Sheltered 1-acre garden: solar-heated swimming pool, putting, croquet. Function facilities. Children over 10 allowed. 10 bedrooms. B&B £75–£83 per person; D,B&B £105–£113. Packages available.

IRELAND

BALLINTOY Co. Antrim
Map 6:A6

Whitepark House, 150 Whitepark Road, BT54 6NH. Tel 028-2073 1482, www.whiteparkhouse.com. Hospitable owners Bob and Siobhan Isles offer B&B guests a cup of tea on arrival at their crenellated 18th-century house, four miles east of the Giant's Causeway. Their home, above the spectacular sandy beach of Whitepark Bay, is cosily furnished and contains many artefacts from their travels. There are peat fires, spacious rooms, Irish breakfasts (vegetarians catered for), and a folly in the garden. Sitting room, conservatory. No background music. Wi-Fi. 3 bedrooms. B&B £60–£80 per person.

BALLYVAUGHAN Co. Clare
Map 6:C4

Gregans Castle Hotel. Tel 00 353 65-707 7005, www.gregans.ie. Donkeys, ducks and a pony roam the extensive grounds surrounding Simon Haden and Frederieke McMurray's 'magical' 18th-century country house overlooking Galway Bay. Public rooms are furnished with antiques, 'gorgeous, squashy sofas', and jugs of garden flowers; elegant bedrooms are decorated in sage and grey. David Hurley has taken over as chef this year, serving 'creative' modern Irish dishes. A children's early dinner is available by arrangement. 'We would go back tomorrow.' Drawing room, *Corkscrew* bar (background jazz), restaurant. 15-acre grounds: ornamental pool; croquet. No TV. Wi-Fi. Wedding facilities. Children welcomed (no under-6s in dining room at night), also dogs (in 2 bedrooms). 21 bedrooms (some on ground floor). B&B €102.50–€122.50 per person; D,B&B €157.50–€180. Closed mid-Nov–early Feb. Restaurant closed Sun.

BELFAST
Map 6:B6

Malmaison, 34–38 Victoria Street, BT1 3GH. Tel 028-9022 0200, www.malmaison-belfast.com. Occupying a converted 1860s seed warehouse, this centrally located hotel retains many original features (carved stone gargoyles, iron pillars and beams). Well-appointed bedrooms have a CD-player, take-home toiletries and free gym access. (Rooms facing the main street can be noisy.) Chef Ip Wai Cheong serves classic dishes in the high-ceilinged brasserie; the moody, low-lit bar is popular with locals. Lounge, bar, brasserie; gym. Background music. Lifts. Wedding/function/business facilities. Wi-Fi. Children welcomed. 64 bedrooms. Rooms £105–£400 per person.

The Old Rectory, 148 Malone Road, BT9 5LH. Tel 028-9066 7882, www.anoldrectory.co.uk. Furnished with heirlooms and antiques, Mary Callan's B&B, in a leafy conservation area (ten minutes by bus from the centre), is a Victorian Church of Ireland rectory with original tiled floors and fireplaces and stained-glass windows. The drawing room has a library specialising in local history and Irish houses and interiors. A copious breakfast (home-made breads and spreads, good vegetarian options) is 'enough to set you up for the whole day'. A small supper menu is available Mon to Fri. No background music. Drawing room. Garden. Wi-Fi. Parking. Children welcomed. 5 bedrooms (1 on ground floor). B&B £44–£54 per person.

Ravenhill House, 690 Ravenhill Road, BT6 0BZ. Tel 028-9020 7444, www.ravenhillhouse.com. Guests are welcomed with tea, coffee and biscuits on arrival at Roger and Olive Nicholson's B&B, in a restored Victorian house in a leafy suburb two miles from the city centre. Bedrooms in this comfortable family home have locally handcrafted furniture; the sitting room has a computer for guests' use and a library of local-interest books. Breakfast has freshly baked Irish wheaten bread and home-made granola and muesli (good vegetarian options). Shops, pubs, restaurants and a park within walking distance. Sitting room, dining room; small garden. Occasional background music; Radio 3 at breakfast. Wi-Fi. Parking. Children welcomed. 5 bedrooms. B&B £37.50–£60 per person. Closed Christmas, New Year, early July.

BUSHMILLS Co. Antrim
Map 6:A6

Bushmills Inn, 9 Dunluce Road, BT57 8QG. Tel 028-2073 3000, www.bushmillsinn.com. Movies are screened on Thursday nights at Alan Dunlop's quirky old coaching inn and adjoining mill house, parts of which date back to the 17th century. Rustic features include a grand staircase, a 'secret' library and a web of interconnecting public rooms with turf fires, oil lamps and ancient wooden booths. Drawing room, gallery, oak-beamed loft. The restaurant ('new Irish' cuisine) overlooks the garden courtyard; there is live music in the *Gas* bar. It is two miles from the Giant's Causeway. Conference facilities, 30-seat cinema, treatment room; 3-acre garden. Wi-Fi. Parking. Children welcomed (family rooms). 41 bedrooms (some on ground floor; spacious ones in *Mill House*, smaller ones in inn). B&B £64–£199 per person. Dinner £40–£45.

CALLAN Co. Kilkenny
Map 6:D5

Ballaghtobin Country House. Tel 00 353 56-772 5227, www.ballaghtobin.com. Catherine Gabbett provides friendly B&B accommodation in her 18th-century ancestral home, on a site where 14 generations of the Gabbett family have lived. There is a ruined Norman church opposite. Set in informal gardens, the house is within a 500-acre farm producing cereals, blackcurrants and Christmas trees. Country house-style rooms in soothing colours are elegantly furnished with paintings and antiques. Drawing room, dining room, study, conservatory. No background music. Tennis, croquet, clock golf. Children and dogs welcomed. 3 bedrooms. B&B €50–€60 per person. Closed Nov–Mar.

CARLINGFORD Co. Louth
Map 6:B6

Ghan House. Tel 00 353 42-937 3682, www.ghanhouse.com. In walled gardens near the interesting medieval town, this Georgian house is run in 'hands-on' style by the owners Paul Carroll and his mother, Joyce. It has an 'atmospheric' bar, a 'comfortable' sitting room and a 'very elegant dining room with a grand piano' (also background music 'when required'). Robert Read is the chef: 'Very good cooking with a decent helping of vegetables.' Home-made bread and muesli, freshly squeezed orange juice and 'Joyce's jam' at breakfast in separate room. 12 bedrooms (8 in annexe). B&B €65–€115 per person; D,B&B €99–€155. Closed Christmas/New Year.

CASTLEBALDWIN Co. Sligo
Map 6:B5

Cromleach Lodge, Lough Arrow. Tel 00 353 71-916 5155, www.cromleach.com. In the hills above Lough Arrow, this hotel has been owned by Moira and Christy Tighe for 35 years. 'Modern, clean and spacious' bedrooms are divided between the main building and a new block accessible via enclosed walkways. Deluxe rooms have a private balcony overlooking the lough, with views to the Bricklieve Mountains. Lounge, bar, restaurant, spa (sauna, steam room, outdoor whirlpool; treatment rooms). 30-acre grounds: forest walks, private access to Lough Arrow (fishing, boating, surfing), hill climbing. Background music. Wedding/function facilities. Good walks from the front door. Children and dogs welcomed (dog-grooming parlour). 57 bedrooms (1 suitable for ♿). B&B €37–€100 per person; D,B&B €77–€139. Closed Mon and Tues, May–June, Sept–Dec; Christmas.

CONG Co. Mayo
Map 6:C4
LISLOUGHREY LODGE, The Quay. Tel 00 353 94-954 5400, www.lisloughrey lodge.com. A former gamekeeper's home, this country hotel overlooking Lough Corrib has welcomed fishermen, huntsmen and nature walkers since the late 19th century. Individually decorated bedrooms have imposing bedheads and striking wallpaper; duplex suites have a fireplace and private terrace. (Families have a choice of suite options.) The *Quay* bar and brasserie has a wood-burning open fire; *Wilde's at the Lodge* restaurant serves 'contemporary country cuisine'. Background music. Vault with pool table, games room, private screening room. Spa suite, beauty treatments; gym. Wi-Fi. Wedding/function facilities. Children welcomed (playroom). 50 bedrooms. B&B €47.50–€80 per person. Dinner €38.

CORK Co. Cork
Map 6:D5
CAFÉ PARADISO, 16 Lancaster Quay. Tel 00 353 21-427 7939, www.cafeparadiso.ie. Denis Cotter, acclaimed chef and author of four cookery books, owns this vegetarian restaurant-with-rooms, which he runs with Geraldine O'Toole. His inventive meat-free dishes, based on seasonal, organic produce from Gort na Nain Farm nearby (visits arranged), are colourful, with an emphasis on texture and flavour. The spacious bedrooms have a CD-player, a coffee machine and a supply of board games and books; no TV. A buffet-style breakfast is served in the room on Sundays. Background music. Wi-Fi. Restricted parking. 2 bedrooms (1 faces the river). D,B&B €100 per person. Restaurant open Tues–Sat.

DERRY Co. Londonderry
Map 6:B6
BEECH HILL COUNTRY HOUSE, 32 Ardmore Road, BT47 3QP. Tel 028-7134 9279, www.beech-hill.com. 'A genuine taste of Irish hospitality.' Patsy O'Kane's 'impressive' 18th-century house stands in 'stunning' 32-acre grounds with waterfalls and a working waterwheel. Bedrooms have antiques and period decoration; some are in a modern wing. Chef Trevor Hambley serves modern dishes in the wood-floored conservatory. Background music. 2 lounges, *Ardmore* restaurant. Lift. Wedding/function facilities. Wi-Fi. 4 miles from city centre. Children welcomed; dogs by arrangement. 32 bedrooms (2 suitable for ♿). B&B £47.50–£117.50 per person. Dinner £19.95–£21.95.

SERENDIPITY HOUSE, 26 Marlborough Street, BT48 9AY. Tel 028-7126 4229, www.serendipityrooms.co.uk. Helpful hosts Paul and Stephen Lyttle, a father-and-son team, run this B&B on a hill overlooking the city walls. (Top-floor bedrooms have good views.) The town centre, with its restaurants, bars and tourist sites, is within walking distance. Lounge, dining room (background music at breakfast); panoramic sun deck. Wi-Fi. Children welcomed. 5 bedrooms. B&B £17–£35 per person.

DONEGAL Co. Donegal
Map 6:B5
Harvey's Point, Lough Eske. Tel 00 353 74-972 2208, www.harveyspoint.com. In extensive grounds in the hills of Donegal, this country hotel has been owned by the Gysling family since 1989. Large bedrooms in the main house are traditionally designed (dark wood furniture, oriental rugs); some have a four-poster bed. A turf fire burns in the cocktail bar, where locals and guests gather. In the restaurant overlooking Lough Eske, chef Paul Montgomery serves a modern menu showcasing local produce. Activity breaks (canoeing, golf, walks, archery) available. Lounge, bar, restaurant, ballroom (resident pianist; Irish/classical background music); beauty treatments. Lift. Wedding/conference facilities. Wi-Fi. 4 miles from town. Children (babysitting, early supper) and dogs welcomed. 74 bedrooms (some in courtyard). B&B €89–€320 per person. Dinner €59.

DUBLIN
Map 6:C6
The Cliff Town House, 22 St Stephen's Green, Dublin 2. Tel 00 353 1-638 3939, www.theclifftownhouse.com. Gerri and Barry O'Callaghan's small hotel occupies a handsome Georgian town house (the former home of one of the oldest private members' clubs in Ireland) on St Stephen's Green. Bedrooms have antique writing desks or dressing tables; most deluxe rooms overlook the green. In the bright restaurant, chef Sean Smith's menu specialises in seafood. Bar, restaurant, private dining room. 'Subtle' contemporary background music. Wi-Fi. Wedding/function facilities. Children welcomed. 10 bedrooms. B&B €67.50–€97.50 per person; D,B&B €107.50–€137.50. Closed Christmas.
25% DISCOUNT VOUCHERS

Waterloo House, 8–10 Waterloo Road, Dublin 4. Tel 00 353 1-660 1888, www.waterloohouse.ie. Twin red doors welcome guests to Evelyn Corcoran's B&B, which occupies two Georgian town houses in a quiet yet 'very central' location. Reception is 'slightly eccentric but helpful'; some bedrooms can be compact, though 'more than adequate' for a short stay. A 'good' breakfast (full Irish; 'catch of the day'; freshly baked croissants) is served in the raspberry dining room or adjoining conservatory. Lounge (classical background music), dining room, conservatory; garden. Lift; ramp. Wi-Fi. Parking. Children welcomed. 17 bedrooms (some suitable for ♿). B&B €44.50–€110 per person.

DUNLAVIN Co. Wicklow
Map 6:C6
Rathsallagh House. Tel 00 353 45-403112, www.rathsallagh.com. Turf and log fires burn in the bar and drawing rooms of the O'Flynn family's country hotel, in extensive parkland an hour's drive from Dublin. The grounds include a walled garden and an 18-hole golf course and driving range; a potager provides the kitchen with seasonal herbs and vegetables. Breakfast has home-baked bread, home-made preserves and fruit compotes. 2 drawing rooms, bar, dining room (background music), snooker room; 500-acre grounds (golf, tennis, croquet, clay-pigeon shooting, archery); sauna with spa bath and steam room, massage and spa treatments. Wi-Fi. Wedding/conference

facilities. Children over 6 allowed. Dogs welcomed (heated kennels). 29 rooms (20 in courtyard). B&B €105–€120 per person.
25% DISCOUNT VOUCHERS

GALWAY Co. Galway
Map 6:C4
The g Hotel, Wellpark. Tel 00 353 91-865200, www.theghotel.ie. Spacious bedrooms, vibrantly decorated public areas and attentive staff attract return guests to this Philip Treacy-designed hotel overlooking Lough Atalia. Rooms have 'comfortable' beds and tea trays; public spaces have 'thick carpet and rich wallpaper'. Bedrooms overlooking the Zen garden are 'particularly quiet and private'. Children are welcomed with milk and cookies on arrival. 3 lounges, cocktail bar, restaurant; spa (indoor swimming pool, treatments); bamboo Zen garden. Lift. Background music. Wedding/function facilities. Parking. Children welcomed (babysitting, DVD and games library). 101 rooms. B&B €75–€300 per person. Dinner €29.50–€36.

GOREY, Co. Wexford
Map 6:D6
Woodlands, Killinierin. Tel 00 353 402-37125, www.woodlandscountryhouse.com. Dedicated hosts John and Philomena O'Sullivan welcome guests to their creeper-covered Georgian house with hot scones and home-made preserves. The traditionally decorated B&B is furnished with antiques; the large gardens include orchards, a vegetable plot and water features. Breakfast has freshly baked soda bread, fresh seasonal fruits and hot dishes cooked to order. Mrs O'Sullivan holds home-baking classes (brown bread, soda bread, scones, tarts). Lounge, study, dining room; courtyard; 2-acre garden. No background music. Children welcomed. 6 bedrooms (2 with balcony overlooking the garden). B&B €50–€60 per person. Closed Oct–Mar.

KENMARE Co. Kerry
Map 6:D4
Brook Lane Hotel. Tel 00 353 64-664 2077, www.brooklanehotel.com. Una and Dermot Brennan own this modern, small hotel in a pretty heritage town on the bay. Superior bedrooms are simply decorated in earth tones; deluxe rooms have striking wallpaper and organic bath products. In the restaurant, chef Benny Scannell serves 'contemporary Irish' dishes; sister restaurant *No. 35* is a 15-minute walk away. Lift; library, bar/restaurant, private dining room; garden. Background music. Wedding/conference facilities. Golf, walking, cycling breaks. Wi-Fi. Parking. Children welcomed (family rooms). 20 bedrooms (1 suitable for ♿), plus *Studio* 2-bedroom apartment. B&B €50–€85 per person; D,B&B €85–€100. Dinner €20–€25.95. Closed Christmas.
25% DISCOUNT VOUCHERS

KILKENNY Co. Kilkenny
Map 6:D5
Rosquil House, Castlecomer Road. Tel 00 353 56-772 1419, www.rosquilhouse.com. Phil and Rhoda Nolan's 'well-run' guest house is in a 'pleasing modern house', a 20-minute walk from town. There are large, pristine bedrooms and a comfortable sitting room. 'Excellent' breakfasts, served in a spacious, light dining room,

include home-baked bread, scones and cakes; home-made granola, jam and marmalade. Lounge; small garden. No background music. Wi-Fi. Children welcomed. Close to Kilkenny Golf Club. 7 bedrooms (1 suitable for ♿), plus *The Mews* self-catering apartment. B&B €35–€50 per person.
25% DISCOUNT VOUCHERS

KILLARNEY Co. Kerry
Map 6:D4
The Dunloe, Beaufort. Tel 00 353 64-664 4111, www.thedunloe.com. Overlooking the Gap of Dunloe, this family- and dog-friendly hotel sits in extensive grounds encompassing gardens, farmland and the ruins of the 12th-century Dunloe Castle. There is complimentary fishing on the River Laune; the kitchen will prepare and cook guests' catch for their dinner. Children are made very welcome, with movie nights, a kids' club and many other facilities (playground, games room, indoor tennis, pony riding). 3 lounges, bar, *Garden* café, *Oak* restaurant, 64-acre grounds. Background music. Heated indoor pool, tennis courts, sauna, steam room, treatment rooms. Wedding/function facilities. 102 bedrooms (20 smoking, 1 suitable for ♿). B&B €90–€287.50 per person; D,B&B €130–€159. Closed mid-Oct–mid-Apr.

KINSALE Co. Cork
Map 6:D5
The Old Presbytery, 43 Cork Street. Tel 00 353 21-477 2027, www.oldpres.com. Once a priests' residence attached to the nearby St John the Baptist church, this 200-year-old house in a coastal town is today run as a B&B by Philip and Noreen McEvoy. Traditionally decorated bedrooms have antique brass beds; some superior rooms have a balcony. A substantial breakfast (vegetarian options available) features local produce. Lounge, dining room, sun patio. Classical/Irish background music. Parking. Children welcomed. 9 bedrooms (3 suites, 2 self-catering). B&B €45–€90 per person. Closed mid-Nov–Feb.

LAHINCH Co. Clare
Map 6:C4
Moy House. Tel 00 353 65-708 2800, www.moyhouse.com. In large grounds with mature woodland and a river, this 19th-century country house has uninterrupted views over Lahinch Bay. Bedrooms are individually designed; the Signature Suite has a private conservatory, and an original well in the bathroom. Chef Gerard O'Connor's 'modern Irish' dinners are served in the candlelit conservatory restaurant overlooking the ocean. Library, drawing room (honesty bar), restaurant (background music), 15-acre grounds. Children welcomed. 9 bedrooms. B&B €92.50–€180 per person; D,B&B €150–€190. Closed Nov–Mar. Restaurant closed Sun and Mon off-season.

LONGFORD Co. Longford
Map 6:C5
Viewmount House, Dublin Road. Tel 00 353 43-334 1919, www.viewmounthouse.com. The former home of the Earl of Longford, this restored Georgian house, now run as a guest house by Beryl and James Kearney, sits in large landscaped gardens. Individually decorated bedrooms have antique beds and country views; the former kitchen,

with its vaulted ceiling, is now a cosy sitting room with Chesterfields in front of an open fire. Reception room, library, sitting room, breakfast room, dining room; courtyard, gardens (Japanese garden, knot garden, orchard). Gary O'Hanlon is the chef in the *VM* restaurant in the grounds; he serves Irish dishes with a modern twist; background music. Wedding facilities. Children welcomed. 12 bedrooms (7 in modern extension, some on ground floor). B&B €55–€65 per person; D,B&B from €108.
25% DISCOUNT VOUCHERS

MAGHERAFELT Co. Londonderry
Map 6:B6
LAUREL VILLA TOWNHOUSE, 60 Church Street, BT45 6AW. Tel 028-7930 1459, www.laurel-villa.com. Eugene and Gerardine Kielt run a guest house at their Victorian home in the centre of this small town. They offer coffee and home-made scones on arrival, and expect a guest to 'come as a stranger and leave as a friend'. The atmosphere is warm, intimate and decidedly literary, with a rich collection of Seamus Heaney memorabilia on display, and comfortable bedrooms named after Ulster poets. The host, a Blue Badge guide, arranges poetry readings and tours of 'Heaney country'. No background music. 2 lounges, dining room. Children welcomed. 4 bedrooms. B&B £40–£60 per person.

MOYARD Co. Galway
Map 6:C4
CROCNARAW COUNTRY HOUSE. Tel 00 353 95-41068, www.crocnaraw.co.uk. Lucy Fretwell is the 'terrific' hostess in this Georgian country house set in eight acres of gardens and fields. Individually decorated bedrooms are 'full of light'; 'a bathroom radiator was a lovely luxury in an Irish July'. Afternoon tea (home-made scones and jams) is taken in front of the peat fire in the drawing room. Breakfast is roundly praised: home-made Irish bread, produce from the kitchen garden. Fishing, angling, golf nearby. Dining room, drawing room, snug; garden, orchard. No background music. Children welcomed. Dogs allowed in some bedrooms. 6 bedrooms. B&B €35–€58 per person.

NEWTOWNARDS Co. Down
Map 6:B6
BEECH HILL COUNTRY HOUSE, 23 Ballymoney Road, Craigantlet, BT23 4TG. Tel 028-9042 5892, www.beech-hill.net. In the Holywood hills, with a 'lovely view over rolling countryside', Victoria Brann's white Georgian-style house is decorated in period fashion with 'lots of places to sit and read'. Locally sourced produce is a priority here, and water is heated by solar power. Drawing room, dining room, conservatory. No background music. Wi-Fi. Dogs welcomed. 3 bedrooms (on ground floor; *The Colonel's Lodge* is available for self-catering). B&B £55–£60 per person.

PORTSTEWART Co. Londonderry
Map 6:A6
THE YORK, 2 Station Road, BT55 7DA. Tel 028-7083 3594, www.theyorkportstewart.co.uk. Guests praise the views of the water and the Inis Eoghain peninsula from this modern guest house by the sea. Bedrooms are simply decorated in unassuming shades of brown and sand. Several rooms have

sea views; superior suites have a private balcony as well. The *Grill Bar* restaurant (piano, juke box) serves pub classics (burgers, steaks, fish and chips); a children's menu is available. Bar, terrace/ conservatory. Lift. Wi-Fi. Children welcomed. 8 bedrooms (1 suitable for ♿). B&B £57.50–£72.50 per person.

RAMELTON Co. Donegal
Map 6:B5

FREWIN, Rectory Road. Tel 00 353 74-915 1246, www.frewinhouse.com. Decorated 'with flair', this B&B retains its Victorian period features, carefully preserved by owners Regina and Thomas Coyle. An old rectory, the house stands in mature wooded grounds on the outskirts of a historic Georgian port. Inside, there are stained-glass windows, an elegant staircase and antiques. Afternoon tea is served in the cosy library with an open fire. Breakfast is taken communally at a large table. Candlelit dinners are by arrangement. No background music. Sitting room, library, dining room; 2-acre garden. 4 bedrooms, plus 1-bedroom cottage in the grounds. B&B €55–€75 per person. Dinner €45–€50.

RATHMULLAN Co. Donegal
Map 6:B5

THE WATER'S EDGE, Ballibo. Tel 00 353 74-915 8182, www.thewatersedge.ie. On the banks of Lough Swilly, this restaurant-with-rooms, owned by Neil and Mandy Blaney, has 'superb' views across the water to Inishowen. Floor-to-ceiling windows in the dining room make the most of the view; individually decorated bedrooms also overlook the water. The modern bar is popular with locals and visitors (live piano music at weekends). Wedding facilities. Children welcomed. 10 bedrooms. B&B €60 per person. Dinner from €30.

RATHNEW Co. Wicklow
Map 6:C6

HUNTER'S HOTEL, Newrath Bridge. Tel 00 353 404 40106, www.hunters.ie. Said to be the oldest in Ireland, this former coaching inn has been run by the same family for five generations. Bedrooms have antiques, prints, creaking floorboards; many overlook the gardens on the River Vartry. The public areas are traditionally decorated, with polished brass and open fires. Afternoon tea and drinks can be taken in the award-winning gardens in warm weather. Sitting room, lounge, bar, restaurant; 2-acre garden. No background music. Children welcomed. 16 bedrooms (1 suitable for ♿). B&B €65–€85 per person; D,B&B from €100. Closed Christmas.
25% DISCOUNT VOUCHERS

RECESS Co. Galway
Map 6:C4

LOUGH INAGH LODGE, Connemara. Tel 00 353 95-34706, www.loughinagh lodgehotel.ie. 'A lovely, peaceful lodge with warm fires and delicious food', Máire O'Connor's small hotel, on the shores of a freshwater lough beneath the Twelve Bens mountain range, is run with 'a pleasant informality'. The public rooms and some bedrooms have been refurbished this year. Seafood and game dishes feature on Julie Flaherty's Irish ('with European flair') menus. The chef was 'very accommodating' with a guest's young children. Good walks, fishing. Bar, sitting room, library, dining room (no background music); 5-acre grounds.

Wedding facilities. Children and dogs welcomed. 13 bedrooms (4 on ground floor; 4 smoking). B&B €62.50–€90 per person; D,B&B €99–€135. Closed mid-Dec–Mar.
25% DISCOUNT VOUCHERS

STRANGFORD Co. Down
Map 6:B6
THE CUAN, 6–10 The Square, BT30 7ND. Tel 028-4488 1222, www.thecuan.com. 'Friendly' hosts Peter and Caroline McErlean run this guest house in a conservation village on the shores of Strangford Lough (a World Heritage site). Its location by the ferry terminal makes it a convenient choice for guests arriving by boat. The bedrooms are comfortable and simply decorated; some overlook the village square. The restaurant's speciality is a locally sourced seafood platter, accompanied by Mr McErlean's home-made wheaten bread. 2 lounges, bar, restaurant (traditional background music). Wedding/function facilities. Wi-Fi. Children welcomed. 9 bedrooms (1 suitable for ♿). B&B £40–£60 per person; D,B&B £55–£75.

THOMASTOWN Co. Kilkenny
Map 6:D6
BALLYDUFF HOUSE. Tel 00 353 56-775 8488, www.ballyduffhouse.ie. 'A wonderful place of real style and friendliness.' In a 'fabulous situation' amid farmland and gardens on the River Nore, this Georgian house is run in personal style by the owner, Breda Thomas. She looks after guests with 'grace and warmth; she shared a bottle of wine with us after we returned from a concert'. An elegant lounge is furnished with family antiques; a book-lined library is 'a gem'; a 'delicious' breakfast is taken in the dining room. No background music. Children are welcomed; pets allowed by arrangement. 5 bedrooms. B&B €50 per person.

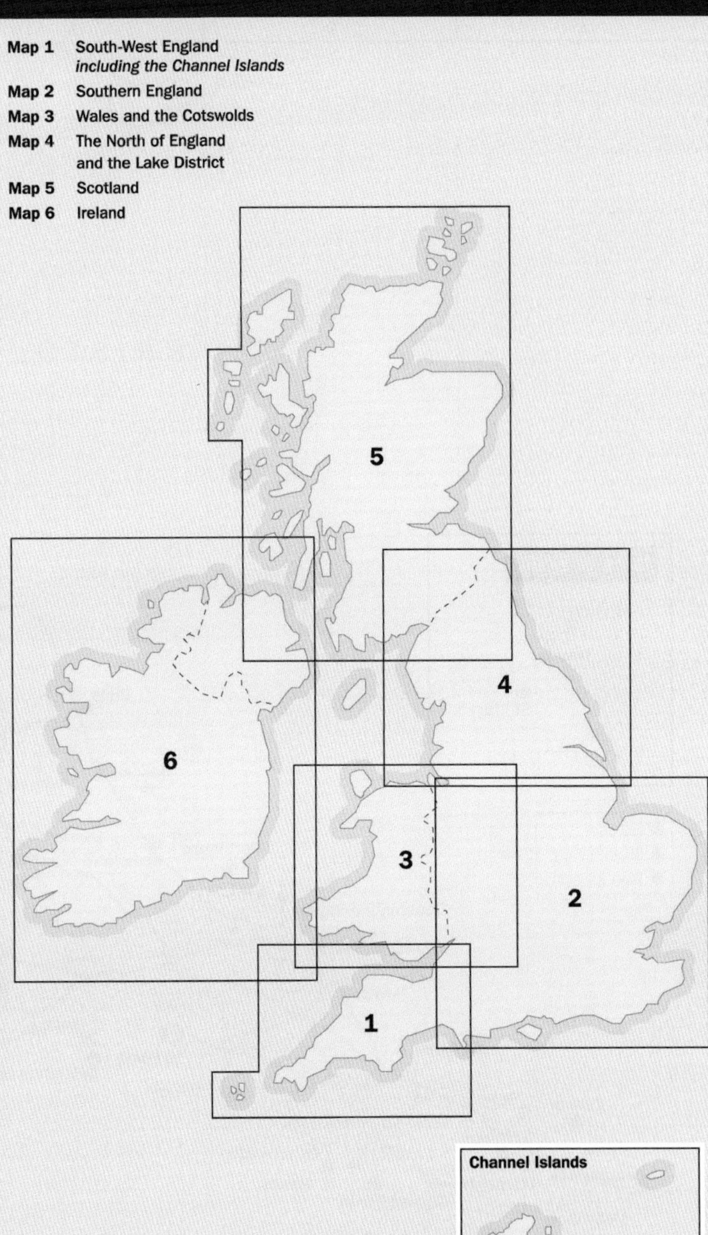

Channel Islands

1

Not to scale

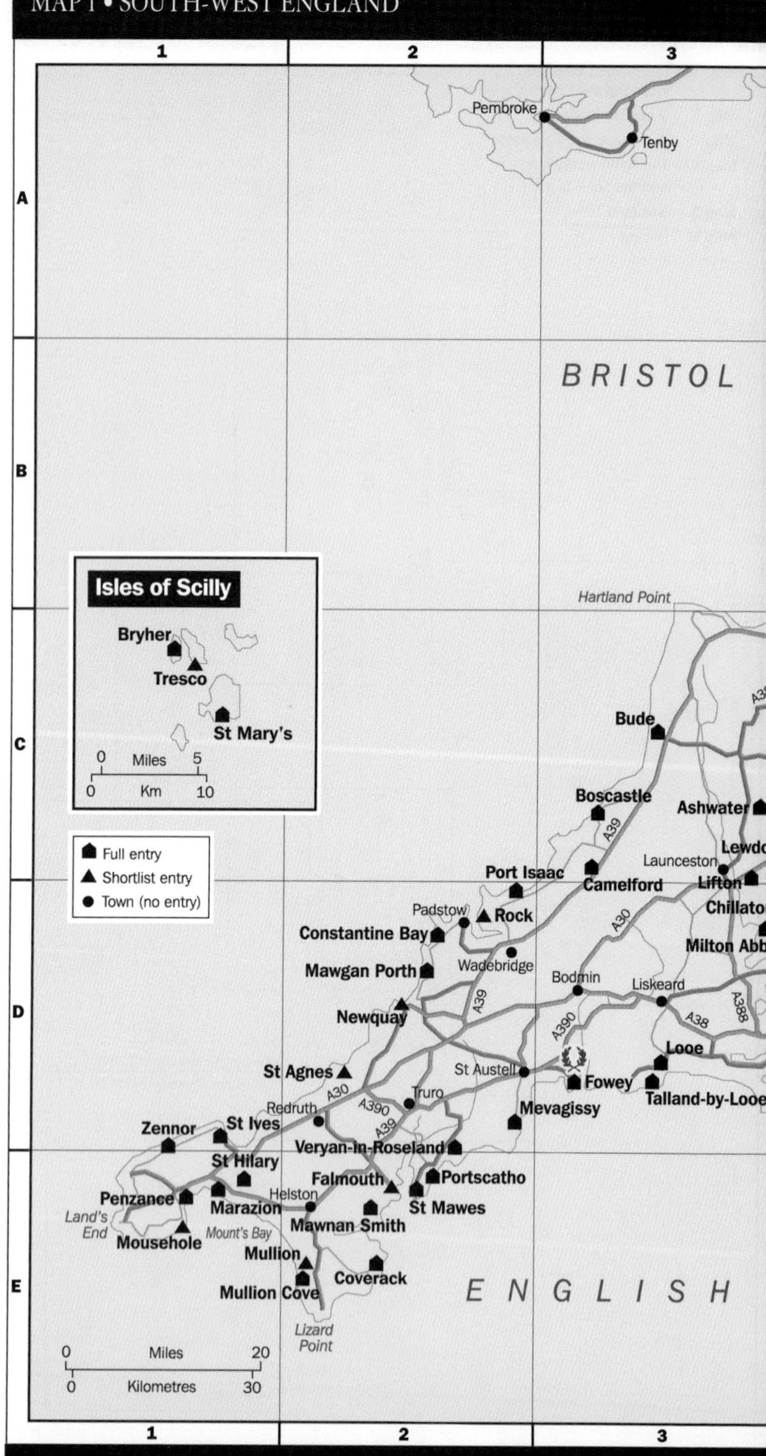
1
2
3
A
B
C
D
E
Pembroke
Tenby
BRISTOL
Isles of Scilly
Bryher
Tresco
St Mary's
0 Miles 5
0 Km 10
Full entry
Shortlist entry
Town (no entry)
Hartland Point
Bude
Boscastle
Ashwater
Lewdo
Launceston
Lifton
Port Isaac
Camelford
Padstow
Rock
Chillator
Constantine Bay
Milton Abb
Wadebridge
Mawgan Porth
Bodmin
Liskeard
Newquay
A39
A30
A390
A38
A388
Looe
St Agnes
St Austell
Fowey
Talland-by-Looe
Truro
Redruth
A390
Mevagissy
Zennor
St Ives
Veryan-in-Roseland
St Hilary
Portscatho
Falmouth
Helston
St Mawes
Penzance
Marazion
Land's End
Mawnan Smith
Mousehole
Mount's Bay
Mullion
Coverack
Mullion Cove
E N G L I S H
Lizard Point
0 Miles 20
0 Kilometres 30

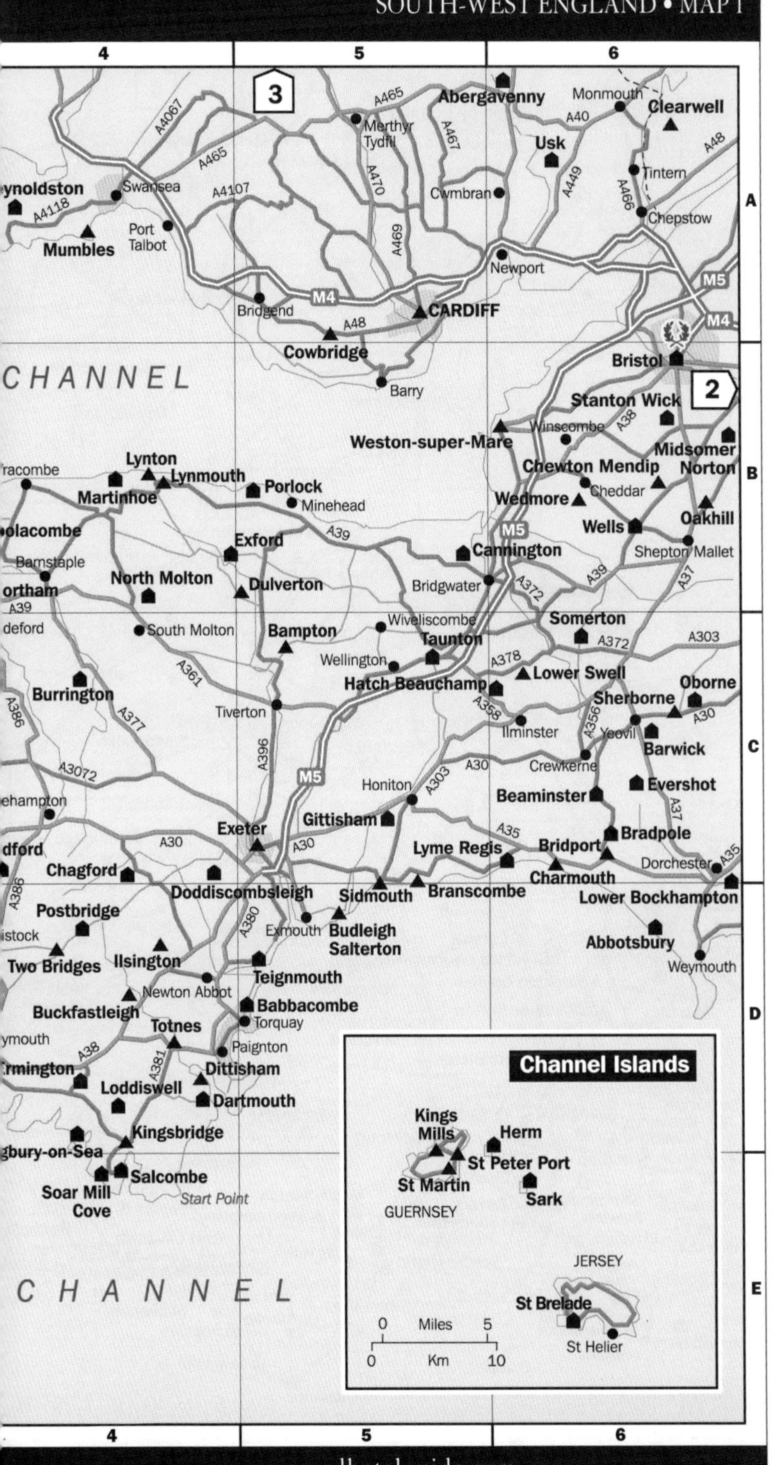
4
5
6
3
2
A
B
C
D
E
Abergavenny
Monmouth
Clearwell
Merthyr Tydfil
Usk
Tintern
Swansea
Reynoldston
Mumbles
Port Talbot
Cwmbran
Chepstow
Newport
Bridgend
CARDIFF
Cowbridge
Barry
Bristol
CHANNEL
Stanton Wick
Winscombe
Weston-super-Mare
Midsomer Norton
Chewton Mendip
Cheddar
Lynton
Lynmouth
Ilfracombe
Martinhoe
Porlock
Minehead
Wedmore
Oakhill
Wells
Woolacombe
Exford
Cannington
Shepton Mallet
Barnstaple
North Molton
Dulverton
Bridgwater
Northam
Bideford
South Molton
Bampton
Wiveliscombe
Taunton
Somerton
Wellington
Lower Swell
Hatch Beauchamp
Oborne
Burrington
Sherborne
Tiverton
Ilminster
Yeovil
Barwick
Crewkerne
Honiton
Evershot
Beaminster
Okehampton
Gittisham
Exeter
Bradpole
Lyme Regis
Bridport
Chagford
Dorchester
Charmouth
Doddiscombsleigh
Sidmouth
Branscombe
Lower Bockhampton
Postbridge
Exmouth
Budleigh Salterton
Abbotsbury
Tavistock
Weymouth
Two Bridges
Ilsington
Teignmouth
Newton Abbot
Babbacombe
Buckfastleigh
Torquay
Totnes
Plymouth
Paignton
Ermington
Dittisham
Loddiswell
Dartmouth
Kingsbridge
Bigbury-on-Sea
Salcombe
Soar Mill Cove
Start Point
CHANNEL
Channel Islands
Kings Mills
Herm
St Peter Port
St Martin
Sark
GUERNSEY
JERSEY
St Brelade
St Helier
0 Miles 5
0 Km 10
M4
M5
A465
A467
A470
A469
A4067
A4107
A4118
A48
A40
A449
A466
A38
A39
A37
A372
A361
A377
A386
A396
A3072
A30
A303
A378
A358
A356
A35
A380
A381

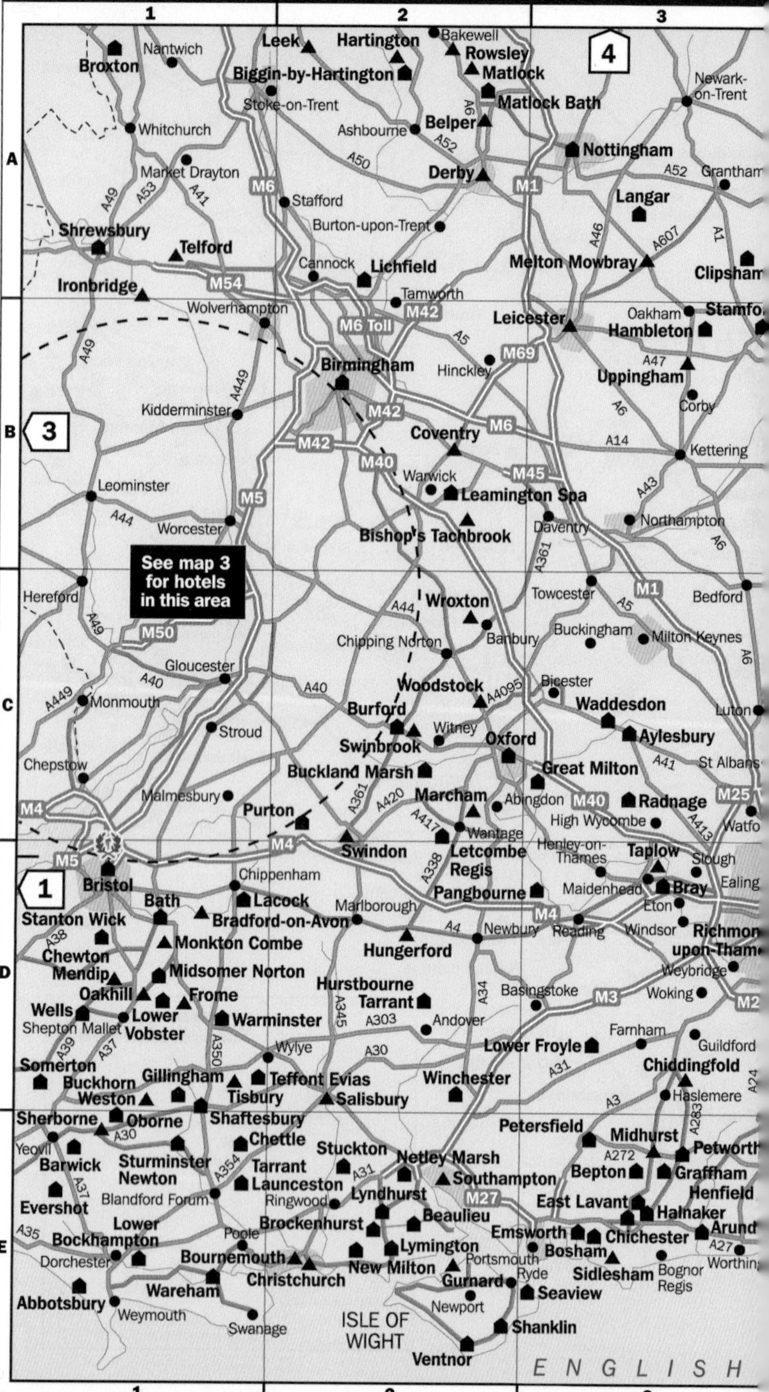

1 2 3

A
B
C
D
E

4
3
1

Broxton
Nantwich
Leek
Hartington
Bakewell
Rowsley
Biggin-by-Hartington
Matlock
Stoke-on-Trent
Matlock Bath
Newark-on-Trent
Whitchurch
Ashbourne
Belper
A6
A52
Nottingham
A50
Market Drayton
Derby
A52
Grantham
A49
A53
A41
M6
M1
Stafford
Langar
Burton-upon-Trent
A46
A607
A1
Shrewsbury
Telford
Cannock
Lichfield
Melton Mowbray
Clipsham
Ironbridge
M54
Tamworth
Wolverhampton
M42
Oakham
Stamfo
M6 Toll
Leicester
Hambleton
A5
A49
M69
A47
Birmingham
Hinckley
Uppingham
A449
M42
Corby
Kidderminster
A6
Coventry
M6
A14
M42
Kettering
M40
Warwick
M45
Leominster
A43
Leamington Spa
M5
A44
Daventry
Northampton
Worcester
Bishop's Tachbrook
A6

See map 3 for hotels in this area

A361
Towcester
M1
Hereford
Bedford
Wroxton
A44
A5
A49
M50
Banbury
Buckingham
Milton Keynes
Chipping Norton
A6
Gloucester
A40
Woodstock
Bicester
A40
A4095
A449
Monmouth
Waddesdon
Burford
Luton
Stroud
Witney
Swinbrook
Oxford
Aylesbury
Chepstow
Buckland Marsh
Great Milton
A41
St Albans
A361
A420
Malmesbury
Marcham
Abingdon
M40
Radnage
M25
M4
Purton
A417
High Wycombe
A413
Watfo
Wantage
M4
Swindon
Letcombe Regis
Henley-on-Thames
Taplow
M5
Slough
A338
Chippenham
Bristol
Maidenhead
Bray
Ealing
Bath
Lacock
Pangbourne
Eton
Stanton Wick
Bradford-on-Avon
Marlborough
M4
A38
A4
Newbury
Reading
Windsor
Richmond upon-Tham
Monkton Combe
Hungerford
Chewton Mendip
Weybridge
Midsomer Norton
Hurstbourne Tarrant
A34
Basingstoke
M3
Oakhill
Frome
A345
Woking
M2
Wells
Lower Vobster
Warminster
A303
Andover
Shepton Mallet
A350
Farnham
A39
A37
Wylye
A30
Lower Froyle
Guildford
Somerton
A31
Chiddingfold
A24
Buckhorn Weston
Gillingham
Teffont Evias
Winchester
Tisbury
Salisbury
Haslemere
Sherborne
Oborne
Shaftesbury
A3
A283
A30
Chettle
Petersfield
Yeovil
Midhurst
Stuckton
Netley Marsh
A272
Petworth
Barwick
Sturminster Newton
Tarrant Launceston
A354
A31
Southampton
Bepton
Graffham
A37
Ringwood
Lyndhurst
Henfield
Blandford Forum
M27
East Lavant
Evershot
Halnaker
Lower Bockhampton
Beaulieu
Brockenhurst
Emsworth
Chichester
Arund
A35
Poole
A27
Lymington
Bosham
Dorchester
Bournemouth
Portsmouth
Worthin
New Milton
Ryde
Sidlesham
Bognor Regis
Christchurch
Gurnard
Wareham
Seaview
Abbotsbury
Newport
Weymouth
Swanage
ISLE OF WIGHT
Shanklin
Ventnor
ENGLISH

1 2 3

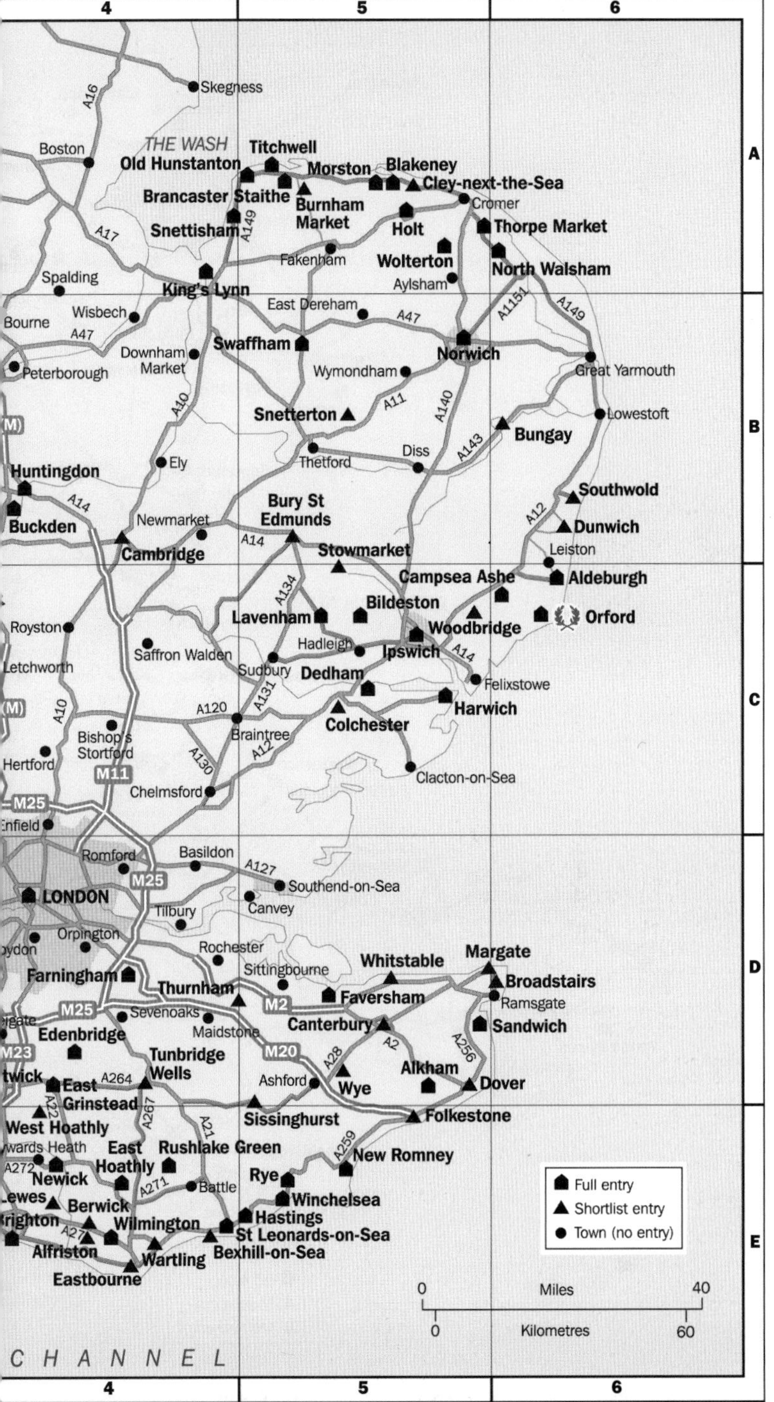
4
5
6
A
B
C
D
E
Skegness
Boston
THE WASH
Titchwell
Old Hunstanton
Morston
Blakeney
Cley-next-the-Sea
Brancaster Staithe
Burnham Market
Cromer
Holt
Thorpe Market
Snettisham
Fakenham
Wolterton
North Walsham
Aylsham
Spalding
King's Lynn
Wisbech
East Dereham
Bourne
Swaffham
Norwich
Downham Market
Peterborough
Wymondham
Great Yarmouth
Snetterton
Lowestoft
Bungay
Thetford
Diss
Huntingdon
Ely
Southwold
Buckden
Newmarket
Bury St Edmunds
Dunwich
Cambridge
Stowmarket
Leiston
Campsea Ashe
Aldeburgh
Bildeston
Royston
Lavenham
Woodbridge
Orford
Saffron Walden
Hadleigh
Ipswich
Letchworth
Sudbury
Dedham
Felixstowe
Harwich
Colchester
Bishop's Stortford
Braintree
Hertford
Clacton-on-Sea
Chelmsford
Enfield
Romford
Basildon
Southend-on-Sea
LONDON
Tilbury
Canvey
Orpington
Rochester
Margate
Whitstable
Sittingbourne
Farningham
Broadstairs
Thurnham
Faversham
Ramsgate
Sevenoaks
Canterbury
Sandwich
Maidstone
Edenbridge
Tunbridge Wells
Alkham
Ashford
Wye
Dover
East Grinstead
Sissinghurst
Folkestone
West Hoathly
East Hoathly
Rushlake Green
New Romney
Newick
Rye
Battle
Lewes
Berwick
Winchelsea
Brighton
Wilmington
Hastings
St Leonards-on-Sea
Alfriston
Wartling
Bexhill-on-Sea
Eastbourne
Full entry
Shortlist entry
Town (no entry)
0
Miles
40
0
Kilometres
60
C H A N N E L
A16
A17
A149
A47
A10
A11
A140
A1151
A149
A143
A12
A14
A134
A131
A120
A130
A12
A14
A127
M11
M25
M2
M20
M23
A264
A22
A267
A21
A259
A28
A2
A256
A271
A272
A27

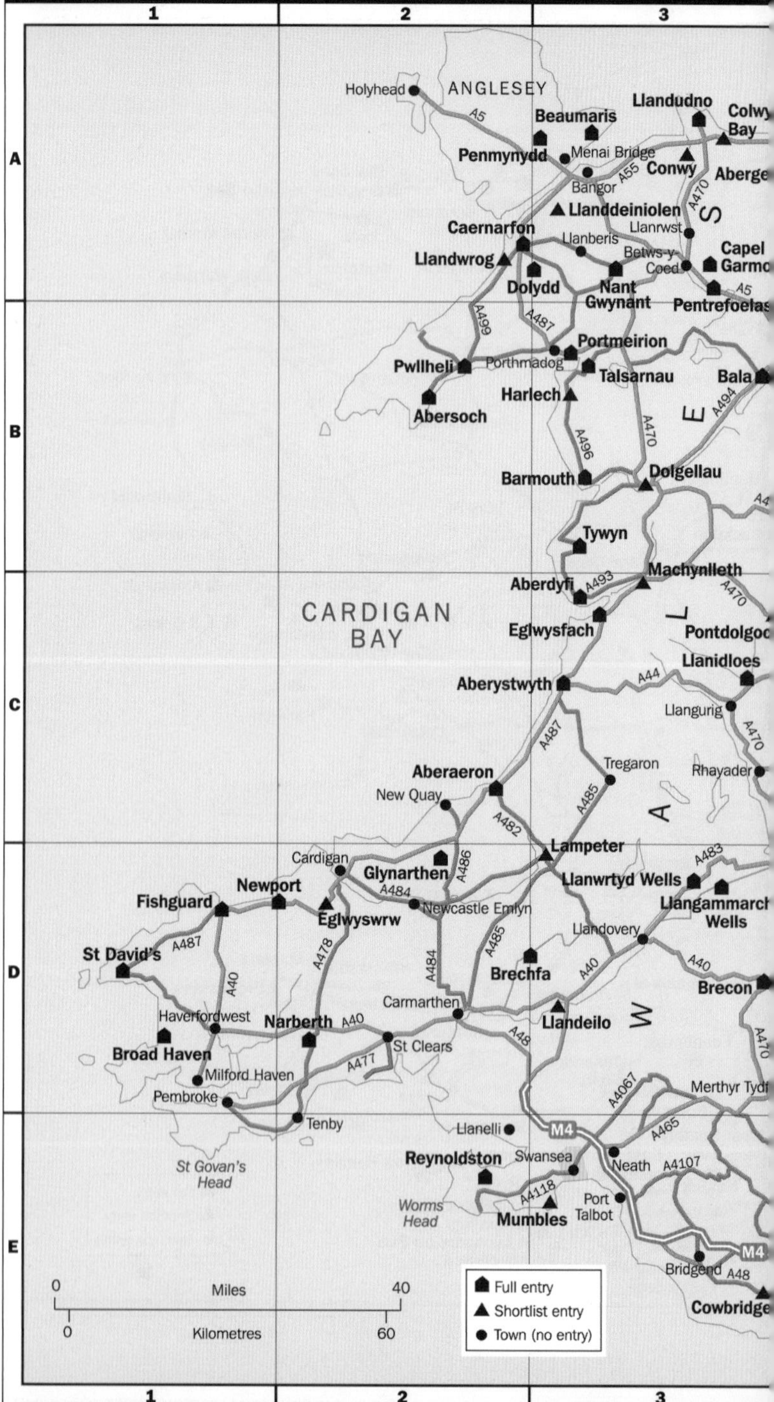

1 2 3

A
ANGLESEY
Holyhead
A5
Beaumaris
Llandudno
Colwyn Bay
Penmynydd
Menai Bridge
Conwy
Abergele
Bangor
A55
Llanddeiniolen
A470
Caernarfon
Llanrwst
Llanberis
Capel Garmon
Llandwrog
Betws-y-Coed
Dolydd
Nant Gwynant
A5
Pentrefoelas

B
A499
A487
Portmeirion
Pwllheli
Porthmadog
Talsarnau
Bala
Harlech
A494
Abersoch
A496
A470
Barmouth
Dolgellau

C
Tywyn
Machynlleth
Aberdyfi
A493
A470
CARDIGAN BAY
Eglwysfach
Pontdolgoch
Llanidloes
Aberystwyth
A44
Llangurig
A487
A470
Tregaron
Aberaeron
Rhayader
New Quay
A485
A482

D
Lampeter
Cardigan
A486
Glynarthen
A483
Llanwrtyd Wells
Newport
A484
Fishguard
Newcastle Emlyn
Llangammarch Wells
Eglwyswrw
Llandovery
A487
A485
St David's
A478
A484
Brechfa
A40
A40
A40
Brecon
Carmarthen
Haverfordwest
Narberth
A40
Llandeilo
Broad Haven
St Clears
A48
A470
A477
Milford Haven
A4067
Merthyr Tydfil
Pembroke

E
Tenby
Llanelli
M4
A465
St Govan's Head
Reynoldston
Swansea
Neath
A4107
A4118
Port Talbot
Worms Head
Mumbles
M4
Bridgend
A48
Cowbridge

0 Miles 40
0 Kilometres 60

Full entry
Shortlist entry
Town (no entry)

1 2 3

W A L E S

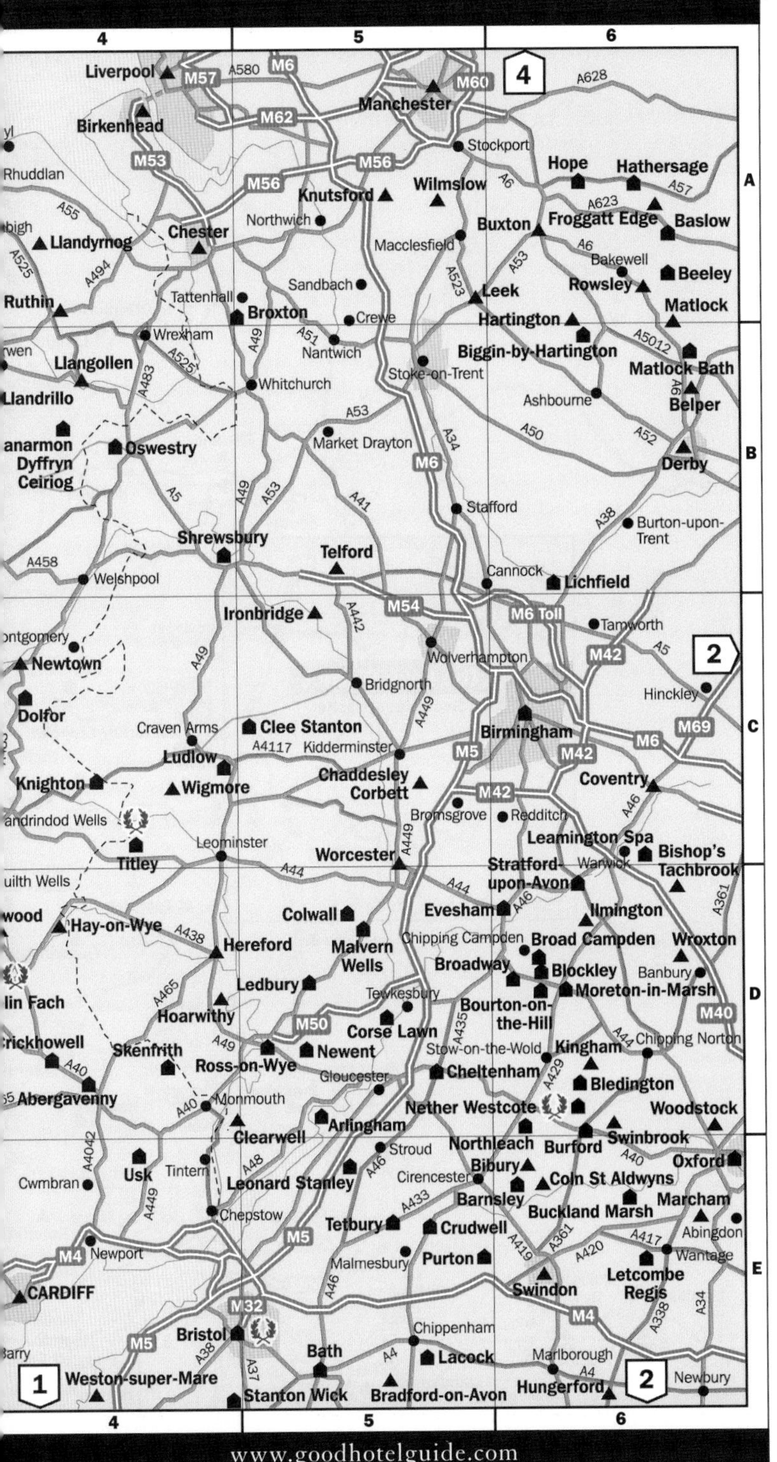
4
5
6
A
B
C
D
E
Liverpool
Birkenhead
Manchester
Stockport
Hope
Hathersage
Rhuddlan
Knutsford
Wilmslow
Northwich
Chester
Llandyrnog
Buxton
Froggatt Edge
Baslow
Macclesfield
Bakewell
Beeley
Sandbach
Rowsley
Ruthin
Tattenhall
Broxton
Crewe
Leek
Hartington
Matlock
Wrexham
Nantwich
Biggin-by-Hartington
Matlock Bath
Llangollen
Stoke-on-Trent
Whitchurch
Llandrillo
Ashbourne
Belper
Market Drayton
Oswestry
Llanarmon Dyffryn Ceiriog
Derby
Stafford
Burton-upon-Trent
Shrewsbury
Telford
Welshpool
Cannock
Lichfield
Ironbridge
Tamworth
Montgomery
Newtown
Wolverhampton
Bridgnorth
Hinckley
Dolfor
Craven Arms
Clee Stanton
Birmingham
Kidderminster
Ludlow
Knighton
Wigmore
Chaddesley Corbett
Coventry
Bromsgrove
Redditch
Llandrindod Wells
Leamington Spa
Leominster
Worcester
Bishop's Tachbrook
Titley
Stratford-upon-Avon
Warwick
Builth Wells
Colwall
Evesham
Ilmington
Hay-on-Wye
Hereford
Malvern Wells
Chipping Campden
Broad Campden
Wroxton
Broadway
Blockley
Banbury
Llanwrtyd Fach
Ledbury
Tewkesbury
Moreton-in-Marsh
Hoarwithy
Bourton-on-the-Hill
Crickhowell
Skenfrith
Corse Lawn
Stow-on-the-Wold
Kingham
Chipping Norton
Ross-on-Wye
Newent
Gloucester
Cheltenham
Bledington
Abergavenny
Monmouth
Nether Westcote
Woodstock
Clearwell
Arlingham
Swinbrook
Stroud
Northleach
Burford
Oxford
Usk
Tintern
Leonard Stanley
Bibury
Coln St Aldwyns
Cwmbran
Cirencester
Barnsley
Marcham
Buckland Marsh
Chepstow
Tetbury
Crudwell
Abingdon
Newport
Purton
Wantage
Malmesbury
Swindon
Letcombe Regis
CARDIFF
Bristol
Chippenham
Barry
Bath
Lacock
Marlborough
Weston-super-Mare
Hungerford
Newbury
Stanton Wick
Bradford-on-Avon
M57
M6
M60
M62
M53
M56
M54
M6 Toll
M42
M69
M5
M40
M50
M4
M32
A580
A628
A6
A57
A623
A55
A525
A494
A53
A523
A51
A5012
A49
A483
A50
A52
A34
A41
A5
A38
A458
A442
A449
A4117
A44
A46
A361
A438
A465
A40
A435
A429
A4042
A48
A433
A419
A420
A417
A4
A338
A37
1
2
4

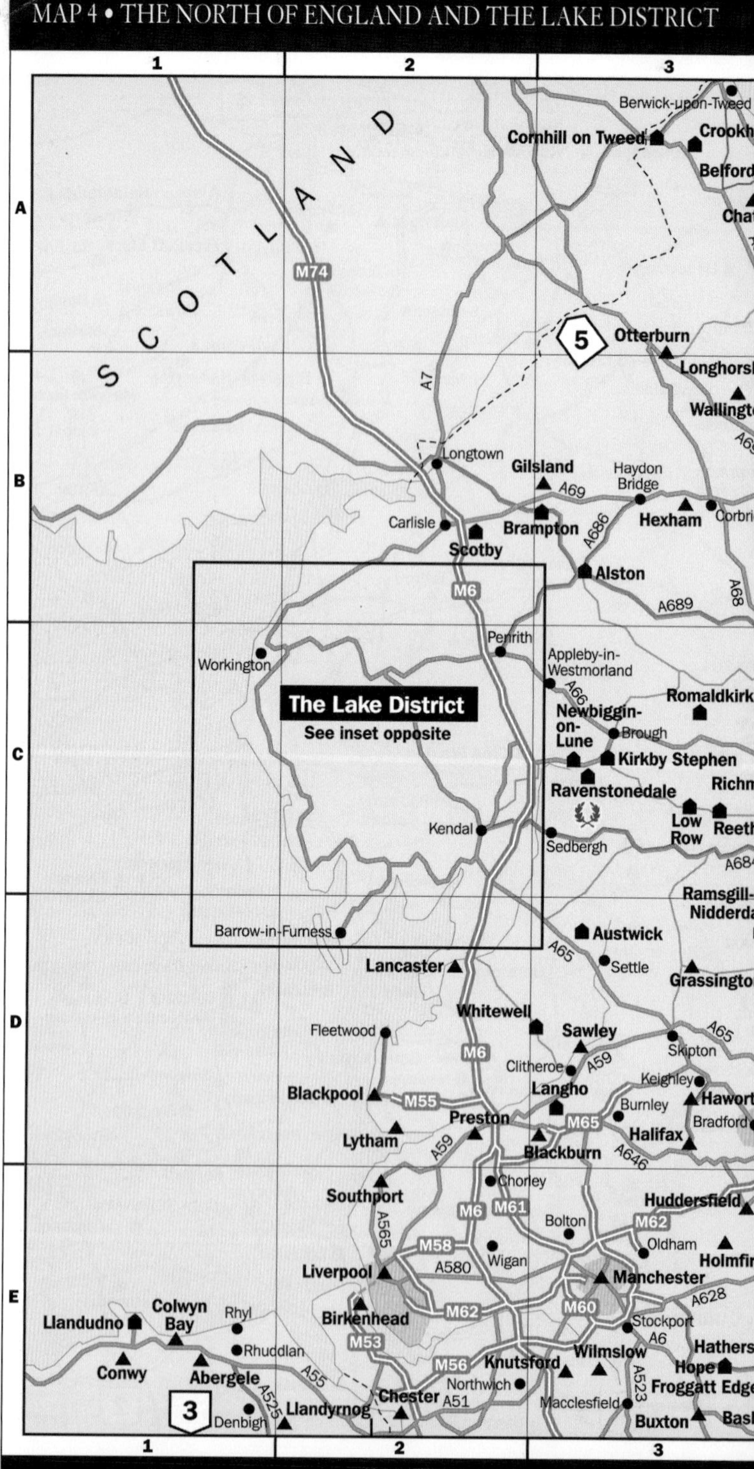
SCOTLAND
Berwick-upon-Tweed
Cornhill on Tweed
Belford
Otterburn
Longtown
Gilsland
Haydon Bridge
Hexham
Carlisle
Brampton
Scotby
Alston
Penrith
Workington
Appleby-in-Westmorland
The Lake District
See inset opposite
Romaldkirk
Newbiggin-on-Lune
Brough
Kirkby Stephen
Ravenstonedale
Low Row
Reeth
Kendal
Sedbergh
Barrow-in-Furness
Austwick
Settle
Grassington
Lancaster
Whitewell
Sawley
Fleetwood
Skipton
Clitheroe
Keighley
Langho
Blackpool
Burnley
Haworth
Preston
Bradford
Halifax
Lytham
Blackburn
Chorley
Southport
Huddersfield
Bolton
Oldham
Wigan
Liverpool
Manchester
Birkenhead
Llandudno
Colwyn Bay
Rhyl
Stockport
Rhuddlan
Wilmslow
Conwy
Abergele
Knutsford
Northwich
Chester
Macclesfield
Froggatt Edge
Denbigh
Llandyrnog
Buxton
M74
A7
A69
A686
M6
A689
A68
A66
A684
A65
A59
M55
M65
A646
M61
M62
A565
M58
A580
M60
A628
M53
A6
M56
A523
A55
A525
A51
5
3
1
2
A
B
C
D
E

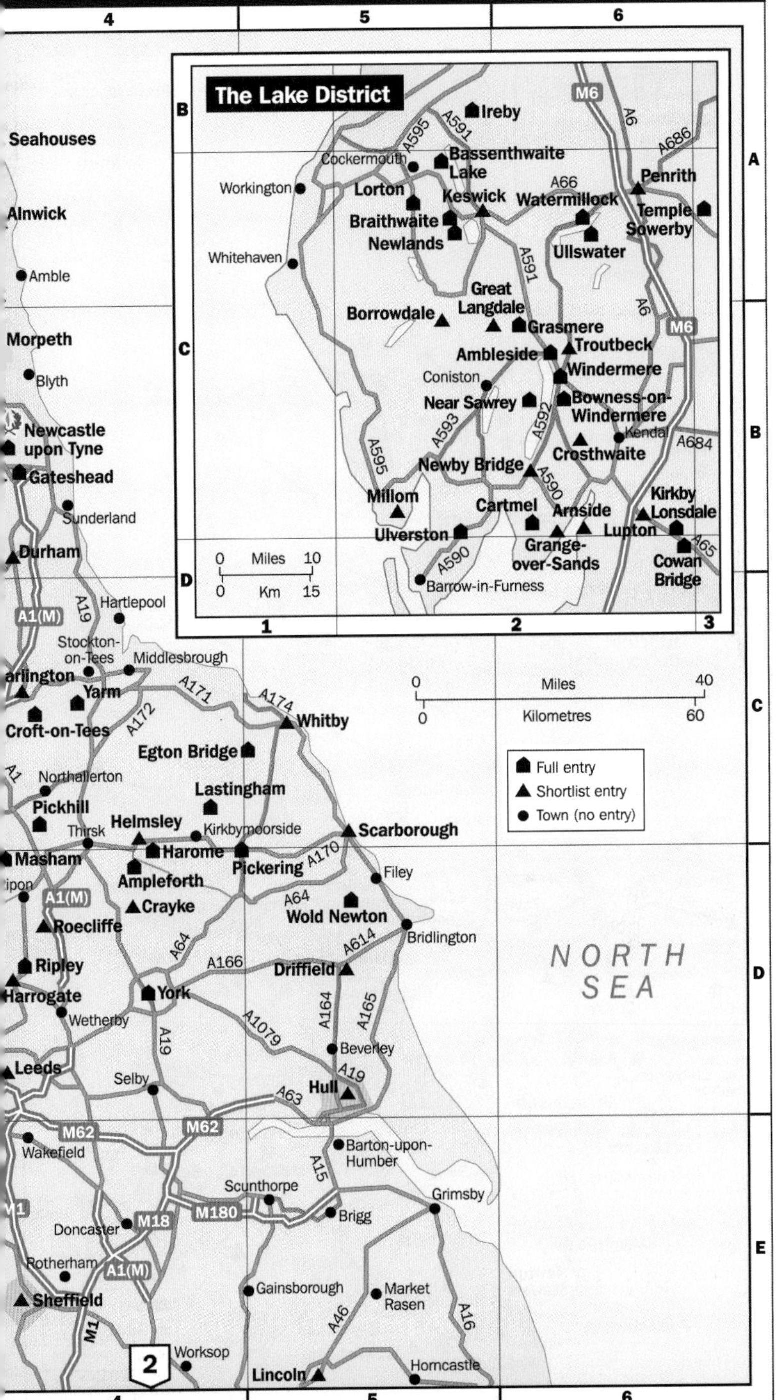

4 5 6

The Lake District

Ireby
Cockermouth
Bassenthwaite Lake
Workington
Lorton
Keswick
Watermillock
Penrith
Braithwaite
Temple Sowerby
Newlands
Whitehaven
Ullswater
Great Langdale
Borrowdale
Grasmere
Troutbeck
Ambleside
Windermere
Coniston
Near Sawrey
Bowness-on-Windermere
Kendal
Crosthwaite
Newby Bridge
Millom
Cartmel
Arnside
Kirkby Lonsdale
Ulverston
Lupton
Grange-over-Sands
Cowan Bridge
Barrow-in-Furness

M6, A6, A686, A591, A595, A66, A592, A593, A590, A684, A65

0 Miles 10
0 Km 15

Seahouses
Alnwick
Amble
Morpeth
Blyth
Newcastle upon Tyne
Gateshead
Sunderland
Durham
Hartlepool
Stockton-on-Tees
Middlesbrough
Darlington
Yarm
Croft-on-Tees
Whitby
Egton Bridge
Northallerton
Lastingham
Pickhill
Helmsley
Thirsk
Kirkbymoorside
Scarborough
Masham
Harome
Pickering
Ripon
Ampleforth
Filey
Crayke
Wold Newton
Roecliffe
Bridlington
Ripley
Driffield
Harrogate
York
Wetherby
Beverley
Leeds
Selby
Hull
Wakefield
Barton-upon-Humber
Scunthorpe
Grimsby
Brigg
Doncaster
Rotherham
Sheffield
Gainsborough
Market Rasen
Worksop
Lincoln
Horncastle

A1(M), A19, A1, A171, A174, A172, A170, A64, A614, A166, A164, A165, A1079, A63, M62, A15, M1, M18, M180, A46, A16

0 Miles 40
0 Kilometres 60

Full entry
Shortlist entry
Town (no entry)

NORTH SEA

2

4 5 6

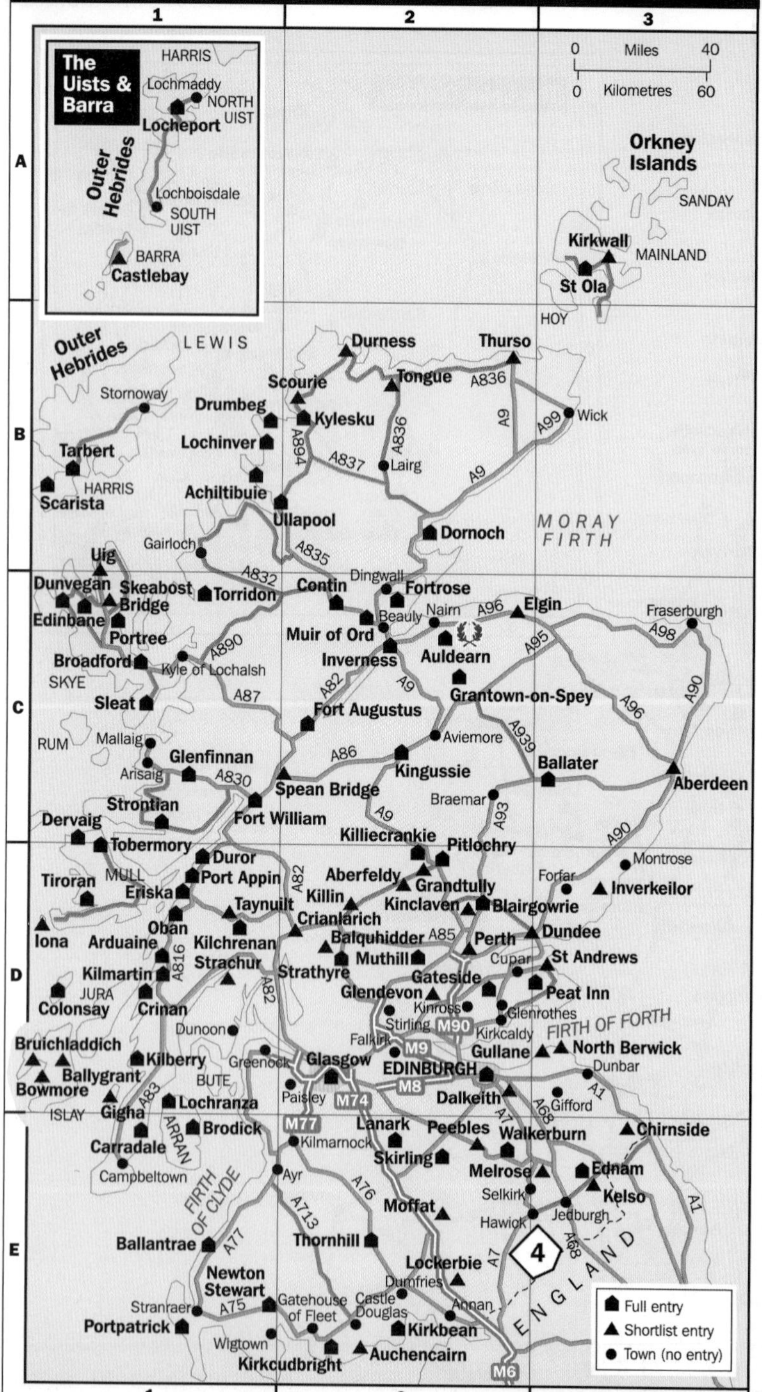

1 2 3

The Uists & Barra

HARRIS
Lochmaddy
NORTH UIST
Locheport
Outer Hebrides
Lochboisdale
SOUTH UIST
BARRA
Castlebay

0 Miles 40
0 Kilometres 60

Orkney Islands
SANDAY
Kirkwall
MAINLAND
St Ola
HOY

A

Outer Hebrides
LEWIS
Stornoway
Tarbert
HARRIS
Scarista
Durness
Thurso
Scourie
Tongue
A836
Drumbeg
Kylesku
A9
A99
Wick
Lochinver
A894
A836
A837
Lairg
A9
Achiltibuie
Ullapool
Dornoch
MORAY FIRTH
Gairloch
A835

B

Uig
Dunvegan
Skeabost Bridge
Edinbane
Torridon
A832
Contin
Dingwall
Fortrose
Beauly
Nairn
A96
Elgin
Fraserburgh
A98
Portree
Muir of Ord
Auldearn
A95
Broadford
A890
Inverness
SKYE
Kyle of Lochalsh
A87
A82
A9
Grantown-on-Spey
A96
A90
Sleat
Fort Augustus
A939
RUM
Mallaig
Aviemore
Glenfinnan
A86
Ballater
Arisaig
A830
Kingussie
Aberdeen
Spean Bridge
Braemar
Strontian
A93
Fort William
A9
Dervaig
Killiecrankie
A90

C

Tobermory
Pitlochry
Duror
Montrose
Tiroran
MULL
Port Appin
A82
Aberfeldy
Forfar
Inverkeilor
Eriska
Grandtully
Killin
Taynuilt
Kinclaven
Blairgowrie
Crianlarich
Iona
Oban
Balquhidder
A85
Perth
Dundee
Arduaine
Kilchrenan
Muthill
Cupar
St Andrews
A816
Strachur
Strathyre
Kilmartin
A82
Gateside
JURA
Glendevon
Peat Inn
Colonsay
Crinan
Kinross
Glenrothes
Dunoon
Stirling
M90
Kirkcaldy
FIRTH OF FORTH
Falkirk
M9
Bruichladdich
Gullane
North Berwick
Kilberry
Greenock
Glasgow
EDINBURGH
Dunbar
Ballygrant
BUTE
Bowmore
Paisley
M8
Dalkeith
A1
M74
Gifford
ISLAY
Gigha
A83
Lochranza
A7
A68

D

M77
Lanark
Peebles
Walkerburn
Chirnside
Brodick
ARRAN
Carradale
Kilmarnock
Skirling
Campbeltown
Ayr
Melrose
Ednam
Selkirk
Kelso
FIRTH OF CLYDE
A76
A713
Moffat
Hawick
Jedburgh
A1
Ballantrae
A77
Thornhill
4
A7
A68
Lockerbie
Newton Stewart
Dumfries
Stranraer
A75
Gatehouse of Fleet
Castle Douglas
Annan
ENGLAND
Portpatrick
Kirkbean
Wigtown
Auchencairn
Kirkcudbright
M6

E

Full entry
Shortlist entry
Town (no entry)

1 2 3

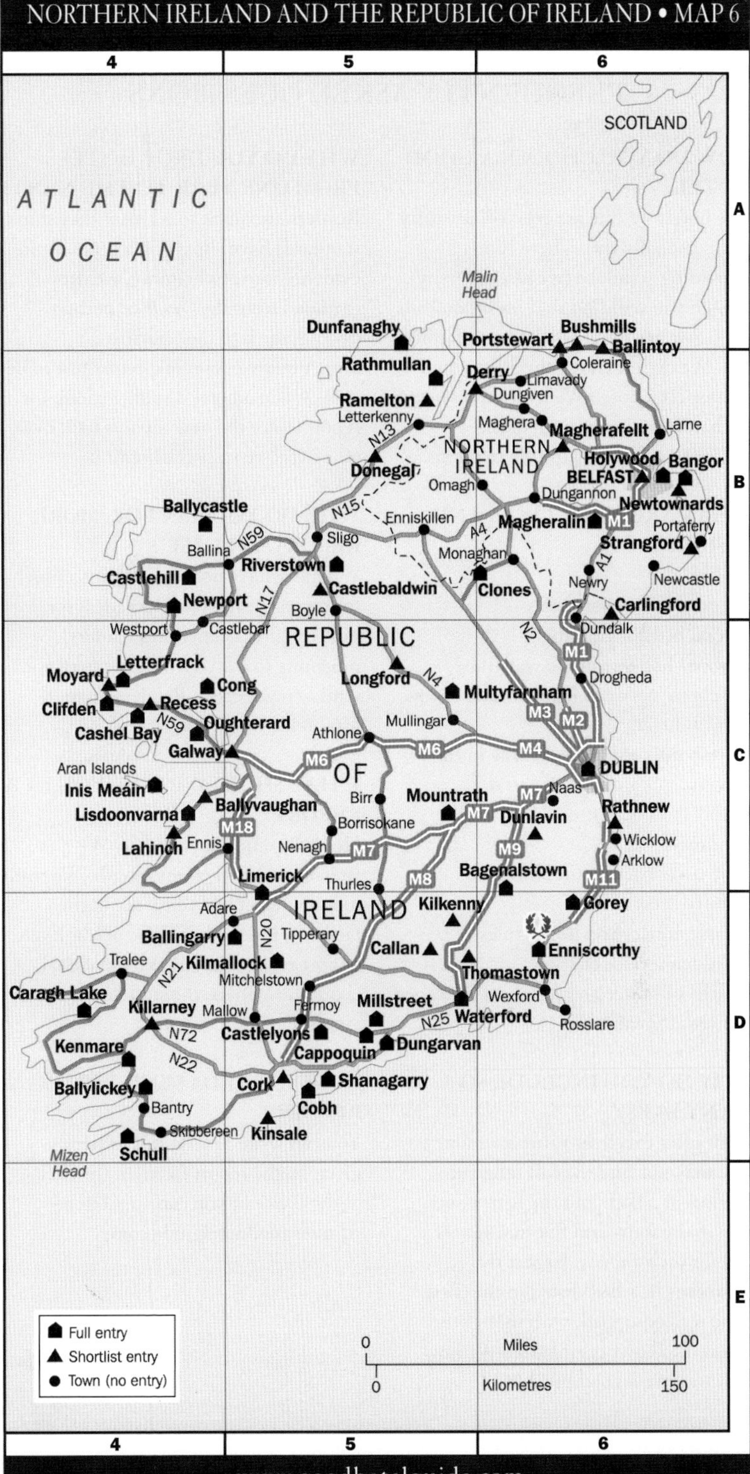
4
5
6
A
B
C
D
E
ATLANTIC
OCEAN
SCOTLAND
Malin Head
Dunfanaghy
Portstewart
Bushmills
Ballintoy
Rathmullan
Derry
Coleraine
Limavady
Dungiven
Ramelton
Letterkenny
Maghera
Magherafelt
Larne
N13
NORTHERN
IRELAND
Donegal
Holywood
Bangor
BELFAST
Omagh
Dungannon
Newtownards
Ballycastle
N15
Enniskillen
Magheralin
M1
Portaferry
N59
Sligo
A4
Strangford
Ballina
Monaghan
Riverstown
A1
Castlehill
Castlebaldwin
Newry
Newcastle
Clones
Newport
N17
Carlingford
Boyle
Westport
Castlebar
REPUBLIC
N2
Dundalk
Letterfrack
M1
Moyard
Longford
N4
Drogheda
Cong
Multyfarnham
Clifden
Recess
M3
M2
Cashel Bay
N59
Oughterard
Mullingar
Athlone
Galway
M6
M4
Aran Islands
M6
OF
DUBLIN
Inis Meáin
Birr
Mountrath
M7
Naas
Ballyvaughan
Rathnew
Lisdoonvarna
M7
Dunlavin
M18
Borrisokane
Wicklow
Lahinch
Ennis
Nenagh
M7
M9
Arklow
Limerick
M8
Bagenalstown
Thurles
M11
Adare
IRELAND
Kilkenny
Gorey
Ballingarry
N20
Tipperary
Callan
Enniscorthy
Tralee
Kilmallock
N21
Thomastown
Mitchelstown
Caragh Lake
Wexford
Millstreet
Waterford
Killarney
Mallow
Fermoy
N25
Rosslare
N72
Castlelyons
Kenmare
Cappoquin
Dungarvan
N22
Shanagarry
Ballylickey
Cork
Cobh
Bantry
Kinsale
Skibbereen
Mizen Head
Schull
Full entry
Shortlist entry
Town (no entry)
0
Miles
100
0
Kilometres
150
4
5
6

FREQUENTLY ASKED QUESTIONS

HOW DO YOU CHOOSE A GOOD HOTEL?
The hotels we like are relaxed, unstuffy and personally run. There is no overriding standard (we like diversity), though you will find that most hotels in the *Guide* are family owned and family run. We do not take a checklist when we inspect a hotel. We look for a sense of character; the warmth of the welcome; a flexible attitude to guests.

WHAT ARE YOUR LIKES AND DISLIKES?
We like
* Flexible times for meals.
* Good bedside lighting.
* Proper hangers in the wardrobe.
* A choice between blankets and sheets and a duvet.
* Fresh milk with the tea tray in the room.

We dislike
* Intrusive background music.
* Stuffy dress codes.
* Bossy notices and house rules.
* Hidden service charges.
* Packs of butter and jam, and packaged juices at breakfast.

WHY DO YOU INCLUDE SO MANY B&BS?
B&Bs offer excellent value for money. You may not find the full range of services in a B&B, but the better ones give many four- and five-star hotels a run for their money. Expect the bedrooms in a B&B listed in the *Guide* to be well equipped, with thoughtful extras. B&B owners invariably know how to serve a good breakfast.

WHY DO YOU DROP HOTELS FROM ONE YEAR TO THE NEXT?
Readers are quick to tell us if they think standards have slipped at a hotel. If the evidence is overwhelming, we drop the hotel from the *Guide* or perhaps downgrade it to the Shortlist. Sometimes we send inspectors just to be sure. When a hotel is sold, we look for reports since the new owners took over, otherwise we inspect or omit it.

WHY DO YOU ASK FOR 'MORE REPORTS, PLEASE'?
When we have not heard about a hotel for several years, we ask readers for more reports. Sometimes readers returning to a favourite hotel may not send a fresh report. Readers often respond to our request.

WHAT SHOULD I TELL YOU IN A REPORT?
How you enjoyed your stay. We welcome reports of any length. We want to know what you think about the facilities, the food, and the decor. Even a short report can tell us a great deal about the owners, the staff and the atmosphere.

HOW SHOULD I SEND YOU A REPORT?
You can write to us at the address given on the report forms at the back of the *Guide* or you can email us at editor@goodhotelguide.com.

Please send your reports to:
The *Good Hotel Guide*, Freepost PAM 2931, London W11 4BR
NOTE: No stamps needed in the UK.
Letters/report forms posted outside the UK should be addressed to:
The *Good Hotel Guide*, 50 Addison Avenue, London W11 4QP, England, and stamped normally.
Unless asked not to, we assume that we may publish your name. If you would like more report forms please tick ☐

NAME OF HOTEL: ____________________
ADDRESS: ____________________

____

Date of most recent visit: __________ Duration of stay: __________

☐ New recommendation ☐ Comment on existing entry

REPORT:

Please continue overleaf

I am not connected directly or indirectly with the management or proprietors

Signed: ______________________

Name: (CAPITALS PLEASE) ______________________

Address: ______________________

____

Email address: ______________________

Please send your reports to:
The *Good Hotel Guide*, Freepost PAM 2931, London W11 4BR
NOTE: No stamps needed in the UK.
Letters/report forms posted outside the UK should be addressed to:
The *Good Hotel Guide*, 50 Addison Avenue, London W11 4QP, England, and stamped normally.
Unless asked not to, we assume that we may publish your name. If you would like more report forms please tick ☐

NAME OF HOTEL: ____________________
ADDRESS: ____________________
____

Date of most recent visit: __________ Duration of stay: __________

☐ New recommendation ☐ Comment on existing entry

REPORT:

Please continue overleaf

I am not connected directly or indirectly with the management or proprietors

Signed: ______________________________

Name: (CAPITALS PLEASE) ______________________________

Address: ______________________________

____

Email address: ______________________________

Please send your reports to:
The *Good Hotel Guide*, Freepost PAM 2931, London W11 4BR
NOTE: No stamps needed in the UK.
Letters/report forms posted outside the UK should be addressed to:
The *Good Hotel Guide*, 50 Addison Avenue, London W11 4QP, England, and stamped normally.
Unless asked not to, we assume that we may publish your name. If you would like more report forms please tick ☐

NAME OF HOTEL: ______________________
ADDRESS: ______________________
____

Date of most recent visit: ____________ Duration of stay: ____________

☐ New recommendation ☐ Comment on existing entry

REPORT:

Please continue overleaf

I am not connected directly or indirectly with the management or proprietors

Signed: ______________________

Name: (CAPITALS PLEASE) ______________________

Address: ______________________

____

Email address: ______________________

INDEX OF HOTELS BY COUNTY

(S) indicates a Shortlist entry

ALPHABETICAL LIST OF HOTELS

(S) indicates a Shortlist entry